WIRELESS AND MOBILE NETWORKING

IFIP – The International Federation for Information Processing

IFIP was founded in 1960 under the auspices of UNESCO, following the First World Computer Congress held in Paris the previous year. An umbrella organization for societies working in information processing, IFIP's aim is two-fold: to support information processing within its member countries and to encourage technology transfer to developing nations. As its mission statement clearly states,

> *IFIP's mission is to be the leading, truly international, apolitical organization which encourages and assists in the development, exploitation and application of information technology for the benefit of all people.*

IFIP is a non-profitmaking organization, run almost solely by 2500 volunteers. It operates through a number of technical committees, which organize events and publications. IFIP's events range from an international congress to local seminars, but the most important are:

• The IFIP World Computer Congress, held every second year;
• Open conferences;
• Working conferences.

The flagship event is the IFIP World Computer Congress, at which both invited and contributed papers are presented. Contributed papers are rigorously refereed and the rejection rate is high.

As with the Congress, participation in the open conferences is open to all and papers may be invited or submitted. Again, submitted papers are stringently refereed.

The working conferences are structured differently. They are usually run by a working group and attendance is small and by invitation only. Their purpose is to create an atmosphere conducive to innovation and development. Refereeing is less rigorous and papers are subjected to extensive group discussion.

Publications arising from IFIP events vary. The papers presented at the IFIP World Computer Congress and at open conferences are published as conference proceedings, while the results of the working conferences are often published as collections of selected and edited papers.

Any national society whose primary activity is in information may apply to become a full member of IFIP, although full membership is restricted to one society per country. Full members are entitled to vote at the annual General Assembly, National societies preferring a less committed involvement may apply for associate or corresponding membership. Associate members enjoy the same benefits as full members, but without voting rights. Corresponding members are not represented in IFIP bodies. Affiliated membership is open to non-national societies, and individual and honorary membership schemes are also offered.

WIRELESS AND MOBILE NETWORKING

IFIP Joint Conference on Mobile and Wireless Communications Networks (MWCN'2008) and Personal Wireless Communications (PWC'2008), Toulouse, France, September 30 – October 2, 2008

Edited by

Zoubir Mammeri
IRIT – Paul Sabatier University
France

 Springer

Wireless and Mobile Networking

Edited by Zoubir Mammeri

p. cm. (IFIP International Federation for Information Processing, a Springer Series in Computer Science)

ISSN: 1571-5736 / 1861-2288 (Internet)

ISBN: 978-1-4419-4655-3   e-ISBN: 978-0-387-84839-6

Printed on acid-free paper

9 8 7 6 5 4 3 2 1

springer.com

Preface

Research and development in wireless and mobile networks and services areas have been going on for some time, reaching the stage of products. Graceful evolution of networks, new access schemes, flexible protocols, increased variety of services and applications, networks reliability and availability, security, are some of the present and future challenges that have to be met.

MWCN (Mobile and Wireless Communications Networks) and PWC (Personal Wireless Communications) are two conferences sponsored by IFIP WG 6.8 that provide forum for discussion between researchers, practitioners and students interested in new developments in mobile and wireless networks, services, applications and computing.

In 2008, MWCN and PWC were held in Toulouse, France, from September 30 to October 2, 2008. MWNC'2008 and PWC'2008 were coupled to form the first edition of IFIP Wireless and Mobile Networking Conference (WMNC'2008). MWCN and PWC topics were revisited in order to make them complementary and covering together the main hot issues in wireless and mobile networks, services, applications, computing, and technologies.

A total of 81 papers were submitted (50 to MWCN and 31 to PWC) by authors from 22 countries. Submitted papers were evaluated by program committee members assisted by external reviewers. Each paper was reviewed by three reviewers. 37 papers (22 from MWCN submissions and 15 from PWC submissions) were then selected and included in this book. The selected papers illustrate the state of the art, current discussions, and development trends in the areas of wireless and mobile networks and services. The contributions published in this book underline the international importance of the related field of research. They cover a variety of topics including: Wireless LANs, Sensor networks, Ad hoc networks, UMTS networks, Cellular networks, Mobility, Localization, Routing, Quality of service, IMS, Network management, Energy efficiency, and Security.

We heartily thank the steering committee, the program committee, and the external reviewers, for their efforts and hard work. Without their support, the program organization of this conference would not have been possible. We would like to thank all the authors for their paper submission, as well as Springer publishing service for their good cooperation during the preparation of this book. We are also indebted to many individuals and organizations that made this conference possible: Paul Sabatier University, IRIT, ISAE, LAAS, and IFIP. Finally, many thanks to the local organizers and all the other people who helped with the conference organization.

September 2008   *Michel Diaz, Zoubir Mammeri, Patrick Sénac*

                                        MWCN'2008 and PWC'2008 General Co-Chairs

Table of Contents

Part I: *Mobile and Wireless Communications Networks (MWCN'2008)*

Routing

Energy Efficiency

Wireless Networks, WLANs

Ad hoc and Sensor Networks

Part II: *Personal Wireless Communications (PWC'2008)*

Wireless LANs, Sensor Networks

UMTS and Cellular Networks

Mobility and Location

Network Management, Security

Part I

10th IFIP International Conference on Mobile and
Wireless Communications Networks (MWCN'2008)

Part I

MWCN'2008 Committees

General Co-chairs

Michel Diaz, LAAS-CNRS (France)
Zoubir Mammeri, Paul Sabatier University (France)

Steering Committee

Georg Carle, University of Tübingen (Germany)
Pedro Cuenca, Universidad de Castilla La Mancha (Spain)
Guy Pujolle, University of Paris 6 (France)
Tadao Saito, Toyota Info Technology Center (Japan)
Jan Slavik, TESTCOM (Czech Republic)
Otto Spaniol, University of Technology of Aachen (Germany)
Cormac J. Sreenan, University College Cork (Ireland)

Technical Program Committee

Dominique Barthel, Orange Labs (France)
Georg Carle, University of Tübingen (Germany)
Hakima Chaouchi, Telecom Sud Paris (France)
Jyh-Cheng Chen, National Tsing Hua University (Taiwan)
Luis Correia, Technical University of Lisbon (Portugal)
Pedro Cuenca, Universidad de Castilla-La Mancha (Spain)
Mieso Denko, University of Guelph (Canada)
Michel Diaz, LAAS-CNRS (France)
Otto Duarte, Universidade Federal do Rio de Janeiro (Brazil)
Mario Freire, University of Beira Interior (Portugal)
Eva Hladka, Masaryk University (Czech Republic)
Zbigniew Hulicki, Cracow Univ. of Science and Technology (Poland)
Babak Jafarian, Ortiva Wireless Inc (USA)
Shengming Jiang, University of Glamorgan (United Kingom)
Farouk Kamoun, University of Manouba (Tunisia)
Shou-Chih Lo, National Dong Hwa University (Taiwan)
Pascal Lorenz, University of Haute Alsace (France)
Zoubir Mammeri, Paul Sabatier University, Toulouse (France)

Organizing Committee

Environmental Monitoring Aware Routing in Wireless Sensor Networks

Bernd-Ludwig Wenning, Dirk Pesch, Andreas Timm-Giel and Carmelita Görg

Bernd-Ludwig Wenning, Andreas Timm-Giel, Carmelita Görg
Communication Networks, University of Bremen, Germany, e-mail: (wenn,atg,cg)@comnets.uni-bremen.de

Dirk Pesch
Centre for Adaptive Wireless Systems, Cork Institute of Technology, Ireland, e-mail: dirk.pesch@cit.ie

Abstract Wireless Sensor Networks (WSNs) are designed for many monitoring and surveillance tasks. A typical scenario category is the use of WSNs for disaster detection in environmental scenarios. In disasters such as forest fires, volcano outbreaks or flood disasters, the monitored events have the potential to destroy the sensor devices themselves. This has implications for the network lifetime, performance and robustness. While a fairly large body of work addressing routing in WSNs exists, little attention has been paid to the aspect of node failures caused by the sensed phenomenon itself. This contribution presents a routing method that is aware of the node's destruction threat and adapts the routes accordingly, before node failure results in broken routes, delay and power consuming route re-discovery. The performance of the presented routing scheme is evaluated and compared to AODV based routing in the same scenario.

1 Introduction

The majority of wireless sensor network applications are designed to monitor events or phenomena, that is the temperature in a room, the humidity in a particular space, the level of contaminants in a lake, the moisture of soil in a field, etc. A specific monitoring application for wireless sensor networks is monitoring of areas which are of risk of geological, environmental or other disasters. Examples of such disasters are natural events such as floods, volcano outbreaks, forest fires, avalanches, and industrial accidents such as leakages of harmful chemicals.

These disasters have one aspect in common, that they all bear the potential to destroy the very sensor nodes that are monitoring the area to detect the desaster events. This means that sensor nodes are not available for routing of data anymore once they have detected the event, e.g. they have burned in a forest fire for example,

Please use the following format when citing this chapter:

Wenning, B.-L., Pesch, D., Timm-Giel, A. and Görg, C., 2008, in IFIP International Federation for Information Processing, Volume 284; *Wireless and Mobile Networking*; Zoubir Mammeri; (Boston: Springer), pp. 5–16.

and therefore routes have to be changed or re-discovered to adapt to these changed conditions.

However, most existing routing protocols consider the lifetime of a sensor node as being dependent only on the energy resources of the node, i.e. a node is assumed to only fail when the battery is depleted. Well known routing protocols such as LEACH [4], PEGASIS [5], TEEN [6], Directed Diffusion [8], SPIN [7], Maximum Lifetime Energy Routing [10], and Maximum Lifetime Data Gathering [9], all focus on energy as the primary objective to making routing decisions. While energy conservation is critical for wireless sensor networks that are deployed in the environment, it is not always the best approach in particular when sensing hazardous phenomena.

Here we present EMA (Environmental Monitoring Aware) routing, a routing method that is "context-aware" in the sense that it adapts its routing tables based on the iminent failure threat due to the sensed phenomenon. While EMA also attempts to be power efficient, it proactively avoids route breaks caused by the disaster-induced node failures and thus increasing network reliability. In order to evaluate EMA routing, we have simulated a forest fire scenario within an OPNET simulation model and compared results with standard AODV based routing. Simulation results show that the proposed approach results in a more resilient network and lower end-to-end delays compared to other well known protocols.

The remainder of the paper is structured as follows; related work is presented in section 2, the proposed routing algorithm is described in section 3. Section 4 introduces the disaster scenario, which we have introduced to evaluate the routing algorithm. The simulation setup and results are shown in section 5 and discussed in section 6. The paper ends with a conclusion and outlook in section 7.

2 Related Work

Routing protocols that consider the "context", include the Sensor Context-Aware Routing protocol (SCAR) [11] which utilizes movement and resource predictions for the selection of the data forwarding direction within a sensor network. It is an adaptation of the Context-Aware Routing protocol (CAR) [12] to wireless sensor networks. In SCAR, each node evaluates its connectivity, collocation with sinks and remaining energy resources. Based on the history of these parameters, a forecast is made and the forecasted values are combined into a delivery probability for data delivery to a sink. Information about this delivery probability and the available buffer space is periodically exchanged with the neighbor nodes. Each node keeps an ordered list of neighbors sorted by the delivery probability. When data are to be sent, they are multicasted to the first R nodes in the list, thus exploiting multiple paths to increase the reliability of delivery.

Energy and Mobility-aware Geographical Multipath Routing (EM-GMR) [13] is a routing scheme for wireless sensor networks that combines three context attributes: relative distance to a sink, remaining battery capacity and mobility of a node. The mobility is only used in a scalar form indicating the speed, but not the direction of movement. Each of the three context attributes is mapped to three fuzzy levels (low, moderate, high), leading to a total of $3^3 = 27$ fuzzy logic rules. The result of these rules - the probability that the node will be elected as forwarding node - is a fuzzy set with 5 levels: Very weak, weak, moderate, strong, very strong. Each node maintains a neighbor list which is sorted by these 5 levels, and it chooses the topmost M nodes as possible forwarding nodes from the list. Then it sends a route notification (RN) to these nodes requesting whether they are available. Upon receipt of a positive reply, the data is sent.

The protocols discussed above utilize context attributes such as relative position, remaining energy, mobility or connectivity to make routing decisions. While the algorithm proposed in this paper also uses different context attributes, it extends the current work in the lietrature in that it uses measurements of an external influence, the phenomenon the nodes sense, to adapt the routes to external threats.

3 Proposed routing method

The intention of the work reported in this paper is to create a routing method that can adapt to external node threats, the very threats that are being sensed/monitored. The node's health, affected by the sensed phenomenon, is the most relevant routing criterion here. Additionally, there have to be criteria that allow efficient routing when all nodes are equally healthy. These are parameters that indicate the connectivity and the direction to the destination.

Based on these requirements, the parameters used as routing criteria in the proposed EMA approach are the health status, the RSSI (Received Signal Strength Indicator) and the hop count of the respective route.

The health status is defined to be a value between 0 and 100, with 0 being the worst and 100 the best health. If the node's temperature is below a lower threshold, the health status is 100, if it is (or has been) above an upper threshold, the health status is 0, indicating that the node is likely to fail within a very short period of time. Between the two thresholds, the health is linearly dependent on the temperature. This setting clearly is a simplified one, but the main focus of this work is not an elaborated modelling of the nodes' health with respect to temperature.

3.1 Route update signaling

The sink initiates route updates in the network by sending out a beacon. This *sink beacon* contains information about the sink's health and a hop count of 0. A sensor node which receives a sink beacon determines the RSSI and updates an internal *sink table* with the new information, including the measured RSSI value. It then increases the hop count by 1 and compares its own health to the health value in the received beacon. The lower of these two health values is put into the beacon so that the beacon contains the lowest health value on the route. Additionally, the RSSI value is added to the beacon so that a quality indication of the path is available for the next nodes. After these changes, the beacon is rebroadcast.

The rebroadcast beacons (*neighbor beacons*) can then be received by nodes that are not in direct communication range of the sink. Upon receipt of a neighbor beacon, the node compares the current information about health, RSSI and hop count to the information it might already have about the sending neighbor node and updates its internal *neighbor table* accordingly. Then it elects its best neighbor node. If there is a change related to the best neighbor, the beacon is rebroadcast with updated health, RSSI and hop count information. A "change related to the best neighbor" actually means that one of the following conditions is fulfilled:

- a new best neighbor is elected,
- a new beacon was received from the current best neighbor.

If there is no change related to the elected best neighbor, the neighbor beacon is not rebroadcast to save energy and to reduce network load. As new beacons from the current best neighbor are always forwarded, new sensor nodes that are joining the network can easily be integrated as there are beacons occuring regularly. To avoid that the death of a best neighbor remains undiscovered, a timeout is defined after which a neighbor table entry becomes invalid. In the case of a timeout, a new best neighbor is elected.

3.2 Best neighbor election

The node sorts both its neighbor table and its sink table according to a weighted multiplicative metric. The general form of this metric is

$$M = \prod_{i=1}^{N}(f_{s,i}(p_i)) \tag{1}$$

where p_i is parameter i and $f_{s,i}$ is a shaping function that maps p_i to an interval $[0, 1]$. In the case of the neighbor table, the parameters are the health, the hop count and the RSSI. For these parameters, the following settings were applied:

- **The health** is a parameter which, as stated before, is defined between 0 and 100, a good health is preferable. Therefore, a linear downscaling, dividing by 100, can be used for this criterion.
- **The hop count** can be any non-negative integer value. As low hop counts are preferable, the shaping function should have its maximum for hop count 0 and be 0 for an infinite hop count. A negative exponential shaping function was chosen here.
- **the RSSI value** is given in dBW, and as long as the transmission power of the nodes is below 1 W (which is usually the case in wireless sensor networks), the

RSSI always has a negative value. A high RSSI is preferable here. The shaping function chosen here is a positive exponential function, adapted to the usual value range of the RSSI.

The complete metric used here is

$$M = \frac{health}{100} * e^{-hopcount} * e^{\frac{RSSI}{50}}.$$ (2)

For the sorting of the sink table, the metric does not use the hop count, as it is always the same for a direct link to a sink. The health and RSSI are used in the same manner as for the neighbor table.

The best neighbor selection then works as follows:

- **If sinks are in communication range**, the best sink is elected as best neighbor node, thus using direct communication to the sink whenever this is possible.
- **If no sink is in communication range**, a neighbor node has to act as a multi-hop relay towards the sink. In this case, best node from the neighbor table is elected.

3.3 Sensor data transmission

Whenever a sensor node has data to send, communication to the sink takes place on a hop-by-hop basis. The sending node looks up the current best neighbor node in the neighbor table and forwards its data to that node. The receiving node then does the same, and in this way the data packets travel through the network until they reach the destination. Acknowledgments are also transmitted according to this hop-by-hop forwarding: there are no end-to-end acknowledgments, but instead there are acknowledgments on each hop. This is sufficient for most sensor network scenarios where end-to-end acknowledged transmissions are not required. If an application relies on end-to-end acknowledgements, e.g. to fulfill QoS requirements, there has to be an additional end-to-end acknowledgement support, which could be provided by only acknowledging a transmission if the subsequent hop has been acknowledged. In this case, however, acknowledgment timeouts have to be dimensioned according to the expected maximum hop count in the sensor network. In the forest fire scenario, end-to-end acknowledgements do not increase reliability.

4 Scenario description

The proposed routing scheme is studied within a forest fire scenario. A wireless sensor network is assumed to be deployed in a forest area, with one base station being connected to a wireless wide area network and receiving the sensor measurements. All other nodes are identical in that they each have the same sensing, computation and communication capabilities. Temperature sensing is among these capabilities.

Within the simulated area, a fire is breaking out and spreading over the map. When the fire reaches a sensor node, its temperature will rapidly increase and quickly lead to a terminal node failure.

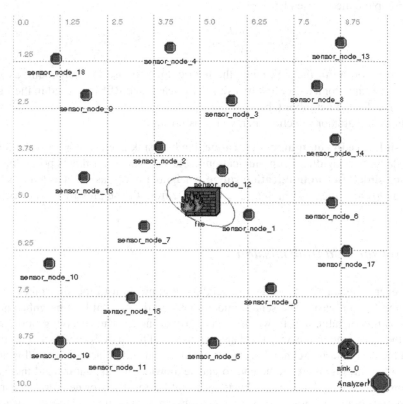

Fig. 1 Scenario Layout

Figure 1 depicts the scenario we studied in the work reported here. The simulated area has a size of 10 km x 10 km. The node in the lower right corner which is labeled "sink_0" is the base station, the 20 small nodes are the deployed sensor nodes. As it can be seen, the fire breakout is exactly at the center of the area.

In the simulation, we consider that the forest fire breaks out 30 seconds after the simulation start. To avoid an unrealistic, circular spread of the fire, but still keeping the scenario simple, an elliptical spread is assumed with a spreading speed of 1 m/s on the minor axis and 2 m/s on major axis of the ellipse. The ellipse's angle (in radians) with respect to the coordinate system is 0.5. The red shape visualizes the ellipse's angle and the ratio between the major and minor axes. When the expanding fire ellipse reaches a node, its temperature increases rapidly. The maximum temperature a node can withstand is set to 130 degrees Celsius, when the value is above this threshold, the node dies (which means it is completely deactivated in the simulation).

The nodes measure the temperature every 15 seconds and transmit the obtained values to the base station as input into a forest fire detection algorithm and fire fighter alerting. We have modelled an individual starting time for a nodes' first measurement to avoid effects caused by synchronous transmissions of all nodes. As the temperature might not be the only data that a node is sending, the measured values are part of a data packet of 1 kBit size. This means each node is transmitting 1 kBit every 15 seconds, resulting in an overall rate of generated data at all nodes of 1.33 kBit/s or 1.33 packets/s.

The transmission power, which is equal for all nodes in the scenario, is chosen so that multiple hops are required to reach the sink. Only the four nodes that are closest to the sink are in direct communication range with it.

5 Computer Simulation

The simulations for the evaluation of the proposed routing method were performed using the network simulator OPNET [3] with the simulation layout described in the previous section of this paper. The MAC (Medium Access Control) and PHY (Physical) layers in the node model are based on the Open-ZB [2] implementation (version 1.0) of the 802.15.4 stack. Different from the original Open-ZB model, the MAC layer was modified to support an ad-hoc mode with unslotted CSMA/CA instead of the original PAN-coordinated mode.

We simulated the scenario for one hour in order to reach a statistical equilibrium. Several statistics were collected and are shown in the following. For comparison, the same scenario was simulated using AODV (Ad-hoc On-demand Distance Vector) [1] as the routing method. Here, the existing AODV implementation of OPNET's wireless module was used and the PHY and MAC layers were replaced with the 802.15.4 layers.

Figure 2 shows the temperature at sensor node 1, a node that is located close to the fire breakout location. It can be clearly seen that the temperature, which initially varies around a constant value (20 degrees Celsius) increases quickly when the fire reaches the node. Within a short time, the maximum temperature threshold is reached and the node dies.

This temperature graph is shown to illustrate the conditions the nodes experience when the fire reaches them. Real temperature curves might have a smoother nature, which would make it even easier for a health-aware routing protocol to adapt to the changing conditions.

Figure 3 shows the packet reception statistics from the individual sources (sensor nodes) at the sink. The values on the ordinate are the IDs of the sensor nodes. Each blue cross marks the reception of an individual packet from the respective source at the sink. A continuous incoming flow of data from each node is visible (although the interarrival times vary in some cases). The flow of data stops abruptly when the node dies.

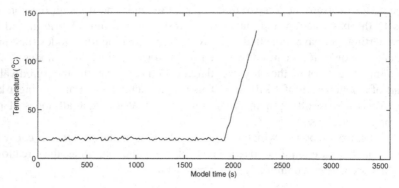

Fig. 2 Temperature at sensor node 1

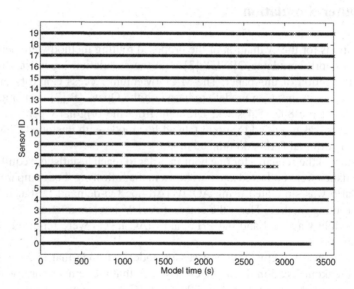

Fig. 3 Incoming packet flows at the sink

The death of nodes leads to less data traffic being generated and being received at the sink. This can be seen in the packet generation and reception rates shown in Figure 4. The blue curve shows the generation rate, the red curve shows the reception rate. It has to be noted that both curves show moving average values in a 250 s time window, so that the curves are smoother and the difference between generation and reception is more visible. For comparison, the packet generation and reception rates were also measured in the AODV simulation and are shown in 5.

One more performance measure that was recorded in the simulations was the end-to-end delays. These were not recorded for each source node separately, but across all source nodes. The results for both routing methods can be seen in Figure

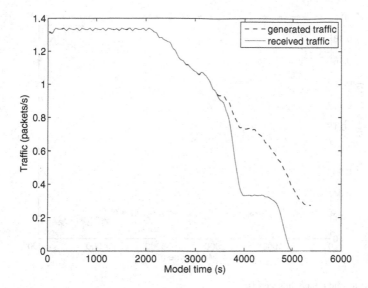

Fig. 4 Traffic generated and received at the sink in packets/s (EMA routing)

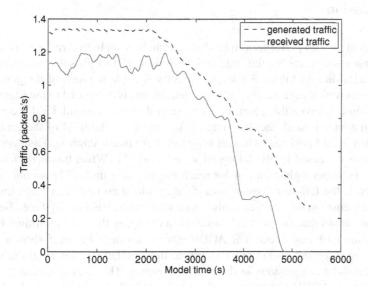

Fig. 5 Traffic generated and received at the sink in packets/s (AODV routing)

6 with the crosses marking the AODV end-to-end delays and the dots marking the delays for EMA. Each cross or dot represents the reception of an individual packet.

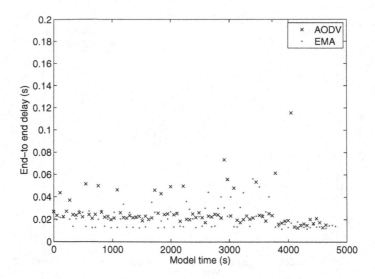

Fig. 6 End-to-end delays in seconds

6 Discussion

The EMA algorithm performs as intended - as can be seen in Figure 3 - as the traffic of all sensor nodes reaches the sink, and the inflow of data packets continues until sensor nodes die. As Figure 3 does not directly show how much of the generated traffic is received at the sink, the incoming packet rate is compared to the generation rate in Figure 4. From this chart, it can be seen that until around 3500 seconds of model time have passed, the incoming packet rate is on the level of the generated rate, which is 1.33 packets/s when all nodes are alive (see section 4). The steep drop that follows is caused by the failure of sensor node 17. When this node fails, the nodes in the upper right area can not reach the sink any more. The second significant drop is the failure of sensor node 5, after which no node can reach the sink any more (sensor node 0, which is also close to the sink, has already failed before). The result shows that the protocol succeeds in changing the routing in time before transmission problems occur. The AODV results shown in Figure 5 show a lower and varying incoming packet rate throughout the simulation. This means there are less successful transmissions in the AODV scenario. This was observed for various settings of AODV parameters such as allowed hello loss, hello intervals, route request TTL settings and so on.

The end-to-end delays, depicted in Figure 6, show that the proposed EMA algorithm in average is also providing slightly lower delays. While the delays are mostly between 20 and 30 ms in the AODV results, the delay results of the new algorithm proposed in this paper often are some ms lower, with a significant portion of them below 20 ms.

The comparisons show clearly that the proposed EMA routing approach is superior to the quite common AODV routing protocol in the given scenario. However, further investigations have to be made though, to prove that these results also hold in different scenarios, and comparison has to be made to other sensor network routing methods, too.

7 Conclusion and Outlook

We have proposed a routing approach that proactively adapts routes in a wireless sensor network based on information on node-threatening environment influences. The approach, called EMA routing, has been evaluated by computer simulation and has shown good performance in the considered forest fire scenario. With respect to the considered network and performance parameters, it outperforms the well known AODV routing algorithm.

Further research will include evaluation in further scenarios, not only scenarios with a single-sink but also multiple-sink scenarios. Based on the neighbor selection/ route evaluation function, the specific routing scenario will be generalized into an approach for context-aware routing in sensor networks, where the evaluation function is not static, but can be modified according to changes in the context.

Acknowledgements Parts of this work were performed under the framework of the Network of Excellence on Sensor Networks CRUISE partly funded by the European Commission in the 6th Framework IST Programme.

References

1. C. Perkins, E. Belding-Royer, S. Das, *Ad hoc On-Demand Distance Vector (AODV) Routing*, IETF RFC 3561, July 2003.
2. Open-ZB, *OpenSource Toolset for IEEE 802.15.4 and ZigBee*, http://open-zb.net, 2007.
3. OPNET, *OPNET Modeler*, http://opnet.com/solutions/network_rd/modeler.html, 2007.
4. W.B. Heinzelman, A.P. Chandrakasan, H. Balakrishnan, *An application-specific protocol architecture for wireless microsensor networks*, IEEE Transactions on Wireless Communications , 1(4): 660-670, October 2002.
5. S. Lindsey, C.S. Raghavendra, *PEGASIS: power efficient gathering in sensor information systems*, in: Proc. IEEE Aerospace Conference, Big Sky, Montana, March 2002.
6. A. Manjeshwar and D.P. Agrawal, *TEEN: A Protocol For Enhanced Efficiency in Wireless Sensor Networks*, in Proceedings of the 1International Workshop on Parallel and Distributed Computing Issues in Wireless Networks and Mobile Computing, San Francisco, CA April 2001.
7. J. Kulik, W. Heinzelman, H. Balakrishnan, *Negotiation based protocols for disseminating information in wireless sensor networks*, ACM Wireless Networks, Vol. 8, Mar-May 2002, pp.169-185.

8. D. Intanagonwiwat, R. Govindan, D. Estrin, J. Heidemann, F. Silva, *Directed diffusion for wireless sensor networking*, IEEE/ACM Transactions on NetworkingIEEE/ACM Transactions on Networking, 11, February 2003.
9. C. Pandana, K.J.R. Liu, *Maximum connectivity and maximum lifetime energy-aware routing for wireless sensor networks*, in Proc. of Global Telecommunications Conference GLOBECOM 2005.
10. K. Kalpakis, K. Dasgupta, P. Namjoshi, *Maximum Lifetime Data Gathering and Aggregation in Wireless Sensor Networks*, in Proc. of the 2002 IEEE International Conference on Networking (ICN'02), Atlanta, Georgia, August 26-29, 2002.
11. C. Mascolo, M. Musolesi, *SCAR: Context-Aware Adaptive Routing in Delay Tolerant Mobile Sensor Networks*, in Proc. of the 2006 International Conference on Wireless Communications and Mobile Computing, 2006, pp. 533-538.
12. M. Musolesi, S. Hailes, C. Mascolo, *Adaptive Routing for Intermittently Connected Mobile Ad Hoc Networks*, in Proc. of the Sixth IEEE International Symposium on a World of Wireless Mobile and Multimedia Networks (WoWMoM) 2005, pp. 183-189.
13. Q. Liang, Q. Ren, *Energy and Mobility Aware Geographical Multipath Routing for Wireless Sensor Networks*, in Proc. of the IEEE Wireless Communications and Networking Conference 2005, pp. 1867-1871.

Comparison of Proposed Path Selection Protocols for IEEE 802.11s WLAN Mesh Networks

Sana Ghannay, Sonia Mettali Gammar and Farouk Kamoun

CRISTAL Lab, National School of Computer Sciences, ENSI, 2010, Manouba e-mail: {sana.ghanlnay,sonia.gammar,frk.kamoun}@cristal.rnu.tn

Abstract IEEE 802.11s wireless LAN mesh network technology is the next step in the evolution of wireless architecture. A WLAN mesh network consists of WLAN devices with relay functions that communicate directly. In this type of networks, path selection is based on two protocols: HWMP and RA-OLSR. This paper presents a detailed study of the performance of the proposed path selection algorithms for IEEE 802.11s WLAN mesh networks based on the current draft standard D1.08 from January 2008 under different scenarios to provide conditions of the applicability of the protocols.

1 Introduction

WLAN wireless mesh networks are anticipated to deliver wireless services for a large variety of applications in personal, local, campus, and metropolitan areas. The main characteristic of wireless mesh networking is the communication between nodes over multiple wireless hops on a network [1]. Indeed, WLAN mesh networks consist of Mesh Point and Mesh Stations, where mesh point have minimal mobility and form the backbone of WLAN mesh network. They provide network access for both mesh and conventional stations. Furthermore, the integration of WLAN mesh networks with other networks such as the Internet, cellular, etc., can be accomplished through the gateway and bridging functions in the Mesh Point [2].

The standardization of WLAN mesh network in IEEE 802.11s is work in progress. The goal of the IEEE 802.11s group is the development of a flexible and extensible standard for wireless mesh network based on IEEE 802.11 [1]. Many research challenges remain in wireless mesh networks such as mesh Medium Access Coordination, mesh security, mesh routing, etc.

One of the key functionalities of IEEE 802.11s is the wireless multi-hop routing, which sets up the paths for the wireless forwarding. For that reason, efficient routing protocols have to provide paths through the wireless mesh and react to dynamic changes in the topology so that mesh nodes can communicate with each other even if they are not in direct wireless range. IEEE 802.11s proposed two path selection protocols HWMP(Hybrid Wireless Mesh Protocol) and RA-OLSR (Radio-Aware Optimized Link State Routing). In this paper, we present HWMP and RA-OLSR, we evaluate their performance and we compare them through simulation.

Please use the following format when citing this chapter:

Ghannay, S., Gammar, S.M. and Kamoun, F., 2008, in IFIP International Federation for Information Processing, Volume 284; *Wireless and Mobile Networking*, Zoubir Mammeri; (Boston: Springer), pp. 17–28.

The remainder of the paper is structured as follows. Section 2 gives a brief overview of IEEE 802.11s future standard. Path selection protocols HWMP and RA-OLSR are explained in section 3. Section 4 presents simulation results and compares the proposed path selection protocols.

2 The IEEE 802.11s standard

The IEEE 802.11s working group specifies an extension to the IEEE 802.11 MAC to solve the interoperability problem by defining an architecture and protocol that support both broadcast/multicast and unicast delivery using "radio-aware" metrics over self-configuring multi-hop topologies [1]. The IEEE 802.11s WLAN mesh network architecture is composed of (Fig. 1) [3]:

- **MP (Mesh Point)**: is a dedicated node for forwarding packets on behalf of other MP that may not be within direct wireless transmission range of their destinations
- **Mesh Access Point (MAP)**: is a particular MP that provides the network access to the clients or stations
- **MPP (Mesh Portal Point)**: is a particular MP that acts as a bridge to access external networks like Internet and WiMax
- **STA (Station)**: is connected via a MAP to the mesh network

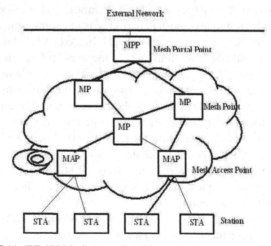

Fig. 1 IEEE 802.11s WLAN Mesh network architecture

3 Path selection protocols

Each network uses a single method to determine paths through the Mesh. The standard includes a default mandatory path selection protocol HWMP to ensure interoperability and an optional routing protocol called RA-OLSR. Moreover, the proposed IEEE 802.11s define a default radio-aware path selection metric called the Airtime Link Metric (ALM). The ALM metric is calculated as [1] :

$$C_a = \left[O + \frac{B_t}{r} \right] \frac{1}{1 - e_f}$$

O and B_t are constant. r is the transmission bit rate. e_f is the frame error rate for the Test Frame of size B_t. ALM estimates the quality of a link by taking into account the packet loss probability as well as the bit rate of the link.

3.1 Hybrid Wireless Mesh Protocol

As a hybrid protocol, HWMP combines the flexibility of on-demand routing with proactive topology tree extension [1]. HWMP contains two operating modes : a reactive mode and a proactive mode. As a hybrid protocol, HWMP combines the flexibility of on-demand routing with proactive topology tree extension [1]. The reactive mode defines RM-AODV which is an extension of AODV using ALM. If the proactive mode is selected, a Mesh Portal Point (MPP) is configured as Root and HWMP sets up a tree to this Root. This second mode of operation of HWMP called the Proactive tree building mode can be performed with Proactive PREQ (Proactive Path REQuest) or Proactive RANN (Proactive Root ANNouncement) depending on the configuration of the root [4].

3.1.1 Reactive routing mode in HWMP

RM-AODV is an adaptation of AODV [5]. In RM-AODV, if a source MP needs a route to a destination, it broadcasts a PREQ (Path REQuest) with the destination MP address specified in the destination field and the ALM metric is initialized to 0. When an MP receives a PREQ, it creates a path to the source or updates its current path if the PREQ contains a greater sequence number or the sequence number is the same as the current path and the PREQ offers a better metric than the current path. Whenever an MP forwards a PREQ, the metric field in the PREQ is updated to reflect the cumulative metric of the path to the PREQ's source. After creating or updating a path to the source, the destination MP sends a unicast PREP back to the source. Intermediate MPs create a path to the destination on receiving the PREP and also forward the PREP toward the source. When the source receives the PREP, it creates a path to the destination. If the destination receives further PREQs with a better metric then the destination updates its path to the source to the new path and also sends a PREP to the source along the updated path. A bidirectional, best metric end-to-end path is established between the source and destination. As long as the route remains active, it will continue to be maintained. A route is considered active as long as there are data packets periodically travelling from the source to the destination along that path. Once the source stops sending data packets, the links will time out and eventually be deleted from the intermediate node routing tables. If a link break occurs while the route is active, the node upstream of the break propagates a route error PERR (Path ERRor) message to the source node to inform it of the unreachable destinations. After receiving the PERR, if the source node still desires the route, it can reinitiate route discovery.

3.1.2 Proactive Tree mode

There are two mechanisms for proactively disseminating path selection information for reaching the Root MP : Proactive PREQ Mechanism and Proactive RANN Mechanism.

Proactive PREQ Mechanism

The PREQ tree building process begins with a proactive Path Request message broadcast by the Root MP. The PREQ contains the path metric set to 0 and a sequence number. The proactive PREQ is sent periodically by the Root MP, with increasing sequence numbers.
An MP hearing a proactive PREQ creates or updates its forwarding information to the Root MP, updates the metric and hops count of the PREQ, records the metric and hop count to the Root MP and then transmits the updated PREQ. Each MP may receive multiple copies of a proactive PREQ, each traversing a unique path from the Root MP to the MP. An MP updates its current path to the Root MP if and only if the PREQ contains a greater sequence number or the sequence number is the same as the current path and the PREQ offers a better metric than the current path to the Root MP.

Proactive RANN Mechanism

The Root MP periodically propagates a RANN message into the network. The information contained in the RANN is used to disseminate path metrics to the Root MP. Upon reception of a RANN, each MP that has to create or refresh a path to the Root MP sends a unicast PREQ to the Root MP via the MP from which it received the RANN. The unicast PREQ follows the same processing rules defined in the on demand mode. The Root MP sends PREP in response to each PREQ. The unicast

PREQ creates the reverse path from the Root MP to the originating MP while the PREP creates the forward path from the MP to the Root MP.

3.2 Radio-Aware Optimized Link State Routing Protocol

RA-OLSR protocol is a proactive link-state wireless mesh path selection protocol based on Optimized Link State Routing (OLSR) [6] protocol and the Fisheye State Routing (FSR) [7] protocol and uses a radio aware metric for forwarding path and multipoint relay set calculation.

OLSR is based on MPR flooding technique to reduce the number of transmission as compared to classical flooding mechanism where each node forward all received packets. In OLSR, a node selects a minimal subset of its one hop neighbors set to cover all its two hop neighbors set to act as multipoint relaying nodes. The process is based on information acquired from Hello messages which are containing list of it neighbors' links. When a node sends/forwards a broadcast Topology Control (TC) message, containing the topology information necessary to build the routing tables, only its MPR nodes forward the message reducing duplicate retransmission. In order to reduce the routing overhead (TC message) of OLSR, RA-OLSR adopts FSR technique.

FSR [7] is a proactive routing protocol based on link state routing. In FSR, information about closer nodes is exchanged more frequently than it is done about further nodes. So each node has the most up to date information about all nearby nodes and the accuracy of information decreases as the distance from node increases.

In RA-OLSR, there are different frequencies for propagating the TC message to different scopes so that the fisheye scope technique allows exchanging link state message at different intervals for nodes within different fisheye scope distance, leading to a reduction of the link state message size.

4 Comparison

In this section, we compare mesh typical routing protocols according to different criterias. (Table. 1) resumes the characteristics of each routing protocols. *Route Computation* indicates when the route is computed. There are two cases: reactive and proactive. *Stored Information* denotes the information stored in each node. As for *Update Period*, it is mainly applicable to proactive protocols and assumes values. The *Update information* is the message used to update routing table entry concerning an *Update destination*.

Table 1 Comparison of Typical Routing Protocols

Characteristic	RM-AODV	Proactive PREQ	Proactive RANN	RA-OLSR
Route computation	Reactive	Proactive	Proactive	Proactive
structure	Flat	Tree	Tree	Flat
Stored information	Next hop for destination	Next hop for Root	Next hop for Root	Entire topology
Update period	Even driven	Periodical	Periodical	Periodical
Update information	PERR	PREQ	RANN	Hello and TC
Update destination	Source	Root	Root	All nodes
Method	Unicast	Tree Broadcast	Tree Broadcast	Broadcast
Routing metric	ALM	ALM	ALM	ALM

5 Performance evaluation

The purpose of our simulations is to uncover in which situations the individual protocols have their strengths and weaknesses, rather than to promote one protocol as
generally better than the others. Thus, in order to avoid getting results which favor
either of the protocols, we apply a strategy of specifying a set of parameters (number
of nodes, number of CBR connections etc), from which a large number of scenarios
are randomly generated. These scenarios will be different, yet have the same overall
characteristics.

In our performance evaluation we have implemented a sub layer called IEEE
802.11s between IP and MAC layers. This sub layer contains two modules: Path
selection module and Measurement module. The Path selection module contains
functions for determining routes to transfer packets to their destination using MAC
address as identifier. The Mesh network Measurement module contains functions
for calculating and advertising radio metric used by routing protocols. It uses two
frames: Test Frame and Link State Announcement frame which are mesh management frames. Test Frame has a fixed size and it is transmitted every Test Frame
interval. Each MP computes the number of received Test Frame in a fixed period of
exchange. It calculates the loss probability as the ratio between the number of received Test Frames and the number of sent Test Frames. Link State Announcement
Frame is used to advertise periodically the loss probability to compute Frame Error
Rate e_f in both the forward and reverse directions to account for data as well as
ACK.

In our implementation, we use the novel MAC frame format described by IEEE
802.11s future standard [1]. This MAC frame format is an extension of the existing
data frame format.

5.1 Simulation parameters

We conduct our simulations using the Glomosim simulator [8]. We base all our scenarios on the following basic parameters (Table. 2):

Table 2 Simulation parameters

Simulation time	200s
Network density	1 over 80m^2
Transmission range	200m
Bandwidth	2 Mbit/s
Node placement	Uniform
Traffic type	CBR
Packet size	512 bytes
Packet rate	10 pkts/s
RANN interval	3s
Proactive PREQ interval	3s
Test Frame interval	1s
Test Frame size	8192 bits
Test Frame period of exchange	16s
Link State Announcement Frame	4s

5.2 Simulation results

Simulations have been conducted with varying number of nodes and varying number of CBR connections to examine the protocols in different scenarios. Comparisons have been done on the following performance metrics: Packet delivery ratio, End to end delay and Routing overhead.

- **Packet delivery ratio**: the ratio between the number of packets delivered to the receiver and the number of packets sent by the source.
- **End to end packet delay**: the mean time in second taken by data packets to reach their respective destinations.
- **Routing overhead**: the number of routing bytes required by the routing protocol to construct and maintain its routes.

We have defined two scenarios. In the first scenario, the traffic is distributed over the network. Source and destination of any CBR connections are distributed among all nodes and are chosen randomly. In the second scenario, all the CBR connections are intended to Root.

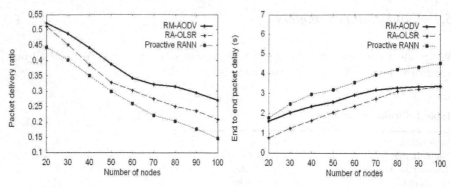

Fig. 2 Packet delivery ratio as a function of number of nodes

Fig. 3 End to end packet delay as a function of number of nodes

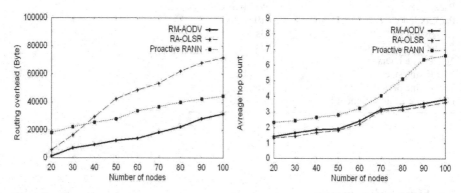

Fig. 4 Routing overhead as a function of number of nodes

Fig. 5 Number of hops in the path as a function of number of nodes

5.2.1 Distributed traffic

In figures 2, 3 and 4, we report the performance in term of packet delivery ratio, end to end packet delay and routing overhead as a function of the number of nodes over RM-AODV, RA-OLSR, and Proactive RANN for 20 CBR connections. We noted that, as the number of nodes increases, the packet delivery ratio decreases while the end to end packet delay increases for all routing protocols. Indeed, as the routing overhead increases, so does the interference and contention.

Fig. 2 presents the packet delivery ratio against the number of nodes. RM-AODV outperforms RA-OLSR because it introduces less routing overhead. In RM-AODV, as the network is without mobility, traffic control is sent only at the beginning of any CBR connection. However, in RA-OLSR, traffic control is sent periodically and it increases as the network dimensions. Moreover, due to the use of the ALM metric instead of the number of hops, we noted that the average routes length for CBR connections established by RA-OLSR and RM-AODV are approximately equal (Fig. 5).

In figure 3, we observe that RA-OLSR consistently presents the lowest delay for

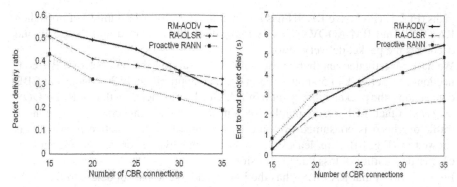

Fig. 6 Packet delivery ratio as a function of number of CBR connections

Fig. 7 End to end packet delay as a function of number of CBR connections

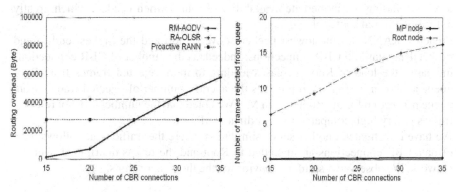

Fig. 8 Routing overhead as a function of number of CBR connections

Fig. 9 Number of frame rejected from queue as a function of number of nodes

successful packets, regardless of number of nodes. This may be explained by the fact that RA-OLSR is a proactive protocol: when a packet arrives at a node, it can immediately be forwarded or dropped. In reactive protocols, if there is no route to a destination, packets to that destination will be stored in a buffer while a route discovery is conducted. This may cause longer delays. The difference between RA-OLSR and RM-AODV decreases regardless the number of nodes. From a certain threshold (80 nodes) both curves get closer. Indeed, in figure 4, we clearly see an important difference in the routing overhead generated by RA-OLSR and RM-AODV. For number of nodes below 40, the control traffic overhead of RA-OLSR is composed of Hello messages only and it gets closer to the routing overhead of RM-AODV. However, as the number of node increases, the broadcast of TC messages introduces a large control traffic overhead.

The Proactive RANN protocol has the worst performance regardless the number of nodes. In fact, all the CBR connections pass through the Root. Besides, Root sends and receives all control traffic. This node becomes overloaded and it rejects incoming packets. Moreover, Proactive RANN has the longest number of hops for CBR paths (Fig. 5) (Proactive RANN has approximately the double number of hops then RA-OLSR and RM-AODV). This increases both the overhead and the delay and decreases the packet delivery ratio.

We have investigated another set of simulations varying the number of CBR connections in a network of 50 nodes. For more than approximately 30 concurrent CBR connections, the packet delivery ratio of RA-OLSR is higher than that of RM-AODV (Fig. 7). In fact, with a large number of concurrent CBR connections, extra control traffic overhead is consumed by route establishment in the reactive protocols (as showed in (Fig. 8)). This leaves less available bandwidth for data traffic and increases probability of loss due to collisions.

Figure 7 shows that RA-OLSR has the lowest end to end packet delay. In fact, RA-OLSR is an optimization over a classical link-state routing protocol, tailored for WLAN mesh networks, as such, it inherits all the benefits of link-state routing protocols, including the immediate availability of routes when needed, which greatly reduces the initial route setup delay.

Proactive RANN has the lowest packet delivery ratio and the highest end to end packet delay until 25 CBR connections. Indeed, as the number of CBR connections increases, the load of Root increases leading to more rejected frames from Root queue as shown in (Fig. 9). It presents the average number of rejected frames from queue per second for the Root and an MP. We noted that the number of Root rejected frames is very high compared to an ordinary MP.

We have investigated another set of simulation where the traffic is as follows: half of data CBR connections are intended to Root and the rest is distributed over the network. We observed a similar behavior for the three algorithms.

5.2.2 Traffic intended to Root

The main purpose of mesh networks is to allow Internet access. By this way, most of traffic is from MP to Root. Therefore, we have defined another scenario where the most of CBR connections are sent to Root. In this scenario, performance of Proactive PREQ protocol is evaluated in addition to RA-OLSR, RM-AODV and Proactive RANN as a function of number of nodes and number of CBR connections. Indeed, Proactive PREQ provides only routes to Root.

Figures 10 and 11 depict the packet delivery ratio and the end to end packet delay respectively regardless the number of nodes. They show that all mode of HWMP outperforms RA-OLSR. Indeed, in RM-AODV, as all CBR connections are intended to Root, the probability to find an existing path established to the root increases leading to less delay and overhead and more delivered packet. As regards Proactive PREQ protocol, it introduces the least routing overhead. In fact, the intention of the Proactive PREQ mode is a "lightweight" HWMP topology formation where the routing overhead for the proactive extension is kept at a minimum. The broadcast PREQ messages set up a tree that contains paths from all mesh points to the Root, but mesh points are not registered proactively at the Root. Besides, we can see in (Fig. 11)that Proactive PREQ introduces less delay than RM-AODV due its

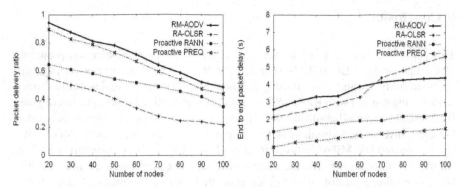

Fig. 10 Packet delivery ratio as a function of number of nodes

Fig. 11 End to end packet delay as a function of number of nodes

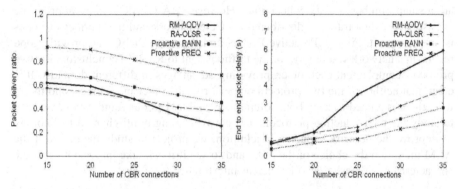

Fig. 12 Packet delivery ratio as a function of number of CBR connections

Fig. 13 End to end packet delay as a function of number of CBR connections

proactive nature. Moreover, Proactive RANN has less delay then RA-OLSR for two reasons . First, Proactive RANN has less routing overhead. Second, in RA-OLSR, MPR are selected by an MP following some conditions. The first condition imposes that all strict two hops neighbors should be reached. The last condition requires that path metric (ALM) toward a strict two hops neighbors may be optimal. The conclusion from this is that, routes selected by RA-OLSR can not be optimal in term of end to end delay.

Figures 12 and 13 present the evaluation of path selection protocols by varying number of CBR connections intended to Root. We observe that the two proactive modes of HWMP have consistently better performance in term of packet delivery ratio and end to end packet delay. Indeed, Proactive PREQ and Proactive RANN are proactive path selection protocols, so routes are immediately available in routing table. In addition, they have less routing overhead then RA-OLSR and RM-AODV.

6 Conclusion

This paper presented a detailed overview of the proposed path selection protocols of the upcoming IEEE 802.11s standard for WLAN mesh networks. In fact, the configurability of the default routing protocol HWMP and the extensibility framework for the routing with RA-OLSR as optional standardized routing protocol gives IEEE 802.11s a broad applicability to many usage scenarios of wireless networks. We have investigated simulations to compare these path selection protocols. We have compared HWMP with its different modes to RA-OLSR. Our experiments and simulations have shown that the choice of a path selection protocol among IEEE 802.11s routing protocols is a difficult task, thus there is no protocol suitable for all cases. Indeed, each protocol improves good performance in certain conditions of network and traffic. For example, RM-AODV is more suitable in case where there are a small number of data connections. However, RA-OLSR is more appropriate in case where data traffic is distributed over the network and the number of nodes is not important. Finally, Proactive RANN and Proactive PREQ can provide good results in a network where most of the traffic is sent to Root. In conclusion, the two protocols complement each other, providing advantages in different domains. It is clear, that neither of the two protocol outperforms the other in all cases, and therefore, there is a need to keep both solutions available. For our future work, we plan to study the path selection protocols in a network using multi-channel technology to improve the network capacity. In addition, we project to study the effect of the ALM metric on the choice of the route and to see if it can take into account all the characteristics of mesh networks such as interference.

References

1. IEEE P802.11s/D1.08, Draft Amendment to Standard for Information Technology, January 2008.
2. Akyildiz, Wang. X and Wang. W: Wireless mesh networks: a survey, *Computer Networks - Elsevier Science*, January. 2005.
3. Aoki, Takeda, Yagyu, and Yamada: IEEE 802.11s Wireless LAN Mesh Network Technology, *NTT DoCoMo Tech J journal*, 2006 .
4. Bahr: Proposed routing for IEEE 802.11s WLAN mesh networks.(2006). In Proceedings of ACM International Conference, 2006.
5. Perkins, Belding-Royer and Das: Ad hoc on-demand distance vector (AODV) routing.(2003). In: IETF RFC 3561, July 2003.
6. Clausen, Jacquet and Laouiti: Optimized Link State Routing Protocol.(2003). In: IETF Internet RFC 3626, 2003.
7. Pei, Gerla, and Chen: Fisheye State Routing in Mobile Ad Hoc Networks.(2000). In Internet-Draft, November 2000.
8. Zeng, Bagrodia and Gerla: GloMoSim: a Library for the Parallel Simulation of Large-scale Wireless Networks (1998). In Proceedings of PADS, 1998.

ETM – An Optimized Routing Protocol for Mobile SSM Sources

Thomas C. Schmidt, Matthias Wahlisch and Maik Wodarz

Thomas C. Schmidt, Maik Wodarz
HAW Hamburg, Dept. Informatik, Berliner Tor 7, 20099 Hamburg, Germany e-mail: t.schmidt@ieee.org, Maik.Wodarz@informatik.haw-hamburg.de

Matthias Wählisch
link-lab, Hönower Str. 35, 10318 Berlin, Germany e-mail: waehlisch@ieee.org
He is also with HAW Hamburg, Dept. Informatik

Abstract Mobility is considered a key technology of the next generation Internet and has been standardized within the IETF. Rapidly emerging multimedia group applications such as IPTV, MMORPGs and video conferencing increase the demand for mobile group communication, but a standard design of mobile multicast is still awaited. The traditional Internet approach of Any Source Multicast (ASM) routing remains hesitant to spread beyond walled gardens, while the simpler and more selective Source Specific Multicast (SSM) is expected to globally disseminate to many users and services. However, mobility support for Source Specific Multicast is still known to be a major open problem. In this paper we introduce the Enhanced Tree Morphing (ETM), an optimized multicast routing protocol for transforming (morphing) source specific distribution trees into optimal trees rooted at a relocated source. Following up on previous results for the initial Tree Morphing, we present enhancements that lead to a simpler protocol with significantly optimized performance values in both, forwarding performance and protocol robustness. Extensive evaluations based on real-world topology data are part of this work.

1 Introduction

Mobile communication today follows the trend to converge with networked applications to a common IP-centric world. Throughout this process, Internet services are expected to extend to mobility management in the near future. The virginal availability of a new, truly mobile IP enabled network layer [9] offers connectivity to nomadic users at roaming devices, while preserving communication sessions beyond IP subnet changes. Voice and video (group) conferencing, as well as large scale content distribution (e.g., IPTV) and massive multiplayer games (MMORPGs) are considered the key applications for the next generation ubiquitous Internet. Inexpensive, point-to-multipoint enabled technologies such as IEEE 802.16 or DVB-H/ IPDC emerge on the subnetwork layer and facilitate large-scale group communi-

Please use the following format when citing this chapter:

Schmidt, T.C., Wahlisch, M. and Wodarz, M., 2008, in IFIP International Federation for Information Processing, Volume 284; *Wireless and Mobile Networking*; Zoubir Mammeri; (Boston: Springer), pp. 29–40.

cation deployment. But unlike point-to-point mobility and despite of ten research years, mobile multicast protocol development is still in a premature state [17].

This paper addresses the issue of mobile Source Specific Multicast routing on the network layer in presenting the Enhanced Tree Morphing protocol (ETM). Source Specific Multicast (SSM) [7], just released as an initial standard, is considered a deployment-friendly variant of group distribution techniques. In contrast to Any Source Multicast (ASM) [3], optimal (S,G) multicast source trees are constructed immediately from (S,G) subscriptions at the client side, without utilizing network flooding or rendezvous points. Source addresses are to be acquired out of band, which a SIP [13] session initiation in conferencing scenarios may facilitate [16].

Conferencing parties request seamless real-time performance of a mobility aware group communication service, thereby attaining the simultaneous roles of mobile multicast listener and source. We discuss session mobility in the context of real-time multicast communication and present an optimized protocol, which adapts to sender mobility with minimal impact on service quality. The Tree Morphing protocol (TM) [14, 15], one of the few approaches to SSM source mobility management, was designed to enable immediate, unencapsulated multicast data transmission subsequent to Mobile IPv6 handovers. Nevertheless, a previously undertaken extensive analysis of the early scheme revealed shortcomings and opportunities for improvement.

As will be shown in the remaining paper, ETM overcomes all issues of the TM and adheres to real-time compliant performance in various, realistic routing topologies. The simplified scheme can be implemented with little overhead, and by applying minimal modifications to current standard protocols for unicast mobility management. In this paper we first discuss the mobile multimedia group conferencing problem and related work. In section 3 we present the core protocol. A thorough evaluation follows in section 4. Finally, section 5 is dedicated to a conclusion and an outlook.

2 The Mobile Source Specific Multicast Problem and Related Work

2.1 Problem Statement

A mobile multicast sender will face the problem of enabling a continuous forwarding of data to its group of receivers, while it undergoes roaming and network layer handovers. Its mobility protocol should facilitate a seamless transmission service and at the same time preserve transparency with respect to network and address changes at the receiver side. Multicast listener applications are frequently source address aware. A mobile multicast source consequently must meet address transparency at two layers: To comply with RPF checks, it has to use an address within the IPv6 basic header's source field, which is in topological concordance with the employed multicast distribution tree. For application transparency, the logical node identifier, commonly the Home Address, must be presented as the packet source address to the transport layer at the receivers.

At the complementary side, network routing must comply with the sender movement without having network functionality compromised. It should realize native forwarding whenever possible to preserve its resources, but needs to ensure routing convergence even under a rapid movement of the sender. Mobility support for multicast sources at the network layer thus poses a significant challenge to the infrastructure. An SSM node submitting data to a group of receivers defines the root of a source specific shortest path tree (SPT), distributing data towards its receivers. Native forwarding along source specific delivery trees will be bound to the source's topological network address due to reverse path forwarding (RPF) checks. A mobile multicast source moving to a new subnetwork is only able to either inject data into a previously established delivery tree, which may be a rendezvous point based shared tree, or to (re-)initiate the construction of a multicast distribution tree compliant to its new location. In the latter case, the mobile sender will have to precede without controlling the new tree development, as it operates decoupled from its receivers.

2.2 Related Work

Three principal approaches to SSM source mobility are presently around.

Statically Rooted Distribution Trees

The MIPv6 standard proposes bi-directional tunneling through the home agent as a minimal multicast support for mobile senders and listeners as introduced by [21]. In this approach, the mobile multicast source (MS) always uses its Home Address (HoA) for multicast operations. Static home agents hide mobility completely from multicast routing at the price of triangular paths and extensive encapsulation.

Following a shared tree approach, [12] propose to employ Rendezvous Points of PIM-SM [4] as mobility anchors. Mobile senders tunnel their data to these "Mobility-aware Rendezvous Points" (MRPs), whence in restriction to a single domain this scheme is equivalent to the bi-directional tunneling. Focusing on interdomain mobile multicast, the authors design a tunnel– or SSM–based backbone distribution of packets between MRPs.

Reconstruction of Distribution Trees

Several authors propose to construct a completely new distribution tree after the movement of a mobile source. These schemes have to rely on client notification for initiating new router state establishment. At the same time they need to preserve address transparency to the client. To account for the latter, Thaler [18] proposes to employ binding caches and to obtain source address transparency analogous to MIPv6 unicast communication. Initial session announcements and changes of source addresses are to be distributed periodically to clients via an additional multicast control tree based at the home agent. Source–tree handovers are then activated on listener requests. Jelger and Noel [8] suggest handover improvements by employing anchor points within the source network, supporting a continuous data reception during client–initiated handovers.

Tree Modification Schemes

Very little attention has been given to procedures, which modify existing distribution trees to continuously serve for data transmission of mobile sources. In the ASM case of DVMRP routing, [2] propose an algorithm to extend the root of a given delivery tree to incorporate a new source location. O'Neill [10] suggests a scheme to overcome RPF–check failures originating from multicast source address changes, by introducing an extended routing information, which accompanies data in a Hop-by-Hop option header.

A routing protocol adaptive to SSM source mobility, the Tree Morphing, has been introduced by the authors in [14]. A mobile multicast source (MS) away from home will transmit unencapsulated data to a group, using its current CoA on the Internet layer, but HoA on the application layer, which is carried in extension headers like in MIPv6. In extension to unicast routing, though, the entire Internet layer, i.e. routers included, will be aware of the permanent HoA. Maintaining binding-cache-like address pairs in router states will enable all routers to simultaneously identify (HoA, G)–based group membership and (CoA, G)–based tree topology. When moving to a new point of attachment, the MS will alter its address from previous CoA (pCoA) to new CoA (nCoA) and eventually change from its previous Designated multicast Router (pDR) to a next Designated Router (nDR). Subsequent to handover it will immediately continue to deliver data along an extension of its previous source tree using source routing from nDR to pDR. All routers along this path will learn the new CoA of MS and implement appropriate forwarding states.

Routers on this extended tree use RPF checks to discover potential short cuts. In the absence of short cuts, routers re-use those parts of the previous delivery tree, which coincide with the new shortest path tree. Only branches of the new shortest path tree, which have not previously been established, need to be constructed. In this way, the previous shortest path tree will be morphed into a next shortest path tree.

2.3 Discussion

Bi-directional tunneling is considered only a minimal solution, operational without explicit multicast mobility support. It introduces considerable overheads from triangular routing and wide spanned encapsulation. Handover assistance via mobility-aware rendezvous points relies on triangular routing and tunneling, as well, and in addition re-introduces RPs, which are not native to SSM routing.

Receiver oriented tree reconstructions in SSM suffer from the problem of receivers being unsynchronized to source handovers. The adoption of a persistent control tree will resolve this issue, but introduces the overhead of an additional multicast tree spanning all receivers. In addition, handover messages distributed via a control tree will require a roundtrip signaling between source and receivers and consequently may be slow in widespread topologies. The MSSMSv6 approach [8] will expedite the handover process, but fails to solve client synchronization. The authors henceforth are leaving the source in case of its rapid movement with an unlimited number of 'historic' delivery trees to be fed simultaneously.

Adaptive tree approaches offer a solution space that addresses both, seamless handovers and sustained receiver contact. In addition, they can take advantage of limited mobility-related changes in the shapes of multicast distribution trees that can be observed [20]. The Tree Morphing protocol complies well with these advantages, but suffers from two significant drawbacks. At first, it relies on an initial source routing of packets, which appears elegant from the perspective of protocol design, but faces severe deployment objections from the perspective of operators. Source routing is considered a general security threat and frequently defeated. At second, extensive simulation studies revealed not only an undesirable delay stretch in initial packet delivery, but a realistic likelihood that the router convergence process will cause packet loss for those packets, initially routed via the previous designated router. For these reasons, we will present an enhanced version of the protocol in the following section that operates without source routing, omits packet loss and attains expedited forwarding and protocol convergence.

3 The Enhanced Tree Morphing Protocol

3.1 Overview

A mobile multicast source (MS) away from home will transmit *unencapsulated* data to a group using its current CoA on the Internet layer, but its HoA on the application layer, which is carried in mobility extension headers defined in MIPv6. In extension to unicast routing, though, the multicast routing layer will be aware of the permanent HoA by maintaining (CoA, HoA, G) address triples in router states.

When moving to a new point of attachment, the MS will alter its address from previous CoA (pCoA) to new CoA (nCoA) and eventually change from its previous Designated multicast Router (pDR) to a next Designated Router (nDR). Subsequent to handover, it will immediately initiate forwarding states on the route from nDR to pDR by submitting a *regular unicast* state update packet (cf. section 3.2) to pDR. As a result, the previous delivery tree will be elongated by $(nCoA, HoA, G)$ states as shown in figure 1(a). MS then continues to deliver data along this extended previous source tree. Delivery is done by including state update message headers in the first data packet(s). All routers along the previous delivery tree will thereby learn MS's new CoA and add appropriate forwarding states.

Routers participating in the ETM protocol will provide two additional functions: The STATE INJECTION ALGORITHM and the EXTENDED FORWARDING ALGORITHM as shown below. State injection is triggered by the state update messages carried in a Hop-by-Hop option header. On each hop the new $(nCoA, HoA, G)$ state is implemented on the forwarding interfaces of the previous $(pCoA, HoA, G)$–state

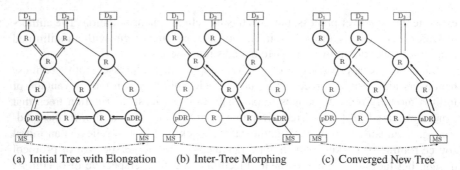

(a) Initial Tree with Elongation   (b) Inter-Tree Morphing   (c) Converged New Tree

Fig. 1 Tree Morphing States Neighboring to the Source with Receiver Domains D_i

tree. Previous states are kept only if the update packet was received on a topological incorrect interface. In detail this algorithm runs as follows:

STATE INJECTION ALGORITHM
    ▷ Upon receiving an $(nCoA, HoA, G)$
    ▷ state update for multicast group G
1   **for** all $(\cdot, HoA, G)$ Forwarding Interfaces
2   **do if** (RPF-CHECK$(nCoA)$ = TRUE)
3   **then** REPLACE all $(\cdot, HoA, G)$-*states*
               by $(nCoA, HoA, G)$
4   **else** ADD $(nCoA, HoA, G)$-*state*
5   INIT TREE_OPTIMIZATION

After the update has been processed, the packet is passed on according to the EXTENDED FORWARDING ALGORITHM explained below. At this stage, the delivery tree does not need to be optimal and packets may fail at standard RPF check. To prevent discarding, incoming packets need to be accepted from any interface, which is a topological member of the current or a previous distribution tree of $(\cdot, HoA, G)$ state.[1] Therefore an extended forwarding, which accounts for all source address states $(\cdot, HoA, G)$, has to be applied until local tree optimization has completed. Packets thereby will be forwarded along an (CoA, HoA, G) tree, provided they arrived at the topologically correct interface for this CoA.

Any router will observe suboptimal routes from packets arriving at a topological incorrect interface (w.r.t. the packet source address). As part of the algorithm it will then dynamically attempt to join to an optimal shortest path tree. When receiving a multicast packet for group $(\cdot, HoA, G)$ with source address $nCoA$ at the wrong interface, a router will immediately submit a join to $(nCoA, G)$. The underlying SSM routing protocol will initiate the construction of a shortest path source specific branch. The router will learn about its completion by $(nCoA, HoA, G)$ traffic arriving

---

[1] Further on we will denote "some state with group address G and home address HoA" by $(\cdot, HoA, G)$, whereas $(*, HoA, G)$ stands for all such states.

at the correct interface and will then prune $(*, HoA, G)$ on all incoming interfaces corresponding to previous CoA addresses. Fig. 1(b) visualizes such an intermediate morphing state.

A tree will be locally optimal, as soon as packets arrive at the topological correct interface. The details of this extended forwarding algorithm read:

EXTENDED FORWARDING ALGORITHM

    ▷ Upon arrival of packet with source address nCoA and
    ▷ in the presence of multiple $(*CoA, HoA, G)$-states

1 **for** each $(\cdot CoA, HoA, G)$ Forwarding Interfaces
2   **do if** (RPF-CHECK($nCoA$) = TRUE)
3   **then** FORWARD_PACKET_ON_INTERFACE
4   REMOVE $(*, HoA, G)$-states
              except $(nCoA, HoA, G)$
5   **else if** (RPF-CHECK($\cdot CoA$) = TRUE)
6   **then** FORWARD_PACKET_ON_INTERFACE
7   **else** DISCARD_PACKET

In applying this forwarding algorithm, the delivery tree thus will not only transport intermediate detouring packets, but will continuously degenerate branches dispensable due to optimization incidences. As soon as $(*, HoA, G)$ forwarding states have reduced to a single $(\cdot, HoA, G)$ entry, the router operations continue as defined by its standard multicast routing protocol without mobility extension.

Finally, state update packets will arrive at the receivers of the $(\cdot, HoA, G)$ SSM group. The mobile IPv6 stack will interpret the binding update and alter its multicast binding cache entry. Thereafter the standard destination option header is processed and data is transparently passed as (HoA, G) to the transport layer.

3.2 Packet Design

The networking layer requires information of state changes, whenever a multicast source address changes after a Mobile IPv6 handover. This signaling is implemented on the network layer by inserting additional headers into the data packets and bears the common risks of a global redirect. The required information, group address, home address and care-of address, as well as proof of authentication can already be extracted of Binding Update messages sent by mobiles to correspondent end nodes subsequent to every unicast handover. The State Update Message needed for multicast can therefore be composed of several Mobile IPv6 headers and there is no need to define a new protocol from scratch. ETM messages can thus be processed transparently with regular, CGA authenticated [1] Binding Updates. Nevertheless they need to be interpreted by routers along the packet's path, which is achieved by a Router Alert Option inserted in a Hop-by-Hop Option Header [11]. This option is used to instruct routers to further inspect packet headers.

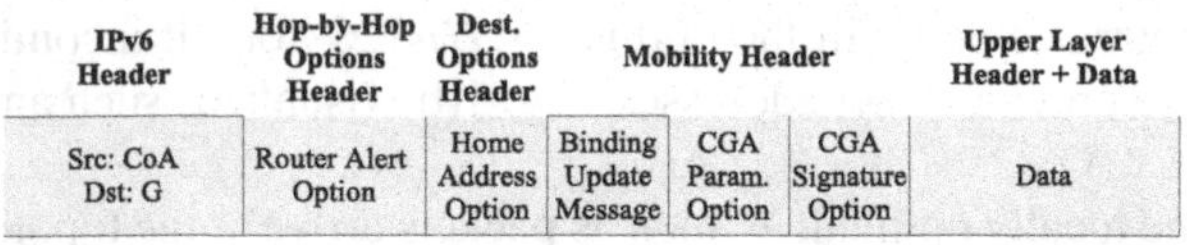

IPv6 Header	Hop-by-Hop Options Header	Dest. Options Header	Mobility Header				Upper Layer Header + Data
Src: CoA Dst: G	Router Alert Option	Home Address Option	Binding Update Message	CGA Param. Option	CGA Signature Option		Data

Fig. 2 ETM IPv6 Header Sequence for Authenticated State Updates of Mobile Multicast Sources

The complete signaling is built by chaining the IPv6 extension headers as to be sent in the initial unicast state update message as well as for piggy-backing with the first data packet(s). Figure 2 shows the combined packet format used after source handover. This mechanism generalizes to an integrated, secure update protocol for mobile multicast sources named 'AuthoCast' in forthcoming work.

3.3 ETM Finite State Machine

The finite state machine of the ETM protocol is derived of the PIM-SSM [4] state machine. The states No Info (NI), Join (J) and Prune Pending (PP) interact as in standard PIM-SSM. The Join state is augmented by an ETM state, which represents the ETM router conditions during mobility management and prior to protocol convergence. Its characteristic lies in a state splitting initiated from state update messages, which in the event of rapid movement may be received multiple times prior to convergence. This is realized via a state counter and allows for a joined treatment of the correlated $(\cdot, HoA, G)$ stated within routers. The FSM has been used to verify the protocol formally.

4 Protocol Evaluation

To evaluate the protocol behavior, we implemented the corresponding functions of routers, sources and receivers within the network simulator platform OMNeT++ 3.3 [19] on top of the IPv6Suite, which is based on the INET framework and already realizes MIPv6 protocol operations. We performed a stochastic discrete event simulation, firstly choosing artificial topologies, which explore the attainable relative network geometry, and several real–world measurements. In detail, the simulation proceeds as follows: The mobile source continuously submits (numbered and time-stamped) packets at a constant bit rate of $15ms$, while performing a handover from one WLAN access point to another. Access points are directly connected to the designated routers. Link delays in our setting have been homogenously chosen to be $10\ ms$.

Our analysis covers packet delay, loss and convergence times. Measurements have been performed with the help of a monitoring function at routers and receivers, which accounts for the maximal delay stretch, i.e., the ratio taken of the slowest packet, delivered during handoff, over the optimal time, a surveillance of packet delivery at the receivers, and a state observation for protocol convergence. It should be noted that there are two relevant convergence times. Prior to a full protocol convergence, i.e., a leave of the ETM state in all routers, packets may be already delivered on optimal paths. This convergence to optimal forwarding has been monitored separately at the receivers.

4.1 Analyzing the Network Topology Space

For a systematic approach to routing analysis, we first proceed in artificially exploring the topology space, i.e., the relative positions of the relevant network entities. The latter are given by the designated routers and the first intersection point (X) of previous and new multicast tree. The degrees of freedom, which only depend on distance ratios, are covered by the two networks displayed in figure 3.

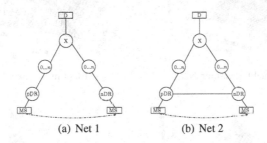

(a) Net 1   (b) Net 2

Fig. 3 Test Networks Covering the Relative Routing Topology

The simulation results for the two test networks as functions of intermediate router hops *DR-to-X chosen between 0 and 30 are given in figure 4. As a striking outcome, test net 1 always delivers optimal forwarding without additional delays. This is due to the immediate discovery of the intersection router X by the EX-TENDED FORWARDING ALGORITHM, which leads to packet delivery on the shortest path directly following a handover. Test net 2 admits similar performance values, but requires a re-routing, whenever the path lengths pDR-X equals nDR-X. This is reflected by a non-normal delay stretch and non-zero convergence time to optimal forwarding along a diagonal of the graph. Note that the characteristic of the delay stretch derives from the changing optimal forwarding times, while the absolute delay excess stems from one additional hop, i.e., nDR-X. In contrast, routing convergence to final states is non-negligible in most cases. Routers along the path from nDR to pDR will change into TM state, the routers on the previous tree, i.e., along X-pDR, will remain therein until a regular PIM prune is received. For test net 2 forwarding states will be simply overwritten, when the distribution tree remains unaltered, i.e., $dist(nDR,X) \neq dist(pDR,X)$. A PIM prune towards pDR is

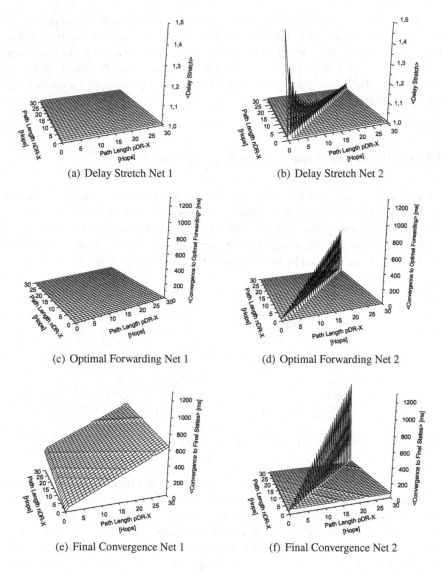

(a) Delay Stretch Net 1

(b) Delay Stretch Net 2

(c) Optimal Forwarding Net 1

(d) Optimal Forwarding Net 2

(e) Final Convergence Net 1

(f) Final Convergence Net 2

Fig. 4 Performance Results for the Test Networks

required for $dist(nDR,X) < dist(pDR,X)$, while for $dist(nDR,X) = dist(pDR,X)$ the tree changes with the result of join and prune operations along the entire paths. No packet loss occurs in any case, why corresponding graphs are omitted.

4.2 Simulations Based on Real-World Topologies

To approximate realistic scenarios, further protocol evaluation has been performed on the basis of real-world topologies. Network data must be considered critical, as key characteristics of multicast routing are dominated by the topology in large networks. We chose the ATT core network [6] as a large (154 core nodes), densely meshed single provider example. For multiple provider Internet data we extracted a sub-samples of 154 and 1.540 core nodes from the "SCAN + Lucent" map [5] project, further on denoted as "Internet" topology.

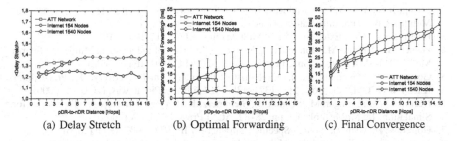

(a) Delay Stretch   (b) Optimal Forwarding   (c) Final Convergence

Fig. 5 Performance Results for Real-World Topologies (Error Bars show Standard Deviation)

Mean performance results are shown in figure 5 as functions of pDR-nDR distance.[2] Packet loss, which is only possible, when initial routing is guided along uneven triangles, did occur at only a couple events. Losses remain invisible in distributions, why the corresponding graphs are again not shown. The initial delay stretches for the topologies vary at an excess rate of about 20 to 35 %, almost independent of access router distance. The convergence times to optimal forwarding remain bound by about 20 ms. At our probe packet rate, the second datagram thus travels an optimal path. Final convergence times clearly represent routing complexity as a function of mobility 'step size' and of topological diversity at comparably low values. Combinedly, the results indicate that the extremal values obtained for the artificial topologies equal out nicely when mixing in realistic topological settings.

5 Conclusions and Outlook

In this article the Enhanced Tree Morphing protocol was introduced and extensively evaluated. ETM is an optimized improvement of the previously developed Tree Morphing. ETM abandons the source routing of packets used in TM and separates control packets from the data in its initial tree elongation phase. These op-

---

[2] The access router distance, the mobility 'step size' in a figurative sense, can be regarded as a measure of complexity inherent to the problem [15]. Values range up to 15 in the Internet topology samples, while the maximum router distance within the ATT network is 5.

timizations significantly advanced the protocol performance, as could be derived from a systematic protocol evaluation. In future work we will focus on analyzing the protocol robustness against network disruptions from strong bursts and packet overflow, as well as on the case of rapid movement of the mobile source. AuthoCast, an integrated secure state update protocol for mobile multicast will be forthcoming.

References

1. Arkko, J., et al.: Enhanced Route Optimization for Mobile IPv6. RFC 4866, IETF (2007)
2. Chang, R.S., Yen, Y.S.: A Multicast Routing Protocol with Dynamic Tree Adjustment for Mobile IPv6. Journ. Information Science and Engineering **20**, 1109–1124 (2004)
3. Deering, S.E.: Host Extensions for IP Multicasting. RFC 1112, IETF (1989)
4. Fenner, B., Handley, M., Holbrook, H., Kouvelas, I.: Protocol Independent Multicast - Sparse Mode (PIM-SM): Protocol Specification (Revised). RFC 4601, IETF (2006)
5. Govindan, R., Tangmunarunkit, H.: Heuristics for internet map discovery. In: Proceedings IEEE INFOCOM 2000, vol. 3, pp. 1371–1380. IEEE Press, Piscataway, NJ, USA (2000).
6. Heckmann, O., Piringer, M., Schmitt, J., Steinmetz, R.: On Realistic Network Topologies for Simulation. In: MoMeTools '03, pp. 28–32. ACM Press, NY, USA (2003)
7. Holbrook, H., Cain, B.: Source-Specific Multicast for IP. RFC 4607, IETF (2006)
8. Jelger, C., Noel, T.: Supporting Mobile SSM sources for IPv6 (MSSMSv6). Internet Draft – work in progress (expired) 00, individual (2002)
9. Johnson, D.B., Perkins, C., Arkko, J.: Mobility Support in IPv6. RFC 3775, IETF (2004)
10. O'Neill, A.: Mobility Management and IP Multicast. Internet Draft – work in progress (expired) 01, IETF (2002)
11. Partridge, C., Jackson, A.: IPv6 Router Alert Option. RFC 2711, IETF (1999)
12. Romdhani, I., Bettahar, H., Bouabdallah, A.: Transparent handover for mobile multicast sources. In: P. Lorenz, P. Dini (eds.) Proceedings of the IEEE ICN'06. IEEE Press (2006)
13. Rosenberg, J., Schulzrinne, H., Camarillo, G., Johnston, A., Peterson, J., Sparks, R., Handley, M., Schooler, E.: SIP: Session Initiation Protocol. RFC 3261, IETF (2002)
14. Schmidt, T.C., Wählisch, M.: Extending SSM to MIPv6 — Problems, Solutions and Improvements. Computational Methods in Science and Technology **11**(2), 147–152 (2005).
15. Schmidt, T.C., Wählisch, M.: Morphing Distribution Trees – On the Evolution of Multicast States under Mobility and an Adaptive Routing Scheme for Mobile SSM Sources. Telecommunication Systems **33**(1–3), 131–154 (2006).
16. Schmidt, T.C., Wählisch, M.: Group Conference Management with SIP. In: S. Ahson, M. Ilyas (eds.) SIP Handbook: Services, Technologies, and Security. CRC Press (2008).
17. Schmidt, T.C., Wählisch, M.: Multicast Mobility in MIPv6: Problem Statement and Brief Survey. IRTF Internet Draft – work in progress 03, MobOpts (2008).
18. Thaler, D.: Supporting Mobile SSM Sources for IPv6. Proceedings of ietf meeting (2001).
19. Varga, A.: The OMNeT++ discrete event simulation system. http://www.omnetpp.org (2007)
20. Wählisch, M., Schmidt, T.C.: Exploring the Routing Complexity of Mobile Multicast - A Semi-empirical Study. In: CoNEXT '07 Proceedings. ACM, NY (2007).
21. Xylomenos, G., Polyzos, G.C.: IP Multicast for Mobile Hosts. IEEE Comm. Mag. **35**(1), 54–58 (1997)

A Synchronous Tiered Based Clustering Algorithm for large-scale Ad hoc Networks

Imen Jemili[1,2], Abdelfatteh Belghith[1], and Mohamed Mosbah[2]

HANA Lab.
N. School of Computer Sciences, Tunisia, e-mail: imen.jemili@cristal.rnu.tn,abdelfattah.
belghith@ensi.rnu.tn

LaBRI
University of Bordeaux I, Talence, France e-mail: {jemili,mosbah}@labri.fr

Abstract Relaying on a virtual backbone formed by the induced hierarchy of a connected dominating set is a widespread solution in ad hoc networks. However, the majority of existing approaches require gathering neighborhood information without considering the loss of information due to collision and the effect of wireless interference and its impact on the accuracy of information used during clustering process. In this paper, we present an improved version of our clustering algorithm, TBCA, operating in layered manner and exploiting the eventual collision to accelerate the clustering process. We prove through simulations that our mechanism outperforms other ones, in terms of effectiveness throughput and per-packet sojourn delay. Conducted simulations show also that it copes better with mobility.

1 Introduction

Clustering is considered as a promising approach to face one of the most critical problems confronting the ad hoc networks: the scalability. Indeed, the dynamic topology, limited mobile node capability and limited link bandwidth pose a challenge for the scalability of these networks.

The clustering process aims to build a hierarchy among the nodes, by organizing nodes into smaller groups called clusters simpler to manage. A virtual backbone can be formed by clusterheads and sometimes gateway nodes in a connected dominating set. A node set is a dominating set (DS) if every node in the network is either in the set or a neighbor of a node in the set. The DS is called a connected dominating set (CDS) if any two nodes in a DS can be connected through intermediate nodes from the DS. The virtual backbone formed by the induced hierarchy of a CDS plays a very important role in routing, broadcasting and connectivity management in wireless ad hoc networks [1, 2]. Many CDS formation algorithms exist in the literature. However, constructing a virtual backbone comes at a cost in terms of the time it takes for CDS building and also the overheads incurred in the additional network traffic generated. In fact, most of the proposed approaches require the knowledge of

Please use the following format when citing this chapter:

Jemili, I., Belghith, A. and Mosbah, M., 2008, in IFIP International Federation for Information Processing, Volume 284; *Wireless and Mobile Networking*; Zoubir Mammeri; (Boston: Springer), pp. 41–55.

the h-hop neighborhood information only with a small h. However, the lack of structure is a characteristic of wireless multi-hop radio networks when being deployed. Every node is unable to know its neighbors or the number of its neighbors without exchanging control messages with its neighborhood. Thus, a discovery phase is required preceding the execution of the algorithm aiming to construct a set of connected dominating nodes. Besides, over time, the dominating set must be updated to reflect the changes occurring in the network topology due to node mobility. The maintenance phase should also require as little communication between mobile nodes as possible. The majority of the proposed approaches gather neighborhood information periodically to maintain the CDS; collecting information takes time and there is a high likelihood of changes in network connectivity before the termination of this gathering phase required for maintenance. The use of explicit message exchange among neighbors in periodic basis can greatly affect the performance of the upper-layers protocols in large scale networks. Further, these algorithms do not take into account the presence of message losses due to eventual collision and the effect of wireless interference.

In this paper, we present an improved version of DCAWNK [3, 4], entitled TBCA (Tiered Based Clustering Algorithm). The main contribution of DCAWNK is that our mechanism does not necessitate any type of neighborhood knowledge, trying to alleviate the network from some control messages exchanged during the clustering and maintenance process. Consequently more bandwidth is left for transporting data traffic. The new version guarantees the construction of a dominating node set. So, we detail the three overlapping phases followed to construct a connected dominating set. The two first phases allow us to select the clusterheads and then gateways. While the third one allows us to verify that all clusterheads are connected through gateway neighbors. Improvements concerning rules for selecting the appropriate candidate for clusterhead and gateway roles are also presented. The rest of the paper is organized as follows. Section 2 reviews the related works; we focus specifically on clustering algorithms based on graph domination. Then, we give an exhaustive description of our clustering algorithm in section 3. We confirm the effectiveness of our algorithm through exhaustive simulations in section 4. In section 5, we conclude.

2 Related works

Many approaches have been proposed to construct a connected dominating set. Wu [5] proposed a distributed algorithm to find a CDS in order to design efficient routing schemes. The first phase allows nodes with at least two unconnected neighbors to be marked as dominator. Then some extension rules are implemented to reduce the size of a CDS generated from the marking process. Wu and Li algorithm was improved in term of message overhead in [6]. An extension of Wu and Li's distributed algorithm has been presented in [7], where the connected dominating set selection is based on the node degree and the energy level of each host. In [2], the authors proceed in the same way. A periodic exchange of hello permits nodes to gather two hop information allowing nodes to verify their eligibility for coordinator role. In [8], a dominating set is firstly constructed, then, the second step permits to connect the dominating set to form a CDS. The authors adopt in [9] the same way, a leader node triggers the construction of a Maximal Independent Set (MIS) by sending its hello message. Selection of others dominators of the MIS is based on the maximum weight in a given neighborhood. In [10], the authors propose a fast interference-aware distributed algorithm for wireless networks which constructs only a dominating set in an asynchronous environment. They assume that the network nodes have no information about their local neighborhood and do not possess a reliable collision detection mechanism. In [11], the authors present local control algorithmic techniques for CDS construction in wireless ad hoc networks which take into account message losses due to collisions from interfering transmissions. One of the described distributed algorithms requires each node to know their three-hop topology, while the second requires the knowledge of the maximum degree and the size of the network. This latest necessitates gathering two hops neighbor information.

Most of previous works have focused on selecting a small virtual backbone for high efficiency. A CDS with small size reduces the number of nodes involved in routing activities which contribute to deplete their energy quickly. It is also important to maintain a certain degree of redundancy in the virtual backbone for fault tolerance and routing flexibility. Besides, all these propositions rely on gathering h-hop neighborhood information, only with a small h. In many mechanisms, no mechanism was specified how to proceed when information loss occurs due to collision between data packets and the control packets or due to effect of interference. Moreover, over time, the CDS must change to reflect the changes in the network topology as nodes move. Many CDS schemes employ explicit message exchange among neighbors in periodic basis for maintaining the backbone structure. They apply local repairs, with the target of enhancing as much as possible the quality and stability of the hierarchy organization, by avoiding any unnecessary structure changes. However, in highly dynamic ad hoc net-works, local repairs are insufficient, since they are based on gathering information, which can be not up-to-date when being used by nodes. Algorithms requiring two hops or more neighborhood knowledge face this drawback, since the propagation of this information necessitate time.

3 Connected Dominating Set construction

Our clustering algorithm DCAWNK is based on the presence of a specific node called the Designated Node (DN). Electing the DN node is out of the scope of this paper. The basic idea is to organize the clustering process into layered stages in order to limit the number of participating nodes at the clustering process at a given instant. In this way, we reduce the eventual collisions between the control messages dedicated to the clustering phase. Through the improved version, TBCA, we guarantee the construction of a connected dominating set formed by elected clusterheads and gateways. Thus, we add a checking phase assuring that all clusterheads can communicate through gateways. Besides, we define new rules for clusterhead selection and gateway declaration in order to allow the most appropriate nodes to gain clusterhead or gateway role. We aim also to minimize the total number of nodes elected as clusterhead or as gateway. At the start of the clustering process, all nodes are unaffected, marked to N. We assume that all the nodes are synchronized thanks to an external agent.

3.1 Clusterhead and member declaration

The DN node triggers the clustering process by sending a cbeacon message exactly at TBTT[1]. The latter is the first declared clusterhead and remains a clusterhead forever. Its immediate neighbors will join its cluster as member nodes (M) and reply after a SIFS [2] by an ACK_BT. To avoid signal attenuation especially in large-scale ad hoc networks, we impose to nodes with odd identity to send their ACK_BT after a SIFS sensing period, while, nodes with even identity will transmit their ACK_BT after 2 SIFS periods. Simultaneous sending of ACK_BT generates hence a collision, considered like a 'Busy Tone' (BT). The busy tone will be intercepted by the two hop neighbors of the DN informing them that they are able to compete to become clusterheads. A node which has heard a cbeacon message is not allowed to participate into the clusterhead election. A node, marked to N, which intercepts a BT collision or an ACK_BT is an eligible candidate for the clusterhead role (candCH). The eligible nodes can concur to gain the clusterhead status in a randomized manner. To compute the backoff time, we prefer to use local information in order to avoid the required collecting information phase which is prone to collisions. So, each candCH node i computes a new boundary D_1^i for the backoff computing delay taking into account the energy factor, as follows:

$$D_1^i = \lceil ((\frac{(D_{1min} - D_{1max})}{E_{max}}) * E_i) + D_{1max} \rceil \qquad (1)$$

Where:

D_{1max}, D_{1min} : The maximal and minimal boundaries imposed for the backoff calculation by eligible candCH nodes

E_{max}, E_i : The maximal and remaining energies at node i

The personalized boundary D_1^i favors the declaration of nodes having sufficient energy, since clusterheads will have to assume additional tasks like routing. Every eligible node will calculate a random delay d_1 uniformly distributed in the range between zero and the new calculated boundary D_1^i. Our aim is to reduce the collision probability between multiple candCHs accessing the medium for announcing their

---

[1] TBTT : Target Beacon Transmission Time
[2] SIFS : Short InterFrame Space

cbeacon. Thus, we fix a minimal boundary different from zero. The random delay d_1 timer is decremented according to the defined CSMA/CA backoff algorithm. A candCH cancels the remaining random delay and the pending cbeacon transmission, if a cbeacon packet arrives before the random delay d_1 timer has expired. So, such a node will be assigned member status while joining the cluster of the cbeacon sender. Otherwise, it declares itself a clusterhead after transmitting its own cbeacon packet. Each node, which receives a cbeacon, sends an ACK_BT in order to inform two hops clusterhead neighbors that are able to candidate to clusterhead role. In this way, the clustering process progress in a layered manner.

To be able to differentiate between collisions which happened between cbeacon messages from collisions which happened between a cbeacon and ACK_BT messages, we force the layering to be centered at the DN. We impose the termination of the clustering process in a specific layer before allowing nodes in the subsequent layer to start the clustering process. Furthermore, nodes in the current layer that have heard cbeacon(s) transmit their ACK_BT at the same time upon the termination of the clusterhead election process at this layer. So, we divided the time in a succession of periods of time, denoted by T_i, i=1..N, where N represents the number of layers needed to cover the entire network. Depending on the context, we consider that T_i denotes also the instant at which period T_i ends. Period T_i defines the time duration required by the execution of the clustering process for layer i. It includes a sub period for the announcements of cbeacon messages followed by a second sub period for the simultaneous transmission of ACK_BT. We denote by T_{iBT} the instant at which this second sub period starts; as shown in Figure 1. Collisions occurring among cbeacons messages (only possible during the first sub period) are called CH collision, and the collisions between ACK_BT messages (happening during the second sub period) are called BT collision.

Let us now express explicitly the T_i, i = 1..N. We define the following quantities:

Txcbeacon : The transmission time of a cbeacon

TxBT : The transmission time of a ACK_BT

SlotTime : The slot time

CWsize : the contention window which is slot count

We get the following expressions for T_i, for i=1...N:

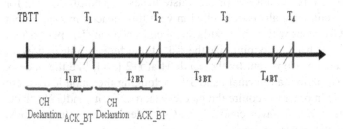

Fig. 1 Time division for clustering process

$$T_1 = SIFS + Txcbeacon + (2 * SIFS) + TxBT \qquad (2)$$

$$T_N = T_1 + (N - 1) * (SIFS + CWsize + Txcbeacon + (2 * SIFS) + TxBT) \qquad (3)$$

And the following expressions for T_{iBT}, i=1.. N:

$$T_{1BT} = SIFS + Txcbeacon \qquad (4)$$

$$T_{NBT} = T_{N-1} + (SIFS + CWsize + Txcbeacon) \qquad (5)$$

Since the beginning of the clustering process, all nodes will be passive, except the DN node. Each node will estimate continuously the instants T_i and T_{iBT} while waiting for clustering process to reach its level. We note that upon the first reception of a cbeacon or an ACK_BT or the detection of a CH collision or BT collision, a node realizes that the current clustering process concerns its layer.

3.2 Gateway declaration

3.2.1 Normal candGW declaration

During the clustering process, a node within layer i, that hears a correct cbeacon message, modifies its status to a Member node and adds the sender node identity to its clusterhead list (CH list). A member node that receives two or more correct cbeacon messages during T_i or T_{i+1} becomes a candidate gateway (candGW), called a normal candGW. This node is eligible to ensure lately the role of a gateway between its clusterhead neighbors. Immediate declaration of a candGW will cause troubles for next layer nodes busy with the clustering process in progress. Thus, a candGW node within layer i must wait a period of time, denoted by TG_i, in such a way to not perturb the clustering process traffic of the layers i and i+1. To this end, computing the period TG_i by a normal candGW at level i is done as follows for i = 1..N:

$$TG_i = T_{i+2} - t \qquad (6)$$

Where, t denote the instant of node declaration as candGW.

In figure 2, the node k is a candGW for the clusterheads i, j and m. Waiting for a period TG_i aims to eliminate all risk of collision with the cbeacon messages that can be sent by candCH nodes within the next layer, such as node m. The period TG_i was also computed in such a way to minimize the risk of interference able to prevent the good receipt of the cbeacons sent by the candCH at i+2 level, like the node o. After waiting the TG_i period, all normal candGW, belonging the same level i, are authorized to compete in order to acquire the gateway status. Each candGW selects a random backoff delay d_2. To favor candGW nodes closer to many clusterheads, each candGW i computes a personalized boundary D_2^i as follows:

$$D_2^i = \left(\frac{D_2}{CH\_Neighbor\_Number}\right) \tag{7}$$

Where D_2 is the maximal boundary used

So, each candGW chooses a random slot number in the range of zero to D_2^i. We note that the personalized boundary D_2^i can't exceed the threshold $D_2/2$, since a node must hear at least two correct cbeacons to obtain the candGW status. Upon expiration of d_2 backoff delay, a candGW is authorized to transmit its declaration to be an effective gateway for the clusterheads in its CH list, if it is steal eligible for this role. An eligible node for gateway role is a candGW with at least one uncovered CH neighbor. Otherwise, it becomes a member node. In fact, at the receipt of other gateway declaration, a candGW is able to verify if its own clusterheads are covered or not. Besides, every normal candGW or gateway renounces to the gateway role if it hears another GW declaring itself for a set of clusterheads that covers its own, the latest is called a dominating gateway. We note that during checking eligibility operation, a candGW or a GW must take into account the declaration of other GWs within the same layer. With this rule, we ensure that enough gateways will be elected to assure communication between clusterheads within adjacent layers.

3.2.2 Declaration of candGW with anonymous CHs

During the step of candCH declarations within a layer i, we can't eliminate completely the risk of collision occurrence. CandGWs with anonymous CHs gather nodes which intercept a CH collision due to a simultaneous transmission of two or more cbeacons from candCH nodes during T_i or T_{i+1}. In this case, the node adds an anonymous clusterhead to its CH list to represent the existence of two or more unknown clusterheads. However, such a node will not be assigned candGW status in all situations.

1) Detection of a CH collision by a node within level i during the first sub period of T_i

During the clusterhead election at level i, a node can be assigned one of these states when intercepting a CH collision: candCH, N node, M node or a candGW node. A candCH node or node, initially marked to N, acquires only member sta-

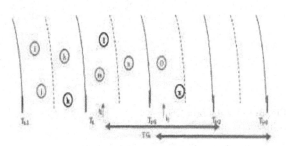

Fig. 2 Waiting period TG_i

tus despite the fact that it is closer to many clusterheads. While a member node conserves also its member status. In such a situation, a candGW node is already an eligible candidate for assuming gateway role. Subsequently, this candGW must indicate the existence of anonymous clusterheads in its list and specify the time of collision occurrence.

We remind that our main objective is to minimize the whole gateways number while guarantying the declaration of enough gateways in order to assure communication inter layers. Thus, communication between clusterheads within the same layer can be done easily through gateways of the previous layer i-1. Moreover, in case of dense ad hoc networks, the collision probability between multiple candCHs accessing the medium is higher. Such collisions may be detected by many nodes within the same layer, like nodes o, m and h (see figure 3). Authorizing all these nodes to acquire candGW status will increase considerably the number of candGW. Besides, no rule is able to differentiate efficiently between such candGWs, since they do not know all their neighboring clusterheads.

2)Detection of a CH collision by a node within level i during the first sub period of T_{i+1}

When the clusterhead election at layer i+1 starts, the clustering process at level i is already stopped. So, only member or candGW nodes, within a layer i, are able to detect a CH collision during T_{i+1}. Such a candGW adds an anonymous clusterhead to its CH list and memorizes to time of collision occurrence, like the node j (see figure 3). Same actions are undertaken by a member node and it declares itself as candGW. However, we must allow normal candGW to candidate for gateway role before authorizing candGWs having an anonymous clusterhead in their CH list also to compete. So, after the waiting period TG_i, such candGWs select a random delay d_2 in the range $D_2/2$ to the maximal boundary D_2. Each candGW must indicate the number of anonymous clusterheads and the times of collision detection. We note that we associate an anonymous CH for each CH collision. Thanks to these indications, other similar candGWs can verify their eligibility to assure gateway role. A such candGW compares the instants of collision detection indicated in the received declaration to their own in order to estimate if they are close to the same clusterheads. Thus, a steal eligible candGW announces its declaration whenever the

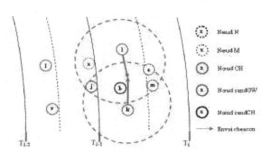

Fig. 3 Detection of a CH collision

backoff delay expires. Otherwise, it cancels the gateway declaration transmission and modifies its status to member (M).

3.3 Checking phase

Thanks to clusterheads and gateways declaration, we aim to form a connected dominating set. In fact, every node will either a member node attached to a clusterhead, or a dominating node assuming a clusterhead or gateway role. In order to avoid any negative impact on the other protocol exploiting the virtual backbone resulting from the clustering process, we must insure that the set formed by gateways and clusterheads is connected. However, the gateway declaration step following clusterhead election one is insufficient in some cases due to information loss. Indeed, the risk of packet loss due to possible cbeacon collision can prevent the member nodes from being aware of clusterhead existence in their neighborhood. While the eventual collision during the gateway election step avoid the correct receipt of gateway declaration by neighbor clusterheads. We note that an eventual mistake when verifying the eligibility for gateway role by a candGW with anonymous clusterhead can lead to a case of disconnected clusterheads within adjacent layers.

To avoid the case of disconnected clusterheads belonging to adjacent levels, we require a checking phase. This step will be realized by all clusterhead nodes, each one shall verify if it has at least one gateway allowing it to communicate with previous layer's clusterheads. Each clusterhead within a layer i should wait the period required for gateways declaration before being able to verify connectivity. Thus, upon sending its cbeacon, each clusterhead estimates the waiting period P_attente. This period P_attente must take into account the periods TG_{i-1} and TG_i required by any candGW within layers i and i-1 before being able to candidate for gateway role. Moreover, the period P_attente must include the necessary time for the declaration of the maximum number of gateways able to be close to a clusterhead. These gateways may belong the layers i or i-1. We aim to estimate the waiting period in terms of period T_i. Thanks to this, every node will maintain a landmark to initiate a given step during the clustering process. Thus, we force a clusterhead to do this checking step in the beginning of a T_i period. Computing the number of period T_i to wait is done as follows:

$$Nbr\_TiGW = \lceil (CWsize + (NumberMax\_gw/CH * TcandGW)/T_i) \rceil \qquad (8)$$

$$T_i = SIFS + CWsize + Txcbeacon + (2 * SIFS) + TxBT \qquad (9)$$

where:

TcandGW : Time for transmitting a gateway declaration

NumbreMax_gw/CH : Maximum number of gateways able to be close the a given clusterhead

Nbr_TiGW : Number of periods T_i necessary for election step of gateways close to the given clusterhead

Consequently, a clusterhead within layer i determines the waiting period P_attente following the formula 10, if it belongs to an odd level. While, other ones within an even level will adopt the formula (11). We try to avoid the problems of collision and interference able to occur due simultaneous cbeacon sending by two disconnected CH within adjacent layers.

$$P\_attente = (T_{i+2} - t) + (Nbr\_TiGW * T_i) \qquad (10)$$

$$P\_attente = (T_{i+2} - t) + (Nbr\_TiGW * T_i) + (3 * T_i) \qquad (11)$$

Where t represents the instant of the given CH election

Upon the P_attente period expires, every CH verifies its connectivity with clusterheads within the previous layer. A a clusterhead, with no intermediate gateway from the previous layer, has to retransmit its cbeacon after a random delay back-off to oblige their neighbours from the previous layer to react. In the beginning of the following period T_i, gateways from the previous layer, which receive the cbeacon, must send again their declaration. They defer their transmission by choosing a random delay selected in the range of 0 to $D_2/2$. Member nodes from the previous layer gain the candGW status. But, they select their random delay in the range of $D_2/2$ to D_2. In this way, we allow the gateways to manifest first minimizing consequently the number of additional gateway declaration. This gateway election step is submitted to the same rules as the normal gateway declaration phase. The checking period Tphase_verif includes a period T_i for the cbeacon retransmission by disconnected clusterheads and a period for gateways and additional candGW declarations. Details are omitted here.

3.4 Maintenance

Providing rapidly a connected dominating set able to be deployed by others upper-protocols is one of the main characteristics of TBCA. This advantage allows us to suspend sending data traffic before starting the clustering process. This temporary data traffic pause allows us to quickly finalize the clustering process. In this way, we avoid also eventual collisions between data packets and control packets exchanged during the clustering process. These eventual collisions can cause loss of information and useless retransmissions and prevent the good progress of the clustering process. We note that any node which has already participate in the clustering process is able to determine the number of T_i period to wait before processing the suspending data packets. Details are omitted here for length limitation.

In order to take onto account up-to-date information, we relinquish the clustering algorithm periodically in order to reconstruct a new CDS. To avoid the construct the overall CDS from scratch and to enhance stability of the clustering infrastructure, we add another stability mechanism. This latest aims to permit re-election of older clusterheads, when they have yet enough resources to assure additional tasks. Besides, we limit the maximal number of consecutive clustering periods for clusterhead re-election in order to rotate the clusterhead role equitably between all nodes. In this context, we define two other boundaries D_{1pmin} and D_{1npmin}. During the first execution of the clustering process, all candCH nodes have the same opportunity to become clusterhead, since they use the rule (1). During subsequent clustering phases, a candCH node computes its personalized boundary D_1^i following the rule below, if it was a clusterhead during the previous clustering period and it does not exceed the maximal number of clustering period as clusterhead :

$$D_1^i = \lceil ((\frac{(D_{1pmin} - D_{1max})}{E_{max}}) * E_i) + D_{1max} \rceil \qquad (12)$$

Other candCH nodes use the rule (1) and they must ensure that d_1 is greater or equal to the new boundary D_{1pmin}. In this way, we give the advantage to older clusterheads able to assure coordinator responsibilities. We guarantee also a certain degree of stability in the CDS structure. To rotate the responsibility among all nodes fairly, we limit the number of successive clustering periods for a node as clusterhead. In this context, we impose to an older clusterhead which has lost this privilege to use the following rule to compute D_1^i, the value of d_1 must be greater or equal to the boundary D_{1min}.

$$D_1^i = \lceil ((\frac{(D_{1npmin} - D_{1max})}{E_{max}}) * E_i) + D_{1max} \rceil \qquad (13)$$

4 Performance evaluation

Constructing a CDS with low communication and computation costs is the main advantage of our new algorithm TBCA. Besides, it provides rapidly a virtual infrastructure able to support other communication algorithms. To show the effectiveness of our algorithm, we conduct exhaustive simulations over several static and mobile topologies. We compare performances of our algorithm against SPAN performances [2]. Similar to our algorithm, SPAN operates at MAC level in a synchronous environment. But, it relies on a periodic exchange of hello message for maintaining the connected dominating set. The two mechanisms were implemented under the J-SIM simulator. During the evaluation phase, we focus on three essential factors which have a direct impact on the performance of the clustering algorithm and consequently on the network performance. The first criterion is the size of the generated connected dominating. Then, we tried to show the impact of periodic control packet exchange on network performance. Finally, we evaluate the impact of mobility on the performances of the two algorithms. All simulations are allowed to run for 300 seconds and the results are averaged over several simulation runs. During all conducted simulations, we assume that every node has a maximum transmission range, which is the same for all nodes in the network. The transmission range is fixed to 250 meters. Any two nodes are considered as neighbors if there are within the maximum transmission range of each other.

a) The size of the connected dominating set

During this first phase, we compare the size of the connected dominating set produced by SPAN and TBCA while varying the node density and the size of the simulation area. The exchange of hello messages is done every 10 seconds in SPAN mechanism. The same interlude is adopted by TBCA for relinquishing periodically the clustering algorithm. In the first step, simulations are done with different topologies chosen randomly in an area of $500 \times 500m$. Figure (4.a) shows that the size of the dominating set generated by TBCA is smaller when of the maximal boundaries D_1 and D_2 are equal to 31. We recall that these boundaries are used during the clusterhead election phase and the gateway declaration phase. When these boundaries are large, the probability of collision occurrence between cbeacon messages and gateway declarations decreases, since the probability of choosing the same backoff by candidate nodes decreases consequently. We notice also a little difference in the size of generated CDS by the two mechanisms. Our mechanism TBCA produced small CDS, despite the lack of neighborhood knowledge.

During the second step, we choose different topologies with variable size in an area of $1000 \times 1000m$. In this stage, we fix the boundaries D_1 and D_2 to 31, since we deal with large-scale topologies and the probability of collision occurrence increases with density. The results exposed in figure (4.b) confirm that TBCA outperforms by far SPAN.

In this phase, we proved by simulations that density has no impact on the performance of our mechanism, since it keeps the size of the dominating set as low as possible without requiring any periodic control message exchange for gathering neighborhood information. Involving more nodes in routing contribute to deplete their energy, this can cause network partitioning.

b) Impact of the additional overhead dedicated to clustering

To illustrate the impact of the additional overhead introduced for clustering maintenance purpose on the network performance, we opt for geographic forwarding. We assume that nodes can obtain the geographic position of others neighbors through a low-power Global Position System (GPS) receiver or through some other ways. The source verifies if the destination is in its neighborhood. In such case, the source sends directly the data packet to the destination. Otherwise, it determines the closest

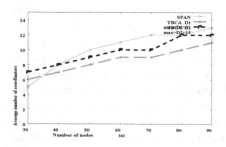
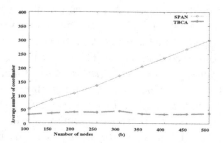

Fig. 4 Average number of coordinator

neighbor coordinator to the destination and sends to it the packet. The coordinator also operates in the same manner. We note here, that forwarding is done through coordinator nodes only. We choose ten sources which send packets to ten destinations. Sources and destinations are chosen at the boundary of the simulation area in order to allow multi hop communication. Each CBR flow includes 512 bytes packets.

During the first step, we choose different random topologies of 100 nodes confined in a square area of $500 \times 500m$. The periodicity for clustering update is fixed to 5 beacon intervals. We vary the traffic load in order to evaluate the impact of the periodic exchange of control messages on data traffic. Figure (5. a) illustrates that the number of delivered packets using our clustering mechanism is higher than the number measured when using SPAN, since we do not require periodic control messages which throttle the actual data traffic. The figure (5. b) exposes the average sojourn delay measured during all simulations, we notice that the sojourn delay increases with the data traffic load for both mechanisms. However, the sojourn delay measured for SPAN is always greater than our algorithm delay, since the periodic hello messages contend with data traffic.

The figure (6.a) consolidates this result, since it exposes the number of delivered packets while varying the updating interval used for periodic exchange of hello

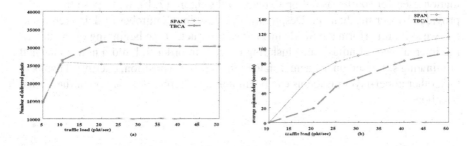

Fig. 5 (a) Average number of delivered packets regarding variable traffic load, (b) Average sojourn delay regarding variable traffic load

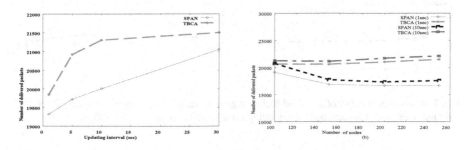

Fig. 6 (a) Average number of delivered packets regarding variable updating interval, (b) Average number of delivered packets regarding variable updating interval and variable number of nodes

message. In these simulations, every source injects 20 packets per second during the 200 seconds. We remark that performance of SPAN improves as the updating interval becomes longer. However, our algorithm still outperforms it.

During the second step, we simulate different topologies with variable size in a fixed square region of $500 \times 500m$ to evaluate the impact of density on performance of the network. Every CBR flow sends 50 packets per second. In these simulations, we vary also the updating interval for exchanging hello messages for SPAN and relinquishing clustering process for TBCA. We notice through results illustrated in figure (6. b) that TBCA is unaffected by the variation of density or updating interval. While the performances of SPAN degrade when the number of nodes increases, since the control overhead of hello messages increases also.

c) Impact of mobility

In the second phase, we consider random topologies of 100 mobiles nodes. Only the sources and destinations are stationary. To evaluate the impact of mobility, we measure the number of delivered packets under different speeds. The figure (7.a) shows that the performances of SPAN degrade when the updating interval for clustering maintenance increases. In fact, gathering 2 hop neighborhood information takes time, so the collected information may be not up to date when be used by nodes. We remark also that the performances of SPAN are badly in highly dynamic environment, particularly when the updating interval is large, since routing information used for routing is not up to date. In the figure (7. b), we expose the results provided by our mechanism. Despite the decrease in the number of delivered packets, we still outperform the SPAN mechanism. In fact, at the beginning of the updating interval, we relinquish the clustering process in order to build a new connected dominating set based on the actual state of the network (position, energy). Thanks to this, other upper-layer protocols can be implemented efficiently on top of the virtual backbone.

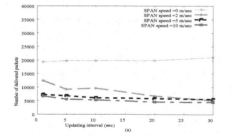 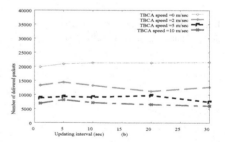

Fig. 7 (a) Average number of delivered packets regarding variable updating interval for SPAN, (b) Average number of delivered packets regarding variable updating interval for TBCA

5 Conclusion

In this paper, we detail the three phases of our clustering algorithm TBCA. Our goal is to construct a connected dominating set while taking into consideration the eventual occurrence of collision. Besides, we exploit this situation for doing the clustering process in an organized layered manner. No neighborhood knowledge is needed for node to be able to decide locally on the role to take. Conducted simulations show first that our algorithm outperforms by far other clustering techniques for CDS construction in terms of the average number of delivered packets and per-packet sojourn delay, especially in case of heavy loaded networks. Moreover, we notice that it copes better with mobility.

References

1. Das, B., Sivakumar, R., Bhargavan, V.: Routing in ad hoc networks using a spine. Proceedings of ICCCN. pp. 1-20 (1997).
2. Chen, B., Jamieson, K. Balakrishnan, H., Morris, R.: Span: an energy efficient coordination algorithm for topology maintenance in ad hoc wireless networks. ACM Wireless Networks J. 8 (5). pp. 481-494 (2002).
3. Belghith, A. Jemili, I., Mosbah, M. : A Distributed Clustering Algorithm without an Explicit Neighborhood Knowledge. International Journal of Computing and Information Sciences, Vol. 5, number 1, pp. 24-34 (2007).
4. Jemili, I., Belghith, A., Mosbah, M. : Algorithme Distribu de Clusterisation sans connaissance du voisinage : principe et valuation. Proceeding NOTERE'2007, Marrakech, June (2007).
5. J. Wu, H..L. Li (1999) On calculating connected dominating set for efficient routing in ad hoc wireless networks. Proceedings of the 3rd ACM International Workshop on Discrete Algorithms and Methods for Mobile Computing and Communications. PP 7-14.
6. I. Stojmenovic, M. Seddigh and J. Zunic (2001) Dominating sets and neighbor elimination-based broadcastings in wireless networks. IEEE Transactions on Parallel and Distributed Systems, 13(1):14-25, January 2001.
7. J. Wu, M. Gao, I. Stojmenovic (2002) On calculating power-aware connected dominating sets for efficient routing in ad hoc wireless networks. Journal of Communication and Networks, March 2002.
8. Wan, P.-J., Alzoubi, K., Frieder, O. : Distributed construction of connected dominating-set in wireless ad hoc networks. In IEEE INFOCOM (2002).
9. Theoleyre, F., Valois, F. : A self-organization structure for hybrid networks, Ad Hoc. Netw. (2007). doi:10.1016/j.adhoc.2007.02.013
10. Kuhn, F., Moscibroda, T., Wattenhofer, R. : Initializing newly deployed ad hoc and sensor networks, in: 10th Annual International Conference on Mobile Computing and Networking (MOBICOM), (2004).
11. Gandhi, R., Parthasarathy, S. : Distributed algorithms for connected domination in wireless networks. Journal of Parallel and Distributed Computing, Volume 67, Issue 7, pp. 848-862 July (2007).

A Novel Power Counting Mechanism for Enhanced MBMS Performance in UMTS Networks

Antonios Alexiou[1,2], Christos Bouras[1,2] and Evangelos Rekkas[1,2]

[1] Computer Engineering and Informatics Dept., Univ. of Patras, Greece

[2] Research Academic Computer Technology Institute, 26500 Rio, Patras, Greece

alexiua@cti.gr, bouras@cti.gr, rekkas@cti.gr

Abstract One of the key objectives of Universal Mobile Telecommunications System (UMTS) is the realization of enhanced end-user experience through the provision of rich multimedia services, ensuring in parallel an economical delivery cost for service providers. Multimedia Broadcast/Multicast Services (MBMS) framework of UMTS epitomizes the increasing popularity of such applications by efficiently delivering multimedia traffic to a large number of users and optimizing the radio interface of UMTS networks. For exploiting resource efficiency, MBMS specifications consider the Counting Mechanism which decides whether it is more economic to deliver MBMS multicast traffic over point-to-point (PTP) or point-to-multipoint (PTM) bearers. However, the necessity to further improve MBMS resource efficiency and integrate new technologies such as High Speed Downlink Packet Access (HSDPA) stresses the need for an advanced Counting Mechanism. To this direction, in this paper we propose a novel Power Counting Mechanism which performs optimal power resource utilization and incorporates the HSDPA broadband extension of UMTS for enhanced performance.

1 Introduction

The major challenge that the mobile telecommunications industry faces today is how to offer a wide range of appealing multimedia services, such as Mobile TV, to mobile users. The expected high penetration of such services translates into optimal resource allocation strategies and improved network performance. A significant step to compensate for these requirements was the introduction of the MBMS framework in the Release 6 UMTS architecture [2], [3]. In MBMS data is transmitted from a single source entity to multiple destinations.

Please use the following format when citing this chapter:

Alexiou, A., Bouras, C. and Rekkas, E., 2008, in IFIP International Federation for Information Processing, Volume 284; *Wireless and Mobile Networking*; Zoubir Mammeri; (Boston: Springer), pp. 57–68.

The main requirement during the provision of MBMS services is to make an efficient overall usage of radio and network resources. Under this prism, a critical aspect of MBMS performance is the selection of the most efficient radio bearer for the transmission of MBMS multicast data. In the frame of switching between different radio bearers, MBMS specifications consider the Counting Mechanism [8] which decides whether it is more efficient to deploy PTP or PTM bearers. Counting Mechanism is an open issue in today's MBMS infrastructure mainly due to its catalytic role in radio resource management (RRM). Current specifications of Counting Mechanism suffer from two major performance inefficiencies. On the one hand Counting Mechanism may lead to significant power wasting, while on the other hand it is characterized by the absence of broadband characteristics.

According to existing Counting Mechanism, the decision on the threshold between PTP and PTM bearers is based on the number of serving MBMS users [8]. However, this criterion for channel type switching may result to significant wasting of the expensive power resources, since it does not take into account the base station's downlink transmission power. Power in UMTS networks is the most limited resource and may lead to significant capacity decrease when misused.

Another inefficiency of the current Counting Mechanism is the absence of key technologies, such as HSDPA. HSDPA introduces a new transport channel, named High Speed-Downlink Shared Channel (HS-DSCH), which optimizes the air interface to support higher data rate services [4], [7]. Although Release '99 transport channels have already been standardized for MBMS transmissions, MBMS over HS-DSCH is an open research topic. More specifically, in PTP mode multiple Dedicated Channels (DCHs) may be used, while in PTM mode a Forward Access Channel (FACH) is configured [8]. However, all the broadband features of HS-DSCH constitute it an ideal candidate for the delivery of MBMS data.

In this paper we propose a novel Power Counting Mechanism that confronts all the above inefficiencies and enhances MBMS performance. Actually, in this paper we further extend and optimize our previous work presented in [9] in order to better utilize power resources and enrich MBMS with broadband characteristics in the frame of 3G evolution. The proposed Power Counting Mechanism maximizes power efficiency and simultaneously gets advantage of the HSDPA improved performance. We evaluate the proposed mechanism based on a theoretical analysis of downlink power consumption during MBMS multicast transmission. In addition, in order to prove our proposed mechanism's superiority against the current form of Counting Mechanism we present an explicit comparison between the two approaches. Finally, our investigation steps over the conventional macrocellular analysis and focuses on microcellular environments too.

The paper is structured as follows: Section 2 is dedicated to the functional description of the Power Counting Mechanism, while in Section 3 an extended power profile analysis of the three types of radio bearers (DCH, FACH and HS-DSCH) is provided. Section 4 is devoted to the presentation of the evaluation results. Finally, concluding remarks and planned next steps are briefly described in Section 5.

2   Power Counting Mechanism

Power Counting Mechanism improved performance relies on the exploitation of power resource efficiency and on the integration of HSDPA technology. The proposed mechanism adopts downlink transmission power as the optimum criterion for radio bearer selection. The transport channel with less power consumption is preferred for the delivery of multicast content. Furthermore, in order to enrich MBMS with broadband characteristics, HS-DSCH transport channel is introduced as a multicast bearer in PTP mode. HS-DSCH brings more capacity and enables the mass-market delivery of MBMS services to end users.

Next in this section, we present the architecture and the functionality of the proposed Power Counting Mechanism. The block diagram of the mechanism is illustrated in Fig. 1. The mechanism comprises three distinct operation phases: the parameter retrieval phase, the power level computation phase and the transport channel selection phase. A periodic check is performed at regular time intervals.

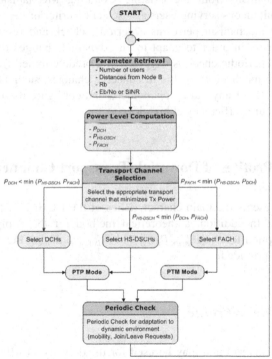

Fig. 1 Power Counting Mechanism

During the parameter retrieval phase (Fig. 1) the mechanism retrieves parameters of the MBMS users and services in each cell. These parameters are the number of users requesting a specific MBMS session, their distances from the base station and their QoS requirements. This information is received from the

Radio Network Controller (RNC) through appropriate uplink channels. In addition, we assume that the MBMS bit rate service is already known through the Broadcast Multicast-Service Center (BM-SC) node of the MBMS architecture.

The power level computation phase processes the information received from the parameter retrieval phase. In this phase, the required power to be allocated for MBMS session delivery in each cell is computed. The computation is based on the assumption that the transmission of the multicast data can be performed over multiple DCHs, HS-DSCHs or over a single FACH. Consecutively, P_{DCH}, $P_{HS\text{-}DSCH}$ and P_{FACH} power levels are computed respectively for each type of transport channel, according to the method that is presented in Section 3.

In the transport channel selection phase, the appropriate transport channel for the transmission of the MBMS multicast content is selected. The P_{DCH}, the P_{FACH} and the $P_{HS\text{-}DSCH}$ are compared. The algorithm decides which case consumes less power and consequently, chooses the corresponding transport channel for the session. This is a key point of our mechanism that actually differentiates Power Counting Mechanism from the existing Counting Mechanism (that uses the number of simultaneous serving users as a selection criterion).

Finally, our mechanism performs a periodic check and re-retrieves user and service parameters in order to adapt to any dynamic changes during the service provision. This periodic check is triggered at a predetermined frequency rate and ensures that the mechanism is able to conceive changes, such as users' mobility, join/leave requests or any fading phenomena and configure its functionality so as to maintain resource efficiency at high levels.

3   Power Profiles of Downlink Transport Channels

This section presents the main characteristics of the DCH, FACH and HS-DSCH power profiles. In addition, a theoretical method for the computation of their power consumption levels (P_{DCH}, P_{FACH} and $P_{HS\text{-}DSCH}$) during the MBMS multicast transmission is provided.

3.1   DCH Power Profile

DCH is a PTP channel and may be used for the delivery of MBMS services to a small number of users. The total downlink transmission power allocated for all MBMS users in a cell that are served by multiple DCHs is variable. It mainly depends on the number of serving users, their distance from the base station, the bit rate of the MBMS session and the experienced signal quality E_b/N_0 for each user. Equation (1) calculates the base station's total DCH transmission power (P_{DCH}) required for the transmission of the data to n users in a specific cell [5].

$$P_{DCH} = \frac{P_P + \sum_{i=1}^{n} \frac{(P_N + x_i)}{\frac{W}{(E_b/N_0)_i R_{b,i}} + p} L_{p,i}}{1 - \sum_{i=1}^{n} \frac{p}{\frac{W}{(E_b/N_0)_i R_{b,i}} + p}} \tag{1}$$

where P_{DCH} is the base station's transmitted power, P_P is the power devoted to common control channels, $L_{p,i}$ is the path loss, $R_{b,i}$ the ith user transmission rate, W the bandwidth, P_N the background noise, p is the orthogonality factor ($p = 0$ for perfect orthogonality) and x_i is the intercell interference observed by the ith user given as a function of the transmitted power by the neighboring cells $P_{Tj}, j=1,\ldots K$ and the path loss from this user to the jth cell L_{ij}.

3.2 FACH Power Profile

FACH is a PTM channel and must be received by all users throughout the MBMS service area of the cell. A FACH essentially transmits at a fixed power level that should be high enough to serve the user with the worst path loss, i.e. the user with the higher distance from the base station. This is another important difference between Power Counting Mechanism and its current form. Existing Counting Mechanism is not scalable and transmits at a power level so as to provide full cell coverage, irrespective of users' location, while Power Counting Mechanism dynamically adjusts its downlink power to a level high enough to serve only the desired cell coverage area.

Table 1. FACH Tx Power Levels vs. Cell Coverage – Macrocell

% Cell Coverage	Tx Power (W) - 64 Kbps
10	1.4
20	1.6
30	1.8
40	2.0
50	2.5
60	3.0
70	3.6
80	4.8
90	6.4
100	7.6

Table 1 presents some indicative FACH downlink transmission power levels obtained for varying cell coverage areas in a macrocell environment, without assuming any diversity techniques. Depending on the distance of the user with the worst path loss from the serving base station, the RNC dynamically sets FACH transmission power at one of the levels presented in Table 1 [6].

3.3 HS-DSCH Power Profile

HS-DSCH is a rate controlled rather than a power controlled transport channel. In HSDPA fast power control (characterizing Release '99 channels) is replaced by the Link Adaptation functionality, including techniques such as dynamic Adaptive Modulation and Coding (AMC), multicode operation, fast scheduling, Hybrid ARQ (HARQ) and short Transmission Time Interval (TTI) of 2ms.

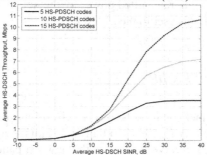

Fig. 2 Actual Cell Throughput vs. SINR

In this paper we employ a dynamic method in order to provide only the required, amount of HS-DSCH power so as to satisfy all the serving users and, in parallel, eliminate system interference. A major measure for HSDPA link budget planning is the HS-DSCH Signal-to-Interference-plus-Noise Ratio (SINR) metric. SINR for a single-antenna Rake receiver is calculated from equation (3):

$$SINR= SF_{16} \frac{P_{HS-DSCH}}{pP_{own} + P_{other} + P_{noise}} \tag{3}$$

where $P_{HS-DSCH}$ is the HS-DSCH transmission power, P_{own} is the own cell interference experienced by the mobile user, P_{other} the interference from neighboring cells and P_{noise} the Additive Gaussian White Noise (AGWN). Parameter p is the orthogonality factor ($p = 0$ for perfect orthogonality), while SF_{16} is the spreading factor of 16.

There is a strong relationship between the HS-DSCH allocated power and the obtained MBMS cell throughput. This relationship can be disclosed in the three following steps. Initially, we have to define the target MBMS cell throughput. Once the target cell throughput is set, the next step is to define the way that this throughput relates to the SINR (Fig. 2). At this point, it is worth mentioning that as the number High Speed-Physical Downlink Shared Channel (HS-PDSCH) codes increases, a lower SINR value is required to obtain a target MBMS data rate (Fig. 2). Finally, we can describe how the required HS-DSCH transmission power ($P_{HS\text{-}DSCH}$) can be expressed as a function of the SINR value and the user location (in terms of Geometry factor - G) through equation (4) [7]:

$$P_{HS-DSCH} \geq SINR[\, p - G^{-1}] \frac{P_{own}}{SF_{16}}$$
(4)

The Geometry factor indicates the users' position throughout a cell (distance from the base station). Geometry is given by the relationship between P_{own}, P_{other} and P_{noise} and is defined from equation (5). A lower G is expected when a user is located at the cell edge. Moreover, in microcells MBMS users experience a better (higher) G due to the better environment isolation.

$$G = \frac{P_{own}}{P_{other} + P_{noise}}$$
(5)

4   Performance Evaluation

For the purpose of the Power Counting Mechanism evaluation we consider the delivery of a typical 64 Kbps MBMS service. Furthermore, both macro and micro cell environments are examined, with parameters presented in Table 2 [1], [10].

Table 2. Macrocell and Microcell Simulation Parameters

Parameter	Macrocell	Microcell
Cellular layout	Hexagonal grid	Manhattan grid
Number of cells	18	72
Site-to-site distance	1 Km	360m (4 blocks)
Maximum BS Tx power	20 W	2 W
Other BS Tx power	5 W	0.5 W
CPICH Power	2 W	0.2 W
Common channel power	1 W	0.1 W
Propagation model	Okumura Hata	Walfish-Ikegami
Multipath channel	Vehicular A (3km/h)	Pedestrian A (3Km/h)
Orthogonality factor (0 : perfect orthogonality)	0.5	0.1
E_b/N_0 target	5 dB	6dB

Initially, we present some indicative results concerning the operation of the transport channel selection phase in order to highlight the key role of power control in MBMS and HS-DSCH's contribution in further enhancing MBMS performance. Next, we address the superiority of the proposed mechanism through an explicit comparison, on power and capacity performance, between the Power Counting Mechanism and the existing form of Counting Mechanism.

4.1 Efficient MBMS Transport Channel Selection

In this section, we present performance results concerning the most critical aspect of the Power Counting Mechanism: the transport channel selection phase. The mechanism computes the transmission power required for all types of channels and selects the transport channel with less power requirements. This power efficient channel deployment is illustrated in Fig. 3. Transmission power levels for DCH, HS-DSCH and FACH channels are depicted both for macrocell (Fig. 3a) and microcell (Fig. 3b) environments. These power levels, actually, constitute the overall output of the power level computation phase. Users are assumed to be in groups (of varying population each time), located near the cell edge which results to the worst case scenario, in terms of transmission power.

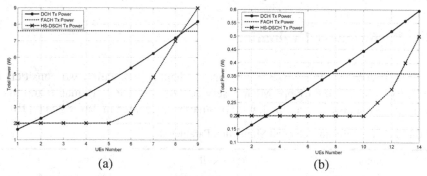

(a)   (b)

Fig. 3 MBMS Power Allocation 64Kbps, 100% coverage (a) Macrocell, (b) Microcell

Regarding the macrocell case we observe, from Fig. 3a, that HS-DSCH is less power consuming for a multicast population with less than 8 users and, thus, it should be preferred for MBMS content transmission (PTP mode). On the other hand, for more than 8 users, FACH is more power efficient and should be deployed (PTM mode). For such a high coverage in macrocells HS-DSCH outperforms the performance of DCH and is the optimal channel in PTP mode. The power gain of HS-DSCH against the DCH reaches 2.5 W when serving 5 multicast users. Similar results can be extracted in the case of a microcell. However, in microcells it is observed that DCH is the optimal choice for a small multicast group of less than 3 users. For 4-12 users HS-DSCH should be deployed, while for even more users, FACH is the appropriate bearer.

In general, in cases where the number of users is small, PTP transmissions are preferred. DCH and HS-DSCH are both PTP channels; however, the results prove that for very small multicast user population DCH is preferred, while, for relatively more users HS-DSCH is the most appropriate. Therefore, our mechanism does not only decide to use PTP or PTM transmissions (as the existing Counting Mechanism does), but it makes a further distinction between DCH and HS-DSCH in PTP mode.

However, the most important notice, extracted from Fig. 3, is that the HSDPA technology provides significant power savings in MBMS PTP mode, when serving a few multicast users, since HS-DSCH appears to be less power consuming than DCH in most cases. This power gain can, in turn, lead to a significant gain in capacity which enables the mass-market delivery of higher bit rate services to end users. As a consequence, it is imperative that HSDPA technology should be integrated in MBMS specifications in order to benefit both operators and mobile users and further improve MBMS resource efficiency.

4.2   Power Counting Mechanism vs. current Counting Mechanism

In the previous section, we presented that the Power Counting Mechanism can efficiently utilize power resources. However, the superiority of the mechanism can be better illustrated if we compare the performance of our approach with the current form of the Counting Mechanism. For a more realistic performance comparison, both mobility issues and varying number of serving users are taken into consideration and investigated.

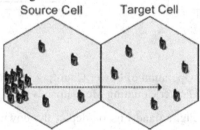

Fig. 4 Simulation Topology

At this point it should be reminded that current Counting Mechanism specifications consider a static switching point between PTP and PTM modes, based on the number of MBMS serving users. Such a reasonable threshold for a macrocell environment would be 8 multicast users. That means that for less than 8 users in PTP mode, multiple DCHs (and no HS-DSCH) would be transmitted, while for more than 8 multicast users in PTM mode, a single FACH, with such power so as to provide full coverage would be deployed.

For the purpose of the evaluation we set up a simulation scenario which considers the provision of a MBMS multicast session in a segment of a UMTS macrocellular environment. We examine the performance of both approaches for two neighboring cells (called source cell and target cell) as depicted in Fig. 4. A 64 Kbps MBMS session with 2000 sec time duration is delivered in both cells. Simulation results are depicted in Fig. 5 (source cell) and Fig. 6 (target cell).

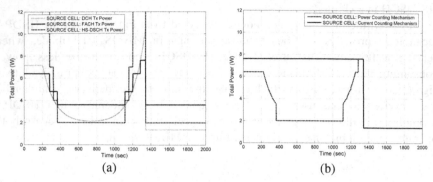

(a)   (b)

Fig. 5 Source Cell: (a) Operation of Power Counting Mechanism,
(b) Power Counting Mechanism vs. UE Counting Mechanism

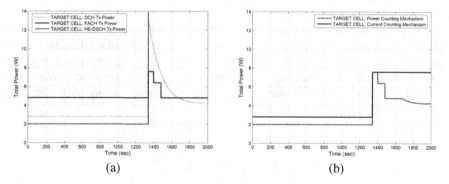

(a)   (b)

Fig. 6 Target Cell: (a) Operation of Power Counting Mechanism,
(b) Power Counting Mechanism vs. UE Counting Mechanism

More specifically, Fig. 5a and Fig. 6a depict the downlink power of the three transport channels, as extracted from the power level computation phase, in source and target cells respectively. Fig. 5b and Fig. 6b depict the transmission power of the transport channel that is actually deployed both for the Power Counting Mechanism and the current Counting Mechanism, in source and target cell respectively. In case of Power Counting Mechanism, this power level represents the power consumed by the channel selected in the transport channel selection phase. Regarding the existing Counting Mechanism this power level is either the total DCH power as computed in equation (1) for less than 8 users, or the fixed FACH power, equal to 7.6 W for full cell coverage, for more than 8 users.

The source cell initially consists of 14 multicast users, while 6 users are residing in the target cell. During the first 200 sec of the simulation time, all users in both cells are static. In source cell, the Power Counting Mechanism favors the transmission of MBMS content over FACH with power set to 6.4 W in order to serve users with the worst path loss, located at a distance of 90% cell coverage as depicted in Fig. 5a. On the other hand, current Counting Mechanism uses a FACH with 7.6 W to achieve full cell coverage, since it does not take into account the users' location, resulting in a power wasting of 1.2 W (Fig. 5b) in the source cell. Target cell is a PTP cell, since it serves less than 8 users. However, HS-DSCH has better performance than DCH, thus, Power Counting Mechanism performs better than the existing Counting Mechanism in the target cell.

A group of 10 users in the source cell, which is located near the cell edge (90% cell coverage), starts moving at time instance 201 sec towards the target cell, according to the trajectory depicted in Fig. 4, while the rest users remain static. This group leaves the source cell and enters the target cell at time instance 1341 sec. During the time period 201-1341 sec we can make the following observations in the source cell. Power Counting Mechanism is able to track users' location, thus, it dynamically computes power allocation for all transport channels (including the FACH scalable power level). When multicast users get close to the source cell's base station, PTP bearers (DCH and HS-DSCH) are less power consuming than PTM bearer (FACH) even for a large number of serving users. Similarly, when users reside near the cell edge, FACH is more efficient. Existing Counting Mechanism fails to deal efficiently with users' mobility, in the absence of any adaptive procedure, and uses exclusively FACH since simultaneous users receiving the MBMS service exceed the threshold of 8 users. As a result, we observe that a significant power budget (approaching 5.6 W) is wasted. Counting Mechanism and Power Counting Mechanism have identical performance only when moving users are on the cell border (a FACH is deployed in both cases).

Finally, at time instance 1341 sec, the group of 10 moving users enters the service area of the target cell. At this point, according to current Counting Mechanism, the source cell switches to PTP mode (multiple DCHs) since it serves only 4 users. Power Counting Mechanism also uses DCHs and, thus, both approaches have similar performance. At the same time, the target cell switches to PTM mode (a single FACH) and serves 16 users. However, as the moving group in the target cell keeps moving towards the base station, Power Counting Mechanism appropriately adapts its functionality and leads to better utilization of power resources in contradiction to the static transport channel assignment of the existing MBMS specifications.

Conclusively, from Fig. 5b and Fig. 6b it is obvious that the proposed Power Counting Mechanism is prevailing over the current Counting Mechanism. The power based criterion for switching between different transport channels as well as the deployment of the HS-DSCH strongly optimizes resource allocation and enhances MBMS performance. Similar results can also be extracted in the case of microcells. However, in microcells results are even more optimistic due to the fact that HS-DSCH performs better than in macrocells (Fig. 3). In addition, in microcells the higher cell isolation (which entails better geometry distribution) and the less multipath propagation ensure the provision of higher MBMS data rate services.

5   Conclusions and Future Work

In this paper we proposed a novel Power Counting Mechanism for the efficient transport channel selection in MBMS enabled UMTS networks. The proposed mechanism integrates the HSDPA mobile broadband technology as a part of the overall architecture and defines downlink power as the undisputable switching criterion between different radio bearers. This novel mechanism is capable of conceiving dynamic changes in such wireless environments and optimally adapting its functionality in order to maximize resource efficiency. Simulation results prove that Power Counting Mechanism strongly outperforms current Counting Mechanism of MBMS specifications, by exploiting high power and capacity efficiency.

The step that follows this work is to further examine and optimize the provision of MBMS over HSDPA through experiments conducted in the ns-2 simulator. In addition, power saving techniques that can further improve MBMS performance over HSDPA will be investigated.

References

1. Holma, H., Toskala, A.: WCDMA for UMTS: HSPA Evolution and LTE. 4th edition, John Wiley & Sons (2007)
2. 3GPP, TS 22.146 V7.1.0. Technical Specification Group Services and System Aspects; Multimedia Broadcast/Multicast Service; Stage 1 (Release 7)
3. 3GPP, TR 23.846 V6.1.0. Technical Specification Group Services and System Aspects; Multimedia Broadcast/Multicast Service; Architecture and functional description (Release 6)
4. 3GPP, TS 25.308 V5.4.0. Technical Specification Group Radio Access Network; High Speed Downlink Packet Access (HSDPA); Stage 2 (Release 5)
5. Perez-Romero, J., Sallent, O., Agusti, R., Diaz-Guerra, M.: Radio Resource Management Strategies in UMTS. John Wiley & Sons (2005)
6. 3GPP TS 25.803 V6.0.0, Technical Specification Group Radio Access Network; S-CCPCH performance for MBMS, (Release 6)
7. Holma, H., Toskala, A.: HSDPA/HSUPA for UMTS: High Speed Radio Access for Mobile Communications. John Wiley & Sons (2006)
8. 3GPP, TS 25.346 V7.2.0. Introduction of the Multimedia Broadcast Multicast Service (MBMS) in the Radio Access Network (RAN), Stage 2, (Release 7)
9. Alexiou, A., Bouras, C., Rekkas, E.: A Power Control Scheme for Efficient Radio Bearer Selection in MBMS. IEEE International Symposium on World of Wireless, Mobile and Multimedia Networks (WoWMoM) (2007)
10. 3GPP, TR 101.102 V3.2.0. Universal Mobile Telecommunications System (UMTS); Selection procedures for the choice of radio transmission technologies of the UMTS (UMTS 30.03 version 3.2.0)

Detours Save Energy in Mobile Wireless Networks

Chia Ching Ooi and Christian Schindelhauer

Chia Ching Ooi · Christian Schindelhauer
Albert-Ludwigs-Universität Freiburg, Computer Networks and Telematics, Georges-Köhler-Allee 51, 79110 Freiburg, Germany, e-mail: {ooi, schindel}@informatik.uni-freiburg.de

Abstract Autonomous robotic systems have been gaining the attention of research community in mobile ad hoc network since the past few years. While motion cost and communications cost constitute the primary energy consumers, each of them is investigated independently. By taking into account the power consumption of both entities, the overall energy efficiency of a system can be further improved. In this paper, the energy optimization problem of radio communication and motion is examined. We consider a hybrid wireless network that consists of a single autonomous mobile node and multiple relay nodes. The mobile node interacts with the relays within its vicinity by continuously communicating high-bandwidth data, e.g. triggered by a multimedia application like video surveillance. The goal is to find the best path such that the energy consumption for both mobility and communications is minimized. We introduce the Radio-Energy-Aware (*REA*) path computation strategy by utilizing node mobility. Given the starting point, the target point and the position of the relays, our simulation results show that the proposed strategy improves the energy efficiency of mobile node compared to the Motion-Energy-Aware (*MEA*) path constructed based only on the mobility cost.

1 Introduction

With the unprecedented growth of wireless communication technologies witnessed over the past two decades, intensive researches [1] have been conducted to improve the performance of communications in mobile wireless network. Among them, a number of improvements were achieved [2, 3] through the extensive investigation of node mobility. However, most of the existing literature assumes that mobility cannot be controlled. A mobile node in a wireless network can be a mobile handheld device, a manned or unmanned vehicle, a mobile robot, or a combination of them. Among them, the artificial mobile nodes are capable of controlling their own movement but the natural mobile nodes are not.

Recently, networked robotics has been gaining increasing interest among robotic and mobile networking research community. Many modern mobile robots are already equipped with networking capabilities [4, 5], using either radio frequency, or infra-red communications. Multi-robot systems (MRS) [6, 7, 8, 9] take the ad-

Please use the following format when citing this chapter:

Ooi, C.C. and Schindelhauer, C., 2008, in IFIP International Federation for Information Processing, Volume 284; *Wireless and Mobile Networking*; Zoubir Mammeri; (Boston: Springer), pp. 69–82.

vantage of collective and cooperative behavior of robot team through inter-robot communications. Swarm robotics [10, 11] is an example of MRS that deploys and coordinates large number of relatively simple physical robots to complete the assigned tasks as a team.

The co-location of the motion and task control systems with the communications mechanisms in a robot enables the co-exploitation of individual subsystems, providing a completely new kind of networked autonomy. However, only little on-going researches make use of this advantage. Our paper explores this uniqueness of an artificial mobile node to achieve energy optimization.

The remainder of the paper is organized as follows. Section 2 reviews related work. In Section 3, we present the system and the energy models used in our research and define the problem of computing the minimal-energy detour for a mobile robot. Based on these foundations, we propose an optimal-energy path computation strategy and analyze the algorithm in Section 4. The proposed scheme is evaluated through simulation described in Section 5. Lastly, we make concluding remarks and discuss future works.

2 Related Work

A mobility control scheme is proposed in [12] to improve the communication performance. They show that controlled mobility increases network performance through extensive evaluations on its feasibility. However, this scheme mandates all relay nodes to move to the optimal configurations in order to optimize the communications performance. Therefore, it can not be applied to certain applications that consist of static node or node restricted to move.

The authors of [13] have similar objectives and another approach. They focus on optimizing the positions of relay nodes for a single source-destination pair. Both works involve high number of relays, and consequently, high power efficiency can be achieved in the entire network. We propose a different approach by making use of node mobility of the source to optimize its energy consumption, given that the relay node is restricted from moving, for instance, due to the assigned task.

In [14], Liu et al. proposed a resource-aware movement strategy to achieve energy conservation by guiding the nodes movement and utilizing node heterogeneity. However, motion cost for mechanical movement is not taken into consideration as they assume all communication devices are carried by people moving on foot.

Our work is motivated by the natural fact that radio energy degrades over the transmission range, and the limited energy resource carried by most mobile nodes. A study of mobile ad hoc networks based on *Khehera* [21] provide the practical insights that in certain environments, motion cost and communications cost constitute the primary energy consumers. While the mobility cost increases linearly, the communication cost grows at least quadratically with the communication distance. Thus, it is advantageous to move a robot towards its communicating node at a certain radio range.

Recently, the optimization problem of motion and communication cost was stud-ied in [15]. Taking a single-robot single-base station scenario, they solved the prob-lem by using a proposed approximation algorithm based on Dijkstra's algorithm to compute the minimal energy path, and show that up to nearly 50% of total energy can be saved. However, it can be achieved only if the robot is allowed to move more than half of the transmission distance relative to its originally planned path, which is not applicable to many scenarios.

In this paper, we study how a minimal-energy detour can be computed to op-timize the energy consumption of a mobile robot in a multiple relay wireless network. Motivated by the emergence of the promising wireless technology like IEEE 802.11n [16] and wireless multimedia sensor network [17], we are interested in the applications in which a team of mobile robots has to exchange a high volume of data over the wireless medium among themselves, or to its base station through multiple relays. We concentrate on optimizing the energy consumed by both mobil-ity and communications.

3 Preliminaries

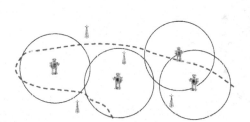

Fig. 1 Mobile Robots and Relay Stations

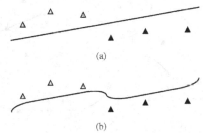

Fig. 2 Energy-Aware Paths **(a)** A *MEA* Path **(b)** A *REA* Path

As shown in Fig. 1, we consider a hybrid wireless network that consists of a team of autonomous mobile robots and multiple relays. All nodes can communicate with each other wirelessly. The lifetime of a robot is limited to the energy resource it carries along. Every robot is assigned with different task(s): searching, exploring, sensing, foraging, and so on. Some are required to transmit the mission-specific data directly or via relay(s) to a target node. The relay can be either a static node such as a base station or an access point, or a mobile node. An example scenario is that a robot is deployed to collect data from sensors [18] and transmit them to the target via single- or multi-hop communications, forming a robot-assisted wireless sensor network. Another potential application is the robot surveillance system [19].

We assume that every point on the robot navigation area is covered by at least one relay. The positions of the relays are known prior to path computation. The robot knows the Euclidean distance to the relay within its vicinity, which serves as the destination of the data transmission.

On the other hand, at any instant, a mobile robot is assumed to know its route towards its next destination, which is planned based only on the motion cost and equal to the Euclidean distance between a robot's start point and target point. We call this route a motion-energy-aware (*MEA*) path. A *MEA* path is a straight line because moving on Euclidean distance costs minimal motion energy. *MEA* path is not necessarily the optimal energy path since the robot consumes the energy not only for the movement but also for the wireless communications. A minimal energy path constructed based on both the communication and motion cost is called a Radio-Energy-Aware (*REA*) path in the rest of the paper. Fig. 2 shows the examples of both *MEA* and *REA* paths.

3.1 System Model

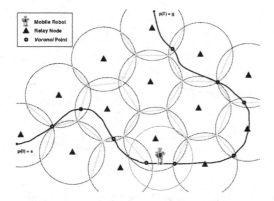

Fig. 3 Navigation Area of Mobile Robot in a Multi-relay Network

The navigation area of a mobile robot is modeled on a two dimensional Euclidean space as illustrated in Fig. 3. The node position is indicated as a continuous function of time $p : [0,T] \mapsto \mathbb{R} \times \mathbb{R}$ such that the position of the mobile robot at time t in Cartesian Coordinates is $p(t) = (p_x(t), p_y(t))$. At the beginning, we have $p(0) = s$ where s denotes the start position of the node. At the end, we have $p(T) = g$, where g is the target position. Both positions are obtained from *MEA* path. When we compute the path, we approximate the path by k sub-paths of constant speed $P = ((t_0, x_0, y_0), (t_1, x_1, y_1), \dots, (t_k, x_k, y_k))$ for $t_0 < t_1 < \dots < t_k$ where the corresponding path function is given by

$$p(t) = \left(x_i + \frac{(t - t_i)(x_{i+1} - x_i)}{t_{i+1} - t_i}, y_i + \frac{(t - t_i)(y_{i+1} - y_i)}{t_{i+1} - t_i} \right),$$

for $t \in [t_i, t_{i+1})$.

A set of static relays is defined as $R = \{r_1, ..., r_m\}$, where m represents the number of relays interacting with mobile robot moving on path P, and $r_i = (r_{i,x}, r_{i,y})$. Let the maximum radio range of all nodes be R_{max} and the relay in use at t be r_i. The transmission range between robot and relay for all $t \in [0, T] : ||p(t) - r_i||_2 \leq R_{max}$, where $||u - v||_2 = \sqrt{(u_x - v_x)^2 + (u_y - v_y)^2}$. Due to the limited radio range, the robot needs to switch to different relay whenever it moves out of the vicinity of current relay. The switching of relay happens at a set of positions on *MEA* path, indicated by a set of *Voronoi* points, $V = \{v_1, ..., v_{m+1}\}$, where $v_1 = s$ and $v_{m+1} = g$.

Every consecutive *Voronoi* point pair, v_i and v_{i+1}, defines a path segment, s_i, and a relay, r_i. Robot moving on s_i communicates only with r_i, which transmission range, $R_i = ||p(t) - r_i||_2 \leq ||p(t) - r_j||_2$ for $j \neq i$ and $1 \leq j \leq m$. Therefore, this link has the lowest transmission cost given that the radio condition of the transmission medium between robot and all relays in range are the same. While the robot communicates with relay r_i, all other relays of set R are free for communications with other nodes.

A *MEA* path, P_{mea} is composed of multiple fragments f and defined as $P_{mea} = \{f_1, ..., f_k\}$, where k is the number of fragments. Meanwhile, a fragment consists of multiple segment s, and is defined as $f_j = \{s_{j,1}, ..., s_{j,q_j}\}$, where the total number of segments on P_{mea} is given by $m = \sum_{i=1}^{k} q_j$. We explain how to determine a fragment from a *MEA* path in Section 4.

3.2 Energy Models for Robot

As the robot communicates with relays while moving, its energy model comprises mobility cost and communication cost. For robot motion, we adopt the energy model $E_m = m \cdot d_m$, where d_m is the distance traversed by the robot in *meter* and the movement parameter, m, in *Joule/meter*, is a constant value determined by the mass of the robot, the friction to the surface, gravity and acceleration. This model is suitable for wheeled robot [12], and is adopted by [13, 15, 20].

We refer to [13, 15, 22] for the communications energy models. The transmit energy model $E_{tx}(\ell, d_c) = \ell \cdot (d_c^{\alpha} \cdot e_{tx} + e_{cct})$ is used for transmission of ℓ bits data over d_c measured in *meter*, where e_{tx} is the energy consumed by the power amplifier of transceiver to transmit one bit data over one meter, and e_{cct} is the energy used by the transceiver to transmit or receive one bit, measured in *Joule/bit*. Depending on the condition of wireless transmission medium, α ranges from 2 to 6. On the other hand, the energy consumption for receiving ℓ bits data is defined as $E_{rc}(\ell) = \ell \cdot e_{cct}$, which is independent of the distance between communicating nodes.

3.3 Multi-Relay Communications Model

We modify the Position-critical Communications Model (PCM) of [15] designed for single relay communication. A sequence of tasks $Q_1, ..., Q_n$ is defined for the mobile robot. Each task $Q_i = (A_i, B_i)$ consists of a region A_i from which the robot may choose a point $p_i \in A_i$ and the size of data B_i the robot needs to transmit. A robot path solves the task $Q = ((A_1, B_1), \ldots, (A_n, B_n))$ at points $(x_1, \ldots, x_n)$ if $\exists t_1 < t_2 < t_3 < \cdots < t_n$ with $p(t_i) = x_i$ and $x_i \in A_i$.

Based on the energy models described in Section 3.2, the energy consumption of a robot with path p and solution points $x = (x_1, \ldots, x_n)$ is then defined as:

$$E_{pcm}(Q, p, x) := E_{tx}(Q, p, x) + E_m(p) ,$$

where $E_{tx}(Q, p, x) = \sum_{i=1}^{n} B_i \cdot (||x_i - r_c||_2)^{\alpha} \cdot e_{tx}$, $E_m(p) = m \cdot D$, and D is the path length of p. In $E_{tx}(Q, p, x)$, r_c is the current relay node interacting with robot at x_i. In a multi-relay network, we are interested in the accumulated energy consumption of the mobile robot moving from s to g, denoted as $E_{total}(p)$. Using the system model defined in Section 3.1, we have:

$$E_{total}(p) = \sum_{j=1}^{k} E_{pcm,j}(Q, p, x) ,$$

where $E_{pcm,j}(Q, p, x) = \sum_{w=1}^{q_j} \sum_{i=1}^{n} (B_{i,w} \cdot (||x_{i,w} - r_c||_2)^{\alpha} \cdot e_{tx} + m \cdot D)$.

3.4 Minimal-Energy Detour Problem Statement

The minimal-energy detour is also called the *REA* path. In this problem, the location of relay nodes, the initial and target position of the mobile robot are given. The mobile robot communicates with multiple relays while moving towards its target position. The goal is to find the optimal energy path to reach the given target point.

Definition. *The path optimization problem for multi-relay communications model. Given a sequence of tasks $Q = ((s, 0), (A_1, B_1), \ldots, (A_w, B_w), (g, 0))$ and a set of relay, R, the mobile robot has to find a (discrete) path $(s, x_1, \ldots, x_w, g)$ that solves the tasks, i.e. $x_i \in A_i$ for all $i \in \{1, \ldots, w\}$, and minimizes the total energy $E_{total}(p) = \sum_{j=1}^{k} E_{pcm,j}(Q, p, x)$.*

4 Algorithms

We introduce *REA* path computation strategy described in Fig. 4. The resulting *REA* path, P_{rea}, has minimum total cost of motion and communication for mobile robot.

Fig. 6 shows the breakdown of a *MEA* path into fragments and segments defined in Section 3.1. Let ρ_{r_i} be the polarity of the relay r_i. To determine which fragment a segment s_i belongs to, ρ_{r_i} must be first determined based on the position of r_i relative to *MEA* path as follows: Taking $p(0) = (0, 0)$, $\rho_{r_i} = 1$ for $r_{i,y} > p_y(t)$ at $r_{i,x}$, $\rho_{r_i} = 0$ for $r_{i,y} = p_y(t)$ at $r_{i,x}$, and $\rho_{r_i} = -1$ for $r_{i,y} < p_y(t)$ at $r_{i,x}$. Successive relays

Radio-Energy-Aware Path Computation
  Obtain *MEA Path*, P_{mea}
  Identify *Voronoi* point set, V
  Obtain relay node set, R and its polarity, ρ_R
  $i, j \leftarrow 1$
  $f_j.sp \leftarrow v_i$
  while $i \leq m$
      if $\rho_{r_i} \neq \rho_{r_{i+1}}$
          $f_j.ep \leftarrow v_{i+1}$
          $f_{j+1}.sp \leftarrow v_{i+1}$
          if $\rho_{r_i} = 0$
              $f_j \leftarrow \{s_{f_j.sp}, \ldots, s_i\}$
          else
              Run modified PCM-Dijkstra-
                Refinement algorithm
              $f_j' \leftarrow p_{\varepsilon'}$
          end of if
          Increment j
      end of if
      Increment i
  end of while
  return *REA Path*, $P_{rea} \leftarrow \{f_1', \ldots, f_k'\}$

Fig. 4 *REA* Path Computation

Modified PCM-Dijkstra-Refinement
  Obtain relay node set, R
  Obtain $f_j.sp$ and $f_j.ep$
  $s \leftarrow f_j.sp$
  $g \leftarrow f_j.ep$
  Carefully choose parameters $c, k > 1$
  $\varepsilon' \leftarrow \frac{\|s, g\|_2}{c}$
  Construct $G_{\varepsilon'}$
  Use Dijkstra's algorithm to compute
      optimal path $p_{\varepsilon'}$ in $G_{\varepsilon'}$
  while $\varepsilon' > \varepsilon$
      $\varepsilon' \leftarrow \varepsilon'/c$
      Refine around $p_{\varepsilon'}$:
          Construct graph $G_{\varepsilon'}$
          Erase all nodes in $V_{\varepsilon'}$ which are not
              within $k \cdot \varepsilon'$ distance to a node of p
          Erase all edges adjacent to erased
              nodes
      Use Dijkstra's algorithm to compute
          optimal path $p_{\varepsilon'}$ in resulting graph $G_{\varepsilon'}$
  end of while
  return $p_{\varepsilon'}$

Fig. 5 Modified PCM-Dijkstra Algorithm

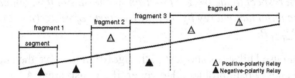

Fig. 6 Fragment, Segment and Polarity of Relay Node relative to *MEA* Path

having the same ρ_{r_i} are grouped into the same fragment. Given the set of relay R, once ρ_{r_i} for all relays are determined, the *REA* path computation strategy constructs a set of fragment F of a given *MEA* path, P_{mea}. For each fragment f_j, a modified PCM-Dijkstra-Refinement algorithm explained next is used to compute a minimal-energy detour, f_j'. The final output of the strategy is an optimal-energy *REA* path, $P_{rea} = \{f_1', \ldots, f_k'\}$.

The PCM-Dijkstra-Refinement algorithm [15] was designed to cope only with one-robot one-relay scenario. As showned in Fig. 5, we modified it to solve the optimal energy path problem in multiple relay communications. The algorithm is invoked for each fragment that composes the *MEA* path, with fragment f_j as an input and the optimal-energy fragment, f_j' as the output. A fragment f_j may contain multiple segments, and thus, multiple relays. Therefore, before running the algorithm, we need to determine fragment start point, $f_j.sp$, fragment end point, $f_j.ep$, and set of relays, R.

According to the PCM-Dijkstra-Refinement algorithm in [15], a finite candidate set $V_{i,\varepsilon} = y_{i,1}, y_{i,2}, \ldots \in A_i$ has to be selected such that for all $u \in A_i$ within the transmission range of a relay node, a candidate $y_{i,j}$ exists within distance ε. This is done by using a two-dimensional grid positions with distances of at most

$\frac{\varepsilon}{\sqrt{2}}$. This candidate can be placed with distance ε if the task areas are lines. To construct a graph $G_\varepsilon = (V_\varepsilon, E_\varepsilon)$, the node set $V_\varepsilon = \bigcup_{i \in \{1,...,n\}} V_{i,\varepsilon}$ and the edge set $E_\varepsilon = \bigcup_{i \in \{1,...,n-1\}} V_{i,\varepsilon} \times V_{i+1,\varepsilon}$ are defined. The weight function for the edges is defined as below:

$$w(y_{i,j}, y_{i+1,k}) = B_i \cdot (||y_{i,j} - r_c||_2)^\alpha \cdot e_{tx} + m \cdot ||y_{i,j}, y_{i+1,k}||_2$$

for $i < n - 1$ and all j, k. For $i = n - 1$, we define the weight function, $w(y_{n-1,j}, y_{n,k}) = (B_{n-1} \cdot (||y_{n-1,j} - r_c||_2)^\alpha + B_n \cdot (||y_{n,j} - r_c||_2)^\alpha) \cdot e_{tx} + m \cdot ||y_{n-1,j}, y_{n,k}||_2$. Note that the weight of $w(p)$ represents the energy consumption of a mobile robot on this path. Now, let p_{min} be the minimal-energy path in the original problem. By the definition of G_ε, a path p exists in G_ε such that $||p_{min,i} - p_i||_2 \leq \varepsilon$. Thus,

$$|E_m(p_{min}) - E_m(p)| \leq m \cdot \varepsilon \cdot (n-1) .$$

It indicates that $|E_{tx}(p_{min}) - E_{tx}(p)| \leq e_{tx} \cdot \varepsilon \cdot \alpha \cdot (R_{max} + \varepsilon)^{\alpha-1} \cdot \sum_{i=1}^n B_i$, where R_{max} is the maximum transmission distance of the relay node. Therefore, the theorem below follows:

Theorem 1. *With respect to the weight function w, the minimal weighted path in G_ε approximates the minimum energy by an additive term of $m \cdot \varepsilon \cdot (n-1) + e_{tx} \cdot \varepsilon \cdot \alpha \cdot (R_{max} + \varepsilon)^{\alpha-1} \cdot \sum_{i=1}^n B_i$.*

Therefore, we can use Dijkstra's shortest path algorithm to solve the approximation of the minimum energy path problem. However, if the task areas A_i are regions, i.e. containing some small-sized disk, the number of nodes of G_ε grows proportional to $\Theta(\frac{1}{\varepsilon^2})$ and the size of the edge set grows by $\Theta(\frac{1}{\varepsilon^4})$, which is the decisive term of Dijkstra's algorithm.

Introducing the heuristic refinement strategy shown in Fig. 5, we can improve its running time considerably. The following theorem shows that this algorithm is very efficient.

Theorem 2. *The PCM-Dijkstra-Refinement algorithm has an asymptotic running time of $\mathcal{O}(n \cdot \log(\frac{1}{\varepsilon}))$ for general task areas aiming at an additive error bound of $\mathcal{O}(\varepsilon)$.*

5 Performance Evaluation

In this section, we study the impact of various parameters on the performance of the proposed scheme and compare it with that without using our approach. Two main criteria of our evaluation are the percentage and the total energy saving that can be achieved by the mobile robot using the proposed scheme. The first criterion shows the performance gain of *REA* path, while the latter is important to determine if *REA* path computation is beneficial for different scenarios.

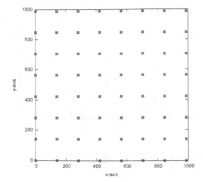

Fig. 7 Location of Relays in Simulation

Simulation Environment Parameter	Value
Field size, (m²)	1000 1000
Number of relay node	64
Maximum transmission range, R_{max} (m)	100

Parameter	Value(s)
Energy consumed by transceiver circuitry to transmit or receive a bit, e_{cct} (Joule)	10^{-7}
Energy consumed by transceiver amplifier to transmit one bit data over one meter, e_{tx} (Joule)	10^{-12}
Energy to receive a bit, e_{rc} (Joule)	10^{-7}
Path loss exponent, α	3, 4
Data size, B (MB)	1, 2, 3
Maximum detour gap allowed, G (m)	1 to 10
Energy to move robot over one meter, m (Joule)	1, 2

Fig. 8 Simulation Parameters

5.1 Simulation Environment Setup

We simulate 64 static relays on an area of 1000m   1000m as illustrated in Fig. 7. This simplified simulation model is sufficient to provide various situations that require a robot to interact with multiple relays while traveling towards a target. The robot needs to switch to the best relay at a number of *Voronoi* points as explained in section 3.1.

At the beginning, a *MEA* path is constructed by randomly selecting a start point on the left edge and an end point on the right edge of the simulated area. A mobile robot is deployed to travel from the start point to the end point while transmitting mission-specific data to selected relays. The maximum transmission range of all nodes are assumed to be 100m, which is applicable to most 802.11 standards [23]. Simulation results shown in [15] indicate that higher maximum radio range yields more energy saving. The transmission range between robot and relay changes based on the instantaneous robot position on the path, relative to the location of the relay in use.

Fig. 8 shows the simulation parameters. e_{cct} e_{tx} e_{rc}, are assigned according to [22]. A robot may perform its assigned tasks in indoor or outdoor environment. To simulate different environments, the path loss exponent α is varied from 3 to 4. We eliminate $\alpha = 2$ because it is hardly achieved in realistic environment. The data size used, B, ranges from 1 to 3 MB, and is suitable for multimedia data transmission for the applications stated in Section 1. We simulate the robot to transmit B data at each meter of *MEA* path within its task region.

Moreover, depending on the application, robot movement is restricted within a task-specific area between the relay and a *MEA* path. We introduce the parameter G to indicate the maximum gap allowed between *REA* and *MEA* path. It also serves as the tuning parameter for applications with specific delay tolerance if a robot moves on a longer path, as a balance of energy and delay trade-off needs to be achieved. Lastly, we vary the motion power constant m between 1 and 2*J/m*. These values are applicable to wheeled robots weighed between 10 to 20kg travelling on a flat

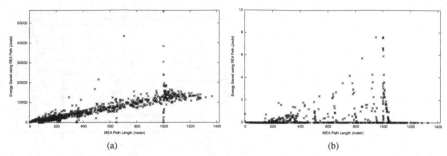

(a)   (b)

Fig. 9 Overall Energy Saving Achieved using *REA* Path (**a**) Maximum energy saved (α=4, B=3, G=10, m=1) (**b**) Minimum energy saved (α=3, B=1, G=1, m=2)

surface [15], for instance, *Khepera II* at 80g to 250g, and *Khepera III* at 690g to 2kg [4], *s-bot* at 660g [11], and *e-puck* at 150g [5]. Robots at lighter weight (lower m) further improve the performance of *REA* path. By using various combination of these parameters, we perform 100 simulation runs for each combination and compute the total and percentage of energy saved by the robot.

5.2 Simulation Results

In every simulation run, total energy saved is recorded at the end point of each fragment, $f_{i}.ep$ and the target position, g. Different *MEA* path length can be simulated up to the maximum length of $\sqrt{2 \cdot 1000^2}$, based on the size of the simulated area.

Fig. 9 shows the two simulations producing the maximum and minimum energy saved. In both cases, the highest energy saving is observed when a straight path appears at a certain distance in parallel to a row of relays. In Fig. 9(a), α, B, G are set to the maximum values, while m at its minimum. On the contrary, in Fig. 9(b), α, B, G are at the minimum values, while m at its maximum. We will describe how α, B, G contribute to the performance gain of the proposed strategy. Moreover, in order to determine if the *REA* path computation is worth running, it is important to note the overall minimum energy saved in our simulation. More about it will be elaborated at the end of the section.

Impact of Path Loss Exponent, α. Fig. 10 illustrates the effect of varying α on the energy saving by using different *MEA* path lengths. First, in Fig. 10(a), by fixing the parameters B=3, G=10, m=1, the *REA* paths save around 30% and 7% on average for α=4 and α=3 respectively. We will observe later that the impact of α is comparably high among all parameters. Next, to illustrate the total energy saved, we choose the combination of parameters that produces two best results when α=3 and α=4. Using B=3, G=10, m=1, the impact of α is illustrated in Fig. 10(b). It shows the very large difference of energy saving with various α. We further analyze the impact of α by selecting the combination of parameters (B=1, G=1, m=2) that produces the minimum energy saving for α=4, and comparing it with that of α=3

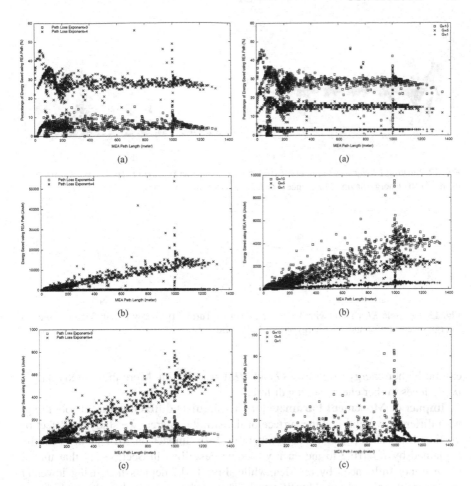

Fig. 10 Varying Path Loss Exponent **(a)** Percentage of Energy Saving (B=3, G=10, m=1, α=4 vs. α=3) **(b)** Maximum Energy Saving Difference (B=3, G=10, m=1, α=4 vs. α=3) **(c)** Minimum Energy Saving Difference (α=4, B=1, G=1, m=2 vs. α=3, B=3, G=10, m=1)

Fig. 11 Varying Maximum Detour Gap Allowed **(a)** Percentage of Energy Saving for G_1, G_5, G_{10} (α=4, B=3, m=1) **(b)** Energy Saving Difference for G_1, G_5, G_{10} (α=4, B=1, m=1) **(c)** Energy Saving Difference for G_1, G_5, G_{10} (α=3, B=1, m=1)

in the first case. As shown in Fig. 10(c), the energy saving difference is lower, but still high compared to the influence of other parameters to be described next.

Impact of Maximum Detour Gap Allowed, _G_. Fig. 11 shows the impact of varying _G_ on the performance of _REA_. As explained in Section 5.1, a task region A_i is application-dependent. To simulate various sizes of A_i, we introduce a set of $G = \{G_1, G_2, \ldots, G_{10}\}$, where $G_i = i$. First, we show in Fig. 11(a) the percentage of energy saved for G_1, G_5, G_{10} when α=4, B=3, m=1. The impact is observed to be lower than that of α. Next, we show the total energy saved for varying _G_ under the influence of α in Fig. 11(b) and Fig. 11(c) using α=3, 4, B=1, m=1. Both results

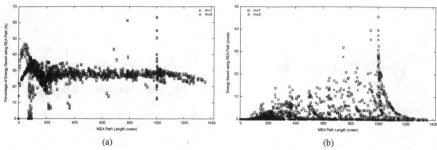

(a)   (b)

Fig. 12 Varying Movement Parameter **(a)** Percentage of Energy Saving (α=4, B=3, G=10, m=1 vs. m=2) **(b)** Energy Saving Difference (α=3, B=1, G=5, m=1 vs. m=2)

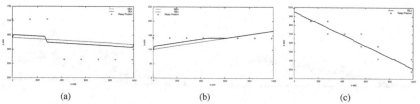

(a)   (b)   (c)

Fig. 13 Example *REA* Paths with Various Number of Turns **(a)** Energy saved: 365.66 Joule **(b)** Energy saved: 4.95 Joule. **(c)** Energy saved: 1.47 Joule

exhibit higher energy saved over *G* and *MEA* path length. More importantly, larger α produces higher energy saving difference.

Impact of Movement Parameter, *m*. To simulate different types of robot (e.g. with different weight) and the surface of the simulated area, we study the effect of *m*. Fig. 12(a) shows that *m* has comparably little impact on *REA* path. It can be explained by referring to the energy models described in Section 3.2 that unlike *G*, *m* is not influenced by α. Meanwhile, Fig. 12(b) depicts that using lower *m* increases total energy saved by *REA* path. This is also supported by the study of the tradeoff between mobility energy and communication cost [12]. Furthermore, we observe some *REA* paths falling on *MEA* paths when the mobility energy consumed is much higher than the communication cost, resulting in zero energy savings. It occurs mostly on short *MEA* paths. Higher communication cost (higher *B* or α) is needed to compensate *m*. However, since we simulate the lowest *m*=1, our approach is applicable to all lightweight robots mentioned in Section 5.1 using *m* <1*J/m*, leading to higher energy saving than our simulation results.

Next, we show some example *REA* paths with the total energy saved in Fig. 13. The objective of this analysis is to determine if a *REA* path is worth computing. Fig. 13(a) presents a scenario that achieves a total energy saving of 365.66 Joule, representing one of the strong *REA* paths. On the other hand, the two example paths in Fig. 13(b) and Fig. 13(c) illustrate the weak *REA* paths. In the first weak path, the total energy saved is at merely 4.95 Joule but the robot needs to make three distinct turns traveling on it. The second path shows an even weaker path with more turns. Turning needs extra energy for controlling the motion of robot wheels. Let the additional energy needed to move on *REA* path be β, which includes energy to compute *REA* path and control robot wheels. If the energy saving is too low to compensate β, it is unnecessary to trigger *REA* path computation. The robot can decide if a particular turn on *REA* path is worth making in terms of its energy efficiency.

With the simulation results explained above, we show the impact of each parameter and different combination of the parameters on the performance gain of *REA* path. Overall, the total energy saved increases with higher α, G, B, the length of *MEA* path and its fragments. Higher m reduces the amount of energy saved, though its impact is less than the others. Analysis on the percentage of energy saving shows that the path loss exponent has the most significant impact. If the communication takes place in free space, the robot will always move on *MEA* path.

6 Conclusions and Future Works

In this paper, we study the energy optimization problem for an artificial mobile node in a multiple relay wireless network. We propose a novel energy-aware movement strategy that computes a minimal-energy detour by considering both the motion cost and the communication cost of a mobile node. The mobile node takes the full advantage of the optimal-energy path to prolong its lifetime while working towards its mission. By analyzing the impact of different parameters, we show the simulation results, which are promising in improving the energy efficiency of future networked robot system. For further exploration, the proposed *REA* strategy can be incorporated into other aspects, such as improving the performance of wireless communications in terms of its Quality of Service, through utilizing the benefits of controllable node mobility. Lastly, a thorough study on the trade-off between the energy and time consumption to produce an optimal path is significant to time-critical applications.

Acknowledgements This research is partially supported by *DFG-Sonderforschungsbereich SPP 1183: Organic Computing. Smart Teams: Local, Distributed Strategies for Self-Organizing Robotic Exploration Teams.*

References

1. V. Rodoplu and T. Meng, "Minimum energy mobile wireless networks," in *Proceedings of IEEE ICC*, vol. 3, 1998, pp. 1633–1639.
2. W. Su, S. Lee, and M. Gerla, "Mobility prediction in wireless networks," in *Proceedings of the IEEE Military Communications Conference (MILCOM)*, 2000.
3. A. Jardosh, E. Belding-Royer, K. Almeroth, and S. Suri, "Towards realistic mobility models for mobile ad hoc networks," in *Proceedings of ACM MobiCom*, 2003.
4. *K-Team Corporation.* http://www.k-team.com, 2007.
5. *EPFL Education Robot.* http://www.e-puck.org, 2007.

6. A. Farinelli, L. Iocchi, and D. Nardi, "Multirobot systems: A classification focused on coordination," *IEEE Trans. Syst., Man, Cybern.*, 2004.
7. D. Koutsonikolas, S. M. Das, Y. C. Hu, Y.-H. Lu, and C. S. G. Lee, "Cocoa: Coordinated cooperative localization for mobile multi-robot ad hoc networks," in *the 26th IEEE ICDCSW*.
8. M. Powers, T. Balch, and B. Lab, "Value-based communication preservation for mobile robots," in *IEEE ICRA*, 2004.
9. S. M. Das, Y. C. Hu, C. G. Lee, and Y.-H. Lu, "An efficient group communication protocol for mobile robots," in *IEEE ICRA*, 2005.
10. *Swarm-robotics.org.* http://www.swarm-robotics.org/, 2007.
11. *Swarm-bots Project.* http://www.swarm-bots.org, 2007.
12. D. K. Goldenberg, J. Lin, A. S. Morse, B. E. Rosen, and Y. R. Yang, "Towards mobility as a network control primitive," in *Proceedings of the 5th ACM MobiHoc*, 2004, pp. 163–174.
13. C. Tang and P. K. McKinley, "Energy optimization under informed mobility," *IEEE Trans. Parallel Distrib. Syst.*, vol. 17, no. 9, pp. 947–962, 2006.
14. W. Liu, Y. Zhang, K. Lu, and Y. Fang, "Energy conservation through resource-aware movement in heterogeneous mobile ad hoc networks," *IEEE Trans. Parallel Distrib. Syst.*, vol. 11, no. 1, pp. 7–20, 2006.
15. C. C. Ooi and C. Schindelhauer, "Minimal energy path planning for wireless robots," in *ROBOCOMM*, 2007.
16. *Status of Project IEEE 802.11n - Standard for Enhancements for Higher Throughput.* http://grouper.ieee.org/groups/802/11/Reports/802.11_Timelines.htm, 2007.
17. I. F. Akyildiz, T. Melodia, and K. R. Chowdhury, "A survey on wireless multimedia sensor networks," *Comput. Networks*, vol. 51, no. 4, pp. 921–960, 2007.
18. C.-H. Wang, Yu Wu, "Robot-assisted sensor network deployment and data collection," in *CIRA*, 2007, pp. 467–472.
19. Y.-C. Tseng, Y.-C. Wang, K.-Y. Cheng, and Y.-Y. Hsieh, "imouse: an integrated mobile surveillance and wireless sensor system," vol. 40, no. 6.   IEEE Computer, 2007.
20. Y. Mei, Y.-H. Lu, H. Y.C., and L. C.S.G., "A case study of mobile robot's energy consumption and conservation techniques," in *12th IEEE ICAR*, 2005, pp. 492– 497.
21. Gruenewald, M., Rueckert, U., Schindelhauer, C., Volbert, K.: Directed power-variable infrared communication for the mini robot khepera. In: Proceedings of the 2nd International Conference on AMIRE, pp. 113–122 (2003)
22. A. T. Hoang and M. M., "Exploiting wireless broadcast in spatially correlated sensor networks," in *IEEE ICC*, 2005, pp. 2807– 2811.
23. *IEEE 802.11 WIRELESS LOCAL AREA NETWORKS - The Working Group for WLAN Standards.* http://www.ieee802.org/11/, 2007.

Enhancing Power Saving Mechanisms for Ad hoc Networks

Wafa Akkari and Abdelfettah Belghith

Wafa Akkari
HANA Research Group, ENSI, University of Manouba, Tunisia 2010, e-mail: wefa.akkari@gmail.com

Abdelfettah Belghith
HANA Research Group, ENSI, University of Manouba, Tunisia 2010, e-mail: abdelfattah.belghith@ensi.rnu.tn

Abstract According to PSM, each station must announce traffic before its transmission. PSM requires for this purpose a rather large handshaking period to complete the required announcements. This functional behavior puts a heavy constraint on the size of the announcement period and consequently on throughput, delay and more importantly on power consumption. This paper proposes an optimization of some functional properties of PSM in order to improve its performances. Our proposed UTA-PSM (Unicast Topology Aware Power Saving Mechanism) aims to reduce the number of exchanged announcement frames in order to reduce the announcement period. Conducted simulations show that UTA-PSM outperforms superbly PSM and power saving mechanisms such as the DCS-ATIM that dynamically adjusts the handshaking period according to the traffic load. We show that UTA-PSM delivers more throughput with a smaller average delay yet yielding a much better power saving and robustness.

1 Introduction

As wireless networks become an integral component of the modern communication infrastructure, energy efficiency becomes an important challenge due to the limited battery life of mobile terminals. Two different operational modes are defined in IEEE802.11 [2], the dominating WLAN technology today: the infrastructure network in which a specific central entity manages communications between stations, and the ad hoc network where spontaneous mobile nodes (we shall use interchangeably the word node or station) communicate with each other over multiple wireless hops [2, 8]. As each mobile node in an ad hoc network performs routing functionalities to assist other node communications, even one or few mobile hosts' energy exhaustion might cause the disruption of the entire network [16]. Therefore, there has been an increased interest in energy efficient communication protocols for the ad hoc networking environment [6, 25, 13, 22, 7] and numerous energy efficient MAC

Please use the following format when citing this chapter:

Akkari, W. and Belghith, A., 2008, in IFIP International Federation for Information Processing, Volume 284; *Wireless and Mobile Networking*; Zoubir Mammeri; (Boston: Springer), pp. 83–94.

protocols have being proposed [5, 10, 24, 3, 4]. These protocols are virtually all based on turning off the nodes' radio transceivers (hence putting the transceiver in the so called sleep or Doze state) to reduce energy consumption whenever they are not involved in communication. Neither a transmission nor a reception is allowed when a node is in this inactive state thus resulting in little energy consumption. The IEEE 802.11 DCF (Distributed Coordination Function) standard [2] also incorporates such a power saving mechanism (PSM) that uses Awake and Doze states. In 802.11 PSM, time is divided into specific periods called Beacon intervals and each node tries to synchronize with its neighbors to ensure that all nodes wake up at the same time. Any node can announce its pending data information during the sub-period called the ATIM window using the ATIM (Announcement Traffic Indication Map) frames which must each be acknowledged by an ATIM-ACK frame. During the period following ATIM window (we here denote this period as the Beyond-ATIM window or period), nodes having sent an ATIM or an ATIM-ACK frame must remain in an Awake state and perform data communication based on Carrier Sense Multiple Access with Collision Avoidance (CSMA/CA) mechanism, whereas all other nodes switch to Doze state. It should be stressed here that the number of ATIM frames may be very important as each station needs to announce its pending traffic. The required ATIM window may take a huge fraction of the Beacon period leaving insufficient Beyond-ATIM period to transmit the announced data frames. A compromise between the length of the ATIM period and the Beyond-ATIM period is surely needed and several research works have tackled such an issue. The central question here is how can we lessen this ATIM window to its minimum, yet allowing the maximum of announcements and data traffic exchange. To this end, we propose a new protocol coined UTA-PSM (Unicast Topology Aware-PSM) that thrives to decrease the ATIM window period. This is accomplished by making each node aware of the already known nodes that will stay Awake during the following Beyond-ATIM period. Indeed all nodes are readily Awake during the ATIM window and hence they are inspecting all transmitted ATIM and ATIM-ACK frames that are transmitted within their respective vicinities. These control frames readily provide the needed information about which nodes have already agreed to stay Awake for the data transmission phase. UTA-PSM simply allows a node to maintain such an information and abandon its ATIM transmission if the destined node of the ATIM is already sensed to stay anyway active. In this way and as we shall later show, we can significantly reduce the handshaking control traffic and consequently a substantially smaller ATIM period is needed. A smaller ATIM window not only implies that more time is left for the data exchange phase but more importantly that more announcements could be made which clearly amounts to a better throughput. To our best of knowledge no one has used this context aware handshaking in ad hoc networks. We shall show that this will provide a better throughput and smaller delays, yet amounts to much better energy saving than some of the most reputed protocols.

The rest of the paper is organized as follows. In section (2), we present a quick survey on recent research related proposals. We purposely put the accent on proposed energy saving protocols that dynamically adjust the ATIM period as a function of the traffic load. We devote section (3) to introduce and explain our proposed

UTA-PSM. Section (4) explains our experimental set up and results. Finally, section (5) presents some concluding remarks and future directions.

2 Related work

Power save protocols take a variety of forms. IEEE 802.11 PSM [2] attempts to conserve energy on idle nodes by powering off their wireless interfaces for a specific period of time. Nodes are assumed to be synchronized and should get Awake at the beginning of each Beacon interval. The synchronization is established by exchanging specific management frame called Beacon according to the TSF (Timing Synchronization Function) function [2]. At every Beacon interval, each node must even send a Beacon or receive at least one. TSF uses timestamped Beacon transmitted to synchronize clocks among nodes.

After waking up at the beginning of the Beacon interval, each node stays on for a period of time called the ATIM window (Ad hoc Traffic Indication Message window). During the ATIM window, since all nodes are guaranteed to be listening, queued data frames are advertised by sending a Unicast ATIM frame. Upon reception of an ATIM frame, a station replies by sending an ATIM-ACK. The transmission of the ATIM frame is performed using the CSMA/CA mechanism specified in IEEE 802.11. No data is sent during the ATIM window. Upon the termination of the ATIM window, any station that has transmitted ATIM frames (of which at least one is acknowledged) or an ATIM-ACK remains active during the entire current period and attempts to send its announced data frames before the next Beacon interval. Any node that has not transmitted an ATIM or an ATIM-ACK frame enters the Doze state at the end of the ATIM window until the start of the next Beacon interval. Figure 1 above illustrates a typical data transfer in a three nodes ad hoc network. Station A sends an ATIM to station B which responds by sending an ATIM-ACK during the same period. Both stations A and B must remain Awake for the whole

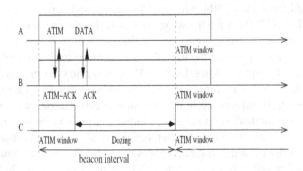

Fig. 1 Power management in an ad hoc network using PSM.

Beacon interval. Station C can switch to sleep state at the end of the ATIM window since it has not sent or received any ATIM frame. This means that, in a dense network, with many traffic flows, we need to have a large announcement period (ATIM window) so that all sources can send their ATIM frames and receive the correspondent ATIM-ACK. However, for a predetermined Beacon interval period, increasing the ATIM window period leads to the decrease of the Beyond-ATIM window period and consequently the time devoted to data transmission is reduced. This way of functioning can degrade the throughput and increase the delay.

In [9], the authors proposed an adaptive scheme to reduce power consumption and forwarding delay in an ad hoc network. APSM (Adaptive Power Saving Mode) allows stations to have multiple Awake instants during the same Beacon interval. The Awake instants are decided by the station receiving the ATIM during the ATIM window and includes them into the ATIM-ACK. Both stations know when to get Awake to handle their data traffic. The number of the Awake instants can be adjusted using traffic information. The problem with APSM is that having many Doze-to-Awake transitions may consume an important amount of energy. In fact, the transition from the Doze state to the Awake state consumes more energy than transmitting [20, 23].

In [4], the others argue that having a fixed ATIM window the same for all nodes may not be efficient. The size of this window can be too small to receive and send all announcements or too large for the Beacon interval to be able to deliver all data traffic. They presented DPSM (Dynamic Power Saving Mechanism) as an improvement to PSM that allows to a node to dynamically and locally choose a suitable size for its own ATIM window. In particular, they showed that the ATIM window depends on both the traffic load and the number of nodes in the network. However, the procedure of dynamically choosing the ATIM window size works perfectly only in a fully connected network (i.e., just one cell) and fails to be efficient for multi-hop networks.

IPSM (Improved Power Saving Mechanism) first presented in [12] and then in [11] stipulates that the ATIM window ends when the channel is idle for a specified amount of time. However, IPSM only works in single-hop networks since it relies on a node and all its neighbors having the same consistent view of channel activity. Some nodes (all the nodes of the network in some cases) can increase their ATIM window period to ATIMmax for the wrong reasons: the channel can be idle because of other's data transmission or simply interference.

In [18], the authors propose the use of carrier sensing to dynamically adjust the size of the advertisement windows. DCS-ATIM (Dynamic Carrier Sense-ATIM) allows nodes to have different values of ATIM window depending on the amount of traffic that needs to be advertised in the current window. Carrier sensing is used as an energy efficient method to let neighbors know if a node intends to advertise any packets in the upcoming window. Carrier sensing is also used as a mechanism for nodes to keep track of whether their neighbors have already stopped listening for advertisements and possibly returned to sleep. The authors show that DCS-ATIM can significantly reduce the energy consumption of 802.11 PSM with a slight increase in latency. The authors stipulated to the contrary of IPSM, that DCS-ATIM stays efficient even in multi-hop networks. We shall show in the following sections that DCS-ATIM is only effective when traffic load is extremely light. For other traffic conditions even very moderate, DCS-ATIM delivers worse than PSM due to time it takes for sensing.

In [10], they proposed an extensible on demand power management scheme that adapts to traffic load. Nodes maintain timers to determine power management transitions. They proposed to monitor routing control messages and data transmissions to set and update the timers. Nodes that are not involved in data delivery may then enter the Doze state.

SPAN [5] elects a group of nodes, called `coordinators` to be responsible for forwarding the traffic to active connections. Thus, the `coordinators` must stay Awake however, the non-coordinator nodes follow the power saving mechanism in IEEE 802.11 PSM. The `coordinators` are periodically changed to face the problem of mobility and battery depletion. SPAN defines a new advertisement traffic window following the ATIM window. During this window, the announced packets (during the ATIM window) can be transmitted in addition to the traffic among `coordinators`. After this window, only traffic among `coordinators` can be transmitted. It is worth here mentioning that the clustering phase needed to select `coordinators` and the time needed to maintain the clustered topology would greatly affect the performance of SPAN. The authors just assumed that this is done with no traffic taken into account in their evaluations.

3 Proposed UTA-PSM scheme

We now present our proposed scheme, UTA-PSM (Unicast Topology Aware Power Saving Mechanism). The main difference between UTA-PSM and PSM is that nodes can transmit data frames even if they didn't sent any announcement frame during ATIM window. Each station maintains an active neighbors table (ANT) that contains the identities of the neighbors learned to stay Awake during the Beyond-ATIM window of the current Beacon period. ANT is initialized to be empty at the start of each Beacon period. During the ATIM period, whenever a station hears an announcement frame (ATIM or ATIM-ACK) it adds, to its ANT, the identity of the transmitting node if it is not already here. A station refrains to transmit an ATIM frame to any station indicated in its ANT since anyway that station will surely be Awake. The ATIM and the ATIM-ACK transmitting nodes are considered as Awake neighbors for the entire current Beacon interval. However, we recall that the ATIM frame contains both the source and the destination identities but the ATIM-ACK contains only the ATIM-ACK receiving station address [2]. Consequently, we propose to modify the ATIM-ACK frame to also include the ATIM-ACK source address. This simple modification allows nodes to be aware of the state of all their neighbors being in Doze or Awake state. Being Awake results from the transmission of at least one ATIM or ATIM-ACK frame. A station receiving an ATIM frame destined to itself must, after performing the required updating to its ANT, send an

ATIM-ACK frame and consequently stays Awake for the entire Beacon period. A station sends its ATIM if it is destined to a node not yet included in its ANT. Finally, a station goes into the Doze state if it has no data frame to send and it has not acknowledged any ATIM frame.

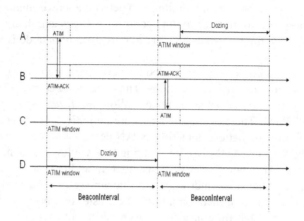

Fig. 2 Power management in an ad hoc network using UTA-PSM.

Using Figure 2, we will explain how UTA-PSM works. All stations are supposed for the sake of simplicity to be in line-of-sight. During the first Beacon interval, stations A and C have packets to send to node B. Both A and C prepare an ATIM frame to be sent to B according to the underlying CSMA/CA scheme. In Figure 2, we suppose that A transmits first to B. B, C and D being all neighbors of A will firstly update their ANTs by including A's identity. Then, B directly acknowledges the received ATIM frame by sending an ATIM-ACK frame to A. A, C and D will then update their ANTs by including B. Exactly at the same time, node C aborts its pending transmission to B. Station D however, having no traffic to announce, can switch to the Doze state at the end of the ATIM window. At the end of this Beacon period all ANTs at the different nodes will be flushed. For the second Beacon period, we suppose that node B sends its announcement ATIM frame before D. The rest of the scenario continues in the same way.

UTA-PSM may significantly reduce the number of exchanged announcement frames in comparison to PSM and DCS-ATIM. This will certainly allow to specify a much smaller ATIM window. We can further improve UTA-PSM by making it more sensitive to the traffic load. To carry out this objective, we referred to the work presented in [1]. In this work, the authors investigated in particular enhancement called the Traffic Aware Power Saving Mechanism (TA-PSM) that allows nodes to enter the Doze state in the middle of a Beacon period when they are no more involved in data delivery even if they have already sent an ATIM or an ATIM-ACK. TA-PSM reduces the energy consumption by making PSM more sensitive to the current traffic. First, they added a one bit MoreData field into the frame header to indicate to the receiving station that further pending data frames are buffered. If the MoreData bit is set in the received frame, both the transmitting and the receiving stations stay Awake; otherwise, they can switch to the Doze state. Our scheme consists on reducing the energy consumption by making UTA-PSM more sensitive to the traffic load in the same way TA-PSM does. Thus, the same idea is applied on UTA-PSM and all stations having finished their data transmission without having sent an ATIM or an ATIM-ACK may switch to the Doze state to save energy. Stations having sent an ATIM or an ATIM-ACK cannot switch to the Doze state during the Beyond-ATIM period because other stations rely on them.

4 Simulation results

We implemented our simulated models using J-Sim [14, 21]. We simulate the proposed UTA-PSM scheme, the PSM scheme, the DCS-ATIM mechanism proposed in [18] and IEEE 802.11 without power saving. For these schemes, we use the following abbreviations:

- WOPSM: This is the IEEE 802.11 protocol with no power saving mechanism.
- PSM: This is the standard IEEE 802.11 protocol with power saving enabled.
- UTA-PSM: Our proposed protocol described in Section 3.
- DCS-ATIM: This is 802.11 PSM with the dynamic ATIM modification for multi-hop networks described in [18].

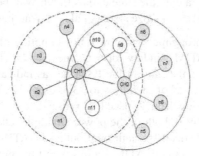

Fig. 3 The network topology.

We use four metrics to evaluate the proposed UTA-PSM and compare its performance with the others:

- Aggregate Throughput: represents the total number of data frames delivered to all destined stations at the end of the simulation. This metric is useful to verify whether power saving mechanisms degrade throughput or not.

- Delay: represents the average time a data frame spent in the network from its generation at the source station to its delivery to the destination station.
- Power consumed: representing the total energy consumed by all stations during the simulation time.
- Power consumed per delivered data frame: represents the total energy consumed divided by the number of delivered data frames.

Each simulation run is performed for 200 seconds. We used CBR traffic models with different data rates, a fixed data frame size of 512 bytes, a wireless channel bit rate of 2 Mbps. The transmission range is fixed to 240m. We considered the network example depicted on Figure 3. The data flows are defined as follows: n1-CH1-CH2-n7, n2-CH1-CH2-n8, n10-CH1-n4, n11-CH2-n5, n4-CH1-n11, n5-CH2-n8, n9-CH1-n3 and CH1-CH2. Stations CH1 and CH2 are the `clusterheads` and the rest of stations of the network are just ad hoc mobile stations. We choose to emulate a clustered network to show best the contribution of UTA-PSM. In fact all the defined flows have to be forwarded through CH1, CH2 or both of them which concentrate traffic through this two particular stations. Having all stations involved in data transmission in a clustered topology is more in favor of UTA-PSM than of DCS-ATIM because the advantage of UTA-PSM is especially shown when the topology of the network presents a centrifugal architecture. We consider a Beacon interval of 0.1 seconds which is the default value specified for PSM in [6]. We assume an initial energy equal to 1000 Watt per station. The energy consumption model used throughout the simulations is defined as follows:

- Energy consumption rate in transmit state equals 0.660 Watt per second.
- Energy consumption rate in receive state equals 0.395 Watt per second.
- Energy consumption rate in idle state equals 0.296 Watt per second.
- Energy consumption rate in Doze state equals 0.0 Watt per second.

We first tested the throughput and power consumption of PSM and UTA-PSM to fix the appropriate ATIM window for each mechanism. The ATIM window attributed to DCS-ATIM is the same value PSM has as indicated in [18]. For these tests, we fixed the traffic load of each flow to 13 pkt/sec (52 kbps) and we varied the length of the ATIM window from 2 msec to 25 msec.

As shown in Figure 4(a), both of the power saving mechanisms naturally show an increase followed by a decrease in throughput as the ATIM window is increased. If the ATIM window is too small, ATIM frames won't be sent so no data frame will be sent. On the other hand, if the ATIM window is too large, there won't be enough time to transmit the announced data frames and hence throughput decreases. More importantly, we observe that UTA-PSM delivers far more aggregate throughput than does PSM since UTA-PSM needs a much shorter ATIM period. On the other hand, Figure 4(b) portrays the total power consumed by the two schemes. It is clear that UTA-PSM consumes far more power since it delivers far more data frames. Recall that the energy consumption rate in transmit state is the highest. These two curves allow us to set the adequate ATIM window corresponding to each of the two schemes. Hereafter, we shall then use these typical values of the ATIM window 15 msec for PSM and 6 msec for UTA-PSM.

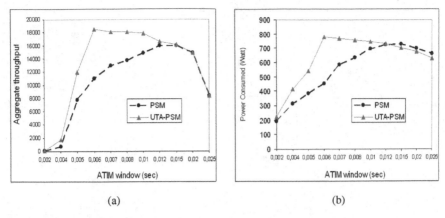

Fig. 4 (a)(b): Aggregate Throughput and Power consumed vs ATIM window.

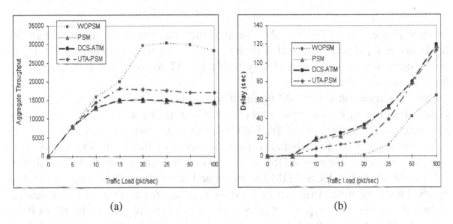

Fig. 5 (a)(b): Aggregate Throughput and Delay vs Traffic Load.

Now let us consider the same topology (Figure 3) and vary the data rate of all the defined flows from 5pkt/sec to 100pkt/sec. We clearly observe that PSM and DCS-ATIM yield the same throughput: the corresponding curves are completely super-posed in Figure 5(a). However, UTA-PSM performs significantly better than both PSM and DCS-ATIM but not better than WOPSM that offers the highest through-put. This difference between WOPSM and all other protocols is readily justified by the influence of the ATIM window during which no data frame is sent.

Now, let us consider the delay of all received frames. Figure 5(b) portrays the delay and shows that PSM and DCS-ATIM still have almost superposed curves (slightly less for PSM). The difference between the delay for DCS-ATIM and the delay provided by PSM is relatively constant in the range of 800 msec to 1 sec. This small increase in DCS-ATIM latency comes from the fact that that packets arriv-ing after the ATIM window is expired will not be announced until the next ATIM

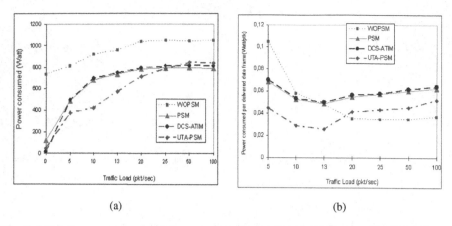

(a)   (b)

Fig. 6 (a)(b): Power consumed and Power consumed per delivered data frame vs Traffic Load.

window in the case of DCS-ATIM. Another fact that makes the difference in delay between PSM and DCS-ATIM is the extra carrier sensing period. UTA-PSM, on the other hand, outperforms clearly both DCS-ATIM and PSM. It delivers more throughput and yields less delay.

Now, we focus on UTA-PSM main efficiency as a power saving mechanism. In Figure 6(a) below, we show the total power consumed by all nodes in the network as a function of the traffic load. DCS-ATIM consumed energy is less than that consumed by any of the other schemes for very extremely small traffic loads only. This is indeed due to its dynamic ATIM window which is kept smaller than even that of UTA-PSM. However, DCS-ATIM leverages and from above the energy consumed by PSM when the traffic load gets larger than 5 packets per second per traffic source. In fact, the energy consumption of DCS-ATIM converges from above to that of PSM since it additionally needs the overhead for carrier sensing. However, we observe that UTA-PSM outperforms DCS-ATIM and surely PSM when the traffic load gets larger than 2 packets per second. This is somehow remarkable for back to Figure 5(a) we see that UTA-PSM delivers more throughput also. That is to say: despite the energy consumed by transmitting more packets (recall that transmitting energy consumption rate is the largest), UTA-PSM consumes less energy. To this end, we consider in Figure 6(b) the average power consumed per delivered data frame as a function of the traffic load. This is just the total energy consumed by all nodes divided by the total network throughput. This figure shows that UTA-PSM clearly outperforms PSM and DCS-ATIM which have almost the same power consumed per delivered data frame. At light traffic conditions, where any energy saving mechanism is supposed to save the most, we notice the clear efficiency of UTA-PSM, a substantial gain of more than 40% over both PSM and DCS-ATIM (at a traffic load of 5 packets per second). As the traffic load increases, the gain decreases a little bit until reaching a limiting value which indicates the gain accomplished by the reduction of the number of announcement frames exchanged during ATIM window. It is also worth noticing that at high traffic loads it becomes better not to use any power saving mechanism. In this region we readily see that WOPSM outperforms all the studied schemes and for that matter any power saving mechanism as nodes are kept Awake all the time. Nevertheless, it is interesting to notice that UTA-PSM can save energy where the others fail completely.

5 Conclusion and future directions

IEEE 802.11 PSM and the like that base their saving mechanisms on a handshaking period whether this period is predefined and fixed or dynamic do not yield as expected good performances. The crux of this is that the number of announcements should be lowered at its maximum to give more time to data frames and in turn obtain more throughput. This is exactly what our proposed UTA-PSM is about. Lowering the handshaking period is shown to allow more announcements and more throughput. This in turn yielded a much better data frame average delay. Conducted simulations portrayed that UTA-PSM outperforms not only PSM but more importantly schemes such as DCS-ATIM that dynamically adjust their ATIM period. The later has been shown to behave as poorly as PSM since when traffic load is not extremely light the ATIM window gets at least the same value as that used by PSM. Our simulations were based on a network topology that is supposed to be clustered. This indeed let traffic flows trough certain nodes, namely the clusterheads. Other scenarios could use routing algorithms that have a similar effect of concentring traffic through certain nodes such as the OLSR algorithm. Unquestionably more simulations are needed to better ascertain the excellent efficiency of UTA-PSM. Furthermore efforts are underway to integrate the DCS-ATIM approach into our UTA-PSM scheme.

References

1. Abdelfattah Belghith, Wafa Akkari and Jean Marie Bonnin: Traffic Aware Power Saving Protocol in Multi-hop Mobile Ad-hoc networks. JOURNAL OF NETWORKS, Volume 2, Issue 4, Pages 1-13(2007)
2. ANSI/IEEE Standard 802.11: Wireless LAN Medium, Access Control (MAC) and Physical, Layer (PHY)Specifications. (1999)
3. A. Sheth and R. Han: Adaptive power control and selective radio activation for low-power infrastructure-mode 802.11 LANs. Proceedings of 23rd International Conference on Distributed Computing Systems (ICDCSW'03), Providence, Rode Island, USA, 5: 812-817 (2003)
4. B. Awerbuch, D. Holmer and H. Rubens: The pulse protocol: energy efficient infrastructure access. IEEE INFOCOM'04, Hong Kong (2004)
5. B. Chen, K. Jamieson, H. Balakrishman and R.Morris: Span: An energy-efficient coordination algorithm for topology maintenance in ad hoc wireless networks. in MOBICOM 2001 (2001)
6. C.E. Jones, K. Sivalingam, p. Agrawal and J Chen: A survey of energy efficient network protocols for wireless networks. ACM Journal Wireless Networks , 15: 343–358 (2001)

7. Changsu Suh, Young-Bae Ko and Jai-Hoon Kim: Enhanced Power Saving for IEEE 802.11 WLAN with Dynamic Slot Allocation. LNCS, Vol. 3794, 11: 466-477 (2005)
8. Conference on Mobile Computing and Networking. San Diego, California, USA, September 14-19, (MobiCom 2003)
9. D.Y. Kim and C.H. Choi: Adaptive power management for IEEE 802.11 based ad hoc networks. in World Wireless Congress, San Francisco, USA (2004)
10. E.S. Jung and N.H. Vaidya: An energy efficient MAC protocol for wireless LANs. INFOCOM 2002,New York , USA (2002)
11. Eun-Sun Jung and N. H. Vaidya: Improving IEEE 802.11 Power Saving Mechanism. University of Illinois at Urbana-Champaign, Tech. Rep (2004)
12. Eun-Sun Jung and Nitin H. Vaidya: Improving IEEE 802.11 power saving mechanism. Published online: 4 January 2007, Springer Science+Business Media, LLC (2007)
13. H. Zhu and G. Cao: A power-aware and QoS-aware service model on wireless networks. IEEE INFOCOM'04, Hong Kong (2004)
14. J-Sim simulator: on-line at www.j-sim.org, last visited in 23-05-2005
15. J. So: Design and Evaluation of Multi-channel Multi-hop Wireless Networks. Ph.D. Dissertation, University of Illinois at Urbana Champain (2006)
16. J. Zhu, C. Qiao and X. Wang: A comprehensive minimum energy routing scheme for wireless ad hoc networks. IEEE INFOCOM'04, Hong Kong (2004)
17. L. Huang and T. lai: On the scalability of the IEEE 802.11 Ad HOC Networks. In the proceedings of the ACM MOBIHOC (2002)
18. Matthew J. Miller and N. H. Vaidya: Improving Power Save Protocols Using Carrier Sensing for Dynamic Advertisement Windows. University of Illinois at Urbana-Champaign, Tech. Rep (2005)
19. N. Bulusu, J. Heidemann, and D. Estrin.: GPS-less low cost outdoor localization for very small devices. IEEE Personal Communications Magazine, 5:28-34 (2000)
20. Paul J.M.Havinga and Gerard J.M.Smit: Energy-Efficient TDMA meduim access control protocol scheduling. in Proc.Asian International Mobile Computing Conference AMOC'02 (2000)
21. R. S. Nair: JSIM: A Java-Based Query Driven Simulation and Animation Environment. Masters Thesis (M.S. in CS Degree) (1997)
22. R. Zheng and R. Kravets: On-demand Power Management for Ad Hoc Networks. Proc. of IEEE INFOCOMM 2003, San Francisco (2003)
23. Tajana Simunic, Haris Vikalo, Peter Glynn and Giovanni De Micheli: Energy efficient design of portable wireless system. in International Symposium of Low Power Electronics and Design (ISLPED) (2000)
24. T. Simunic and S. Boyd: Managing power consumption in networks on ships. ACM DATE (2002)
25. T. Zhang, P. Gurung: E. Van Den Berg, S. Madhani and A. Muttreja, Silent networking for energy constrained nodes. in press in Computer Communications, Elsevier (2006)

An Analysis of Alterations to the SCTP RTO Calculation Mechanism for WLAN Environments

Sheila Fallon[*], Paul Jacob[*], Yuansong Qiao[*], Liam Murphy[**],
Enda Fallon[*], and Austin Hanley[*]

sheila.fallon@gmail.com, pjacob@ait.ie, ysqiao@ait.ie, liam.murphy@ucd.ie, efallon@ait.ie,
ahanley@ait.ie

Software Research Centre, Athlone Institute of Technology, Ireland[*]

Performance Engineering Laboratory, University College Dublin, Ireland[**]

Abstract As a connection oriented transport layer protocol the Stream Control Transmission Protocol (SCTP) inherits many of the features of the Transmission Control Protocol (TCP) including the mechanism by which Retransmission Timeout (RTO) is calculated. Previous investigations have established that the mechanism through which SCTP calculates RTO is inappropriate in Wireless LAN (WLAN) environments. This paper investigates the performance implications of changes to the SCTP RTO calculation mechanism. In particular alterations to the parameters α, *the smoothing factor*, and β, the *delay variance factor* are investigated. Results indicate that performance improvements are achievable through careful selection of α and β values. Throughput improvements of 63% over the default mechanism defined in RFC 4960 are described. These performance improvements however, while significant, still can not address the switchover delays which result from the distortions caused by continuously increasing RTT values in WLAN environments.

1 Introduction

In recent years there has been a significant increase in the availability of wireless and mobile networks capable of supporting IP communication. The diversity of these networks in terms of signal coverage and transmission capability has made it essential to employ a transparent network migration strategy which can seamlessly

Please use the following format when citing this chapter:

Fallon, S., Jacob, P., Qiao, Y., Murphy, L., Fallon, E. and Hanley, A., 2008, in IFIP International Federation for Information Processing, Volume 284; *Wireless and Mobile Networking*; Zoubir Mammeri; (Boston: Springer), pp. 95–108.

migrate from one network to another without a perceived degradation in quality from an end user. Significant research efforts are ongoing to investigate if SCTP [1], which was originally designed as a transport protocol for Signaling System 7 (SS7) data across IP networks, can support seamless network migration. As a transport layer protocol SCTP shares some of the features of TCP, as well as introducing enhancements to support network mobility. Foremost amongst these enhancements is its support for multi-homing - the ability to implement an end to end communication session transparently over multiple physical paths where the end point of each path is identified by an IP address.

As a connection oriented transport layer protocol SCTP inherits many of the features of TCP including the mechanism by which RTO is calculated. For a traditional connection oriented protocol such as TCP the selection of an appropriate RTO value is a tradeoff between: (a) setting a large value which may degrade performance by allowing excessively long periods before retransmitting a lost packet (b) setting a conservative value which mistakenly retransmits valid packets, known as *spurious retransmissions*. In addition to the tradeoff between (a) excessive retransmission delay and (b) spurious retransmissions, SCTP must also consider the effect of RTO selection on switchover.

Previous investigations undertaken [2] have established that the current SCTP mechanism for calculating RTO values is inappropriate in WLAN environments, since increased Round-Trip Time (RTT) significantly distorts RTO calculations. It was illustrated that SCTP behaves in a counterintuitive manner which allows more time for switchover as network conditions degraded: delays of up to 187 seconds were experienced before switchover occurred. This paper investigates if it is possible to alleviate the switchover performance deficiency experienced in WLAN environments through configuration of the parameters α, *the smoothing factor,* and β, the *delay variance factor*.

This paper is organized as follows. Section 2 details related work in the area. Section 3 describes SCTP path management functionality. Section 4 describes the SCTP RTO calculation mechanism and illustrates the importance of the parameters α and β. In Section 5 some background is provided on how increased RTT in can affect SCTP RTO calculation. In Section 6 results are presented which illustrate the performance implications of changes to α and β. Finally conclusions and future work are discussed in Section 7.

2   Related Work

The mechanism by which SCTP calculates the value of a retransmission timer is inherited from TCP. The TCP mechanism itself is defined in [3] and has developed over time. In response to Internet "congestion collapse" of the mid 1980s it was suggested [4] that a back off mechanism be employed when congestion was detected. The suggested alterations were formally adopted [5] in 1989. In [4] the values .25 and .125 were suggested for the estimator gains and variation weight respectively. In [6] Karn's algorithm suggested that RTT measurements should not be taken for retransmitted packets. In [7] it was suggested that TCP connections utilizing large congestion windows should, if possible, take at least one RTT measurement per RTT in order to improve estimation. A mechanism which TCP should employ to begin sending after RTO expiration is outlined in [8].

With the advent of wireless networking a number of investigations have focused on accurate RTO estimation. In [9] results are presented which indicate that the optimal RTO, which maximizes TCP throughput, should take into consideration the TCP window size as well as RTT. In [10] the impact of variable transmission delays, as experienced in wireless and mobile networks, on TCP performance are investigated. In particular TCPs RTT estimation for bulk data traffic over wireless links is analysed. The results indicate that the RTT sampling rate has a significant impact on performance. In [11] optimizations for a TCP sender in the presence of delay spikes are discussed. The authors recommend timing every segment and restarting the retransmit timer to achieve a more conservative RTO estimate. In [12] the behaviour of TCP during vertical network switchover from a high capacity to low capacity network is investigated. The investigation concentrates on the TCP timeout problem caused by increased network RTT. Three schemes; fast response, slow response and ACK delay are evaluated. Simulation results presented demonstrated that these schemes can improve the performance of TCP during soft vertical handover. In [13] the performance of SCTP, TCP, and Eifel are compared during delay spikes. Results indicate that in the presence of delay spikes without packet loss, SCTP and TCP Reno have similar performance. This paper does not consider continuously increasing RTT.

A number of studies have been undertaken which investigate the performance of SCTP switchover. In [14] an analytical study of SCTP failover is undertaken which indicates that the current mechanism for calculating the duration of an SCTP switchover is unsatisfactory. Two additional parameters are introduced to the SCTP failover strategy in order to more accurately reflect the exact time at which catastrophic primary path failure occurs. In [15] performance implications of the use of heterogeneous wireless networks with differing bandwidths are presented. In [16] it is suggested that the SCTP handover strategy is reactive in nature and a more proactive approach where handover is based on path delays should be introduced in order to pre-empt and avoid path failures. In [17] it is suggested that SCTP path failure detection is inadequate for wireless networks. A new path failure detection method which utilises cycle sampling rather than the single sampling method as suggested in [1] is evaluated. Results presented indicate that the cycle sampling method can increase performance. In [18] a new scheme for primary path management for the mobile terminals during SCTP handover is evaluated. The proposed scheme utilises the absolute gap and relative ratio of the RTT of the primary and alternate paths in the switch decision. The proposed scheme implements conservative and aggressive modes of operation depending on the absolute gap of the measured RTTs in the network. The results presented indicate that a conservative scheme is preferred for a network where the gaps of the measured RTTs are small, whereas an aggressive scheme needs to be considered in a network when the gaps of RTTs are relatively large.

3   SCTP Path Management

SCTP identifies a path by the IP address of the destination. During the protocol startup stage, each SCTP endpoint selects one of its peer's IP addresses as a primary path for data transmission. When the primary path fails, a backup path will be selected as primary path. SCTP sends heartbeat packets periodically to an idle address to detect the reachability of the address. SCTP defines "idle address" as: no data chunks are sent within the current heartbeat interval. An address is considered active if the sender received the expected acknowledgement from its peer within a designated period. Otherwise, if the number of consecutive transmission timeouts exceeds the protocol parameter Path.Max.Retrans (PMR), it means the address is inactive. If this inactive address is current primary path, a handover will occur. The SCTP parameters which are used to implement the switch over management strategy are; RTO.Initial = 3 seconds, RTO.Min = 1second, RTO.Max = 60 seconds and Path.Max.Retrans = 5 attempts.

4   RTO Calculation in SCTP

RTO is the time that elapses after a packet has been sent until the sender considers it lost and retransmits it. In this way RTO is a prediction of the upper limit of RTT. If an SCTP sender does not receive a response for an SCTP data chunk from its receiver within the time of RTO, the sender will consider this data chunk lost. According to [1] RTO is calculated for each destination address separately based on the Smoothed Round-Trip Time (SRTT) and Round-Trip Time Variation (RTTVAR) of the path. It is initialized with RTO.Initial which is an SCTP parameter and can be configured by the user:

RTO = RTO.Initial   (3.1)

SRTT and RTTVAR of a path are calculated by the measurement of RTT of the path. The RTT measurement for a path is made for every round trip. When SCTP gets the first measurement of RTT: RTT.1st, SRTT and RTTVAR are initialized as:

SRTT = RTT.1st (3.2)

$$RTTVAR = {RTT.1st}/{2}   (3.3)$$

And RTO is updated to

RTO = SRTT+4 x RTTVAR   (3.4)

For each time SCTP gets a new measurement of RTT: RTT.new, SRTT and RTTVAR will be updated as follows:

RTTVAR.new = (1-β) x RTTVAR.old+ β x (SRTT.old- RTT.new)   (3.5)

SRTT.new = (1- α) x SRTT.old+ α x RTT.new   (3.6)

Where β and α are constants and their recommended values are 1/4 and 1/8 respectively. Then the new RTO is:

RTO = SRTT.new + 4 x RTTVAR.new   (3.7)

If the new RTO is less than RTO.Min, it will be set to RTO.Min. If the new RTO is greater than RTO.Max, it will be set to RTO.Max. Every time a transmission timeout occurs for an address, the RTO for this address will be doubled:

RTO = RTO x2   (3.8)

And if the new RTO is greater than RTO.Max, RTO.Max will be used for the new RTO. If the sender gets a response from the receiver and a new RTT is measured, SCTP will use this new RTT to calculate RTTVAR, SRTT and finally RTO by the equations (3.5) to (3.7).

5   An Illustration of the Effect of Increased RTT on SCTP RTO Calculation

In this section a brief illustration of the effect of increased RTT experience in a WLAN environment on RTO estimation in SCTP is presented. A more complete description of the performance implications of increased RTT on SCTP RTO can be found in [2]. In the following example a mobile node is communicating with a back end server through a Linksys WRT54GL 802.11g access point. The test starts with the mobile node adjacent to the access point. The mobile node then moves at slow walking pace away from the access point. As the mobile node moves from the coverage area of the AP signal strength degrades and results in intermittent network connectivity. After 100 seconds the RTT increases significantly. Figure 1 details the increased RTT and illustrates its affect on RTO calculation through the SRTT (3.6) and RTTVAR (3.7) parameters.

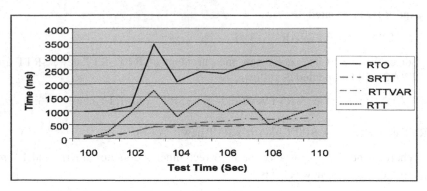

Fig. 1 RTT and RTO Values for Time 100-110 Secs

For the period shown the calculation of RTO is based on the recorded RTT value by applying (3.5) (3.6) and (3.7). As a result of the continuously high RTT value the baseline RTO value also increases significantly. As the packet retransmission failures occur (3.8) is applied which doubles an already high baseline RTO value.

After 100 seconds the RTO was 1000ms, SRTT was 107ms, RTTVAR was 79ms and the recorded RTT was 7ms. Within a period of 10 seconds the RTO has increased from 1000ms to 2802ms. The average RTO between 100 and 250 seconds was 3.148 seconds. If a retransmission timeout occurred during this time period (3.8) would be applied. This would double the RTO to 5602ms. Using the default PMR value of 5 it would take 2.8+5.6+11.2+22.4+44.8+60=146.8 seconds for switchover to occur. Even using more aggressive PMR values of 0, 1 and 2 excessive delays of 2.8, 8.4 and 19.6 seconds respectively are experienced.

6   Results

In order to investigate the performance implications of changes to α, *the smoothing factor,* and β, the *delay variance factor* on SCTP RTO estimation and performance a number of studies were undertaken as follows:

- An experimental study which illustrates that mobility can result in continually increasing RTT in a WLAN environment
- An analytical study which considers the optimal configuration of α and β for a traditional TCP oriented trade off between (a) excessive retransmission delay and (b) spurious retransmissions in the presence of continuously increasing RTT.
- A simulated study which considers the optimal configuration of α and β when the effects of SCTP path switchover are considered in the presence of continuously increasing RTT.

The aim of these investigations was to determine if the performance deficiencies relating to path switchover highlighted in [2] could be addressed through careful configuration of the α, and β parameters employed in the estimation of RTO.

6.1   *Experimental Illustration of Increased RTT in WLAN*

From equations (3.2) to (3.6) in can be seen that RTO is significantly dependent on RTT. In order to estimate RTT and loss rates in wireless environments 25 tests were undertaken which utilized Ixia's IXChariot [19] network analysis software which transmitted RTP data using H263QCIF service quality at a constant bit rate of 3.75 Mbps. The tests were initiated adjacent to the access point. The mobile client then moved at slow walking pace, approximately 1m/sec, away from the access point. Figure 2 illustrates the average RTT and loss rates for 25 tests.

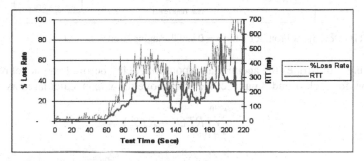

Fig. 2 Average RTT and Loss Rates in WLAN Environment

Figure 2 illustrates that as the mobile node moved from the coverage of the access point the RTT and loss rate increased significantly, particularly after 60 seconds.

6.2   *A TCP Oriented Analysis of the Optimal Configuration of α and β With Increasing RTT in WLAN*

In order to analyse the optimal configuration of α and β in TCP oriented manner and to address the tradeoff between (a) excessive retransmission delay and (b) spurious retransmissions for a WLAN environment an analytical study was undertaken. This analytical study used the average RTT estimated by the experimental study, illustrated in Figure 2, as input. The analytical study employed the following configurations of α and β pairs:

$$\alpha = i, \beta = j \;\; \{i, j \in 0, .1, .2, \ldots, 1.0\ \}$$

As an example, Figure 3 illustrates how different configurations of α and β affect RTO estimation. It illustrates how the estimated RTO deviates from RTT. The X-axis represents the baseline RTT values illustrated in Figure 3. Positive values indicate that the RTO estimation is greater than the actual RTT, in such a scenario excessive delays occur before lost packet retransmission. Negative values indicate that the RTO estimation is less than actual RTT, in such a scenario spurious retransmissions result.

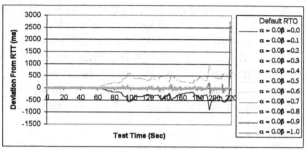

Fig. 3 RTO Deviations From RTT for $\alpha = 0$ and β ranging from 0, .1, ... 1

Figure 4 illustrates the accumulated potential delay before lost packet retransmission, for each α and β pair i.e. the area above the x-axis, calculated as follows:

$$\sum_{i=0}^{i=220} (RTO_i - RTT_i)$$

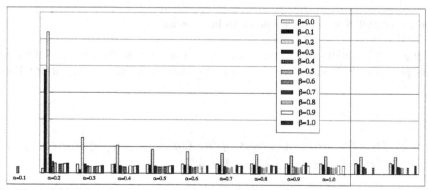

Fig. 4 Potential Delay Before Lost Packet Retransmission for α and β pairs

Figure 4 illustrates that $\alpha = .1\ \beta = .1$ and $\alpha = 0\ \beta = 0$ were the most effective test pairs with potential delays of 2.59 and 3.4 seconds respectively. The test pairs with the greatest delay were $\alpha = 0\ \beta = .1$ and $\alpha = 0\ \beta = .2$ with delays of 76.74 and 105.11 seconds respectively.

Figure 5 is concerned with the estimation of the total number of spurious retransmissions. It illustrates the potential number of seconds in which spurious retransmission would occur and is calculated as follows:

$$\sum_{i=0}^{i=220} if\,(RTO_i < RTT_i)1,else0$$

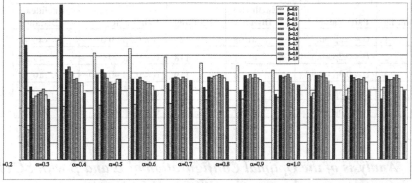

Fig. 5 Number of Seconds in which Spurious Retransmissions Occur for α and β pairs

Figure 5 illustrates that the test pairs with least number of spurious retransmissions were $\alpha = 0.0$ $\beta = 0.2$, $\alpha = 0.1$ $\beta = 0.2$ and $\alpha = 0.2$ $\beta = 0.2$ with 35, 62 and 63 seconds of spurious retransmissions respectively. The test pairs with the most seconds of spurious retransmissions were $\alpha = .1$ $\beta = .1$, $\alpha = 0$ $\beta = 0$ and $\alpha = .1$ $\beta = .1$ with 178, 169 and 138 seconds of spurious retransmissions respectively.

In order to determine the optimal selection of α and β each of the test pairs were graded from 1 to 121 in terms of efficiency relating to lost packet retransmission delay and spurious retransmission. As an example the test pair $\alpha = 0.0$ $\beta = 0.2$ had the least number of spurious retransmissions (x=0) yet the highest potential delay before lost packet retransmission (y=120) thus resulting in the point (0,120). Figure 6 illustrates the performance distribution of test pairs.

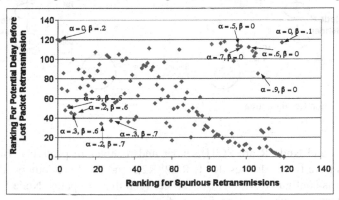

Fig. 6 Performance Distribution for α and β pairs

For each test pair the Euclidean distance from the origin was calculated. Table 1 illustrates that the test pairs likely to provide the optimal tradeoff between excessively long periods before retransmitting a lost packet and spurious retransmission of valid packets were $\alpha = 0.2$ $\beta = 0.7$, $\alpha = 0.2$ $\beta = 0.6$ and $\alpha = 0.3$ $\beta = 0.6$.

Table 1 Performance Ranking for α and β pairs

Ranking	Pair Values	Euclidean Distance	Ranking	Pair Values	Euclidean Distance
1	$\alpha = 0.2\beta = 0.7$	41.05	117	$\alpha = 0.5\beta = 0.0$	148.92
2	$\alpha = 0.2\beta = 0.6$	44.91	118	$\alpha = 0.9\beta = 0.0$	149.20
3	$\alpha = 0.3\beta = 0.6$	45.54	119	$\alpha = 0.7\beta = 0.0$	149.24
4	$\alpha = 0.3\beta = 0.7$	46.40	120	$\alpha = 0.6\beta = 0.0$	150.81
5	$\alpha = 0.3\beta = 0.5$	48.17	121	$\alpha = 0.0\beta = 0.1$	166.88

6.3 Analysis of the Optimal Configuration of α and β with SCTP Path Switchover and Increasing RTT in WLAN

The analytical study described in Section 6.2 suggested optimal configurations for α and β parameters in order to provide a tradeoff between (a) excessive retransmission delay and (b) spurious retransmissions. The analytical study however, did not consider the affect of path switchover on performance. In this section the effect of path switchover is considered.

The same α and β pair configurations as in the analytical study were evaluated using the University of Delewares [20] SCTP module for NS2 [21]. The simulation topology is detailed in Figure 7.

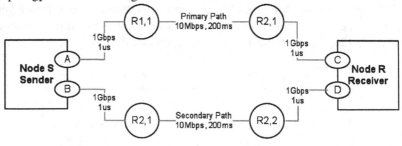

Fig. 7 Simulation Configuration

Node S and Node R are SCTP sender and receiver respectively. Both SCTP endpoints have two addresses. R1,1, R1,2, R2,1 and R2,2 are routers. The implementation is configured with no overlap between the two paths. Node S begins to send FTP data to Node R after 0.5 seconds.

As with the analytical study the simulations used the average RTT values, illustrated in Figure 2 as input. Since α and β are not configurable SCTP parameters their alteration required updates to and recompilation of [20] for each test. Each test pair was ranked by its performance in relation to the total amount of data transmitted. Table 2 illustrates the variation in performance for a representative sample of the configurations, between the analytical study and the simulated investigation.

Table 2 Performance Comparison for α and β pairs for Analytical and Simulated Study

Pair Values	Ranking		Pair Values	Ranking	
	Simulated	Analytical		Simulated	Analytical
$\alpha = 0.7\beta = 0.7$	1	104	$\alpha = 0.8\beta = 0.5$	117	49
$\alpha = 0.9\beta = 0.7$	2	121	$\alpha = 0.0\beta = 0.7$	118	96
$\alpha = 1.0\beta = 0.7$	3	105	$\alpha = 0.9\beta = 0.9$	119	65
$\alpha = 0.1\beta = 0.8$	4	100	$\alpha = 0.5\beta = 0.7$	120	35
$\alpha = 0.2\beta = 0.8$	5	89	$\alpha = 0.0\beta = 0.3$	121	53

The results illustrated in Table 2 indicate that there is a significant variation in performance when the effect of path switchover is considered. For SCTP the selection of an appropriate RTO value is not only a tradeoff between (a) excessive retransmission delay and (b) spurious retransmissions. As a multi-homed protocol SCTP is significantly affected by the RTO value as it is used as a mechanism to determine when switchover is initiated.

Figure 8 graphs the performance rankings of the α and β pairs from the most effective $\alpha = 0.7\beta = 0.7$ to the least effective $\alpha = 0.0\beta = 0.3$. The results indicate an inverse relationship between data throughput and switchover time; as switchover times increase data throughput degrades.

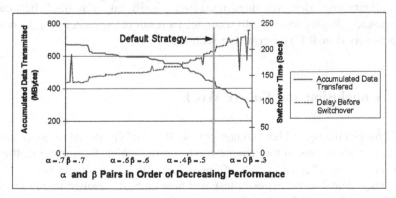

Fig. 8 Performance Comparison of Analytical and Simulated Results for α and β pairs

The default RTO calculation, which utilises the values $\alpha=.125$, $\beta = .25$, transmitted 412 Mbytes of data. The 3 pair configurations which were selected by the analytical study as the optimal tradeoff between (a) excessive retransmission delay and (b) spurious retransmissions $\alpha = .2$, $\beta =.7$, $\alpha = .2$, $\beta =.6$ and $\alpha = .3$, $\beta =.6$ transmitted 527, 527 and 359 MBytes respectively.

When the effects of switchover were considered by the simulated study the 3 most effective strategies were $\alpha = .7$, $\beta =.7$, $\alpha = .9$, $\beta =.7$ and $\alpha = 1$, $\beta =.7$. These configurations transmitted 673, 672 and 671 Mbytes respectively which was significantly more than the default configuration. Figure 9 compares the performance of the default strategy against the 3 most effective configurations from the analytical and simulated studies.

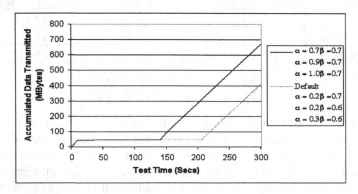

Fig. 9 Accumulated Data Transmitted for Selected α and β pairs

Figure 9 illustrates that alteration of α and β pairs from the default have the potential to improve SCTP throughput by up to 63%. This performance improvement is achieved through reduced switchover time due the altered α and β configurations. However there remains a significant *"flat line"* between approximately 30 seconds and 140 seconds as a result of the switchover delay due to excessively large RTO described in Section 5.

7   Conclusion and Future Work

This paper investigated how changes to the SCTP RTO calculation mechanism, in particular alterations to the parameters α, *the smoothing factor,* and β, the *delay variance factor* affected SCTP performance in a WLAN environment.

Experimental investigations illustrated how mobility resulted in continually increasing RTT in a WLAN environment. Using these results as input an analytical study was undertaken that considered the optimal configuration of α and β in the presence of continuously increasing RTT. The analytical study considered the traditional TCP oriented trade off between (a) excessive retransmission delay and (b) spurious retransmissions. The results indicated the optimal configurations for α and β in the presence of continuously increasing RTT. These optimal values of $\alpha = .2, \beta = .7, \alpha = .2, \beta = .6$ and $\alpha = .3, \beta = .6$ differ significantly from the default values of $\alpha = .125, \beta = .25$.

For SCTP however, the selection of an appropriate RTO value is not only a tradeoff between (a) excessive retransmission delay and (b) spurious retransmissions, SCTP must also consider the effect of RTO selection on switchover. Therefore a simulated study was then undertaken to consider the optimal configuration of α and β when the effects of SCTP path switchover were considered in the presence of continuously increasing RTT. The results indicated a significant variation in performance between the analytical and simulated studies. Two of the three α and β configurations which were selected as optimal by the analytical study were found to be more effective than the default strategy. However, the three most effective configurations suggested by the simulated study were $\alpha = 0.7 \beta = 0.7, \alpha = 0.9 \beta = 0.7$ and $\alpha = 1.0 \beta = 0.7$. These configurations transmitted significantly more than the configurations suggested by the analytical study and up to 63% more data than the default configuration as defined in RFC 4960.

While the results indicate that performance improvements are possible as a result of reduced switchover time through careful α and β configuration there remains a significant switchover delay due to excessively large RTO.

Future work will investigate optimized mechanisms for SCTP path management in WLAN environments. One mechanism may involve an SCTP switch management algorithm which will recognize continuously increasing RTT as an indicator of imminent path failure in a WLAN environment. Another approach may investigate a cross layer switch management strategy which utilizes received signal strength as a parameter in the path selection decision.

References

1. R. Stewart et al. Stream Control Transmission Protocol, RFC 4960, Sep. 2007.
2. Fallon, S et al. A "SCTP Switchover Performance Issues in WLAN Environments", IEEE Consumer Communications & Networking Conference (CCNC) 2008
3. Allman, M., Paxson V. "Computing TCP's Retransmission Timer" RFC 2988 November 2000
4. Jacobson, V., "Congestion Avoidance and Control", Computer Communication Review, vol. 18, no. 4, pp. 314-329, Aug.
5. Braden, R., "Requirements for Internet Hosts - Communication Layers", RFC 1122, October 1989.
6. Karn, P. and C. Partridge, "Improving Round-Trip Time Estimates in Reliable Transport Protocols", SIGCOMM 87.
7. Jacobson V.Braden R. Borman. D "TCP Extensions for High Performance" May 1992
8. Allman, M., Paxson V. and W. Stevens, "TCP Congestion Control", RFC 2581, April 1999.
9. Kesselman, A, Mansourz, Y, "Optimizing TCP Retransmission Timeout", 4th International Conference on Networking, Reunion Island, France 2005

10. Scharf, M, Necker, M, Gloss, B, "The Sensitivity of TCP to Sudden Delay Variations in Mobile Networks" Lectute notes in Computer Science 2004
11. Gurtov, A, "Effect of Delays on TCP Performance" IFIP Personal Wireless Communications 2001, Lappeenranta, Finland
12. Huang, H, Cai, J, "Improving TCP performance during soft vertical handoff", 19th International Conference on Advanced Information Networking and Applications, 2005.
13. Fu, S, Atiquzzaman, M, Ivancic, W, "Effect of delay spike on SCTP, TCP Reno, and Eifel in a wireless mobile environment" Conference on Computer Communications and Networks, 2002.
14. Budzisz L et al. "An Analytical Estimation of the Failover Time in SCTP Multihoming Scenarios" Wireless Communications and Networking Conference (WCNC) 2007
15. Qiao Y et al. "SCTP Performance Issue on Path Delay Differential", Wired/Wireless Internet Communications (WWIC) 2007
16. Kelly, A, et al. "Delay-Centric Handover in SCTP over WLAN", Transactions on Automatic Control and Computer Science, 49, 63 (2004), 1--6.
17. Min-Chin, C, Jen-Yi, P, Ting-Wei, H, "A Smart Path Failure Detection Method for SCTP in Wireless Network" International Conference on Wireless Communications, Networking and Mobile Computing, 2007. WiCom 2007.
18. Kim, D, Koh, S, Kim, Y, "A Scheme of Primary Path Switching for Mobile Terminals Using SCTP Handover" 2007 annual Conference on International Conference on Computer Engineering and Applications
19. IXChariot Console version 6.50 www.ixia.com
20. A. Caro, et al : ns-2 SCTP module, Version 3.5, www.armandocaro.net/software/ns2sctp/.
21. G. Combs, et al : Wireshark network protocol Analyzer, Version 0.99.5, www.wireshark.org

Efficient Joint Unicast/Multicast Transmission over IEEE 802.11e WLANs

José Villalón, Pedro Cuenca and Luis Orozco-Barbosa

Albacete Research Institute of Informatics

Universidad de Castilla-La Mancha 02071 Albacete, Spain

{josemvillalon,pcuenca,lorozco}@dsi.uclm.es

Abstract Multimedia communications over WLAN is widely acknowledged as one of the key, emerging applications for wireless LANs. As with any multi-service network, there is the need to provision the WLANs with the QoS mechanisms capable of guaranteeing the requirements of various services. The IEEE 802.11e (EDCA) standard defines the required QoS mechanisms into the protocol architecture of IEEE 802.11 WLANs. However, recent studies have shown that EDCA performs poorly when the medium is highly loaded due to the high collision rate. Numerous proposals have been reported in the literature aiming to overcome this main drawback. However, EDCA and the proposed mechanisms continue to have a serious problem with a specific type of application: the multicast traffic. In EDCA (as in DCF) the multicast service is defined as an unreliable service, i.e., it does not include the use of ACK frames. Furthermore, different to the unicast service, the multicast service makes use of a single rate out of the various rates included in the Basic Service Set (BSS) defined by the IEEE 802.11 standard. This situation has led many researchers to design techniques aiming to improve the multicast transmission such as Auto Rate Selection mechanism for Multicast (ARMS) and Hierarchical-ARSM (H-ARSM). In this paper we present a comparative performance evaluation when supporting different services, such as, voice, video, best-effort, background and in presence of multicast traffic. Our simulation results show the benefits present in multimedia applications when the unicast and multicast traffic are sent efficiently.

1 Introduction

A wide range of enterprise organizations have realized significant productivity increases by deploying mobile data applications using WLAN networks [1]. Motivated by the success, the organizations are now looking to further enhance the

Please use the following format when citing this chapter:

Villalón, J., Cuenca, P. and Orozco-Barbosa, L., 2008, in IFIP International Federation for Information Processing, Volume 284; *Wireless and Mobile Networking*; Zoubir Mammeri; (Boston: Springer), pp. 109–121.

productivity of their mobile workers and leverage their WLAN network invest-ments by deploying more applications into their networks. Multimedia communi-cations is one of the leading applications that benefit from the mobility and in-creasing bit rates provided by current and emerging WLAN technologies. However, multimedia applications are not only characterized by their high band-width requirements, but also impose severe restrictions on delay, jitter and packet loss rates. In others words, multimedia applications require Quality of Service (QoS) support. Guaranteeing those QoS requirements in IEEE 802.11 is a very challenging task due to the QoS-unaware operation of its MAC layer. This layer uses the wireless media characterized by the difficulties faced by the signal propa-gation. Thus providing QoS to IEEE 802.11 has been and it is an active research area giving rise to numerous service differentiation schemes.

The IEEE 802.11e Working Group has worked hard on the specification of IEEE 802.11e standard [2]. The IEEE 802.11e defines the mechanisms for wire-less LANs aiming to provide QoS support to time-sensitive applications, such as, voice and video communications. However, many studies have shown that the IEEE 802.11e (EDCA) scheme performs poorly under heavy load conditions. The severe degradation is mainly due to high collision rates. This reason has led many researchers to design new techniques aiming to address the shortcomings of the current standard.

Furthermore, EDCA and the proposed mechanisms to improve the QoS only have been designed to enhance the performance of unicast applications. In these schemes (as in DCF) the multicast service is defined as an unreliable service, i.e., it does not include the use of ACK frames. Furthermore, due the absence of a feedback, the multicast service makes use of a single rate out of the various rates included in the Basic Service Set (BSS) defined by the IEEE 802.11 standard. This situation has led many researchers to design techniques aiming to improve the multicast transmission.

In this paper, we address the two aforementioned issues by enhancing the mul-timedia communications over IEEE 802.11 WLANs. Our main objective has been to check the behavior of some QoS and multicast schemes proposed, in presence of uplink unicast traffic and downlink multicast traffic. The unicast traffic support different service, *such as, voice, video, best-effort, background.* For the downlink traffic, the access point transmits a video stream to the multicast receivers. The rest of the paper is organized as follows. Section 2 provides an overview of the IEEE 802.11 and the IEEE 802.11e WLAN standard, and some of the most rele-vant QoS proposals recently reported in the literature. In Section 3, we present an overview of some schemes to provide reliable multicast transmission in IEEE 802.11 WLAN. In Section 4, we carry out a comparative performance evaluation when supporting different unicast services, such as, voice, video, best-effort, back-ground and in presence of multicast traffic. Finally, Section 5 concludes the paper.

2 The IEEE 802.11 DCF and QoS Enhancements

The basic access function in IEEE 802.11 is the *Distributed Coordination Function* (DCF). A station operating under the DCF scheme should first sense the state of the channel before initiating a transmission. A station may start to transmit after having determined that the channel is idle during an interval of time longer than the *Distributed InterFrame Space* (DIFS). Otherwise, if the channel is sensed busy, once the transmission in course finishes and in order to avoid a potential collision with other active (waiting) stations, the station will wait a random interval of time (the *Backoff_Time*) before starting to transmit. As long as no activity is detected in the channel, a backoff counter, initially set to *Backoff_Time*, is decremented on an *aSlotTime* by *aSlotTime* basis. Whenever activity is detected, the backoff counter is frozen and reactivated once again when the channel has remained idle during an interval of time longer than DIFS. The station will be able to begin transmission as soon as the backoff counter reaches zero. In case of an unsuccessful transmission, the station will have a finite number of attempts, using a longer backoff time after each attempt.

Even though DCF is a simple and effective mechanism, DCF can neither support QoS nor guarantee to meet the multimedia applications requirements. It is for this reason that many researchers have proposed techniques the provisioning of QoS mechanisms into the DCF mode of operation. The description of such mechanisms is out of the scope of this work. An overview of many of the different QoS enhancements mechanisms for the IEEE 802.11 standards can be found in [3]. The need for a better access mechanism with an aim for providing service differentiation has led Task Group E of the IEEE 802.11 working group to come up with an extension to the IEEE 802.11 standard called IEEE 802.11e [2].

The IEEE 802.11e standard specifies the mechanisms enabling the provisioning of QoS guarantees in IEEE 802.11 WLANs. In the IEEE 802.11e standard, a third coordination function has been added: the *Hybrid Coordination Function* (HCF). HCF incorporates two new access mechanisms: the contention-based *Enhanced Distributed Channel Access* (EDCA) and the *HCF Controlled Channel Access* (HCCA).

EDCA has been designed to be used with the contention-based prioritized QoS support mechanisms. In EDCA, two main methods are introduced to support service differentiation. The first one is to use different IFS values for different ACs. The second method consists in allocating different CW sizes to the different ACs. Each AC forms an EDCA independent entity with its own queue and its own access mechanism based on an DCF-like mechanism with its own *Arbitration Inter-Frame Space* defined by $AIFS[AC]=SIFS+AIFSN[AC] \times aSlotTime$ and its own CW[AC] ($CWmin[AC] \leq CW[AC] \leq CWmax[AC]$), where $AIFSN[AC]$ is the *Arbitration Inter Frame Space Number*. If an internal collision arises among the queues within the same station, the one having higher priority obtains the right to transmit. The queue getting the right to access to the channel obtains a transmission opportunity. The winning queue can then transmit during a time interval whose length is given by *TXOPLimit*.

Many on-going research efforts are focusing on the evaluation of the IEEE 802.11e standard [4]-[6]. Many studies have revealed that the poor performance exhibited by the standard is mainly due to the high collision rates encountered when a large number of stations attempt to access the channel. Numerous proposals have been reported in the literature aiming to overcome this main drawback. In the following, we undertake the analysis of three of the most prominent ones.

In this regard, the *Fast Collision Resolution Mechanism* FCR [7] aims to shorten the backoff period by increasing the contention window sizes of all active stations during the contention resolution period. To reduce the number of wasted (idle) slots, the FCR algorithm assigns the shortest window size and idle backoff timer to the station having successfully transmitted a packet. Moreover, when a station detects a number of idle slots (static backoff threshold), it starts reducing the backoff timer exponentially, instead of linearly as specified by the EDCA standard. To address the provisioning of QoS mechanisms, the authors further introduce an enhanced version of the FCR algorithm, namely, the *Real Time Fast Collision Resolution* (**RT-FCR**) [7] algorithm. In this algorithm, the priorities are implemented by assigning different backoff ranges based on the type of traffic. In their study, the authors have considered three main traffic types: voice, video, and best-effort (data) traffic.

Under this scheme, voice packets hold the highest priority to access the channel by setting $CW = CW_{min}$. All the other flows have to wait, at least, eight backoff slots before being allowed to gain access to the channel. The video traffic is assigned the second highest priority by using a smaller maximum CW size than the one assigned to the best-effort data traffic.

In [8], *Mali et al.* go a step further by introducing a new scheme called *Adaptive Fair EDCF* (**AFEDCF**). This mechanism uses an adaptive fast collision resolution mechanism (similar to the FCR mechanism) when the channel is sensed idle. In contrast with the FCR mechanism, AFEDCF computes an adaptive backoff threshold for each priority level by taking into account the channel load.

However, the main deficiency of these mechanisms comes from its inability to provide the proper QoS to the video service in scenarios comprising legacy DCF-based and IEEE 802.11e stations. This is due to the fact that, under theses schemes, the video packets have always to wait for a minimum of eight backoff slots in order to comply with the highest priority assigned to the voice traffic. Under these schemes, the presence of voice and DCF stations may even result in starvation to the video flows. Moreover, the implementation of these mechanisms implies incompatible modifications to the IEEE 802.11e specifications.

Based on limitations of these mechanisms, in [9] we proposed a new IEEE-802.11e (called **B-EDCA**) based QoS mechanism compatible with the IEEE 802.11e specifications and capable of providing QoS support, particularly to video applications. Based on the results obtained in one of our previous studies we found out that the IFS (denoted AIFS in the EDCA standard) is the most important and critical parameter enabling the provisioning of QoS to multimedia applications. Our proposal has been based in using the minimum waiting time necessary to continue decrementing the backoff counter of the multimedia flows.

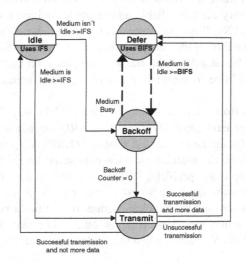

Fig. 1 B-EDCA Proposed Mechanism.

In order to introduce our proposal, we toke a closer look at the mode of operation of the DCF and EDCA schemes, and particularly on the role played by the IFS (AIFS) parameter. The IFS (AIFS) is used in the idle and the backoff states (see fig. 1). According to the current DCF and EDCA standards, the same values for the IFS parameter should be used regardless of the state in which the station is. In B-EDCA we propose to use a different set of IFS values depending on the state in which the station is. We have however to ensure not to compromise the operation of the HCF. We then propose the following parameter setting:

1. In the **Idle** state. The stations will use the IFS values as specified in the IEEE 802.11e standard including the Hybrid Coordination Function. This also ensures compatibility with the IEEE 802.11 (DCF) mechanism.
2. In every transfer from the **Defer** state to the **Backoff** state, we propose to use a different parameter, equivalent to the IFS, denoted from now on by BIFS. We then propose setting up this parameter to one, i.e., BIFS = 1, for the voice and video services. In this way, we improve considerably the performance of voice and video applications, increasing their priorities with respect to other flows. This setting also ensures that the HC will keep the highest priority. According to this mechanism, the stations must wait at least one additional slot during the backoff procedure before being allowed to transmit since the backoff interval is set within the [1, CW+1] range. We then propose using the set of values for BIFS to 1-1-3-7 for voice, video, best-effort and background traffics, respectively.

3 Multicast transmission over IEEE 802.11

Multicasting in IEEE 802.11 WLAN is specified as a simple broadcasting mechanism that does not make use of ACK frames. There are two main issues to be addressed to effectively deploy reliable and scalable multicast services over IEEE 802.11 wireless LANs. First, the absence of a feedback mechanism has a strong impact on the reliability of the service provided to the user. Second, according to the IEEE 802.11a/b/g standards, all frames with multicast and broadcast *Receiver Address* (RA) should be transmitted at one of the rates included in the basic rate set.

Most research efforts on multicasting in IEEE 802.11 WLANs have focused on improving the service reliability by integrating ARQ mechanisms into the protocol architecture. In [10], the *Leader-Based Protocol* (**LBP**) ARQ mechanism has been introduced to provide the multicast service with some level of reliability. To address the ACK implosion problem, LBP assigns the role of group leader to the multicast receiver exhibiting the worst signal quality in the group. The group leader holds the responsibility to acknowledge the multicast packets on behalf of all the multicast group members, whereas other MTs may issue *Negative Acknowledgement* (NACK) frames when they detect errors in the transmission process.

Recently, the *Rate Adaptive Multicast* (**RAM**) scheme has been proposed in [11] for reliable multicast delivery. Similar to the LBP scheme, the transmitter has first to send a RTS frame to indicate the beginning of a multicast transmission. However, in RAM the RTS frame is used by all the multicast receivers to measure the *Receiver Signal Strength* (RSS). Then, each multicast receiver has to send a variable length dummy CTS frame whose length depends on the selected PHY transmission mode. Finally, the transmitter senses the channel to measure the collision duration and can adapt the PHY rate transmission of the multicast data frame accordingly. Thus, RAM adapts the PHY transmission rate of the multicast data frames to the channel conditions. However, the overhead introduce by this mechanism is very high. In fact, the RTS/CTS option is disabled in most 802.11 products currently available in the market.

For reduce this overhead, we presented in [12] a novel mechanism named *Auto Rate Selection* mechanism for *Multicast* (**ARSM**) in multirate wireless LAN. Basically, the ARSM mechanism dynamically selects the multicast data rate based on the channel conditions perceived by the MTs. The main idea behind our proposal is to identify the AP to MT channels exhibiting the worst conditions, expressed in terms of the SNR ratio. The AP assigns the role of group leader to this MT. The group leader holds the responsibility of acknowledging the multicast packets on behalf of all the multicast group members, whereas other MTs may issue NACK frames when they detect errors in the transmission process, in that case the AP retransmit the frame. The mechanism to discover this station is named *Multicast Channel Probe Operation* (MCPO). In order to reduce the amount of processing to be carried out by the MTs, we proposed a *Dynamic Multicast Data Transmission* procedure by making use of several multicast PHY data rates. Under this scheme, the AP can be found in one of two different states depending on the feed-back received.

1. While the AP successfully delivers multicast data frame, the MCPO is deactivated. In this state, the AP will adapt its PHY data rate using the SNR value contained in the received ACK coming from the group leader.
2. If the AP shows a failure of N_{th} consecutive multicast transmissions (detected via NACKs), it initiates the MCPO.

Even though ARSM has proved to be effective as reported in [12], such setting heavily penalizes those MTs exhibiting better channel conditions. For this reason, we presented in [13] an enhancing the ARSM scheme to address the aforementioned issues. This second mechanism is named *Hierarchical ARSM* (**H-ARSM**). In this scheme, we focus our attention to its use in multicast video services. Under H-ARSM, the video is expected to be encoded into two layers, namely the base and enhancement layers. The packets containing the base layer of the video are sent to all the members of the multicast group following the rules as established by ARSM. In this way, the mechanism should guarantee a minimum video quality to all users. In the case of the enhancement layer, the operating mode is quite similar to the one used by the ARSM scheme, i.e., the AP has to first select a group leader for the enhancement layer, whose main mission is to acknowledge (ACK) the packets sent to the group. The other MTs may issue NACK frames when they detect errors in the transmission process, in that case the AP retransmit the frame. The main difference for enhancement layer comes from the fact that instead of selecting one of the members with the lowest SNR as the group leader, this new mechanism selects one of the members with the highest SNR. Furthermore, the enhancement layer is sent at a rate no lower than 5.5Mbps

4 Performance Evaluation

In this section, we carry out a performance analysis of our proposed mechanism. Our main objective is show the performance of our proposed schemes for QoS and multicast transmission (B-EDCA, ARSM and H-ARSM) in presence of multicast traffic and different unicast applications. We compare the performance of EDCA with the compatible B-EDCA mechanism as access model to the channel. Concern to the multicast mechanism, in [12] we showed that the standard is unable to effectively provide multicast services, and ARSM enhance the performance of LBP and RAM mechanism. For this reason, we study ARSM and H-ARSM as method to send the multicast traffic. Table I shows the different combinations studied in this paper.

Table 1. Combinations used to access the channel and for the multicast traffic.

	Access Model	Multicast scheme
ARSM-EDCA	EDCA	ARSM
ARSM_BEDCA	B-EDCA	ARSM
HARSM-EDCA	EDCA	H-ARSM
HARSM-BEDCA	B-EDCA	H-ARSM

Throughout our study, we have made use of the OPNET Modeler tool 11.5 [14], which already integrates the IEEE 802.11 simulator. We have integrated into it the EDCA, B-EDCA, ARSM and H-ARSM mechanisms.

In our simulations, we model an IEEE 802.11b WLAN consisting of an AP, nine multicast wireless MTs receivers, and eight unicast wireless MTs. We have varied the network size expressed in terms of the area covered by the AP and multicast MTs. The network size has been initially set to a geographical area of 50m x 50m. We have then increased the network size in both dimensions by 10m x 10m to a maximum network size of 140m x 140m. The access point is located in the center of the BSS. The cell size is changed throughout the different scenarios under study. The multicast MTs move randomly within the BSS at a constant speed of 5 km/h, whereas the unicast MTs are static and placed close to the access point. We assume that the unicast packets are always transmitted at 11 Mbps.

In our scenarios, we have assumed the use of two types of traffic flows: downlink multicast traffic and uplink unicast traffic. For the downlink traffic, the access point transmits a video stream to the multicast MTs. For the video streaming source, we have used traces generated from a variable bit-rate H.264 video encoder [15]. We generate two types of traces corresponding to the use or not of the hierarchical video coding scheme presented in [13]. We have used the sequence *Mobile Calendar* encoded on CIF format at a video frame rate of 25 frames/s. When the hierarchical coding is used, the base layer accounts approximately for 30% of the total video data (209 Kbps). Throughout our experiments, we have confirmed that an acceptable video quality in the base layer can be obtained while the amount of data traffic pertaining to the enhancement layer is in the order of 70 % (489 Kbps). The average video transmission rates used has been around 650 Kbps and 700 Kbps corresponding to the use or not of the hierarchical video coding.

For the unicast traffic our scenarios have eight unicast stations, with the following ratio: 2 voice, 2 video, 2 BE and 2 BK stations. We assume the use of constant bit-rate voice sources encoded at a rate of 16 kbits/s according to the G.728 standard [16]. The voice packet size has been set to 168 bytes including the RTP/UDP/IP headers. For the video applications, we have made use of the traces generated from a variable bit-rate H.264 video encoder. We have used the sequence mobile calendar encoded on CIF format at a video frame rate of 25 frames/sec. The average video transmission rate is around 480 kbits/s with a packet size equal to 1064 bytes (including RTP/UDP/IP headers). The best-effort and background traffics have been created using a *Pareto* distribution traffic model. The average sending rate of is 128 kbit/s, using a 552 bytes packet size (including TCP/IP headers). All traffic sources are randomly activated within of the interval [1,1.5] seconds from the start of the simulation. Throughout our study, we have simulated two minutes of operation of each particular scenario.

In our study, we have been interested in assessing the performance in terms of the following metrics: Normalized throughput, packet loss rate and video quality. To be able to compare the results at different loads (traffic patterns of different applications), we have preferred plotting the normalized throughput rather than the absolute throughput. The normalized throughput is calculated as the percentage of the offered load actually delivered to destination.

In order to limit the delay experienced by the unicast video and voice applications, the maximum time that video packet and voice packet may remain in the transmission buffer has been set to 100ms and 10ms, respectively. For the multicast video traffic (video streaming), we are selected 2s. These time limits are in line with the values specified by the standards and in the literature. Whenever a video or voice packet exceeds these upper bounds, it is dropped. The loss rate due to this mechanism is given by the packet loss rate due to deadline.

Finally, one of the most important metrics in multimedia communications is the quality of the received signal as perceived by the end user. This has been evaluated using the *Video Quality Metric* (VQM) [17] for the video signal. These metrics have been proved to behave consistently with the human judgments according to the quality scale that is often used for subjective testing (MOS, *Mean Opinion Score*) in the engineering community (see Table **II**).

Table 2. Quality scale (MOS)

Rating	Impairment	Quality
5	Imperceptible	Excellent
4	Perceptible, not annoying	Good
3	Slightly	Fair
2	Annoying	Poor
1	Very annoying	Bad

Fig. 2 shows the normalized throughput obtained for the Vo, Vi, BE and BK services and the global throughput when making use of each one of combinations being considered. From the results, it is clear that H-ARSM offers better results than the ARSM scheme. When H-ARSM is used to send the multicast traffic, the unicast normalized throughput for all the traffic is 100%. In H-ARSM, the base layer is sent at low rates (the same rate used in ARSM) while the enhancement layer is sent at a rate no lower than 5.5Mbps. For this reason, H-ARSM need less time to send the multicast video streaming, and the other applications can to send more data packets. Figure also shows that the B-EDCA mechanism outperforms the EDCA mechanism when the multicast traffic is sent to ARSM. B-EDCA use the minimum waiting time necessary to continue decrementing the backoff counter of the voice and video flows. B-EDCA introduces a new reserved slot to the voice and video traffic, and reduces the collision present between these applications and the other traffic.

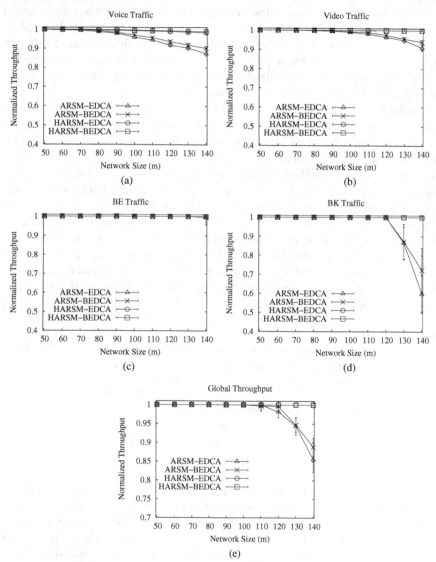

Fig. 2 Unicast Normalized Throughput: a) Voice, b) Video, c) Best-Effort d) Background and e) Total Traffic.

In the case of the multicast traffic, in Figure 3.a it is clear that the H-ARSM scheme is capable of sending all the traffic associated to the base layer (H-ARSM.HP[1]) independently of the network size. However, the throughput of the enhancement layer (H-ARSM.LP) decreases as the network size is increased. The reduction experienced by the enhancement layer is due to the decrease of the MTs pertaining to the enhancement layer as the network size increase. Figure 3.b shows the packet loss rate for the different scenarios. In the case of H-ARSM, the only packets being lost belong to those carrying the enhancement layer and being addressed to the stations not belonging to the enhancement multicast group. The H-ARSM scheme guarantees the correct delivery of all the packets containing the base layer to all the members of the multicast group (H-ARSM.HP). The scheme also guarantees the correct delivery of all the packets of the enhancement layer to all the members of the enhancement group. In the case of the ARSM and scheme, all the packet losses are due to excessive delay by the packets while waiting to be transmitted. H-ARSM limits the packet losses (belongs to enhancement layer) to those stations exhibiting the worst channel conditions, i.e., those stations belonging only to the base layer multicast group. With ARSM, all the members of the multicast group are affected.

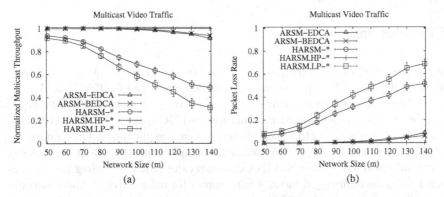

Fig. 3 Multicast Traffic: a) Normalized Throughput and b) Multicast Packet Loss Rate.

Finally, Figure 4 shows the video quality for unicast and multicast video traffic. The figure 4.a shows that when H-ARSM is used to send de multicast video streaming, the quality of the unicast video received is not dependent on network size. However, when ARSM is used, this quality decrease when the network size increase. In the case of the multicast traffic, when ARSM mechanism is used, the figure 4.b shows a video quality around 4.2 (corresponding a quantization factor equal to 26) as long as no packet losses are reported. However, the video quality drastically falls as the packet loss rate increases (network sizes beyond 90 m) as a

---

[1] HARSM-*, HARSM.HP-* and HARSM-LP-* symbolize the H-ARSM, H-ARSM base layer and H-ARSM enhanced layer respectively used whit EDCA and B-EDCA mechanism

result of missing the packet delivery deadlines. In the case of the H-ARSM, a minimum video quality is always guaranteed since the base layer is always delivered.

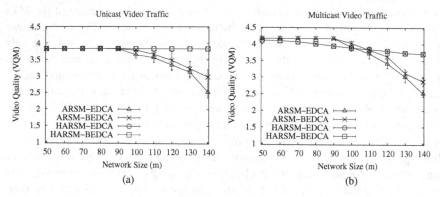

Fig. 4 Video Quality (VQM): a) Unicast Video and b) Multicast Video.

5 Conclusions

In the first part of this paper, we have overviewed some of the most relevant works in the area of QoS provisioning and reliable multicast for IEEE802.11 wireless LANs. Our main objective has been to show the performance of our proposed schemes for QoS and multicast transmission (B-EDCA, ARSM and H-ARSM) in presence of multicast traffic and different unicast applications. Our results obtained have shown that B-EDCA mechanism outperforms the EDCA mechanism. Our results also have shown that H-ARSM carry out efficient sending for the multicast traffic, maximizing the available resources for unicast traffic. The results obtained have shown that H-ARSM outperforms the ARSM mechanism for unicast and multicast traffic.

Acknowledgments

This work was supported by the Ministry of Science and Technology of Spain under CONSOLIDER CSD2006-46 and CICYT TIN2006-15516-C04-02, the Council of Science and Technology of Castilla-La Mancha under project PAI06-0106 and FEDER

References

1. LAN MAN Standards Committee of the IEEE Computer Society, ANSI/IEEE Std 802.11, "Part 11: Wireless LAN Medium Access Control (MAC) and Physical Layer (PHY) Specifications", 1999 Edition.
2. IEEE 802 Committee of the IEEE Computer Society, ANSI/IEEE Std 802.11e, "Part 11: Wireless LAN Medium Access Control (MAC) and Physical Layer (PHY) Specifications: Medium Access Control (MAC) Quality of Service (QoS) Enhancements", Nov. 2005.
3. F. Mico, P. Cuenca and L.Orozco Barbosa "QoS Mechanisms for IEEE 802.11 Wireless LANs". Lecture Notes in Computer Science. Vol. 3079. pp. 609-623, 2004.
4. D. Vassis and G. Kormentzas, "Delay Performance Analysis and Evaluation of IEEE 802.11e EDCA in Finite Load Conditions". Wireless Personal Communicat., vol. 34. pp. 29-43. 2005.
5. Z.K.Tsang, D.H.K. Bensaou and B. D. Gao, "Performance Analysis of IEEE 802.11e Contention-based Channel Access". IEEE Journal on Selected Areas in Communications. vol. 22 .pp. 2095-2106. 2004.
6. Q.Ni, "Performance Analysis and Enhancements for IEEE 802.11e Wireless Networks". IEEE Network. vol.19. no.4. pp. 21-26. 2005.
7. Y. Kwon, Y. Fang and H. Latchman, "Design of MAC Protocols with Fast Collision Resolution for Wireless Local Area Networks". IEEE Trans. on Wireless Communicat., vol. 3, no.3. pp. 793-807, May 2004.
8. M. Malli, Q. Ni, T. Turletti and C. Barakat "Adaptive Fair Channel Allocation for QoS Enhancement in IEEE 802.11 Wireless LANs", in Proceedings of IEEE ICC, Paris, Jun. 2004.
9. J. Villalón, P. Cuenca and L. Orozco-Barbosa "B-EDCA: A New IEEE 802.11e-based QoS Protocol for Multimedia Wireless Communications" Lecture Notes in Computer Science. Vol. 3976. pp. 6148-159, 2006.
10. Joy Kuri and Sneha Kumar Kasera, "Reliable Multicast in Multi access Wireless LANs", ACM Wireless Networks, Volume 7, Issue 4, Pages 359 - 369, 2001.
11. A. Basalamah, H. Sugimoto and T. Sato "Rate Adaptive Reliable Multicast MAC Protocol for WLANs", Proc. of VTC, Melbourne, Australia, May 2006. pp 1216-1220.
12. J. Villalón, Y. Seok, T. Turletti, P. Cuenca and L. Orozco-Barbosa, "ARSM: A Cross-Layer Auto Rate Selection Multicast Mechanism for Multi-Rate Wireless LANs". IET Communications, Vol. 1-5. pp. 893-902. October 2007.
13. J. Villalón, Y. Seok, T. Turletti, P. Cuenca and L. Orozco-Barbosa, "Cross-Layer Architecture for Adaptive Video Multicast Streaming over Multirate Wireless LANs". IEEE Journal on Selected Areas in Communications, Vol. 25-4. pp. 699-711, May 2007.
14. Opnet.Technologies.Inc. OPNET Modeler 11.5 (c)1987-2006. http://www.opnet.com.
15. ITU-T Recommendation H.264, "Advanced Video Coding For Generic Audiovisual Services". May 2003.
16. ITU-T Recommendation G.728, "Coding of Speech at 16 kbit/s using Low-Delay Code Excited Linear Prediction", Std., September 1992.
17. S. Wolf and M. H. Pinson, "Video Quality Measurement Techniques". NTIA Report 02-392. June 2002.

Content-Aware Selective Retransmission Scheme in Heavy Loaded Wireless Networks

Árpád Huszák and Sándor Imre

Budapest University of Technology and Economics, Department of Telecommunications, Mobile Communications and Computing Laboratory, Magyar Tudósok krt.2., H-1117 Budapest, Hungary

Tel.: +36 70 514 5925, Fax: + 36 1 463-3263

Email: huszak@hit.bmc.hu, imre@hit.bme.hu

Abstract Streaming media is becoming increasingly prominent on the Internet, although multimedia applications have very stringent bandwidth, delay and loss requirements. In mobile environment the limited bandwidth and the higher error rate arise as an obstacle of its popularity. In many cases retransmission-based error recovery can be an attractive solution to improve the quality of the video stream, because it requires minimal network bandwidth and processing cost. In this paper we propose a content-aware selective retransmission scheme which allows the retransmission of all packets when the risk of congestion is low, but as it rises the retransmission is disabled step-by-step, but not all at once, in order of packet importance. In this work the heterogenity of H.264 streams were utilized for the determination of packet importance. The advantage of this transmitter controlled procedure is that all the needed information is available at the source due to DCCP transport protocol and its congestion control algorithm. The effectiveness of the proposed method was examined in Ns2 network simulator.

1 Introduction

Real-time multimedia applications are gaining prominence on the Internet. These applications are not only used in reliable wired networks but also in wireless environment where the obstacles of the expansion are the higher bit error ratio of the radio link and the limited bandwidth of the mobile links. The loss of packets in a video frames leads not only to reduce the quality of video but also results in the propagation of distortion to successive frames, because inter-frame-video compression algorithms such as MPEG exploit temporal correlation between frames to achieve higher compression. To minimize the end-to-end packet loss ratio the packet loss should be either prevented or subsequently handled.

Please use the following format when citing this chapter:

Huszák, A. and Imre, S., 2008, in IFIP International Federation for Information Processing, Volume 284; *Wireless and Mobile Networking*; Zoubir Mammeri; (Boston: Springer), pp. 123–134.

Traditional error control mechanisms generally use retransmission to provide reliability at the expense of latency. For the retransmission to be successful, retransmitted packet must arrive at the receiver in time for playback. To minimize the probability of wastefully retransmitted packets, a playout buffer is usually set up at the receiver side.

The reason of packet loss can be either the overload of the network or the bad channel conditions. In order to avoid congestion collapse of the network and to minimize the packet loss, multimedia applications may use congestion control. The performance of congestion control protocols may significantly degrade over wireless links because they confuse wireless losses with congestion losses and unnecessarily reduce the throughput. To solve this problem new congestion control were developed, like ARC [1] and WLED-ARC [2].

In this paper a selective retransmission method is introduced which efficiently manages the retransmission process in heavy loaded network. Our proposal is that we disable the retransmission of less important packets step-by-step, as the network load increases and approaches to congestion state. With disabling the retransmission of packets with specified content, we are able to control the overall stream bitrate between certain limits in order to avoid congestion. We notice that the proposed algorithm is acceptable only for pre-recorded and one-way real-time video streams, when the retransmission delay can be tolerable.

The rest of the paper is organized as follows. A review of related work in selective retransmission is presented in Section II. In Section III we introduce our content-aware selective retransmission method for multimedia applications. The obtained results are presented in Section IV. Finally, we summarize our paper and make the conclusions in the last section.

2   Related work

Many papers deal with QoS control, but packet losses remain inevitable because the network condition between the server and the client changes dynamically and drastically during playout. The method of these previous works can be divided to content based and network characteristic based selective retransmission algorithms.

Our work focuses on content based schemes, which basic idea is to retransmit only the important data of the bitstream, taking advantage of the motion prediction loop employed in most motion compensation based codecs. Several proposals have described retransmission schemes for recovering lost streaming packets. One of the most popular schemes, based on RTP (Real-Time Transport Protocol)[3], was proposed in [4-6]. In the scheme, when the client detects packet losses, it transmits a retransmission request packet to the server. The server then retransmits the lost packets to the client.

Feamster and Balakrishnan [7] analyzed this approach with SR-RTP [8]. This RTP extension provides semantics for requesting the retransmission of independently processible portions of the bitstream and a means for reassembling fragmented portions of independently processible units. They have shown that, by recovery of only the most important data in the bitstream, significant performance gains can be achieved without much additional penalty in terms of latency.

In [9] the selective retransmission of MPEG stream was analyzed with DCCP. This transport protocol provides indispensable information to apply semi-reliable transfer of MPEG video. The results show that the effectiveness of this protocol is considerable when selective retransmission is deployed. In [10] a semi-reliable multicast protocol is analyzed based on the IP multicast protocol and retransmission request messages. Zheng and Atiquzzaman [11] proposed a new selective retransmission scheme for multimedia transmission over noisy wireless channel using the ATM ABR service. They analyzed the system requirements and minimum receiver.

In most of the related works the receiver controls the retransmission procedure. The decision algorithm is implemented at the receiver therefore additional administration messages must be sent to the sender. Most of the prior works use NACK (Negative ACKnowledgement) or Retransmission Request messages. In our proposal no administration messages are needed because the decision procedure is located at the transmitter. The other advantage of the transmitter side decision is that the input parameters of the decision algorithm (RTT, estimated link bandwidth, etc.) are available at the source using the DCCP [12] transport protocol.

3   Content-Aware Selective Retransmission Scheme

Loss-tolerant real-time multimedia applications prefer UDP or UDPLite [13] but in our proposal we applied DCCP (Datagram Congestion Control Protocol) as transport protocol because it uses sequence numbering, acknowledgements and congestion control algorithms. Sequence numbers and acknowledgement are needed to identify the lost packets while the congestion control algorithms (TCP-Like Rate Control [14], TCP Friendly Rate Control [15], ARC [1], WLED-ARC [2]) manage the actual sending rate. To determinate the sending rate the congestion control algorithms estimates the round-trip-time (RTT) and the packet loss probability of the link. The packet loss probability is an important variable for our content-aware selective retransmission algorithm too.

The DCCP protocol makes it possible to identify the lost packets; therefore we can manage the retransmission of these packets. Retransmitting packets will increase the bandwidth used for the video stream transmission. The additional load due to retransmissions highly depends on the overall packet loss ratio. We can easily verify that with the increase of the packet loss probability, the needed bandwidth will be higher due to retransmissions. The expected value of the overall bandwidth can be calculated as follows, where μ is the video bitrate, μ' is the additional bitrate due to retransmissions and p is the loss probability:

$$\mathsf{E}(\mu + \mu') = \mu + \mu p + \mu p^2 + ... = \mu + \mu \frac{p}{1-p} = \mu \frac{1}{1-p} \tag{1}$$

The retransmission delay can also limit the number of retransmissions if we enable multiple retransmissions, that means we allow to retransmit a lost packet when it was already retransmitted and lost. If we want to provide reliable transmission we have to allow multiple retransmissions. In other words, the number of retransmission is infinite. In this case the expected value of the delay (d) due to retransmission can be calculated using the formulas of geometrical progression:

$$\mathsf{E}(d) = \frac{RTT}{2}(1-p) + \frac{3RTT}{2}(1-p)p + \frac{5RTT}{2}(1-p)p^2 + ... \tag{2}$$

$$\mathsf{E}(d) = \frac{RTT}{2}(1-p) \cdot \sum_{n=0}^{\infty}(2n+1)p^n = \frac{RTT}{2} \cdot \frac{1+p}{1-p} \tag{3}$$

If we also consider the loss detection delay (τ) the expected value of the retransmission delay is:

$$\mathsf{E}(d) = \frac{RTT}{2}(1-p) + \left(\frac{3RTT}{2} + \tau\right)(1-p)p + \left(\frac{5RTT}{2} + 2\tau\right)(1-p)p^2 + ... \tag{4}$$

$$\mathsf{E}(d) = \frac{RTT}{2} \cdot \frac{1+p}{1-p} + \tau \frac{p}{1-p} \tag{5}$$

In our proposed content-aware retransmission scheme we have taken only the bandwidth constrains into consideration. The estimated available bandwidth in the network is considered as the proposed sending rate of the congestion control algorithm. In order to avoid congestion the overall bandwidth should not exceed the proposed sending rate. In case when the overall video stream bitrate is higher then the calculated sending rate (X_{cc}), the retransmissions must be disabled, because it makes no sense to retransmit any packet that will be lost again.

$$\mu(t) + \mu'(t) > X_{cc}(t) \quad \Rightarrow \quad \text{retransmission disabled} \tag{6}$$

In a heavy loaded wireless network the packets should loss due to congestion and the due to bad wireless channel conditions. To efficiently estimate the available bandwidth alternative congestion control algorithm must be used. The TFRC protocol can not distinguish congestion loss and wireless loss; therefore, during wireless losses, the sending rate will be lower than the really achievable rate. Using alternative congestion control methods (ARC and WLED integrated with ARC (WLED-ARC)) which effectively estimates the congestion loss, the performance of transmission can be improved. ARC [1] is the first congestion control algorithm that models the behavior of the "ideal" TCP that doesn't react to wireless losses. ARC is a rate-control scheme that uses the following equation:

$$S = \frac{1}{RTT}\left(3 + \sqrt{25 + \frac{24}{p_c}}\right), \tag{7}$$

where S is the sending rate in packets per second and p_c is the congestion loss probability. The latter is related to the total packet loss probability π and the wireless loss probability ω through the expression:

$$p_c = \left(\frac{\pi - \omega}{1 - \omega}\right) \tag{8}$$

The parameter π is easily estimated from the total packets received and the total packets lost, by looking at the sequence numbers. To calculate ω, ARC relies on the MAC layer to get this loss probability. However, this approach violates the end-to-end paradigm and will not work if there is no way to obtain the wireless loss probability from lower layers.

The proposed selective retransmission scheme uses the calculated sending rate of the congestion control algorithms to decide whether to enable the retransmission of a lost packet or not. In same network conditions when the wireless loss is high, the ARC-based congestion control algorithms provide significantly higher sending rates than TFRC.

As we declared before, the retransmission must be disabled when the calculated sending rate (X_{cc}) descend under the overall video bitrate ($\mu + \mu'$). In some cases the difference between X_{cc} and the video bitrate (μ) is too low to enable the retransmission of all the lost packets. In general:

$$E(\mu') = \mu \frac{p}{1 - p} < \lambda, \tag{9}$$

where $\$$ is the bound of the difference, when the retransmission of all lost packets can be enabled.

For the real-time decision algorithm:

$$X_{cc}(t) - \mu(t) < \lambda \tag{10}$$

In cases when retransmission of all lost packets is not possible, we should consider which packets should be retransmitted. Our recommendation is that the packet content must be used to select the packets for retransmission. The MPEG video frame structure gives a good opportunity to efficiently select the lost packet for retransmission. If we utilize this feature of the MPEG, we can allow the retransmission step-by-step. When the difference of the calculated sending rate and the video bitrate (X_{cc}-μ) is decreasing and not all the lost packets can be retransmitted, first the retransmission of packets that contains B frames must be disabled. In second step, when the difference is too small to retransmit I and P frames, P frame retransmission must be disabled. For the decision, the additional load due to the retransmissions should be estimated.

The extra load (μ_I') due to the I frame retransmission is:

$$\mu_I' = \rho_I \cdot p \cdot \mu, \tag{11}$$

where ϱ_I is the I-frames data ratio in the GOP, and can be calculated as:

$$\rho_I = \frac{\text{total size of I frames in the GOP}}{\text{GOP size}} \tag{12}$$

The calculation of corresponding P and B frame ratios are similar, hence $\rho_I + \rho_P + \rho_B = 1$. Similarly to (11) the extra loads for I+P and all frame types retransmission can be calculate as follows:

$$\mu_{I+P}{}' = (\rho_I + \rho_P) \cdot p \cdot \mu \tag{13}$$

$$\mu_{all}{}' = p \cdot \mu \tag{14}$$

The decision process will enable or disable different frame type retransmission according to the additional load and the currently proposed congestion control sending rate. In some cases there is no possibility to determinate the current ratio, we can set the frame ratios $\rho_I = \rho_P = \rho_B = 0.33$ or 0.5, but as we will see in the simulation section, there is no significant difference between the two parameter setup. The stipulation of retransmitting I, I+P and all the frames are as follows:

Table 1. Frame type retransmission

	General ratio ($\varrho_{50\%}$=0.5)	Ratios of the actual video ($\varrho_I, \varrho_P, \varrho_B$)
I frames	$\mu < X_{cc} < \mu + \mu'_{50\%}$	$\mu < X_{cc} < \mu + \mu'_I$
I+P frames	$\mu + \mu'_{50\%} < X_{cc} < \mu + 2\mu'_{50\%}$	$\mu + \mu'_I < X_{cc} < \mu + \mu'_{I+P}$
all frames	$X_{cc} > \mu + 2\mu'_{50\%}$	$X_{cc} > \mu + \mu'_{all}$

With the proposed method we can utilize the available bandwidth in the most efficient way, because when the bandwidth is not enough to retransmit all the lost packets, the packet selection for the retransmission is done according to packet importance. We used the calculated sending rate (X_{cc}) of the ARC congestion control protocol.

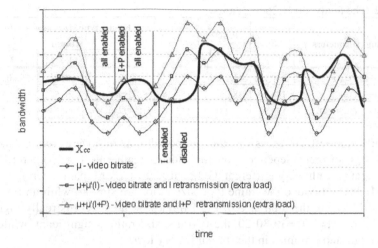

Fig. 1 The decision algorithm of the proposed content-aware retransmission method

The figure clearly illustrates the decision function. The bandwidth difference between the retransmission limits linearly depend on the overall packet loss ratio. When the packet loss is higher, the difference is becoming more and more significant. Our method can be effective when the calculated sending rate of the congestion control algorithm is similar to the video bitrate. This situation can occur when the available channel bandwidth is low like in heavy loaded networks.

4   Simulation results

In this section we explore the performance of the proposed ARC-based adaptive content-aware retransmission scheme in Ns2 [16]. We used dumbbell topology with 1Mbps links and 10ms link delays. The wireless packet link was the bottleneck of the analyzed network. We have used a simple random drop model to introduce losses, with the given loss probability. In order to analyze the proposed method in heavy loaded network WWW background traffic were set up. Each WWW connection was transmitting random size of files and after the TCP transmission of the webpage, random idle interval was inserted. The idle time was determined, using exponential distribution with average value of 5 seconds, while webpage size was generated using the Pareto distribution (mean value was set to 10kB). To analyze the quality of the H.264 video stream (reference video "mother and daughter"), the PSNR (Peak Signal to Noise Ratio) objective quality parameter was used. In order to emphasize the improvement of the proposed method we have generated three ~155kbps H.264 video streams with different frame type ratios.

Table 2. The analyzed H.264 streams

Coding parameters	kbps	PSNR Y [dB]	Kbps	Frame type size ratios in the stream		
				I [%]	P [%]	B [%]
N=24 M=3 Q=10	159,77	41,24	159,77	31,93974	42,65924	25,40102
N=6 M=3 Q=15	154,36	38,25	154,36	80,05087	10,36654	9,582596
N=6 M=3 Q=30-30-20	155,07	31,33	155,07	12,99754	1,290237	85,71222

Of course the effectiveness of the proposed content-aware retransmission method was different depending on the video stream. We have generated the video streams with very different GOP structures (N/M parameters). In the N=24 M=3 Q=10 video the frame type size ratios are similar, while in the N=6 M=3 Q=15 video, the total size of the I frames in the stream is really high. In case of N=6   M=3 Q=30-30-20, the B frame size ratio is significant, while the total size of I and P frames in the stream is very low.

To achieve quality improvement successfully retransmitted packets are needed. We have made simulations with X_{cc} determined by TFRC and ARC congestion control algorithm. According to the simulation results, the TFRC is not effective for our content-aware retransmission method, because the calculated sending rate (X_{cc}) is too low; therefore the estimated free bandwidth ($X_{cc}-\mu$) is not enough for the additional load due to retransmissions. When the total loss probability is low, the number of lost packet is also very low. The proposed selective retransmission method is developed for transmission in high loss probability networks. In case of high total loss probability, we should examine more possibilities: high wireless loss – high congestion loss, low wireless loss – high congestion loss and high wireless loss – low congestion loss. In all these cases the TFRC sending rate (X_{cc}) is very low, but in case of ARC the sending rate will not decrease when the wireless loss is high. When the congestion loss is high we can not retransmit lost packets neither with ARC nor TFRC.

In the simulations we have analyzed the number of retransmitted packet in case of content-aware retransmission scheme and without content-aware (frame) differentiation. Selective retransmission without frame differentiation is means that the retransmission is enabled if the congestion control rate is higher then the video bitrate ($X_{cc}>\mu$) and disable when $X_{cc}<\mu$. We have made the simulation with five different wireless loss probability setup (0.1%, 1%, 5%, 10%, 15%, 20%) and twelve different background load setup (number of WWW is from 5 to 60). The total number of simulation tests for each video stream was 60. In order to efficiently present the results and the overall performance of the proposed method, we have calculated the average of the measured values.

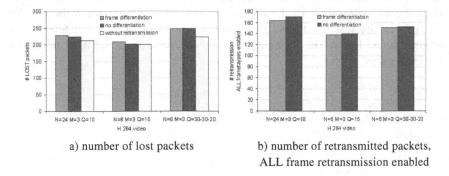

a) number of lost packets

b) number of retransmitted packets, ALL frame retransmission enabled

Fig. 2 The average number of lost and retransmitted packets using the content-aware (frame differentiation) method compared with methods without content differentiation and retransmission

Transmitting more packets on the link will increase the number of lost packets too, as Fig. 2 a) shows. According to Fig. 2 b) the number of retransmitted packets, when all frame type retransmission is enabled is a little bit higher, because in case of content-aware retransmission the I and I+P frame retransmissions are not included. If we add the number of I and I+P retransmission to it, the total number of retransmissions will be very similar.

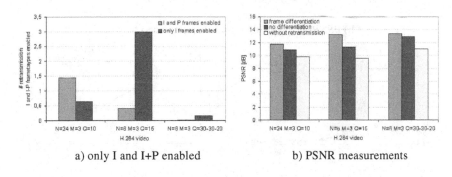

a) only I and I+P enabled

b) PSNR measurements

Fig. 3 Average number of retransmissions, when only I and I+P frame type retransmission is enabled

According to the average number retransmissions, when only I and I+P frames but no B frames were retransmitted, we were suspecting that the highest quality improvement will achieved in case of N=3 M=6 Q=15 video stream. As the PSNR measurements show, the protection of I frames effectively improves the quality.

We have analyzed the PSNR improvement of the proposed retransmission scheme from the wireless loss and congestion loss point of view. In order to efficiently illustrate the general impact of the proposed method, we have calculated the average values of the measurements. For example when the wireless loss probability was fixed, twelve measurements were done with different background traffic loads. The averages of the measured values are used in the following figures.

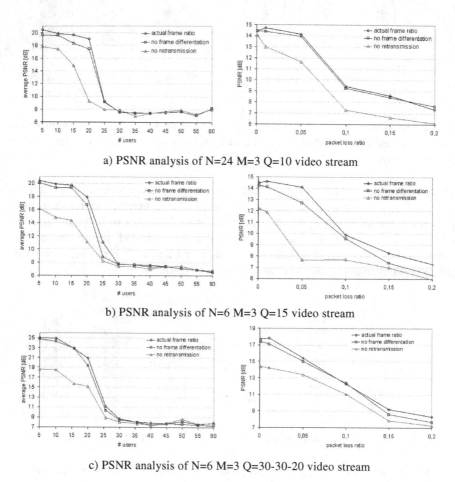

a) PSNR analysis of N=24 M=3 Q=10 video stream

b) PSNR analysis of N=6 M=3 Q=15 video stream

c) PSNR analysis of N=6 M=3 Q=30-30-20 video stream

Fig. 4 PSNR measurements

As we can see the retransmissions can gain significant quality improvement, but using frame differentiation further PSNR improvement can be achieved. The differences in the PSNR values were not varying significantly when the packet loss was changed, while increasing the background load leads to congested state. In this state the proposed method has no effect. In the simulations 30 WWW users were overloaded the network and made not possible to retransmit any lost packet.

5 Conclusion

Bad channel conditions in wireless networks, not only degrade the video quality, but render the current congestion control algorithms that back-off on every loss. We have shown that, by recovery of the data in the bitstream considering the current state of the network, significant performance gains can be achieved without much additional penalty in terms of latency. We have integrated the ARC congestion control scheme with an adaptive re-transmission scheme in order to selectively retransmit some lost video packets. When the network utilization is very high, the extra load due to retransmissions can not be delivered. In this situation content-aware differentiation is an alternative solution to maximize the overall quality of the transmitted video stream.

Acknowledgement

This work was supported by the frame of Mobile Innovation Centre's integrated project Nr. 1.1., supported by the National Office for Research and Technology (Mobile 01/2004 contract), the Celtic-BOSS project under the framework of the EUREKA Celtic Program and the NKTH Déri Miksa project.

References

1. O. B. Akan and I. F. Akyildiz, "ARC: the analytical rate control scheme for real-time traffic in wireless networks", IEEE/ACM Transactions on Networking, vol. 12, no. 4, pp. 634–644, 2004.
2. Kamal D. Singh, David Ros, Laurent Toutain and César Viho. "Improving Multimedia Streaming over wireless using end-2-end estimation of Wireless Losses", IEEE 64th Vehicular Technology Conference, Montreal, Canada, September 2006.
3. Schulzrinne, H., Casner, S., Frederick, R., and Jacobson, V.: "RTP: A Transport Protocol for Real-Time Streaming Protocol", Internet Engineering Task Force, RFC 3550, July 2003
4. Miyazaki, A., Fukushima, H., Hata, K., Wiebke, T., Hakenberg, R., Burmeister, C., Takatori, N., Okumura, S., and Ohno, T.: "RTP Payload Formats to Enable Multiple Selective Re-transmissions", draft-ietf-avt-rtp-selret-05.txt, June 2002
5. Ott, J., Wenger, S., Sato, N., Burmeister, C., and Rey, J.: "Extended RTP Profile for RTCP-based Feedback (RTP/AVPF)", draft-ietf-avt-rtcp-feedback-05.txt, February 2003
6. Rey, J., Leon, D., Miyazaki, A., Varsa, V., and Hakenberg, R.: "RTP Retransmission Payload Format", Internet Engineering Task Force, RFC 4588, July 2006
7. M. Feamster, H. Balakrishnan, "Packet Loss Recovery for Streaming Video", 12th International Packet Video Workshop, Pittsburgh, PA, April 2002.
8. A. Miyazaki, A. H. Fukushima, K. Hata, T. Wiebke, R. Hakenberg, C. Burmeister, Matsushita, "RTP payload formats to enable multiple selective retransmission", Internet Engineering Task Force, draft-ietfavt-rtp-selret-04.txt, Nov. 2001.
9. A. Huszak, S. Imre," Selective Retransmission of MPEG Video Streams over IP Networks", CSNDSP 2006, Patras, Greece, July 2006.

10. Christiane Montenegro Bortoleto, Lau Cheuk Lung, Frank A. Siqueira, Alysson Neves Bessani, Joni da Silva Fraga: "A Semi-reliable Multicast Protocol for Distributed Multimedia Applications in Large Scale Networks", MMNS 2005, LNCS 3754, Barcelona, Spain, October 24-26

11. Bing Zheng, Mohammed Atiquzzaman, "Network Requirement for Management of Multimedia over Wireless Channel", Lecture Notes In Computer Science Vol. 2496, Proceedings of the 5th IFIP/IEEE International Conference on Management of Multimedia Networks and Services: Management of Multimedia on the Internet, London, UK, 2002.

12. Kohler, Handley, Floyd, "Datagram Congestion Control Protocol", Internet Engineering Task Force, RFC 4340, March 2006.

13. Larzon, Degermark, Pink, "The Lightweight User Datagram Protocol", Internet Engineering Task Force, RFC 3828, July 2004.

14. S. Floyd and E. Kohler, "Profile for DCCP Congestion Control ID 2: TCP-like Congestion Control", draft-ietf-dccp-ccid2-10.txt, March 2005.

15. S. Floyd, E. Kohler, and J. Padhye, "Profile for DCCP Congestion Control ID 3: TFRC Congestion Control", draft-ietf-dccp-ccid3-11.txt, March 2005.

16. Ns-2 – Network Simulator, http:///www.isi.edu/nsnam/ns/index.html

Request Mechanisms to Reduce the Contention Period in 802.16: A Comparison

Jesús Delicado, Francisco M. Delicado and Luis Orozco–Barbosa

Instituto de Investigación en Informática de Albacete (I³A)
Universidad de Castilla–La Mancha (UCLM)
02071–Albacete, Spain
e-mail: {jdelicado,franman,lorozco}@dsi.uclm.es

Abstract Nowadays, a large number of applications characterized by stringent end–to–end requirements are on high demand. The development of Broadband Wireless Access (BWA) should enable the ubiquitous and cost-effective deployment of such applications. The IEEE 802.16 standard is currently one of the promising BWA technology under development. The IEEE 802.16 defines the principles of the Physical and Medium Access Control mechanisms to be implemented by the standard. Under the proposed MAC protocol, the Base Station (BS) is responsible of allocating the bandwidth required by the Subscriber Stations (SS). A SS issues its bandwidth request during a pre–defined contention period. Since the user data and signalling data are transmitted over the same band, the design of efficient signalling mechanism aiming to reduce the time and space length of the contention period is nowadays the main focus of a large number of studies. In this paper, we introduce and evaluate two novel bandwidth request mechanisms and compare their performance with the signalling mechanisms proposed by the standard.

1 Introduction

Nowadays, there is an increasing demand for high–speed Internet wireless access mainly due to the use of applications characterized by stringent time requirements. The IEEE 802.16 standard is currently one of the most promising proposals Broadband Wireless Access technologies [7]. An upgrade from fixed BWA systems to mobile service to vehicular speeds was ratified in December 2005, IEEE 802.16e [8].

The MAC protocol of the IEEE 802.16 Standard defines a set of connection–oriented services and distinguishes two types of devices: the Base Station (BS) and the Subscriber Stations (SSs). The former is responsible of allocating on–demand the bandwidth required by the all active SSs. The SSs enable the connectivity between the end-user equipments and the BS. According to the MAC protocol, a SS should request to the BS the required bandwidth before actually transmitting a data unit over the wireless channel. The request mechanisms to be employed by the SS depend on the QoS requirements of the application. It is therefore clear that the signalling protocol plays a central element on the QoS guarantees offered by the

Please use the following format when citing this chapter:

Delicado, J., Delicado, F.M. and Orozco–Barbosa, L., 2008, in IFIP International Federation for Information Processing, Volume 284; *Wireless and Mobile Networking*; Zoubir Mammeri; (Boston: Springer), pp. 135–147.

IEEE 802.16 Standard. The signalling protocol should allow the SSs to request the bandwidth according to the needs of active connections associated to the SSs. In turn, the BS should comprise the signalling mechanisms to respond to the various SSs requirements.

In this work, we present two signalling proposals whose main aim is to reduce the number of signalling messages. We also conduct a comparative study of these two proposals and the signalling mechanisms defined by the standard. The paper is organized as follows: Section 2 briefly describes the IEEE 802.16 Standard. Section 3 overviews previous efforts reported in the literature related to our proposals. Our proposals are described in Section 4. In Section 5, we conduct a comparative performance study of the three different signalling schemes. Section 6 draws our conclusions and future work plans.

2 IEEE 802.16

In this section, we provide an overview of the IEEE 802.16 physical (PHY) and the medium access control (MAC) layers. The IEEE 802.16 proposes a PMP (Point–to–MultiPoint) topology, and optionally a mesh topology [4]. Under the PMP mode, the standard supports a range of frequencies from 2 to 66 GHz, including the licensed and license–exempt bands. Depending on the range of frequencies there may be necessary line–of–sight (LOS) or non–line–of–sight (NLOS) between the communicating entities. Three types of modulation can be used: QPSK (Quadrature Phase–Shift Keying), 16–QAM (Quadrature Amplitude Modulation) and 64–QAM, but only QPSK is mandatory. Through the different releases of the standard, three different physical air interface specifications are proposed: SC/SCa (Single Carrier), OFDM (256–carrier Orthogonal–Frequency Division Multiplexing) and OFDMA (2048–carrier OFDM scheme).

The MAC is a centralized and connection–oriented mechanism, i.e., the BS allocates the resources and provides the system with QoS–aware mechanism according to the required needs of the various applications while the SSs request the needed bandwidth on a frame by frame basis.

The communication between the BS and the SSs is carried out by means of fixed–length frames and is time multiplexed by means of TDMA (*Time Division Multiplexing Access*), divided into two subframes: the downlink subframe (from the BS to the SSs) and the uplink subframe (from the SSs to the BS). Both subframes are multiplexed using time–division duplexing (TDD) or frequency–division duplexing (FDD).

The downlink subframe begins with a Frame Start Preamble (FSP), which is used for synchronization and equalization at the PHY layer. This is followed by the Frame Control Section (FCS), which is composed of management messages. Two of these messages are the downlink and uplink maps (DL-MAP and UL-MAP, respectively), which are comprised by the bandwidth allocations for SSs, and their corresponding burst profiles, in both downlink and uplink directions, respectively. Following these maps, other important management messages are the DCD and UCD, which indicate the physical characteristics of the physical channels in both directions. Finally, a time–division multiplexing (TDM) portion is introduced, organized into bursts on a decreasing robustness.

The uplink subframe is divided into three periods. The initial period is used by the SSs requiring access to the network. This part is followed by another contention period reserved to convey the BW-request messages sent by each active connection to request their bandwidth needs to the BS. These two contention periods are divided into slots. Finally, the last period is used by the SSs to send their user data to the BS (uplink). Each transmission is separated by SS Transition Gaps in order to properly synchronize the channel activity.

The sizes of the downlink and uplink subframes are determined dynamically by the BS on a frame to frame basis. This information is broadcasted by the BS to the SSs through DL-MAP and UL-MAP messages, respectively. The BS is also responsible node of controlling the number of transmission opportunities given to the SSs during the first two periods and the data transmission through the UL-MAP. The Tx/Rx Transition Gap (TTG) and the Rx/Tx Transition Gap (RTG) are used to switch from transmission to reception and vice versa.

2.1 Grants

According to the first release of the IEEE 802.16 Standard [6], the bandwidth grants to be issued by the BS should be associated to a specific connection by explicitly indicating its CID (Connection IDentifier) in the grant message. This mechanism is called GPC (*Grants Per Connection*) and it requires that the BS issues a grant in response to a request.

The 2004 release of the Standard [7] defines the GPSS (*Grants Per Subscriber Station*) mechanism. Under this mechanism, the bandwidth is granted to the SS through its Basic CID and not explicitly to each and every individual CID associated to the SS. In this way, the number of needed signalling messages is reduced to one grant per SS. Under this mechanism, the SSs are charged of distributing the granted bandwidth among their backlogged connections.

2.2 Requests

According to the IEEE 802.16 Standard, the bandwidth requests have to be issued by the SSs on a connection by connection basis. Since potential channel access conflicts may arise during the contention period reserved in the uplink subframe for this purpose, the standard defines a conflict resolution mechanism, namely the *truncated binary exponential backoff* algorithm. This mechanism is put in place to resolve potential conflicts due to simultaneous access to this period by different

SSs. Under this mechanism, the initial time slot to be used by a SS to transmit a request message is randomly selected from a set of consecutive slots, referred as a window. Once having issued its request, the SS activates a timer and waits for its confirmation for a maximum time period defined by the initial value of the timer. If the timer expires before the SS receives the confirmation, the SS resends the message during a time slot determined from a window size. In this second attempt, the size of the window is set to twice the value of the one having been used in the previous transmission. This procedure is repeated as long as a conflict arises, i.e., the SS does not get a confirmation within the time period defined by the timer and up to a given number of attempts defined by the standard, whatever it arises first. It is clear that as the number of active connections increases the collision probability also increases. This condition will adversely affect the network performance. In the following, we will review the various proposals being put forward to limit the number of signalling messages being used to convey the bandwidth requests.

3 Related work

Many research efforts on the performance of IEEE 802.16 contention algorithm have been carried out through the past few years. In [5], a dynamic mini–slot allocation scheme has been introduced based on an estimate of the maximum number of data packets that can be transmitted through a frame. In [14], the authors try to minimize the delay for transmitting the requests, by identifying the number of active SSs and by uniformly distributing the transmission attempts over the available random access slots. The authors of [12] have concluded that the optimal size of the contention period is $2M - 1$, where M is the number of SSs (users). In [1], the authors have determined the size of the contention period aiming to maximize the throughput. In this case, the result is a contention period equal to the number of competing SSs. In the previous papers, the length of the contention period is fixed by the number of active SSs. However, they do not take into account the statistics of the various applications which may potentially be exploited to improve the overall system performance. The authors of [15] have developed a novel random access method. They have compared the random access method with centralized polling and station–grouping mechanisms, and introduce an adaptive switching mechanism between both methods depending on the request arrival rate. In [11] a new algorithm has been introduced, called Multi–FS–ALOHA, which divides the contention period into two parts: the first is used by the SSs issuing bandwidth request for the first time while the second part is used by the SSs having previously attempted to transmit without success. These two parts are dynamically fixed on a frame by frame basis. A cross–layer design has been developed in [16] to design the optimal size of the contention period with various classes of services. As conclusion, a contention period size, which is approximately equal to the number of the SSs, is used to optimize all classes of service performance. In [3] the authors have conducted a general study on the contention period in IEEE 802.16. They have analyzed the impact of the contention period resolution mechanisms over the data transmission period, in terms of the achievable data throughput and packet delay.

In all the previous studies reported, the IEEE 802.16 standard request mechanism has been used. However, they do not make an in–depth analysis of the bandwidth required to convey the request messages. Obviously, this bandwidth increases as the contention period increases, limiting the amount of bandwidth available for data transmission. In this work, we propose some simple enhancements to the request mechanism defined by the standard, aiming to reduce the length of the contention period.

4 Our Proposals

In order to reduce the introduced overhead during the contention period, we proposed a new request bandwidth mechanism in [2], called RGPSS (*Requests and Grants Per Subscriber Station*). In it, each SS only sends one request with the needed amount of bandwidth of all the active connections belonging to this SS.

Although the RGPSS reduces the contention period, the received information by the BS about the needed resources for each service flow is null. So, the method defined by the standard (GPSS) gives better information about the needs of each connection individually, allowing that the BS allocates the resources of the system using QoS criteria. However, the information sent by the GPSS method is too much, because it uses a request per connection while the grants are made per SS. In this way, a lot of requests are sent by each SS, depending on its active connections, increasing the collision probability. On the other hand, as the bandwidth is granted to each SS and not to individual connections, the BS only needs to know the requirements of each service flow in each SS (as aggregation of the requirements of all connections of each service flow, associated with a SS) to implement a scheduler, which could classify and prioritize service flows applying QoS criteria.

So, we have proposed a new requesting mechanism, called RPSF (*Requests Per Service Flow*). In it, each SS sends one request per service flow aggregating the required amount of bandwidth to transmit all enqueued data in all connections which belong to this service flow. In this way, the RPSF reduces the number of requests with regard to the GPSS, introducing more overhead than the RGPSS, but giving the necessary information to the BS to allocate the resources of the system using QoS criteria. At the same time, the RPSF gives the same information to the BS as the GPSS, but reducing the number of requests when more than one active connection belongs to the same service flow. That is, the GPSS uses more BW-request messages to give the same information to the BS as the RPSF does.

To use this mechanism according to the standard, each SS will select one fixed CID among every active connection which belongs to this service flow to send its request, and this fixed CID will always be used to request bandwidth of this kind of connections. When the BS receives a request with this fixed CID, it will be interpreted like a request according to the service flow and not the individual connec-

Table 1 Traffic characterization

	BE - BG	Voice	Video
Start (sec.)	0	uniform(0, 0.024)	uniform(0, 0.5)
ON period (sec.)	pareto(1, 1.9)	always	
OFF period (sec.)	pareto(1, 1.25)	never	
Interarrival time (sec.)	0.0215	0.024	
Packet size (bytes)	138	384	396
Average rate	21 Kbps	16 Kbps	75 Kbps
Trace			Jurassic Park
Frame rate			25 fps

tion. Another possibility is to assign a specific CID to each service flow, which will always be used to request bandwidth like the Basic CID. In both cases, an interpretation of CIDs inside the request messages is only required.

5 Performance Evaluation

In this section, we carry out a performance analysis of our proposals jointly with the standard method (GPSS). Throughout our study, every simulation is conducted using an IEEE 802.16 model implemented in the OPNET Modeler v11.5 tool [13].

In our simulations, we consider an IEEE 802.16 wireless network describing a point–to–multipoint (PMP) system consisting of a BS and a different number of SSs in each simulation. Each SS runs voice, video, best–effort (BE) and background (BG) applications, which are modelled as described in Table 1. These four applications are assigned to four different service flows whose priorities in descending order are: voice, video, best–effort and background. The rate corresponding to each kind of service flow is constant in each scenario and corresponds to a quarter of the overall demand.

All nodes operate at 28 MHz, with a symbol rate of 22.4 MBaud. All transmissions are done using QPSK modulation with a bit rate of 44.8 Mbps. According to the standard, a frame duration of 1 ms is used. The mode of operation is FDD. We assume ideal channel conditions and a system operating in a steady–state, where the number of connections does not change over time.

The BS and each SS use a priority scheduling discipline. The highest priority is assigned to the voice and video applications, followed by the best–effort applications and finally the background applications. Within a given service class, the connections are served in a FCFS order (*First Come First Server*).

The initial values for initial and maximum backoff window in the contention resolution algorithm are 4 and 10, respectively.

Throughout our study, we have simulated 15 seconds of operation of each particular scenario, collecting statistics after a warm–up period of 4 seconds. Each point in our plots is an average over 32 simulation runs, and error bars indicate 95% confidence interval.

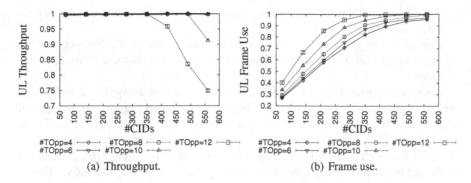

Fig. 1 Throughput and frame use in RPSF mode (*Campus Connectivity* scenario).

Due to the nature of the WiMAX standard, it is possible to consider a wide range of applications and usage scenarios, over a broad range of markets and geographies [9]. We consider two scenarios: the *Campus Connectivity* scenario and the *Individual Connectivity* scenario.

5.1 Campus Connectivity scenario

In this scenario, there are a limited number of SSs with a large number of connections per SS and all kind of applications are used. Each SS is usually used to provide buildings with connectivity on the Internet through the BS.

This scenario is composed of a fixed number of SSs. Five in our case. In each SS runs all kind of applications as described before. Initially, 5 voice, 1 video, 4 BE and 4 BG applications are running, and they are increased in the same proportion, obtaining 14, 28, 42, 56, 70, 84, 98 and 112 connections per SS.

Every connection requests bandwidth through the contention period independently from their service flow. This mainly responds to our interest in reducing the size of contention period. The size of the contention period (#TOpp) is set, according to [2], to 8 and 4 in the case of GPSS and RGPSS, respectively. For RPSF, the #TOpp value is elected after an evaluation, in which #TOpp is increased by 2 from 4 to 12 transmission opportunities.

5.1.1 RPSF parametrization

To select the optimum #TOpp value in the RPSF case, a study increasing its value from 4 to 12 is done.

Figure 1 shows the uplink throughput and frame use in the RPSF mechanism. Regarding the throughput, in all data except for the largest contention period, all the data is effectively transmitted. This is mainly due to reduced available capacity for data transmission.

Figure 1.b. We can see as the frame use increases with the #TOpp, because the uplink subframe for data is reduced, and so, the frame is totally used with less connections.

Another important aspect to analyze is the end–to–end delay (Ete delay) of the critical applications, voice and video. They are depicted on Figure 2. Both types of applications keep their respective deadlines higher than the obtained values in the simulations. These deadlines are 10 ms and 100 ms for voice and video, respectively, in line with specified values by standards and in literature [10]. A decrease of the delay is appreciated when the number of connections is increased. This is because when a grant is received by a SS, it allocates resources in descending order of priority. As the number of connections increases, it is possible that new incoming high priority connections takes advantages of the allocated resources to the SS regardless of their class.

With the study of these previous figures, we can conclude that, for the RPSF mechanism, if we select the smallest value from transmission opportunities (#TOpp=4) the traffic load of the network can totally be transmitted and the critical applications keep their deadlines.

5.1.2 GPSS, RGPSS and RPSF comparative

In this section, we will compare the performance of these different mechanisms under study using the best values. In Figure 3.a shows the uplink throughput. The GPSS mechanism is not capable of keeping the network in good conditions when the traffic load is high. Regarding the collision probability, see Figure 3.b, the RGPSS mechanism exhibits the best results. This is not surprising since this mechanism requires the least number of signalling packets to operate.

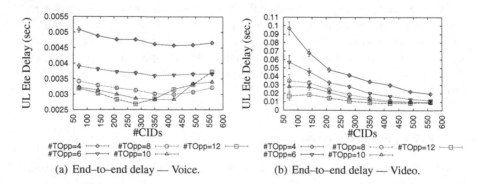

(a) End–to–end delay — Voice.   (b) End–to–end delay — Video.

Fig. 2 End–to–end delay in RPSF mode (*Campus Connectivity* scenario).

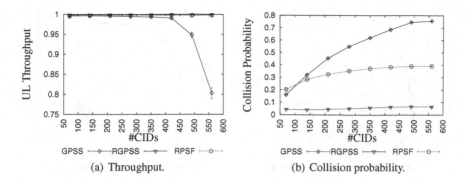

(a) Throughput.

(b) Collision probability.

Fig. 3 Throughput and collision probability of GPSS, RGPSS and RPSF (*Campus Connectivity* scenario).

Figure 4 shows the mean of the end–to–end delay of the two time critical applications under study, voice and video. Initially, the RPSF mechanism shows the best results for voice while the RGPSS mechanism proves to be better for video applications. However, a closer look to the Cumulative Distribution Function (CDF) of the end–to–end delay of these applications in the case of the largest number of connections (Figure 5), the RPSF mechanism is considered to be the best, that is, it reduces the size of the contention period and at the same time it keeps the deadlines of these applications.

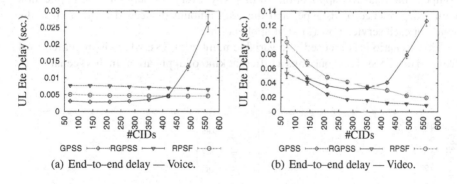

(a) End–to–end delay — Voice.

(b) End–to–end delay — Video.

Fig. 4 Uplink end–to–end delay of voice and video applications of GPSS, RGPSS and RPSF (*Campus Connectivity* scenario).

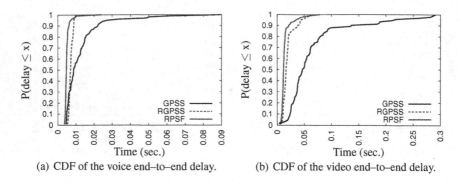

(a) CDF of the voice end–to–end delay.   (b) CDF of the video end–to–end delay.

Fig. 5 CDF of end–to–end delay of GPSS, RGPSS and RPSF — #CID=112 (*Campus Connectivity* scenario).

5.2 Individual Connectivity scenario

In this case, the BS is located in the control center or head office, allowing each SS (or user) to connect directly to the BS. We consider a variable number of SSs in this scenario. This number is increased by 4. One of these four SSs only runs a voice application, which is an aggregating application, that is, the resulting voice application is composed of 15 voice applications similar to the voice applications describe above. For a video application, the aggregation is 16 video applications. BE application is composed of 12 original BE applications, and finally 13 BG applications compose the final BG application. In this way, every SS only has one application with independence of its type, and the total amount of needed bandwidth is the same for each service flow (kind of application).

This scenario is composed of a variable number of SSs, which is increased by 4 from 20 to 48 SSs. Each one runs a different kind of application. In this scenario, we

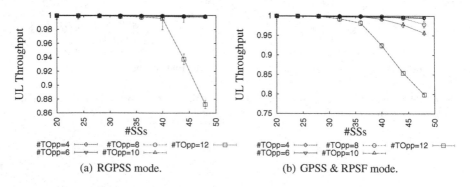

(a) RGPSS mode.   (b) GPSS & RPSF mode.

Fig. 6 Throughput (*Individual Connectivity* scenario).

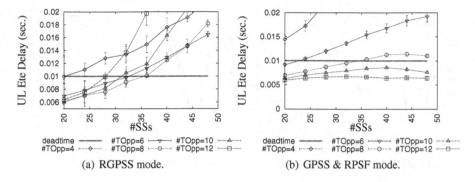

(a) RGPSS mode.

(b) GPSS & RPSF mode.

Fig. 7 End–to–end delay — Voice (*Individual Connectivity* scenario).

increase the #TOpp by 2 from 4 to 12, in order to evaluate the performance of each request method (GPSS, RGPSS and RPSF) as function of the contention period.

The behavior of the GPSS and RPSF mechanism is similar through the simulations. This result is expected, since each SS supports only one connection. In other words, the number of request to be sent by service flow and by connections are the same.

Regarding the uplink throughput, Figures 6.a and 6.b, the best behavior is exhibited by the RGPSS mechanism, because only with the highest value of the contention period this mechanism is not able to transmit all data. However, if we analyze the end–to–end delay of the two critical applications (Figures 7 and 8), we observe that the RGPSS mechanism is unable to meet their deadlines, which are depicted on the figures with a horizontal line in their maximum values. However, the GPSS and RPSF mechanisms can meet these voice and video deadlines of voice and video if #TOpp values are higher than 8. This is due to the fact that in the RGPSS method, the bandwidth request does not inform of the service flow associated to each connection. The requests are served in a FCFS order. On the other hand, the GPSS and

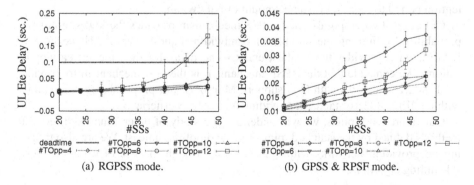

(a) RGPSS mode.

(b) GPSS & RPSF mode.

Fig. 8 End–to–end delay — Video (*Individual Connectivity* scenario).

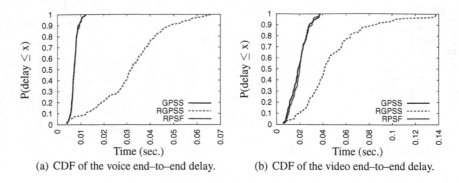

(a) CDF of the voice end–to–end delay.   (b) CDF of the video end–to–end delay.

Fig. 9 CDF of end–to–end delay of GPSS, RGPSS and RPSF — #SS=48 (*Individual Connectivity* scenario).

RPSF methods provide the BS with information on the service flow of the connections which request bandwidth. For that, the BS can prioritize the requests, and then, it firstly grants resources to the most important connections.

In Figure 9, the CDF of the end–to–end delay for voice and video are represented. When #TOpp=10 is used and the number of SSs is equal to 48, we can see that the GPSS and RPSF mechanisms maintain the video and the voice end–to–end delays below of their deadline values, and their variations are minimal. In the case of the RGPSS method, we can see that every data voice received exceeds the deadline of this type of service flow.

6 Conclusions

In this paper, we have presented a comparative study of various to bandwidth request mechanisms for the IEEE 802.16 networks. It has been shown that our proposals exhibit better behavior than the mechanism proposed by the standards: shorter contention period to request the same amount of bandwidth.

Out of our two proposals, the RGPSS mechanism provides the lowest collision probability by limiting the number of bandwidth requests per SS. However, the RPSF method provides the smallest end–to–end delay for the time critical applications. We conclude that the RPSF mechanism is the best mechanism to provide IEEE 802.16 networks with QoS support. Moreover, our proposals are compatible with the IEEE 802.16 standard, providing higher QoS criteria.

Our future work plans, we will undertake the study of other bandwidth request methods defined by the standard: piggyback and polling unicast. We are also thinking on providing networks with QoS support through the use of a more robust scheduling algorithm.

Acknowledgements This work has been jointly supported by the Spanish MEC and European Comission FEDER funds under the grants "Consolider Ingenio–2010 CSD2006–00046" and "TIN2006–15516–004–02"; by JCCM under the project PAI06–0106 and the grant 05/112.

References

1. Cho, D.H., Song, J.H., Kim, M.S., Han, K.J.: Performance Analysis of the IEEE 802.16 Wireless Metropolitan Area Network. In: 1st International Conference on Distributed Frameworks for Multimedia Applications (DFMA'05), pp. 130–137 (2005)
2. Delicado, J., Delicado, F.M., Orozco-Barbosa, L.: Study of the IEEE 802.16 Contention-based Request Mechanism. In: Personal Wireless Communications (PWC'07), vol. 245, pp. 87–98 (2007)
3. Doha, A., Hassanein, H., Takahara, G.: Performance Evaluation of Reservation Medium Access Control in IEEE 802.16 Networks. In: IEEE International Conference on Computer Systems and Applications, pp. 369–374 (2006)
4. Eklund, C., Marks, R.B., Stanwood, K.L., Wang, S.: IEEE Standard 802.16: A Technical Overview of the WirelessMAN^{TM} Air Interface for Broadband Wireless Access. IEEE Communications Magazine **40**(6), 98–107 (2002)
5. Hawa, M., Petr, D.W.: Quality of Service Scheduling in Cable and Broadband Wireless Access Systems. 10th IEEE International Workshop on Quality of Service pp. 247–255 (2002)
6. IEEE: IEEE 802.16 Standard—Local and Metropolitan Area Networks—Part 16: Air Interface for Fixed Broadband Wireless Access Systems (IEEE Std 802.16–2001) (2002)
7. IEEE: IEEE 802.16 Standard—Local and Metropolitan Area Networks—Part 16: Air Interface for Fixed Broadband Wireless Access Systems (IEEE Std 802.16–2004) (2004). Revision of IEEE Std 802.16–2001
8. IEEE: IEEE 802.16 Standard—Local and Metropolitan Area Networks—Part 16: Air Interface for Fixed Broadband Wireless Access Systems—Amendment 2: Physical and Medium Access Control Layers for Combined Fixed and Mobile Operation in Licensed Bands and Corrigendum 1 (IEEE Std 802.16e–2005) (2006). Amendment and Corrigendum to IEEE Std 802.16–2004
9. Inc., W.C.: Can WiMAX Address Your Applications? WiMAX Forum (2005)
10. Karam, A., Tobagi, F.: On the Traffic and Service Classes in the Internet. In: In Proc. of IEEE GLOBECOM'00 (2000)
11. Kobliakov, V.A., Turlikov, A.M., Vinel, A.V.: Distributed Queue Random Multiple Access Algorithm for Centralized Data Networks. In: 10th International Symposium on Consumer Electronics (ISCE'06), pp. 1–6 (2006)
12. Oh, S.M., Kim, J.H.: The Analysis of the Optimal Contention Period for Broadband Wireless Access Network. In: Proceedings of the 3rd International Conference on Pervasive Computing and Communications Workshops (PerCom'05 Workshops), pp. 215–219 (2005)
13. OPNET Technologies, I.: OPNET Modeler 11.5 (2005)
14. Vinel, A., Zhang, Y., Lott, M., Tiurlikov, A.: Performance Analysis of the Random Access in IEEE 802.16. In: Proceedings of the 16th International Symposium on Personal, Indoor and Mobile Radio Communications (PIMRC'05), vol. 3, pp. 1596–1600 (2005)
15. Vinel, A., Zhang, Y., Ni, Q., Lyakhov, A.: Efficient Request Mechanism Usage in IEEE 802.16. In: Proccedings of the IEEE GLOBECOM'06 (2006)
16. Yan, J., Kuo, G.S.: Cross–layer Design of Optimal Contention Period for IEEE 802.16 BWA Systems. In: IEEE International Conference on Communications (ICC'06), vol. 4, pp. 1807–1812 (2006)

Optimization of a QoS Aware Cross-Layer Scheduler by Packet Aggregation

Andreas Könsgen, Md. Shahidul Islam, Andreas Timm-Giel
and Carmelita Görg

Communication Networks
Center for Computing Technologies (TZI)
University of Bremen
Germany
e-mail: {ajk|msi|atg|cg}@comnets.uni-bremen.de

Abstract In this paper, the performance of a QoS-aware two-stage cross-layer scheduler utilising a MIMO channel for transmission is considered along with TDMA, OFDMA and SDMA channel access methods which serves a number of users with QoS-constrained data flows. OFDMA and SDMA allow a parallel transmission of packets which can have different transmission durations due to varying physical bit rates and packet lengths. The data flow with the longest packet slows down the other flows because they have to wait until the transmission is complete. This paper proposes packet aggregation where waiting times are reduced by transmitting more than one packet per user if airtime is left. It is shown that this method significantly enhances the QoS parameters throughput and delay. For constant-size packets, shorter delays can be achieved than for variable-size packets. Aggregating non-consecutive packets further enhances the performance, however the packets have to be buffered at the receiver to put them into the correct order.

1 Introduction

Wireless LANs have to meet increasing requirements nowadays and in the future: high data rates for each user, high spectral efficiency in the sense of a high total capacity and meeting several types of QoS requirements for different applications.

Up to now, most protocols stacks are designed according to the OSI model which defines seven layers from the physical layer up to the application layer, with an increasing degree of abstraction from the physical hardware. In legacy protocol stacks, these different protocol layers have been optimised independently of each other. This separation is in particular problematic for the design of the two lowest layers, which are the MAC and the PHY layer, because there are close mutual dependencies between these two layers. The QoS requirements have already to be considered by selecting the physical transmission method. Moreover, the actual channel conditions and the effects of these conditions for a QoS aware transmission have to be known when selecting a particular packet for the transmission.

Please use the following format when citing this chapter:

Könsgen, A., Islam, M.S., Timm-Giel, A. and Görg, C., 2008, in IFIP International Federation for Information Processing, Volume 284; *Wireless and Mobile Networking*; Zoubir Mammeri; (Boston: Springer), pp. 149–160.

To cope with these requirements, in the framework of the xLAYER project funded by the German Research Foundation (DFG), a cross-layer transmission system for wireless LANs was introduced in [9] and extended by QoS support in [10]; the OFDMA/SDMA platform which means the parallel transmission to multiple users was introduced in [5].

The cross-layer transmission system is located in the access point which has full control of the channel access, similar to the Hybrid Coordination Function Controlled Channel Access (HCCA) specified in IEEE 802.11e. In this paper, only the downlink from the access point to the mobile stations is considered.

In the previous investigations mentioned above, a number of boundary conditions were simplified. The number of users was assumed to be constant and the load of each user as well as the packet size was assumed to be time-independent. In practice, such idealised conditions do not apply. Typical applications such as voice-over-IP (VoIP) have variable packet size and also can have varying load dependent on the used codec. This paper investigates the properties of the previously introduced QoS scheduler considering that the above-mentioned parameters can be variable. In addition, the efficiency of the scheduler is increased: When packets for different data flows are transmitted simultaneously using OFDMA or SDMA, the packet for one flow might be transmitted faster than for another flow due to different packet lengths and channel conditions. In the previous investigations, the faster flow then had to wait for the slower flow because transmission for all flows starts at the same time. The scheduler is now enhanced in the way that the faster flow can transmit one or more additional packets in the remaining time until the slower flow has finished its transmission.

Methods of legacy scheduling schemes which do not consider application requirements are discussed in [14, 8]. Schedulers which are specialized on video applications are discussed in [7, 13, 6, 2]. The metric to optimize the transmission is the quality of the video image at the mobile station. The optimum transmission is achieved by selecting the most suitable type of video codec as well as adjusting parameters in the MAC and the PHY layer. The approach given in this paper is independent on the particular application, however QoS requirements specified by the application are considered.

In [16], it is pointed out that Video-On-Demand can cope with relatively large delays which should however be constant, i. e. a low jitter is required. From the view of the QoS scheduler discussed in this paper, the jitter is kept small by enforcing a short delay. Low jitter means that a packet always has to be sent inside a short time frame, regardless if this has to be done immediately or after a certain delay. Two scheduling concepts are analyzed in [1], where one has a better support for QoS and the other one has a better support for the total throughput. In this paper, the aim of the scheduler is to satisfy the QoS requirements for a maximum number of users, because meeting the QoS requirements is the criteria which results in the highest satisfaction for the user. A user does not get personal benefit if a system optimizes the total throughput, but the performance of the own application is poor. The scheduling concept presented in [4, 3] is specially designed for OFDM-TDMA transmissions and integrates the channel state into the MAC layer scheduling. In the

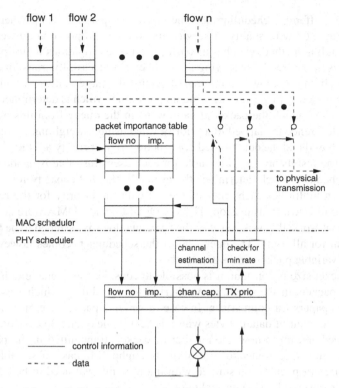

Fig. 1 Design of the parallelised cross-layer scheduler

approach presented in this paper, the PHY scheduling is separated from the MAC scheduling, however the schedulers communicate through an abstract interface, i. e. providing an importance metric instead of giving detailed information about packet lifetime etc.

The method of aggregating packets is for example used in IEEE 802.11n to avoid loss of airtime due to contention periods and acknowledgements [15]. The aggregated packets are treated as one large packet.

2 Scheduling for Varying Load Conditions

Fig. 1 shows the design of the cross-layer scheduler introduced in [9] which is used for the investigations described in this paper. The scheduler includes a hardware-independent stage in the MAC layer and a hardware-dependent stage in the PHY layer. In the hardware-independent stage, each data flow of a user is assigned its own queue. In each turn of the scheduling process, the MAC scheduler assigns a priority to the data packet at the top of each queue according to a certain scheduling scheme. Different scheduling schemes were compared in [10], where also a scheduling method with quality-of-service support was proposed and investigated. In this scheduling method, which is also used for the investigations in this paper, the throughput is monitored by observing the number of successfully transmitted packets inside a sliding window and compared against the target value. The maximum delay of the packet is mapped to its remaining lifetime, which is determined by subtracting the time which the packet already waits in the queue from this maximum delay. The difference is mapped to a priority value using a weighting function. The throughput-based and the delay-based contribution to the priority are then added for each user. The results are kept in a table for each user; this table is handed over to the PHY scheduler which determines the available channel capacity for each user which is then multiplies each entry of the list with the priority for the respective user. For the physical transmission, TDMA, OFDMA and SDMA were considered in [11]. In that work, the packet size of the user data flows is assumed to be the same and constant for all users. The operation of the scheduler becomes however more complex if variable packet size is assumed.

If the packet size is constant, it is possible to consider the queue length, i. e. the number of packets in the queue as a criterion for scheduling which was done in the previous papers for comparison. In case of variable packet size, it is needed to consider the amount of data in bytes which is kept in the queue. In case of the QoS enabled scheduler, up to now, the number of packets transmitted in the past were compared against a reference to control the throughput. In case of variable packet sizes, the sizes of packets transmitted within a time interval need to be added and compared against a reference throughput.

In case of a parallelised transmission, it was up to now assumed that exactly one packet is transmitted for each user in each turn of the scheduling process. This is not optimum even if the packet size is the same for all flows, because the users can face different channel capacities so that a user with a fast channel has to wait for a user with a slower channel until his packet was transmitted. The problem increases if the packet sizes of the users are different. For this reason, the scheduler needs to be extended: if the packet for data flow A is transmitted within a shorter time than the packet for data flow B, then the remaining time can be used to transmit other packets for A until the transmission for B is finished.

The above-mentioned task is performed by the algorithm given below, where $S_{i,1}$ is the size of the packet at the top of the queue of user i and and C_i is the channel capacity of that user.

Select the flows for which a packet should be transmitted
according to the legacy scheme:
for all flows i **do**
    calculate the transmission time $T_{i,1} = S_{i,1} C_i$
end for
find flow j which needs maximum time for transmission:
$j = \arg\max_i T_{i,1}$.
for all users $i \neq j$ **do**

calculate the remaining transmission time:
$T_{\text{rem},i} = T_j - T_{i,1}$
$n =$ packet no in queue i
for $k = 2$ to n **do**
   $T_{i,k} = S_{i,k} \cdot C_i$
   if $T_{i,k} < T_{\text{rem},i}$ **then**
      append packet i,k to packet $i,1$
      $T_{\text{rem},i} = T_{\text{rem},i} - T_{i,k}$
   end if
end for
end for

By this method, more than one packet can be sent for a user within one scheduling process. However, the packets might be taken from the queue non-consecutively. Assuming the packet at the top of the queue (no. 1) was taken and the next packet (no. 2) is too big, the search continues until the end of the queue is reached. If no. 3 is also too big, but 4 and 5 fit into the gap, then packets 1, 4 and 5 are transmitted. Since the order of the packets must not be changed when being handed over to the upper protocol layers, only packet 1 may be handed over; 4 and 5 have to be kept inside the buffer until the missing packets 2 and 3 were received.

The case that the data flow uses constant-size packets is easier. In this case, consecutive packets can be taken from the queue until the gap is filled.

3 Simulation Setup

The channel capacities are determined based on the IEEE 802.11 TGn radio channel model proposed in [5] which is deployed here to implement a MIMO transmission with $M = 2$ transmit antennas at the base station and $N = 2$ receive antennas at each of the mobile stations, $K = 8$ users and $L = 52$ subcarriers. The model considers a typical indoor environment where the signal transmitted by the sender is reflected at a number of objects so that a large amount of signal components arrive at the receiver. Based on this model, the channel matrices are calculated for each user. Due to the OFDM based transmission, this matrix calculation has to be done for each subcarrier.

For TDMA, OFDMA and SDMA, the throughput and delay is compared between data flows with variable and constant packet size. In case of variable packet size, the size is uniformly distributed between 500 and 1500 bytes.

For OFDMA and SDMA, the effect of packet aggregation is compared against the case of transmitting individual packets for each user.

The simulator used for the investigations discussed in this paper is called WARP2; it implements the IEEE 802.11 protocol stack and has been extended with the two-stage MAC/PHY scheduler as described above. The simulated scenario includes an access point which serves a number of stations. The stations move between 5 m and 15 m distance towards and away from the access point with a speed of 2 m/s. They start at a randomly selected point and change the direction when one of the boundaries was reached. Each station is assigned one user with a certain traffic category. The load generator generates CBR traffic for the users 1, 2 and 4 and Poisson traffic for the other users; the traffic load is configured individually for each user. The packets for each user are stored in the respective queue until they are served by the MAC scheduler. The MAC scheduler works with the QoS enabled scheduler mentioned before.

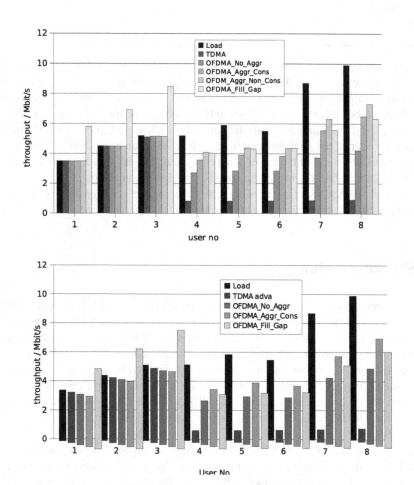

Fig. 2 Per-flow throughput for OFDMA. Up: variable, down: constant packet size

4 Results and Discussion

Fig. 2 shows the throughput for the eight routes for different OFDMA access methods and variable resp. constant packet size. For each user, the bar on the left depicts the offered traffic load. The throughput achieved by TDMA is shown right to the load bar for comparison. Four different OFDMA scenarios are considered: transmitting a single packet without aggregation (OFDMA_No_Aggr), aggregation of consecutive packets (OFDMA_Aggr_Cons) and, in case of variable packet size, aggregation of non-consecutive packets (OFDM_Aggr_Non_Cons). Finally, for comparison, the theoretical case is given that the gap is completely filled with a packet that exactly has the size of the gap. For the idealised case where the distribution function of the packet size and of the channel capacity is uniform or exponential, it was shown in [12] that the simulation results can be well described by analytical means. The results in Fig. 2 show that all OFDMA techniques yield better performance than TDMA by a factor of about 2.5 due to the parallel transmission for different users. The TDMA throughput is almost the same for all non-time-critical flows. Packet aggregation increases the throughput by another 20% due to the reduced gap size. If the packets are aggregated non-consecutively, another enhancement can be observed because the chance is higher that a packet can be found in the queue which still fits into the gap. In the theoretical case of filling the gap completely, the throughput is lower than for variable packet size for users 7 and 8. On the other hand, for the time-critical users 1 to 3, the throughput is higher than the offered load, which is due to the assumption taken in this case that the entire gap is filled with additional data not contained in the queue.

Fig. 3 shows the delay for the same scenario. Users 1 to 3 are served according to their QoS requirements. The delay for the other users inversely corresponds to the throughput, i.e. the higher the throughput for a user is, the lower is the delay. This fact is explained by the lower queueing delay which a packet experiences if the queue service rate is higher. The delay is lower for constant packet size, because for eight user data flows, it is likely that there is at least one of them which has to transmit a long packet so that the scheduling interval will be long.

In Fig. 4, the per-user throughput is shown for SDMA in case of variable and constant packet size, respectively. The different cases are the same as for OFDMA, i.e. transmission without aggregation, with consecutive and non-consecutive aggregation and filling the entire gap. The results are similar than for OFDMA, which is that packet aggregation enhances the throughput and variable-size packets result in a better throughput than constant-size packets. Also, for idealised filling the gap, the throughput is in case of users 7 and 8 lower than for packet aggregation. For the time-critical users 1 to 3, the QoS criteria are always met. For the other users, the achieved throughput is higher than in case of OFDMA. The throughput for variable packet size is about the same than the throughput for constant packet size if the variable-size packets are aggregated non-consecutively. In case of consecutive packet aggregation, the throughput for variable-size packets is lower than for constant-size packets. This is explained by the fact that in case of consecutive variable-size packets, it is less likely to fill the gap effectively than for constant-size

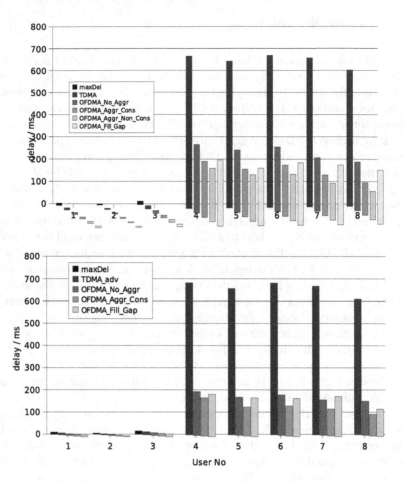

Fig. 3 Delay for OFDMA, up: variable, down: constant packet size

or non-consecutive variable-size packets. The delay is reduced for a particular user when the throughput is increased as demonstrated in Fig. 6 in a similar way as observed for OFDMA. The delay for constant packet size is always smaller than for variable packet size.

Fig. 5 depicts the behaviour of the total throughput in the different transsission configurations which is similar to the per-user throughput for the non-time-critical flows.

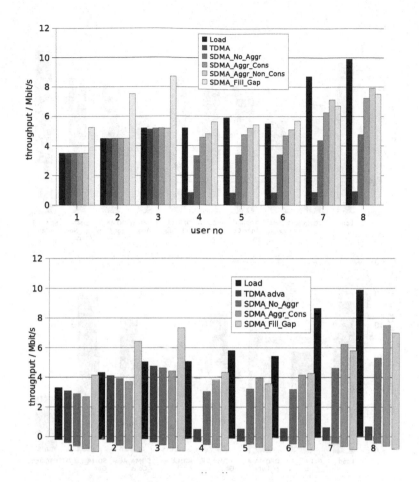

Fig. 4 Per-flow throughput for SDMA. Up: variable, down: constant packet size

5 Conclusion and Outlook

In this paper, the effect of packet aggregation on the throughput and delay performance in a wireless LAN with parallel transmission between the access point and the mobile stations was investigated by simulations. Due to variable packet length and channel capacity, airtime remains unused for a legacy transmission because a user with a good channel has to wait until the transmission of slower users is complete. This remaining airtime can be used by aggregating more than one packet from the users' queues in order to improve the Quality-of-Service parameters. In case of consecutive packet aggregation, the amount of enhancement is higher for traffic with constant packet size than for traffic with variable packet size. If non-consecutive aggregation is used, the throughput for variable and constant packet size

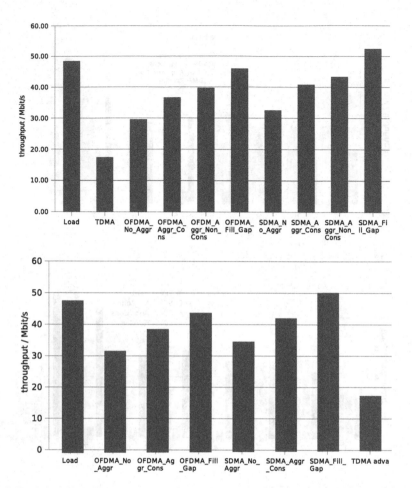

Fig. 5 Total throughput for different access methods, up: variable, down: constant packet size

is approximately the same. Along with the throughput enhancement, the queueing delay is also reduced due to the higher service rate of the queues. The packet aggregation enhances non-time-critical data flows for which the scheduler does not enforce guaranteed QoS parameters. Users with QoS-constrained transmission are in any case correctly served due to the properties of the scheduler.

Further investigations will consider the behaviour of the system in case of imperfect channel knowledge. In this case, packets can be dropped because the channel was overestimated which requires ARQ to recover the lost data. If the channel is underestimated, the physical bit rate selected for the packet transmission is unnecessarily low which reduces the achievable throughput. Thus the robustness of the scheduler against these imperfections needs to be investigated.

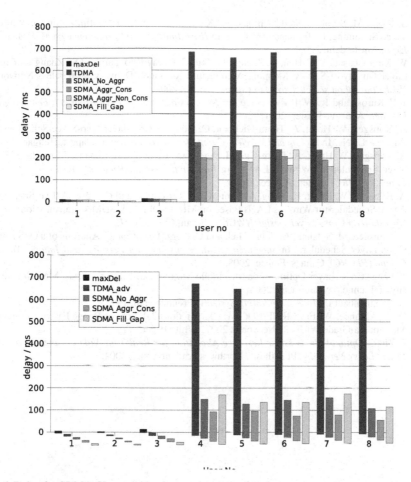

Fig. 6 Delay for SDMA. Up: variable, down: constant packet size

References

1. B. Chen, F. Fitzek, J. Gross, R. Grünheid, H. Rohling, and A. Wolisz. Framework for Combined Optimization of DLC and Physical Layer in Mobile OFDM Systems. In *6th Int. OFDM Workshop*, Hamburg, 2001.
2. L.-U. Choi, W. Kellerer, and E. Steinbach. Cross-Layer Optimization for Wireless Multi-User Video Streaming. In *IEEE International Conference on Image Processing (ICIP)*, Singapore, 2004.
3. M.A. Haleem and R. Chandramouli. Adaptive Stochastic Iterative Rate Selection for Wireless Channels. *IEEE Comm. Letters*, 8(5), 2004.
4. M.A. Haleem and R. Chandramouli. Adaptive Downlink Scheduling and Rate Selection: A Cross-Layer Design. *IEEE Journal on selected areas in communications*, 23(6), 2005.
5. J. P. Kermoal, L. Schumacher, K. I. Pedersen, P. E. Mogensen, and F. Frederiksen. A Stochastic MIMO Radio Channel Model with Experimental Validation. *IEEE Journal on Selected Areas in Communications. Work supported by IST project I-METRA IST-2000-30148*, 20(6), 2002.

6. S. Khan, M. Sgroi, E. Steinbach, and W. Kellerer. Cross-Layer Optimization for Wireless Video Streaming: Performance and Cost. In *IEEE International Conference on Multimedia & Expo*, Amsterdam, 2005.
7. W. Kumwilaisak, Y. T. Hou, Q. Zhang, W. Zhu, C.-C. Jay Kuo, and Ya-Qin Zhang. A Cross-Layer Quality-of-Service Mapping Architecture for Video Delivery in Wireless Networks. *IEEE Journal on selected areas in Comm.*, 21(10), 2003.
8. J. F. Kurose and K. W. Ross. *Computer Networking: A Top-Down Approach Featuring the Internet*. Addison-Wesley, 2001.
9. A. Könsgen, W. Herdt, A. Timm-Giel, and C. Görg. A Crosslayer Two-Stage Scheduler for Wireless LANs. In *Mobile and Wireless Communications Summit*, Budapest, Hungary, 2007.
10. A. Könsgen, W. Herdt, A. Timm-Giel, H. Wang, and C. Görg. An Enhanced Crosslayer Two-Stage Scheduler for Wireless LANs. In *Int. Symposium on Personal and Indoor Wireless Comm. (PIMRC)*, Athens, Greece, 2007.
11. A. Könsgen, W. Herdt, H. Wang, A. Timm-Giel, R. Böhnke, and C. Görg. A Two-Stage QoS Aware Scheduler for Wireless LANs Based on MIMO-OFDMA-SDMA Transmission. In *Int. Workshop on Cross-Layer Design (IWCLD)*, Jinan, China, 2007.
12. A. Könsgen, M. S. Islam, A. Timm-Giel, and C. Görg. Performance Analysis of a QoS Aware Cross-Layer Scheduler. In *Submitted to Int. Symposium on Personal and Indoor Wireless Comm. (PIMRC)*, Cannes, France, 2008.
13. Y. Peng. Cross-Layer Optimization for Mobile Multimedia. Master's thesis, Munich University of Technology, Germany, 2004.
14. A. S. Tanenbaum. *Modern Operating Systems*. Prentice Hall, 1992.
15. Wi-Fi Alliance. Wi-Fi CERTIFIED(TM) 802.11n draft 2.0: Longer-Range Faster Throughput Multimedia-Grade Wi-Fi(R) Networks, 2007. White Paper.
16. F. Zhai. *Optimal Cross-Layer Resource Allocation for Real-Time Video Transmission over Packet Lossy Networks*. PhD thesis, Northwestern University, 2004.

MANET Protocols Performance in Group-based Networks

Jaime Lloret[1], Miguel García[2], Fernando Boronat[3] and Jesus Tomás[4]

Department of Communications, Polytechnic University of Valencia

Camino Vera, s/n, Valencia 46022, Spain

[1]jlloret@dcom.upv.es, [2]migarpi@posgrado.upv.es, [3]fboronat@dcom.upv.es, [4]jtomas@upv.es

Abstract   Many routing protocols for ad-hoc and sensor networks have been designed, but none of them are based on groups. It is known that grouping nodes gives better performance to the group and to the whole system, thereby avoiding unnecessary message forwarding and additional overhead. In this paper we show the efficiency of the MANET routing protocols when the nodes are arranged in groups. In order to do it, first, we study the advantages of grouping nodes in each individual protocol for both fixed and mobile networks (nodes with random mobile behaviour). Then, the routing protocols will be compared to analyse which one has the best performance when it is used in a group-based network. This paper shows that group-based systems applied to ad-hoc networks provides better performance than when they are not arranged in groups.

1 Introduction

MANET networks [1] are a type of ad-hoc networks much more studied and mature than Wireless Sensor Networks (WSN) [2]. Independently of the medium access method used [3], in the recent years many routing protocols have been developed for MANET networks [4] [5]. The nodes' mobility, the lack of stability of the topology, the lack of a pre-established organization and performing of the wireless communications are reasons for not using the routing protocols developed for fixed networks. There are standardized routing protocols for MANET networks used by different fixed or mobile devices.

Depending on the information type exchanged by the nodes and on the frequency they do it, the routing protocols in ad-hoc networks are divided into three types: proactives, reactives and hybrids. The proactive protocols update the routing tables of all the nodes periodically, even though no information is being exchanged. When a topology change occurs, the routing table is updated and the

Please use the following format when citing this chapter:

Lloret, J., García, M., Boronat, F. and Tomás, J., 2008, in IFIP International Federation for Information Processing, Volume 284; *Wireless and Mobile Networking*; Zoubir Mammeri; (Boston: Springer), pp. 161–172.

routing protocol finds the optimum route to forward the information. A periodical control protocol message exchange allows this, but consumes bandwidth and energy (batteries). The reactive protocols only maintain routing routes in their tables when a node has to communicate with another node in the network. With these protocols, when a communication starts, as the right route is unknown, a route discovering message is sent. When the response is received, the route is included in the routing tables and the communication is now possible. The main disadvantage of these protocols is the latency at the beginning of the communications (route discovery time) but they improve the network and energy resources use. Inside this kind of protocols, we can find the source-based protocols and hop-by-hop protocols. Finally, the hybrid protocols are a combination of the other two types, taking the advantages of both types. These protocols divide ad-hoc networks into different zones, and then near nodes use proactive routing meanwhile far nodes use reactive routing.

Current IETF standardized protocols are AODV (Ad-Hoc On-demand Distance Vector) [6], DSR (Dynamic Source Routing Protocol) [7] and OLSR (Optimized Link State Routing Protocol) [8]. So, we are going to analyze and study their performance in this paper.

AODV is a routing protocol for Mobile ad-hoc networks and is a reactive protocol. It has a minimalist behaviour because it hardly overloads the ad-hoc network and needs very few memory comparing with other protocols. It works over IP protocol.

DSR is a reactive protocol developed specifically for ad-hoc networks. It only sends information when it is required, saving bandwidth, energy and battery. The protocol has two mechanisms: route discovering and route maintenance. It also includes a mechanism to avoid loops. It is compatible with IPv6 (IP, version 6). It has the following disadvantages: the excessive initial latency while discovering the route; and, as a source-based protocol, the size of the packet header increases each time it goes through a node, affecting to the bandwidth consumption.

OLSR is a proactive protocol in which each node knows permanently the network state and the number, availability and addresses of the nodes. This performs a faster routing protocol. OLSR optimizes the time of response when a change is detected in the network, by reducing the period time of the control messages transmission. As routes for all the destinations are maintained, it has a quite good performance in networks with random and sporadic traffic in large groups of nodes. As disadvantages we can point the followings: the nodes require more memory resources and it overloads the network with routing control packets. OLSR was developed to work, in an independently way, with other protocols, bringing versatility to use it in any scenario. The most important key in this protocol is MPR (Multipoint Relay) node, it optimizes the number of control messages in the network.

There are several works published that compare MANET routing protocols [9] [10] [11] [12], but none of them have compared MANET routing protocols from the group-based network point of view. In order to do our comparison, we have used the version Modeler of OPNET simulator [13]. Our goal is to evaluate the performance of three MANET routing protocols from the point of view of some parameters such as: network load when the network is stable, network load when there are topology changes, convergence time, number of updates, correct sent/received packets, wrong sent/received packets, etc.

This paper is structured as follows. Section 2 explains group-based networks benefits, describes some group-based protocols and explains where group-based protocols could be implemented. Our simulations, analysis and comparison are shown in section 3. Finally, section 4 gives the conclusions and future works.

2 Group-based networks benefits and related works

A group is referred as a small number of interdependent nodes that interact in order to share resources or computation time and produce joint results. In a physical group-based architecture neighboring groups could be connected if border nodes from different groups are close. A group-based network is capable of having different types of topologies and protocols inside every group. There are some works in the literature where nodes are divided into groups and links between nodes from different groups are taken into account, but all of them have been developed to solve specific issues and none of them for MANET networks. Rhubarb system [14] organizes nodes in a virtual network, allowing connections across firewalls/NAT, and efficient broadcasting. Rhubarb system has only one coordinator per group and coordinators could be grouped in groups in a hierarchy. A Peer-to-Peer Based Multimedia Distribution Service was presented in [15]. Authors propose a topology-aware overlay in which nearby hosts or peers self-organize into application groups. End hosts within the same group have similar network conditions and can easily collaborate with each other to achieve QoS awareness. There are some architectures, such as [16] and [17], were nodes are structured hierarchically and parts of the tree are grouped into groups. In some cases, some nodes have connections with nodes from other groups although they are in different layers of the tree, but the information has to be routed through the hierarchy.

Finally, we want to emphasize that the cluster-based networks are a subset of the group-based networks, because every cluster could be considered as a group. A cluster can be made up of a Cluster Head node, Cluster Gateways and Cluster Members ([18] [19]). The Cluster Head node is the parent node of the cluster, which manages and checks the status of the links in the cluster, and routes the information to the right clusters. The rest of the nodes in a cluster are all cluster members and don't use to have inter-cluster links. The size of the cluster is usually about 1 or 2 hops from the Cluster Head node while a group could be as large as we want. All the clusters have the same rules, however, a group-based network is capable of having any type of topology inside the group, not only clusters.

Group-based networks provide some benefits for the whole network such as:

- Spreads the work to the network in groups giving more flexibly, efficiently and lower delays.
- Content availability will increase because it could be replicated to other groups.
- Anyone could search and download from every group using only one service.
- It provides fault tolerance. Other groups could carry out tasks from a failed one.
- It is scalable because a new group could be added to the system easily.
- Network measurements could be taken from any group.

Group-based networks have many application areas. They could be used when it is wanted to setup a network where groups could appear and join the network anytime or by networks have to be split into smaller zones to support a large number of nodes, that is, any system where the devices are grouped and there must be connections between groups. The main goal in a group-based topology is the network protocol and the group management, that is, the design of an efficient algorithm for a new node to find its nearest (or the best) group to join in. The performance of the network highly depends on the efficiency of the nearby group locating process and on the interaction between neighboring groups.

The following list gives several group-based ad-hoc networks application areas:
1. Let us suppose a job where all human resources need to be split into groups to achieve a purpose (such as fire fighter squads for putting out the fire). Now, let's suppose that all people involved in that activity need a device that has to be connected with other devices in the same group to receive information from the members within the group, and closer groups have to be connected to coordinate their efforts. Currently coordination between groups is done through a wireless connection to the command center or using satellite communications. But, some times neither of those solutions can be used because a free of obstacles line of sight is needed, because there are too many wall looses or because more gain or power is needed to reach the destination.
2. Groups could also be established because of geographical locations or unevenness. It happens in rural and agricultural environments. A group-based topology in this kind of environment could be useful to detect plagues or fire and to propagate an alarm to neighbor lands. It will provide easier management and control for detecting fires and plagues as well as allowing scalability.
3. It could be used in any kind of system in which an event or alarm is based on what is happening in a specific zone, but conditioned to the events that are happening in neighbor zones. One example is a group-based system to measure the environmental impact of a place. It could be better measured if the measurements are taken from different groups of nodes, but those groups of nodes have to be connected in order to estimate the whole environmental impact.
4. Group-based virtual games. There are many games where the players are grouped virtually in order to perform a specific task. Interactions between groups in virtual reality should be given by interactions between players from different groups to exchange their knowledge.

3 Group-based ad-hoc networks analysis

This section describes how are the test bench and the traffic used for simulations, in the regular and the group-based topologies, to take measurements.

3.1 Test bench

We used the same test-bench for all the evaluated protocols using OPNET Modeler [13]. We varied the number of nodes and the coverage area in an open environment. The nodes in the topology have the characteristics of an ad-hoc node (40 MHz processor, 512 KB memory card, radio channel of 11 Mbps and 2.4 GHz as the work frequency). The MAC protocol was CSMA/CA. We chose nodes with a 50 meters maximum coverage radius. This is a conservative value, so the simulations presented in this work give us an adequate view for the worst case.

We simulated 4 scenarios for each protocol: the first one with fixed nodes; the second one with mobile nodes and failures; the third one with grouped nodes; and, the fourth one with grouped mobile nodes and failures. For each topology, we simulated for 100 and 250 nodes, to observe the system scalability.

Instead of a standard structure we chose a random topology where the nodes are mobile and change their position constantly. The groups are created by physical coverage area. When a node moves into a new coverage area, it belongs to the new group. 100 nodes topology has a 750x750 m^2 area (density $\approx 0.18 \cdot 10^{-3}$ nodes/m^2) and 250 nodes topology has a 1 Km^2 area (density $\approx 0.25 \cdot 10^{-3}$ nodes/m^2). We forced failures at t=200 sec., t=400 sec. and t=1200 sec. in each network, with a recovering process of 300 sec., to take measurements when the physical topology changes. We are going to study how several network-level protocols perform when failures and recoveries happen in this kind of networks.

We created 6 groups for the 100 nodes topology, each group covers a circular area of 150 meter radius. They were arranged to cover the whole area. There were approximately 16 or 17 nodes, in each group in the initial process. The number of nodes in each group varied because of the node's random mobility, so in one instant a node could belong to a group and in another instant to another one. We created 12 groups with 15 or 16 nodes per group for the 250 nodes topology. The group's coverage areas were similar for both areas. The routing protocol used inside the group will be the same as the one used between groups.

The traffic load used for the simulations is MANET traffic generated by OPNET. We inject this traffic 100 seconds after the beginning. The traffic follows a Poisson distribution (for the arrivals) with a mean time between arrivals of 30 seconds. The packet size follows an exponential distribution with a mean value of 1024 bits. The injected traffic has a random destination address, to obtain a simulation independent of the traffic direction. We have simulated the four scenarios for DSR, AODV and OLSR protocols.

3.2 Simulation results and analysis for DSR protocol

In figures 1 and 2 we can see the MAC level mean delay experimented by traffic using CSMA/CA. In figure 1, the group-based topology has a mean delay of 250 μs independently of the number of nodes in the network. The regular topology converges around 1.1 ms. The difference between both cases is about 850 μs; therefore the MAC level mean delay decreases a percentage of 23% in both cases. In figure 2, we can see that the delays are lower. It is mainly because of the network mobility. In this case, we appreciate that there are differences between 100-node and 250-node topologies. In group-based topologies the MAC level mean delay is around 100 μs for both topologies, so they converge faster.

When we study the network throughput consumed (figures 3 and 4), we observe that group-based topologies give a much lower value than the one obtained in regular topologies. For the 100-node topology (figure 3), the mean throughput varies from 225 Kbits/s to 100 Kbits/s in the group-based topology (a 56% improvement). In the 250-node topology we obtain 460 Kbits/s of throughput for the regular topology and 190 Kbits/s of throughput for the group-based one (a 59% improvement). Moreover, when we compare figures 3 and 4, we can conclude that the throughput in group-based topologies has a very low variation regarding a fixed or mobile scenario. The obtained improvement is quite important. We can see in figure 4 that, after 1200 seconds, the obtained throughput in 250-node topology is similar to the obtained throughput in the 100-node regular topology.

Observing figures 5 and 6, we conclude that the MANET traffic load through the network is lower for group-based topologies. In both figures we can see that when the number of nodes increases the traffic decreases. This is due to the existence of more nodes working as routers and therefore the probability of a packet to reach the destination is higher. The 100-node group-based topology (figure 5) gives a 77% improvement regarding the regular 100-node topology, but the improvement decreases when the number of nodes increases (in 250-node cases the improvement is about 60%). This behavior varies when the topology has mobility, errors and failures (figure 6). In this case, the 100 node group-based topology also has improvement (around 77%) regarding to the 100-node regular one. This improvement is higher (80%) in 250-node topologies.

We have also compared the routing traffic sent (figures 7 and 8). In figure 7 we observe that the traffic is quite stable due to the characteristics of the network, because it is a fixed network without errors and failures. The traffic sent in 250-node topology is around 225 Kbits/s, but when we group the nodes this traffic decreases to 100 Kbits/s (a 60% improvement). The value obtained in a 100-node topology is also improved when we group the nodes (50 Kbits/s, therefore a 50% improvement). In figure 8 we observe a similar behavior. In this case we conclude that when there are errors and failures in the network (interval from 600 to 800 seconds and around 1200 seconds) the traffic fluctuates and is less stable. We appreciate the instability is much lower in group-based topologies.

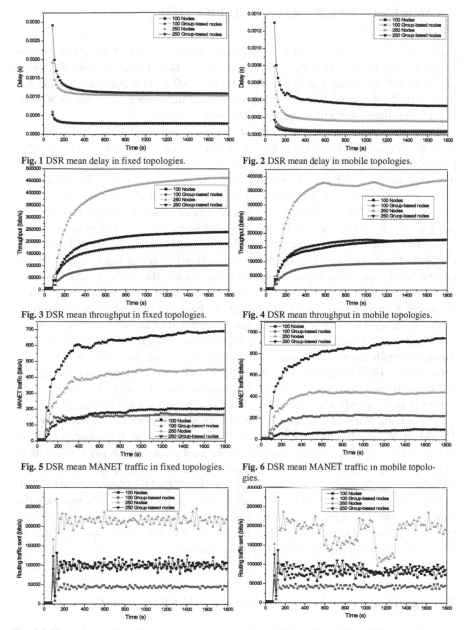

Fig. 1 DSR mean delay in fixed topologies.

Fig. 2 DSR mean delay in mobile topologies.

Fig. 3 DSR mean throughput in fixed topologies.

Fig. 4 DSR mean throughput in mobile topologies.

Fig. 5 DSR mean MANET traffic in fixed topologies.

Fig. 6 DSR mean MANET traffic in mobile topologies.

Fig. 7 DSR routing traffic in fixed topologies.

Fig. 8 DSR routing traffic mobile topologies.

3.3 Simulation results and analysis for AODV protocol

Figures 9 and 10 show the MAC level mean delay for AODV protocol simulations. We can observe that the delay has no strong dependence of both the topology type and the number of nodes. For 100 and 200-node topologies we obtain a delay stabilized around 1 ms, but for group-based topologies this value is 300 µs. Therefore it decreases a percentage of 70% in both cases.

Figure 11 shows the mean throughput for fixed topologies. The 100-node scenario gives a 200 Kbits/s mean value, but a value of 120 Kbits/s is obtained for the group-based scenario (a 40% improvement). In the 250-node case, we obtain mean values of 425 Kbits/s for the fixed scenario and of 225 Kbits/s for the group-based scenario (a 47% improvement). Figure 12 shows the results for mobile topologies with errors and failures. The improvement, obtained by grouping nodes, decreases in the 100-node case (37%), but it doesn't vary in the 250-node cases.

Figures 13 and 14 show the evolution of the MANET traffic for different scenarios. In figure 13, the traffic of the 100-node fixed topology has a mean value of around 600 bits/s, but it decreases to 180 bits/s for the 100-node group-based scenario, giving a 70% of improvement. In the 250-node topologies, it has varied from 480 Kbits/s (fixed) to 50 Kbits/s (group-based), obtaining a 90% improvement. In figure 14 we appreciate the improvement (not too relevant as in above case) and we can see the fast convergence of group-based topologies for mobile topologies with errors and failures. In the 100-node case the traffic doesn't converge before 1400 seconds, but it converges in 200 seconds when there are group of nodes. It also happens in the 250-node topologies: the regular topology converges in 600 seconds while the group-based one converges in 180 seconds.

The routing traffic measured in each simulated scenario can be seen in figures 15 and 16. We observe that the routing traffic is independent of the node mobility. In figure 15 we can see that the routing traffic goes from 200 Kbits/s for 250-node case to 125 Kbits/s when there are group of nodes (a 37% improvement). In the 100-node cases, it goes from 90 Kbits/s to 50 Kbits/s (a 45% improvement). When there are mobility, errors and failures (see figure 16), in the 250-node topology the values go from 190 Kbits/s to 110 Kbits/s in the group-based scenario (a 42% improvement). We obtained 85 Kbits/s for the regular 100-node topology and 50 Kbits/s for the group-based one (a 41% improvement).

3.4 Simulation results and analysis for OLSR protocol

Figure 17 shows the MAC level mean delay in fixed topologies. In the 250-node regular topology we obtained a value around 920 µs and a value around 250 µs in the group-based one (a 73% improvement). With 100 nodes there is no a significant improvement in the group-based topology (both values are around 260 µs).

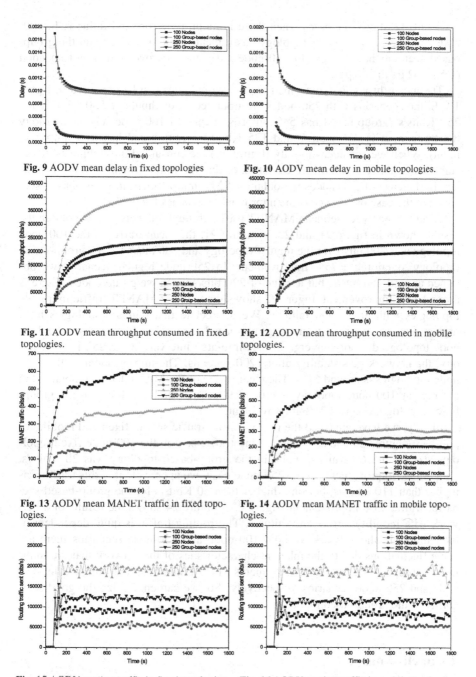

Fig. 9 AODV mean delay in fixed topologies

Fig. 10 AODV mean delay in mobile topologies.

Fig. 11 AODV mean throughput consumed in fixed topologies.

Fig. 12 AODV mean throughput consumed in mobile topologies.

Fig. 13 AODV mean MANET traffic in fixed topologies.

Fig. 14 AODV mean MANET traffic in mobile topologies.

Fig. 15 AODV routing traffic in fixed topologies.

Fig. 16 AODV routing traffic in mobile topologies.

Figure 18 shows the cases when there is mobility, errors and failures. In 100-node topologies, the regular topology has a mean value of 268 µs and the group-based scenario has 262 µs. In 250-node case, the improvement is not so good (from 262 µs to 260 µs).

The mean throughput consumed in fixed topologies can be observed in figure 19. In the scenarios with 250 nodes we obtained throughputs of 550 Kbits/s and 250 Kbits/s (group-based has 54% improvement). In 100-node regular topology the throughput is 325 Kbits/s and 125 Kbits/s (group-based has 61% improvement). When we consider mobility (figure 20) the consumed throughput is not so stable as in above case but, we can observe that the improvements are quite similar. In the case of 250 nodes we obtain a 52% improvement in group-based scenario; in the case of 100 nodes the improvement reaches the 60%.

When we analyze the mean MANET traffic through the network, we obtain the results shown in figure 21 and 22. In figure 21, the mean traffic in the 100-node topology was 700 bits/s for the regular topology and 180 bits/s for the group-based topology, obtaining a 75% improvement. In 250-node regular scenario, we obtained around 450 bits/s, but a value of 220 bits/s when we group nodes. There is around 51% improvement. Figure 22 shows the value of MANET traffic in mobile topologies with errors and failures. We appreciate that regular topologies have higher convergence time than the group-based topologies. In this case, the 100-node topology did not converge in the simulated interval. In the 250-node topology, the network gets stability after 1200 seconds. The improvement of the 250-node topologies is around 51%. The mean value of the MANET traffic obtained in the regular 100-node topology is around 900 bits/s and 215 bits/s in the group-based topology, giving a 76% improvement.

Finally, we have analyzed the mean routing traffic sent in fixed and mobile topologies (figures 23 and 24). The routing traffic sent in the 100-node fixed topology was around 60 Kbits/s, while in the group-based topology was 28 Kbits/s, with a 53% improvement. In the 250-node case, we appreciate that this traffic was higher than 110 Kbits/s, but only higher than 60 Kbits/s for the group-based scenario, with a 45% improvement (figure 23). Figure 24 shows the results of a network with mobility, errors and failures. The routing traffic is quite dependent of the failures in the network. In both 100-node and 250-node scenarios there are some fluctuations due to the inherent characteristics of the network that are minimized grouping the nodes. Improvements of 45% and 53% are obtained in 100-node and 250-node scenarios, respectively. So, we can emphasize the good scalability of the group-based topologies.

4 Conclusions

In this work we have shown the benefits of using a group-based topology in ad-hoc networks and we have shown several examples where they can be used.

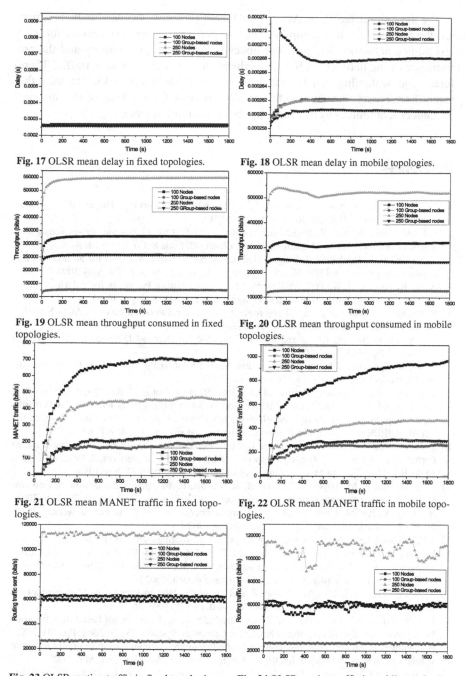

Fig. 17 OLSR mean delay in fixed topologies.

Fig. 18 OLSR mean delay in mobile topologies.

Fig. 19 OLSR mean throughput consumed in fixed topologies.

Fig. 20 OLSR mean throughput consumed in mobile topologies.

Fig. 21 OLSR mean MANET traffic in fixed topologies.

Fig. 22 OLSR mean MANET traffic in mobile topologies.

Fig. 23 OLSR routing traffic in fixed topologies.

Fig. 24 OLSR routing traffic in mobile topologies.

We have simulated DSR, AODV and OLSR protocols with and without groups and the results show that group-based topologies give better performance for wireless ad-hoc networks. So, grouping nodes increases the productivity and the performance of the network with low overhead and low extra network traffic. Therefore, good scalability can be achieved in group-based networks. On the other hand, the protocol that gives better results has been OLSR because this protocol introduces less routing traffic and it has behavior more regular.

References

1. M. Frodigh, P. Johansson, P. Larsson. "Wireless ad hoc networking. The art of networking without a network". Ericsson Review, No. 4, 2000.
2. I. F. Akyildiz, W. Su, Y. Sankarasubramaniam and E. Cayirci. "A survey on sensor networks". Communications Magazine, IEEE. Volume 40, Issue 8. Pp. 102- 114. Aug 2002.
3. S. Kumar, V. S. Raghavan, J. Deng. "Medium Access Control protocols for ad hoc wireless networks: A survey". Ad Hoc Networks. Volume 4, Issue 3, Pp. 326-358. May 2006.
4. E. M. Royer and C.-K. Toh, "A Review of Current Routing Protocols for Ad Hoc Mobile Wireless Networks," IEEE Personal Communications, April 1999, pp. 46-55.
5. R. Rajaraman, "Topology control and routing in ad hoc networks: a survey". ACM SIGACT News. Volume 33, Issue 2, Pp. 60-73. June 2002.
6. C. Perkins, E. Belding-Royer and S. Das, "Ad Hoc On-Demand Distance Vector (AODV) Routing". RFC 3561. July, 2003.
7. D. Johnson, Y. Hu, D. Maltz. "The Dynamic Source Routing Protocol (DSR) for Mobile Ad-hoc Networks for IPv4". RFC 4728. February, 2007.
8. T. Clausen and P. Jacquet. "Optimized Link State Routing Protocol". RFC 3626. Oct. 2003.
9. Josh Broch, David A. Maltz, David B. Johnson, Yih-Chun Hu, Jorjeta Jetcheva, "A Performance Comparison of Multi-Hop Wireless Ad Hoc Network Routing Protocols". Proc. of the 4th ACM/IEEE int. conf. on Mobile computing and networking. Pp. 85-97. 1998.
10. P. Johansson, T. Larsson, N. Hedman, B. Mielczarek, and M. Degermark, "Scenario-Based Performance Analysis of Routing Protocols for Mobile Ad Hoc Networks". Proc. of the 5th ACM/IEEE int. conf. on Mobile computing and networking. Pp. 195-206. 1999.
11. C. E. Perkins, E. M. Royer, S. R. Das, M. K. Marina, Performance Comparison of Two On-Demand Routing Protocols for Ad Hoc Networks, IEEE Personal Com. Pp. 16-28. Feb. 2001.
12. X. Hong, K. Xu, M. Gerla. "Scalable routing protocols for mobile ad hoc networks". IEEE Network. Volume 16, Issue 4, Pp. 11-21. Jul/Aug 2002.
13. OPNET Modeler website. At, http://www.opnet.com/solutions/network_rd/modeler.html
14. Wierzbicki, A., Strzelecki, R., Swierczewski, D. and Znojek, M. Rhubarb: a Tool for Developing Scalable and Secure Peer-to-Peer Applications. Second IEEE International Conference on Peer-to-Peer Computing (P2P2002), Linöping, Sweden, 2002.
15. Xiang, Z., Zhang, Q., Zhu, W., Zhang, Z. and Zhang, Y. Peer-to-Peer Based Multimedia Distribution Service, IEEE Transactions on Multimedia 6 (2) (2004).
16. L. Hongjun, L. P. Luo, Z. Zhifeng. A structured hierarchical P2P model based on a rigorous binary tree code algorithm, Future Generation Computer Systems 23 (2). 2007. Pp. 201-208.
17. B. Thallner, H. Moser. Topology control for fault-tolerant communication in highly dynamic wireless networks. 3rd Wrk. on Intelligent Solutions in Embedded Systems. May 2005.
18. M. Jiang, J. Li, Y.C. Tay. "Cluster Based Routing Protocol (CBRP)". Internet-draf, draft-ietf-manet-cbrp-spec-01.txt, National University of Singapore, 14 August 1999.
19. Chiang, C.C., Wu, H.K., Liu, W., Gerla, M., "Routing in Clustered Multihop, Mobile Wireless Networks with Fading Channel", IEEE SICON, Kent Ridge (Singapore). April 1997.

Performance Analysis of Reservation MAC Protocols for Ad-hoc Networks

Ghalem Boudour, Cédric Teyssié and Zoubir Mammeri

IRIT, Paul Sabatier University

Toulouse, France

{boudour, cedric.teyssie, mammeri}@irit.fr

Abstract Multimedia and real-time applications require bandwidth guarantees, which may be achieved by resource reservation. However, resource reservation in ad-hoc networks is a very challenging task due to the instability of radio channels, node mobility and lack of coordination between mobile nodes. Proposed reservation MAC protocols like CATA, FPRP, R-CSMA and SRMA/PA have limitations and are suitable only for particular situations. In this paper, we propose a comparative analysis of the most representative reservation MAC protocols. We identify the major issues unresolved by reservation MAC protocols. A performance evaluation and comparative analysis with the IEEE 802.11e are achieved through the NS-2 simulator.

1 Introduction

Mobile ad-hoc networks (MANETs) are collections of mobile nodes forming temporary networks without any infrastructure support. They can be set up anywhere anytime owing to their easy deployment and self-organization ability. As a result, MANETs become the primary mean of communication in several domains where the deployment of wired infrastructure is difficult. Such domains include battle fields, forestry fire, and disaster recovery.

The characteristics of MANETs like the lack of centralized coordination, node mobility and resource availability make the Quality of Service (QoS) support in MANETs a very challenging task. MAC protocols for MANETs define the manner channels are shared between mobile nodes. They have significant impacts on the overall system performances and their design is a very challenging issue.

Many solutions have been proposed to support QoS at the MAC sub-layer. Those solutions attempted to improve the channel access mechanism to provide QoS guarantees to multimedia and real-time applications. Proposed solutions may be classified into two categories: contention-based and reservation-based schemes.

Contention-based protocols are non deterministic and nodes compete to get access to the channel for the transmission of each data packet. The aim of these

Please use the following format when citing this chapter:

Boudour, G., Teyssié, C. and Mammeri, Z., 2008, in IFIP International Federation for Information Processing, Volume 284; *Wireless and Mobile Networking*; Zoubir Mammeri; (Boston: Springer), pp. 173–186.

protocols is to avoid packet collisions, and resolve the hidden and exposed terminal issues. This is achieved through carrier sensing, handshaking and backoff mechanisms. Carrier sense ensures that nodes compete to access the channel only when the channel is detected idle. The handshake mechanism uses short control frames (RTS/CTS) to avoid the hidden and exposed terminals issues. The IEEE 802.11 standard is the most known example of contention-based protocols.

Reservation protocols seem to be attractive solutions for QoS provisioning in ad-hoc networks. Their characteristics such as the contention free medium access and the reduced collision rate are very interesting for MANETs. In this paper we provide a comparative analysis of these protocols and the major issues encountered in designing such protocols. Particularly, we analyze the effects of mobility on the performance of reservation MAC protocols. We also compare these protocols with the IEEE802.11e standard.

The rest of this paper is organized as follows. In section 2, we give an overview of the IEEE 802.11e standard and reservation MAC protocols. In section 3 we highlight the major challenges and limitations of reservation protocols. In section 4 we give a performance evaluation of reservation protocols. Section 5 gives our conclusions.

2   Background and Related Work

Channel access protocols in MANETs can be classified into two categories: contention-based and reservation-based protocols. The IEEE 802.11 [1] is the most known example of contention-based protocols. The IEEE 802.11 standard is considered as the de-facto MAC protocol for wireless networks. The DCF mode is based on the Carrier Sense Multiple Access with Collision Avoidance (CSMA/CA). It uses two mechanisms to avoid collision: the physical carrier sensing and the virtual carrier sensing. The physical carrier sensing is used to detect the presence of signal on the common physical channel. The virtual carrier sensing uses the duration field of the MAC frame header to indicate the duration during which a node will reserve the channel.

DATA transmission in DCF is accomplished following the RTS / CTS / DATA / ACK handshake. A station which has a DATA packet to send waits the channel to be idle for the duration of DIFS (DCF Inter Frame Space). If the channel lasts idle for DIFS, the station transmits an RTS packet. Otherwise, the station enters in a backoff period, by choosing a backoff timer. The backoff timer is decremented for each idle time-slot. The station transmits its RTS packet when the backoff timer expires. When the receiver receives successfully the RTS packet, it waits for SIFS (Short InterFrame Space) before replaying with a CTS packet. Both the RTS and CTS packets contain the Duration field which is used in order to prevent neighbours from accessing the channel during the RTS / CTS / DATA / ACK handshake.

Unfortunately, the contention-based access of the IEEE 802.11 makes it unable to fit the requirements of multimedia applications over multi-hop networks. In [11], authors discovered that the IEEE 802.11 did not function well in a wireless multihop environment. The results revealed that the standard suffers from serious throughput degradation and unfairness. Performance degradations are mainly due to the hidden and exposed terminals problems, and the binary exponential backoff scheme. The IEEE 802.11e standard [12] enables deterministic QoS guarantees through MAC level service differentiation. However, the throughput of IEEE 802.11e is expected to degrade at high traffic load. Authors in [11] showed that the performance of MANETs running EDCF are not optimal, and the collision rate increases quickly when the number of contentions to access the medium is high.

On the other hand, reservation MAC protocols seem to be very suitable for multimedia and real-time applications since they reserve the required bandwidth to each source. The basis of these protocols is to give to each node a guaranteed periodic access to the wireless channel. In these protocols, channel is segmented into super-frames, and a global synchronization between nodes is assumed. The MAC protocol reserves a slot to each real-time node. Once the reservation is done, the node uses the same slot in subsequent super-frames without contention. Examples of protocols in this category are FPRP, D-PRMA [3], CATA, and R-CSMA. These protocols mainly differ in the super-frame structure and the medium access control mechanism adopted to reserve time-slots.

In FPRP [4], the super-frame is composed of a reservation frame (RF) followed by several information frames (IF). Each RF is composed of N reservation slots (RS), and each IF is composed of N information slots (IS). In order to reserve an IS, the nodes must make reservations during the corresponding RS. Each RS is composed of M reservation cycles (RC), and, in each RC, a five-step reservation process is followed to make a reservation in the current RS. These five steps are: Reservation Request, Collision Report, Reservation Confirmation, Reservation acknowledgement, and Packing and Elimination. These five phases are undertaken by each node to compete to reserve a time-slot, and to inform neighbors about the result of the competition (reservation success of failure). A node which fails in reserving the slot in a RC, enters in competition to reserve the slot in another RC. However, FPRP incurs a significant amount of overhead for slots reservation.

CATA [5] protocol divides time into equal size super-frames, and each super-frame is composed of S slots. Each slot is composed of four control mini-slots and one Data mini-slot (DMS). Control mini-slots are used to establish reservations, and prevent neighbors from using already reserved slots. The advantage of CATA over other reservation protocols is it permits to establish unicast / multicast / broadcast reservations. Its major drawback is the waste of bandwidth due to control mini-slots. Reserving four mini-slots in each slot reduces the available bandwidth dedicated for the transmission of data packets.

SRMA/PA [7] adopts the same concepts as CATA. The added feature is that it distinguishes higher-priority nodes from lower-priority nodes. It permits to a higher-priority node to grab reservation from lower-priority nodes.

In R-CSMA [6], time is segmented into super-frames. Each super-frame is composed of a contention period (CP) and a set of TDMA slots. A node which wants to establish a reservation follows a three way handshake during the CP in order to negotiate reservations with the receiver. Neighbor nodes record the reservation thus preventing any collision during reserved slots. The major advantage of R-CSMA against FPRP, CATA and SRMA/PA is that it doesn't reserve any bandwidth for control packets. R-CSMA doesn't allocate any control slot since control packets are transmitted only once at the reservation request step.

RTMAC [2] is a reservation MAC protocol that doesn't need global synchronization between mobile nodes. Each super-frame consists of a number of reservation-slots (resv-slots). The duration of each resv-slot is twice the maximum propagation delay. A node that has real-time packets for transmission, reserves a block of consecutive resv-slots, which is called connection-slot on a super-frame and uses the same connection-slot to transmit in successive super-frames. The reserved connection-slot is repaired using relative times of starting and ending times of the connection-slot. With relative time of connection-slots, RTMAC eliminates the need of time synchronization. Each node maintains a reservation table that records for each reservation the pair of sender and receiver identifiers, and the starting and ending time of the reserved connection-slot.

Despite their advantages, previously proposed reservation MAC protocols have many limitations. The most challenging issue with these protocols is mobility of nodes. These protocols consider that nodes are static and no mobility considerations are taken into account. When nodes are mobile, collisions may occur during reserved slots. This phenomenon is called reservation clash and must be handled at the MAC sub-layer. The other issues with reservation MAC protocols are the important control traffic overhead, the support of multimedia applications with different QoS requirements, and the lack of fairness between traffic flows. These issues and possible solutions are discussed in the next section.

3   Discussion of reservation MAC protocols

Reservation protocols provide some bandwidth guarantees for real-traffic sources. However, they suffer some drawbacks: the waste of bandwidth due to control traffic, reservation clash in case of mobility, lack of support of heterogonous classes of traffic, inefficiency of the reservation release scheme, and lack of fairness. These issues will be discussed in detail in this section.

3.1 Control traffic overhead

One important parameter in the performance of reservation MAC protocols is the control traffic overhead. The control traffic overhead determines the amount of control packets transmitted by mobile nodes in order to maintain coherent reservations. The transmission of control traffic results in an increase of energy consumption. In addition, increasing the amount of bandwidth reserved for control traffic results in decreasing the effective bandwidth offered to real-time traffic sources to transmit their data packets.

CATA allocates four control mini-slots (CMS1, CMS2, CMS3, and CMS4) on each slot. After reservation is successfully established, CMS1 is used by the receiver to provide a "busy tone" to senders attempting to reserve the slot for transmission. CMS2 is used by the sender to jam any possible RTS addressed to its neighbors. CMS3 and CMS4 are used only at the reservation setup. Once the reservation is established, these two slots are not used. However, the use of four control mini-slots in each slot incurs a significant overhead.

In FPRP, each RS is composed of M reservation cycle (RC), and a five control mini-slots are associated with each RC to establish reservation. If a node successfully reserves a slot during one of the RCs, the remaining RCs are not used any more for contention. Hence, depending on the number of RC associated with each reservation slot (RS), the control traffic overhead of FPRP may be high, and the waste of bandwidth may be significant.

Like CATA, SRMA/PA allocates four control mini-slots (SR, RR, RC, and ACK) in each slot. The SR is used by the sender to indicate the reservation to its neighbors once the reservation is established. Hence, only the SR slot is used to indicate the slot reservation in subsequent frames, the other control slots (RR, RC) are used only during the reservation handshake. However, allocating three control mini-slots in each slot to coordinate reservations results in a significant overhead.

The major advantage of R-CSMA and RTMAC against FPRP, CATA and SRMA/PA is that they don't reserve any bandwidth for control packets. Control packets are transmitted only at the reservation request step. Instead of allocating control mini-slots to prevent neighbor nodes from reserving already reserved slots, R-CSMA and RTMAC use reservation tables that include for each slot its state "reserved" or "available".

As bandwidth is limited in MANETs, the effective bandwidth offered to real-time traffic sources must be increased, and the wasted bandwidth must be reduced as much as possible. An efficient MAC reservation protocol should permit to maintain coherence of reservations with less control traffic overhead.

3.2 Heterogeneous classes of traffic support

The second drawback with almost all the reservation MAC protocols is that they consider that real-time traffic sources have the same QoS requirements, and the varying requirements of heterogeneous sources of traffic are not considered. They reserve a slot to each real-time traffic source, with the assumption that the traffic source will use the reserved slot in each frame to transmit its data packets.

Reserving one slot to each real-time traffic source is not efficient, especially when heterogeneous traffic streams are characterized by different QoS requirements. According to the encoding and compression techniques used to represent multimedia sources, traffic streams will have widely varying traffic characteristics (bit-rate, delay). Reserving one slot to each traffic stream (TS) results in a waste of bandwidth mainly when the packet inter-arrival time is greater than the super-frame length.

A well designed MAC protocol should provide an efficient mechanism to share the limited bandwidth resource and satisfy the heterogeneous and usually contradictory QoS requirements of each traffic class (voice, video, data ...). The reservation MAC protocol should ensure that each reserving node will be allocated exactly its required share of bandwidth. To achieve such adaptive scheme, we need QoS mapping scheme which determines the quantity of bandwidth to reserve to each class of traffic in function of the considered channel structure (i.e. super-frame length and the number of slots per super-frame).

3.3 Efficiency of reservation release scheme

The reservation release scheme is a key component in reservation MAC protocols. Reservation release is required when the source of real-time traffic has finished its data transmission. At the end of a real-time session, the sender should inform the receiver and its neighbors about the end of transmission. The receiver also is required to inform its neighbors that the slots are no more reserved for reception.

The role of the reservation release scheme is to permit neighbors of the sender and receiver to reserve the slots that have been released. However, the efficiency of the reservation release scheme impacts performance of the reservation protocol. A flaw in the reservation release scheme may result in a saturation of the network where slots can not be reserved while they where released.

The reservation release schemes proposed by reservation protocols are inefficient because there exist situations in which some nodes (receiver, sender neighbors, or receiver neighbors) are not informed about the reservation release. Authors of R-CSMA consider that reserved slot is released automatically when it is left empty. However, this scheme is not efficient because reserving nodes may not use all their reserved slots periodically to send data packets, especially when the inter-packets arrival time is greater than the super-frame length. If a reserving node has no data packet to transmit in the current super-frame while it has not finished the transmission, the node loses its reservation, and the slot is available for reservation by other nodes. The node is required to re-establish reservation each time the reserved slot is not used for transmission. Another issue with the reservation release of R-CSMA is that only the sender is able to signal reservation release to its neighbors by leaving the reserved slot empty. The receiver has no way to indicate the reservation release to its neighbors. The slot will remain reserved from the viewpoint of the receiver's neighbors.

Authors of RTMAC use explicit reservation release packets to inform neighbors about the reservation release. At the end of transmission, the sender informs the receiver and its neighbors by sending a ResvRelRTS packet. When the receiver receives the ResvRelRTS packet, it sends a ResvRelCTS packet. The purpose of the ResvRelRTS and ResvRelCTS packets is to request neighbours of the sender and receiver to release the reserved connection-slot. However, since the ResvRelease packets are transmitted using contention, they may collide with other transmitted packets. Consequently, there may be situations in which either the receiver or neighbors of the sender/receiver don't receive the ResvRelease packet. In FPRP, CATA, and SRMA/PA no reservation release scheme is defined.

An efficient reservation MAC protocol should ensure that at the end of real-time session both the receiver and all nodes around the sender and the receiver receive correctly the reservation release. In addition the MAC protocol should ensure reuse of slots once these slots are released.

3.4 Impacts of the super-frame length

Unlike the IEEE 802.11e where nodes are enabled to transmit each time they wine contention to the wireless channel, nodes in reservation MAC protocols can transmit only on their reserved slots. A node which has the opportunity of transmission at time t, can transmit the next packet only after $t+T_{super-frame}$, where $T_{super-frame}$ is the super-frame length. The super-frame length (in term of number of slots per frame) affects the bandwidth and delay offered to real-time and multimedia traffic sources.

There is a trade-off between the super-frame length and delay and bandwidth requirements of real-time traffic sources. On one hand, choosing a small number of slots per super-frame guarantees a small delay equal to the super-frame length. This scheme is suitable for multimedia traffic sources with a short inter-packet arrival time and stringent delay requirements. However, the call acceptance ratio (the ratio of accepted reservations) is low since each real-time source reserves exclusively one slot on the super-frame. On the other hand, choosing a too large super-frame length results in more established connections, but does not meat the delay requirements of multimedia applications with stringent delay requirements.

Performances of reservation MAC protocols are strongly affected by the super-frame length. The impact of the super-frame length and the number of slots by frame should be carefully taken into account at network configuration step.

3.5 Mobility handling and reservation break detection

Unlike contention based protocols where mobility of nodes has not a strong impact on the MAC protocol performance, the mobility factor is a challenging issue in the design of reservation MAC protocols. When nodes are mobile, conflicts between reservations and collisions may occur during reserved slots. This phenomenon is called reservation clash and must be handled at the MAC layer. The reservation clash phenomenon due to mobility is illustrated in the following scenario. In fig. 1, nodes B and C establish reservation with A and D respectively on the same slot s. As long as A and C are far away from each other, no collision occur in reserved slots. If nodes C and D move toward A, reservation clash will occur at A. Both of B and C transmit on the reserved slot s and collision occur during slot s. Reservation clash has drastic consequences on the QoS, especially in highly mobile nodes. Reserving nodes affected by reservation clash will suffer excessive packets collisions and dropping.

Almost all proposed reservation MAC protocols are suitable only for static ad-hoc networks. They consider that nodes are static and no mobility considerations are taken into account. Reservation MAC protocols must provide efficient mechanisms to face mobility of nodes, and reduce the degradation of performance in dynamic ad-hoc networks. Particularly, reservation protocols should provide a reservation clash detection mechanism. In addition, a reservation recovery mechanism must be defined in order to permit to nodes that lost their reservations due to mobility to release their reservations and establish new reservations.

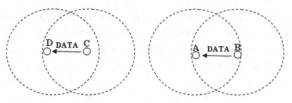

Fig. 1 Reservation clash due to mobility.

3.6 Fairness

Fairness is another parameter in the performances of MAC protocols. Proposed reservation MAC protocols lack the definition of mechanisms to ensure fairness between traffic flows, and between different service classes. In FPRP, CATA, SRMA/PA, and RTMAC there is no limit on the maximum bandwidth that can be reserved by a real-time traffic source. In addition, there is no limit on the amount of bandwidth that can be reserved to the real-time traffic class. Real-time traffic sources are allowed to reserve time slots as long as there are free slots in the super-frame. However, this scheme is not efficient since real-time traffic sources can monopolize all the available bandwidth leading to starvation of other classes of traffic like best effort traffic sources. Unlike, FPRP, CATA, and SRMA/PA, R-CSMA allocates a fraction of the super-frame for the transmission of best effort packets. Best effort traffic sources have always the chance to transmit their data packets during the contention period regardless the offered traffic load since no traffic class is authorized to monopolize the contention period.

Much attention should be paid on the bandwidth that can be allocated to real-time applications. Reservation MAC protocols should define a limit on this bandwidth, and the available bandwidth should be well partitioned between the different classes of service to avoid starvation of low priority traffic classes.

4   Simulations

We compare the performance of previously presented reservation protocols (R-CSMA, CATA, FPRP, and IEEE 802.11e). Particularly, we are interested in analyzing how these protocols provide QoS guarantees to voice and video traffic flows. Particularly, we analyze their control traffic overhead, their efficiency in regard to mobility and their control overhead. The comparative analysis is performed through a set of tests using the network simulator NS-2. We use the IEEE 802.11e simulation model of Wiethölter and Hoene available at [13].

We consider an ad-hoc network composed of 100 nodes randomly distributed on a 1 km^2 area. The wireless channel is 11Mb/s. We assume that the wireless channel is noise and distortion free. Nodes are considered equipped with omni-directional antenna with a 250 meters transmission range.

In our simulations we consider two voice traffic models (G.711 and G.723 models), and two video models (MPEG-4 and H263 video models). Table 2 summarizes the TSpec parameters for the classes of considered traffic. Each station can generate a G.711, a G.723 audio, an MPEG-4, or an H263 video flow. The TSpec parameters of G.711 and G.723 are taken from [8]. For MPEG-4 and H263, the TSpec parameters are extracted from traces of films available at [9].

Table 1. TSpec parameters for the considered traffic classes

Parameter	Traffic models			
	G.711	G.723	MPEG-4	H.263
ϱmin (kbps)	64	6.4	150	270
ϱmax (kbps)	64	6.4	1600	2300
average frame size (bytes)	160	24	770	1278
Mean inter-frame arrival time (ms)	20	30	40	40

Table 2. Simulation parameters

Parameter	Value
Channel bit rate (Mbps)	11
Slot payload size (bytes)	160
UDP/IP header (bytes)	8+20
MAC header (bytes)	38
PHY layer overhead (PLCP header+preamble) (bits)	8+48
Slot length (ms)	0.18
Guard time between slots (µs)	20
Super-frame length (ms)	5
Number of slots per super-frame	25
Simulation time (s)	1000s

The maximum payload of a slot is set to 160 bytes in our simulations. Each slot consists of the transmission time of a real-time packet (including different layer overheads), and the round trip propagation time. With 11Mbps channel bit-rate, the slot length is 0.18ms. Simulation parameters are shown in table 2.

Because video frames are larger than the payload of a TDMA slot, video frames are fragmented into several packets. After fragmentation, MPEG source generates one packet every 10ms, H263 generates a packet every 5ms, G.711 generates one packet every 20ms, and G.723 generates one packet every 30ms. The super-frame length is set to the smallest packet inter-arrival time (i.e. the packet inter-arrival time of H263 source) which is 5ms.

4.1 Analysis of the impact of the super-frame length and traffic load

We analyze the impact of the traffic load on the performances of the considered protocols in a static ad-hoc network. In this analysis we increase the traffic load by increasing the number of best effort (BE) and real-time (RT) sessions (MPEG, H263, G711, and G723) in equal numbers. The maximum number of sessions is 100, and sessions are uniformly distributed among the 100 nodes.

Fig. 2.a shows the reservation acceptance ratio of CATA, FPRP, and R-CSMA versus the increase of traffic load. The figure shows that the reservation acceptance ratio remains above 90% as long as the number of sessions is less than 40 sessions. When the number of sessions exceeds 40 sessions, the reservations acceptance ratio decreases linearly because the number of sessions become much higher than the number of slots per super-frame. Some sessions will be rejected because of the unavailability of resources. R-CSMA has a lower reservations acceptance ratio than the other protocols at high traffic load because of the portion of the super-frame allocated to the contention period. We don't give the reservation acceptance ratio of the IEEE 802.11e because this protocol doesn't make explicit reservations.

Fig. 2.b shows the throughput achieved by FPRP, CATA, R-CSMA, and the IEEE 802.11e versus the increase of traffic load. The Figure shows that at low traffic load the considered protocols have approximately the same throughput. At high traffic load, reservation protocols achieve higher throughput than the IEEE 802.11e. Fig. 3.a shows the packets delivery ratio (i.e. the percentage of packets received by their destinations) of RT packets offered by FPRP, CATA, R-CSMA, and IEEE 802.11e versus the increase of traffic load. The figure shows that reservation protocols offer better packets delivery ratio than the IEEE 802.11e at high traffic load. The low throughput and packets delivery ratio of the IEEE 802.11e is due to the increase of contention and collision rate at high traffic load. The high delivery ratio of FPRP, CATA, and R-CSMA results from that packets in these protocols are transmitted periodically on reserved slots in collision-free way. Consequently, the probability of collision and packet dropping is very low.

Fig. 3.b shows the average RT packets delay with FPRP, CATA, R-CSMA, and IEEE 802.11e versus the increase of traffic load. The figure shows that reservation protocols give deterministic delay regardless the traffic load, while IEEE802.11e diverges with the increase of traffic load. At low traffic load, the IEEE802.11e outperforms the other protocols because low level of contention results in a small number of collisions and short backoffs. At high input load, IEEE 802.11e nodes experience more contention, and thus more collisions and wider backoff windows, and consequently the access delay increases drastically. Reservation protocols provide quasi-constant delay because real-time packets are transmitted at regular intervals once the reservations established.

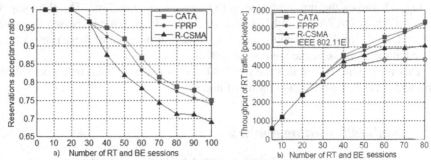

Fig. 2   a) Reservations acceptance ratio versus the increase of traffic load
b) Throughput of RT traffic versus the increase of traffic load

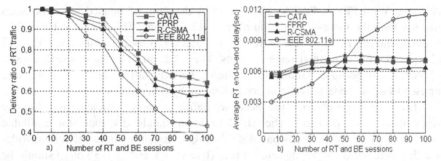

Fig. 3   a) RT traffic delivery ratio versus the increase of traffic load.
b) Average end-to-end delay of RT traffic versus the increase of traffic load.

4.2 Analysis of the effect of mobility

For mobility of nodes, we use the RWP (Random Walk Point) model. Each mobile node chooses randomly its next position and moves toward that position with a velocity uniformly distributed between *Vmin* and *Vmax*. We choose *Vmin=1 m/s and Vmax=10 m/s*. The node stays in its new position for a time *dt* (set to 30 seconds in our simulations) after witch it chooses another position.

Fig. 4.a shows that the packet dropping rate with CATA, FPRP and R-CSMA increases drastically with the increase of the number of mobile nodes. The packet dropping rate of IEEE 802.11e remains very low compared to other protocols. The drastic packets dropping ratio of FPRP, CATA, and R-CSMA is due to the reservation clash, and the high number of collisions. As mobility increases, reservations clashes increase and nodes start losing their reservations. Since no reservation recovery mechanism is defined, reserving nodes have no way to establish new reservations, and reserving nodes continue sending their data packets on their reserved lost slots. The IEEE 802.11e is less affected by mobility of nodes because nodes are required to compete and acquire the channel for the transmission of each data packet no matter of their positions.

Fig. 4.b shows the throughput with the increase of mobility. The throughput with R-CSMA, CATA and FPRP decreases drastically with the increase of mobile nodes. Like the packets dropping rate, the reduced throughput of these protocols is linked to the increase of the number of collision slots.

This section has shown that the IEEE 802.11e is more efficient than reservation protocols in the case of high mobility of nodes.

4.3 Bandwidth wasting analysis

We analyze the waste of bandwidth incurred by reservation schemes, especially when heterogeneous classes with different QoS requirements are considered. Fig. 5.a shows the ratio of unused reserved slots with the increase of the number RT sessions. With FPRP, CATA, and R-CSMA the ratio of unused slots increases linearly with the increase of the number of RT sessions. This waste of bandwidth is due to the low rate of voice sources. G711 and G723 sources consume only 3/12 (2/12 respectively) of their reserved slots. The IEEE 802.11e doesn't suffer waste of bandwidth because bandwidth is shared between all nodes, and bandwidth unused by some node is available for utilization by other nodes.

This section points out the need to define a more efficient and flexible reservation MAC protocol. The MAC protocol should distribute the available bandwidth to reserving nodes based on their QoS requirements so that bandwidth wasting is reduced. Low data rate sources (like G.711 and G.723 voice) should be allocated less bandwidth than the high data rate sources such as video.

4.4 Control traffic overhead

Fig. 5.b shows the control traffic generated by nodes as a function of the number of RT sessions. On one hand, we observe that the amount of control traffic generated by R-CSMA remains very low. This is because R-CSMA does not use any control slots to coordinate reservations. Control packets are transmitted only at the reservations setup. On the other hand, we observe that CATA and FPRP and IEEE 802.11e generate high quantity of control traffic. CATA requires each reserving node to transmit RS and RTS packets on each reserved slot. FPRP requires the repetition of the five-phase reservation steps on each Reservation Frame. The IEEE 802.11e requires the transmission of the RTS and CTS packets before the transmission of each data packet.

This section reveals that CATA and FPRP and IEEE 802.11e suffer significant control traffic overhead when the number of traffic streams in the network is high.

R-CSMA has the advantage that it uses less control traffic.

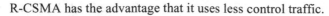

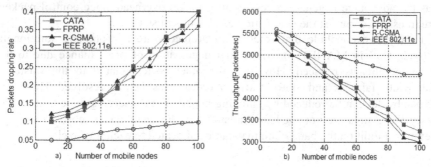

Fig. 4 a) Packet dropping rate versus the increase of number of mobile nodes.

b) Throughput versus the increase of number of mobile nodes.

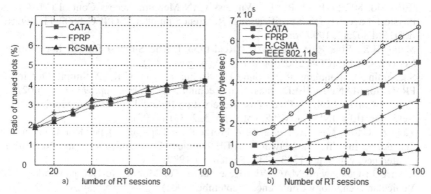

Fig. 5 a) Ratio of unused slots versus the increase of number of RT sessions.

b) Control traffic overhead versus the increase of number of RT sessions.

5 Conclusion

In this paper we analyzed the advantages of reservation-based protocols against their counter-part contention-based protocols, especially the IEEE 802.11e standard. Also, we provide a detailed analysis of the main drawbacks, and challenging issues

First, we found that reservation MAC protocols perform well in static ad hoc networks. Simulation results show that these protocols outperform the IEEE 802.11e standard in low mobility scenarios. However, the performances of these protocols are expected to degrade as mobility of nodes increases. All reservations which are being built since the initialization of the network overlaps one with each other and collisions during reserved slots appear. In these situations the IEEE 802.11e is more efficient since no permanent transmission scheduling is established. Nodes compete to get access to the channel no matter their positions in regard to their neighbors. Second, we found that some protocols like FPRP,

CATA, and IEEE 802.11e suffer significant control traffic overhead. R-CSMA has the advantage it generates less control traffic overhead since control packets are transmitted only at the reservation establishment step.

Finally, we conclude that reservation protocols are a promising solution to provide QoS in MANETs provided that degradation of performance due to the node mobility is reduced. However, the other issues related to the waste of bandwidth, fairness, and control traffic overhead must be also resolved. The waste of bandwidth can be reduced by allowing neighbors of reserving node to use slots when these slots are not used for transmission. Fairness can be ensured through defining a limit on the bandwidth that can be allocated to each traffic class.

References

1. IEEE Std. 802.11-1999, Part11: Wireless LAN Medium Access Control (MAC) and Physical Layer (PHY) Specifications, Reference number ISO/IEC 8802-11:1999(E), IEEE Std 802.11, 1999 edition.
2. Manoj B.S., Siva Ram Murthy C.: Real-time Traffic Support for Ad hoc Wireless Networks, IEEE ICON 2002, pp. 335-340 (August 2002).
3. Shengming J., Jianqiang R., Dajiang H., Xinhua L., Chi, C.K.: A Simple Distributed PRMA for MANETs, IEEE Trans. Veh. Technol., vol.51, no.2, pp.293–305 (2002).
4. Zhu C., Corson M.S.: A Five-Phase Reservation Protocol (FPRP) for Mobile Ad hoc Networks, IEEE INFOCOM'98, vol.1, pp. 322–331 (1998).
5. Tang Z., Garcia-Luna-Aceves J. J.: A Protocol for Topology-Dependent Transmission Scheduling in Wireless Networks, IEEE Wireless Communications and Networking Conference, vol. 3, pp. 1333-1337 (September 1999).
6. Inwhee J.: Qos-Aware MAC With Reservation For Mobile Ad-Hoc Networks, IEEE Vehicular Technology Conference (September 2004).
7. Ahn C.W., Kang C.G., Cho Y.Z.: Soft Reservation Multiple Access with Priority Assignment (SRMA/PA): A Distributed MAC Protocol QoS-guaranteed Integrated Services in Mobile Ad-hoc Networks, IEICE Transactions on Communications, vol. E86-B, no. 1, pp. 50-59 (January 2003).
8. Sharafeddine S., Riedl A., Glasmann J., and Totzke J.: On Traffic Characteristics and Bandwidth Requirements of Voice over IP Applications, IEEE International Symposium on Computers and Communication (ISCC'03) (July 2003).
9. Video Traces for network Performance Evaluation, available at http://www.tkn.tu-berlin.de/research/trace/trace.html
10. Hsieh H.-Y., Sivakumar R.: IEEE 802.11 over Multi-hop Wireless Networks: Problems and New Perspectives, Proc. IEEE VTC 2002 Fall (September 2002).
11. Romdhami L., Ni Q., Turletti T.: Adaptive EDCF: Enhanced Service Differentiation for IEEE 802.11 Wireless Ad-Hoc Networks, IEEE Wireless Communications and Networking Conference (WCNC), New Orleans, USA (March 2003).
12. IEEE 802.11WG. Drat Supplement to Standard for Telecommunications and Information Exchange Between Systems-LAN/MAN Specific Requirements-part11: MAC Enhancements for Quality of Service (QoS). IEEE 802.11e Standard Draft/D13.0 (January 2005).
13. Wiethölter S., Hoene C., Wolisz A.: Perceptual Quality of Internet Telephony over IEEE 802.11e Supporting Enhanced DCF and Contention Free Bursting, TKN–04-11 Technical Report Series, Technische Universität Berlin (September 2004).

Evaluation of WiseMAC on Sensor Nodes

Philipp Hurni and Torsten Braun

Universität Bern, Switzerland

Abstract The WiseMAC protocol is one of the most energy-efficient medium access control protocols for wireless sensor networks. However, in many typical wireless sensor network scenarios, throughput is limited when high traffic occurs, e.g., if many sensors simultaneously detect and report an event to the base station. The paper proposes to improve the traffic-adaptivity of WiseMAC by extending the more bit mechanism supporting transmissions of frame bursts in WiseMAC. It allows bottleneck nodes to stay awake in situations of high traffic and temporarily abandon the periodic sleep-wake pattern. We evaluate WiseMAC's energy efficiency and compare the original and extended more bit by simulations as well as measurements in a real sensor experiment test-bed.

1 Introduction

The Wireless Sensor MAC (WiseMAC) 1 protocol is based on low duty cycles, periodic wake-ups and preamble sampling. Performance evaluations show that the required energy increases linearly with the traffic rate. However, the throughput is rather limited and packet loss already occurs with rather low traffic rate. The reason is that in tree-based wireless sensor network scenarios, nodes receiving traffic from several sources might become bottleneck nodes in case they wake up strictly in a periodic way. The more bit mechanism of WiseMAC allows exchanging additional traffic between a pair of nodes, but this only supports the exchange of large messages or frame bursts in point-to-point scenarios. This paper evaluates the more bit mechanism as well as the proposed extension to allow a bottleneck node to temporarily adapt its duty cycle in case of high traffic.

Section 2 describes the basic WiseMAC protocol and its more bit mechanism. Section 3 introduces the extended more bit mechanism. Section 4 presents simulation results, while section 5 discusses performance evaluation results from real-world experiments. Section 6 concludes the paper.

Please use the following format when citing this chapter:

Hurni, P. and Braun, T., 2008, in IFIP International Federation for Information Processing, Volume 284; *Wireless and Mobile Networking*; Zoubir Mammeri; (Boston: Springer), pp. 187–198.

2 WiseMAC

WiseMAC is based on short, unsynchronized duty cycles and preambles exceeding the time of a node in sleep state (Fig. 1). When transmitting a frame, a preamble of variable length is used to alert the receiving node in its wake-up interval not to return to sleep state, but to stay awake for the upcoming transmission. When the receiver's wake-up pattern is still unknown, the duration of the preamble equals the full basic cycle duration T, as illustrated in Fig. 1 in the first transmission. The own schedule offset is then piggybacked to the frame and transmitted to the receiver.

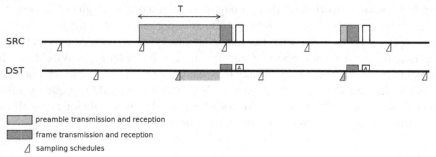

■ preamble transmission and reception
■ frame transmission and reception
◿ sampling schedules

Fig. 1 WiseMAC

After successful frame reception, the receiver node piggybacks its own schedule to the respective frame acknowledgement. Received schedule offsets of all neighbor nodes are subsequently kept in a table and are periodically updated. Based on this table, a node can determine the wake-up intervals of all its neighbors and minimize the preamble length for upcoming transmissions. It waits for its neighbor's wake-up and sends the frame just in the appropriate moment, only prepending a small preamble that compensates for the maximum clock drift that the two involved node's clocks may have developed since the last schedule exchange.

To increase the maximum achievable throughput in case of packet bursts and higher traffic load, WiseMAC suggests an optional fragmentation scheme called more bit mode. WiseMAC sets a flag (more bit) in a unicast MAC frame whenever a node has more packets to send. The more bit in the frame header signals to the receiving node that it shall not turn off the transceiver after receiving the frame, but switch to the receive mode again after frame acknowledgement in order to receive the next packet, cf. Fig. 2. A sender does not need to wait for the next wake-up of the receiver to transmit the next frame. This increases the throughput. The scheme proved to be very effective in scenarios with varying traffic, especially with packet bursts generated by single nodes.

The more bit scheme only serves to improve traffic adaptivity between one sender and one destination. In a wireless sensor network scenario, there are often nodes that have to forward data from large sub-trees. Such bottleneck nodes will have to forward messages generated by many other nodes. The more bit scheme does not help at all if several nodes aim to simultaneously transmit a packet to the same bottleneck node, as it can happen in a tree scenario as depicted in Fig. 3. One node after the other will have to wait for a wake-up of the bottleneck node in order to forward a frame. The duty cycle of the bottleneck node, however, is not increased with the more bit scheme.

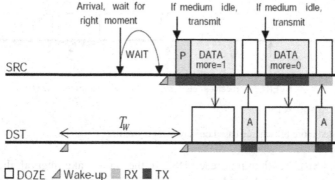

Fig. 2 More bit in WiseMAC

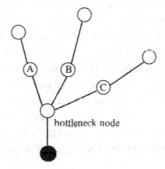

Fig. 3 Tree structure in a wireless sensor network

3 Extended WiseMAC More Bit Scheme

We proposed a scheme, where nodes will automatically stay awake for a longer time than just the awake period when more traffic has to be handled and tell this to all nodes waiting to forward traffic to it 8. Therefore, we extended the semantics of the more bit to a so-called stay awake promise bit. This is also called extended more bit hereafter. Fig. 4 shows two sources SRC1 and SRC2 simultaneously aiming to transmit some packets to the same node DST, possibly because an event has occurred in their vicinity.

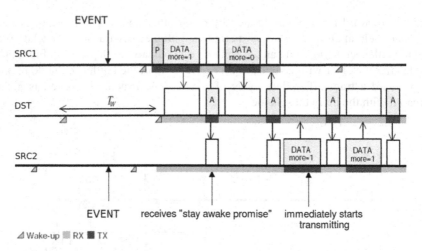

Fig. 4 Extended more bit scheme based on stay awake promise

If SRC1 and SRC2 both aim to reach DST in the same wake interval, the medium reservation preamble will decide who is first. SRC1 wins the contention and sends its first two frames with the more bit set. The destination node acknowledges the more bit in the ACK packet and stays awake for at least a basic wake interval T. As SRC2 has lost the contention, it will wait and overhear the transmission from SRC1 to DST. By hearing the stay awake promise in the ACK, SRC2 knows that it can start sending its own data frames right after SRC1 has finished its transmissions. The advantage of this scheme is that no time is wasted for waiting, because the transmission of SRC2 can start immediately after the transmission of node SRC1. The mechanism is only activated when there is a node buffering more than one frame that requests its destination to stay awake for one next packet, which is an indication of increased load. The scheme is not applied after every unicast transmission, as this would lead to unnecessary energy consumption.

4 Simulations

4.1 Performance Evaluation Scenario

For performance evaluation by simulation, we used 90 nodes uniformly distributed in an area of 300 m x 300 m. Traffic using a Poisson model is generated for 1 hour at each node and sent towards a single sink. We use static shortest path routing. Each node uses a basic interval T = 250 between two wake-ups and a duty cycle of 5 %. We used the OMNeT++ network simulator 2 and the mobility framework 3, which supports simulations of wireless ad hoc and mobile networks on top of OMNeT++. The energy consumption model is based on the amount of energy that is used by the transceiver unit. CPU processing costs are considered as negligible. We used an energy consumption and state transition model with three operation modes sleep, receive and transmit, and applied the respective energy consumption values and state transition delays of the transceiver manufacturer 4. Table 1 indicates the input current and the state transition delays of the simulations. The energy consumption during the state transition is assumed to be equal to the consumption of the respective higher state.

Table 1. Simulation parameters

carrier frequency	868 MHz
bit rate	19.2 kbps
packet size including header	160 bits
transmitter power	0.1 mW
SNR threshold	4 dB
sensitivity	-101.2 dBm
sensitivity carrier sensing	-112 dBm
communication range	50 m
packet loss coefficient α	3.5
carrier sensing range	100 m
supply voltage	3V
current	
transmit	12 mA
receive	4.5 mA
sleep	5 μA
state transition delays	
receive to transmit	12 μs
transmit to receive	12 μs
sleep to receive	518 μs
receive to sleep	10 μs
transmit to sleep	10 μs
packet queue length	15

4.2 Simulation Results

The good traffic adaptivity of WiseMAC is clearly visible in Fig. 5, which depicts the overall energy consumption with the original WiseMAC approach dependent on the traffic rate. With no traffic, the energy consumption remains very low. With linear increase of traffic, WiseMAC is able to react with a more or less linear increase of the total energy consumption.

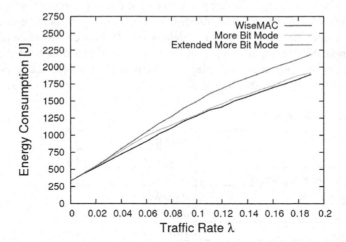

Fig. 5 Energy consumption

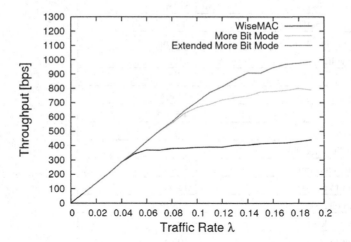

Fig. 6 Throughput

Problems arise when dealing with packet bursts and when neighboring stations are also intending to send traffic. When a node wants to reach a station in its wake interval, but fails to access to the medium, it is quite likely that the preamble sampling period is missed and that the destination node goes back to sleep too early. The very short duration of the duty cycles to sense the carrier has an impact on the maximum traffic rate. The boundary values for the maximum traffic rate are limited by the duration of the sleep intervals to only a few percent of the cycle interval. Therefore, the bandwidth achievable with the basic WiseMAC scheme is limited and exceeding that limit results in higher packet loss. Fig. 6 shows that an increase of maximum throughput is possible with the (extended) more bit, but the improved throughput comes with higher energy costs. But when we consider the ratio of throughput and energy, the extended scheme is even better than the more bit scheme for high traffic 8.

5 Measurements in Real Test-Beds

5.1 Experimentation Environment

In order to examine the real-world behavior of the simulated wireless sensor network mechanisms, we implemented the original WiseMAC mechanism and the (extended) more bit on Embedded Sensor Boards (ESB). ESBs run the sensor node operating system ScatterWeb 5 and are equipped with a micro-controller MSP430, various sensors and communication interfaces such as an 868.35 MHz wireless transceiver. ESBs run with 3 AA batteries or external power source. The input voltage must be in the range of 3-5 V. The embedded voltage controller of the ESB then tailors the input voltage to 3V. The different sensors and the communication interfaces can be turned on and off. Depending on the operation mode of the sensors and the microcontroller, the ESB nodes have different energy consumption levels: Average power consumption for the ESB running with all communication interfaces is 45 mW. When all sensors are turned off and the TR1001 transceiver module is transmitting data, power consumption is 29 mW in average. With all sensors shut off and radio in sleep mode the ESB still consumes 14 mW.

5.2 Measurement Methodology

Measuring the current of a small device such as the ESB can be done with some inaccuracy using a cathode-ray oscilloscope. However, these devices are not intended to record and sum up the current and the energy consumption over a longer period of time. Equipping all nodes with replaceable or rechargeable AA batteries is not a suitable approach, because measurements of battery capacities have shown that the variance can be huge. The capacities of rechargeable batteries that have just been charged up also vary heavily, especially if some of them are new and some have already been used for many charging cycles. It is too impractical to use batteries or rechargeable batteries to make lifetime and energy-consumption measurements. With energy-saving sensor nodes, the respective lifetimes can last for days, weeks, or even months.

We therefore used another well-tested and established measurement methodology to investigate the energy consumption of the ESB nodes. The methodology was already applied by the developers of the ESB in 7 and likewise used in the investigation on different MAC protocols in 6. The methodology uses so-called gold cap capacitors. These capacitors are a special kind of capacitors that come with high capacity of 1 Farad in our case. They can be charged quite quickly and power a sensor node for a reasonable amount of time. Such a capacitor stores up to 15 J for a charging voltage of 5.5 V. When charged with the same initial amount of energy, a node with a lower overall energy consumption can live longer. The methodology allows answering the question how much energy could actually be saved when applying energy-efficiency measures on the ESBs.

We charged the 1 Farad capacitors for a charging time of 120 seconds with a supply voltage of 5.5 V. Shutting down all sensors and unplugging the nodes from the RS232 Interface makes sure that only CPU and transceiver consume energy, besides some small amount of energy spent for the circuits on the board. We observed the supply voltage of the capacitor with a multi-meter. When unplugging the capacitor from the charging source, the voltage of the capacitor continuously keeps falling. We measured the time until the voltage drops below 3 V, which is the supply voltage the embedded voltage controller requires to power the node. Below this threshold, the node still runs for some small amount of time, but its behavior is unpredictable. By applying this methodology, we obtained robust and stable results with low variance, which allow comparing the ESB node's energy consumption in different operation modes. This allowed quantifying the energy efficiency gains for different traffic load levels.

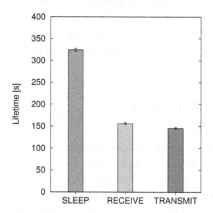

Fig. 7 ESB operation modes

Fig. 7 depicts the lifetime of an ESB node, when the transceiver is constantly in one of the three transceiver states sleep, receive and transmit. When comparing the sleep mode with the respective states receive and transmit, it is obvious that approximately half the energy of the capacitor is being used to power the ESB circuit, microcontroller unit, and memory. A node that is constantly in the sleep mode can live approximately twice as long as a node that is constantly in the receive state. The lifetime of nodes being constantly in the sleep state gives us upper boundary values for the energy measurements.

5.3 Measurement Results

5.3.1 Power Consumption

Fig. 8 depicts the measured lifetime of an ESB node when applying the methodology described in Section 5.2. The lifetime of a node applying the WiseMAC medium sampling technique with basic cycle duration T = 500 ms and 10% duty cycle is almost equal to the lifetime of a node with the permanently switched-off transceiver. Considering that the mechanism still allows reaching nodes within 500 ms, the cost for this connectivity is quite reasonable. When comparing the lifetime of the WiseMAC node to the lifetime of simple ScatterWeb CSMA, which keeps the transceiver permanently in the receive state, the lifetime could be increased by approximately 120 %.

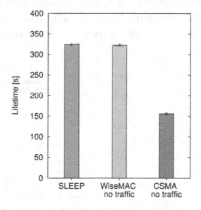

Fig. 8 Power consumption for sleep mode, WiseMAC, ScatterWeb CSMA (receive mode)

The implementation parameters of the power saving WiseMAC protocol on ESB nodes listed in Table 2 led to stable and quite robust functioning of the prototype implementation on the ESB. We also implemented the more bit scheme and the extended more bit scheme using the stay awake promise on ESB nodes. Signaling to stay awake is achieved by altering a single bit in the MAC header. The buffer space for storing packets has been limited due to the small RAM in ESBs, and allows to store 20 frames. In case of buffer overflows, packets passed from the application layer are simply discarded.

Table 2. ESB prototype parameters

Basic interval duration T	500 ms
awake ratio	1%
retries	3
minimum preamble	5 ms
medium reservation preamble	uniform [0,6] ms
baud rate	19'200 bps
bit rate	9'600 bps
MAC header	104 bit
payload	96 bit
packet queue length	20

We measured the lifetime of WiseMAC in a chain scenario consisting of six nodes. Fig. 9 depicts the lifetime of the selected ESB node 5 as a function of the traffic rate r when being charged with the initial amount of energy. As the node's energy consumption increases with increasing traffic along the chain, a more or less linear decrease of the node's lifetime can be observed. The lower curve in Fig. 9 displays the lifetime of a node using ScatterWeb CSMA. ScatterWeb CSMA keeps the transceiver constantly in the receive state, applying no energy-saving scheme such as periodic switching between sleep and active states. As sending and receiving is more or less equally expensive, the traffic has no big impact on the lifetime of nodes.

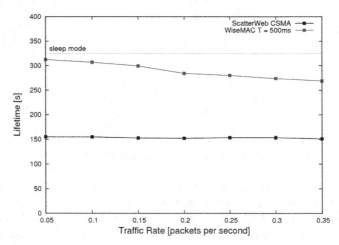

Fig. 9 Lifetime of WiseMAC

5.3.2 Throughput

In another experiment, we measured the throughput of the two schemes more bit and extended more bit when generating traffic of equal rate from two senders to one receiver. When both senders aim to concurrently forward packets to the receiver, the receiver becomes a bottleneck, as both nodes aim to concurrently transmit their packets during the limited wake-up intervals. With the extended more bit scheme, the receiver node promises to stay awake for at least $T = 500$ ms by a single bit in the acknowledgement frame. Fig. 10 shows the measured throughput in the given scenarios. The x-axis corresponds to the traffic generated by each of the two nodes.

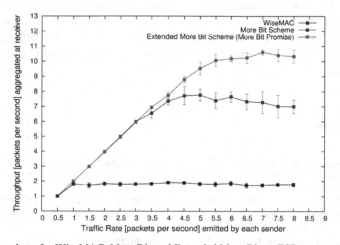

Fig. 10 Throughput for WiseMAC, More Bit and Extended More Bit on ESBs

The WiseMAC protocol without the more bit scheme can only deliver one packet per wake-up, and therefore, throughput is limited to two packets per second with a basic cycle duration $T = 500$ ms. When increasing the rate, packets are subsequently queued in the buffer. When the buffer is full, packets are simply dropped.

When two stations apply the (extended) more bit scheme, they can alternately empty their transmit buffers by packet bursts for increasing traffic. More than one packet can be sent during each wakeup interval of the receiver. The sending station receives packets from its application layer and buffers them until the receiver node's next wake-up. The sender then transmits frames with the more bit set, listens for the acknowledgement and continues sending the next packet in line, until its buffer is empty.

By applying the (extended) more bit scheme, we could increase the throughput to much higher values. The throughput reaches nearly 8 packets per second for the more bit scheme and exceeds 10 packets for the extended more bit scheme using the stay-awake promise bit. The throughput increase for the extended more bit scheme compared to the original more bit scheme exceeds 20 %. The throughput

improvement of 20 % is similar to what has been achieved in the simulation scenario as shown in Fig. 6, although the measurement scenario is much simpler.

6 Conclusions

The paper evaluated WiseMAC and extensions on ESB sensor nodes. The measurement results underline and usefulness of the energy-conserving WiseMAC
compared to a MAC scheme without integrated power saving mechanism. The paper evaluated two schemes to improve throughput in scenarios with multiple senders and bottleneck destination nodes. The results obtained in simulation and sensor testbed confirm that the extended more bit basing on the so-called stay-awake-
promise performs better than the original WiseMAC more bit scheme. The superior performance of 20% has been found similar in both simulation and real-world
experiments.

References

1.   El-Hoiydi, A.; Decotignie, J.-D.: WiseMAC: An Ultra Low Power MAC Protocol for Multihop
      Wireless Sensor Networks, ALGOSENSORS 2004, First International Workshop on Algorithmic
      Aspects of Wireless Sensor Networks
2.   András   Varga: The   OMNeT++   Discrete   Event   Simulation   System
      (http://www.omnetpp.org), European Simulation Multiconference (ESM'2001), Pra-
      gue, Czech Republic, June 2001
3.   Mobility Framework for OMNeT++ (http://mobility-fw.sourceforge.net)
4.   RF Monolithics: Datasheet for TR1001 868.35 MHz hybrid transceiver,
      http://www.rfm.com/products/data/TR1001.pdf
5.   Schiller, J. Liers, A. Ritter, H. Winter, R. Voigt, T.: ScatterWeb - Low Power Sensor
      Nodes and Energy Aware Routing, 38th Annual Hawaii International Conference on
      System Sciences, 2005
6.   Staub T., Bernoulli T., Anwander M., Waelchli M., Braun T.: Experimental Lifetime
      Evaluation for MAC Protocols on Real Sensor Hardware, ACM Workshop on Real-
      World Wireless Sensor Networks REALWSN, 2006
7.   Ritter H., Schiller J., Voigt T., Dunkels A., Alonso J.: Experimental evaluation of life-
      time bounds for wireless sensor networks, European Workshop on Wireless Sensor
      Networks EWSN, 2005
8.   Philipp Hurni, Torsten Braun: Increasing Throughput for WiseMAC, IEEE/IFIP
      WONS 2008 , Garmisch-Partenkirchen, Germany, January 23 - 25, 2008

Boosted Incremental Nelder-Mead Simplex Algorithm: Distributed Regression in Wireless Sensor Networks

Parisa Jalili Marandi[1] and Nasrollah Moghadam Charkari[1]

[1]Parallel Processing Lab, Electrical and Computer Engineering Department, Faculty of Engineering, Tarbiat Modares University, Tehran, Iran

{parisa.jalili, charkari}@modares.ac.ir

Abstract   Wireless sensor networks (WSNs) have been of great interest among academia and industry due to their diverse applications in recent years. The main goal of a WSN is data collection. As the amount of the collected data increases, it would be essential to develop some techniques to analyze them. In this paper, we propose an in-network optimization algorithm based on Nelder-Mead simplex to incrementally do regression analysis over distributed data. Then, we improve the resulted regressor by the application of boosting concept from machine learning theory. Simulation results show that the proposed algorithm not only increases accuracy but is also more efficient in terms of communication compared to its gradient based counterparts.

1 Introduction

A wireless sensor network (WSN) comprises a group of sensors. Sensors usually have low power supply, limited computational capacity and memory. The main use of WSNs is for data collection. As the amount of collected data increases, some methods to analyze them are required [1, 2]. Machine learning approaches are good solutions, in this regard. Transmitting all the collected data to a fusion center for centrally analyzing the behavior of data and modeling it leads to a high accuracy in the final result. But, since communication capabilities of sensors are limited, this central approach significantly drains the energy of each node and decreases the life time of the network as a whole. In order to deviate with this problem, in-network approach is adapted which eliminates the need for transmitting data to the fusion center [3]. In-network processing increases local computation to prevent energy wasting through a large amount of communications required in central approach. Based on [3] a learning problem can be converted into one of optimization which is much easier to be dealt with. Accordingly, we aim to propose an incremental optimization algorithm to do regression analysis over distributed data which should also adapt to the limitations of WSNs. Distributed optimization for WSNs based on gradient optimization has been previously studied in [1, 4, and 5]. For the algorithm proposed in [1] a Hamiltonian cycle is set on sensors prior to optimization. Then, the estimate for parameter vector is transmitted from one neighboring sensor to the other and each sensor, using incremental sub-

Please use the following format when citing this chapter:

Marandi, P.J. and Charkari, N.M., 2008, in IFIP International Federation for Information Processing, Volume 284; *Wireless and Mobile Networking*; Zoubir Mammeri; (Boston: Springer), pp. 199–212.

gradient optimization, adjusts the parameters. The algorithm in [4] shows that clustering the network and setting a Hamiltonian cycle within each cluster not only increases the accuracy of final parameters but also makes the algorithm more robust to failures compared to the algorithm proposed in [1]. While [4] sets a Hamiltonian cycle among nodes of each cluster, [5] sets a Hamiltonian cycle among cluster heads and adapts an approach for each sensor to transmit compressed data to the head of the cluster to which it belongs. This algorithm is much more efficient in terms of accuracy, communication cost, and network latency compared to the previously proposed algorithms. In optimization community, when the form of the objective function is known and it is differentiable, the best decision is to use the first order class of optimization algorithms, where incremental sub-gradient is one of them. However, we have some reasons to apply NM simplex to optimization problem in WSNs which has not been studied previously in the field. In this paper, we first develop an incremental version of NM simplex algorithm for WSNs. According to simulation results, although the accuracy achieved with Incremental NM Simplex algorithm is acceptable, yet it is far from the centralized accuracy and a method is required to improve it. The method applied here is the boosting from the machine learning theory. Boosting was originally developed for binary classification [6]. Later, some versions of it were proposed for multi-class classification [7-9]. Other studies such as [10-13] boosted regressors instead of classifiers. Some parallel and distributed versions of boosting have also been proposed in [14-16]. Our experiments show that boosting really improves the accuracy of the regressor, obtained from Incremental NM Simplex. *Thus the main contributions of this paper are: a) to apply NM simplex rather than gradient based optimization and b) to improve the regression accuracy by boosting, in the context of WSNs.* The rest of this paper is organized as follows. Section 2 provides an overview of supervised learning and its application to WSNs and basics about NM simplex optimization. In section 3, assumptions and problem statement are stated. The motivations to use NM simplex are discussed in section 4. In section 5, we present the proposed algorithm. Experimental results are presented in section 6. Finally, in section 7 we conclude the paper and state some of the future works intended.

2   Preliminaries

In this section required basic knowledge are provided.

2.1   *Supervised Learning and its Application to WSNs*

According to [17], Supervised, Semi-supervised, and Unsupervised are three types of learning. Supervised learning, being the least intelligent, requires a labeled data set indicated as Eq. (1).

$$GD = \{(x_1, y_1)..., (x_N, y_N)\} \tag{1}$$

Where $X = \{x_k\}_{k=1}^{W}$ and $Y = \{y_k\}_{k=1}^{W}$ are feature and label sets, respectively. Features describe data and labels indicate the class to which data belongs. The goal of supervised learning is to learn a function (f) to map X to Y such that $y = f(x)$. There are several algorithms for supervised learning one of which is regression, which fits a model to existing data. For further information about regression refer to [18]. Sensors collect lots of data spatially and temporally. In order to gain benefit of the collected data, there must be some analyzing methods. If we consider these data as a kind of labeled data then supervised learning can easily be applied. Throughout this paper, we will consider a network of sensors distributed in an environment which can measure temperature temporally and localize themselves using an existing efficient localization algorithm such as [19]. Here the labeled dataset includes time and location as features and temperature as the label. Thus supervised learning has to discover the function which given a location in the space and a time epoch can predict the temperature with least possible error.

2.2 Nelder-Mead Simplex Algorithm

NM simplex which was first proposed in 1965 [20] is a local optimization algorithm. There are some works done to free NM simplex from local optima such as [21]. NM simplex employs a regular pattern of points in the search space sequentially to obtain the optimizer. Computationally it is relatively uncomplicated, hence easy to implement and quick to debug [22]. One of the major drawbacks of NM simplex is the lack of convergence proof. Further research, study and experimental results are expected to help understand its behavior. Details of NM simplex algorithm implemented in the experiments of this study are the same as [23] where for termination criterion the approach proposed in [24] is employed.

3 Assumptions and Problem Statement

This section introduces the assumptions and outlines the problem.

3.1 Assumptions

The following assumptions are considered throughout the paper:

1. There are n sensors as $S = \{s_1, ..., s_n\}$, each of which has collected m data.
2. i, j indices are used to refer to i^{th} sensor and j^{th} data in an arbitrary sensor, respectively ($x \in \{1, .., n\}$, $j \in \{1, ..., m\}$). Thus $(x_{i,j}, y_{i,j})$ indicates j^{th} data from i^{th} sensor.
3. Sensors are distributed in a bi-dimensional area. Coordinates of s_i are indicated by dx_i, dy_i.
4. Three features and one label are chosen for describing data such that $x_{i,j} = \lfloor dx_i, dy_i, time_{i,j} \rfloor$ and $y_{i,j} = temperature_{i,j}$, where $time_{i,j}$ and $temperature_{i,j}$ indicate the time of jth measurement and j^{th} temperature in s_i, respectively.

5. Local dataset of s_i is indicated by LD_i, where $|LD_i| = m$.

6. Global dataset, which is the dataset that could be obtained if transmission over long distances was possible, is denoted by GD, where $GD = \bigcup_{i=1}^{n} LD_i$ and $|GD| = N$, where $N = n \times m$.

7. A Hamiltonian path is set among nodes (a distributed algorithm to set a Hamiltonian cycle is described in [25]). This is the routing scheme used in [1]. We selected it because of its simplicity and ability to clarify the main points of the proposed algorithm. Fig. 1 depicts this path. Here we have set a Hamiltonian path rather than a Hamiltonian cycle over the nodes. As every such a cycle can be converted to a Hamiltonian path by removing one of its edges, so the algorithm in [25] is applicable. The reason to set a path rather than a cycle is stated in section 5.2. We assume that s_1 and s_n are the head and the tail nodes of the Hamiltonian path, respectively.

8. As NM simplex is a heuristic method [22], it builds several simplexes to reach the optimizer. The number of local simplexes formed in s_i, which might be different from one sensor to another and depends on the LD_i, is denoted by c_i.

9. Before learning starts, a query dissemination process distributes to all the sensors in the network the user's desired model to fit data. We have followed [26] in fitting a model to data, which suggests some polynomial models among which we chose 'Linear space and quadratic time' which will be called 'quadratic' in the remaining of the paper.

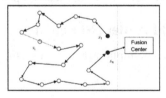

Fig. 1 A Hamiltonian path over the network nodes. Two adjacent nodes on the path can communicate with each other in any direction.

3.2   Statement of the Problem

The goal of the proposed algorithm is to incrementally fit a model to the collected data. Considering the quadratic modeling of the data from section 3.1-Assumption 9, where temperature is to be stated in terms of location and time of measurements, the model is as Eq. (2)

$$F(dx, dy, time) = R[1] \times (dx) + R[2] \times (dy) + R[3] \times (time)^2 + R[4] \times (time) + R[5] \qquad (2)$$

, in which R is a vector of unknown constants. Given a set of basis functions as $(1, time, time^2, dx, dy)$ the algorithm aims to estimate their coefficients such that the final model fits data with less possible error (Similar to the approach used in [26]). Based on [1, 3], the learning problem of F can be converted to an optimization problem to compute R, such that applying least-square error Eq. (3) is minimized:

$$G(R) = \frac{1}{n}\sum_{i=1}^{n}\frac{1}{m}\sum_{j=1}^{m}\left(\begin{array}{l} R[1]\times(dx_i) + R[2]\times(dy_i) + R[3]\times(time_{i,j})^2 + R[4]\times(time_{i,j}) \\ + R[5] - temperature_{i,j}\end{array}\right)^2 \quad (3)$$

That is to say, we would like to determine R in a way that the final model fits all the data with the least possible error. Here, optimization is the same as minimization. So, for quadratic modeling of temperature the problem of learning is converted into a minimization problem with five parameters. As mentioned previously in section 1, it is impossible or at least difficult to centrally compute G, as Eq. (3) is highly dependent on individual data and their transmission to fusion center is energy-consuming. So, it is not feasible to have this formula centrally, but distributed. In fact, there are n sub formulas in the form of Eq. (4):

$$g_i(R) = \frac{1}{m}\sum_{j=1}^{m}\left(\begin{array}{l} R[1]\times(dx_i) + R[2]\times(dy_i) + R[3]\times(time_{i,j})^2 + R[4]\times(time_{i,j}) \\ + R[5] - temperature_{i,j}\end{array}\right)^2 \quad (4)$$

, which when added up give the central formula of Eq. (3). Following this consideration, Eq. (3) is rewritten as Eq. (5):

$$G(R) = \frac{1}{n}\sum_{i=1}^{n}g_i(R) \quad (5)$$

Where $g_i : \Re^L \to \Re$, $G : \Re^L \to \Re$ and L, the length of R, is the number of parameters to be estimated. So, the goal of the proposed algorithm is to do the regression analysis by fitting a pre-specified model to the existing data in a distributed manner and to compute the final parameters as a vector R_G $(|R_G| = L)$.

4 Motivations

The reason to use gradient methods in the previous works was the fact that when the objective function is in hand, having the formula of its first derivative is inevitable. Thus, there is a compelling reason to apply gradient-based optimization. But, examining the previous works revealed some deficiencies that made us to apply another optimization algorithm. Here we have listed the shortcomings encountered:

1. For the incremental sub-gradient method to work, there must be an estimate of Θ, a non-empty, closed, and convex subset of $\Re^L$ in which optimizer is expected to exist [1, 4]. Determining such a subset prior to algorithm execution seems to be a difficult job and the distributed nature of the data makes it even worse.
2. If in any stage of the algorithm execution, the estimate falls out of Θ, a projection must be done to keep the value in the boundary. The experiments showed that the final results highly depend on the projection procedure.
3. In incremental gradient method, at the end of the cycle, parameters suffer from an error. Experiments show that the obtained accuracy for our objective func-

tion is far from the central results. It must be stated that the behavior of optimization methods depends on the objective function and hence, inaccurate results of one method over a special function does not label it as a non efficient method.

4. When the objective function is quadratic, [1] estimates that often one cycle suffices to find the optimizer with a low error. However, their experiments showed that, in one special function, 45 cycles led to the answer, which means large energy consumption.

Based on these, it is desired to propose an algorithm which reduces the final error and frees the user or programmer from specifying Θ as well as the projection procedure. Reduction of communication in the expense of computation increase is another goal followed. NM simplex is selected to fulfill these desires. One of the reasons for applying NM simplex rather than any other optimization method was its popularity among practitioners, despite the absence of any general proof for its convergence. So, further experiments will be helpful to discover the nature of NM simplex. The other main reason to choose NM simplex was its computationally light procedure, which is consistent with the sensors limited computational capacity.

5   Proposed Algorithm

Based on fundamentals of NM simplex described in section 2.2 and the motivations of section 4, in this section we describe the proposed algorithm.

5.1   IS: Incremental NM Simplex

Incremental NM Simplex algorithm, IS henceforth, is illustrated in Fig. 2. Starting from the first sensor on the path, each sensor runs a NM simplex algorithm on the local data and sends the computed parameters to the neighboring sensor. The neighboring sensor uses received parameters as the start point for its local simplex execution. In step II of Fig. 2 the notion of R_{i,c_i} indicates the coefficients of the final local regressor in s_i. As mentioned in section 3.1-Assumption 8, there are c_i locally built simplexes in s_i numbered through 1 to c_i, where $c_i{}^{th}$ simplex leads to the final local optimizer. At the end of the algorithm, s_n includes $R_G = R_{n,c_n}$ and $N = N_{\{1,...,n\}}$. Let's rename R_G as $R_{G,(IS)}$ to distinguish it from global regressor obtained from BIS in the next section. Also the need to calculate N is explained in the next section.

5.2   BIS: Boosted Incremental NM Simplex Algorithm

Although IS solves deficiencies of incremental gradient, yet the accuracy achieved needs to be improved. The idea here is to apply boosting in order to reduce regression error.

```
IS ()

        For i = 1, ..., n:  s_i does the followings:

    I.      Computes g_i, the same as Eq. (4), based on LD_i.
    II.     Runs a local NM simplex, the same as section 2.2, over LD_i, where g_i
            is the local objective function. (starting point for s_i's local simplex
            algorithm is R_{i,0} = R_{i-1,c_{i-1}},  which indicates coefficients of the final
            regressor in s_{i-1}, and R_{1,0} = R_0 is any arbitrary vector in ℜ ).
            If (i ≠ 1)
    III.    Computes N_{(1,...,i)} = N_{(1,...,i-1)} + |LD_i|, where N_{(1)} = |LD_1|.
            If (i ≠ n)
    IV.     Transmits R_{i,c_i} as well as N_{(1,...,i)} to s_{i+1}.
```

Fig. 2 Steps of Incremental NM Simplex (IS) algorithm.

5.2.1 Motivation to apply Boosting

The main idea of boosting as an ensemble learning method is to train several weak learners serially and to combine them in some way in order to compute a final strong learner [8]. Features mentioned in this sentence, were the motivation for the application of boosting to regression in WSNs. In these networks, sensors collect data independently of each other and don't have access to each others' datasets. Therefore, in case each sensor is to train a regressor individually, that regressor will behave weakly over global dataset which could be obtained centrally if transmission of data over long distances was possible. Serial behavior of boosting on the one hand, and setting a Hamiltonian path among nodes on the other, was the second motivation for proposing this method. Based on [15], there are three types of errors present in a learning algorithm which threaten the accuracy of the learner and can be reduced by the boosting. One is the systematic error of prediction technique which is called bias and the other of these three is variance that is engaged with the sample set. The third error is not of interest here (for more information refer to [15]). Boosting is applied to simplex method as it suffers from both bias and variance. The former is due to the dependence of simplex on the starting point and as the objective function is made up of local samples, the latter type is also present. This is the third compelling reason to apply boosting in this paper.

5.2.2 Boosting Procedure

In boosting, the first regressor is trained over the entire dataset where all data are equally important [12]. Then this regressor is evaluated over the entire dataset and weights are assigned to data so that correctly learned data get smaller weights while higher weights are assigned to wrongly learned data (If the weight assigned to a correctly learned data is zero, it means that these data are simply eliminated from the dataset). Then a second regressor is trained over the new weighted dataset which mostly concentrates over data with higher weights. This procedure continues until a desired level of accuracy is achieved. Furthermore, for each weak learner a weight is assigned which expresses its ability in global regression. Finally, all the regressors are combined to compute the global regressor which is much more accurate than any of the individual models [8]. Now, if boosting is to be applied to regression in WSNs, this procedure must be simulated in some way.

5.2.3 Simulation of Boosting Procedure in WSNs

Before simulating the boosting procedure in a WSN, an important point must be highlighted: the difference between the first weak learner and the others. For the first learner, all data are equally important, whereas, the others pay more attention to some partitions of the entire dataset. Since as mentioned in section 5.2.2, for a new weak learner, the dataset is reweighed according to the previous learners' behavior such that the weights of correctly learned data are decreased while the weights of the remaining are increased. Assuming a weight of zero is assigned to correctly learned data, this can be viewed as for the new learner the correctly learned data with the previous regressors is omitted. Therefore, instead of the entire dataset, the learners other than the first consider only one partition of dataset.

5.2.3.1 Simulation of the First Regressor

For the first step of boosting procedure to be simulated in a WSN, all the data must be present in a single node; nevertheless it is not possible because of the restricted power supply of small sensors. The simulation of this step is the IS from section 5.1, which aims at incrementally obtaining a global regressor. Although the result of this simulation is not as accurate as that of the central approach in the first step of boosting, yet it is an appropriate estimation. Now in order to arrive at the weighted dataset needed in the next step, $R_{G,(IS)}$ must be evaluated over the entire dataset, a weight must be assigned to it and the correctly learned data must be eliminated from the sensors (assuming a weight of zero is assigned to correctly learned data). To accomplish these goals a second pass over the nodes is started in which each sensor's dataset is shrunk to exclude correctly learned data with $R_{G,(IS)}$. Each sensor also calculates a partial weight for $R_{G,(IS)}$ by evaluating it over the local dataset and then by giving the partial weight to its neighbor on the path contributes at computing a global weight for $R_{G,(IS)}$, the sum of all the partial weights.

5.2.3.2 Simulation of Next Regressors

If in a WSN partitions mentioned at the beginning of this section could be obtained, the rest of the boosting procedure would also be simulated. If we assume that each sensor monitors its own range of region, then the local data of one will be distinct from that of the others. Based on this, we can further assume that each local dataset (which is now shrunk due to evaluation of $R_{G,(IS)}$) is the same as a partition in the boosting procedure and thus a local regressor obtained over a shrunk dataset matches a weak learner. Let's refer to this as isolated learning in each sensor. But in reality there might be some common parts among different sensors observation areas in such a way that a larger part of a region is monitored by s_i and a smaller part by s_{i+a} $(a \mid a+i \in \{1,...,n\})$, thus in order to train a more perfect local weak learner in s_i, it is desirable to transfer the data collected from smaller part of the region by s_{i+a} to s_i. Similarity in observations is usually among adjacent sensors, leading to data exchange over short distances. However, as the transmission of data is costly even over the short distances, it was decided to transfer the regressors forward instead of transmitting data backward, which was somehow similar to the approach used in [14]. This means that a regressor is computed in s_i and then transmitted to s_{i+a}. Obviously if s_{i+a} includes any similar data to that of s_i, the regressor will fit them correctly. If such data exists, s_{i+a} simply excludes these data from its local dataset, avoiding unnecessary training of another regressor over repeated data. Such a procedure was tested against isolated learning in each sensor. The increased accuracy of the former was negligible in contrast to drained energy, so it was decided not to do this transfer and simply to run a local regressor in individual nodes. Thus to simulate next steps of the boosting procedure:

1. A second pass over the network is started from s_n back to s_1. (This is the same started in the simulation of first regressor in subsection 5.2.3.1).

2. $R_{G,(IS)}$ is evaluated over s_i's local dataset (LD_i) and each local dataset is shrunk to exclude correctly learned data leading to $Shrunk(LD_i)$.

3. A local NM simplex is run over the shrunk dataset and a weak regressor is obtained (R_{i,c_i}).

4. Each weak regressor is evaluated and is assigned a weight in relation to global dataset, whose size is calculated during the first pass over the network in IS.

5. Each sensor also takes part at computing $R_{\{n,...,i\}}$, the partial combination of weighted local regressors.

```
BIS ()

    1. R_G,(IS) = IS()   (from section 5.1,figure 2)
    2. For i = n,...,1:   s_i does the followings:
        I.     Computes W(R_G,(IS))_i = RWP(R_G,(IS),LD_i,N).  (s_n knows N ,global dataset
               size, as IS() is first executed over the network.)
        II.    Shrinks LD_i to include those data wrongly learned by R_G,(IS) and
               refers to new local dataset as Shrunk(LD_i).
        III.   Runs  a  local  NM  simplex  over  Shrunk(LD_i)  and  computes
               R_i,c_i. (Starting point for s_i's local simplex algorithm might be
               any arbitrary point independent of other sensors, and R_i,c_i is
               the regressor obtained after c_i execution of local NM simplex
               in s_i over Shrunk(LD_i)).
        IV.    Computes W(R_i,c_i) = RWP(R_i,c_i,Shrunk(LD_i),N).
               If (i ≠ n)
        V.     Computes W(R_G,(IS))_{n,...,i} = W(R_G,(IS))_{n,...,i+1} + W(R_G,(IS))_i.W(R_G,(IS))_{n} = W(R_G,(IS))_n.
        VI.    Computes R_{n,...,i} = R_{n,...,i+1} + R_i,c_i × W(R_i,c_i) , R_{n} = R_n,c_n × W(R_n,c_n).
               If (i ≠ 1)
        VII.   Transmits R_G,(IS) ,  W(R_G,(IS))_{n,...,i} , R_{n,...,i} , N  to  s_{i-1} as the Hamiltonian
               path is being traversed in the reverse order.
               If (i = 1)
        VIII.  Computes R_G,(BIS) = R_G,(IS) × W(R_G,(IS))_{n,...,1} + R_{n,...,1}.
```

Fig. 3 Steps of Boosted Incremental NM Simplex (BIS) algorithm.

Finally s_1 computes $R_{G,(BIS)}$, the final strong learner in the boosting procedure, as the sum of weighted local regressors and weighted $R_{G,(IS)}$ and transmits it to the fusion center. Boosted Incremental NM Simplex algorithm, BIS henceforth, has two steps and is illustrated more formally in Fig. 3. As IS terminates in s_n, second step of BIS starts from it, thus avoiding an extra direct communication from s_n to s_1 for transmitting two values of $N, R_{G,(IS)}$. Even though this seems to be a minor saving in energy consumption, it is valuable in WSNs context. This is why a Hamiltonian path is set over the nodes rather than a Hamiltonian cycle. Accuracy of each regressor is reflected in its weight, which is the fraction of correctly learned data in relation to the global dataset. We have used a pre-specified threshold to decide if the data is learned correctly. This weighing procedure is suggested in [10] and is illustrated in Fig. 4. So the reason to calculate N in IS from section 5.1 is for computing weights of regressors in the second step of BIS. Also calls to RWP () in Fig. 3, refer to the weighting procedure of Fig. 4.

RWP (R, D, DatasetSize)

- If the number of correctly learned data with R over D is C, then: $W(R) = \dfrac{C}{DatasetSize}$

Fig. 4 Regressor Weighting Procedure

6   Experimental Results

We used the publicly available Intel Lab dataset which contains data collected from 54 sensors deployed in the Intel Berkeley Research Lab. Mica2Dot sensors with weather boards has collected time stamped topology information, along with humidity, temperature, light and voltage values once every 31 seconds [27]. Fig. 5 depicts relation between temperature and time epochs for an arbitrary sensor. All the sensors in the network show the same behavior. It is evident from the figure that except some noisy measurements, a polynomial model, repeated over time intervals, relates temperature to time epochs. Here we evaluate algorithms over such a randomly selected interval. $n = 48$ sensors which contained uniformly distributed measurements over the interval were selected. For each sensor $m = 20$ data were selected. Obviously a single sensor's measured temperatures are constantly related to its location. But for multiple sensors distributed over an area, temperature varies with changes in location. We have decided to consider a linear model for location. Thus the intended model is comprised of some basis functions as ($1, time, time^2, dx, dy$) which is also shown in Eq. 2 in section 3. 2. Additional basis functions such as $time^3, time^4$ ... might improve the regression accuracy. But the important is the relative accuracy of different algorithms, which is independent of the fitting model and depends on the nature of the algorithms applied.

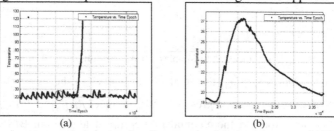

(a)   (b)

Fig. 5 (a) Temperature variation over time for a randomly selected sensor. (b) Temperature over a randomly selected time interval which is also shown by an oval in (a).

6.1   Regression Accuracy

Fig.6 (a) depicts Root Mean Square error (RMS) of regressors obtained from IS, BIS, Incremental Gradient (IG), and Centralized approach. Results shown for IG are for one pass over the network. As it was repeated for more passes, minor improvements were achieved in contrast to consumed energy.

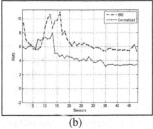

(a)   (b)

Fig. 6 (a) RMS of the final regressor for IG, Centralized approach, IS and BIS. As it is evident from the curves BIS has the least RMS compared to its distributed counterparts. (b) RMS of the BIS and the Centralized approach. For the Centralized curve, RMS in s_i is for the regressor

trained over $\bigcup_{k=1}^{i} LD_k$.

A better accuracy was achieved for 36 more passes over the network, and improved very little after that, which was yet far from that of others. As it is evident from the figure, BIS is superior to its distributed counterparts. Fig. 6 (b) depicts the accuracy of BIS and Centralized algorithm. As it is expected, in both methods, except in some sensors, the overall RMS is decreasing as parameters reach the last sensor, which means that dataset is growing and more data is included. Although RMS of the BIS is not as good as that of the Centralized approach, yet it is better than any other distributed algorithm. The curve of IS in Fig. 6 (a) is also more stable in contrast to that of IG.

6.2   Computation Requirements for IS and BIS

At the first glance, it seems that local computation for the proposed algorithm is much more than that of the IG, but experimental results show that in average, the number of local simplexes formed is low. For IS, the average number of local simplexes formed was 3. For BIS, some additional computations were required in the second step, which had an average of 15 local simplexes produced. Other computations include simple addition and multiplication which are compatible with sensors limited computational capacity. So, altogether computation burden of the proposed algorithms is affordable for sensors.

6.3   Communication Requirements

There are two parameters transmitted among the nodes in IS:

1. Partial global dataset size, which is an integer denoted by $N_{\{1,...,i\}}$.

2. Coefficients of a locally obtained regressor which is a vector of size L .

And four parameters in the second step of BIS:

1. Coefficients of the regressor obtained from IS, which is a vector of size L
2. Partial weight of $R_{G,(IS)}$, which is a double denoted by $W\left(R_{G,(IS)}\right)_i$.
3. Global dataset size which is an integer denoted by N.
4. Partial weighted combination of local regressors which is a double denoted by $R_{\{n,...,i\}}$.

Hence $L+1$ and $L+3$ parameters in IS and in the second step of BIS are transmitted between two adjacent nodes respectively. In IG there is one parameter transmitted: Local regressor which is a vector of size L. Let's denote the number of passes over the network for IG algorithm by P. In the Central approach there are N vectors transmitted from sensors to the fusion center each of which has a size of 3 for assumed labeled dataset as stated in section 2.1. Following [28] and considering the case where n nodes are uniformly distributed in a unit square, the average distance between two successive nodes over a Hamiltonian path is: $O\left(\sqrt{\log^2 n/n}\right)$. Whereas in the Centralized approach the average distance between a sensor and the fusion center is 1 over the unit square. Based on these considerations, Table. 1 shows communication order of four algorithms. Upon termination of BIS, IS, and IG there is a transmission of the final regressor from the last node on the path to the fusion center. As this is common in all three algorithms, it is eliminated from Table. 1. If $P > 1$ and $L > 1$ then $P \times L \geq (L+2) > (L+1)$, thus BIS and IS are more efficient in terms of communication than IG and as usually $L << m$, BIS, IS, and IG are much more efficient than Centralized approach. Compression of transmitted data and other similar strategies can decrease energy consumption even more. Thus in BIS, with two passes over the network a good estimation of regerssor parameters are obtained, which is more accurate than parameters obtained from several passes of IG over the network. Thus a good balance point for the tradeoff between energy consumption and regression accuracy is achieved.

Table 1. Communication order of Centralized approach, (IG), IS, BIS.

Algorithm	Communication Cost
Centralized	$O(3mn) \cong O(mn)$
IG	$O\left(P \times L \times \sqrt{\log^2 n/n}\right)$
IS	$O\left((L+1) \times \sqrt{\log^2 n/n}\right)$
BIS	$O\left(2(L+2) \times \sqrt{\log^2 n/n}\right) \cong O\left((L+2) \times \sqrt{\log^2 n/n}\right)$

7   Conclusions

In this paper we proposed an in-network optimization technique for distributed regression in WSNs. To overcome deficiencies of incremental gradient optimization, NM simplex was applied and an incremental version of it (IS) was developed. Although, the accuracy of IS was higher than that of the incremental gradient, yet improvements were needed. Hence boosting was applied, and the global accuracy did really improve. Experiments also illustrated the actual effect of boosting in improving the accuracy. Efficiency of the proposed algorithm was also analyzed from the point of computation and communication. The conclusion is that, the proposed BIS algorithm is more efficient in terms of accuracy, communication cost, and local computations compared to its gradient based predecessors. Although the accuracy of BIS is closer to that of the central approach, further improvements are required. We have used the least-square error for converting regression to optimization; other error functions which are more robust to noise might be applied. Other optimization algorithms rather than NM simplex should be considered, as well. Examining the evolutionary algorithms and comparing their performance with that of this paper is put for a later time.

Acknowledgements. The authors wish to thank Iran Telecommunication Research Center (ITRC) for partial funding for this research and the PhD candidate Muharram Mansoorizadeh for his constant help during the research. And also thanks to Intel Berkeley Lab for collected data.

References

1. Rabbat, M., Nowak, R.: Distributed optimization in sensor networks. In International Symposium on information processing in sensor networks, ACM Press, Berkley California USA, (2004)
2. Wang, B., He, Z.: Distributed Optimization Over Wireless Sensor Networks using Swarm Intelligence. In: IEEE International Symposium on Circuits and Systems, pp. 2502 - 2505, (2005)
3. Predd, J. B., Kulkarni, S. R., Poor, H. V.: Distributed Learning in Wireless Sensor Networks. J. Signal Processing, vol. 23, pp. 56-69. (2006)
4. Son, S. H., Chiang, M., Kulkarni, S. R., Schwartz, S. C.: The value of clustering in distributed estimation for sensor networks. In: Proceedings of International Conference on Wireless Networks, Communications and Mobile Computing, pp. 969–974, vol. 2, IEEE, Maui, Hawaii, (2005)
5. Charkari, N. M., Marandi, P. J.: Distributed Regression based on gradient optimization in Wireless sensor networks. In: proceedings of first Iranian Data Mining Conference, Tehran, Iran, (2007)
6. Schapire, R.: The strength of weak learnability. J. Machine Learning, vol. 5, pp. 197-227. (1990)
7. Freund, Y., Schapire, R.: A decision Theoretic generalization of on-line learning and an   application to boosting. J. Computer and System Sciences, vol. 55, pp.119-139. (1995)
8. Freund, Y., Schapire, R.: Experiments with a new boosting algorithm. In: Proceedings of 13th International Conference on Machine Learning, Morgan Kaufmann Press, pp. 148-156. (1996)
9. Li, L.: Multiclass boosting with repartitioning. In: Proceedings of the 23rd international conference on Machine learning, ACM Press, vol. 148, pp. 569 - 576. (2006)
10. Solomatine, D. P., Shrestha, D. L.: AdaBoost.RT: a Boosting Algorithm for Regression Problems. In: IEEE International Joint Conference on Neural Networks, IEEE Press, vol. 2, pp. 1163 - 1168. (2004)

11. Wang, L., Zhu, X.: A Modified Boosting Based Neural Network Ensemble Method for Regression and Forecasting. In: 2nd IEEE Conference on Industrial Electronics and Applications: IEEE Press, pp. 1280-1285 (2007)
12. Avnimelech, R., Intrator, N.: Boosting regression estimators. J. Neural Computation, vol. 11, pp. 491--513. (1999)
13. Drucker, H.: Improving Regressors using Boosting Techniques. In: Proceedings of the 14th International Conference on Machine Learning, pp. 107--115. (1997)
14. Lazarevic, A., Obradovic, Z.: Boosting Algorithms for Parallel and Distributed Learning. In: Distributed and Parallel Databases, Kluwer Academic Press, vol. 11, pp. 203–229. (2002)
15. Yu, C., Skillicorn, D. B.: Parallelizing Boosting and Bagging. Technical Report, Queen's University, Kingston, Ontario, Canada K7L 3N6 February (2001)
16. Lozano, F., Rangel, P.: Algorithms for parallel boosting. In: Proceedings. Fourth International Conference on Machine Learning and Applications, (2005)
17. Chapelle, O., Scholkopf, B., Zien, A.: Semi Supervised Learning. MIT Press, (2006)
18. Draper, N. R., Smith, H.: Applied Regression Analysis. Wiley Press, (1998)
19. Langendoen, K., Reijers, N.: Distributed localization in wireless sensor networks: a quantitative comparison. In: J. Computer and Telecommunications Networking, vol. 43, pp. 499-518. (2003)
20. Nelder, J. A., Mead, R.: A simplex method for function minimization. J. *Computer* vol. 7, pp. 308-313. (1965)
21. Pedroso, J. P.: Simple Metaheuristics Using the Simplex Algorithm for Non-linear Programming, vol.4638, pp. 217-221. Springer Berlin, (2007)
22. Reklaitis, G. V., Ravindran, A., Ragsdell, K. M.: Engineering Optimization: Methods and Applications. John Willey Press, (1983)
23. Lagarias, J. C., Reeds, J. A., Wright, M. H., Wright, P. E.: Convergence properties of the Nelder-Mead simplex method in low dimensions. *SIAM J. Optima,* vol. 9, pp. 112-147. (1998)
24. Padmanabhan, V., Rhinehart, R. R.: A Novel Termination Criterion for Optimization. In: Proceedings of the Americal Control Conference, vol. 4, pp. 2281 - 2286. Portland, OR, USA, (2005)
25. Petit, J.: Hamiltonian cycles in faulty random geometric networks. In: proceedings of International Workshop on Approximation and Randomization Algorithms in Communication Networks, BRICS Aarhus, Denmark., (2001)
26. Guestrin, C., Bodi, P., Thibau, R., Paskin, M., Madde, S.: Distributed regression: An efficient framework for modeling sensor network data. In: proceedings of third international symposium on Information processing in sensor networks, ACM Press, pp. 1–10. Berkeley, California, USA, (2004)
27. "http://berkeley.intel-research.net/labdata/."
28. Rabbat, M., Nowak, R.: Quantized Incremental Algorithms for Distributed Optimization. IEEE J.Sel Areas Commun, Vol.23, no. 4, pp. 798-808. (2005)

UMTS HSPA and R99 Traffic Separation

Xi Li, Richard Schelb, Carmelita Görg and Andreas Timm-Giel

Xi Li, Carmelita Görg and Andreas Timm-Giel
TZI-ikom, Communication Networks, University of Bremen, Germany,
e-mail: xili I cg I atg@comnets.uni-bremen.de

Richard Schelb
Nokia Siemens Networks GmbH & Co. KG, Germany, e-mail: richard.schelb@nsn.com

Abstract This paper presents a general traffic separation approach to transmit HSPA traffic in the existing ATM-based UMTS network, together with Release 99 (R99) traffic. The traffic separation technique enables QoS differentiations of HSPA and R99 traffic, while at the same time aims to achieve a maximum utilization of the transport resources in the radio access network. The potential benefit of applying traffic separation and its impact on the performance of the transport network as well as the end users are explored in this paper. The quantitative evaluations are provided by means of simulations. The results presented are obtained from a UMTS simulation model developed in this work which transmits both HSPA and R99 traffic, either with traffic separation enabled or disabled.

1 Introduction

Universal Mobile Telecommunication Systems (UMTS) is a key standard of the third-generation (3G) WCDMA-based cellular network. With the development and expansion of 3G cellular networks, UMTS evolution continues to unfold, with the range of the offered services rapidly extending from primarily voice telephony to a variety of appealing data and multimedia-based applications. It is expected that data services like Internet access, email, FTP upload/download, will constitute a dominant traffic share in UMTS networks. In order to significantly improve the support of such delay-tolerant data services with enhanced resource efficiency and service quality, High Speed Downlink Packet Access (HSDPA) [1] and High Speed Uplink Packet Access (HSUPA) also named as Enhance Uplink [2] are introduced by 3GPP Release 5 and Release 6 individually, as the evolution of UMTS to enhance the transmission of data packet traffic on the downlink and uplink separately. They offer a much higher data rate (up to 14.4 Mbps in the downlink with HSDPA and 5.76 Mbps in the uplink with HSUPA), lower latency,

Please use the following format when citing this chapter:

Li, X., Schelb, R., Görg, C. and Timm-Giel, A., 2008, in IFIP International Federation for Information Processing, Volume 284; *Wireless and Mobile Networking*; Zoubir Mammeri; (Boston: Springer), pp. 213–224.

increased system capacity and thus facilitate improved data services. HSDPA and HSUPA are jointly referred to as High Speed Packet Access (HSPA) [3]. So far, HSPA services have been already supported in the existing ATM-based UMTS networks to enhance data transmissions. Besides, the UMTS system still accommodates a significant amount of Release 99 (R99) traffic such as voice telephony. In R99, user traffic is transported via Dedicated Channels (DCHs) over the radio interface. For HSPA traffic, in order to support their new features like fast Hybrid Automatic Repeat Request (HARQ), fast NodeB scheduling, and using a shorter 2ms Transmission Time Interval (TTI) (mainly for HSDPA and optionally for HSUPA), HSDPA establishes a new downlink transport channel called High-Speed Downlink Shared Channel (HS-DSCH) that is shared by all HSDPA UEs in the cell. In HSUPA, for each UE a new uplink transport channel called E-DCH (Enhanced Dedicated Channel) is used to provide high-speed uplink traffic transmission. HSPA traffic is characterized by high peak data rates and high burstiness. To support such HSDPA traffic on the downlink and HSUPA traffic on the uplink, not only the UMTS air interface but also the backhaul of the UMTS access network, namely UMTS Terrestrial Radio Access Network (UTRAN), will require considerably high transport capacity for the provisioning of high-speed transmission of packet data. In addition, R99 and HSPA services have rather different QoS requirements: R99 mainly carries delay sensitive traffic like voice or streaming services; whereas HSPA traffic is primarily interactive and background traffic which is insensitive to the delay. Thus, how to efficiently transport R99 and HSPA traffic in the same radio access network while guarantying their individual QoS requirements is a big challenge for designing the evolved UMTS network.

This paper introduces a general traffic separation approach to transmit both HSPA and R99 traffic in the existing ATM-based UMTS networks, providing a differentiated QoS support for each type of traffic according to its individual QoS requirements. The traffic separation technique is based on using separate ATM Virtual Paths (VPs) or Virtual Circuits (VCs) for transmitting different types of traffic each with a different ATM QoS class. The major contribution of this paper is to investigate how much performance gain can be achieved by applying traffic separation in terms of user throughput, packet losses, and link layer transport efficiency, and in addition what will be the impact on the dimensioning of the transport network, i.e. the Iub interface between the RNC and the NodeB. To achieve a cost-efficient dimensioning for the transport network, an optimum configuration shall be desired. For the performance analysis, we take the HSDPA and R99 traffic scenario as an example for the investigations in this paper, where only HSDPA and R99 traffic are transmitted. The rest of the paper is organized as follows: Section 2 describes the problem of carrying HSDPA and R99 traffic without any traffic separation. Section 3 introduces the basic concept of traffic separation. Section 4 addresses configurable parameters for the traffic separation, and possible traffic separation configurations for transmitting R99, HSDPA and HSUPA traffic in the same radio access network. Section 5 presents the simulation results and the performance analysis. The end gives conclusions and the future work.

2 Problem Description

Figure 1 illustrates the evolved UMTS system with integrated R99 and HSPA services. It is seen that one UMTS cell supports (1) normal UMTS R99 users like traditional voice users; (2) HSDPA users who require HSDPA service for high-speed data transfer on the downlink, e.g. Internet access; (3) HSUPA users who only uses HSUPA service for uplink data transmissions, e.g. FTP upload; (4) or HSPA users who use HSUPA on the uplink and HSDPA on the downlink simultaneously. HSPA technology is integrated directly into the existing UMTS nodes, i.e. NodeB and RNC, via software/hardware updates. Thus, the Iub interface between the RNC and NodeB carries both HSPA and R99 traffic.

R99 and HSPA traffic have different delay requirements on the transport network. There is an extremely strict delay constrain on the Iub interface for DCH channels of R99, not only due to the delay requirements of the user traffic itself but also because of the requirements derived from supporting radio control functions such as outer-loop power control and soft handover. The excessively delayed Frame Protocol packets (their delay is larger than predefined delay boundaries) will be discarded at the NodeB as they become too late to be sent over the air interface for the allocated time slot. However, HSPA traffic has significantly lower delay requirement on the Iub interface. Because for both HSDPA and HSUPA a fast scheduling is introduced at the NodeB which reserves the time slot on the air interface replacing the scheduling at RNC in R99, and furthermore there is buffering in the NodeB which supports fast HARQ. Thus, the delay requirements for HSPA are essentially only due to the service itself, which are mainly delay-tolerant best effort services that have loose constraints on the delay and delay variations. Thanks to the R99 traffic having a much more stringent delay requirement on the Iub interface, the R99 traffic is usually given a higher priority to transmit over the HSPA traffic.

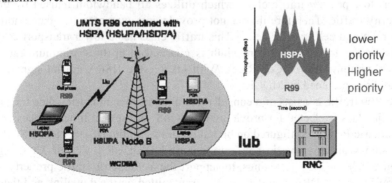

Fig. 1 UMTS Network supporting R99 and HSPA traffic

In the currently deployed UMTS system, the UTRAN transport network is ATM-based. In the case without using any traffic separation at the Iub interface, the R99 traffic and HSPA traffic are carried within a single, end-to-end ATM CBR (Constant Bit Rate) VP (Virtual Path). Without traffic separation, there are two major problems: (1) the transport network treats all UTRAN traffic with equal priority. Thus, the stringent delay requirements of the R99 traffic can not be guaranteed as it strongly depends on the behavior of HSPA traffic. Moreover, in case of congestion on the Iub link, the network will discard ATM cells irrespective of their importance, e.g. high priority R99 or inband signaling traffic could be skipped in favor of low priority HSDPA or HSUPA data. (2) With CBR for the common VP, a fixed transport bandwidth is reserved without considering any potential multiplexing gain. Thus the high quality ATM service category CBR is overspecified for the transport of Best Effort HSPA traffic, and this causes unnecessary cost in terms of leased ATM bandwidths.

3 Concept of Traffic Separation

The basic idea of traffic separation technique is to apply separate ATM Virtual Paths (VPs) or Virtual Circuits (VCs) with different ATM QoS categories to transmit different traffic types. One example of using traffic separation to transmit R99, HSDPA and HSUPA traffic at the Iub interface is depicted in figure 2. In this example, each traffic type is carried by one individual ATM VP. R99 traffic is transported with ATM CBR (Constant Bit Rate) [4] service category. It is defined as high priority traffic class, where bandwidth is reserved up to requested Peak Cell Rate (PCR) with guaranteed cell loss ratio and cell transfer delay. This also means a high transport cost. While the transport of Best Effort HSDPA and HSUPA traffic uses ATM traffic class UBR (Unspecified Bit Rate) [4] or UBR+ [5][6]. UBR is a best effort service and is the lowest class of service in ATM. It is defined as low priority traffic class, which utilizes all bandwidth unused by the high priority traffic. Therefore it does not provide any guarantees for bandwidth, cell loss ratio and cell transfer delay. This traffic class has a lower transport cost. UBR+ is similar to UBR, but bandwidth is guaranteed up to a minimum rate - MDCR (Minimum Desired Cell Rate). With UBR+, the HSPA inband signaling traffic can be guaranteed by MDCR.

As the R99 traffic consists of a considerable amount of symmetric voice traffic, CBR traffic class is elected for providing high QoS for the real time services and also symmetric PCR is configured on both directions. On the HSDPA and HSUPA path, it allows an asymmetric configuration of UBR/UBR+ VPs or VCs, e.g. asymmetric PCR or MDCR settings, to support the asymmetric traffic property of HSPA traffic, i.e. HSDPA user data is only transmitted on the downlink and there is a small amount of inband signaling traffic on the uplink, and HSUPA user data is only transmitted on the uplink with a small amount of inband signaling on the downlink.

With traffic separation, the network transmission cost for the low priority

HSPA traffic will be reduced. The transport of Best Effort HSDPA/HSUPA traffic with UBR/UBR+ allows the low priority HSPA traffic to use any free bandwidth in the transport network. Depending on the structure of transport network, significant multiplexing gain can be achieved for the HSDPA/HSUPA path(s). Moreover, by separating the HSPA and R99 traffic on different ATM paths, data loss in the Realtime R99 path can be avoided in case of network congestion, e.g. during bursts of Best Effort HSPA traffic. By using different ATM service categories for R99 traffic and HSPA traffic, the transport network is able to handle the R99 and HSPA traffic with different priorities and during congestion it can preferably discard the Best Effort HSPA traffic. Thereby, the QoS of the R99 traffic is protected from the bursty HSPA traffic.

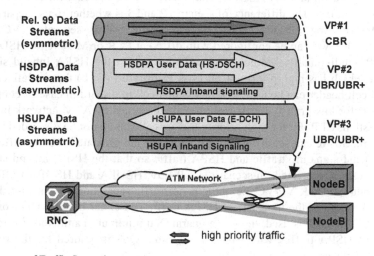

Fig. 2 Concept of Traffic Separation

4 Configuration of HSPA and R99 Traffic Separation

For setting up a traffic separation scenario, we need to configure the following ATM parameters:
- PCR (Peak Cell Rate) is the upper limit of the traffic that can be submitted to the link.
- MDCR (Minimum Desired Cell Rate) defines a minimum guaranteed cell rate on UBR VC. It is optionally configured on either a VC or VP connection.

PCR is required to configure for both ATM CBR and UBR/UBR+ service categories. Maximum allowed bandwidth can be set different for the uplink and downlink by means of an asymmetric PCR configuration of VPs and VCs. MDCR is only configurable for UBR+ VP/VCs.

To transport HSDPA, HSUPA and R99 traffic simultaneously in the UTRAN transport network, there are mainly four possible scenarios to be considered:

1. 3 VPs: 1 CBR VP for R99, 1 UBR/UBR+ VP for HSDPA, 1 UBR/UBR+ VP for HSUPA;
2. 2 VPs: 1 CBR VP for R99, 1 UBR/UBR+ VP for HSPA with separated VCs to transmit HSDPA and HSUPA;
3. 2 VPs: 1 CBR VP for R99, 1 UBR/UBR+ VP for HSPA without separated VCs to transmit HSDPA and HSUPA;
4. 1 VP: 1 Common CBR VP or VC to carry all traffic types.

Scenario 1 applies three VPs each transferring one traffic type. Scenario 2 and 3 uses two VPs: 1 VP is assigned for R99 and the other one for the HSPA traffic. For these two cases, the HSDPA data traffic will be mixed with HSUPA inband signaling traffic and the HSUPA data traffic will be mixed with HSDPA inband signaling traffic. The difference of scenario 2 and 3 is whether to use separate VCs for transmitting HSDPA and HSUPA traffic. With separated VCs, each UBR/UBR+ VC can be configured with different PCR or MDCR for HSDPA and HSUPA individually. Moreover, in order to protect the HSPA inband signaling traffic which has high priority, Cell Loss Priority bit (CLP) that is defined in the ATM cell header can be used to select which cell to discard in case of congestion: CLP=1: for low priority traffic, cell may be discarded by ATM network in case of congestion; CLP=0: for high priority traffic, cell should not be discarded by ATM network. So we can set different CLP value for the separated VCs to differentiate the inband signaling traffic and HSPA traffic so that the HSPA inband signaling traffic can be protected. In scenario 4, all R99, HSUPA and HSDPA traffic share one common CBR VP/VC, i.e. there is no traffic separation in this case. For scenario 1, 2 and 3, the transport of HSPA traffic can either be on a UBR or UBR+ VP. If UBR+ VP is used, there is a guaranteed minimum bandwidth for transmitting the HSPA traffic, with which a minimum QoS is assured for the requested HSPA services.

5 Result Analysis

This section presents the simulation results. For the analysis of traffic separation, following we take the HSDPA and R99 traffic scenario as an example in this paper for the investigations. In the following part, the results of applying traffic separation to transport both HSDPA and R99 at the Iub interface is presented and compared to the scenario without traffic separation. The parameter settings for the traffic separation and its impact on the dimensioning will be also discussed. Additionally one example of the Iub dimensioning with traffic separation and without traffic separation is given and their transmission efficiency is compared. Though the case of transporting HSDPA, HSUPA and R99 traffic will not be presented in this paper, the general impact of applying traffic separation on the performance and the Iub dimensioning will be similar.

5.1 Simulation Scenario Description

The simulation scenario consists of one NodeB and one RNC. As mentioned above, in this paper we focus on the HSDPA and R99 traffic scenario for the performance analysis. The simulation model of HSDPA and R99 were developed in OPNET [11]. R99 model implements all functions and radio protocols according to the 3GPP specifications. In the HSDPA model, a Round Robin air interface scheduler is used in the simulations. In addition, in order to protect the congestion on the Iub link, flow control and congestion control schemes are applied in the Iub. The HSDPA traffic is modeled with 20 Internet users browsing the web. The web traffic model is defined by ETSI standards [7], the traffic model parameters are given in Table 1. Each user requests multiple pages where the inactive time between pages follows the geometric distribution. The same traffic model is used for generating the R99 traffic where multiple Packet Switched (PS) Radio Access Bearers (RABs) are available for transmitting the data.

When no traffic separation is applied in the Iub interface, R99 and HSDPA traffic are sharing one common ATM CBR VP, where the AAL2 priority is applied which assigns higher priority to R99 traffic over the HSPA traffic. While in the case of using traffic separation, two ATM VPs are established: the transport of R99 traffic is over one ATM CBR VP and the transport of HSDPA traffic is on an ATM UBR+ VP. Here UBR+ VP is set to low priority.

Table 1. ETSI Traffic Model

Page Interarrival Time (IAT) (Reading Time)	Geometric distribution mean interarrival time = 5 seconds
Page size	Pareto distribution parameters: Shape=1.1, location=4.5 Kbyte, max page size = 2 Mbyte mean page size = 25 Kbyte

The following metrics are used for performance evaluation:
- Application Throughput: the average throughput of transferring a web page at the application layer, excluding reading time period. The normalized application throughput is given in simulation results defined as the ratio of the application throughput under certain Iub link bandwidth to the maximum application throughput under an ideal Iub capacity.
- Cell Discard Ratio: in case of congestion of the Iub link, the ATM cells are discarded. The packet discard ratio is measured as the ratio of discarded ATM cells to the total ATM cells sent to the Iub link.
- TCP Retransmission Counts: the total number of TCP retransmissions.
- Link Utilization: the Iub link throughput over the given Iub link bandwidth. The link throughput includes transport network overheads as well as all TCP/RLC retransmissions.

5.2 Impact of Traffic Separation

In this section, the influence of traffic separation (TS) is investigated by comparing to the scenario without traffic separation technique in use in the transport network. In this example, there is in average 815.9kbps HSDPA traffic and 968.7kbps R99 PS traffic on the Iub link. In both with and without traffic separation cases, the offered HSDPA and R99 traffic is fixed while the common Iub link rate is step by step increased. For the configuration with traffic separation, the PCR of CBR VP for transport of the R99 traffic is set to 1600kbps, whereas the MDCR of UBR+ VP for transmitting the HSDPA traffic is increased from 0kbps up to 1400kbps which results in the increase of the total Iub link bandwidth.

Figure 3 compares the performance difference of using and not using traffic separation. It shows that with the usage of traffic separation technique, the end user application throughput is improved while the cell losses and resultant TCP retransmissions are reduced significantly. The major reason is that traffic separation provides a minimum bandwidth guarantee for HSDPA traffic, thus the HSDPA traffic will get less influence from the R99 traffic. Though the link utilization is similar in both scenarios, there is more link load contributed by RLC and TCP retransmissions in the case of no traffic separation.

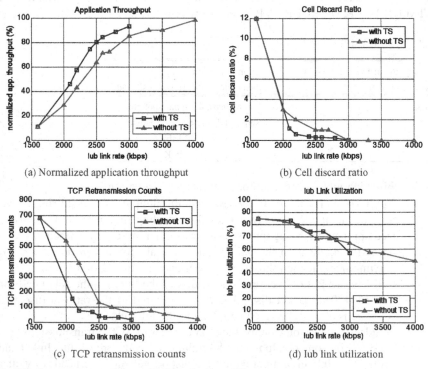

(a) Normalized application throughput

(b) Cell discard ratio

(c) TCP retransmission counts

(d) Iub link utilization

Fig. 3 Performance comparisions: with TS and without TS

From these results, we can conclude that to achieve the same application through-put or cell discard ratio target, using traffic separation needs less bandwidth on the Iub link, which means a more efficient utilization of the transport resources. For example, to achieve 90% normalized application throughput, applying traffic separation requires 2800kbps while no traffic separation requires 3300kbps on the Iub link. The obtained bandwidth saving is 15%. To guarantee less than 1% cell discard ratio, using traffic separation requires minimum 2100kbps bandwidth while no traffic separation requires minimum 2500kbps on the Iub link. The obtained bandwidth saving is 16%.

5.3 Impact of MDCR Settings for UBR+ VP/VC

This part discuses the influence of MDCR settings of ATM UBR+ VP/VC on the overall performance, based on the results of the traffic separation scenario in the above example shown in figure 3. As the PCR of CBR VP for transport of the R99 traffic is fixed to 1600kbps, the MDCR of UBR+ VP (MDCR = the total Iub link rate – allocated bandwidth on R99 path) for transmitting the HSDPA traffic varies from 0kbps up to 1400kbps. It can be observed from figure 3 that with the increased MDCR rates the end user application performance is improved considerably: the normalized application throughput is increased from 11% to 95%. Because with a higher MDCR rate, there is more bandwidth reserved for HSDPA traffic, and therefore the performance is better. Besides the improvement of application performance with a higher MDCR setting, the network performance is also enhanced. It is observed that RLC delays, cell discard ratio, number of TCP retransmissions are all decreased when MDCR increases. But on the other hand, the link utilization drops down due to a higher Iub link bandwidth caused by larger MDCR rates is configured to transfer the same offered traffic. Therefore, MDCR should be chosen as a compromise of the system performance and the Iub link utilization. That means, MDCR rate should be set properly to achieve the maximum link utilization while stratifying the QoS target.

Moreover it is observed that the application performance is much more sensitive to the MDCR setting than transport network performances. When MDCR is larger than 500kbps (i.e. Iub link rate = 2100kbps), the transport network performance such as cell discard ratio, TCP retransmissions, has been improved drastically. And afterwards, with further increased MDCR rate, the pace of the improvement is reduced and becomes more stable. But the application throughput is still quite low with 500kbps MDCR rate: only 46% of normalized application throughput is achieved. In order to achieve more than 90% of the application throughput, the MDCR need to be set higher than 1200kbps. So it is basically a choice of network operation to decide the MDCR rate based on its predefined QoS target. If the transport network performance is more important, then a smaller MDCR is adequate. If the end user application performance is the main target of the dimensioning, the MDCR rate needs to be configured to a relative higher value.

5.4 Dimensioning Results

This section presents the results of dimensioning of the Iub link, which transmits the HSDPA and R99 traffic either with or without Traffic Separation (TS) technique. In the following example, R99 traffic contains 50% web traffic (web traffic model is defined in Table 1) and 50% voice traffic with AMR codec. The voice model consists of a series of ON and OFF periods with a service rate of 12.2kbps with Adaptive Multi-Rate (AMR) codec specified by 3GPP. ON and OFF states are exponentially distributed with a mean duration of 3 seconds [8]. HSDPA consists of purely web traffic (Table 1). In the following results, we fix the R99 traffic load and gradually increase the offered HSDPA traffic to the Iub link, and investigate the bandwidth demand for transferring the combined HSDPA and R99 traffic satisfying the predefined QoS targets of both traffic types. In this example, the QoS target for R99 traffic is 1% packet discard ratio and for HSDPA 95% normalized application throughput.

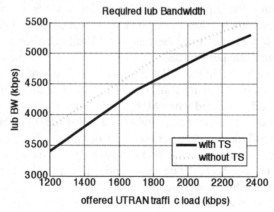

Fig. 4 Required Iub Bandwidth for different UTRAN load

Figure 4 shows the required Iub link bandwidth over different offered UTRAN traffic loads in kbps. The offered UTRAN traffic is the total sum of traffic entering UTRAN network including HSDPA and R99. It shows that with the increased traffic demand, the required Iub bandwidth to achieve the predefined QoS targets is increasing. It can be also obviously seen that, the required Iub bandwidth for the traffic separation scenario is much lower than that for the case without traffic separation. Therefore it is concluded that applying the traffic separation technique brings a significant bandwidth saving for the Iub dimensioning, which reduces the transport cost.

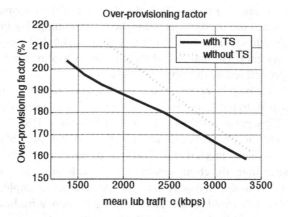

Fig. 5 Over-provisioning factor over Iub link throughput

The required capacity can be also expressed in terms of "Over-provisioning factor", β, which relates the capacity in the link (C) to the aggregated mean bit rate R_{iub} on the Iub link as given in the formula: $C = \beta \cdot R_{iub}$ [9]. This parameter indicates in addition to the mean traffic load on the Iub link how much extra bandwidth is needed in order to fulfill the QoS requirements. Figure 5 shows the obtained over-provisioning factor in percentage of the mean Iub traffic. As observed from figure 5, the degree of over-provisioning decreases for higher traffic load on the Iub link in both with TS and without TS scenario. That means, with a larger traffic load a higher multiplexing gain is achieved which results in decreased over-provisioning factor. Furthermore, with traffic separation technique less extra bandwidth is required for transmitting the same amount of the traffic on the Iub link. And moreover, at the lower traffic load range, the over-provisioning factor of without traffic separation is much higher than that of the traffic separation scenario, and with the increase of the aggregated traffic load their gap is slowly reduced. This implies the traffic separation is able to achieve more bandwidth savings (compared to without traffic separation) at a lower mean Iub traffic load, where the room for the potential multiplexing gain is more.

6 Conclusion

This paper proposes using a traffic separation approach to transmit HSPA and R99 traffic transport in the same radio access network. We investigated the impact of using traffic separation, and explored its advantage compared to the case without traffic separation by analyzing the example of HSDPA and R99 traffic scenario. The simulation results show that the using traffic separation technique greatly improves the end user performance as well as the transport network performance, which in turn saves the bandwidth on the Iub link for achieving the same QoS level. Therefore, it brings a more efficient utilization of the transport resources in UTRAN and reduces the transport cost for the dimensioning. By investigating the different MDCR settings, it is concluded that MDCR should be chosen as a compromise of the system performance and the Iub link utilization, and also dependent on the QoS target defined by the network operator.

In this paper, we mainly present the traffic separation results for HSDPA and R99 traffic scenario. In the future work, we will further evaluate the performances of applying traffic separations for the transport of HSDPA, HSUPA and R99 traffic in the UTRAN transport network, according to the four possible traffic separation scenarios introduced in section 4. Traffic separation approach is a generic approach for transmitting different services (each with different QoS constrains) over different paths in the transport network. As another example, it can be also applied in a Carrie Ethernet-based UTRAN (using Pseudo-Wire Emulation (PWE) [10] to emulate the ATM service over Ethernet as the transport network), a UBR path can be used for transmitting the best effort data service while the delay sensitive real time service like voice telephony is transmitted over a CBR path.

Acknowledgments This work is carried out within the research project Mature (**M**odeling and **A**nalysis of the **T**ransport Network Layer in the **U**TRAN Access Network **RE**search). The partner of this work is the Nokia Siemens Networks GmbH & Co. KG, Germany.

References

1 3GPP TS 25.855 High Speed Downlink Packet Access (HSDPA): Overall UTRAN description (Release 5)
2 3GPP TS 25.309 V6.3.0, FDD Enhanced Uplink; Overall description (Release 6)
3 Erik Dahlman, "3G Evolution: HSPA and LTE for Mobile Broadband"
4 ATM Forum UNI 3.1, UNI 4.0
5 ATM Forum, Addendum to TM 4.1: Differentiated UBR. CA. Juli 2000.
6 ATM Forum, Addendum to TM 4.1 for an Optional Minimum Desired Cell Rate Indication for UBR. CA. Juli 2000
7 ETSI, Universal Mobile Telecommunications System (UMTS): Physical layer aspects of UTRA High Speed Downlink Packet. 3GPP TR 25.848
8 IST-2000-28088 Project: Models and Simulations for Network Planning and Control of UMTS (MOMENTUM)
9 H. Galeana-Zapién, R. Ferrús, J. Olmos, "Transport Capacity Estimations for Over-provisioned UTRAN IP-based Networks", IEEE WCNC, 2007
10 X. Li, Y.Zeng, B. Kracker, R.Schelb, C.Görg and A. Timm-Giel, "Carrier Ethernet for Transport in UMTS Radio Access Network: Ethernet Backhaul Evolution", 2008 IEEE 67th Vehicular Technology Conference VTC2008-Spring, May 2008, Singapore, 2008
11 Thushara Weerawardane, Xi Li, Andreas Timm-Giel and Carmelita Görg, "Modeling and Simulation of UMTS HSDPA in OPNET", OPNETWORK 2006, September, 2006, Washington DC, USA

Measuring Quality of Experience of Internet Access over HSDPA

Manuel Álvarez-Campana, Enrique Vázquez, Joan Vinyes and Víctor Villagrá

Dept. Ingeniería de Sistemas Telemáticos, ETSI Telecomunicación

Ciudad Universitaria s/n; 28040 – Madrid (Spain)

{mac, enrique, vinyes, villagra}@dit.upm.es

Abstract   High-Speed Downlink Packet Access (HSDPA) is being introduced by mobile operators as a solution both for increasing the downlink throughput and for achieving a more efficient usage of the radio resources. This work analyses the quality of experience of HSDPA users, based on experiments and measurements over a commercial network. The effect of multiple users sharing the overall capacity of the cell is explicitly evaluated. The results show that the HSDPA user experience for Internet access is satisfactory and in some cases comparable to that achievable over fixed access technologies such as ADSL. In addition, we explore the impact of TCP configuration on the HSDPA performance and suggest suitable parameter values.

1   Introduction

UMTS (Universal Mobile Telecommunication System) networks based on 3GPP Release 99 specifications provide a maximum downlink throughput for packet-switched (PS) services of 384 kbit/s. From the user point of view, this bit rate may provide an acceptable quality of experience for Internet applications such as web browsing and e-mail, although lower than in fixed access technologies (e.g. ADSL or cable).

From the operator's perspective, however, the way UMTS Rel 99 PS services are provided over the radio interface is far from efficient. The reason is that these services are supported over dedicated radio channels (despite shared channels were defined in the specifications). This limits the maximum number of PS users that can be simultaneously served by an UMTS cell, especially at 384 kbit/s (5 or 6 users at most). In addition to that, considering the high burstiness of many Internet applications, dedicated radio channels are often underutilized.

Please use the following format when citing this chapter:

Álvarez-Campana, M., Vázquez, E., Vinyes, J. and Villagrá, V., 2008, in IFIP International Federation for Information Processing, Volume 284; *Wireless and Mobile Networking*; Zoubir Mammeri; (Boston: Springer), pp. 225–234.

Fortunately, 3GPP Release 5 specifications introduce the HSDPA (High-Speed Downlink Packet Access) technology [1]. Besides increasing the downlink throughput, a key aspect of HSDPA is the use of the High-Speed Downlink Shared Channel (HS-DSCH). This new channel allows for a better utilization of radio resources for packet data services, especially when considering applications that generate intermittent traffic. However, the fact that the HS-DSCH channel is a shared resource requires considering the impact of multiple users simultaneously competing for the channel capacity.

The performance of HSDPA has been investigated in the last years. Most of the studies, however, rely on analytical models or simulation techniques [2], in general following a theoretical approach. As the number of HSDPA networks in operation grows and users start utilizing them, there is a lack of knowledge about the real performance provided by this technology. Some recent papers present results based on measurements in laboratory [3], in scenarios that clearly differ from the real conditions found in a live network. A few studies based on measurements on commercial HSDPA networks have been published [4, 5]. These studies, however, focus on measurements related to one HSDPA user only, without taking into account the influence of other simultaneous users sharing the capacity of the cell. While this aspect can be neglected in early network deployments, as the number of users increases it should definitely be taken into account.

One of the main contributions of our work is the realization of measurements in a scenario with multiple HSDPA users simultaneously accessing to the same cell. The results led us to investigate the impact of the TCP configuration parameters on the observed performance.

The rest of the paper is organised as follows. Section 2 introduces the main aspects that influence the performance of HSDPA networks. Section 3 describes the measurement scenario and the experiments carried out. Sections 4 and 5 present and discuss the results of the measurements with multiple HSDPA users. Section 6 analyzes the performance improvement that can be achieved by tuning some TCP configuration parameters. Conclusions and plans for future work are given in section 7.

2 HSDPA performance issues

HSDPA technology represents the first of a number of enhancements that increase the bit rates offered through 3GPP radio access networks. More specifically, it focuses on increasing the downlink throughput for packet based services, while at the same time providing a more efficient usage of radio resources than in UMTS Release 99. The fist goal is achieved by combining several advanced capabilities including AMC (Adaptive Modulation and Coding), HARQ (Hybrid-ARQ), and fast scheduling mechanisms. The second goal is based on using a common channel, HS-DSCH (High-Speed Downlink Shared Channel), shared among the HSDPA users of the cell.

The maximum downlink throughput achievable by one HSDPA user depends on several issues. Propagation conditions limit the efficiency of AMC and H-ARQ mechanisms. The downlink bit rate is also limited by the terminal category, which determines the modulation scheme and the maximum number of simultaneous OVSF (Orthogonal Variable Spreading Factor) codes that the terminal can use. Currently, most operators support terminals of category 12 (1.8 Mbit/s) and category 6 (3.6 Mbit/s), although other categories (e.g. category 8 with 7.2 Mbit/s) providing higher speeds are expected soon. These bit rates are defined at physical layer, without considering the overhead of the protocol stack above the radio layer. In any case, note that these bit rates surpass the maximum of 384 kbit/s offered with dedicated channels in UMTS Release 99.

Another limiting factor to consider is the number of OVSF codes allocated to the HS-DSCH channel in the cell. The HDSPA specifications allow assigning up to 15 codes to HS-DSCH. However, the number of available codes depends on whether the HSDPA service is offered over a dedicated 5 MHz WCDMA carrier or over an existing carrier providing conventional UMTS services as well. The later option is adequate for early phases of HSDPA deployment, provided that the overall traffic load in the cell is low. In this case, the overall capacity of the cell is distributed between UMTS and HSDPA services, with a number of OSVF codes reserved for each traffic type. Currently, many cells in operation are shared by UMTS and HSDPA services, typically with only 5 OSVF codes allocated to HS-DSCH. As HSDPA gains popularity, a dedicated carrier for HSDPA traffic may be more appropriate, particularly in areas with high traffic load (e.g. business areas). This solution allows up to 15 OVSF codes for the HS-DSCH channel.

As the number of users concurrently using the HS-DSCH channel increase, the maximum throughput achievable by each one decreases. Initial users did not observe this effect, because there were few HSDPA terminals in operation and the probability of having other competing users in the same cell was low. However, as the total number of HSDPA subscribers increases, this probability becomes higher and the capacity sharing effect must be taken into account.

Another relevant issue when evaluating the performance of HSDPA for Internet access is the behaviour of TCP. It is a well-known fact that the performance of TCP connections worsens over wireless networks. This is true also for HSDPA, as discussed in section 6.

3 Measurement scenario

In order to evaluate the performance of HSDPA in a real network, the measurement scenario depicted in Fig. 1 was arranged. The measurements were performed in one of the teaching laboratories at Universidad Politécnica de Madrid, which is in the coverage area of an HSDPA/UMTS macro cell located in the university campus. The cell has five OVSF codes allocated for HSDPA and a backhaul link formed by 3 E1 lines using IMA (Inverse Multiplexing over ATM). We were not able to exclude other users in the same cell during our experiments. However, in normal conditions this particular cell is lightly loaded, so during the test periods most of the traffic was generated by our terminals. Additionally, note that our goal was to assess the user experience during normal network operation, not the maximum performance achievable in ideal conditions. In future tests, we plan to repeat the measurements in other cells with heavier load values and compare the results obtained.

A total of 28 students distributed into two shifts participated in the measurements campaign. The measurements were performed from 11:00 to 14:00, and repeated during five days, from Monday to Friday.

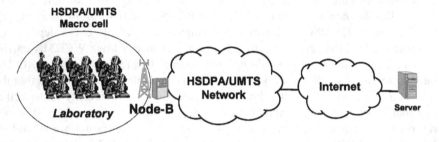

Fig. 1 Measurement scenario.

To perform the measurements, each student had a desktop computer with a Category 6 (3.6 Mbit/s) HSDPA modem. The students performed several basic experiments including web navigation sessions, web-based on-line speed tests, and file downloads.

4 Web navigation experiments

The first experiment consisted in a five minute web navigation session. In order to quantitatively evaluate the HSDPA performance, a basic throughput measurement software was running in the laboratory desktops. Fig. 2 shows the probability density function (PDF) and the complementary cumulative distribution function (CDF) for the downlink peak rate observed in the experiments.

The download peak rate was between 128 kbit/s and 1750 kbit/s, with an average value of 870 kbit/s. The complementary CDF graph indicates that 85% of the users got a download peak rate above 550 kbit/s. These values correspond to net bit rates measured at application level. Taking into account the overhead added by the protocol stack, the non-optimum indoor propagation conditions at the laboratory, and, of course, the high number of HSDPA users simultaneously active in the cell (up to 14), the results obtained are satisfactory.

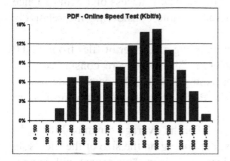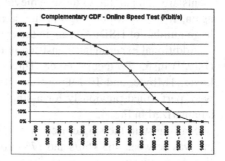

Fig. 2 Downlink peak rate results for web navigation experiments

In order to make a subjective evaluation of performance, the students rated the quality of the HSDPA service between 1 and 5, resulting in an average score 3.4. For comparison purposes, the same experiment was performed using the fixed broadband access infrastructure of the laboratory, giving an average score of 4.3.

5 File transfer experiments

In a second set of experiments, we used a well-known Spanish web portal that offers an on-line speed test application. Residential users with broadband Internet access lines utilize this type of test applications to get an indication of the access speed actually provided by their ISP (which often is well below the maximum speed values advertised by the provider.) The speed test normally consists in exchanging a number of web pages (or files) with different sizes between the user and the server in both directions. In our case, students performed the speed test over HSDPA with the results shown in Fig. 3.

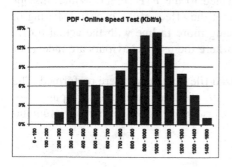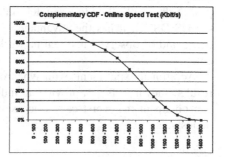

Fig. 3 Results for on-line speed tests

Downlink speed values ranged from 234 kbit/s to 1338 kbit/s, with an average value of 826 kbit/s. 85% of the users got values above 560 kbit/s. These measurements are comparable to those achievable with an ADSL access of 1 Mbit/s. Once again, it is worth pointing out the satisfactory results considering the relatively large number of HSDPA users in the cell.

Additional experiments consisted in downloading a number of files from a FTP (File Transfer Protocol) server. Three different file sizes were considered: 100 kbyte, 1Mbyte, and 10 Mbyte. For comparison purposes, the same experiments were performed previously for a single HSDPA user in the cell. The results are summarized in Fig. 4.

Starting with the single user case (Fig. 4, left), the average download throughput was between 465 kbit/s and 1734 kbit/s, depending on the size of the file. Note that the results are considerably better for large file sizes. This aspect will be analyzed in section 6.

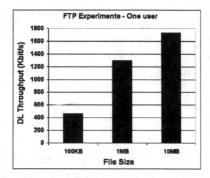 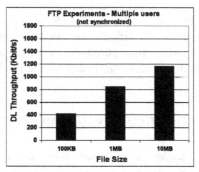

Fig. 4 Summary of results for file transfer experiments

For the scenario with multiple users (Fig. 4, right), the average download throughput was between 422 kbit/s and 1165 kbit/s. When interpreting these results, it is necessary to observe that the experiments were not synchronized. That is, students performed freely the file downloads without taking into account how many of them were simultaneously connected to the FTP server. While this approach does not allow to accurately interpret the effect of the capacity sharing in the HS-DSCH, it has the advantage of being more in line with the actual traffic that could be observed in a real network, where the user behaviours are independent.

Additional experiments with synchronized file downloads were performed. The results, shown in Fig. 5, provide an indication of the minimum throughput a user can obtain in the worst case when several users are downloading files simultaneously.

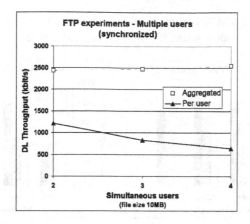

Fig. 5 Results for synchronized file transfer experiments

6 TCP configuration

As mentioned in section 2, the degradation of TCP over wireless networks is a well known issue. On the one hand, packet losses in the radio path are misinterpreted as congestion by TCP, causing a temporal reduction of throughput. On the other hand, the relatively large delays in the wireless link have a direct influence on the duration of slow start and congestion recovery phases. While HSDPA includes a number of features aimed to reduce both packet loss and delay, both effects are still present and negatively affect the performance of TCP.

A number of solutions have been proposed to cope with this type of impairments in wireless networks, and therefore may be applied to HSDPA: modified TCP stacks, performance enhancing proxies, cross-layering mechanisms and TCP parameter tuning. In our experiments, we opted for the last approach as it simply requires adjusting the TCP configuration settings of the operating system in the user desktop computers.

Among the different TCP configuration parameters, we focused on the TCP receive window size and the selective acknowledgement (SACK) option. In the first case, the idea is to use large window sizes in order to allow filling the "pipe" during long transfers. The reasoning behind this is that while delay in HSDPA is lower than in previous systems (GPRS or UMTS Rel 99), this reduction is compensated with higher bit rates, making the overall bandwidth-delay product (BDP) or "pipe size" bigger. Using large window sizes makes it advisable to activate the SACK option in order to avoid retransmitting large amounts of packets in the event of packet losses.

To evaluate the impact of the TCP configuration on the HSDPA performance, we repeated the FTP experiments for the single user case varying the receive window size, with the SACK option on and off. The results are summarized in Fig. 6 for the following window sizes: 17, 64, 128, and 256 kbyte.

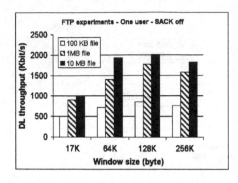
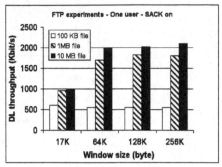

Fig. 6 Impact of TCP receive window size and SACK option in FTP downloads

The smallest window size, 17 kbyte, is clearly insufficient for the bandwidth-delay product of the HDSPA connection and therefore gives low throughput values. Nevertheless, it should be noted that there are still many computers that use this TCP receive window size. In fact, this was the default TCP configuration found in the laboratory computers where the experiments were performed. More recent versions of operating systems use larger window sizes, typically 64 kbyte. The graphs show that a 64 kbyte window provides a much better performance, close to the optimum. Larger window sizes, such as 128 or 256 kbyte, provide marginal improvements only, or may even cause a degradation of throughput due to retransmissions. This effect is corrected by activating the SACK option, as shown in Fig. 6. For example, in our experiments with 1 Mbyte file and SACK off, the maximum throughput is obtained for the 128 kbyte window. Doubling the window size to 256 kbyte results in a lower throughput, but turning on the SACK option this effect is corrected.

The performance improvement obtained by increasing the window size is more noticeable for the larger file sizes: 1 and 10 Mbyte. For small files, using large TCP windows and SACK does not seem to provide a performance improvement. The explanation is that for small files the TCP connection setup hand-shake procedure and the slow start mechanism prevent the full use of the capacity available in the HSDPA link. In other words, the connection may finish without having reached the maximum achievable throughput.

This observation is relevant for the web navigation experiments as well. Recent studies report a typical web page size of around 130 kbyte [6], which is close to the smallest file size considered in our experiments. Therefore, we can conclude that for web navigation, if the user is browsing pages in different servers the moderated size of the web pages themselves does not permit to fully exploit the high bit rates provided by HSDPA. However, there is a growing trend in using web navigation programs for downloading files or reading e-mail messages with attachments. In those cases, the downloaded objects may be considerably bigger (1 Mbyte or more), therefore making large TCP receive windows and SACKs highly recommendable.

Finally, the students repeated the on-line speed test experiments using different window sizes and turning on and off the SACK option. The results are shown in Fig. 7.

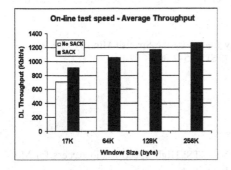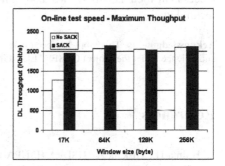

Fig. 7 Impact of TCP receive window size and SACK option in on-line speed tests

The best combination of TCP parameter settings in our experiments is a receive window of 256 kbyte with the SACK option active. This configuration gave an average downlink throughput of 1270 kbit/s. This represents an improvement of around 80% compared with the worst case, corresponding to a receive window size of 17 kbyte without SACKs. As indicated above, a 64 kbyte window gives reasonably good throughput values.

7 Summary and conclusion

This work evaluates the quality of experience of Internet access over HSDPA based on measurements made in a commercial network. A main contribution is the realization of measurements in a scenario with multiple HSDPA users simultaneously accessing to the same cell. Several experiments were performed, including web navigation and file transfer with different file sizes, with up to 14 simultaneous users. Despite the high variability of the results, overall the experiments showed that performance and user-perceived quality are quite satisfactory. For example, in one of the experiments reported above we measured downlink throughput values between 234 kbit/s and 1338 kbit/s, with an average value of 826 kbit/s. In this particular case 85% of the users got throughput values above 560 kbit/s. Other experiments described in the paper produced similar results.

Another set of experiments focused on evaluating the performance impact of the TCP receive window size and the Selective ACK option. The results prove that, for file sizes above 1 Mbyte, large receive window sizes (64 kbyte or more)

with SACK lead to higher download throughputs (up to 80% increase in some experiments).

Future work currently under consideration includes repeating the experiments in several cells with different background traffic load, measuring delay and jitter, and experiments with HSDPA category 8 devices. Taking into account the operators' plans for the imminent introduction of HSUPA (High Speed Uplink Packet Access) in their networks, we also consider extending the measurements to that technology.

Acknowledgments. This work has been partially funded by the Spanish Ministry of Education and Science under the project CASERTEL-NGN (TSI2005-07306-C02-01).

References

1. Holma H., Toskala A.: HSDPA/HSUPA for UMTS: High Speed Radio Access for Mobile Communications, John Wiley & Sons, June 2006.
2. Assaad M., Jouaber B., Zeghlache D.: TCP Performance over UMTS-HSDPA System, Telecommunication Systems, vol. 27, no. 2-4, pp. 371-391, Springer, October 2004.
3. Holma H., Toskala A.: 3GPP release 5 HSDPA measurements, 17th Annual IEEE International Symposium on Personal, Indoor and Mobile Radio Communications (PIMRC), Helsinki, 2006.
4. Derksen J., Jansen R., Maijala M., Westerberg E.: HSDPA performance and evolution, Ericsson Review, No. 3, 2006.
5. Jurvansuu M., Prokkola J., Hanski M., Perälä P.: HSDPA Performance in Live Networks, IEEE International Conference on Communications, ICC'07, June 2007.
6. Levering R., Cutler M.: The Portrait of a Common HTML Web Page, Proceedings of the 2006 ACM symposium on Document engineering, DoEng'06, October 2006, Amsterdam.

Impacts of Air Interface Call Admission Control on UTRAN Transport Simulations

Yi Chen, Xi Li, Richard Schelb, Carmelita Görg and Andreas Timm-Giel

Yi Chen, Xi Li, Carmelita Görg and Andreas Timm-Giel
TZI-ikom, Communication Networks, University of Bremen, Germany,
e-mail: chenyi|xili|cg|atg@comnets.uni-bremen.de

Richard Schelb
Nokia Siemens Networks GmbH & Co. KG, Germany, e-mail: richard.schelb@nsn.com

Abstract This paper investigates the potential impacts caused by Call Admission Control (CAC) mechanism of the air interface on simulations carried out for the transport network domain of UMTS Radio Access Network. Independent from the TNL CAC mechanism of the transport network which is in charge of Iub link bandwidth, the Radio CAC function deals with the highly non-linear resources needed for an attempted connection depending on its specific propagation and interference situation. The consideration of the air interface acting as bottleneck results into a less challenging amount of traffic for the transport domain. In this work, a simulation model with Radio CAC mechanism is implemented to study this correlation, and evaluate the UTRAN transport network performance given a limited radio capacity. The analysis on the impact of the Radio CAC is derived from qualitative simulations.

Key words: UMTS, UTRAN, Iub, CAC, RRM, Dimensioning

1 Introduction

In Wideband Code Division Multiple Access (WCDMA) networks like Universal Mobile Telecommunication System (UMTS) network, Call Admission Control (CAC) plays an essential role for the network capacity allocation and prevents the network from being overloaded. Consequently, it guarantees Quality of Service (QoS) requirements of different types of services. As one of the important Radio Resource Management (RRM) functions, CAC is being used to protect the ongoing connections by limiting the capacity utilization below a certain level [1].

As specified in 3GPP [2], in addition to the CAC at the air interface (between UE and NodeB), there is also admission control required at the transport network of UMTS Terrestrial Radio Access Network (UTRAN), especially at the Iub interface (between NodeB and RNC) where the transport resource is scarce. Accordingly, the terms of Radio CAC and Transport Network Layer (TNL) CAC are used in the

Please use the following format when citing this chapter:

Chen, Y., Li, X., Schelb, R., Görg, C. and Timm-Giel, A., 2008, in IFIP International Federation for Information Processing, Volume 284; *Wireless and Mobile Networking;* Zoubir Mammeri; (Boston: Springer), pp. 235–246.

rest of this paper for the CAC algorithm locating at the air interface to protect the radio resource and at the Iub interface for the protection of ATM link bandwidth, respectively.

So far a lot of research has been ongoing to study the impact of CAC algorithms. [3] [4] present a work of estimation the required radio capacity of WCDMA in downlink, and [5] investigates the effects of the TNL CAC algorithm on Iub dimensioning. But the work from the current research is lack of investigating the effects caused by the coexistence of Radio CAC and TNL CAC. Therefore, a UMTS simulation model with both Radio CAC and TNL CAC is implemented in OPNET modeler and their impacts on the UTRAN transport network performance are studied in this paper.

The rest of the paper is structured as follows: Sect. 2 introduces the system model, including the principles of Radio CAC algorithm and examples of how to estimate the required transmission power in downlink at NodeB; The simulation results and analysis are presented in Sect. 3, where the impacts of Radio CAC are sensitively studied; finally, conclusions are given.

2 System model

2.1 Model Overview

CAC algorithm is composed of TNL CAC and Radio CAC, which manage the transport and radio resources respectively. The transport resource at the Iub interface is the allocated link bandwidth and the radio resource is represented in the total transmission power of base station. TNL CAC function is applied in UTRAN transport network to control the traffic load entering the Iub interface [5]. At the transport layer, each new Dedicated Channel (DCH) connection reserves certain bandwidth in order to protect the QoS. TNL CAC will check whether there is still enough bandwidth for this connection by comparing of the offered Iub link bandwidth with the sum of required bandwidth of this new connection and the already allocated bandwidth. If the requirement of a new connection exceeds the offered Iub link bandwidth, it will be rejected by TNL CAC, and no new connections are allowed until the link resource is released by other admitted connections.

Beside TNL CAC, another limiting factor of CAC is the radio interference, when considering a WCDMA radio interface. An interference-based admission control strategy, Radio CAC is introduced in the UTRAN model, which estimates the power increment caused by the requested radio access bearer and limits the total power consumption not over than the transmission power of base station.

Usually, the downlink capacity is expected to be more important than the uplink capacity because of a majority of asymmetric downloading type of traffic in UMTS. Therefore, within this work only downlink interference-based CAC is implemented.

Assuming each NodeB in this UTRAN model has a maximum transmission power, which indicates its radio capacity. The power consumption caused by a connection request is from two aspects: one is the intercellular interference from adjacent cells, as variable scrambling codes are not as "orthogonal" as the own-cell signal; the other one is the power needed to overcome path loss. To avoid this overloading radio CAC needs to check that power increase caused by the admittance will not exceed the predefined limitation before admitting a connection request. Once the required power is over the predefined level, the connection request will be rejected by Radio CAC.

To estimate the power increase of a connection request, two steps are needed. One is to estimate power consumption as a function of interference; the other one is to find an appropriate propagation model to evaluate the path loss. These two steps are explained in the following part.

2.2 Estimation of Required Transmission Power of NodeB

Firstly, it starts from the assumption that due to the fast power control the UEs are able to obtain exactly the minimum average E_b/N_o required for the service. It also assumes that UEs are uniformly distributed in each cell and thus cells are equally loaded, and the total transmit power of different NodeBs is equal. The generic link quality equation [3] for the downlink connection i is expressed by:

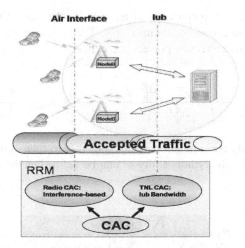

Fig. 1 shows the location of CAC algorithm. The first restriction of the system is from radio interface. Only the traffic accepted by the radio interface is the offered load of access network. After that, TNL CAC manages the Radio CAC allowed traffic and controls the traffic into access network. Therefore, the remaining traffic in the access network is the admitted part of TNL CAC.

$$\rho_i = \frac{W p_i / L_{m,i}}{R_i \left((1 - \alpha_i) P / L_{m,i} + P \sum_{n=1, n \neq m}^{N} 1 / L_{n,i} + P_N \right)}, \; i = 1, \dots, I. \tag{1}$$

The description of the parameters in Equ. 1 is shown in the table below:

Table 1 Parameters used in generic link quality equation in downlink

Parameter	Description
p_i	The required transmit power at NodeB m for the connection i, $i = 1, \dots, I$ Where I is the number of radio link (RL) connections in the cell.
P_N	The thermal noise power, which is set to $-101.2dBm$ in this work.
R_i	The bit rate, determined by RAB rate of different service type.
W	The chip rate, in this work, WCDMA chip rate $W = 3.84Mcps$.
P	The required total transmission power of the NodeB, which indicates the radio capacity.
$L_{m,i}$	The path loss from the serving NodeB m to UE i.
$L_{n,i}$	The path loss from another NodeB n to UE i.
ρ_i	The E_b/N_o requirement for the UE i, including the SHO combining gain and the average power raise caused by fast power control.
N	The number of relevant neighboring NodeBs.
v_i [1]	The effective channel activity for the UE i, which is set to value 0.5 for speech and value 1 for data service.
α_i	The orthogonality factor, which depends on multi-path propagation conditions in downlink.

[1] appears only in later equations

To solve the Equ. 1 a function p_i of an individual required transmit power at NodeB m for the connection i is obtained [3]. The total transmission power P is a sum of the individual connection powers in a cell.

$$P = \frac{P_N \sum_{i=1}^{I} \frac{\rho_i R_i v_i}{W} L_{m,i}}{1 - \sum_{i=1}^{I} \left[\frac{\rho_i R_i v_i}{W} \left((1 - \alpha_i) + f_{DL,i}\right)\right]}, f_{DL,i} = \frac{L_{m,i}}{L_{n,i}} \tag{2}$$

In order to simplify the simulation model, the other-to-own-cell interference ratio in downlink $f_{DL,i}$ and the orthogonality α_i can be defined as the average. Thus the Equ. 2 becomes:

$$P = \frac{P_N \sum_{i=1}^{I} \frac{\rho_i R_i v_i}{W} L_{m,i}}{1 - \sum_{i=1}^{I} \left[\frac{\rho_i R_i v_i}{W} \left((1 - \alpha) + f_{DL}\right)\right]} \tag{3}$$

From the above Equ. 3 the path loss $L_{m,i}$ from the serving NodeB m to UE i can be estimated by using an extended COST-231HATA model with the frequency band $1500 <= f(MHz) <= 2000$ [7] using a set of predefined parameters: working frequency f, distance d between UE and antenna, base station antenna height h_{Base} and the height of the mobile antenna h_{Mobile}.

Note that in this Radio CAC implementation the connection does not occupy any radio resource when it is in Common Channel (CCH). That means the transmission power needed to overcome the interference caused by CCH is negligible.

In a summary, the parameters used to estimate the required transmission power of NodeB in downlink direction are the distance between UE and NodeB antenna, the required Radio Access Bearer (RAB) rate and its associated E_b/N_o value, and channel activity for different services. All these parameters vary according to the changes of mobile environment.

3 Simulation results and analysis

3.1 Simulation Configuration

The simulation model developed in [6] is extended with Radio CAC algorithm. The simulation scenario is composed of one NodeB and one RNC and in between is the Iub interface, on which the system performance is investigated. Web users are simulated using the web traffic model with Pareto distributed page size of an average value $50kbyte$. User data transmission uses HTTP1.1 over TCP Reno. The reading time between pages is exponentially distributed with a mean of 5 seconds. Http application is generated on a $2Mbps$ E1 link where $1.6Mbps$ is actually used for user plane data transfer.

An additional information UE location is needed in radio CAC. The location information is the distance between UE and its serving NodeB with a cell range of $(1km, 5km]$.

In this radio CAC algorithm each NodeB supports three cells, and the cell index is equally distributed among the connected users. If the new connection is admitted, the cell index, together with UE location information are recorded since radio CAC deals with cell specific power and interference.

3.2 Performance Metrics

As the changing of RAB rate affects the required transmission power estimation CAC algorithm is considered when:

- Connection establishment
- Channel Type Switching (CTS) between DCH and FACH/RACH
- Bit Rate Adaptation (BRA)
- Handover (hard/soft handover)

For evaluating radio CAC function and its impacts on the UTRAN network, the statistics Radio CAC reject connection ratio and TNL CAC reject connection ratio are defined as the number of connections rejected by the CAC algorithm over all over connection requests. For each different RAB request, it has its own Radio CAC and TNL CAC reject ratio.

Other metrics also need to be considered to evaluate the whole system performance, like the end-to-end application delay at application layer, packet discard ratio which reflects the transport layer performance and ATM link throughput as well.

3.3 System Performance with Varying Radio Capacity

The system performance is observed with a varying radio capacity from $35dBm$ to $100dBm$ under traffic load 40%, 50% and 70%.

Reject ratios of Radio CAC and TNL CAC are shown in Fig. 2 presents the system capacity restriction is migrating from radio capacity to a limited Iub link bandwidth when the maximum transmission power of NodeB increasing from $35dBm$ to $100dBm$. Higher reject ratio of CAC means less traffic is allowed to enter into the access network. Therefore, most traffic is rejected by Radio CAC at the point of $35dBm$ transmission power as radio capacity is quite low and limits the traffic. Since the traffic is mainly constrained by Radio CAC at the air interface, the Iub link capacity is relatively large thus no traffic is rejected by TNL CAC.

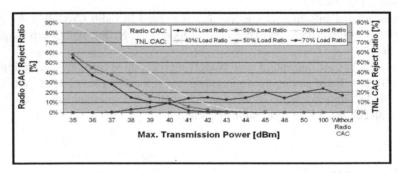

Fig. 2 Reject Ratios of Radio CAC and TNL CAC

High Radio CAC reject ratio leads less traffic in the transport network, thus the transport layer performance is better due to less congestion, consequently, a higher application delay at application layer. Fig. 3(a) and Fig. 3(b) illustrate the system performance at application layer and transport layer respectively.

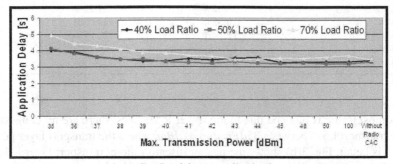

(a) Application delay at application layer

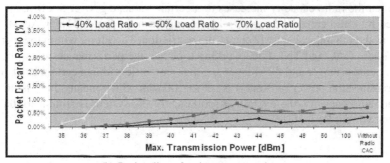

(b) Packet discard ratio at transport layer

Fig. 3 System performance at application layer and transport layer

In spite of the variation of traffic load, application delay in Fig. 3(a) has the same tendency that a long application delay is caused by low radio capacity and it decreases when transmit power is increased from $35dBm$ to $41dBm$. However, the application delay does not substantially decrease afterwards since the restriction moves from radio capacity to Iub link capacity. As the Iub link capacity is fixed, the application delay is in a stable state.

The long application delay means the requested application data are transmitted with a low speed in the lower layers. By comparing the RAB ratio in Tab. 2 with maximum transmission power $35dBm$ and $50dBm$ respectively, we can see that at a low radio capacity lower RAB rate sets are used for the data transferring as more transmission power is required when switching to higher RAB rates. This causes the data transferring using lower RAB rates, e.g. ratio of RAB type $PS8/8$ is 9.96% and $PS64/256$ is 1.84% with $35dBm$ radio capacity, and they change to 0.00% and 10.16% respectively when radio capacity increases to $50dBm$.

Table 2 RAB rate ratios of maximum transmission power of $35dBm$ and $50dBm$

RAB Rate Ratio ($UL-rate/DL-rate$) [kbps]	Max. Transmission Power	
	$35dBm$	$50dBm$
PS 8/8	9.96%	0.00%
PS 32/32	26.88%	10.01%
PS 32/64	29.02%	27.20%
PS 64/64	19.55%	27.50%
PS 64/128	12.74%	22.69%
PS 64/256	1.84%	10.16%
PS 64/384	0.02%	2.44%

As most traffic is blocked due to the lower RAB rates, there are no congestions in the transport layer between $35dBm$ and $41dBm$, where the transport layer performance is better. Fig. 3(b) shows the packet discard ratio at transport layer is lower than 3% when transmission power is not larger than $41dBm$.

When the radio capacity increases to a certain value, e.g. over 50dBm, the limit caused by radio capacity is getting lower; on the other hand, TNL CAC starts to work as the Iub link capacity becomes the restriction. Therefore, within the region of both Radio CAC and TNL CAC working together, the performances of application layer, transport layer and ATM layer are changing little within a certain level. When the transmission power of NodeB is set to $100dBm$ which means there is no limit on the radio capacity, the overall performance of the system is similar to that of a system without Radio CAC.

3.4 Correlation of Radio CAC and System Performance

Based on the measurements in the Sec. 3.3, the association between Radio CAC reject ratio and system performance under different layers can be evaluated by calculating their correlation coefficient (c.c.) values. Taking an example of the correlation calculation between Radio CAC and application delay, the radio CAC reject ratio and application delay, two measurement sets are observed by varying radio capacity from $35dBm$ to $100dBm$. So the strength of linear association of these two measurement sets can be calculated using the standard measure correlation coefficient.

As illustrated in Fig. 4(a), from the sign of the c.c. values two RAB rate changing cases (new connection requesting and channel type switching) have a same linear relationship with the system performance. However the strength of association varies under different layers. The sign of the c.c. values represent the effects are positive or negative, i.e. when Radio CAC reject ratio increases it has a higher application delay, lower packet discard ratio at transport network and less ATM link throughput. In other words, higher Radio CAC reject ratio leads a worse performance in application layer but a better performance at transport layer.

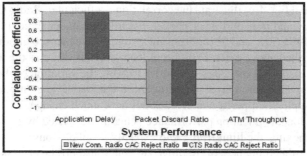

(a) Radio CAC and system performance

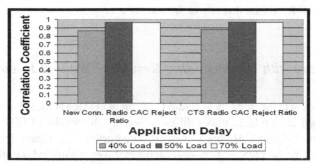

(b) Radio CAC and application delay

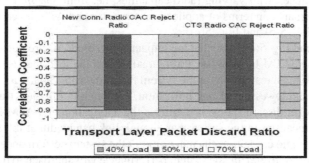

(c) Radio CAC and transport layer packet discard ratio

Fig. 4 Correlation coefficient values

If Radio CAC reject ratio increases, the application delay increases at the same time as they has positive c.c. value. That means the reduction of radio capacity will make the application performance worse as only lower RAB rate set is allowed. The contrast is the transport layer and ATM link performance which have negative c.c. values. The more radio capacity is offered, the more congestion is caused in lower layers. And transport layer is more sensitive to the Radio CAC reject ratio than ATM link layer, if we compare their c.c. values that transport layer has a c.c. value -0.9 which is smaller than the ATM link layer c.c. value -0.8.

Fig. 4(b) and Fig. 4(c) illustrate the correlation coefficient of Radio CAC with application delay and transport layer packet discard ratio under three different traffic load levels: 40%, 50% and 70%. From these figures we can see although the relationship described above exists in different load levels, it varies as the load changes.

When the load level increases from 40% to 50%, the variation of the effect from Radio CAC on application layer is significant. If the load level continues increasing to 70%, the application performance does not have much change. The main reason is under high load, application performance is mainly restricted by Iub link capacity and at the same time the limit from radio capacity is not obvious.

Obviously, the influence of Radio CAC on transport layer is significant in Fig. 4(c), and increases when the load level increasing, since Radio CAC affects the selection of RAB rate directly in the transport layer.

3.5 Compare with Dimensioning Results of Without Radio CAC

In order to evaluate the impacts of Radio CAC on the UTRAN dimensioning results, the traffic load is simulated under different levels. The results of UTRAN dimensioning without Radio CAC are shown in blue curves which have recommended bandwidth where the QoS of Transport Network layer is satisfied, i.e. the transport layer packet discard ratio is less than 1%. Based on the dimensioning results, Radio CAC is introduced with varying radio capacities, i.e. from $35dBm$ to $50dBm$. The system performance in terms of application, transport and ATM layer are observed in Fig. 5(a), Fig. 5(b) and Fig. 5(c).

Fig. 5(a) and Fig. 5(c) show that the impacts of Radio CAC are not significant in application and ATM layer at low traffic load. When the load increases, low radio capacity is the main restriction for the system that shown $35dBm$ has a highest application delay and lowest ATM link utilization. Although in Fig. 5(b) transport layer has lower packet discard ratios, it sacrifices the application and ATM layer performance. This means even the system has enough link bandwidth at Iub interface the relative small radio capacity is the main limit to the system performance. If the radio capacity increases to $50dBm$ the system performance will approach to the blue curve where the restriction moves to Iub link bandwidth. As it is seen from Fig. 5(c) the link utilization is identical when the maximum transmission power is set to $50dBm$. However, the application and transport layer performances are not identical, especially the packet discard ratio which is lower than the blue curve. This difference shows even the restriction of the system is from the Iub link bandwidth, the limit of radio capacity still can affect the selection of high RAB rates. This impact is shown in Fig. 5(a), application delay still increases while Iub bandwidth increasing to $5100kbps$, as data traffic is transmitted using lower RAB rates in transport layer.

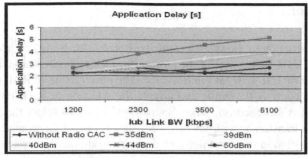

(a) Application delay

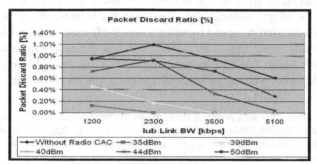

(b) Packet discard ratio

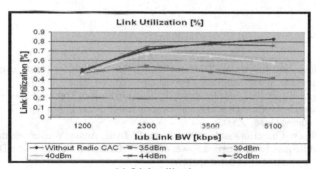

(c) Link utilization

Fig. 5 Comparison of dimensioning results

Base upon the analysis of system performance, Radio CAC controls the traffic offering onto the access network further limits the traffic bursty therefore has a better transport layer performance, however the application performance gets worse as data are transmitted using lower RAB rates.

4 Conclusion

As another restriction to the system capacity, Radio CAC brings an additional bottleneck to the UTRAN network at the air interface with a limited radio capacity and is independent of TNL CAC at Iub interface. The introduction of Radio CAC to the system model controls the traffic and affects the selection of RAB rates when the BRA function is switched on. Since Radio CAC limits to select the higher RAB rates, data are transferred with lower speed, thus it has a higher application delay and less congestion in transport network domain. Additionally, the impacts are not identical in different layers. The experience shows it has more influences on transport layer than ATM layer as Radio CAC can affect the selection of RAB rates directly and the effects will increase along with the increase of traffic load. As it limits the data transferring speed by using lower RAB rates, transport layer performance are getting better. Therefore, by comparing the dimensioning results from the system without Radio CAC, the system with Radio CAC can achieve a better QoS in transport layer but with the sacrifice of a worse application performance.

Acknowledgements This work is carried out in the master thesis which is supported by the Nokia Siemens Networks Project Mature (Modeling and Analysis of the Transport Network Layer in the UTRAN Access Network REsearch). The partner of this work is Nokia Siemens Networks in Berlin, Germany.

References

1. Harri Holma, Antti Toskala: WCDMA for UMTS: Radio Access for Third Generation Mobile Communications. Wiley Technology Publishing, 1 edition (June 7, 2000)
2. 3GPP TS 25.401 v3.10.0, 3rd Generation Partnership Project; Technical Specification Group Radio Access Network; UTRAN Overall Description (Release 1999). Wiley Technology Publishing, 1 edition (June 7, 2000)
3. Kari Sipil, Zhi-Chun Honkasalo, Jaana Laiho-Steffens, Achim Wacker: Estimation of Capacity and Required Transmission Power of WCDMA Downlink Based on a Downlink Pole Equation. VTC 2000, P1002-1005, 2000
4. Chie Dou, Yu-Hua Chang: Class-based downlink capacity estimation of a WCDMA network in a multiservice context. Computer Communications 28 (2005) 1443-1455
5. Xi Li, Richard Schelb, Andreas Timm-Giel and Carmelita Görg: Dimensioning of UTRAN Iub Links for Elastic Internet Traffic with Multiple Radio Bearers. 13th GI/ITG Conference Measuring, Modelling and Evaluation of Computer and Communication Systems, Nrnberg, March 2006.
6. Thushara Weerawardane, Xi Li, Andreas Timm-Giel and Carmelita Görg: Modeling and Simulation of UMTS HSDPA in OPNET. OPNETWORK 2006, September, 2006, Washington DC, USA
7. Robert Akl, Manju Hegde, Alex Chandra: CCAP: CDMA Capacity Allocation and Planning. Washington University, Missouri, USA, April 1998

Definition of a Web 2.0 Gateway for 3rd Party Service Access to Next Generation Networks

N. Blum[*], D. Linner[*†], S. Krüssel[*], T. Magedanz[*†] and S. Steglich[*†]

[*]Fraunhofer Institute for Open Communication Systems (FOKUS),

Kaiserin-Augusta-Allee 31, 10589 Berlin, Germany

{niklas.blum|david.linner|steffen.kruessel|thomas.magedanz}@fokus.fraunhofer.de

[†]Technische Universität Berlin,

Sekr. FR 5-14, Franklinstrasse 28/29, 10587 Berlin, Germany

{thomas.magedanz|stephan.steglich}@tu-berlin.de

Abstract   Modern telecommunication networks and classical roles of operators are subject to fundamental change. Many network operators are currently seeking for new sources to generate revenue by exposing network capabilities to 3rd party service providers. At the same time we can observe that applications on the World Wide Web (WWW) are becoming more mature in terms of the definition of APIs that are offered towards other services. The combinations of those services are commonly referred to as Web 2.0 mash-ups. This report describes our approach to include Next Generation Networks (NGN)-based telecommunications application enabler into Web 2.0 mash-ups by defining a JavaScript-based service exposure API that allows easy and straight forward integration of telecommunications enablers into such mash-ups. The platform is validated through an application including telecommunications-based services as conferencing, rich presence and location, as well as the community portal Facebook and Google maps.

1   Introduction

Telecommunications is at crossroads, the convergence of fixed and mobile telecommunications, cable networks, as well as the Internet leads into a global all-IP based Next Generation Network (NGN). Through this ongoing process of the convergence of access networks and the existence of new players in the telecommunications market, traditional operators and carriers are seeking for new business models to increase their revenue. The reuse of an extensible set of existing service components to rapidly create new market driven applications is a key aspect of telecommunications platforms since many years and gains a new momentum with the definition of dedicated application enablers for NGNs. One real-life example is

Please use the following format when citing this chapter:

Blum, N., Linner, D., Krüssel, S., Magedanz, T. and Steglich, S., 2008, in IFIP International Federation for Information Processing, Volume 284; *Wireless and Mobile Networking*; Zoubir Mammeri; (Boston: Springer), pp. 247–258.

British Telecom's BT Web21C SDK [1] solution that defines an API to expose telecommunications specific core network functionalities to 3rd party service developers using Web Services.

This paper describes our approach of the realization of a service access gateway for applications based on a JavaScript API to address the specific needs of Web 2.0 developers. It is validated within a prototyped application for the community portal Facebook [2] offering access to functionalities such as conference management, location, SMS, MMS and rich presence.

The paper is structured as follows: Section 2 provides a brief state of the art overview of the NGN functionality namely the IP Multimedia Subsystem (IMS) with focus on application enablers and technologies associated to the term Web 2.0. Section 3 describes our concept of a service enabler access gateway for Web 2.0 mash-ups. Section 4 provides an overview of the prototype application. We end the paper with a conclusion and outlook in section 5.

2   Related Standards and technology Overview

The following subsections describe emerging standards as the IMS, IMS enablers, related technologies to the term Web 2.0 like Ajax and the mash-up service architectures. Furthermore it shortly depicts existing solutions in the area of service exposure for Web-based applications.

2.1 The IP Multimedia Subsystem

The IP Multimedia Subsystem (IMS) [3] has been defined from the 3rd Generation Partnership Project (3GPP) Release 5 specifications on as an overlay architecture on top of the 3GPP Packet Switched (PS) Core Network for the provisioning of real time multi-media services. It is based on Internet Engineering Task Force (IETF) protocols like the Session Initiation Protocol (SIP) [4] for session control and Diameter [5] for Authentication, Authorization and Accounting (AAA) and charging purposes. The basic IMS architecture is depicted in figure 1.

Due to the fact that the IMS overlay architecture is widely abstracted from the air interfaces, the IMS can be used for any mobile access network technology as well as for fixed line and cable access technology as currently promoted by ETSI TISPAN (TIPHON (Telecommunications and Internet Protocol Harmonization over Networks) and SPAN (Services and Protocols for Advanced Networks)) within the Next Generation Network (NGN) reference architecture definition [6].

The IMS provides easy and efficient ways to integrate different services, even from third parties. Interactions between different value-added services are anticipated. It enables the seamless integration of legacy services and is designed for consistent interactions with circuit switched domains. Furthermore it supports a mechanism to negotiate Quality of Service (QoS) in different access networks. The IMS also provides appropriate charging mechanisms for online and offline charging. Thus you can realize different business models and charge for specific events using an appropriate scheme.

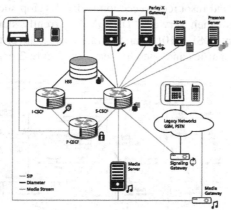

Fig. 1 Basic IMS Architecture

The particular techniques and methodologies that are required to gain the advantages of these key functionalities are not completely new, but the IMS provides the first major integration and the interaction of all key functionalities.

2.2 IMS Enabler

Similar to Service-Independent Building Blocks (SIBs) which form part of the conceptual model for Intelligent Networks, the Open Mobile Alliance (OMA) defined during the last years service enablers for the IP Multimedia Subsystem. The ideas was initially born during the specification of a Push-to-Talk over Cellular (PoC) [7] service, a walkie-talkie like communication service between several mobile peers based on the Internet Protocol (IP) using the SIP, Real-time Transfer Protocol (RTP) and Real-time Transfer Control Protocol (RTCP). PoC uses Presence, Group Management and Instant Messaging as enablers to provide information to the users as well as to the PoC service. This led alongside the standardization of PoC to the definition of Presence SIMPLE [8] for Presence and Instant Messaging and XML Documents Management (XDM) [9] for group and list management.

PoC as a public available service never received real acceptance besides the U.S. market, but the concept of abstract application enablers is by now widely used.

Service developers for next generation network based applications, especially those offered by 3rd party service providers will want to make use of the advanced multimedia communication functionalities offered by IMS-based applications. But core communication functionality like voice- and video call control as well as legacy messaging and location will reside at the operator's domain for security reasons and a well-defined integration of the service platforms into the operator's charging and provisioning functionality. Most application developers will also not have the capability and resources to economically develop such complex communication features into their services. The OMA currently standardizes the OMA Service Environment (OSE) [10] as an abstract enabler layer that serves as an access gateway for 3rd parties and operator services. Figure 2 depicts the OSE architecture:

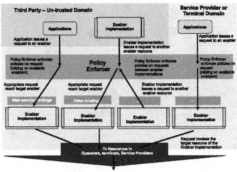

Fig. 2 OSE Architecture.

The OSE has been introduced to enable operators with the functionality to provide their communication and application capabilities to users without the need for the application developer to implement such functionality into their applications themselves. The OSE provides various functions such as process monitoring, software life cycle management, system support, operation, management and administration controls the enablers

2.3 The WWW and Web 2.0

The WWW is by nature community-driven, not only with regard to content, but also from a technical point of view. Simple protocols such as HTTP, description languages as HTML and CSS, and architecture paradigms (e.g. Representational State Transfer - REST) made the Web successful and simplicity is the decisive factor for the developer community's acceptance of extensions to the Web technology stack. Web 2.0 is less a question of novel technologies in the Web technology stack, but rather a question of how existing technologies are applied to create services tailored to user communities.

In this respect, client-side active scripting and the inherent capability of HTML to integrate content from different sources play a major role. Active scripts are shipped along with the web content to control content presentation and interactivity. The object based programming language ECMAScript [11], better known as JavaScript, is today's mostly used scripting language for Web pages. In addition to operations on the associated document, all noteworthy Web browsers allow active scripts to self-reliantly utilize the HTTP client interface in a pared-down configuration. This feature of active scripts to access their origin server for the exchange any of messages is referred to as Asynchronous Java Script (Ajax) [12]. Although the Ajax API introduces with the XMLHttpRequest [13] just one new language construct the amount of available developer tools based on Ajax show its current importance.

The varieties of client-server interaction, given to active scripts through Ajax include Remote Procedure Call (RPC) and Publish-Subscribe. The representatives for RPC over HTTP in favor of the developer community are XML-RPC [14] and JSON-RPC [15]. The major difference between both can be found in the representation of request and response, i.e. marshalling of method calls and objects. While JSON-RPC utilizes a light-weight, non-standard syntax, XML-RPC is based on W3C's XML. However, RPC frameworks for Ajax usually require a respective counterpart on the server-side. In practice, tool support for the selected backend platform (e.g. .NET, J2EE, PHP) is often the decisive criterion for the selection of a RPC framework.

The same holds for message passing and publish-subscribe approaches based on Ajax and the support of HTTP 1.1 for continuous connections. Respective development patterns and the message protocol Bayeux [16] are summarized to a concept named Comet. Bayeux messages are represented in JSON (JavaScript Object Notation) syntax and marshaled within the entity bodies of HTTP requests and responses. Comet allows a Web server to notify events almost synchronous to Web page embedded active scripts. Hence, applying Comet within a Web application has a positive impact on the application's interactivity, which is especially appreciable in a Web 2.0 context.

The above technologies comprise a powerful client-side foundation for a novel approach of creating web applications, called mash-up. A mash-up is a composition of 3rd party service building blocks to a new, customized web application. Examples for such 3rd party service building blocks can be found in the open APIs of Google Maps [17], Yahoo search [18], Youtube [19], or Facebook [20]. While the outgoing web server of a mash-up provides the description of the composition and thus the actual services adding value to the building blocks, the rendering and execution of the mash-up happens at the client-side. Consequently, mash-ups potentially decrease the need for intelligent web servers and avoid bottle necks, since utilized 3rd party service building blocks are accessed by the mash-up clients directly. Furthermore, mash-ups enable the rapid creation of powerful applications, even with limited engineering skills. By today, *programmableweb* [19] lists more than 2500 serious mash-up applications on the web, tendency growing. Our *Telco / Web 2.0 Gateway for 3rd Party Service Access to Next Generation Networks* aims at creating a novel application building block that brings telecommunication services to mash-ups.

2.4 Existing Solutions / Related Work

With respect to the above mentioned correlation of simplicity and developer acceptance, a key objective of our efforts is to create opportunities for fast and easy customization of telecommunications services in the Web. British Telecom's Web21c [1] project follows a similar motivation, while providing APIs and respective SDKs to utilize services of their network within custom applications. The list of supported service comprises, messaging, voice call, conference call, authentication, inbound SMS, and call flow. The provided APIs are currently tailored to the integration with .NET and Java.

An interface to NGN services that is suitable for the creation of mash-ups is the SIPGate API [22]. Therein, XML-RPC is utilized to basically control calls and conference calls, obtain data from the phone book, check the account balance or the status of unified messaging.

A much smaller, but nonetheless charming exposition of a telephony network service for usage on the Web is realized by Skype4Web [23]. Web references to dynamic images allow obtaining users' presence states in the network. Skype also provides professional APIs to access network services such as call control, messaging, and presence, but due to the peer-to-peer nature of the underlying network the service access is integrated with the network client.

3   Telco / Web 2.0 Service Exposure Gateway

In this section we describe our design and implementation of a service enabler access gateway for Web 2.0 mash-ups using telecommunications enablers.

3.1 Parlay X Gateway

The OCS-X [24] is an implementation of the Parlay X Web Services specification for telecommunication networks. These interfaces provide a network abstraction through a very simple and easy to use API based on Web Services technology, which can be used remotely from 3rd party domains and service providers. The OCS-X uses the current Parlay X Version 2.2 [25]. Parlay X defines a set of powerful yet simple, highly abstracted, building blocks of telecom capabilities that developers and the IT community can both quickly comprehend and use to generate new applications. Each building block will be abstracted from the set of telecom capabilities exposed by the Parlay X APIs. The capabilities offered by a building block may be homogeneous (e.g. call control only) or heterogeneous (e.g. mobility and presence). A building block will usually not be application-specific. In order to use them from within the Web 2.0 domain a gateway has been developed, which allows access to the Parlay X API via JavaScript.

3.2 JSON-to-Web Services Gateway

Calling a Web Service from within an Ajax application is restricted to local Web Services, due to the Same Origin Policy enforced by modern web browsers. However, Web Services are used to be consumed beyond server limits at external endpoints. In order to call external Web Services from JavaScript, the service request has to be routed via some server component, which is called *gateway* in the following and is illustrated in figure 3. This gateway provides an interface for the client-side JavaScript, mapping it to the particular interface of the external Web Service. Thus, all parameters of an incoming Ajax request are passed on to the Web Service endpoint. The Java Script client does access a single server as usual, whereas the server may call Web Services remotely.

Web Services are typically accessed via SOAP messages that are difficult to handle with Java Script. The utilization of a gateway allows replacing SOAP by any protocol, as the protocol can be translated within the gateway. Therefore, more convenient data description formats, such as JSON and simple XML [26], can be used to ease the Web Service access.

Furthermore, the Web Service access can be simplified by abstracting the actual Web Service interface. Thereby, underlying Web Service business logic can be hidden from the Java Script developer as well as offered functionality can be expanded at the server side. For example, security constraints could be achieved by the gateway transparently.

In order to realize a gateway functionality in the mentioned fashion, different components are required that are depicted figure 3.

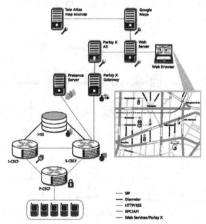

Fig. 3 Architecture of a telco-enabled Web.

The actual web application is stored on a regular web and connected to a database for consistent data management that is available via Ajax. Furthermore, 3rd party JavaScript APIs can be used within the web application (e.g. Google Maps) for mash-up.

In addition, an application server is required for the actual Web Service access. This server has to be connected to a Web Services platform offering multiple Web Services (e.g. OCS-X). The service access is again encapsulated within a simple API that can be used to extend existing Web 2.0 applications, such as the community portal Facebook. In order to use certain notification possibilities that could be offered by certain Web Services (e.g. in the IMS), Web Services endpoints have to be available on the gateway. Therefore, a Web Services engine as Apache Axis2 [27] has been established at the server-side. Moreover, the application server has to be connected to the Web Services engine to exchange incoming information passing it on to the web application via Ajax.

This configuration allows the fast development of complex mash-ups composed of Ajax APIs as well as open Web Services. Within the following section a concrete implementation of such a mash-up is introduced as a proof-of-concept.

3.3 Implementation of JSON-to-Parlay X Gateway

The realization of the above architecture has been transferred to Parlay X Web Services enabling IMS functionality. An overview about this concrete gateway is depicted in figure 4. The implementation is Java- and JavaScript based and the communication between client and gateway has been realized using JSON-RPC. Therefore, the open Java to JavaScript Object Broker (*jabsorb*) [28] is used on the client-side in order to transparently send JSON requests to remote Java objects. On the server-side, the jabsorb framework is used providing a particular Servlet that makes simple Java objects accessible via JSON-RPC that are automatically called on the accordant request.

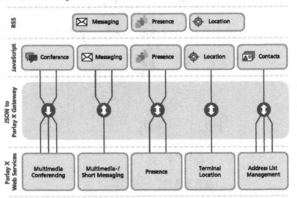

Fig. 4 JSON-to-ParlayX Gateway.

The Web Service access is done in each of those Java objects in order to request the required information. Indeed, the addressed IMS Enabler can be requested periodically to keep information up to date, it is intended that arising changes (e.g. location changes) are published automatically and not requested (pulled) manually. Therefore, the gateway must provide a Web Services endpoint itself to be notified from the Parlay X gateway. These Web Services are setup on the Axis2 engine [27] with their interfaces followed the Parlay X specification [25].

However, the classical Web model only allows for periodic polling, which makes server-push communications difficult. In order to make directly use of the notification mechanisms provided by the IMS the JavaScript client has to be extended by the Comet approach, which has been realized with the help of the HTTP-based publish/subscribe framework Pushlets [29]. This framework enables a direct forward of notifications to the client without periodic polling.

In order to forward incoming notifications, they must be available in the web server, since it holds the only connection to the client. Thus, the web server is connected to the Web Services engine that retrieves the particular information. The connection between web server and Web Services engine is done via cross-context communication [30] to share information between different web containers.

Based on this gateway, typical IMS features, like Instant Messaging, Conference Management and Rich Presence have been integrated into one of the largest online community platforms on the Internet – Facebook. A typical Web 2.0 mash-up composed of Facebook-Userdata, Google Maps and IMS Core functionalities emerged that demonstrates the easy and fast usage of the created gateway and its use for modern web development.

Facebook itself renders the development of a community application without building up the entire community platform from scratch. Moreover, already existing personal data had been easily integrated for further accretion. The visual presentation of location and presence data has been realized with the help of the Google Maps API. While Facebook is used through a PHP API, Google Maps is a pure JavaScript library that are both described in more detail in the following section.

4   Demonstrator / Validation

The demonstration of our Telco / Web 2.0 service exposure gateway, introduced above, is based on one of the largest Internet community portals with almost 65 million active users so far – Facebook. Facebook provides an API that allows developer to easily plug their applications into the portal getting access to Facebook user data, for example, retrieving information about all buddies of a user. The access on community-related information allows an easy mash-up of telecommunications features with user data. However, other APIs, such as Googles OpenSocial [31] could have also been used, but has been missed out due to its immatureness at the time of development. An overview is depicted in figure 5 that shows the current application and its embedding into the IMS infrastructure via the developed gateway.

In order to demonstrate a meaningful way to use information from within the IMS a map has been integrated into the application to present presence and location information in the Web. For this integration the Google Maps API has been used, but could have been exchanged by any other map API (e.g. Yahoo Maps). Additionally, user information from Facebook has been merged into the map to follow the Web2.0 idea of information mash-up.

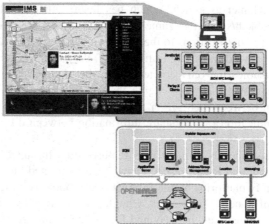

Fig. 5 Architecture of the Facebook Demonstrator.

Telecommunications specific-features have been realized in the following modules that each encapsulates a single functionality:

- **Multimedia Conference**: Voice conferencing through IMS. Participants can be contacted within the Public Switched Telephone Network (PSTN) as well as all-IP Next Generation Networks (NGN).
- **Presence**: Rich presence information, such as online/offline status and mood, of a certain user is published.
- **Terminal Location**: Request location information of a certain user from the IMS. It is necessary that the user provides location information from the IMS client, for example, with the help of a GPS receiver.
- **Short Messaging**: Sending simple text messages (SMS).
- **Multimedia Messaging**: Sending and receiving multimedia messages (MMS), consisting of plain text as well as application data. These messages are sent instantly and are also used for Instant Messaging (IM). A feedback channel has been also realized for this module to receive incoming messages.
- **Address List Management**: Transfer existing user- and group-information from the Web- to the Telco-domain and vice versa.

As a typical Web 2.0 feature, the integration of News Feeds has been also realized. However, the concept has been expanded on the telco side. The user can subscribe to different feeds that are collected within a single feed. The user than is being informed about every new entry. Furthermore, this feed is extended by location information out of the IMS. Therefore, user data at Facebook can be combined by interesting places.

Nevertheless, the developed application does not replace an IMS client, since it is only possible to handle certain management issues (e.g. call setup) or simple functions (e.g. messaging), but it is not possible to act as a communication end-point sending and receiving RTP streams. In fact, a typical IMS client is necessary for the provisioning of location and presence information as well as for the actual call setup. Therefore, the OpenIC IMS client [32] that is illustrated in figure 6 has been extended by Web 2.0 features like a RSS module for writing own RSS feeds as well as a map module that shows one's current location in a Web 2.0 like fashion. Moreover, all information published by the Address List Management component of the gateway can be received by the client as well, which contains information about the friends of a Facebook user and makes that information available in the IMS. Finally, an auto-provisioning mechanism has been implemented that allows for the subsequent integration of client modules triggered from within the Web.

Fig. 6 Web 2.0 enabled IMS Client.

5   Conclusions and outlook

In this report, we described our implementation of a Web 2.0 API gateway for telecommunications services and a proof-of-concept integration as a Facebook application. Our focus was on the creation of a very high level API that meets the needs and programming paradigms of developers from the WWW community. On the other hand it was important to us to integrate and achieve full interworking with existing legacy devices. Another emphasis was the reuse of existing IMS enablers and to keep the implementation as generic as possible in regard of reusability of the components.

Architecture-wise, our service infrastructure is acting on top of a mobile operator infrastructure and offers operator core services like SMS and call control with enhancements through Web 2.0 features on the presentation layer provided by a mash-up. The implementation is part of the Open SOA Telco Playground at

Fraunhofer FOKUS [33] and provides the Web 2.0 Telco Enablers and the Web 2.0 API gateway.

Future work will be done on security issues related to exposing core network capabilities to the WWW. Furthermore the integration of an OMA compliant Policy Enforcer as part of OSE will be implemented to provide flexible mechanisms for Service Level Agreements (SLAs) between an operator and the service provider using the gateway.

References

1. BT. Web21C SDK. http://web21c.bt.com/.
2. Facebook. http://www.facebook.com/.
3. 3GPP. *TS 23.228. IP Multimedia Subsystem (IMS). Stage 2 v.7.10.0.* 2007.
4. H. Schulzrinne, et al.. IETF RFC 3261. *SIP: Session Initiation Protocol.* 2002.
5. P. Calhoun. IETF RFC3588. *Diameter Base Protocol.* 2003.
6. ETSI. http://www.etsi.org/tispan/.
7. Open Mobile Alliance (OMA). *Enabler Release Definition for Push-to-talk over Cellular. Candidate Version 2.0 – 11 Dec 2007.* 2007.
8. Open Mobile Alliance (OMA). *Presence SIMPLE Architecture Document. Approved Version 1.0.1 – 28 Nov 2006.* 2006.
9. Open Mobile Alliance (OMA). *XML Document Management Architecture. Candidate Version 2.0 – 24 Jul 2007.* 2007.
10. Open Mobile Alliance (OMA). *OMA Service Environment. Approved Version 1.0.4 – 01 Feb 2007.* 2007.
11. ECMAScript Language Specification, 3'rd Edition, 1999, http://www.ecma-international.org/publications/standards/Ecma-262.htm
12. J. J. Garrett. *Ajax: A new Approach to Web Applications.* 2005.
13. The XMLHttpRequest Object, W3C Working Draft, October, 2007 http://www.w3.org/TR/XMLHttpRequest/
14. D. Winer; XML-RPC Specification, June, 1999, http://www.xmlrpc.com/spec
15. JSON-RPC Specification 1.1, Working Draft, August, 2006, http://json-rpc.org/wd/JSON-RPC-1-1-WD-20060807.html
16. A. Russel, G. Wilkins, D. Davis, M. Nesbitt, Bayeux Protocol 1.0 draft 1, 2007, http://svn.xantus.org/shortbus/trunk/bayeux/bayeux.html
17. Google Maps API, http://code.google.com/apis/maps/
18. Yahoo Search API, http://developer.yahoo.com/search/web/
19. Youtube Data API, http://code.google.com/apis/youtube/overview.html
20. Facebook API, http://developers.facebook.com/
21. Programmableweb, http://www.programmableweb.com/
22. SIPGate API, http://www.sipgate.co.uk/user/download_api.php
23. Skype4Web, https://developer.skype.com/Docs/Web
24. FOKUS Open Communication Server, http://www.open-ims.org/ocs-x
25. Parlay X. http://www.parlay.org/en/specifications/pxws.asp, 2008
26. W3C, Extensible Markup Language (XML). http://www.w3.org/XML/
27. Apache Software Foundation. Apache Axis2. http://ws.apache.org/axis2/
28. Jabsorb Framework. http://jabsorb.org/
29. Pushlets Framework. http://www.pushlets.com/
30. Apache Software Foundation. Apache Tomcat Configuration Reference (Cross-Context). http://tomcat.apache.org/tomcat-6.0-doc/config/context.html
31. Google Inc. OpenSocial API. http://code.google.com/apis/opensocial/
32. A. Motanga, A. Bachmann, T. Magedanz, *Requirements for an Extendible IMS Client Framework*, Mobilware'08, February 12-15, 2008, Innsbruck, Austria, ACM 978-1-59593-984-5/08/02
33. Open SOA Telco Playground, http://www.opensoaplayground.org

Validation of the Signaling Procedures of a Delivery Platform for IMS Services

Juan Miguel Espinosa Carlin and Dirk Thissen

Juan Miguel Espinosa Carlin
Communication and Distributed Systems, RWTH Aachen University, 52064 Aachen, Germany,
e-mail: `espinosa@i4.informatik.rwth-aachen.de`

Dirk Thissen
Communication and Distributed Systems, RWTH Aachen University, 52064 Aachen, Germany,
e-mail: `thissen@i4.informatik.rwth-aachen.de`

Abstract Defined by the 3rd Generation Partnership Project (3GPP), the IP Multimedia Subsystem (IMS) is becoming the de facto overlay architecture for enabling service delivery in converged environments. In order to explore and to further develop the service delivery mechanisms defined by the IMS, there is the need to enable a reliable testing environment that allows to experiment with these new approaches, in order to correctly evaluate their impact in the standards already defined. With this goal in mind, this paper presents an evaluation of conformance of the session control mechanisms of an IMS testbed based on the UCT IMS Client developed at the University of Cape Town and the Open IMS Core implementation of the Fraunhofer FOKUS Institute at Berlin.

1 Introduction

Nowadays, users want to be able to access their services in a uniform way without regard of the type of subscription they have (e.g. fixed, mobile, data), the device / terminal that they are using for connecting to the network, or the network connectivity existing in their environments (e.g. WLAN, GPRS, UMTS) [10]. One of the main constraints imposed by this paradigm is the need to enable a unified service control architecture that allows the delivery of rich multimedia services that satisfy the expectations of the users. With this goal in mind, the 3rd Generation Partnership Project (3GPP) introduced the IP Multimedia Subsystem (IMS) as a service control architecture aimed to realize network and service convergence.

Because the IMS is already in trial phases with operators adopting the standard worldwide, research efforts in the field are likely to gain support within a broad audience. In order to enable the development of IMS services and of trial of concepts around core the IMS elements, it is necessary to have a testing environment that allows evaluating the impact of the proposed approaches to the 3GPP standards. The aim of this paper is to evaluate the basic session signaling mechanisms of an

Please use the following format when citing this chapter:

Carlin, J.M.E. and Thissen, D., 2008, in IFIP International Federation for Information Processing, Volume 284; *Wireless and Mobile Networking*; Zoubir Mammeri; (Boston: Springer), pp. 259–270.

IMS testbed based on the UCT IMS Client [12] and on the Open IMS Core Project [2].

The rest of this paper is structured as follows. Section 2 gives an overview of the IMS architecture and of the IMS service delivery mechanisms. Then, Sect. 3 describes the hardware and software environment in which the tests were applied. Section 4 presents and analyzes the SIP dialogs traced in the testbed for basic registration, session set up, presence updating and messaging mechanisms. Finally, the conclusions and pointers towards future work are given on Sect. 5.

2 The IP Multimedia Subsystem

The IMS is based on protocols developed by the Internet Engineering Task Force (IETF). The basic ones are the Session Initiation Protocol (SIP) for session control and signaling, and the Diameter protocol for doing Authentication, Authorization, and Accounting (AAA). For an IMS core interconnecting only IP-based networks, the simplified architecture of the system is depicted in Fig. 1.

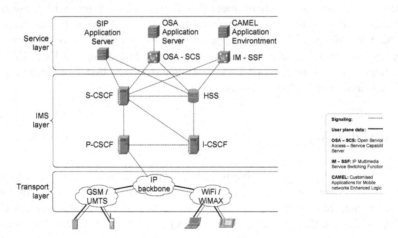

Fig. 1 Simplified IMS Architecture.

As shown, the lowest transport layer groups all the IP-based networks that allow users to access their services via the main IP backbone. For each one of these access networks, a specific technology is defined, and the device / terminal used to interact with the service must be compatible with these definitions (e.g. GSM, UMTS, WiFi, WiMAX).

Next, the IMS layer includes all the functions that implement the logic for enabling AAA and for allowing service delivery in the system. The main nodes in this level are:

One or more SIP-based servers, collectively called Call / Session Control Functions (CSCF's), which are the essential nodes in charge of processing all the SIP signaling in the IMS. Depending on its role, a CSCF can be categorized as a Proxy-CSCF (P-CSCF) when it is the first point of contact between the IMS terminal and the network, as an Interrogating-CSCF (I-CSCF) when it is a proxy located at the edge of an administrative domain, or as a Serving-CSCF (S-CSCF) when it performs session control and provides routing services.

One or more Home Subscriber Servers (HSS's), which are the repositories for the related subscriber information required to handle multimedia sessions.

Finally, the service layer contains the AS's that implement the services that will be delivered to the end users.

3 Evaluation Environment

This section gives an overview of the software components used for the testbed.

3.1 Open IMS Core Project

The Open Source IMS Core Project [2] is an implementation of the CSCF's and a lightweight HSS, which together form the core elements of all IMS architecture as specified by the 3GPP. The four components are all based on Open Source software. The central entities are the Open IMS CSCF's (Proxy, Interrogating, and Serving) which were developed as extensions to the SIP Express Router (SER) [7]. Since even basic signaling routing functionality for IMS requires information look-up in the HSS, the FOKUS Home Subscriber Server (FHoSS) is also part of the Open Source IMS Core project.

The testbed was configured with the default parameters for listening SIP requests: 4060 for the P-CSCF, 5060 for the I-CSCF and 6060 for the S-CSCF. Additionally, a DNS server was set up to properly resolve the default domain on which the testbed is running: open-ims.test. For the case of the HSS, the two IMS subscribers included by default (Alice and Bob) were used for the tests. For both of them, the proper service profiles were defined and a default iFC was configured with the proper service triggers for forwarding the SIP requests when doing the tests with the presence server.

3.2 UCT IMS Client

The *UCT IMC Client* [12] is developed by the Communications Research Group at the University of Cape Town, South Africa. The client was used with the default configuration for both Alice and Bob. For the case of Alice, the IMS configuration parameters are the following:

Public User Identity: `sip:alice@open-ims.test`
Private User Identity: `alice@open-ims.test`
Proxy CSCF: `sip:pcscf.open-ims.test:4060`
Realm: `open-ims.test`
QoS: `Mandatory`
QoS Type: `Segmented`
Access Network: `IEEE-802.11b`

3.3 OpenSER

OpenSER [8] is an open source SIP server that can act as SIP registrar, proxy or redirect server. For the aim of the tests, the OpenSER was configured as a presence server. The necessary configuration changes were done in order for the OpenSER to support the necessary functions to correctly process the `PUBLISH` and `SUBSCRIBE` SIP requests, and to enable the persistent storage of subscriptions information in a database. The server was configure to listen requests at `localhost:5065`.

3.4 Testing Scenario

The architecture of the networking scenario is shown in Fig. 2.

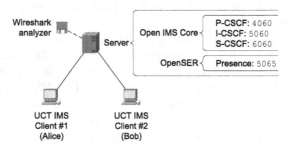

Fig. 2 Networking scenario deployed out for testing

To test the conformance of the testbed regarding the IMS SIP session control mechanisms, it is necessary to have a close look to the SIP flows that exchanged between the parties involved in the signaling. The tool used for this purpose, was Wireshark [11], a known protocol analyzer that features live capture and offline analysis of network streams.

4 Conformance Results

4.1 IMS Registration with Presence Service enabled

The *IMS Registration* procedure is defined in 3GPP TS 24.229 [4], and it is the first step that has to be done by subscribers in order for them to be able to access their services. The following assumptions were done during this test:

Alice is an authorized subscriber in the network (i.e. a valid HSS profile exists).
Neither Alice nor Bob are registered in the network.
Alice is doing the Registration from the home network.
Alice has her *Presence Service* enabled and has Bob in her buddy list.

The SIP sequence traced for Alice (or Bob) when registering in the testbed is shown in Fig. 3. This flow shows the SIP messages exchanged when Alice registers with the testbed. First, the UCT IMS Client #1 sends the proper REGISTER (1) request to the contact point with its IMS network, which as configured, is the P-CSCF running in the server at port 4060. Then, the P-CSCF forwards the request to the I-CSCF (2), which performs the first authorization step and determines if a S-CSCF is already assigned to Alice. This authorization is achieved by exchanging the proper Diameter messages with the HSS (for simplicity, not shown in Fig. 3). Because dealing with a new registration, no S-CSCF has been yet assigned to Alice, so the I-CSCF performs a S-CSCF selection procedure according to the information received by the HSS, and proxies the request to the selected P-CSCF (3). In order to authenticate Alice, the P-CSCF contacts the HSS for downloading her authentication vectors. Additionally, it registers itself in the HSS, so that further queries to the HSS related to Alice are properly routed back to the S-CSCF. Then, the S-CSCF sends back a 401 Unauthorized (4) SIP message that includes a challenge that must be correctly answered. This request is received by the I-CSCF which then forwards it to the P-CSCF (5). Finally, the P-CSCF sends the request Alice's IMS device (6).

After receiving the challenge, the Alice answers and its IMS device sends another REGISTER (7) with this information. After receiving it, the P-CSCF forwards it to the I-CSCF (8), which then sends it to the S-CSCF (9). It is important to mention that before forwarding the message, the I-CSCF queries the HSS to find out which S-CSCF has been assigned to Alice when the first REGISTER was sent (these Diameter messages are not shown in Fig. 3). After receiving the request, the S-CSCF verifies the answer given by Alice to the challenge and, if successful, sends back an 200 OK (10) to confirm the registration. This request is forwarded by the I-CSCF (11) and finally by the P-CSCF (12).

An IMS requirement inherited from the GSM age, consists on letting Alice know whether or not she is reachable. Because the core SIP specification offers not solution to cope with this problem, the IETF created a registration package for the SIP event framework [9], which allows the IMS terminal to subscribe to its own registration information stored in the S-CSCF. After receiving the confirmation of

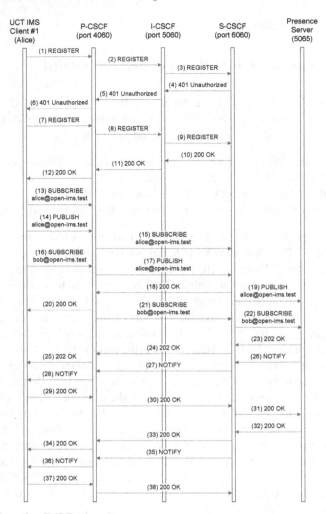

Fig. 3 SIP flow of an IMS Registration

the registration procedure, Alice's IMS terminal sends a SUBSCRIBE request for the reg event (13) addressed to the same PUI that the S-CSCF just registered. This request is directly forwarded from the P-CSCF to the S-CSCF (15), and upon reception, the S-CSCF installs the subscription and positively replies to user with the corresponding 200 OK via the P-CSCF (18 and 20). Additionally, the S-CSCF sends a NOTIFY request (35) that contains the registration information. The request is forwarded to Alice (36) and answered by her client with the corresponding 200 OK (37 and 38).

Because Alice has presence enabled on her device, two additional signaling sequences are traced. The first one consists on Alice publishing her information in the Presence Server. This is achieved by Alice's client sending a PUBLISH (14) request, which is then forwarded by the P-CSCF (17) and by the S-CSCF (19). When receiving the request, the Presence Server updates Alice's information and confirms her with the correspondent OK 200 (32), which is sent back by the CSCF's (33 and 34).

The second sequence is the one dealing with subscribing to Bob's presence information. For achieving this goal, Alice's device sends a SUBSCRIBE (16) to the Presence Server to indicate that Alice wants to be notified about Bob's presence information. This SUBSCRIBE request is forwarded to the Presence Server as usual (16, 21 and 22). When the Presence Server receives this subscription it checks if Bob has already published some information. Then, the Presence Server sends the corresponding 202 OK back to Alice (23, 24 and 25) for confirming the subscription. Additionally, the Presence Server sends Alice the corresponding NOTIFY related to Bob's installed subscription (26, 27 and 28). Upon reception of this notification, Alice's client sends back the corresponding 200 OK (29, 30 and 31) to the Presence Server.

As it can be seen, based on the assumptions already given, the Registration procedure executed by the testbed complies with the rules defined in the correspondent standards of the 3GPP, and satisfies the constraint of executing registration in two round trips.

4.2 Session Setup with Mandatory QoS Requirements

The procedure that is usually followed by users after successfully registering is to establish sessions with other users in the IMS network. The operations done by each node in the IMS network for the aim of setting up a session are also described in 3GPP TS 24.229 [4]. This test consisted on Alice inviting Bob to take part in a voice call. The following assumptions were done:

Alice and Bob have successfully registered in the testbed.
The client configuration of both Alice and Bob is the same.
The supported video and audio codecs are the same for both IMS clients.

The SIP sequence traced in the testbed from the point in which Alice invites Bob to the point in which Bob's client starts the mechanism to negotiate QoS of the session, is shown in Fig. 4.

The procedure starts with Alice's IMS device sending a INVITE (1) request directed to Bob. This request includes a SDP body describing the type of session that Alice's client wants to create. After receiving the request, the P-CSCF replies Alice with a 100 Trying message (2), confirming that the session set up was started. Then, the INVITE request is forwarded by the P-CSCF to the S-CSCF (3), which replies the P-CSCF also with a 100 Trying (4). Because Bob is registered at the same P-CSCF as Alice, the request is send by the S-CSCF to itself (5), and is answered with the proper 100 Trying (6). The INVITE is further forwarded by the S-CSCF to Bob (7) via the P-CSCF (9). Each INVITE is answered with its

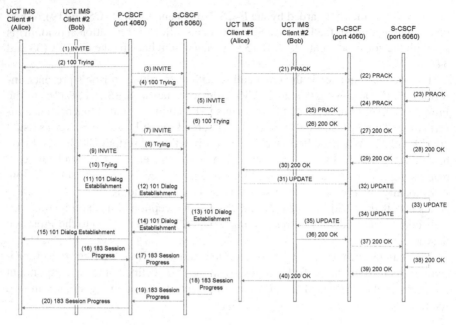

Fig. 4 Basic session setup, part 1

correspondent 100 Trying (8 and 10). Then, Bob's client sends a 101 Dialog Establishment message to inform about the set up status. This message is first sent to the P-CSCF (11) and then forwarded to the S-CSCF (12). As already mentioned, because both Alice and Bob are being served by the same S-CSCF, the 101 Dialog Establishment is sent by the S-CSCF to itself (13) and is further forwarded to the P-CSCS (14) and finally to Alice's IMS device (15).

Because the session requires QoS negotiation as described in [1], Bob's client sends back an additional 183 Session Progress provisional response. This message also includes a SDP [6] body, which contains the media streams and codes that Bob is able to accept for this session. At this point, Bob's client can start its resource reservation, because it knows the parameters needed for it. As in the case of the 101 Dialog Establishment message, the 183 Session Progress response is routed back to Alice via the same route (16, 17, 18, 19 and 20). The provisional response is received by Alice and, assuming that both clients agreed on the codes used, Alice sends a PRACK request including the definitive SDP configuration for the session. In parallel with the generation of this request, Alice's client starts at this point the mechanisms for resource reservation. The PRACK request is sent to Bob traversing the required proxies (21, 22, 23, 24 and 25). When the request is received by Bob, his client generates the corresponding 200 OK for confirming the media streams and codecs that will be used for the session. At this time, Bob's terminal may still be involved in its resource reservation process, and most likely it will not yet be complete. Additionally, the 200 OK response indicates Alice's client that Bob's client wants to receive an indication when Alice is ready with her resource reservation. The 200 OK is then sent back to Alice (26, 27, 28, 29 and 30).

Once that Alice's terminal has finished with its resource reservation, it sends an UPDATE request to inform Bob's client that the procedures on its side are finished. This is indicated through a specific SDP body added to the request. The request is routed to Bob via the same proxies as before (31, 32, 33, 34 and 35). Upon reception, Bob's client generates the corresponding 200 OK and, assuming that it has already finished with the resource reservation procedures on its side, it send the response back to Alice (36, 37, 38, 39 and 40).

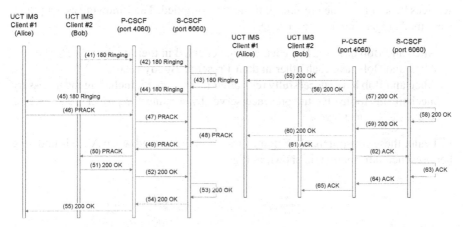

Fig. 5 Basic session setup, part 2

The SIP flow continues as shown in Fig. 5. The next step consists on Bob's IMS device alerting him about the incoming request. This action is indicated to Alice by sending her a 180 Ringing message (41) with a SDP body for indicating Alice about the characteristics accepted by Bob's client. This notification is forwarded by the P-CSCF (42), twice by the S-CSCF (43 and 44), and by the P-CSCF (45) to Alice. After receiving this message, Alice's client will likely generate a locally stored tone to indicate Alice that Bob's terminal is ringing. Additionally, Alice's client sends back a PRACK message (46), which is routed back to Bob (47, 48, 49 and 50). When received, Bob's device sends back a 200 OK confirmation. This message is routed back to Alice following the usual SIP signaling path (51, 52, 53, 54 and 55). After accepting the call, Bob's device sends a 200 OK message (56) that is forwarded to Alice by the P-CSCF (57), twice by the S-CSCF (58 and 59), once more by the P-CSCF (60). Finally, Alice's client generates the last ACK to confirm that the generation of media-place traffic with the agreed codecs can be started. This request travels back to Bob through the usual path (61, 62, 63, 64 and 65). At this point the session setup is complete, and both Alice an Bob can generate their respective audio and video media streams.

As described above, the session set up process done by the testbed, subject to the mentioned restrictions, complies with the procedures described by the 3GPP when dealing with establishing a session with specific QoS requirements.

4.3 Presence Service

The architecture for supporting the *Presence Service* in the IMS is defined in 3GPP TS 23.141 [3]. As in the Internet, the Presence Service in the IMS can be considered as the cornerstone for service provisioning, due to the fact that most of the other services benefit from the presence information supplied. The following assumptions were made regarding the presence tests:

Alice and Bob have the Presence Service enabled in their devices.
Alice and Bob have each other in their Presence Buddy Lists.
Alice and Bob have successfully registered in the testbed, including the necessary mechanisms to involve the presence server by sending the proper SUBSCRIBE and NOTIFY messages.

Under these constraints, the SIP flow traced in the testbed when Alice is updating her presence information, in shown in Fig. 6.

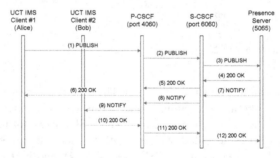

Fig. 6 Publishing presence information

In order to notify the system about a change in her presence status, Alice's client sends a PUBLISH request (1) to the PUI assigned to her during the registration phase. The request is received by the P-CSCF and then forwarded to the S-CSCF (2). Once received, the S-CSCF forwards the message to the Presence Server (3). The Presence Server sends a 200 OK (4) back to Alice to inform her that the request arrived. This message is further forwarded by the S-CSCF (5), and finally sent to Bob (6). Additionally, the Presence Server determines which users have subscribed to changes in the presence status of Alice. Because Bob is included in this list, the Presence Server send the proper NOTIFY (7) to him, routing the request through the S-CSCF (8) and the P-CSCF (9) to finally deliver it to Bob (9). To acknowledge the receipt of the notification, Bob's client sends a final 200 OK, that is routed back to the Presence Server (10, 11 and 12).

From these results, it can be concluded that the basic presence management mechanisms implemented by the testbed comply with those described by the 3GPP.

4.4 Messaging

The last procedure evaluated in the testbed was the *Messaging* service. It is defined in 3GPP TS 24.247 [5], and it allows a user to send some content to another user in almost real time. The basic content in an instant message is text, although it can be any other kind of media. For the aim of the results presented in this paper, only text-based messages were taken into account. This test assumes the following facts:

Alice and Bob have successfully registered in the testbed.
The client configuration of both Alice and Bob is the same.
Alice and Bob authorized each other to use the messaging service.

The SIP flow found in the testbed when Alice and Bob exchange one instant message each, is depicted in figure 7.

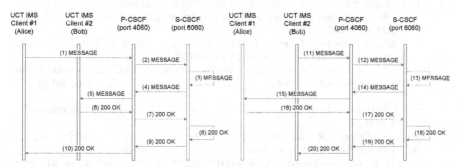

Fig. 7 Instant Messaging

As shown, the process is really simple, and the first step consists on Alice's client sending a MESSAGE request to Bob. This request is routed through the P-CSCF (2), twice through the S-CSCF (3 and 4), and finally sent to Bob (6). When Bob's device receives the request, it notifies Bob about the message sends and a 200 OK reply. Finally, when Bob answers the message, the same procedure is done but in the opposite direction. The MESSAGE is sent by Bob (11, 12, 13, 14 and 15) and the correspondent reply is sent by Alice (16, 17, 18, 19 and 20) upon reception.

5 Conclusions and Future Work

This paper presented a conformance evaluation of the SIP signaling mechanisms realized by an IMS testbed based on well known software components. The tests were performed for the registration procedure, the initialization of a session between two registered users, the updating of presence information, and the sending of instant messages. It was shown that a testbed set up with the chosen software tools complies with the procedures developed by the 3GPP for the IMS regarding session signaling. Future work in the field includes further evaluation of the testbed for complex roaming scenarios and for scenarios involving the invocation of multiple services.

References

1. Camarillo, G., Marshall, W., Rosenberg, J.: Integration of Resource Management and Session Initiation Protocol (SIP). RFC 3312 (Proposed Standard) (2002). URL http://www.ietf.org/rfc/rfc3312.txt. Updated by RFCs 4032, 5027
2. Fraunhofer FOKUS: OpenIMSCore.org — The Open IMS Core Project. http://www.openimscore.org (2007). Last retrieved on the 20.04.2008
3. 3rd Generation Partnership Project: Presence service; Architecture and functional description; Stage 2. 3GPP TS 23.141 (2006)
4. 3rd Generation Partnership Project: Internet Protocol (IP) multimedia call control protocol based on Session Initiation Protocol (SIP) and Session Description Protocol (SDP); Stage 3. 3GPP TS 24.229 (2007)
5. 3rd Generation Partnership Project: Messaging service using the IP Multimedia (IM) Core Network (CN) subsystem; Stage 3. 3GPP TS 24.247 (2007)
6. Handley, M., Jacobson, V.: SDP: Session Description Protocol. RFC 2327 (Proposed Standard) (1998). URL http://www.ietf.org/rfc/rfc2327.txt. Updated by RFC 3266
7. iptel.org: SIP Express Router. http://www.iptel.org/ser (2006). Last retrieved on the 15.11.2007
8. OpenSER.org: OpenSER - the Open Source SIP Server. http://www.openser.org (2007). Last retrieved on the 20.04.2008
9. Rosenberg, J.: A Session Initiation Protocol (SIP) Event Package for Registrations. RFC 3680 (Proposed Standard) (2004). URL http://www.ietf.org/rfc/rfc3680.txt
10. Schonhowd, R.: Telecom And IT Strategists Must Pursue Converged Service Delivery To 2010 And Beyond. Forrester Research Report. Available from http://www.forrester.com/Research/Document/Excerpt/0,7211,41543,00.html (2007). Last retrieved on the 25.03.2008
11. The Wireshark Team: Wireshark. http://www.wireshark.org (2007). Last retrieved on the 15.11.2007
12. University of Cape Town: UCT IMS Client. http://uctimsclient.berlios.de (2007). Last retrieved on the 15.11.2007

Trust Negotiation Protocol Support for Secure Mobile Network Service Deployment

Daniel Díaz-Sánchez, Andrés Marín, Florina Almenarez, Celeste Campo, Alberto Cortés and Carlos García-Rubio

Universidad Carlos III de Madrid, Avda, de la Universidad 30, 28911 Leganés (Madrid), e-mail: {dds,amarin,florina,celeste,alcortes,cgr}@it.uc3m.es

Abstract User-centric services might enforce requirements difficult to be endorsed by visited networks unless tight coupled trust relations are previously established among providers. Maintaining those fixed trust relations is costly and unmanageable if the number of providers increases. Moreover, it requires providers to use a common security model, credentials, policies.... Trust Negotiation can be the solution to this problem since allows to negotiate gradually a security state enabling multiple factor authentication and authorization even for "strangers" by exchanging various credentials. However, there are still two problems to solve, the first one is the delay introduced by the trust negotiation messages if used as bootstrapping in every interaction; the second one is the lack of protocol support. In this article we address those problems by presenting an extension to TLS that enables trust negotiation and credential issuing (to speed-up following interactions) over a secure channel.

1 Introduction

Mobile and legacy networks are converging to "beyond 3G networks" to provide user-centric services regardless the access network. Users might use various Network Access Providers, Internet Service Providers, and services performing horizontal o vertical handover spontaneously depending on the traffic demand of their applications, as described in [1].The required degree of cooperation among providers can be achieve in two ways: by forcing providers to use the same security model, policies, credentials and protocols, requiring tight coupled trust relations among them; or allowing flexible on-demand trust negotiation. Obviously, those fixed trust relations are costly and unmanageable when the number of providers increases.

Different trust management and access control systems have been proposed for distributed authentication/authorization, like PolicyMaker [2, 3], KeyNote [4], SPKI/SDSI, or the Generic Authorization and Access-control API [5]. Other works like [6] focus on providing trust management systems with adequate semantics so that the policies are correctly defined, understood, and can be proven so. Since finding a common access control solution is not a simple solution, it is necessary a way to combine information from different access control systems. Trust negotiation [7]

Please use the following format when citing this chapter:

Díaz-Sánchez, D., Marín, A., Almenarez, F., Campo, C., Cortés A. and García-Rubio, C., 2008, in IFIP International Federation for Information Processing, Volume 284; *Wireless and Mobile Networking*; Zoubir Mammeri; (Boston: Springer), pp. 271–286.

[8] can be used to find a solution to this problem since allows to negotiate gradually a security state enabling multiple factor authentication and authorization even for "strangers". This is done by exchanging various credentials: following a path of credential disclosure, users can increase the level of security gradually until the level needed for accessing a service is reached.

The initial problem of trust negotiation is how different credentials and policies, from different providers and languages, can be combined. This problem is discussed and solved in [9] and [6]. [9] shows how a sequential disclosure path can be built respecting user's privacy and avoiding abuse. That article demonstrate how different requirements, extracted from policies belonging to different actors and perhaps written in different languages can be combined using a single decision engine.

Furthermore, other problems of trust negotiation need to solved: the first one is the delay introduced by the trust negotiation messages if used as bootstrapping in every interaction; the second one is the lack of protocol support. In this article we concentrate on how attribute certificates [10] can be requested and issued, as "trust tickets", after a successful trust negotiation, using TLS, to speed-up future interactions. Although there are similarities with identity certificates acquiring process, we deal also with delegation issues which do not appear in authentication. Regarding protocol support, looking to the authentication problem in service and network access, we can probably agree that the situation has been clarified by extensive use of the TLS/SSL protocol for services and EAP-TLS protocol for network access. In this paper we support that TLS can also play a similar role in trust negotiation as it does in authentication.

The rest of the article is organized as follows: in Sect. 2 we describes the extensions done to TLS. Sect. 2.1 briefly explains the architectural changes done to TLS and Sect. 2.2 describes the additions to the handshake and protocol messages to support trust negotiation over TLS. In Sect. 2.3 the attribute certificate request format is presented. Then, Sect. 2.4 shows how attribute certificate issuing can be requested with TLS. Finally, Sect. 3 presents related work and conclusions.

2 Trust negotiation and authorization issuing over TLS

This section starts with a brief description of our Privilege and Trust Negotiation Layer for TLS. Sect. 2.2 discusses on architectural issues and TLS handshake handshake extensions for Trust Negotiation are defined in Sect. 2.1. Then, to handle the use of trust tickets, we will show our proposal for an Attribute Certificate Request Format, in section Sect. 2.3; and its usage with TLS in Sect. 2.4.

2.1 Privilege and Trust Negotiation Layer for TLS

TLS provides one-round mutual authentication. As discussed in previous section, multiple factor authentication and authorization is needed in complex environments for fine grained access control. Fortunately, TLS can be extended as described in [11, 12]. The generic extension mechanism is based on the handshake client and server hello messages. The extension mechanism is designed to be backwards compatible: servers should ignore unsupported extensions. In this section we describe a mechanism to negotiate trust over TLS. Before going further in the proposed TLS extension, we briefly describe TLS internals.

TLS architecture: TLS defines the *TLS Record Protocol* as a layered protocol. The clients of this layer provides fields for length, description and content. Messages are fragmented in manageable blocks, optionally compressed, encrypted and authenticated using a Message Authentication Code (MAC)as described in *Connection State*. *Connection State* specifies, among others, the MAC algorithm, the bulk encryption algorithm, the compression algorithm and the master-secret key. The TLS standard defines four client layers of the *TLS Record Protocol*: the handshake protocol which initially derives a key for secure message exchange; the alert protocol which produces messages conveying the severity of an alert and a description; the *change cipher spec* protocol which signals changes on the current *Connection State*; and the application protocol, for instance HTTP, FTP or SMTP. *Connection State* is negotiated during a handshake phase. A symmetric key is securely derived from random data sent by peers by using a an asymmetric algorithm (RSA or Diffie Hellman). Once the key is derived, the new *Connection State* is used to protect TLS Record Protocol messages against eavesdropping.

Handshake: The client initiates the handshake sending a *Client Hello* message and a set of optional extensions. In this message the client provides random data, a time stamp, session identification and a set of cipher suites and compression mechanisms. The server answers with a *Server Hello* message, providing also random data and selecting one cipher suite and compression method from the set provided by the client. The *Server Hello* message can be followed by a set of optional extensions. The server optionally sends a certificate or a *ServerKeyExchange* message that will be used to perform the secure key exchange (using certificates or Diffie-Hellman). Optionally, server side can also request a certificate from the client (sending a *CertificateRequest* message).

The client optionally sends its certificate, if requested by the server, and sends the mandatory *ClientKeyExchange* message, which exchanges the pre-master key that will be used to derive the final symmetric key. The *ChangeCipherSpec* and *Finished* messages signals that a new symmetric key is ready for use in *Connection State*, to protect upcoming application messages.

Proposed architecture: To identify the involved entities, consider a mobile device governed by a set of policies. Those policies are controlled by different access control engines (ACEs). Every ACE processes the policies it understands, extracting **requirements** and **policy items** from them. A **policy item** is a formal definition for a requirement so it can be used by other peer to find out which credential should be disclosed in order to satisfy a requirement. ACEs register requirements and policy items to the **decision engine** as explained in [9]. Fig. 1 shows the architecture.

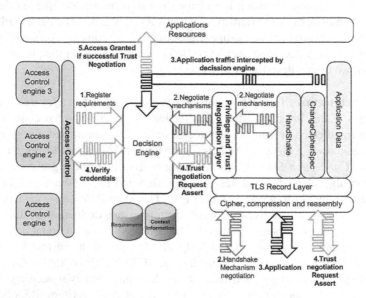

Fig. 1 Access control engines and its relation to the privilege and trust negotiation layer of TLS.

To accomplish trust negotiation in TLS, the handshake protocol module must support a new extension. Besides, a new layer is defined: the *Privilege and Trust Negotiation Layer*(PTN Layer), client of the *TLS record layer*. Fig. 1 illustrates the TLS client layers.

2.2 Trust Negotiation over TLS protocol

The TLS extension described here allows to negotiate trust. We have defined our extension with the intention to allow client and server to negotiate first which policy languages, credentials and mechanisms will be used later, during trust negotiation. This initial negotiation is performed in a mutual agreement basis during the TLS handshake. Once the secure channel is established, the Trust Negotiation starts. The proposed message exchange for the Privilege and Trust Negotiation Layer is the following (optional fields and messages are marked with *):

```
Client                                    Server
--
ClientHello
```

```
<PTLNExtension*>
<AuthRequestExt*>              -------->
                                          ServerHello
                                          <PTLNExtension*>
                                          <AuthRequestExt*>
                                          Certificate*
                                          ServerKeyExchange*
                                          CertificateRequest*
                               <--------   ServerHelloDone
Certificate*
ClientKeyExchange
CertificateVerify*
[ChangeCipherSpec]
Finished                       -------->
                                          [ChangeCipherSpec]
                               <--------   Finished
Handshake ends. Trust Negotiation Messages exchange starts in
parallel to Application Data and Authorization Issuing Requests
TrustNegotiationMessage*       -------->
                               <-------   TrustNegotiationMessage*

ACRequest*                     ------->
                               <-------   ACResponse*

Application Data               <------->  Application Data
```

Let us further describe the additions to the original TLS handshake:

1. The client advertises the list of Trust Negotiation mechanisms it supports by sending the PTLN extension at the end of the *Client Hello* message. This message contains information about which policies, authentication and authorization credentials and mechanisms can be used.
2. If the server understands the extension, it is redirected to the *Privilege and Trust Negotiation Layer*. The server sends to the client, at the end of the *Server Hello* message, a selection of mechanisms provided by the client (Fig. 1).
3. The TLS handshake continues as defined in the standard until a secure channel is established -after the server sends the *Finished* message.
4. At this point, the application layer traffic flows in parallel to trust negotiation protocol message exchange. As can be seen in Fig. 1, application traffic is intercepted by an enforcement point and redirected to the decision engine. The decision engine decides if the client, identified by the TLS session identifier, has a security state higher enough to access a given application or resource.

   - If security state is not enough, the decision engine conveys to the PTN layer the policy item that describes the next requirements to be fulfilled. The PTN server layer sends to the PTN client Layer a *TrustNegotiationMessage* containing a *Request* command. Then, it waits until client sends a *TrustNegotiationMessage* with an *Assert* command containing the credentials. Since trust negotiation messages are managed by the PTN layer, applications do not need to be aware of the underlying access control layers.
   - Otherwise, if the security state is adequate, the application traffic is not blocked.

The structure of the Trust Negotiation extension is the following:

```
struct {
    TrustNegotiationMechanisms TrustN_avail_mechs<0..2^16>;
```

```
}PTNLExtension

struct {
    TrustObjectType trust_object_type;
    opaque      Uri<0..2^16-1>;
    opaque      OID<0..2^16-1>;
} TrustNegotiationMechanisms

enum{
    policy(0), credential(1), strategy(2),...
} TrustObjectType;
```

TrustN_avail_mechs contains a list of supported trust negotiation mechanisms or objects, so both sides can determinate if they "speak" the same language (policies and credentials). For instance, the client might express that he understands XACML policy items and X.509, SAML and KeyNote credentials.

Trust negotiation protocol messages handle three different lists of messages (*TrustNegotiationMessage*): assertions, requirements and information. Thus, in a single message, an entity can request credentials to the other part and also fulfill requirements previously sent by the other side (assertions).

```
struct{
    Message assertion_list<0..2^16-1>;
    Message requirement_list<0..2^16-1>;
    Message information_list<0..2^16-1>;
}TrustNegotiationMessage;
struct{
    Type type;
    Object      PayLoad_list<0..2^16-1>;
    Parameter   Parameters<0..2^16-1>;
}Message;
struct{
    Type type;
    opaque  PayLoad<0..2^16-1>;
}Parameter;
struct{
    opaque OID<0..2^16-1>;
    opaque URI<0..2^16-1>;
}Type;
```

The parameters of *Message* structure allows to combine different policy items using operators or logic expressions.

2.3 Attribute Certificate Request Format

This section describes an Attribute Certificate Request Message Format (ACRM) based in RFC2511 [13], that describes the Certificate Request Message Format. RFC2511 describes the message format used to convey a public key certificate request to a Certification Authority. It requires the client to provide a *Proof of Possession (PoP)* of the private key associated with the certificate's public key. The PoP can be done in different ways, depending on the key type: using a signature or a password based MAC. In addition we have considered different types of authorization issuing:

- Direct issuing: an entity **A** requests an attribute certificate directly to the *SoA* or through the *Registration Authority (RA)*. The *RA* is the entity that should verify the request before the AC is issued by the *SoA*, obviously, the *RA* should be trusted by the *SoA*. The *RA* can be also the entity which receives the payment for a service and the attribute certificate the ticket that gives access to the service.
- Indirect issuing: an entity **B** requests an attribute certificate to a *SoA* (or through a *RA*) on behalf of other entity **A**. This kind of indirect delegation might be useful for limited devices only able to perform some cryptographic primitives.
- Delegation: an entity **A** requests an attribute certificate to another entity **B**. If **B** accepts it delegates the privilege to **A**.

Since ACs can be bound to a PKI certificate or public key, the ACRM should contain the PKI certificate or the key that identifies the user. The proof of possession contained in a ACRM should proof the possession of the associated private key. PKI certificate request messages provide the necessary means for the user to prove possession of private key, but no mechanisms are specified to convey the request from the RA to CA, this is done out-of-band. However, we provide a procedure for any involved entity to assert it agrees with the request by enveloping it and signing it. Fig. 2 shows an example. The ASN.1 syntax of an Attribute Certificate Request Message is the following[1]:

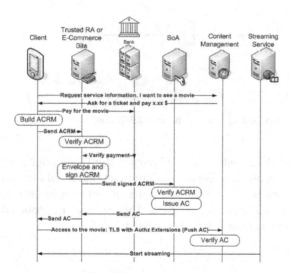

Fig. 2 Request access to a multimedia content

```
AttCertReqMessages ::= SEQUENCE SIZE (1..MAX) OF
AttCertSignedRequestMsg
```

---

[1] the ASN.1 syntax uses implicit tagging and imports the same as in RFC 2511 and also PKIX-AttributeCertificate iso(1) identified-organization(3) dod(6) internet(1) security(5) mechanisms(5) pkix(7) id-mod(0) id-mod-attribute-cert(12)

```
AttCertSignedRequestMsg ::= SEQUENCE {
    -- signature-chained message
    -- allows involved entities to assert the validity of a request
    reqMsg   CHOICE {
    -- at least one attCertReqMsg or attCertSignedReqMsg shall be present.
        attCertReqMsg [0]  AttCertRequestMsg,
        attCertSignedReqMsg [1] AttCertSignedRequestMsg}

    authInfo CHOICE {
        signer         [0] GeneralName,
    -- used only if an authenticated identity has been established for the signer:
    -- an RA or other entity known by RA or SoA asking for a certificate
        delegationAttCertPath SEQUENCE SIZE (1..MAX) OF ACPathData } OPTIONAL,
    -- used only if an entity with delegated privileges ask for a certificate
    on behalf of other signatureAlgorithm AlgorithmIdentifier OPTIONAL,
    signatureValue       BIT STRING OPTIONAL}

ACPathData  ::=  SEQUENCE {
    certificate                [0]  Certificate  OPTIONAL,
    attributeCertificate       [1]  AttributeCertificate  OPTIONAL
}
```

The recursive definition of *AttCertSignedRequestMsg* allows involved entities to envelope and sign requests if they agree with the content. For indirect issuing, the
entity that indirectly delegates a privilege must include its PKI certificate and the
attribute certificate that includes the delegated privilege (see Fig. 3)

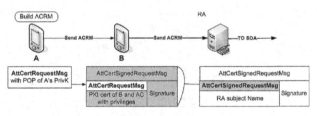

Fig. 3 ACRM envelope and signature for indirect delegation

AttCertRequestMsg contains the AC request itself, an optional proof of possession and a set of optional registration information that should be considered in the
same terms as done in RFC 2511. The request might contain the client PKI certificate or the key to which the AC is bound. This parameter is optional since the RA
or CA can obtain this information out-of-band.

```
AttCertRequestMsg :: = SEQUENCE {
    attCertReq      AttCertRequest,
    pop             ProofOfPossesion OPTIONAL,
    regInfo         SEQUENCE SIZE (1..MAX) of AttributeType And Value OPTIONAL
    -- regInfo: can contain information of publishing, payment...
}

AttrCertRequest ::= SEQUENCE {
    attCertReqID    Integer,
    boundCert       Certificates OPTIONAL, -- PKI certificate of entity
    attCertTmpl     AttCertTemplate,
    controls        Controls OPTIONAL
}

Certificates ::= SEQUENCE {
```

```
        userCertificate   Certificate,
        certificationPath CertPath OPTIONAL
}
```

The cert template provides the necessary information to issue the AC. *Holder*, *AttCertIssuer* and *Attribute* syntax is the same as described in [10] and [14]. The rest of the parameters should be treated as in RFC 2511.

```
AttCertTemplate ::= SEQUENCE {
    version         [0]   Version OPTIONAL,
    serialNumber    [1]   Integer OPTIONAL,
    signatureAlg    [2]   AlgorithmIdentifier OPTIONAL,
    holder          [4]   Holder OPTIONAL,
    issuer          [3]   AttCertIssuer OPTIONAL,
    -- syntax for issuer and holder
    validity        [5]   Validity OPTIONAL,
    attributes      [6]   SEQUENCE SIZE(1..MAX) of Attribute OPTIONAL,
    extensions      [7]   SEQUENCE SIZE(1..MAX) of Extension OPTIONAL
}
```

The PoP depends on the key type. For instance, with RSA keys any PoP can be used. For *keyAgreement*(only) keys, the field *thisMessage* is used for PoP. This field contains a MAC (over the DER-encoded value of the *attCertReq* parameter in *AttCertReqMsg*, based on a key derived from the end entity's private DH key and the CA's public DH key and calculated as explained in RFC 2511.

```
ProofOfPossession ::= CHOICE {
    signature          [0] POPOSigningKey,
    keyAgreement       [1] POPOPrivKey
}

POPOSigningKey ::= SEQUENCE {
    algorithmIdentifier    AlgorithmIdentifier,
    signature              BIT STRING }
    -- signature MUST be computed on the DER-encoded value of attCertReq

POPOPrivKey ::= CHOICE {
    thisMessage        [0] BIT STRING,
    subsequentMessage  [1] SubsequentMessage,
    -- possession will be proven in a subsequent message
    dhMAC              [2] BIT STRING }
```

2.4 Authorization Request with TLS

In this section we describe a TLS extension that allows to securely request an AC to a RA, SoA or any entity able to issue it as, for example, a consequence of a successful trust negotiation. This protocol extension considers protocol messages to cover any proof of possession procedure, including TLS handshake with mutual authentication. Figs. 4(a) and 4(b) show two scenarios where this request mechanism over TLS can be used: the client starts sending a Client Hello message containing the *AuthzRequestExtension*, thus it discovers whether the server supports issuing over TLS or not. If the server understands the extension, it should send the same content back to the client.

The *AuthzRequestExtension* indicates that the client might request an attribute certificate during the TLS connection. Any required information will be given using the Attribute Certificate Request Message (ACRM) format. The client asks the server to request client certificate, for PoP, during handshake, by setting *use-ClientCert* to true: if the AC to be issued should be bound to the certificate used during handshake, no proof of possession is required in ACRM (a successful TLS handshake with mutual authentication already demonstrates the possession). Moreover, to distinguish among different SoAs, targeted by the same RA, the client can indicate the target SoA in *targetSoA* field. The syntax of the TLS extension is the following:

```
struct{
    Boolean useClientCert,
    opaque  targetSoA -- Optional
}AuthzRequestExt;
```

The new protocol messages added to TLS are:

```
struct{
    Boolean useClientCert,
    opaque  targetSoA -- Optional
}AuthzRequestExt;

struct{
    ACReqType acReqType,
    opaque    ACRMs<0..2^16-1>
}ACRequest;

enum{ SendACRM(0), ForwardApprovedACRM(1), RequestKeyExchange(2),..
}
struct{
    opaque payload<1..2^16-1>
}challenge_Response;

struct{
    opaque  ASN1.AC<1..2^16-1>,
    Boolean encrypted
}ACResponse;
```

Fig. 4(a) shows the message exchange over TLS for an AC request. In this case, the possession of the key is proven with a successful TLS handshake. If no mutual authentication is performed during TLS handshake, see Fig. 4(b) , the client can build an ACRM and include a proof of possession based in a signature key.

If client's key can only be used for key exchange, the client can send a *ACRequest* message with an empty ACRM. The type of the *ACRequest* message sent by the client is *RequestKeyExchange*. This message is immediately followed by a TLS *ClientKeyExchange* and *Finalize* (consumed by the PTN layer at server side) and used to derive a key. The random data exchanged during the TLS handshake will be used in this key exchange using a Diffie-Hellman key to compute the master secret as explained in [11]. Key exchange proof of possession should be used only by clients whose keys cannot be used to sign. Finally, the client can ask for a challenge-response message exchange, using the *SubsequentMessage* field of an ACRM or request the attribute certificate to be encrypted. The proof of possession is proven by sending a hash of the received AC, once decrypted.

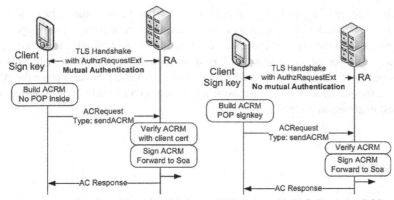

(a) Request with mutual authentication TLS handshake   (b) Request with TLS. Signature POP

3 Conclusions and Related work

We have presented a TLS extension for trust negotiation and other for requesting ACs: we complement other works, as [9], with protocol support. The extensions allows to negotiate trust over an encrypted channel and then request a **"trust ticket"**. We designed a new layer for TLS that allows to perform trust negotiation in parallel to the application protocol. Thus, multiple authentications and authorizations can be performed on demand, depending on the application behavior.

We also have elaborated a message format suitable for requesting ACs over TLS that can reuse TLS mutual authentication to perform the proof of possession. So, as a result of a successful trust negotiation, a credential can be issued to speed up the process in future interactions.

Other works as Farrel [15], and Brown and Housley [16] propose similar extensions. In [15], Farrel defines an approach to the authorization problem. Farrel, uses some extensions on TLS but introduces some protocol messages that are not negotiated using extensions during TLS handshake. This might not work: legacy TLS servers can be broken since there is no prior negotiation before using an application specific protocol message. [16] is a parallel work to ours but only enables authorization over TLS: enables the use of Attribute Certificates and SAML. However, our goal is to enable **multiple factor authentication and authorization regardless the credentials type**. Moreover, they require a double TLS handshake and allows only one credential exchange. Other works on trust negotiation, as [17], allow to exchange credentials using extensions but requires to perform a handshake whenever a credential needs to be exchanged.

Our proposal is more efficient since we only require one handshake. A double handshake implies a double exchange of handshake messages thus, at least 12 messages are exchanged again, if mutual authentication is required. Furthermore, since we rely on an efficient agnostic trust negotiation decision engine, as described in [1], we can deal with multiple credentials and policies types. Regarding to implementation, [16] does not require new protocol messages, but the code has to be changed to allow for adjacent double handshakes. In our proposal, new protocol messages have to be coded, and the state machine has to be modified accordingly. We have developed a toolkit for AC management, based on OpenSSL, compliant with ITU and IETF specifications allowing to build the requests, process them and issue the ACs . We hope that in the near future, network applications can benefit of TLS performing the trust negotiation on their behalf.

References

1. Díaz, D., Marín, A., Almenárez, F., Garcia-Rubio, C., Campo, C.: Context awareness in network selection for dynamic environments. 11th IFIP International Conference on Personal Wireless Communications "PWC06". Lecture Notes In Computer Science Editor: Springer-Verlag GMBH (2006)
2. Blaze, M., Feigenbaum, J., Lacy, J.: Decentralized trust management. In: Proceedings IEEE Symposium on Security and Privacy, 1996, IEEE Computer (1996)
3. Blaze, M., Feigenbaum, J., Strauss, M.: Compliance checking in the policy maker trust management system. In: Financial Cryptography. Number 1465 in Lecture Notes in Computer Science, Springer-Verlag (1998)
4. Blaze, M., Feigenbaum, J., Ioannidis, J., Keromytis, A.: The keynote trust management system version 2. Technical Report RFC 2704, IETF (1999)
5. Ryutov, T., Neuman, C., Kim, D.: The specification and enforcement of advanced security policies. In: Proceedings of the IEEE 3rd International Workshop on Policies for Distributed Systems and Networks, 2002, IEEE Computer (2002)
6. Li, N., Grosof, B.N., Feigenbaum, J.: Delegation logic: A logic-based approach to distributed authorization. ACM Trans. Inf. Syst. Secur. 6 (2003) 128–171
7. Squicciarini, A.C.: Trust negotiation systems. In: EDBT Workshops. (2004) 90–99
8. Bertino, E., Ferrari, E., Squicciarini, A.: X -tnl: An xml-based language for trust negotiations. policy 00 (2003) 81
9. Díaz, D., Marín, A., Almenárez, F.: Enhancing access control for mobile devices with an agnostic trust negotiation decision engine. Personal Wireless Communications. Springer series in Computer Science. ISSN: 1571-5736. (2007)
10. (ITU), I.T.U.: The directory: Public-key and attribute certificate framework. Technical Report X.509, International Telecommunication Union (ITU) (2005)
11. Dierks, T.: The tls protocol. Technical Report RFC 2246, IETF TLS Working Group (1999)
12. Blake-Wilson, S.: Transport layer security (tls) extensions. Technical Report RFC 3546, IETF TLS Working Group (2003)
13. Myers, M., Adams, C., Solo, D., Kemp, D.: Internet x.509 certificate request message format. Technical Report RFC 2511, IETF TLS Working Group (1999)
14. Farrell, S., Housley, R.: An internet attribute certificate profile for authorization. Technical Report RFC 3281, IETF PKIX Working Group (2002)
15. Farrell, S.: Tls extensions for attributecertificate based authorization. Technical Report draft-ietf-tls-attr-cert-01.txt, IETF Transport Layer Security Working Group (1998)
16. Brown, M., Housley, R.: Transport layer security (tls) authorization extensions. Technical Report draft-housley-tls-authz-extns-07.txt, IETF (2006)
17. Hess, A., Jacobson, J., Mills, H., Wamsley, R., Seamons, K., Smith, B.: Advanced client/server authentication in tls (2002)

Part II

13th IFIP International Conference on Personal
Wireless Communications (PWC'2008)

Part II

PWC'2008 Committees

General Co-chairs

Zoubir Mammeri, Paul Sabatier University, Toulouse (France)
Partick Senac, ENSICA (France)

Steering Committee

Khaldoun Al Agha, Paris-Sud University (France)
Robert Bestak, Czech Technical University (Czech Republic)
Pedro Cuenca, Universidad de Castilla La Mancha (Spain)
Sonia Heemstra de Groot, Twente Institute (The Netherlands)
Ignacious Niemegeers, University of Twente (The Netherlands)
Tadao Saito, Toyota Info Technology Center (Japan)
Jan Slavik, TESTCOM (Czech Republic)
Otto Spaniol, University of Technology of Aachen (Germany)
Jozef Woznaik, Technical University of Gdansk (Poland)

Technical Program Committee

Robert Bestak, Czech Technical University (Czech Republic)
Chris Blondia, University of Antwerp (Belgium)
Raouf Boutaba, University of Waterloo (Canada)
Raffaele Bruno, IIT-CNR (Italy)
Carlos Cardeira, IST, Lisboa (Portugal)
Augusto Casaca, INESC (Portugal)
Prosper Chemouil, Orange Labs (France)
Pedro Cuenca, Universidad de Castilla-La Mancha (Spain)
Sonia Heemstra de Groot, University of Twente (The Netherlands)
Geert Heijenk, University of Twente (The Netherlands)
Lukas Kencl, CTU-Ericsson-Vodafone, Prague (Czech Republic)
Francine Krief, LABRI (France)
Maryline Laurent-Maknavicius, GET/INT Evry (France)
Pascal Lorenz, University of Haute Alsace (France)
Zoubir Mammeri, Paul Sabatier University, Toulouse (France)
Pietro Manzoni, Universidad Politécnica de Valencia (Spain)
Dora Maros, Budapest Polytechnic (Hungary)

Ami Marowka, Shenkar College of Engineering and Design (Israel)
Antonin Mazalek, University of Defence in Brno (Czech Republic)
Ali Miri, University of Ottawa (Canada)
Guy Pujolle, University of Paris 6 (France)
Debashis Saha, Indian Institute of Management, Calcutta (India)
Tadao Saito - Toyota Info Technology Center (Japan)
Patrick Senac, ENSICA (France)
Jun-Bae Seo, ETRI (Korea)
Ottio Spaniol, University of Technology of Aachen (Germany)
Dirk Staehle, University of Wuerzburg (Germany)
Ivan Stojmenovic, University of Ottawa (Canada)
Luis Villasenõr González, CICESE (Mexico)
Zuzana Vranova, University of Defence in Brno, Czech Republic
Joerg Widmer, DoCoMO Communications Lab. Europe GmbH (Germany)
Jozef Wozniak, Technical University of Gdansk (Poland)

Organizing Committee

G. Boudour (IRIT, Paul Sabatier University,Toulouse, France)
D. Espes (IRIT, Paul Sabatier University,Toulouse, France)
Z. Mammeri (IRIT, Paul Sabatier University,Toulouse, France)
W. Masri (IRIT, Paul Sabatier University,Toulouse, France)
J. Petit (IRIT, Paul Sabatier University,Toulouse, France)
C. Teyssié (IRIT, Paul Sabatier University,Toulouse, France)

Efficient Handover Scheme for Mobile IPv4 over IEEE 802.11 Networks with IEEE 802.21 Triggers[1]

Przemysław Machań, Józef Woźniak

Gdańsk University of Technology, Faculty of Electronics, Telecommunication and Informatics, Narutowicza 11/12, Gdańsk, Poland

przemac@o2.pl, jowoz@eti.pg.gda.pl

Abstract Handover performance is an important factor for wireless networks, especially nowadays, when multimedia services are becoming increasingly available over the wireless devices. However, users expect uncompromised mobility when using the service. Thus, the support of multimedia services is not possible if handover is inefficient. At the same time it is clear that a strict separation between IP Layer and the Link Layer results in built-in sources of delay. The paper discusses the IEEE 802.11 and Mobile IPv4 handover performance in practical scenarios. We introduce a new simultaneous handover scheme with IEEE 802.21 triggers. In order to verify the handover performance, simulation experiments have been conducted, whose results are also presented and discussed.

1 Introduction

With the growing speed of wireless networks, multimedia services are becoming increasingly available for mobile users. Wireless devices expect service continuity even when they move between points of attachment. Handover performance is a crucial factor for multimedia services support. These types of services are very sensitive to the channel disruption, handover delays or packet losses. All these factors will significantly lower the quality of multimedia services. Because of this, it is not possible to support multimedia services without fast enough and transparent handover procedures.

The network layer protocol - Mobile IPv4 (MIPv4) was designed without any assumptions about the link layer operation and that has negative implications on handover delay. The strict separation between IP Layer and Link Layer (according to the principles of layered architectures design) results in built-in sources of delay. The first reason is that Mobile Host (MH) can only exchange messages with a directly connected Foreign Agent. In consequence the MH cannot communicate

---

[1] The work was supported in part by Polish National Center for Research and Development under project PBZ-MNiSW-02/II/2007.

Please use the following format when citing this chapter:

Machań, P. and Woźniak, J., 2008, in IFIP International Federation for Information Processing, Volume 284; *Wireless and Mobile Networking*; Zoubir Mammeri; (Boston: Springer), pp. 287–298.

with a new FA until layer 2 handover is completed. There are two sources of delay: layer 2 handover and event propagation latency to the IP layer. The second one mainly consists of the Mobile IPv4 Registration process latency. During this period the MH is unable to send or receive any IPv4 packets [8].

The paper is structured as follows. The next section reviews the related work. The following sections describe handover performance in both IEEE 802.11 and MIPv4. Then the IEEE 802.21 draft is discussed. The description of simultaneous handover procedures for layer 2 and layer 3 is subsequently presented. Finally, simulation test-bed is described and results of simulation experiments are presented and discussed.

2 Related Work

There is a large number of MIPv4 handover architectures proposed in the literature. One of the most matured extensions to MIPv4 is Low Latency Handoff (LLH) for Mobile IPv4, described in [7]. There are three techniques presented, however the last one is combination of two previous techniques. Pre-Registration handover method allows MH to prepare its registration state in a new Foreign Agent (nFA) via the old Foreign Agent (oFA), before layer 2 handover commences. The second method is a network-assisted handover that can be either network-initiated or mobile-initiated. Link layer triggers are used on both MH and FA to invoke particular handover events.

Fast Handover for Mobile IPv4 (FMIPv4) is an adaptation of the Fast Handover for Mobile IPv6. The intention is to utilize the same design for IPv4 networks, however new packet formats for MIPv4 should be standardized. The main idea behind Fast Handover is to obtain a new Care-of Address (CoA) prior to carrying out the handover, and start to use this address just after layer 2 handover is completed. The tunnel is established between the old Access Router (oAR) and the new Access Router (nAR) to enable MH to send and receive data while the handover proceeds. The main assumptions about network architecture, for Fast Handover, are related to layer 2 and layer 3 interactions. The Access Router must be able to extract the IPv4 address of the nAR from the layer 2 address of the new Access Point (nAP). Similarly to LLH, MIPv6 Fast Handover stack receives a layer 2 trigger when a nAP is discovered.

Both methods assume tightly coupling of layer 2 and layer 3 protocols. Using Pre-Registration protocol from LLH is questionable with IEEE 802.11 as the scanning phase prevents MH from selecting the new Access Point (nAP) without leaving our current point of attachment [2]. On the other hand, establishing the tunnel between oAP and nAP delays the MIP registration. When the layer 2 handover is completed, the MH remains registered with the oFA. However, packets destined to the MH arrive at the oFA, are tunneled to the nFA and are delivered through the nAP.

Both LLH and FMIPv4 are strongly dependent on unspecified layer 2 trigger when handover begins. This trigger cannot be trustworthy in IEEE 802.11 networks as handover detection is the protocol bottleneck and can take more than one second. This delay can lead to a situation when MH looses its connection with oAP before the Pre-Registration procedure is completed.

The simultaneous handover for Mobile IPv4 over IEEE 802.11 (SMIPv4) was originally proposed in [3]. The author suggested extending the IEEE 802.11 specification with the MIPv4-Registration-Request (MIPv4-Reg-Req) Information Element (IE) that can be conveyed in IEEE 802.11 Association Request or IEEE 802.11 Reassociation Request frames. As the described procedure adheres to both Association and Reassociation frames we will use the (Re)Association name to refer to both cases. The IE is extracted by nAP and sent to the nFA as Registration Request. When Registration Response is received at nAP it is compacted into MIPv4-Registration-Reply (MIPv4-Reg-Repl) IE and send back to the MH along with (Re)Association Response message. The new Information Elements have the same fields as MIPv4 Registration related messages.

There are some architectural implications related to the proposed solution. Mobile Host MIP layer must be able to pass its parameters to MAC layer on request. Layer 2 must be able to construct MIPv4 Information Elements. Mobile Host puts its Home Address, as the source address, in the MIPv4-Req-Req IE. The destination address is the multicast address of Mobile-Agents, as defined in MIPv4 specification [13].

IEEE 802.11 Access Point must be able to extract MIPv4 IEs and send them to nFA. If the nFA is co-located with nAP, the MAC and MIP must be able to exchange MIPv4 IEs. If nAP and nFA functionalities are separated nAP operates as proxy for MH. In this paper we will concentrate on the co-located model.

The authors of [10] optimized the simultaneous handover scheme by allowing the nAP to respond to the Association Request message without waiting on MIPv4 Registration Response. This will eliminate the need for MIPv4-Reg-Repl IE and avoid association timer expiration in MH.

The simultaneous handover scheme has a strong advantage over LLH and FMIPv4 solutions. We will propose the extended solution based on standard layer 2 handover end trigger. The advantage of handover end trigger over the handover begin trigger is that the first one can be determined with a high confidence. Although simultaneous handover procedure has strong architectural dependencies, being the clear and tight coupling of layer 2 and layer 3, it is a necessary compromise for an efficient handover. Moreover, because MIPv4 devices are becoming more and more popular, one can expect IEEE 802.11 and MIPv4 solutions to be available on a "single chip" [6].

3 IEEE 802.11 Handover

The handover process has the following phases: detection, search, authentication and association. The handover delay can be expressed by formula (1).

$$T_{802.11} = T_{802.11\text{-detect}} + T_{802.11\text{-scan}} + T_{802.11\text{-auth}} + T_{802.11\text{-(re)assoc}} \tag{1}$$

The detection phase is the time needed for MH to determine when handover must be performed. During this period the network connection can deteriorate or become unavailable. When the network configuration forces the MH to change the AP before the channel condition deteriorates the detection time will not affect handover delay. However, network configuration is not always optimized for handover performance. IEEE 802.11 standard does not provide a shared control channel for this information distribution, so the client must scan channels for prospective APs. The next step is the handover execution: authentication and association; these procedures are defined in the IEEE 802.11 standard. If stations support the IEEE 802.11e extension the handover can be delayed with QoS messages. Moreover, if WPA or WPA2 procedures are in use the key derivation and exchange messages will additionally influence the handover delay.

The described delays differ between implementations and depend on network equipment interoperability and environment conditions [17]. Empirical studies were conducted to estimate the values of parameters [9] [14] [18]; the corresponding data was collected and is shown in Table 1.

Table 1. IEEE 802.11 Handover procedure delays

Parameter	Value
$T_{802.11\text{-detect}}$	300 – 600 ms
$T_{802.11\text{-scan}}$	58 – 400 ms
$T_{802.11\text{-open-auth}}$	Less then 10 ms
$T_{802.11\text{-(re)assoc}}$	Less then 10 ms

The detection phase delay differs when handover is station-initiated or network-initiated. The AP can initiate handover by sending IEEE 802.11 Deassociation Request message. However, in a typical case the station decides to handover when transmission conditions deteriorate. For station-initiated handover the length of detection phase depends strongly on station algorithm.

The explanation for the maximum detection time presented in Table 1 is as follows. If the transmission fails the station assumes collision and retransmits packet at a lower data rate. If the transmission remains unsuccessful, the station assumes signal fading and sends IEEE 802.11 Probe Request to verify the link state. After several unanswered requests the station starts scanning phase.

Generally, there are two groups of detection algorithms, based on: either failed transmissions or received signal strength reported by PHY layer [18]. An example of the algorithm that belongs to the first class is a case when station detects a loss of the connection with an old Access Point (oAP) after three subsequent frames are not sent successfully. In this case T_{detect} refers to a time needed to send three frames. If the station only receives data or does not send or receive data at all, it can monitor reception of IEEE 802.11 Beacon frames. As typical Beacon frame interval is 100 ms the detection time can be estimated as 300 ms.

The algorithms based on signal strength utilized Received Signal Strength Indicator (RSSI) provided by PHY layer – as defined in IEEE specification [4]. The MH can also use SNR metric. However, a technique to acquire noise level is not covered by the standard. The detection methods based on signal strength typically do not provide the accepted performance because of dynamic nature of wireless channel. Although a number of techniques to shorten detection time is provided in the literature[9][18], this is one of the most important bottlenecks.

The active scanning algorithm is described in IEEE 802.11 standard [4]. This procedure is responsible for a significant part of the handover delay. The station sends Probe Request over a particular channel and waits for either medium busy detection within MinChannelTime or MaxChannelTime timer expiration. The procedure is repeated for each channel to be scanned. However, the standard does not define the timer values and the number of channel to be scanned.

$$T_{802.11\text{-scan}} = \sum_{c=1}^{\text{NumChannels}} (1 - P(c)) \cdot T_{\text{MinChannelTime}} + P(c) \cdot T_{\text{MaxChannelTime}} + T_{\text{switch}} \tag{2}$$

The scanning delay can be represented by equation (2). T_{switch} parameter refers to the switch time to a new frequency, resynchronize and start demodulating packets in a new channel. $P(c)$ is the probability that at least one AP will send Probe Response on the selected channel. The described timers are different between implementations and depends on network equipment interoperability and environment conditions.

The number of algorithms is presented in the literature to limit the scanning delay. For example, the authors of SyncScan [14] configure wireless network that the interval between Beacon frames in neighbour channels is constant. According to this scenario Mobile Host can passively scan the next channel in the limited time.

The time for open authentication and reassociation procedures can be modeled as a trivial frame exchange. The measurements show that each procedure takes no more than 10 ms.

4 MIPv4 Handover

The MIPv4 handover delay (T_{MIPv4}) is expressed by equation (3). The delay consists of detection delay, new CoA acquirement and redirection time [15][16].

$$T_{\text{MIPv4}} = T_{\text{MIPv4-detect}} + T_{\text{MIPv4-coa}} + T_{\text{MIPv4-redirect}} \tag{3}$$

The detection time is defined as an interval between the time instance when link layer connection is reestablished with a new AP and the beginning of CoA acquisition procedure. In the next step the station needs to retrieve information about a new care-of-address and the default gateway to resume communication on the new subnet. The time for this procedure is referred to as $T_{\text{MIPv4-coa}}$. Once the required IP level information is obtained, the station redirects its upstream and downstream flows ($T_{\text{MIPv4-redirect}}$). The timing of MIPv4 handover is presented in Fig. 1.

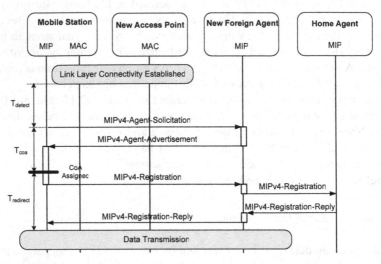

Fig. 1. MIPv4 Handover Timing

To evaluate the handover performance, the more detailed assumptions must be accepted. Detection time depends on the move detection algorithm used. There are three mechanisms proposed for Mobile IPv4 draft: Lazy Cell Switching (LCS), Prefix Matching (PM), and Eager Cell Switching (ECS)[13]. In our experiment the mobile station uses the ECS method. The station records the lifetime received from Agent, with which MH is currently registered. If the lifetime expires until the next Agent Advertisement (AA) is received the station assumes that connectivity with this Agent is lost and the station should perform CoA retrieval procedure. However, MH can attempt to register with another agent if Agent Advertisement from nFA is received before the lifetime of the current Agent expires. Assuming that the advertisement lifetime is $T_{\text{AD-LT}}$ and Agent Advertisements period is T_{AD} the detection time is presented by equation (4). The assumption behind equation (4) is that layer 2 handover is instant. In fact the MIPv4 detection period begins along with IEEE 802.11 handover process, but the first is typically longer.

$$T_{\text{MIPv4-detect(LCS)}} = \frac{\min(T_{\text{AD-LT}}, T_{\text{AD}})}{2} - \frac{\min(T_{\text{AD-LT}}, T_{\text{AD}})^3}{6 T_{\text{AD-LT}} T_{\text{AD}}} \qquad (4)$$

The evaluation of detection time depends directly on Agent Advertisement period. Advertisement lifetime should be at least three times higher then AA period. The AA rate was initially limited to one per second [13] to save the wireless bandwidth. However, with the increasing wireless network speed and the demand for seamless handover, the AA period can be lowered. The authors assumed AA period to be one second. Both $T_{\text{MIPv4-coa}}$ and $T_{\text{MIPv4-redirect}}$ can be modeled as frame exchange and not introduce a significant delay to the MIPv4 handover procedure. The handover phase delays are collected in Table 2.

Table 2. MIPv4 Handover procedure delays

Parameter	Value
$T_{\text{MIPv4-detect(LCS)}}$	100 – 1000 ms
$T_{\text{MIPv4-coa}}$	Less then 10 ms
$T_{\text{MIPv4-redirect}}$	Less then 40 ms

5 IEEE 802.21 Framework

The IEEE 802.21 standard introduces Media Independent Handover (MIH) Function that is considered a shim layer in the network stack of both network node and the network elements that provide mobility support [5]. MIH Function provides abstracted services to the upper layers and communicates with lower layers through technology-specific interfaces. Handover control, handover polices and other algorithms involved in handover decision-making are handled by communication system elements and are not part of the IEEE 802.21 specification.

The scope of IEEE 802.21 standard will include a universal architecture that provides service continuity while a MN switches between heterogeneous link-layer technologies. The MIH Function provides the following services: Media Independent Event Service (MIES), Media Independent Command Service (MICS), and Media Independent Information Service (MIIS).

MIES provides both local and remote events and triggers to the upper layers of MN. Typical events are MIH Link Up or MIH Link Parameters Change, originated in layer 2. MICS provides functions to gather the status of links and invoke commands to control handover process. The commands receiver can be both local and remote. Typical commands are MIH Poll used to poll physical links or MIH Configure used to configure connected links. MIIS defines access to network database that contains information used to aim handover process. The network information is stored in platform independent description language and can be: static and dynamic. Static information examples are network and provider name, whilst dynamic information comprises a channel, security configuration and MAC addresses.

6 Simultaneous Handover with IEEE 802.21 triggers

The concept of simultaneous handover assumes tight coupling of layers 2 and 3 protocols that should result in improved handover efficiency. In the paper we extend the procedure proposed in [10] by the usage of the standard MIH Link Up trigger. This will make it possible to simplify the implementation of protocol on MH. MIPv4 instance does not need to pass parameters to MAC layer and can operate transparently. The handover procedure is depicted in Fig. 2.

The handover procedure begins when Mobile Host MAC detects the handover that is marked as L1 trigger. The active scanning procedure is invoked in the next step. When nAP is selected the Link Up event is passed to the MIH layer and propagated to the MIH Client (MIP). When the event is received the Mobile IPv4 layer sends the Registration Request message. The RR message is transformed into Registration-Request-IE in the MAC layer. The other operations are the same as in the base protocol.

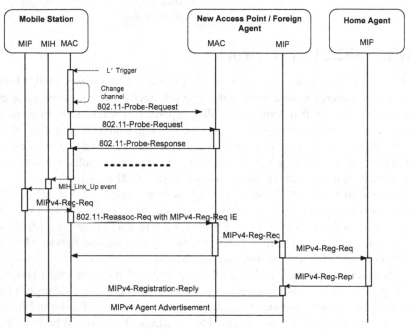

Fig. 2. Simultaneous handoff for IEEE 802.11 and MIPv4

7 Test-bed Implementation

The model of simultaneous handover with our extension was implemented in widely used ns-2 simulator. We based on handover support developed for Seamless and Secure Mobility project [12]. For the purpose of the simulation the model of a "city market" was created, as presented in Fig. 3. There are three Mobile Routers (MR), each of them have both IEEE 802.11 Access Point and MIPv4 Foreign Agent functionalities. The stations move within an area of 180 x 60 meters with the velocity of 1m/s. The number of stations and traffic load was changed to verify correctness of the protocol operation. The experiments were conducted using 10 different, random mobility patterns.

Mobile stations were downloading CBR stream using 1000-bytes-long fixed-size UDP packets. The reason for using UDP, and not TCP, is that TCP infers congestion from packet loss and scales back its send window accordingly. The experiments aimed at how throughput, handover delay and packet loss are affected by handover algorithms, rather than due to protocol-induced throughput reductions. Although TCP is used for many network applications, the majority of real-time multimedia services are based on UDP.

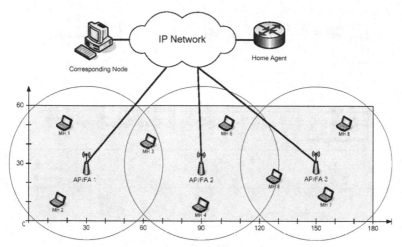

Fig. 3. Simulation scenario for simultaneous handover

8 Simulation Results

The experiments were conducted to compare the handover performance using original and simultaneous handover procedures. The handover delay measurements are presented in Fig. 4. Station number in the experiments is marked in the legend as n. The delay was measured as time between last packet received by MH through the old MR and the first packet received via the new MR. The handover delay does not depend on the network load or the number of stations, but results were presented for consistency. The regular handover scenario is implemented without any handover-optimized mechanisms. MIPv4 handover proceeds independently of IEEE 802.11 handover. The variation of handover delay for regular handover is higher than using simultaneous handover. The reason is that regular MIPv4 handover time is dependent on T_{AD-LT} and T_{AD} timers as described previously.

The detection delay ($T_{SMIPv4-detect}$) is, in the case of simultaneous handover procedure, the time between the IEEE 802.11 (Re)Association Response message is received by MH and MIH Link Up trigger is received by MIPv4 layer. The detection delay strongly depends on internal MH design and its value, in our experiments, was below 1 ms. In turn, the total delay for simultaneous handover ($T_{SMIPv4-802.11}$ = 550 ms) was about 45% lower when compared with the regular scenario ($T_{MIPv4-802.11}$ = 1000 ms). However, the value of $T_{SMIPv4-802.11}$ is still not accepted for multimedia services. Using simultaneous handovers the layer 3 handover delay

T_{SMIPv4} is optimized to less then 30 ms, compared to $T_{MIPv4} = 450$ ms when using the regular protocols. In further investigations we plan to optimize $T_{802.11}$ - the layer 2 handover.

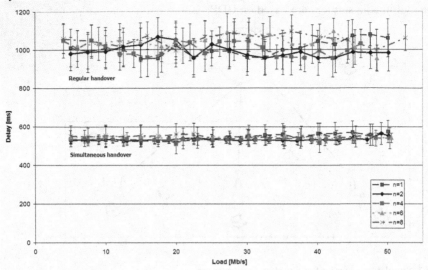

Fig. 4. Handover delay vs. network load

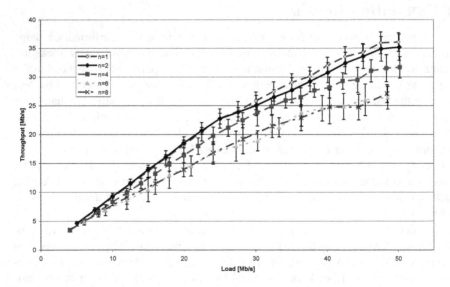

Fig. 5. Data throughput vs. network load in the regular handover scenario

The results of handover delay can be roughly compared with LLH and FMIPv4 performance. The simulation results presented in [1] show that packets sent during the handover with LLH or FMIPv4 experience the delay not longer then 100 ms. Although simulation scenarios were different, we can estimate that SMIPv4 handover delay is shorter compared with the LLH and FMIPv4 protocols.

The data throughput variations vs. network load are presented in Fig. 5 and Fig. 6. The charts show only user data; signal and protocol messages (e.g. IEEE 802.11 Management and Control frames, MIPv4 Registration frames) were not measured. The effective throughput of the network with SMIPv4 handover is slightly higher when compared to MIPv4 case because of the shorter handover delays.

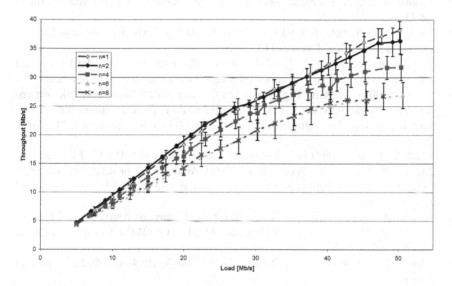

Fig. 6. Data throughput vs. network load in the simultaneous handover scenario

9 Conclusions

The article presents a handover performance analysis with respect to the overall delay. The delay components in each layer were selected and described. The main interest was in the MIPv4 protocols performance. Existing protocols that claim to support fast handovers are based on the layer 2 trigger indicating handover begin. This IEEE 802.21 trigger is unreliable when handover is typically station-initiated, as is the case in IEEE 802.11. We have proposed and described the simultaneous handover procedure that uses the layer 2 handover end trigger. The main advantage of our solution over the previously described is that handover end can be trustfully determined in IEEE 802.11 networks. The simultaneous handover protocol was modeled using ns-2. The results show that layer 3 handover was optimized; the total handover delay was shortened from 1050 ms to 550 ms in typical scenarios.

References

1. Blondia C Casals O Cerdà L Van den Wijngaert N Willems G (2004) Performance Evaluation of Layer 3 Low Latency Handoff Mechanisms. Mobile Netw and Appl 9:633-645
2. De Cleyn P Van den Wijngaert N Cerdà L Blondia C (2004) A Smooth Handoff Scheme Using IEEE802.11 Triggers - Design and Implementation. Comp Netw:345-361
3. Goswami S (2003) Simultaneous Handoff of Mobile-IPv4 and 802.11. Internet Draft
4. IEEE Comp Society (1999) Part11: Wireless LAN Medium Access Control (MAC) and Physical Layer (PHY) Specifications.
5. IEEE Comp Society (2007) P802.21/D05.00: Draft IEEE Standard for Local and Metropolitan Area Networks: Media Independent Handover Services.
6. Love J (2005) Thinking Big: These single-chip switch processors take on enterprise wired/wireless LANs. http://www.eeproductcenter.com /test-measure/review/showArticle.jhtml?articleID=60402054. Accessed 24 March 2008
7. Malki El K (ed) (2007) Low-Latency Handoffs in Mobile IPv4. RFC 4881
8. Matusz P, Machan P, Wozniak J (2003) Analysis of profitability of inter-system handovers between IEEE 802.11b and UMTS. IEEE Conf on Local Comput Netw
9. Mishra A Shin M Arbaugh W A (2003) An Empirical Analysis of the IEEE 802.11 MAC Layer Handoff Process. ACM SIGCOMM Comput Commun Rev:93-102
10. Mun Y Park J (2003) Layer 2 Handoff for Mobile-IPv4 with 802.11. Internet Draft
11. Mun Y Park J (2004) The Layer 2 Handoff Scheme for Mobile IP over IEEE 802.11 Wireless LAN. Springer-Verlag LNCS 3043:1144-1150
12. NIST (2007) Seamless and Secure Mobility. http://www.antd.nist.gov/ seamlessandsecure.shtml. Accessed 01 June 2008
13. Perkins C (ed) (2002) IP Mobility Support for IPv4. RFC 3344
14. Ramani I Savage S (2005) SyncScan: Practical Fast Handoff for 802.11 Infrastructure Networks. IEEE Infocom Conf
15. Rückforth T (2004) AAA Context Transfer for Fast Authenticated Inter-Domain Handover. Swisscom SA Innovations Broadband Network, Bern
16. Vatn J O (2000) Improving Mobile IP handover performance. Royal Institute of Technology, Stockholm
17. Vatn J O (2003) An experimental study of IEEE 802.11b handover performance and its effect on voice traffic. Royal Institute of Technology, Stockholm
18. Velayos H, Karlsson G (2004) Techniques to reduce the IEEE 802.11b handoff time. IEEE Int Conf on Commun

On Enhancing a Hybrid Admission Control Algorithm for IEEE 802.11e EDCA

Mohamad El Masri, Guy Juanole and Slim Abdellatif

Mohamad EL MASRI · Guy Juanole · Slim Abdellatif
LAAS-CNRS ; Université de Toulouse ; 7, avenue du Colonel Roche, F-31077 Toulouse, France
e-mail: {masri,juanole,slim}@laas.fr

Abstract Call Admission Control is one of the main mechanisms allowing an efficient protection of active flows, especially on a wireless network using a distributed access scheme as is the case for IEEE 802.11e EDCA. We proposed in a previous paper [5] a hybrid admission control algorithm (based on analytical model and on measurements) for EDCA which have proven to perform well when compared to another reference algorithm. We present here general modifications to hybrid admission control algorithms. These modifications are applied to our proposed algorithm and analyzed via simulation. Analysis clearly shows the advantages of these modifications.

1 Introduction

Providing quality of service (QoS) within an access network is one of the main challenges facing wireless access networks nowadays. Recent advances in this area include the standardization in 2005 of the QoS amendments to the IEEE 802.11 standard [1] (done by the IEEE 802.11e working group [2]). 802.11e introduced a new access function called the Hybrid Coordination Function (HCF) including one distributed access mechanism (the Enhanced Distributed Channel Access - EDCA) and a centralized polling based mechanism (the HCF Centralized Channel Access - HCCA). EDCA is a CSMA/CA based distributed channel access with traffic differentiation. EDCA classifies packets into 4 access categories with a different access probability each. The 4 access categories (AC) defined by EDCA are: Voice (AC_VO), Video (AC_VI), Best Effort (AC_BE) and Background (AC_BK).
One of the main mechanisms used in order to protect the time sensitive flows using the network from incoming flows is admission control. A flow wishing to use a network in which admission control is applied must first request admission to the network; the admission control's mission is to protect already admitted flows from incoming ones: it thus must decide whether to accept the requesting flow or not based on the incoming flow's specification and on the network's state. The 802.11e working group specifies a framework for admission control algorithms including main procedures and the necessary signaling messages but leaves the specification

Please use the following format when citing this chapter:

El Masri, M., Juanole, G. and Abdellatif, S., 2008, in IFIP International Federation for Information Processing, Volume 284; *Wireless and Mobile Networking*; Zoubir Mammeri; (Boston: Springer), pp. 299–310.

of the algorithm *per se* to manufacturers when deemed relevant.

Several admission control algorithms have been proposed for IEEE 802.11e in literature. Gao et. al. [6] give an overview of some of them. Gao et. al. divide the EDCA admission control algorithms into measurement based algorithms (those basing the admission decision on measurements of network status) and model based (those using an analytical model to assess the behavior of the network).

In [5] we proposed a hybrid admission control algorithm (based both on an analytical model and on measurement of network specific metrics). The algorithm we proposed is made out of three interacting blocks: a parameterized Markov chain model of a saturated Access Category allowing the calculation of a maximum achievable throughput for a given flow; an estimation process of future collision rates and busy probabilities based on actual measurements made on the medium, those estimations are injected to the model in order to make the achievable throughput calculation more accurate; and an admission decision process based on information on the specifications of the flow requiring admission and on the calculated achievable throughput. Extensive simulations were made and the algorithm we proposed proved to perform better than a reference model based algorithm [7]. However, in some cases, the algorithm admitted flows in excess. We propose in this paper enhancements to correct this flaw that can be applied to any similar hybrid algorithm.

The modifications we present here are introduced to both the estimation process and to the decision process. Two main ideas steer those modifications: one is to condition the estimation process and the decision process by the medium state leading to more drastic refusals, the other is to introduce feedback correction to the estimation process of busy probabilities.

The paper presents as follows: the next section details the admission control algorithm we presented in [5] including a brief introduction to the Markov chain model used within the algorithm. The following section presents the enhancements we propose to the algorithm. The fourth section presents, by means of simulation, the analysis and the comparison of the enhancements. Conclusion and future work are given at the end of the paper.

2 The hybrid admission control for EDCA

In this section we present the hybrid admission control algorithm for EDCA. The algorithm was thoroughly presented in [5]. We first briefly present the Markov chain model upon which is based the admission control algorithm for EDCA. We then present the different aspects of the algorithm.

2.1 Introducing the model

We designed a discrete Markov chain model of an EDCA Access Category (AC) behavior. The model included all the standard access functions: differentiated defer- ence and backoff procedure, different collision situations, virtual collision, retrans- missions and drops among other mechanisms. This general model was presented in [3]. The general model was later reduced into a three-useful-state model and pre- sented in [4]. From this reduced model several closed form performance metrics were derived among which is the achievable throughput of a saturated Access Cat- egory Queue in a specified environment (represented by the collision probability p_i and the probability of the medium becoming busy p_b). The synthetic model is shown in figure 1. The synthetic model is composed of three useful states: the Access At- tempt state labeled 1, the successful transmission state labeled 2 and the drop state labeled 3. The Access Attempt state represents the state of an *AC* (which we call AC_i) trying to transmit a packet (going through several unsuccessful transmission attempts, the backoff times preceding those attempts and the backoff time preced- ing the supposedly successful transmission attempt). The successful transmission state and the drop state represent respectively the fact that a packet's transmission was possible or not (the retransmission threshold being reached). The transitions between the states are labeled with the transition probability and the transition time (transition time from state 3 to state 1 is null, we suppose that after a packet drop, the access category proceeds instantaneously with the access attempt of a new packet). T_T is the time it takes AC_i to transit from the Access Attempt state to the Successful transmission state (i.e. the access delay of a successfully transmitted packet), this occurs with probability P_T. T_D is the time it takes AC_i to transit from the Access Attempt state to the Drop state with probability P_D (i.e. the packet's retransmission threshold -noted $m + h$- was reached, the packet is dropped).

This model is a discrete Markov chain. We can evaluate by means of the transition probabilities and the transition times the equilibrium probabilities of states 1, 2 and 3: Π_1, Π_2 and Π_3. We get $\Pi_1 = \frac{1}{2}$; $\Pi_2 = \Pi_1 P_T$; $\Pi_3 = \Pi_1 P_D$. From these probabilities we can conclude the formula of the achievable throughput of a saturated *AC*:

$$Throughput_i =$$

Fig. 1 Abstract model of an
EDCA AC behavior

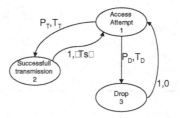

Payload being the number of slots necessary to transmit the payload.

We do not present the detailed formulas of transition times and transition probabilities of the synthetic model because of lack of space and since it is out of the scope of this paper. Note however that they are function of p_i and p_b among other parameters. We highly recommend the reader to check the detailed formulas in our previous work [4, 5].

2.2 The algorithm

We give a quick overview of the functioning of the algorithm and the different mechanisms used in the decision making process.

The algorithm is called when a new flow request arrives at the Access Point's admission controller. Two conditions must apply in order for the algorithm to accept the arriving flow: first the arriving flow must be able to achieve its request in terms of throughput, the second condition being that the admission of the new flow must not degrade the quality of service of already admitted flows. The algorithm bases its admission decision on two parameters:

- estimations made on what each flow's collision rate and the medium busy rate would be if the newly arriving flow was to be admitted (those estimations are made based on actual measurements as explained in next section).
- the maximum achievable throughput of each flow, in the previously estimated collision and medium business conditions, calculated using the Markov chain model of an access category presented earlier.

Algorithm 1 Admission control using the synthetic model

---

  for each *Update_Period* **do**
    Update_Busy_Probability
    Update_Collision_Probabilities
    if *New_Flows* $\neq \emptyset$ **then**
      F_i = Get_New_Flow
      Calculate_Achievable_Throughput(
      Admitted_Flows $\cup F_i$)
      if Check_Throughput (*Admitted_Flows* $\cup F_i$) **then**
        Admit(F_i)
        Admitted_Flows = *Admitted_Flows* $\cup F_i$
      else
        Refuse (F_i)
      end if
    end if
  end for

We define F_i as the flow requesting admission, *New_Flows* is the set of all newly arriving flows, *Admitted_Flows* is the set of active flows. *Update_Busy_Probability* and *Update_Collision_Probabilities* are the procedures giving the admission controller the information he needs on both probabilities (by direct measurement for the busy probability and by piggybacking from the different flows for their collision probabilities). The procedure *Calculate_Achievable_Throughput(SetofFlows)* calculates for each flow (all the active flows and one newly arriving flow) their maximum achievable throughput in the estimated network conditions (i.e. for a given flow, its throughput if saturated, given the estimated busy probability and the estimated collision probability). Procedure *Check_Throughput(SetofFlows)* returns true if, for each of the flows in the set, its achievable throughput is greater that its request: *Calculated_Achievable_Throughput(F)* > *Requested_Bandwidth(F)*. The algorithm is detailed in algorithm 1.

2.3 Estimating the probabilities

In the process of decision making, the values of busy probability p_b and each AC's collision probability are needed. The busy probability can be directly measured by the Access Point. The collision probabilities are calculated by the stations and communicated periodically to the access point by means of piggybacking or management packets (in fact the station will communicate, for each AC, a count of access attempts and of collisions). We figured that since the measurements are made in the actual context of the medium (i.e. having only the already admitted flows active and not those requesting admission), the achievable throughput calculation wouldn't be correct. Thus, an additional process of estimation was added which, based on the actual measurements made and on the specification of the flow requesting to access the medium, will estimate the values of collision probability and busy probability would the requesting flow be admitted.

Let F_i be the flow whose admission is being examined, F_i will be using access category AC_i in station s. We also define τ_i as the probability for AC_i to access the medium on a free slot. We define Γ_s, the probability for station s to access the medium. Among the access categories of a station, only one can access the medium at a specific time slot (the others are either inactive or in backoff procedure or have lost a virtual collision); we can therefore write $\Gamma_s = \sum_{i=0}^{3} \tau_i$.

We define p_b as the probability of the medium becoming busy. We neglect the reasons of business of the medium other than station access, we therefore write

$$p_b = 1 - (1 - \Gamma_1)(1 - \Gamma_2)\ldots(1 - \Gamma_M) = 1 - \prod_{j=1}^{M}(1 - \Gamma_j)$$

M being the number of stations in the medium.

p_{ir} is the probability for AC_i to suffer a real collision when accessing the medium, we can write p_{ir} as follows:

$$p_{ir} = \tau_i(1 - (1 - \Gamma_1)\ldots(1 - \Gamma_{s-1})(1 - \Gamma_{s+1})\ldots(1 - \Gamma_M)) = \tau_i(1 - \prod_{j \neq s}(1 - \Gamma_j))$$

In order to better understand the following, note that all values indexed *old* are measured values (either directly by the access point, or measured by the stations and communicated to the access point). The values indexed *new* are estimated values (estimation of what would the value be if the requesting flow was active).

In the case of the collision probability, we estimate the effect of introducing F_i on real collisions occurring on the medium. Since we consider the admission of one flow at a time, we suppose that the access activity of F_i's station would be the only one to change. Let p_{ir_new} and τ_{i_new} be the estimated real collision probability of AC_i and its estimated access probability if F_i was to be accepted. p_{ir_old} and τ_{i_old} the actual real collision and access probabilities. We have:

$$p_{ir\_new} - p_{ir\_old} = (\tau_{i\_new} - \tau_{i\_old})(1 - \prod_{j \neq s}(1 - \Gamma_{j\_old}))$$

$$p_{ir\_new} = (\tau_{i\_new} - \tau_{i\_old})(1 - \prod_{j \neq s}(1 - \Gamma_{j\_old})) + p_{ir\_old}$$

Let Δ_τ be the difference introduced by F_i to the access category's access probability should F_i be accepted. We have:

$$p_{ir\_new} = (\Delta_\tau)(1 - \prod_{j \neq s}(1 - \Gamma_{j\_old})) + p_{ir\_old}$$

This estimated ratio will be considered as the estimation of what AC_i's real collision probability would be if F_i was to be admitted. In the equation above, the access activities of the stations are communicated to the HC along with the information on the different active flows.

In the same fashion as above, we define p_{b_new} as the estimated busy probability if F_i was to be accepted and p_{b_old} the actual busy probability. Since we consider the admission of one flow at a time, we suppose that the access activity of AC_i would be the only one to change. Hence:

$$\frac{1 - p_{b\_new}}{1 - p_{b\_old}} = \frac{(1 - \Gamma_{1\_old})(1 - \Gamma_{2\_old})\ldots(1 - \Gamma_{i\_new})\ldots(1 - \Gamma_{M\_old})}{(1 - \Gamma_{1\_old})(1 - \Gamma_{2\_old})\ldots(1 - \Gamma_{i\_old})\ldots(1 - \Gamma_{M\_old})}$$

$$= \frac{(1 - \Gamma_{i\_new})}{(1 - \Gamma_{i\_old})}$$

Following the same reasoning as for the estimation of the real probability we have:

$$\frac{1 - p_{b\_new}}{1 - p_{b\_old}} = \frac{(1 - \Gamma_{i\_new})}{(1 - \Gamma_{i\_old})} = \frac{(1 - \Gamma_{i\_old} - \Delta_\tau)}{(1 - \Gamma_{i\_old})}$$

$$1 - p_{b\_new} = (1 - p_{b\_old})\frac{(1 - \Gamma_{i\_old} - \Delta_\tau)}{(1 - \Gamma_{i\_old})}$$

$$p_{b\_new} = 1 - (1 - p_{b\_old})\left(1 - \frac{\Delta_\tau}{(1 - \Gamma_{i\_old})}\right)$$

The only unknown in both estimations is Δ_τ. Δ_τ represents the additional accesses introduced by the new flow which can be additional transmission and possible retransmissions introduced by the flow. Considering only one possible collision per transmitted packet, we use the following to estimate Δ_τ: $\Delta_\tau = (1 + p_{ir})\delta$, δ being the number of accesses introduced by the flow (i.e. the number of packets to be sent during the update period). Both those estimations will be used in the calculation of the achievable throughput during the admission making process.

3 Enhancing the algorithm

Simulations have been made showing that the estimations we make of collision probabilities and of busy probability, although going in the correct direction, are not exact. This is mainly due to the following fact: we consider in our estimations that the new flow will affect the collision rate of its access queue alone; however, it is a fact that all other access queues will be affected by the new flow. The admission control algorithm worked correctly but did, in some cases, wrong admission decisions. Two main ideas drove the enhancements we propose:

- adding information about medium state either to the estimation process or to the decision process.
- correcting the estimations made on the different probabilities with the help of a feedback correction system.

3.1 Additional medium information

3.1.1 added to the estimation process

When estimating what busy probability p_b or collision probability p_i would be if flow F_i was to be accepted, we consider that the new flow will introduce a number of accesses and collisions in correlation with the number of packets it has to send. However, it is clear that the number of collision will be greater with a greater number of flows accessing the medium or with a greater busy rate of the medium. We thus decided to introduce pessimism into the estimation process which will be in correlation with the occupation of the medium: the greater the occupation of the medium, the greater will be the estimated busy probability. This is done as follows: the estimated value of p_b is multiplied by $1 < \alpha < 1.2$ which we will call the pessimism factor. We have $\alpha = 1 + 0.2 * (1 - \frac{totalBandwidth - totalRequests}{totalBandwidth})$. α will be greater with a greater occupation of the medium.

3.1.2 added to the decision process

The change introduced at this level is driven by the intuition that a bad admission decision that could have been avoided is taken when the medium has a high occupation rate. The algorithm should thus be more reluctant to admit with a higher occupation rate of the medium. Our proposal to replace the usual comparison on which is based the decision by the following comparison:
$\alpha Calculated\_Achievable\_Throughput(F) > Requested\_Bandwidth(F)$ where $0 \leq \alpha \leq 1$ and can be written: $\alpha = (1 - \beta) + \beta * \frac{totalBandwidth - totalRequests}{totalBandwidth}$ β will specify the degree of pessimism and was set to 0.2 for the simulations. The greater the requests, the greater α, more pessimistic become the decisions. With β as little as 0.2, the decision will mainly be based on the information given by the model.

3.2 Estimation correction

Since the estimation process we introduced fails in giving correct results in high medium occupation periods, and as said earlier, bad decisions are usually taken in high medium occupation periods, we introduce a simple history-less feedback correction of busy probability estimation where we add to each estimation the error made on the previous one. Let p_{be_k} the kth estimated value of p_b (using the original estimation process), p_{bm_k} the kth measured value of p_b and let $p_{b\_new\_k}$ be the new corrected estimation of p_b. The estimation works as follows:
$p_{b\_new\_k} = p_{be\_k} + (p_{bm\_k-1} - p_{be\_k-1})$.

4 Analyzing the enhancements

We present in this section analysis we made of the three enhancements we propose to the admission control algorithm. The analysis is made by means of simulation using the network simulator (ns-2) [8]. We use the EDCA module contributed by the Telecommunication Networks Group of the Technical university of Berlin [9]. The EDCA module was modified in order to integrate the admission control we propose along with the enhancements. For each scenario we present, 10 simulations with different random number generator seeds were executed, the results we present in this section are sample means. In each simulation, a number of flows will be periodically activated, seeking thus admission to access the network through the

Scenario	Packet Size (Bytes)	Interarrival (s)	Bandwidth (Mbps)
Scenario 1	600	0.002	2.4
Scenario 2	800	0.004	1.6
Scenario 3	600	0.004	1.2

Table 1 Specifying the presented scenarios

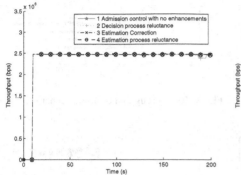
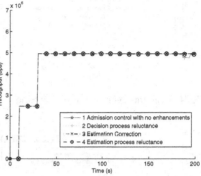

Fig. 2 Mean throughput of flows, scenario 1   **Fig. 3** Total throughput of flows, scenario 1

admission control algorithm (or through the enhanced admission control algorithm). The metrics used for the analysis are the following:

- The total throughput of all the flows in a specific scenario using the algorithm with or without the enhancements.
- The mean throughput of a flow in a specific scenario using the algorithm with or without the enhancements.
- The cumulative distribution function of the delays of all data packets.

Different execution scenarios were tested, we present in the following the results of several representative scenarios. In scenarios 1, 2, and 3: the channel is considered error free, no hidden terminals are present and the stations function at 11 Mbps. One station operates as the Access Point and will execute the admission control algorithm. Within the other stations CBR flows with the traffic specifications described in table 1 will be periodically activated, thus requesting access to the admission controller. The results of those simulations are presented in figures 2-10.

4.1 Analysis

Scenarios 1, 2 and 3 presented here are representative of the different behaviors encountered for different simulation scenarios tested. Note that the bad admission decisions of the original admission control algorithm are not generalized. The algorithm works well but does in some cases bad admission decisions, hence the intro-

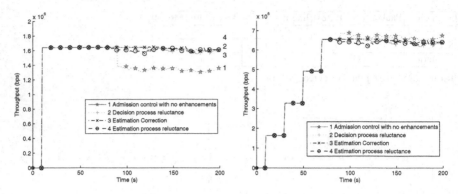

Fig. 4 Mean throughput of flows, scenario 3   **Fig. 5** Total throughput of flows, scenario 3

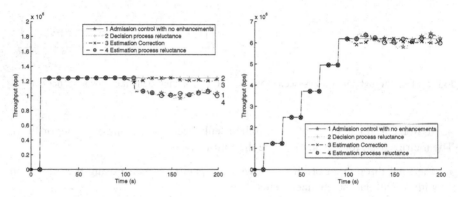

Fig. 6 Mean throughput of flows, scenario 3   **Fig. 7** Total throughput of flows, scenario 3

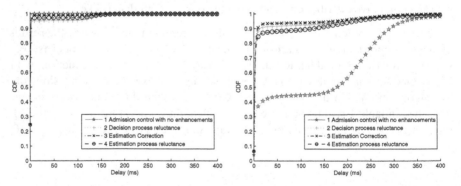

Fig. 8 CDF of delays, scenario 1   **Fig. 9** CDF of delays, scenario 2

duction of the proposed modifications. It can be clearly seen in the following that two of the three proposed modifications achieve a correction of the problems of the original algorithm.

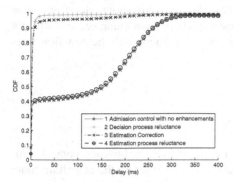

Fig. 10 CDF of delays, scenario 3

Scenario 1

The results are presented in figures 2, 3, 8. Scenario 1 is a case where no bad admission decisions were made by the admission control algorithm. It can be seen that the enhancements proposed did not degrade the service offered by the admission control algorithm. The enhancements admitted the ideal number of flows: maximizing the utilization of the medium without degrading the service offered to the active flows (fig. 2-3). As we said earlier, the main aim of the enhancements is to make admission decisions more drastic in order to avoid a bad admission decision. Here, no bad decisions were taken, neither by the original admission control algorithm nor by the enhanced algorithm: the mean throughput per flow respects each flows request and the delays are minimal (fig. 8).

Scenario 2

The results are presented in figures 4, 5, 9. In scenario 2, the original algorithm will admit one too many flows. The enhancements will correct this flaw. This will result in a better mean throughput per flow (fig. 4) (better in the way it respects the admitted flows requests) and a better distribution of delays (fig. 9) (with the enhancements, depending on the case, 90 % of the packets have delays less than 10 ms whereas it is the case for only 37 % of the packets in the scenario without enhancements). The flow that was admitted in excess by the original algorithm will cause unexpectedly additional collisions which will in turn cause the service provided to be degraded.

Scenario 3

The results are presented in figures 6, 7, 10. The same analysis can be made here with the difference that the estimation process enhancement presented in section 3.1.1 will not correct the admission control algorithm's flaw in this scenario. It is mostly the case with flows with small bandwidth demand requesting admission:

when the admission control algorithm makes a bad decision about admitting a flow with a smaller requested bandwidth the estimation process enhancement will not correct it. This enhancement acting mainly in a way linear with the new flow's request, its effect will be lessened.

5 Conclusion

We have proposed, in this paper, modifications to an hybrid admission control algorithm for IEEE 802.11e EDCA with the objective of rendering the algorithm more reluctant to admit a flow in a high occupancy rate of the medium: so as to avoid bad admission decisions made by the original algorithm. Simulations were made showing the behavior of each of the modifications in varying scenarios. Two of the proposed modifications corrected the original algorithm's problem. We would plead for the busy probability correction modification to be used as it is simpler to implement, more logical and with a better performance in most cases. Future work include implementing the algorithm presented here along with the enhancements and testing it within an experimental WMM (Wireless Multimedia) platform.

References

1. International Standard for Telecommunications and Information Exchange between Systems – LAN/MAN specific Requirements – Part 11: Wireless LAN MAC and PHY specifications, 1999
2. IEEE Standard for Telecommunications and Information Exchange between Systems – LAN/MAN specific Requirements – Part 11: Wireless LAN MAC and PHY specifications – Amendment 8: Medium Access Control QoS Enhancements, November 2005
3. Mohamad El Masri and Guy Juanole and Slim Abdellatif: Revisiting the Markov chain model of IEEE 802.11e EDCA and introducing the virtual collision phenomenon, proceedings of the International Conference on Wireless Information Networks and Systems, WINSYS '07, July 2007
4. Mohamad El Masri and Guy Juanole and Slim Abdellatif, A synthetic model of IEEE 802.11e EDCA, proceedings of the International Conference on Latest Advances in Networks, ICLAN '07, December 2007
5. Mohamad El Masri and Guy Juanole and Slim Abdellatif, Hybrid admission control algorithm for IEEE 802.11e EDCA: analysis, the International Conference on Networks, ICN '08", April 2008
6. Deyun Gao and Jianfei Cai and King Ngi Ngan, Admission control in IEEE 802.11e wireless LANs, IEEE Network, vol. 19, pp. 6-13, July-August 2005
7. Dennis Pong and Tim Moors, Call admission control for IEEE 802.11 contention access mechanism ,IEEE Global Telecommunications Conference, GLOBECOM '03, December 2003
8. The network Simulator - ns-2, http://www.isi.edu/nsnam/ns/
9. An IEEE 802.11e EDCA and CFB Simulation Model for ns-2, http://www.tkn.tu-berlin.de/research/802.11e_ns2/

Study on Intermittent WLAN Consisting of Heterogeneous Multi-radio Devices

Xue Yang, Jing Zhu and Xingang Guo

xue.yang, jing.z.zhu, xingang.guo @ intel.com

Communication Technology Lab, Intel Corporation, Hillsboro, OR, 97124, USA

Abstract It is envisioned that multiple radios may be integrated into a single portable device in the near future. Such multi-radio devices may participate in multiple networks at the same time. In this paper, we consider a 802.11 WLAN network that shares a common set of multi-radio devices with another network, say CO-NETWORK, and we discuss WiMAX as one example of CO-NETWORK. One multi-radio device may not actively operate in WLAN when the same device is transmitting or receiving in the CO-NETWORK. As such, two networks interact with each other via shared multi-radio devices; and scheduling in CO-NETWORK may affect the performance of WLAN. In this paper, we study how the fairness/throughput of a WLAN network may be affected by the scheduling of CO-NETWORK. We further propose some scheduling optimization criteria for CO-NETWORK to minimize such impact. Simulation and analytical results are provided to support our discussions.

1 Introduction

The fast development of wireless technologies in recent years is evidenced by the proliferation of wireless standards such as IEEE 802.11, IEEE 802.16, and IEEE 802.15. As different technologies aim to provide wireless connections in different environments, it is likely that multiple technologies will coexist. Moreover, future wireless devices will likely be equipped with multiple radios of various technologies. We refer to such a device as *Multi-radio Device (MRD)* in this paper. Figure 1 shows several MRDs equipped with both WLAN radios and WiMAX radios.

With MRD, it is often desirable to let all radios equipped on the same device connect to their respective networks at the same time. On the other hand, there can be resource constraints among the co-located radios due to mutual interference or shared hardware component, which prevent them from operating at exactly the same time. For example, WLAN and Bluetooth radios operate at overlapping spectrum and they will interfere with each other when operating simultaneously. When WiMAX operates at 2.5 GHz frequency band, similar problems exist between WLAN and WiMAX radios due to out-of-band emission and receiver

Please use the following format when citing this chapter:

Yang, X., Zhu, J. and Guo, X., 2008, in IFIP International Federation for Information Processing, Volume 284; *Wireless and Mobile Networking*; Zoubir Mammeri; (Boston: Springer), pp. 311–328.

saturation. If simultaneous operations of multiple co-located radios are not possible, time sharing mechanisms can be adopted such that co-located radios operate in TDM (Time-Division-Multiplex) fashion and the MRD frequently switches between different networks (at packet level) to allow perceived concurrent connections. One example of such TDM operations is the Packet Traffic Arbitration (PTA) mechanism defined in IEEE 802.15.2 [2] to resolve the mutual interference between co-located WLAN and Bluetooth radios.

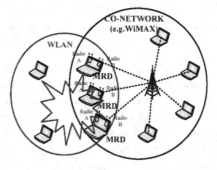

Fig. 1. Multi-radio Devices serve in both WLAN and CO-NETWORK

It is practically possible for MRD to perform TDM operations while maintaining perceived concurrent connections, since typical networks are designed such that no single radio will saturate the network. Since one device will not be busy all the time in one network (NETWORK1), this device can possibly find some time to serve in the second network (NETWOKR2).   Figure 2 illustrates the interleaved activities of **one** MRD, where it serves in NETWORK 1 for some time and switches to NETWORK 2, then switches back to NETWORK 1 again and so on.

TX/RX in NETWORK1	TX/RX in NETWORK2	TX/RX in NETWORK1	TX/RX in NETWORK2

Time

Fig. 2. Interleaved activities of **one** MRD being active in two networks

We refer to networks that consist of MRDs as *Intermittent Networks*. Figure 1 illustrates an intermittent WLAN and an intermittent CO-NETWORK that share a common set of MRDs. It is necessary for MRDs to maintain concurrent connections to both networks in some usage scenarios. For example, a MRD connects to Internet via CO-NETWORK (e.g., WiMAX), while using WLAN to synchronize files with personal devices or connect multi-player gaming devices. In order to maintain concurrent connections in both WiMAX and WLAN networks, the MRD operates in TDM fashion and frequently switches between WLAN and WiMAX networks.

As we know, 802.11 medium access control (MAC) has been designed with the assumption that radios are continuously available for use when needed. Now, given MRD radios with temporal service disruptions (to serve in CO-NETWORK), such assumptions no longer hold and WLAN behavior/performance may be affected. Specifically, with temporal disruptions, a MRD WLAN radio has less time to access the channel compared with a standalone WLAN radio. Consequently, the transmissions a MRD can obtain will be less and it largely depends on the *disruption profile* of WLAN network, which is defined as the relative occurrence time, duration and frequency of disruptions among all MRD radios of the WLAN. Additionally, a MRD WLAN radio will actively compete for the channel access only if it is not in disruption. The more MRD WLAN radios in disruption simultaneously, the fewer radios that compete for channel access in WLAN during that time. Therefore, the channel contention level of WLAN also depends on the disruption profile. Since disruption of a MRD WLAN radio occurs because the MRD needs to serve in CO-NETWORK, scheduling of CO-NETWORK directly affects disruption profile of WLAN, which in turn, affects performance of WLAN network. In this paper, we specifically study how the fairness/throughput of a WLAN network may be affected by the scheduling of CO-NETWORK. We also discuss some scheduling optimization criteria for CO-NETWORK to minimize such impact.

Throughout this paper, we consider a mixed network with both standalone WLAN radios and MRD WLAN radios. In the analysis, we assume a saturated network in which all WLAN radios have packets to transmit all the time. We also assume a MRD WLAN radio will NOT be able to sense the channel during disruptions, thus will have its backoff counter frozen. The rest of this paper is organized as follows. Related work is discussed in Section II. "Soft-fairness" in intermittent WLAN is introduced in Section III. In Section IV, we model two different disruption profiles, i.e., random disruptions and synchronized disruptions, and discuss their different impacts on achieving soft-fairness in WLAN. In Section V, we further discuss a "controlled" disruption profile and show that optimized controlled disruption profile can help reduce the impact of CO-NETWORK on WLAN. The implication of controlled disruption profile on the scheduling of CO-NETWORK, in particular, WiMAX, is also discussed in Section V. Both analytical results and simulation results are presented in Section VI to show that, optimized controlled disruption profile leads to very little impact on WLAN in terms of both throughput and fairness. Section VII finally concludes this paper.

2   Related work

Multi-radio networks have begun to attract attention in the past a few years. In the context of cognitive radio and spectrum sensing, there have been some recent efforts [3] [4] [5] on how to enable coordination among heterogeneous (i.e., using different wireless technologies) transceivers that are located on separate devices. A light-weight cooperative sensing mechanism was proposed in [3] to increase the probability that a secondary user detects a primary user to avoid interference. Reactive /proactive interference avoidance mechanisms were proposed in [4] [5] to address the co-existence of 802.11b and 802.16a networks, by adaptively adjusting transmitter PHY parameters such as frequency, power and time occupancy.

It was suggested in [1] to control protocols, power levels, antenna beam forming, frequency, coding, and timing, in order to mitigate mutual interference among multiple radios that are in close proximity or even on the same platform. The European Ambient Network Project [6] proposes a new architecture to enable the cooperation of heterogeneous networks belonging to different operator or technology domains. A generic link layer is suggested within this architecture to manage dynamic changes of radio access technologies [6]. Gao et al. [7] examined issues in building a ubiquitous QoS framework over the heterogeneous networks. Rossi et al. [8] investigated the issues related to logical device aggregation in heterogeneous networks.

In a more recent work, Zhu and Yang [9] [10] consider radios on a multi-radio device as disruptive radios (due to time sharing operations). Authors studied fairness issues of WLAN networks that consist of disruptive radios and proposed an adaptive credit payback algorithm to compensate the lost transmission opportunities of disruptive radios. In this paper, we further study how different disruption profiles may affect the compensation capability, fairness as well throughput of WLAN networks. We also discuss some scheduling guideline for CO-NETWORK that can help ease the stress on WLAN. To our best knowledge, this is the first paper that addresses the scheduling issues across two different types of networks.

3   Soft-fairness in intermittent WLAN

Using 802.11, a standalone WLAN transmitter will transmit when the channel is sensed idle and its backoff counter reaches zero. On the other hand, for a WLAN radio located on the MRD, it suffers transmission disruption since its channel access procedure can be interrupted by other co-located radios, and it may not be able to transmit if the radio is in disruption (even when the channel is sensed idle and its backoff counter reaches zero). As such, the channel access opportunities a MRD WLAN radio can obtain will be less compared with standalone radios, and they vary with disruption profile of the WLAN network.

For practical purpose, it is often desirable to decouple the channel access opportunities a MRD WLAN radio can obtain from the disruption profile of the WLAN. We define "soft-fairness" for a WLAN network as that, given a sufficiently long period of time, each MRD WLAN radio can obtain its desired share of transmissions (transmissions can succeed or fail), with reference to the amount of transmissions a standalone WLAN radio with the same channel status obtains. More specifically, if a standalone radio with the same channel status obtains Y transmissions, radio j shall obtain $c^{(j)}Y$ transmissions for the same period of time, where $c^{(j)}$ is a predefined parameter and $c^{(j)} \leq 1$ for MRD WLAN radios.

Without loss of generality, we consider two WLAN radios, u and v, which share the same channel status, while radio u is a standalone radio and radio v is a MRD WLAN radio. When there is no disruption, the average number of backoff slots between two consecutive transmissions for stations u and v is denoted as $\overline{X}$. Radio v will obtain fewer transmissions than radio u as it suffers disruptions. However, we can allow some levels of backoff compensation for radio v so that it can regain some of its lost transmission opportunities. More specifically, let $\overline{s}^{(v)}$ be the average number of extra idle slots radio v spends for each transmission obtained (e.g., extra idle slots can include idle slots during disruptions). Also let $r^{(v)}$ be the backoff compensation ratio of radio v and $\overline{x}^{(v)}$ be the average number of backoff slots for station v. Using backoff compensation function $\overline{x}^{(v)} = \dfrac{1}{c^{(v)}}\overline{X}(1 - r^{(v)})$, we have derived in reference [10] the sufficient and necessary condition to achieve soft-fairness in a MIXED intermittent WLAN as follows: $r^{(v)} = c^{(v)}\overline{s}^{(v)} / \overline{X}$ (1)

Equation (1) gives us the optimal compensation ratio for any radio v. In deriving Equation (1), it has been assumed that the backoff compensation does not affect $\overline{X}$. The assumption will hold, for example, when a constant contention window size is applied. This assumption will be relaxed later in Section 6 using exponential backoff.

4   Effect of different disruption profiles on intermittent WLAN network

MRD WLAN radio can regain its desired fair share of channel access opportunities using backoff compensation, as we discussed in previous section. However, backoff compensation effectively reduces backoff slots of MRD WLAN radios and allows them to transmit more aggressively. If the backoff compensation ratios for MRD WLAN radios are large, the collision probability in the network can substantially increase and the overall channel utilization (i.e., the portion of channel bandwidth used for successful transmissions) will degrade. Therefore, it is good to have backoff compensation ratio as small as possible, while, at the same time, achieving desired soft-fairness. In this section, we study two different disruption profiles, i.e., random disruptions and synchronized disruptions. We analytically derive the optimal backoff compensation ratios for each disruption profile, and thus gain some insight on how much disruption profiles can affect the required backoff compensation ratios. The following notations are common for both disruption profiles considered here:

N: the total number of WLAN radios in the network
N_{MRD}: the number of MRD WLAN radios
T_d: disruption period between two consecutive disruptions of a MRD radio
L: length of each disruption interval, assumed to be a constant
M_d: average number of disruptions a MRD WLAN radio encounters between two successive transmissions

4.1 Random Disruption Profile

In the random disruption profile, the disruptions of each MRD WLAN radio occur randomly and independently at each slot with probability p. Each disruption lasts for L duration. Fig. 3 shows the channel access procedure of a MRD WLAN radio. Since a MRD WLAN radio cannot sense the channel status when in disruptions, it will pause its backoff procedure by freezing its backoff counter whenever a disruption occurs. It resumes its normal backoff procedure when the disruption ends. The average duration between two consecutive disruptions of a MRD radio can be written as:

$$E[T_d] = \sum_{i=1}^{\infty}(1-p)^{i-1} \times p \times (L+i-1) = \frac{1}{p} + L - 1 \tag{2}$$

That is, the average period between two consecutive disruptions is $1/p + L - 1$, during which a MRD WLAN radio can access the channel actively for $1/p - 1$ slots and stay in disruption for L slots.

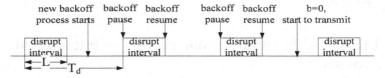

Fig. 3. Channel access procedure of MRD WLAN radios

For a MRD radio v with initial backoff counter set to $\overline{X}(1-r^{(v)})/c^{(v)}$, radio v needs to go through $\overline{X}(1-r^{(v)})/c^{(v)}$ idle slots to reduce its backoff counter to zero before transmitting. Let δ be the average probability of a slot being sensed idle so that the backoff counter may be reduced by 1. Since disruptions of each MRD radio follow i.i.d at each slot, the number of radios in disruptions at each slot will follow the same distribution once entering steady state. As a result, δ is the same for each slot, and $\frac{1}{c^{(v)}}\overline{X}(1-r^{(v)})\frac{1}{\delta}$ is the required average undisruptive duration (idle and busy) between two successive transmissions of radio v. On the other hand, since a radio always has packets to transmit, a new backoff procedure will be initiated immediately after the previous transmission ends. Assuming packet transmission duration T is much smaller than the undisruptive duration so that edge effect may be ignored, we have

$$\frac{1}{2}(\frac{1}{p}-1)+(\frac{1}{p}-1)(M_d-1)+\frac{1}{2}(\frac{1}{p}-1)=\frac{\overline{X}(1-r^{(v)})/c^{(v)}}{\delta} \tag{3}$$

The two $\frac{1}{2}(\frac{1}{p}-1)$ items at the LHS of Eq. (3) account for average undisruptive durations before the first disruption and after the last disruption respectively, while $(\frac{1}{p}-1)(M_d-1)$ accounts for the undisruptive duration in the middle of M_d disruptions. From Eq. (3), we have

$$M_d = \frac{\overline{X}(1-r^{(v)})}{(\frac{1}{p}-1)c^{(v)}\delta} \tag{4}$$

The number of extra idle slots due to disruptions $\overline{s}^{(v)}$ can be represented as

$$\overline{s}^{(v)} = M_d L\delta \tag{5}$$

Combine Eqs. (4) and (5) with Eq. (1) , we have

$$r^{(v)} = L/(L+\frac{1}{p}-1) \tag{6}$$

Equation (6) gives the optimal backoff compensation ratio for random disruptions with disruption probability of p. We define *disruption ratio* as the percentage of time a radio in disruptions. Notice that $L/(L+\frac{1}{p}-1)$ is in fact the disruption ratio for random disruptions.

4.2 Synchronized Disruption Profile

Now we consider a different disruption profile, namely synchronized disruptions, where disruptions to all MRD WLAN radios happen at the same time and they all last for L duration. Additionally, disruptions of each MRD radio repeat with a fixed period of T_d. As shown in Figure 4, within each disruption period T_d, the channel contention status is split into two phases: disruptive phase and undisruptive phase. In the disruptive phase, $N-N_{MRD}$ radios compete for the channel access, while all N radios compete for channel access in the undisruptive phase. As such, the probability of a slot being sensed idle in disruptive phase (denoted as δ_d) is quite different from that probability during undisruptive phase (denoted as δ_{nd}).

Following similar derivation as that for random disruptions, we have the following equation for any MRD radio v:

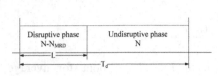

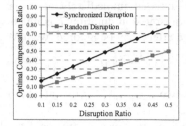

Fig. 4. Synchronized disruptions

Fig. 5. Optimal backoff compensation ratio comparison

$$\frac{T_d - L}{2} + (T_d - L)(M_d - 1) + \frac{T_d - L}{2} = \frac{\frac{1}{c^{(v)}}\overline{X}(1 - r^{(v)})}{\delta_{nd}} \tag{7}$$

M_d can thus be obtained from Eq. (7), and the average number of extra idle slots due to disruptions $\overline{s}^{(v)}$ can be obtained as $\overline{s}^{(v)} = M_d L \delta_d$. As such, we have

$$r^{(v)} = c^{(v)} \overline{s}^{(v)} / \overline{X} = \frac{\delta_d L / T_d}{\delta_d L / T_d + \delta_{nd}(1 - L / T_d)} \tag{8}$$

Equation (8) gives the optimal backoff compensation ratio in the case of synchronized disruptions. Notice that the channel idle time ratio during disruption phase is always higher than that of undisruptive phase (i.e., $\delta_d > \delta_{nd}$). Therefore, we observe that $r^{(v)} > L / T_d$, where L / T_d is the disruption ratio in the case of synchronized disruptions.

4.3 Discussions

Comparing Eqs. (6) and (8), we notice that, even with the SAME disruption ratio, the optimal backoff compensation ratio for synchronized disruptions is always higher than that of random disruptions. Figure 5 shows the optimal backoff compensation ratios for random disruptions (from Eq. (6)) and synchronized disruptions (from Eq. (8)), respectively, assuming a WLAN network consisting of 15 MRD WLAN radios and 5 standalone radios. In calculating Eq. (8), a constant Contention Window size 256 is used. X-axis of Figure 5 is the disruption ratio of MRD radios; y-axis is the optimal compensation ratio r. As we can see, synchronized disruptions lead to much larger compensation ratio than that of random disruptions. In particular, with disruption ratio of 0.5, the optimal compensation ratio for random disruptions is 0.5, while the optimal compensation ratio for synchronized disruptions is 0.78.

5   Control disruptions to improve performance of intermittent WLAN network

5.1 Controlled Disruption Profile

From above discussions, we have seen that disruption profiles have significant impact on the behavior of WLAN network. To achieve soft-fairness, the required backoff compensation ratio resulting from different disruption profiles can be dramatically different. Pure random disruption profile following i.i.d distribution is the ideal case, since it leads to minimal backoff compensation ratio. However, recall that a disruption at a MRD WLAN radio occurs because the MRD needs to serve in CO-NETWORK during that time. Purely random disruptions are practically impossible since disruptions among MRD WLAN radios are often correlated with each other via the scheduling of CO-NETWORK. As such, the question we would like to answer in this section is: what are the scheduling criteria CO-NETWORK should follow such that the required backoff compensation ratio to achieve soft-fairness in WLAN can approach the minimum.

Assuming disruptions of each MRD WLAN radio repeat with a period of T_d, we model a "controlled" disruption profile of WLAN as follows. There are m disruptive intervals within each period of T_d, where $L_{d1}, L_{d2}, ..., L_{dm}$ represent the length of each disruptive interval respectively. Within the k_{th} ($k \in [1, m]$) disruptive interval, an exclusive set of N_{MRD_k} radios will be in disruption, which means only $N - N_{MRD_k}$ radios will compete for the channel access during the k_{th} disruptive interval. Note that a MRD radio will only be in disruption within one interval. Let L_{nd} be the remaining undisruptive interval, during which all N radios compete for the channel access. We have

$$\sum_{i=1}^{m} L_{di} + L_{nd} = T_d; \qquad \sum_{i=1}^{m} N_{MRD_i} = N_{MRD} \qquad (9)$$

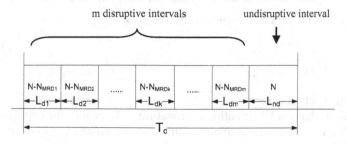

Fig. 6. Controlled Disruption Profile

Figure 6 gives an illustration of the described controlled disruption profile. It should be noted that m disruptive intervals do NOT need to be consecutive as that in Figure 6, and those intervals can appear in any order. The following derivations should not be affected.

Let δ_k be probability of a slot being sensed idle during the k_{th} disruptive interval and δ_{nd} be the probability of a slot being sensed idle during the undisruptive interval. We again consider a MRD WLAN radio v, whose disruption occurs in the k_{th} disruption interval. Using the backoff compensation function $\overline{x}^{(v)} = \frac{1}{c^{(v)}}\overline{X}(1-r^{(v)})$, $\overline{X}(1-r^{(v)})/c^{(v)}$ is the number of channel idle slots radio v has to go through before reducing its backoff counter to zero and transmitting. $L_{di}\delta_i$ gives the number of slots being sensed idle during any i_{th} disruptive interval; and $L_{nd}\delta_{nd}$ gives the number of slots being sensed idle during the undisruptive interval. For radio v, we have

$$M_d\left(\sum_{i=1,i\neq k}^{m}(L_{di}\delta_i) + L_{nd}\delta_{nd}\right) = \overline{X}(1-r^{(v)})/c^{(v)} \tag{10}$$

The average number of disruptions, M_d, can be readily obtained from Eq. (10). The average number of extra idle slots due to disruptions for each transmission of radio v can be approximated as $\overline{s}^{(v)} = M_d L_{dk}\delta_k$. Again, by applying Eq. (1), the optimal compensation ratio for radio v can be obtained as:

$$r^{(v)} = c^{(v)}\frac{\overline{s}^{(v)}}{\overline{X}} = \frac{L_{dk}\delta_k}{\sum_{i=1}^{m}(L_{di}\delta_i) + L_{nd}\delta_{nd}} \tag{11}$$

Intuitively, Eq. (11) says that the optimal backoff compensation ratio of radio v equals to the number of slots sensed idle during radio v's disruption interval L_{dk} divided by the total number of slots sensed idle within the period of T_d. Eq. (11) holds for any MRD WLAN radio in the network. Consider another MRD WLAN radio ϕ, whose disruption occurs in the q_{th} disruptive interval. Based on Eq. (11), we can also write the optimal compensation ratio for ϕ as:

$$r^{(\phi)} = c^{(\phi)}\frac{\overline{s}}{\overline{X}} = \frac{L_{dq}\delta_q}{\sum_{i=1}^{m}(L_{di}\delta_i) + L_{nd}\delta_{nd}} \tag{12}$$

The larger is the backoff compensation ratio, the more aggressively will a MRD radio transmit, thus the larger collision probability. To reduce the collision probability for WLAN, one way is to apply a common compensation ratio to all MRD radios and then find conditions to minimize the common compensation ratio. From Eqs. (11) and (12), it is not hard to see that, in order for

$r^{(1)} = r^{(2)} = ... = r^{(N_{MRD})} = r$,   we need

$$L_{d1}\delta_1 = L_{d2}\delta_2 = ... = L_{dm}\delta_m \qquad (13)$$

Combining Eqs. (11) and (13), we can obtain the common optimal compensation ratio r for all MRD WLAN radios as: $r = \dfrac{1}{m + L_{nd}\delta_{nd} / L_{d1}\delta_1}$

$$(14)$$

Given the constraint $L_{d1}\delta_1 = L_{d2}\delta_2 = ... = L_{dm}\delta_m$, we note that, if each disruptive interval lasts for the same duration (i.e., $L_{d1} = L_{d2} = ... = L_{dm}$), it should be $\delta_{d1} = \delta_{d2} = ... = \delta_{dm}$. As δ_{di} ($i \in [1,m]$) is a function of N_{MRD_i}, Eq. (14) holds only if $N_{MRD_1} = N_{MRD_2} = ... = N_{MRD_m} = N_{MRD} / m$. That is, MRD radios should be evenly distributed into m disruptive intervals. On the other hand, as we will show in Section 6 using simulation results, it is reasonably good to use r given by Eq. (14) as the common compensation ratio for all MRD radios even when $\mathrm{mod}(N_{MRD}, m) \neq 0$. In more general cases, if different disruptive intervals have different lengths, then the number of MRD radios in disruptions at each disruptive interval should be different. A shorter disruptive interval should have more radios in disruption, while a longer disruptive interval should have fewer radios in disruption.

Our ultimate goal is to minimize the common compensation ratio given by Eq. (14). Towards this end, we have the following two lemmas:

Lemma 1. Let r_1 be the common compensation ratio corresponding to WLAN network with m disruptive intervals L_{d1}, L_{d2}, ..., $L_{d(m-1)}$, L_{dm}; and r_2 be the common compensation ratio of WLAN network with m-1 disruptive intervals L_{d1}, L_{d2}, ..., $L_{d(m-1)}$. Then r_1 is always less than r_2.

Proof: In the case of m disruptive intervals, let δ_1 and δ_{nd} be the probability of a slot being sensed idle during the 1st disruptive interval and the undisruptive interval, respectively. The same probabilities in the case of m-1 disruptive intervals are represented as δ_1' and δ_{nd}', respectively. r_1 and r_2 can be written as

$$r_1 = \frac{1}{m + (T_d - \sum_{i=1}^{m} L_{di})\delta_{nd} / L_{d1}\delta_1}, \quad r_2 = \frac{1}{m-1 + (T_d - \sum_{i=1}^{m-1} L_{di})\delta_{nd}' / L_{d1}\delta_1'}$$

With m intervals, the number of MRD radios in disruption within each disruptive interval is no greater than that with m-1 intervals. Lemma 1 can be proved by noting $\delta_{nd}/\delta_1 \geq \delta_{nd}'/\delta_1'$ and $\delta_{nd}/\delta_1 < 1$.

[end of proof]

Lemma 2. Assume the number of disruptive intervals m in the WLAN network is fixed, and the number of MRD radios in disruption within each disruptive interval (i.e., N_{MRD_1}, N_{MRD_2}, ...) is given. Let r_1 be the common compensation ratio corresponding to WLAN network with m disruptive intervals L_{d1}, L_{d2}, ..., L_{dm}; and r_2 be the common compensation ratio of WLAN network with m disruptive intervals $L'_{d1}, L'_{d2}, ..., L'_{dm}$. If $L'_{di} \geq L_{di}$ ($i \in [1, m]$), then r_1 is always less than or equal to r_2.

Proof: Let δ_1 and δ_{nd} be the probability of a slot being sensed idle during the 1st disruptive interval and the undisruptive interval, respectively. $f(r) = \delta_{nd} / \delta_1$ is a function of r. Now consider two curves, $Y_1(r) = m + C_1 f(r)$ and $Y_2(r) = m + C_2 f(r)$, where $C_1 = (T_d - \sum_{i=1}^{m} L_{di}) / L_{d1} \geq C_2 = (T_d - \sum_{i=1}^{m} L'_{di}) / L'_{d1}$

r_1 and r_2 correspond to the points where $Y_1(r)$ and $Y_2(r)$ intersect with the curve $Z(r) = 1/r$, respectively. Lemma 2 can be proved by noting both r_1 and r_2 are no larger than $1/m$. Additionally, $Y_2(r) \leq Y_1(r) < Z(r)$ when $r \to 0$ and $Z(r) < Y_2(r) \leq Y_1(r)$ when $r = 1/m$.   [end of proof]

From Lemma 1 and 2, we have the following theorem:

Theorem 1: Given that constraint in Eq. (13) is satisfied, the common optimal compensation ratio for MRD WLAN radios will decrease when the number of disruptive intervals (i.e., m) increases and the length of each disruptive interval (i.e., L_{d1}, L_{d2}, L_{d3}, ..., L_{dm}) decreases. From theorem 1, we know that synchronized disruption profile discussed in Section 4 has the worst performance. Notice that when $L_{d1} = L_{d2} = ... = L_{dm} = L$ and $mL = T_d$, the optimal compensation ratio of the controlled disruption profile from Eq. (14) exactly equals to the disruption ratio L / T_d. Later in Section VI, we will use numerical results to show that, when m is maximized, the optimal compensation ratio resulting from controlled disruption profile stays very close to the disruption ratio in general.

5.2 System Implication

As we discussed before, different disruption profiles of WLAN map to different scheduling choices for the CO-NETWORK. Consider IEEE 802.16 (WiMAX) based on Orthogonal Frequency Division Multiplexing Access (OFDMA) and Time Division Duplex (TDD) operations as an example of CO-NETWORK. Two dimensions of channel resources can be allocated to each WiMAX radio using OFDMA: one is frequency (vertical axis of Figure 7) and the other is time (horizontal axis of Figure 7). Given five MRD and five standalone (STD) WiMAX devices, Figure 7 illustrates two scheduling options for downlink (DL) operations. In the upper subfigure (Figure 7.a), five MRD WiMAX radios' DL allocations are distributed over the time domain and they are not overlapping with each other in time. Each allocation for a MRD in WiMAX network corresponds to a disruption of this particular device in WLAN network. Therefore, the scheduling in Figure 7.a maps to the case that there are five disruptive intervals (i.e., $m = 5$) in the WLAN network. Another scheduling example for the WiMAX network is shown in Figure 7.b, in which DL-bursts of all five MRDs are allocated within the same time period (occupying different frequencies). Scheduling in Figure 7.b corresponds to the case that WLAN network has synchronized disruption profile.

Our discussions in this section essentially state that, if WiMAX base station follows the scheduling in Figure 7.a rather than that in Figure 7.b, the co-located WLAN network will need less backoff compensation in order to maintain the desired fairness for MRD WLAN radios. Consequently, the co-located WLAN network will suffers less throughput degradation. Theorem 1 provides guidelines for WiMAX base station to schedule MRD WiMAX radios:

a). Allocate a MRD along frequency dimension first, such that its time domain occupancy is as small as possible;

b). Evenly distribute the scheduling of MRDs into m non-overlapping time intervals with equal length;

c). The number of non-overlapping time intervals m should be maximized.

The above guidelines can be applied to scheduling within one frame as well as scheduling across multiple frames. How to design specific scheduling algorithm that follows the above guidelines for WiMAX networks consisting of MRDs without hurting WiMAX performance is an on-going work.

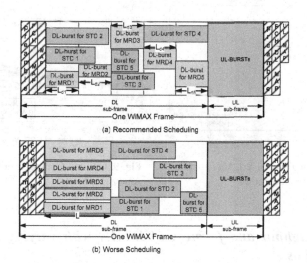

(a) Recommended Scheduling

(b) Worse Scheduling

Fig. 7. Scheduling Choices for Co-located WiMAX Network

6 Numerical Results and discussions

6.1 Simulation Model

We simulate the disrupted channel access behavior of WLAN network using code written in MATLAB™, where time is sliced into slots. A slot is considered as *Success* if only one radio is transmitting; considered as *Collision* if more than one radios are transmitting; and considered as *Idle* if no radio is transmitting. We concentrate on "Saturate Performance", where all WLAN radios always have packets to transmit. To validate our simulator, we have simulated the WLAN network with standalone WLAN radios only, and compared the throughput against the theoretical results from reference [11]. Fig. 8 shows that simulation results match very well with theoretical results from reference [11]. Data points from simulations are obtained with running time sufficiently long to reach steady state. There are two groups of radios in the WLAN network: standalone WLAN radios and MRD WLAN radios. In the simulations, radios in the same group share the same configuration. *Fairness Index* is calculated as the number of transmissions averaged over all MRD WLAN radios divided by the number of transmissions averaged over all standalone WLAN radios. Throughout our simulations, the desired share factor c for all MRD radios is set to 1. Therefore, if the measured fairness index equals to 1, then WLAN achieves perfect soft-fairness.

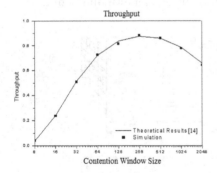
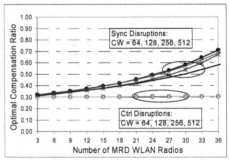

Fig. 8. Throughput of WLAN network with 20 standalone radios

Fig. 9. Optimal Compensation Ratios from Analytical Model

6.2 Throughput and fairness of WLAN with varying number of MRD radios

We consider a mixed WLAN network with total 40 radios. The number of MRD WLAN radio (denoted as N_{MRD}) is increased from 3 to 36 with a step size of 3; the number of standalone radios decreases accordingly. Disruption period T_d is set to

1000 slots; each MRD WLAN radio will be in disruption for 300 slots during each disruption period T_d (i.e., disruption ratio of 0.3 for each MRD radio). Packet transmission duration T is set to 10 slots. Disruptions of all MRD radios occur at the same time in the case of synchronized disruption profile. For controlled disruption profile, MRD radios are evenly distributed into 3 disruptive intervals; there are $N_{MRD}/3$ MRD radios in disruption within each disruptive interval; the remaining undisruptive interval lasts for 100 slots. Figure 9 shows the optimal compensation ratios derived from our analytical models for both synchronized disruption profile and controlled disruption profile, using various constant contention window sizes. In the figure, we marked curves for synchronous profile as "Sync", while the curves for controlled profile as "Ctrl". X-axis is the number of MRD radios while y-axis is the optimal compensation ratio. As we can see, with synchronized profile, the optimal compensation ratio is very sensitive to the contention window size (CW); different CW size leads to different optimal compensation ratio. Additionally, the optimal compensation ratios for synchronized disruption profile increase rather rapidly when the number of MRD radios increases; the value reaches 0.7 with 36 MRD radios, which is much larger than the disruption ratio (i.e., 0.3). On the other hand, the optimal compensation ratios resulting from controlled disruption profile are not sensitive to contention window sizes; four curves corresponding to four different CW sizes override with each other. Furthermore, the optimal compensation ratios for controlled profile remain close to the disruption ratio 0.3 despite the increase of MRD radios.

Figure 10 shows the fairness index obtained from simulations, when applying the optimal compensation ratios in Figure 9 to the corresponding scenarios. X-axis is the number of MRD radios; y-axis is the measured fairness index. Figure 10 serves the purpose of validating our analytical models. As we can see, for both synchronized disruption profile and controlled disruption profile, the fairness index obtained from simulations stays around 1 in all simulated scenarios, which confirms that our analytical models are reasonably accurate in modeling the optimal compensation ratio.

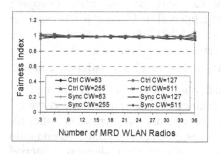

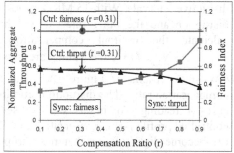

Fig. 10. Fairness Index from Simulations

Fig. 11. Throughput and Fairness of WLAN using Exponential Backoff

We further proceed to enable the exponential backoff for all WLAN radios. That is, whenever a transmission fails, the sender will double its CW size until the maximum CW (CW$_{max}$) is reached. We use CW$_{min}$ = 31 and CW$_{max}$ = 511 in the simulations. We simulated a WLAN network consisting of 33 MRD radios and 7 standalone radios. From Figure 9, we have seen that, for synchronized disruption profile, there is no single compensation ratio that works for all sizes of CW. Therefore, we applied compensation ratio from 0.1 to 0.9 (x-axis) for all MRD radios in the case of synchronized profile, and plotted both normalized aggregate throughput (left y-axis) and fairness (right y-axis) of WLAN in Figure 11. As we can see, when compensation ratio r is increased from 0.1 to 0.9, fairness index improves from 0.32 to 0.88, but aggregate throughput decreases from 0.57 to 0.37 for synchronized profile. In other words, either fairness or throughput will suffer for synchronized disruption profile. On the other hand, for controlled disruption profile, the optimal compensation ratio is insensitive to CW. When we apply r=0.31 to the same WLAN network with controlled disruption profile, we achieved throughput of 0.56 (peak value of synchronized profile) AND fairness index of 0.99 at the same time, as two flat lines in Figure 11 show. That is, controlled disruption profile allows WLAN to maintain good performance in both fairness and throughput.

6.3 Throughput and fairness of WLAN with varying disruption ratios

In this subsection, we study the performance of controlled disruption profile for various disruption ratios. We fix the number of MRD radios as 15 (i.e., N_{MRD} = 15) and the number of standalone radios as 5. Disruption ratio is increased from *0.1* to *0.5* with a step size of *0.05*. The same disruption ratio applies to all MRD radios. For controlled disruption profile, the number of disruptive intervals (i.e., m) should be maximized, and it depends on the value of disruption ratio. For example, if disruption ratio is 0.4, there can only be two non-overlapping disruptive intervals. With 15 MRD radios, one interval will have 8 MRD radios in disruption and the other interval will have 7 MRD radios in disruption. We calculate the optimal compensation ratio based on Eq. (14) using $N_{MRD_1} = \lceil N_{MRD} / m \rceil$, the values are shown in Figure 12 for different constant CW sizes. X-axis of Figure 12 is the disruption ratio; y-axis is the optimal compensation ratio. The disruption ratio in each case is also plotted as a curve for ease of reading. Again, as we can see, the optimal compensation ratio for controlled profile is quite insensitive to CW sizes. The optimal compensation ratio can become slightly larger than the disruption ratio when the undisruptive interval becomes relatively large (e.g., when $L_{nd}=0.3T_d$ with disruption ratio of 0.35); but it stays close to the disruption ratio in general. Comparing Figures 5 and 12, it is also not hard to see that synchronized disruption profile require much larger compensation ratios than controlled disruption profile.

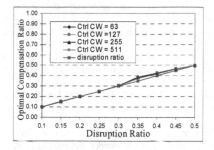

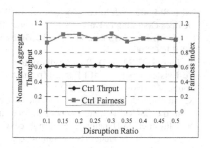

Fig. 12. Optimal Compensation Ratios for Controlled Disruptions

Fig. 13. Throughput and Fairness using Exponential Backoff

The optimal compensation ratio for each disruption radio is average over different CW sizes, and is then applied to all MRD radios in the simulations. Exponential backoff of WLAN is enabled in the simulations. Figure 13 shows the normalized aggregate through (left y-axis) and fairness index (right y-axis) of WLAN at various disruption ratios (x-axis). As we can see, even though it is not possible to evenly distribute MRD radios into m disruption intervals in some cases (since $\text{mod}(N_{MRD}, m) \neq 0$), the compensation ratios calculated from Eq. (14) are reasonably good and fairness index in all simulated scenarios stay close to 1. At the same time, WLAN aggregate throughput is hardly affected by the change of disruption ratios when controlled disruption profile is applied.

7 Conclusions

In this paper, we consider a WLAN network using 802.11 that shares a common set of multi-radio devices with another network CO-NETWORK (e.g., WiMAX). One multi-radio device may not actively operate in WLAN when the same device is transmitting or receiving in the CO-NETWORK. As such, two networks interact with each other via shared multi-radio devices; and scheduling in CO-NETWORK may affect the performance of WLAN. We studied how fairness/throughput of a WLAN network may be affected by different disruption profiles. We show via analytical models and simulation results that, disruptions will have less impact on WLAN performance if disruptions follow the optimized controlled disruption profile discussed in this paper. Our results provide scheduling guideline for the CO-NETWORK to alleviate its impact on WLAN performance. As an example of CO-NETWORK, scheduling in WiMAX network is briefly discussed.

References

1. J. Lansford, "UWB Coexistence and Cognitive Radio", Ultra Wideband Systems, May 18-21, 2004.
2. IEEE Std 802.15.2-2003, "Coexistence of Wireless Personal Area Networks with Other Wireless Devices Operating in Unlicensed Frequency Bands".
3. S. M. Mishra, A. Sahai, and R. W. Brodersen, Cooperative Sensing among Cognitive Radios, IEEE ICC 2006.
4. X. Jing, S.-C. Mau, D. Raychaudhuri and R. Matyas, "Reactive Cognitive Radio Algorithms for Co-Existence between IEEE 802.11b and 802.16a Networks", Proceedings of IEEE Globecom, St. Louis, MO, Nov. 28-Dec. 2, 2005.
5. X. Jing and D. Raychaudhuri, "Spectrum Co-existence of IEEE 802.11b and 802.16a Networks using the CSCC Etiquette Protocol", Proceedings of IEEE DySPAN (International Symposium on New Frontiers in Dynamic Spectrum Access Networks), Baltimore, MD, Nov. 8-11, 2005.
6. N. Niebert, A. Schieder, H. Abramowicz, G. Malmgren, J. Sachs, U. Horn, C.Prehofer, and H. Karl, "Ambient networks: An architecture for communication networks beyond 3g," IEEE Wireless Communications, vol. 11, pp. 14--22, April 2004.
7. X. Gao, G. Wu, and T. Miki, "End-to-end qos provisioning in mobile heterogenous networks," IEEE Wireless Communications, vol. 11, pp. 24--34, June 2004.
8. M. Rossi, L. Badia, P. Giacon, and M. Zorzi, "On the effectiveness of logical device aggregation in multi-radio multi-hop networks," in Proceedings of the 3rd IEEE International Workshop on Mobility Management and Wireless Access (MobiWac 2005), Maui, Hawaii, USA, 2005.
9. J. Zhu, X. Yang and X. Guo, "Disruptive CSMA with Credit Payback (CP) Protocols for Multi-Radio Network," CrownCom 2007, August 2007.
10. X. Yang, J. Zhu and X. Guo, "Using "Scaled Credit Payback" to Achieve Soft-fairness for Disruptive Radios in CSMA Networks", IEEE SECON 2007 poster session.
11. G. Bianchi, Performance Analysis of IEEE 802.11 Distributed Coordination Function, IEEE JSAC, vol. 8, no.3, March 2000.

On QoS Mapping in TDMA Based Wireless Sensor Networks

Wassim Masri and Zoubir Mammeri

IRIT – Paul Sabatier University

Toulouse, France

{Wassim.Masri, Zoubir.Mammeri}@irit.fr

Abstract Recently, there have been many efforts to develop Wireless Sensor Networks (WSN), but no one can deny the fact that QoS support is still one of the least explored areas in this domain. In this paper, we present QoS support in WSN while highlighting the QoS mapping issue, a complex process in which QoS parameters are translated from level to level and we present a case study of a TDMA tree-based clustered WSN, where accuracy and density on the user level are mapped to bandwidth on the network level. We end our paper with simulations that prove our formulas and highlight the relationships between QoS parameters.

1 Introduction

Wireless sensor networks (WSN) were named recently one of eight technologies to save the world [1], side-by-side with nuclear waste neutralizers, and one of ten emerging technologies that will change the world [2]. WSN are being integrated more and more in real world applications, they are used in the medical and healthcare domain, in the musical industry, and in a lot more real world applications.

While there have been many efforts to develop many facets in WSN, including hardware devices, communication protocols, energy consumption [3], and many other issues like time synchronization, geographical location and security, the QoS support remains one of the least explored areas in the WSN domain [4], since most of the research industry is following the actual trend in focusing on the energy consumption problem and the related issues.

In the matter of fact, QoS support in WSN could be seen from different points of view due to the layered architecture of typical distributed systems, so it could be seen as *accuracy, density, precision or lifetime* from the user's point of view, as well as *bandwidth, delay or jitter* from the network's point of view. Due to this

Please use the following format when citing this chapter:

Masri, W. and Mammeri, Z., 2008, in IFIP International Federation for Information Processing, Volume 284; *Wireless and Mobile Networking*; Zoubir Mammeri; (Boston: Springer), pp. 329–342.

diversity in seeing QoS, it is crucial to find the relationships between those different QoS requirements on the different levels, in order to obtain a coherent system. Once the relationships between those different parameters are found, one could translate them correctly from level to level, a process known as *QoS mapping*. QoS mapping is one of the least surveyed issues in the QoS management family, due to its complexity and its application dependency.

In this paper we intend to show the relationships between the density of a WSN (a user level QoS) and the bandwidth reserved for each of its nodes (a network level QoS). We prove the tight coupling between those two parameters on a TDMA tree based clustered WSN, while giving the length of a TDMA superframe as a function of the tree depth. We explore also the different scenarios while increasing the problem complexity. In order to validate our theoretical results, we present simulations that further highlight the relationships between the previously discussed QoS parameters.

In section 2, we present some related work to QoS support in WSN and QoS mapping. In section 3, we present our work on QoS mapping in WSN, and we show our novel approach on how we map user level QoS parameters: density and accuracy, to a network level QoS parameter, the bandwidth. This is achieved by computing the TDMA superframe length in several cases as a function of the network density. In section 4, we present our simulations that validate our formulas presented in section 3, and we discuss the relationships between accuracy, density, reporting period, packet size and bandwidth. As far as we know, no one had explored the relationships between those parameters ever before. We end our paper in section 5 with some perspectives and conclusion.

2   Related Work

QoS support has a wide meaning, because it has not one common definition, beside, it could be seen on different levels and from different points of view.

In [5], QoS was defined to mean sensor network resolution. More specifically they defined it as the optimum number of sensors sending information toward information-collecting sinks, typically base stations. In [6], the authors used the Gur Game paradigm based on localized information to control the number of nodes to power up in a certain area, thus defining their QoS requirements as the optimal number of active nodes in the network. In [7], QoS was defined as the *desired number of active sensors in the network*, and the network lifetime as the *duration for which the desired QoS is maintained*.

We noticed that there are limited research papers about QoS mapping, because it is complex and application specific. For the best of our knowledge, very few works were done concerning QoS mapping in WSN. In [8], the authors presented a formal methodology to map application level SLA (response time) to network performance (link bandwidth and router throughput). In [9], the authors proposed a framework to ease the mapping between different Internet domains, namely between Intserv/RSVP and Diffserv domains. In [10], the authors proposed a framework to map the network packet loss rate to user packet loss rate by determining the location of each lost packet on the packet stream and calculating the impact of the lost packets on the application layer frames sent by a source. In WSN domain on the other hand, the work done concerning QoS mapping is so limited, and it covers mostly the tradeoffs between QoS parameters like energy, accuracy, density, latency, etc. In [11], simulations on QoS parameters in WSN were done, which led to a better understanding of the tradeoffs between density, latency and accuracy. The authors explored also the tradeoff between density and energy. In [12], the authors have identified the following QoS parameters tradeoffs between accuracy, delay, energy and density.

3   QoS Mapping in Tree Based WSN

3.1   Problem Statement and Assumptions

As mentioned earlier, QoS mapping is the process of translating QoS parameters from level to level, which is done by finding the relationship between the different QoS parameters, on the different levels of a distributed system. Typically, an entity in a distributed system has a layered architecture (fig. 1), which includes the user layer at the top, the network layer at the bottom and the application and system layers in the middle.

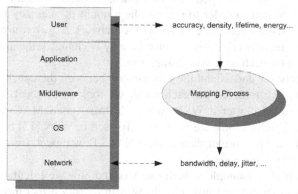

Fig. 1 Layered Architecture in Distributed Systems

On each layer, we could have different QoS requirements, depending on the entities on this layer. Starting from the top of the stack, we have the *User* and the *Application* entities with their QoS requirements as:

1. *Accuracy*: It could be seen as the difference between a set of values assumed as the real values, and the value sensed by the network. Clearly, the number of active nodes in the network has a big impact on this amount of error: when the number of active nodes is increased, the computed error decreases.

2. *Density*: is the number of active nodes in the network divided by the volume. As mentioned above, network density has a direct impact on accuracy.

3. *Energy*: energy consumption is one of the most vital issues in WSN. Due to their small size, sensors suffer from their scarce resources like energy or memory. Thus, energy is usually an important QoS requirement for WSN users.

4. *Lifetime*: network lifetime could be seen as the duration for which a desired QoS is maintained. It could be also seen as the time until the first node (or a subset of nodes) fails, or runs out of energy.

When communication network is of concern, other QoS parameters are distinguished like bandwidth, delay, jitter, etc.

In order to guarantee a User level QoS, e.g. a certain amount of accuracy, we may have to add (or wake up) a number of nodes, thus we should try to answer the following questions: *what does this amount of accuracy equals in terms of network density? And what does this amount of density equals in terms of lower level parameters (network level parameters) so that we can do the suitable reservations on that level?*

Thus there is need to translate User level QoS, to Network level QoS (e.g. the bandwidth allocated for each node).

In the following, we discuss how user QoS requirements like accuracy and density in WSN, could be mapped into network QoS parameters like bandwidth. It has been noticed that in order to change the amount of accuracy (say increasing accuracy), we should add more nodes to the network (e.g. by turning them on), thus changing the network density. Once density is changed, the amount of bandwidth reserved for each node will change too.

In order to better understand the relationship between the density of a network and the bandwidth reserved for each node, we took as a model for our case of study, a tree-based clustered WSN, with a TDMA-based MAC protocol. Tree-based clustered architectures are being widely used in WSN [13] because they are easily scalable and because of their unidirectional flow model, from leaves (sensor nodes) to the root (sink node).

We proceed to an example to better understand how we calculate the length of our TDMA superframe and how the changes in density affect directly the bandwidth reserved for each node. In this example we have a 5-levels tree-based clustered WSN (fig. 2).

Before we start we have to make some assumptions. First of all, nodes which are in the same cluster are considered in the same neighborhood, geographically speaking. Without loss of generality, we assume that initially, all level h clusters in our network have the same number of nodes. This is justified because we want to start our scenario by having a balanced network; nevertheless, our network could evolve by adding or removing nodes from clusters, thus having eventually an unequal number of nodes in level h clusters. Leaf nodes (on level 4 in this example) sense data, and forward it to their parent nodes in each cluster, which in turn forward it to their parent nodes, until the data arrives to the sink (level 0). Intermediate nodes could also be sensors, which means they could perform sensing too. In our case study, we take into account this fact and we compute the amount of time slots needed in the superframe for the intermediate nodes to perform their sensing activity. One could consider the simpler case where intermediate nodes are only relaying data, by simply omitting the part where those flows are computed, so whether intermediate nodes sense data or simply relay data is a choice made at the network implementation.

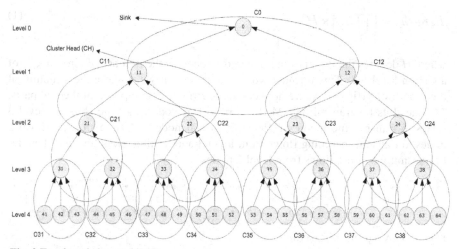

Fig. 2 Tree based clustered WSN

3.2 Bandwidth Allocation

Back to our example, nodes 21 and 22 are in the same cluster, so they are in the same neighborhood. Nodes 21 and 23 aren't in the same cluster, i.e. they cannot hear each other. For each cluster, there is a Cluster Head (CH), which relays data received from its child nodes to its parent node and it could also perform data aggregation if there was data aggregation algorithms implemented on it. Data aggregation is out of the scope of this paper, so it's not considered in our example.

In order to compute the bandwidth available for each node, we have to compute the length of the TDMA superframe in this network first. The superframe must take into account all the flows, from leaf nodes to the sink, because intermediate nodes may share the same clusters, thus sharing the same neighbors. So the problem of overhearing (which often leads to collisions), must be taken into consideration when defining the superframe.

We will proceed with the simplest case, and increase the problem complexity until we reach the most general case.

i) First case: no simultaneous transmissions between clusters, sensing done by leaf nodes only.

First, we consider the case of a WSN where only leaf nodes do sensing, therefore all the intermediate nodes' sensing flows are ignored. All simultaneous transmissions between same level clusters and *"3 hops away nodes"* are also ignored in this case.

The length of the TDMA superframe in a tree based clustered network with a depth equal to H, is obtained by the means of the following formula:

$$Length_H = \left(\prod_{h=1}^{H} n_h\right) \times H \tag{1}$$

where H denotes the depth of the tree and n_h denotes the number of child nodes of a CH on level h-1. This formula would be obvious if we observe the structure of the superframe (fig. 3). As we notice, the superframe is composed of 4 equal parts: 24 time slots for transmitting 24 flows from leaf nodes, 24 time slots for level 3 nodes to transmit the incoming flows from leaf nodes, 24 time slots for level 2 nodes to transmit incoming flows from level 3 and 24 time slots for level 1 nodes to transmit incoming flows from level 2 nodes.

Fig. 3 TDMA superframe (first case)

ii) Second case: simultaneous transmissions by same level clusters, sensing done by leaf nodes only.

Now let us consider the case with simultaneous transmissions knowing that clusters of the same level can transmit their respective flows on the same time slots due to the fact that no overhearing could occur between separate clusters. Formula (1) is thus reduced to:

$$Length_H = \sum_{k=1}^{H}\left(\prod_{h=k}^{H} n_h\right) \tag{2}$$

This is depicted in (fig. 4). As we notice, flows from clusters C31 to C38 are sent on the first, second and third time slots of the superframe because no overhearing could occur between those clusters. When the same rule is applied for each of the levels, we obtain formula (2).

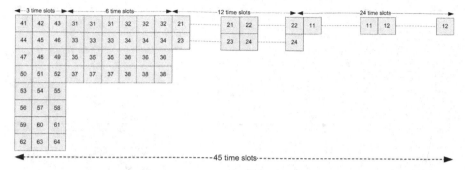

Fig. 4 Reduced TDMA superframe due to simultaneous transmissions (second case)

iii) Third case: simultaneous transmissions by same level clusters and 3 hops away nodes, sensing done by leaf nodes only.

Moreover, further optimization in the superframe length could be applied when taking into account the simultaneous transmissions from 3 hops away nodes. In fact, we noticed that nodes that are 3 hops away (e.g. node 41 and node 22, node 31 and node 12), could also transmit simultaneously without interference. In that case level 4 nodes could transmit their data along with level 2 nodes, and level 3 nodes could transmit their data with level 1 nodes (fig. 5). Clearly, the "*3 hop away nodes*" optimization couldn't be applied on level 2 and level 1.

This rule is obviously applicable on any tree, regardless of its depth H. We could always transmit level h flows with level h-2 flows simultaneously without interference. The formula would thus be the following:

$$Length_H = \prod_{h=1}^{H} n_h + \prod_{h=2}^{H} n_h \qquad (3)$$

This formula is the reduced form of (2). As we can see, we omitted the part concerning the flows from level *3* to level *H*, because they are transmitted simultaneously with each other as explained above.

iv) Fourth case: simultaneous transmissions by same level clusters and 3 hops away nodes, sensing done by leaf nodes and intermediate nodes.

In all of the above cases, intermediate nodes are only relaying data; they don't produce any flows of their own. Now we will consider the most complete case where intermediate nodes are also sensing and transmitting data. In that case, we should add to our formula the part in which we computed the number of time slots for the intermediate nodes to send their own flows. In fact, the number of time slots initially reserved in the superframe for level h nodes should be increased by

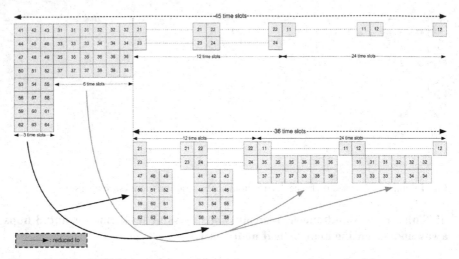

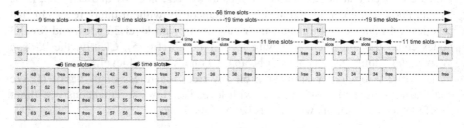

Fig. 5 Optimized TDMA superframe with simultaneous transmissions for 3 hops away nodes (third case)

Fig. 6 TDMA superframe in the complete case (fourth case)

F_h, which corresponds to the number of child intermediate nodes' flows added to level h nodes' own flows:

$$F_h = \sum_{k=h}^{H-1} \left(\prod_{i=h}^{k} n_i \right) \tag{4}$$

In our example, the number of slots we should add to level 2 nodes (*nodes 21* and *22*) is: $F_2 = \sum_{k=2}^{H-1} \left(\prod_{i=2}^{k} n_i \right) = n_2 + n_2 \times n_3 = 2 + 2 \times 2 = 6$ additional slots (3 for each node). This is depicted in (fig. 6), where there are 9 slots reserved for node *21* instead of 6 slots in the previous case. In order to compute the total number of slots added we should do the sum of F_h for every level defining the superframe length, that is level *1* and level *2*. So, the total number of slots added is:

$$F_{total} = \sum_{h=1}^{2} F_h = F_1 + F_2 = \sum_{k=1}^{H-1}\left(\prod_{i=1}^{k} n_i\right) + \sum_{k=2}^{H-1}\left(\prod_{i=2}^{k} n_i\right) = \left(n_1 + n_1 \times n_2 + n_1 \times n_2 \times n_3\right) + \left(n_2 + n_2 \times n_3\right) = 20$$

Hereby, using formulas (3) and (4), the length of the superframe is computed as follows:

$$Length_H = \prod_{h=1}^{H} n_h + \prod_{h=2}^{H} n_h + \sum_{k=1}^{H-1}\left(\prod_{i=1}^{k} n_i\right) + \sum_{k=2}^{H-1}\left(\prod_{i=2}^{k} n_i\right) \qquad (5)$$

The length of the superframe in the most general form is thus:

$$Length_H = \prod_{h=1}^{H} n_h + \prod_{h=2}^{H} n_h + \sum_{k=1}^{H-1}\left(\prod_{i=1}^{k} n_i b_i\right) + \sum_{k=2}^{H-1}\left(\prod_{i=2}^{k} n_i b_i\right) \qquad (6)$$

where b_i is a Boolean which equals 1 if level i nodes are sensing data and 0 if else. Now that we have the superframe length, we can compute the bandwidth ratio allocated for any level h node. From formula (2) and (4) we obtain:

$$B_h = \frac{\left(\prod_{k=h}^{H} n_k + \sum_{k=h}^{H-1}\left(\prod_{i=h}^{k} n_i b_i\right)\right)}{Length_H \times n_h} \qquad (7)$$

Obviously, if we want to add leaf nodes to the network, we have to reschedule the superframe by adding H *slots* for each added node. But, due to the fact that the superframe contains free time slots (fig. 6), we could add (a certain amount of) nodes to the network while just adding 2 additional slots (to the superframe) for each node added (the rest of the flows fit in the free slots). In order to compute the maximum number of leaf nodes, N_H, while preserving this rule, we have to calculate the number of time slots available in level H starting from the number of time slots in level I (using formulas 2 and 4). This is computed as follows:

$$N_H = \begin{cases} v & \text{if } H = 3 \\ \lfloor(\lfloor(v - n_3)/n_3\rfloor ... - n_{H-1})/n_{H-1}\rfloor & \text{if } H > 3 \end{cases} \qquad / v = \prod_{h=2}^{H} n_h + \sum_{k=2}^{H-1}\left(\prod_{i=2}^{k} n_i b_i\right) + b_1 \qquad (8)$$

In our example, all intermediate nodes are performing data sensing, so $b_i = 1 \; \forall i \in [1..H]$. N_4 is computed as follows:

$$N_4 = \left(\left(\prod_{h=2}^{4} n_h + \sum_{k=2}^{3}\left(\prod_{i=2}^{k} n_i b_i\right) + 1 - n_3\right) / n_3\right) = ((2 \times 2 \times 3) + (2 \times 1 + 2 \times 1 \times 2 \times 1)$$

+ 1 x 1 – 2) / 2) = 8 nodes. This means, we can add up to 8 leaf nodes in every cluster, while adding just 2 slots in the superframe for each added node. Beyond this number (N_H), for every node added to the network we will have to add H slots in the superframe. All of this is summarized in rule 9.

$$B_h = \begin{cases} \dfrac{\left(\prod_{k=h}^{H} n_k + \sum_{k=h}^{H-1}\left(\prod_{i=h}^{k} n_i\right)\right)}{Length_H \times n_h} & \textit{if } n_H = n_{H\,init} \\[2em] \dfrac{\left(\prod_{k=h}^{H} n_k + \sum_{k=h}^{H-1}\left(\prod_{i=h}^{k} n_i\right)\right)}{(Length_H + 2) \times n_h} & \textit{if } n_{H\,init} < n_H <= N_H \\[2em] \dfrac{\left(\prod_{k=h}^{H} n_k + \sum_{k=h}^{H-1}\left(\prod_{i=h}^{k} n_i\right)\right)}{(Length_H + H) \times n_h} & \textit{if } n_H > N_H \end{cases} \qquad (9)$$

4   Simulations and Analysis

In order to prove our formulas concerning the mapping between the different QoS parameters, we have conducted several simulations using the Network Simulator 2 (NS-2), with the following settings:

Table 1 Simulations settings

Simulation area	1000 x 1000 m!
Time of simulation	150 seconds
MAC Layer	TDMA
Number of nodes	56 nodes (fig. 6)
Channel bit rate	2 Mbps
Data dissemination interval	0.35 sec
Data sensing interval	0.35 sec
Transmission range	50 m

Below we discuss the main generic forms of relationships between QoS parameters backed up by simulations.

4.1 Relationship Between Network Density and Bandwidth

The relationship between those two parameters is explained in the previous section, where we proved that adding nodes to the network will decrease the bandwidth reserved for each node by an amount computed using rule (9). In rule (9), we presented three different formulas corresponding to three different cases, based on the number of leaf nodes in each H cluster. Practically, it means that adding one more node to the network, will slightly increase the superframe length (i.e. slightly decrease the reporting frequency) thus reducing reserved bandwidth for each node. On one hand we have gained accuracy by increasing network density, and on the other we lost some while decreasing data freshness. A good tradeoff between those values would be having N_H leaf nodes in each cluster, using all the free slots in the superframe and thus increasing accuracy, while slightly decreasing data freshness and bandwidth (2nd case in rule 9). Beyond this number, reporting frequency will highly decrease and thus affecting the data freshness parameter; beside, the bandwidth for each node will also decrease leading for example to the malfunctioning of the network (delay, jitter…).

In fig. 7, we report our simulation result using the example from the previous section, where level *4* clusters contain initially 3 sensors each. Sensors are added on a level *4* cluster, until we reach 12 sensors. We could notice how bandwidth decreases while adding nodes, and how it starts decreasing faster when it exceeds N_H (N_H is computed using formula 8). These results validate our theoretical formulas presented in the previous section (formulas 6, 7, 8 and 9).

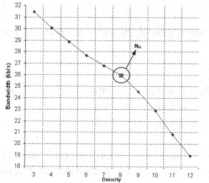

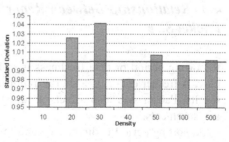

Fig. 7 Relationship between Network Density and Bandwidth

Fig. 8 Relationship between Accuracy and Density

4.2 Relationship Between Accuracy and Network Density

Accuracy could be considered as the difference between the set of the real values and the set of the sensed values. This difference could occur because of the physical nature of sensors, or their distance to the target. This could be represented by the *standard deviation,* computed as follows:

$$Deviation = \sqrt{\frac{1}{N-1} \times \sum_{i=1}^{N} \left(x_i - \overline{x}\right)^2} \tag{10}$$

where x_i is the sensed value, $\overline{x}$ is average value, and N is the number of sensed samples. Obviously, we could minimize this amount of deviation by increasing the network density, i.e. by increasing the number of nodes collecting data, a technique called data redundancy. That could be done either by adding nodes to the cluster or by awaking sleeping nodes.

In our application (*Temperature Sensing*), we have varied the number of nodes sensing temperature, in order to analyze the relationship between the measured accuracy and the number of nodes sensing a certain phenomenon. Our sensed values follow a *Gaussian* distribution, with an average temperature of 25°C, and a standard deviation of 1°C.

In fig. 9, we show how the *standard deviation* of the data samples converges toward the theoretical deviation (of 1°C) as the network density increases.

The small amount of accuracy gained while moving from 100 sensors to 500 sensors for example, may raise the tradeoff issue between the gained accuracy and the cost incurred.

4.3 Relationship Between Reporting Period, Network Density and Packet Size

Reporting period or data freshness is in fact considered as another facet of accuracy. A fresher data (i.e. a shorter reporting period), corresponds to more accurate results. Packet size also affects accuracy: a bigger packet carries more accurate measurements.

Reporting period is directly related to the number of reporting nodes and it depends also on the packet size. In this case, modifying one parameter could affect the others. For example, in order to increase data freshness (i.e. decrease reporting period), we will have to decrease the superframe length, by either removing time slots (i.e. decreasing the number of nodes), or by decreasing the packet size allowed for each node. In both cases, accuracy will be affected negatively. So there is clearly a tradeoff to be done between those parameters.

Fig. 10 shows how reporting period increases when the network density increases, due to longer superframes. We could also notice that nodes allowed to send bigger packets (e.g. 1500 bytes) in their time slots are the most affected by the increase of density. In a WSN with 100 nodes deployed, allowing each to send 1500 bytes in its time slot, the reporting period reaches 0.6 seconds, while it is much shorter (0.04 seconds) when nodes are allowed to send 100 bytes in their time slots. In the first case, data freshness is affected while more accurate results are sent, while in the second case, data is sent more frequently but it's less accurate.

Understanding those relationships or mapping rules, will help us better evaluate the tradeoffs between the different QoS parameters, guaranteeing though a better QoS level for applications by fine tuning those parameters.

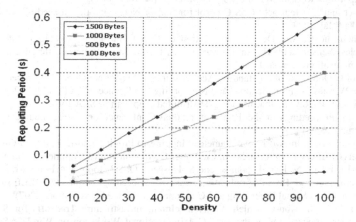

Fig. 9 Relationship between Density, Reporting period and Packet Size

5   Conclusion

QoS Support is one of the least explored tracks in WSN domain, although it has a crucial importance in many kinds of applications (e.g. real-time applications). In this paper we highlight an important issue in QoS Support: the *QoS mapping*. We discuss an approach for mapping user level QoS parameters (density and accuracy) to a network level QoS parameter (bandwidth). This was achieved by computing the TDMA superframe length in different scenarios, and presenting the bandwidth as a function of the superframe length and the network density.

We conduct also several simulations while giving the relationships between the different QoS parameters. Our experiments discuss relationships between density and bandwidth, accuracy and density, and between data freshness, density and packet size. One possible track we will try to explore in the future is to find the relationships between other QoS parameters like between density and delay for example. We will try also to investigate other kinds of MAC protocols like 802.11e.

References

1. S. Datta and T. Woody, Business 2.0 Magazine, February 2007 issue.
2. Technology Review Magazine (MIT), February 2003 issue.
3. G.J. Pottie and W.J. Kaiser: Wireless integrated network sensors. Communications of the ACM (2000).
4. W. Masri and Z. Mammeri: Middleware for Wireless Sensor Networks: A Comparative Analysis. In: Proceedings of the 2007 IFIP International Conference on Network and Parallel Computing – workshops (NPC 2007), China (September 2007).
5. R. Iyer and L. Kleinrock: QoS Control for Sensor Networks. In: Proceedings of ICC 2003, Alaska (May 2003)
6. J. Zhou and C. Mu: Density Domination of QoS Control with Localized Information in Wireless Sensor Networks. In: Proceedings of the 6th International Conference on ITS Telecommunications, China (June 2006)
7. J. Frolik: QoS Control for Random Access Wireless Sensor Networks. In: Proceedings of the IEEE Wireless Communications and Networking Conference, USA (March 2004)
8. B. H. Liu, P. Ray, S. Jha: Mapping Distributed Application SLA to Network QoS Parameters. In: Proceedings of the 10th International Conference on Telecommunications, Tahiti (February 2003)
9. Z. Mammeri: Framework for Parameter Mapping to Provide End-to-End QoS Guarantees in IntServ/DiffServ Architectures. In: Computer Communications, Volume 28, (June 2005)
10. M. Al-Kuwaiti, N. Kyriakopoulos, and S. Hussein: QoS Mapping: A Framework Model for Mapping Network Loss to Application Loss. In: Proceedings of the 2007 IEEE International Conference on Signal Processing and Communications, UAE (November 2007)
11. S. Tilak, N. B. Abu-Ghazaleh, W. Heinzelman: Infrastructure Tradeoffs for Sensor Networks. In: Proceedings of the 1st ACM International Workshop on Wireless Sensor Networks and Applications, USA (September 2002)
12. S. Adlakha, S. Ganeriwal, C. Schurgers, M. Srivastava: Poster Abstract: Density, Accuracy, Delay and Lifetime Tradeoffs in Wireless Sensor Networks – A Multidimensional Design Perspective. In: Proceedings of the ACM SenSys, USA (November 2003)
13. A. Koubaa, M. Alves, E. Tovar: Modeling and Worst-Case Dimensioning of Cluster-Tree Wireless Sensor Networks. In: Proceedings of the 27th IEEE International Real-Time Systems Symposium, Brazil (December 2006).

Minimizing Single TDMA Frame Sizes in Alarm-driven Wireless Sensor Networks Applications

Mário Macedo [1,3], **Mário Nunes** [1,2] and **António Grilo** [1,2]

[1] INESC-ID, Rua Alves Redol, Nº 9,
1000-029 Lisboa, Portugal

[2] IST/UTL, Av. Rovisco Pais,
1096 Lisboa, Portugal

[3] FCT/UNL,
2829-516 Caparica, Portugal

mmm@fct.unl.pt

{mario.nunes, antonio.grilo}@inesc.pt

Abstract Energy-efficiency and latency requirements in alarm-driven Wireless Sensor Networks often demand the use of TDMA protocols with special features such as cascading of timeslots, in a way that the sensor-to-sink delay bound can stay below a single frame. However, this single TDMA frame should be as small as possible. This paper presents a comparative study of timeslot allocation strategies that can be used to attain this goal. The Minimum Single Frame Size Problem is formulated, and the considered slot allocation algorithms are studied based on simulations. The results point to the conclusion that informed depth-first, coupled with a longest-path-first heuristic, can improve significantly the behavior of blind depth-first. Two centralized strategies are also simulated: a longest-paths-first, which allocates the branches by decreasing order of the length of the paths, and a largest-distances-first, which allocates the branches by decreasing distances to the sink that the paths can reach. It is also shown that a largest-distances-first strategy can achieve the smallest single frame sizes, and also the lowest variation of frame sizes. A distributed version of this algorithm (DIST-LDF) is presented, which obtains the same results of its centralized version.

1 Introduction

Wireless Sensor Networks (WSNs) are geographically distributed, self-organized and robustly networked micro-sensing systems that can be readily de-

Please use the following format when citing this chapter:

Macedo, M., Nunes, M. and Grilo, A., 2008, in IFIP International Federation for Information Processing, Volume 284; *Wireless and Mobile Networking*; Zoubir Mammeri; (Boston: Springer), pp. 343–354.

ployed and operated in environments in which more conventional infrastructure-based systems and networks are impractical. WSN are interconnected by means of a wireless communications technology, eventually collaborating to forward the sensorial data hop-by-hop from the source node to the sink nodes, and to external networks and vice versa.

In this paper, we are particularly interested to address critical alarm-driven WSN applications, such as surveillance of sensitive areas (e.g., intrusion detection and tracking). In this kind of WSN applications, traffic generation can be characterized as very sporadic, but the generation of an alarm report demands an immediate response to the event, which makes this kind of traffic very delay-sensitive. However, as WSNs devices have limited energy resources, low duty-cycles are also required. These two goals are usually contradictory, but among the MAC protocol families, TDMA protocols can provide low latency in the convergecast of data from the WSNs nodes to the sink, while still providing low duty-cycles. The quick convergecast of data from the nodes to the sink is usually achieved by constructing a routing tree routed on the sink node, and by ordering the timeslots in the path from a node to the sink, in such a way that the receiving slot(s) number(s) of a given node is lower than its transmitting slot number, while the slot distance between the two is kept as low as possible (a procedure that is called "cascading of timeslots"). On the other hand, low duty-cycle can be achieved by TDMA protocols, since each node only needs to be active during its receiving and transmission slots, while staying asleep for the rest of the TDMA frame. In order to maximize the overall goodput, there is also the need to reutilize the same timeslots in different parts of the network, in a way that allows non-interfering transmissions to take place simultaneously.

While not being a pure TDMA protocol, the Data-gathering MAC (D-MAC) protocol, presented in [1], includes an adaptive duty-cycle, whose main purpose is to minimize the node-to-sink latency in convergecast networks. D-MAC uses staggered synchronization so that a data packet heard by a node, at one level of the tree, is transmitted to the next level in the following time period. The node is then allowed to sleep until the reception period for its level occurs. Nodes at the same level of the tree have to compete for timeslot access and may also interfere with nodes located in the same area. However, support of several sinks in D-MAC is troublesome

The use of TDMA for fast broadcast (a converse problem of convergecast) is a well-known subject (see, [2]). The authors show that the problem of determining optimal channel allocation for fast broadcasting is NP-hard. Two algorithms for tree construction, and slot assignment, are presented, namely a centralized version, and its distributed version. The distributed algorithm begins at the source node, and builds a spanning tree, such that each node has a slot number higher than its parent's slot, but with the smallest possible value. Tree construction and slot assignment is performed depth-first, by means of passing a token to one node at a time, and by exchanging appropriate protocol messages with the neighbor nodes, in order to achieve conflict-free schedules. These protocols are also designed to achieve spatial reuse of the slots, with relatively small TDMA frame sizes.

Another protocol that was designed to achieve TDMA conflict-free schedules is the DRAND distributed slot assignment protocol [3]. As the authors state, the problem of obtaining a minimum slot frame size is NP-hard. DRAND is not particularly suited for fast broadcast or fast convergecast, as slot assignment is random, but it is proved to achieve conflict-free schedules: DRAND assures that nodes in a 2-hop neighborhood do not use the same slot. DRAND also proved to have a message exchanging complexity of $O(\delta)$, where δ is the neighborhood of each node.

References [4] and [5] present two centralized algorithms, namely CTCCAA and CCA, which were specially designed to achieve low latencies in the convergecast process. CTCCAA proceeds with the tree construction and slot allocation processes in a breadth-first top-down manner, while CCA proceeds in a bottom-up manner from the leaves of the tree to the sink node. Both employ cascading slot assignment. The two algorithms differ in the way they establish the neighborhood of each node. These algorithms present the drawback of being centralized.

SS-TDMA [6] is a TDMA protocol designed for convergecast/broadcast applications. Its basic assumption is that the interference range is different from the communication range, and that the relation between them gives an estimation of the number of nodes within interference range that can't have the same slot number. In the slot assignment process, each node receives messages from the neighbors with their assigned slots. The receiving node knows the direction of an incoming message, and adds fixed values to the neighbor's slot number, in order to determine its own slot number. Although being a distributed algorithm, it needs a location service and topological knowledge about the networks, which limits its practical applicability. SS-TDMA also follows a cascading slot allocation, and a 2-hop slot allocation criterion.

More recently, the problems of building routing trees, and minimizing convergecast latency in ZigBee networks, were studied in reference [7]. The authors prove that the problem of obtaining a conflict-free slot assignment that minimizes the convergecast latency is also NP-hard. The distributed version algorithm is essentially a breadth-first tree construction and slot allocation protocol that is based on HELLO messages transmitted by the relay nodes. The main contributions of this protocol are the slot reassignment rules: the nodes that have more interfering neighbors, that stay closer to the sink, or that have a lower ID (identification number), have priority to choose a given slot that minimizes the latency. The interference avoidance procedure of this protocol is also based on a 2-hop neighborhood criterion.

Reference [8] presents a centralized algorithm and two distributed algorithms (namely, the DSA-AGGR algorithm – Distributed CCH for Data Aggregation). All the three algorithms are claimed to achieve a balance between depth-first and breadth-first in the tree slot allocation process. DSA-AGGR is designed to achieve low latency by means of cascading timeslots. DSA-AGGR begins to allocate slots from the sink to the leaves of the network tree, but each node is only eligible to allocate a slot if the following expression results in a value higher than 0.25 for the *color_score*:

$$color\_score = \frac{2.ColoredOneHop + ColoredTwoHop}{2.NumberOneHops + NumberTwoHops} \qquad (1)$$

Reference [9] presents a set of joint routing and slot assignment centralized algorithms that aim to achieve low latencies. However, the procedures have the drawbacks of being computational intensive, while the tree building process being centralized.

Finally, in reference [10] centralized algorithms are presented, which can be used to optimize the energy or the latency of the data collection process. These algorithms are hybrid, being based on genetic algorithms and particle swarm optimization. The centralized nature of these algorithms also limits their potential use.

2 Problem statement

Some of the works mentioned above are concerned with achieving short frame sizes. It is well known that for any greedy coloring algorithm, and also for any slot assignment algorithm, the worst-case of the number of the colors (or respectively the frame size) that are needed is equal to $\Delta+1$, where Δ is the maximum degree of a node, which is the maximum number of possible conflicting neighbors in the network.

As critical alarm-driven WSN applications should only report sporadic abnormal events, they do not to periodically transfer bulk data to the sink. Therefore, achieving high throughputs for these networks is not a specific design requirement. Consequently, the problem addressed in this paper is not to obtain the smallest possible frame sizes, which depend on the maximum degrees of the networks. On the other hand, very small frames sizes also lead to high duty-cycles, and also imply that the transmissions from nodes that are placed away from the sink will potentially have to span several frames. This can originate different delay bounds for each node in the network tree. Finally, we are interested to have similar delay bounds for the alarms transmitted by all the network nodes. This requirement can be accomplished by transmitting the data always in a single TDMA frame, whatever the location of the node. However, since different scheduling algorithms may lead to different single TDMA frame sizes, we are also interested in algorithms that lead to the smallest possible single TDMA frame size in such a way that it is able to accommodate all the network nodes on it. We call this problem the Minimum Single Frame Size (MSFS) problem. To the best of our knowledge, we haven't seen this problem formulated before.

Intuitively, those algorithms will also lead to the lowest maximum slot distance of the network (i.e., the lowest sensor-to-sink delay bound).

Some of the algorithms and protocols mentioned above assume that the building of the routing tree is done simultaneously with the slot allocation procedure, while in others the two processes are done separately. In this paper, it is assumed that the slot assignment procedure, of the network setup phase, is done after the routing tree construction, for example on top of an efficient contention MAC protocol like B-MAC [11].

3 Simulation Model and Scenario

Simulations were carried out considering a 100-node square grid physical topology, where the sink node was placed at the upper-right corner. A logical tree topology was assumed, with the sink being the root node, and each node communicating with a random neighbor, selected among those that were closer to the node, and that offered progress to the sink. In this way, each node was allowed to choose as parent either the node that is closest to it in the West direction, or in the North direction.

In accordance with most references in this subject, a simple free space propagation model was used. The path loss exponent was set to 2, and radio propagation irregularity was not considered [12] for the sake of simplicity.

The dimension of the grid square edges was set to the approximate value of communication distance. The interference graph was built based on a 2-hop neighborhood criterion, as it is customary in the related publications. As each slot was considered bi-directional, the links that were considered as interfering with parent-child communication were all the links established by the 2-hop neighbors of the parent node and of the child node, using the same timeslot.

Slot allocation begins at the sink (which allocates slots to its children) and proceeds independently down the network tree until the leaf nodes are reached. The simulations have considered different slot allocation strategies.

The dimension of each slot was configured to offer three transmission opportunities, in order to attain a sensor-to-sink delay bound of a single TDMA frame with high probability.

4   Slot Allocation Algorithms and Simulation Results

Centralized slot allocation algorithms are potentially more optimal and more predictable in terms of convergence, but present one drawback: they require that the nodes communicate their local topology to the sink (e.g., their neighborhoods, parents, etc.), which is a slow and communication intensive procedure. Additionally, they usually rely on theoretical propagation models to avoid assignment conflicts, being less adaptive to the space-time variability of realistic RF propagation environments. The distributed slot allocation algorithms can be particularly interesting because they do not require the sink node to know the network topology. Therefore, they are more scalable, flexible and adaptive, even if their convergence is less predictable and slower.

In this paper, for the matter of comparison, we did not consider the strategies referred in literature that are centralized, or that perform the building of tree simultaneously with the allocation process. All implemented strategies assume cascading of timeslots, and greedy slot allocation by each node (i.e., always choosing the highest possible slot number that is less than its parent's slot number).

The following slot allocation strategies were firstly considered: the classic depth-first (DF) and breadth-first (BF) [13], RANDOM, DSA-AGGR, and SS-TDMA.

The RANDOM strategy consists in selecting randomly and allocating any node whose parent node has already allocated also a slot. Therefore, the RANDOM strategy can descend the tree in several ways that fall between DF, and BF.

For the SS-TDMA slot allocation protocol, its y parameter was set to 2, meaning that the interference range was twice the communication range. In this way, if a node received a message from its Northern closest neighbor (its parent), it allocated a slot number equal to its neighbor's minus one; if it received a message from its Western closest neighbor, it allocated a slot number equal to its neighbor's minus (y+1), or, in the case, minus 3. The simulations showed that SS-TDMA was able to allocate all slot numbers of a given frame without any unused slots, achieving also the spatial reuse of the slots, and implementing a 2-hop neighborhood interference avoidance criterion.

As the square grid had 100 nodes, and the nodes located at the top edge of the square have always its closest Western neighbor as parent, while the nodes located at the left edge of the square have always its closest Northern neighbor as parent, only 81 nodes can choose one node as parent, among its closest Western neighbor and its closest Northern neighbor. This means that 2^{81} different topologies can be generated, or 2.42×10^{24} different topologies. For each of these different topologies, there are also a huge number of different slot schedules that can be done by each slot allocation algorithm. For instance, DF can descend the tree visiting firstly different branches. These observations suggest that the number of different slot schedules that are possible is a very huge number, it being impossible to look at each of them to find the optimal TDMA frame size. Therefore, for each different slot allocation algorithm, we ran 10,000,000 simulations, each having as input one different random logical tree, and resulting in one different random slot schedule. Although this number is small in comparison with the number of all possible combinations of topologies and slot schedules, it was thought sufficient to assess how the different slot allocation algorithms behave with respect to the TDMA frame size that they can attain. The histogram of frequencies for the respective TDMA frame sizes was then built. Since the RANDOM strategy seems to generate a broader range of slot schedules, the set of simulations was raised to

100,000,000.

Fig. 1 shows the histograms for that set of slot allocation algorithms. The values corresponding to the RANDOM algorithm are the original divided by 10.

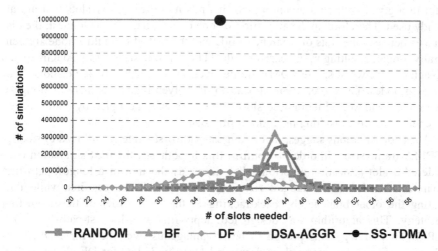

Fig. 1. Histograms of the number of simulations for each TDMA frame size, for the first set of slot allocation algorithms.

These results show that BF has a lower variance than DF, but DF achieves a lower average value, respectively 36.7 slots for DF, and 42.1 for BF (see, Table 1). DSA-AGGR does not behave as being a compromise between BF, and DF, with respect to finding low single TDMA frame sizes. However, the RANDOM algorithm behaves as expected: its histogram falls between those of BF, and DF. It is interesting to note that SS-TDMA achieves always the same number of slots, i.e., 36, whatever the logical topology. This result seems a little bit bizarre but the reason for it is simple to explain: the distances, in terms of slots, between the slot of a given node and the slots of its neighbors are constant, and they depend only on the directions of the neighbors. As the nodes of all simulated grids have always the same coordinates, the frames have always the same size. However, the number of slots that it is achieved with SS-TDMA is not particularly promising, as it is close to the average value that is obtained by DF, and substantially higher than the minimum values of DF.

DF can achieve a lower number of slots because it can descend first on larger branches. The cascading of timeslots in those larger branches results in a set of consecutive slots that can be reused in other adjacent upper and smaller branches of tree network. Inversely, if smaller branches are allocated first, those allocated slots cannot be used in larger adjacent branches, resulting in larger sensor-to-sink slot distances, and therefore larger TDMA frames. Note, however, that the slots that are used on an allocation of the longest branch first are not generally suffi-cient to color all the other network nodes, and that there is a need of some extra slots: for instance, DF achieved a minimum of 23 slots in a given simulation, while the longest path had always a length of just 18 hops. On the other hand, BF achieves higher single TDMA frame sizes, because it allocates the nodes of all the branches at some level in the same round, meaning that when it tries to allocate a slot to a given node in a given branch, it finds more frequently slots that are already used. Therefore, in the allocation of one branch, namely the longest, the distances between the slots of a parent's node and the that of its child's node are generally longer, resulting in increased single TDMA frame sizes. DSA-AGGR seems to achieve the worst single TDMA frame sizes, as it tends to create hotspots of allocated nodes. Therefore, in the allocation of a given branch, namely the longest, the nodes tend to find more used slots, which are even occupied by nodes placed deeper in the tree, resulting in higher frame sizes.

These observations suggest that a longest-path-first strategy will lead to smaller TDMA frame sizes. In order to confirm this hypothesis, the next simulation considered a slot allocation algorithm that descends the tree in a longest-path-first manner when it has to make a decision of which path it chooses first, while allocating the other branches by backtracking in the same order of the depth-first strategy. This algorithm was designated depth-first-with-longest-path-first (DF-LPF). This strategy was proved to be advantageous over the simple DF, as is shown in Fig. 2. Average values decreased from 36.7 slots for DF, down to 27.9 slots for DF-LPF. These values have also resulted from 10,000,000 simulation runs.

Two centralized strategies were also investigated with the objective of achieving even smaller TDMA frame sizes.

The first centralized strategy (CENT-LPF, centralized longest-paths-first) allocates the branches in the descending order of their lengths, breaking the ties with priority for the paths that are situated deeper on the tree, and randomly if this rule is not enough to decide. The rationale for the first breaking ties rule is the same of the DF-LPF algorithm.

The other strategy (CENT-LDF, centralized largest-distances-first) allocates the branches in the descending order of the distances to the sink that the branches can reach, independently of their sizes. Breaking ties rules are the same of CENT-LPF.

Fig. 2 shows that there is a systematic improvement on the number of slots that are needed, when we successively consider DF-LPF, CENT-LPF, and CENT-LDF (which results are the same of its distributed version, DIST-LDF, that we describe later). Average values of the number of slots were respectively 27.9, 25.6, and 24.9, for these three slot allocation algorithms, as it can be seen in Table 1. This last allocation algorithm also produces the smallest range of values, among all the considered slot allocation algorithms. CENT-LDF presents slot numbers that range from 21 to 33 slots, while blind depth-first (DF) presented a much broader range, from 23 to 58 slots.

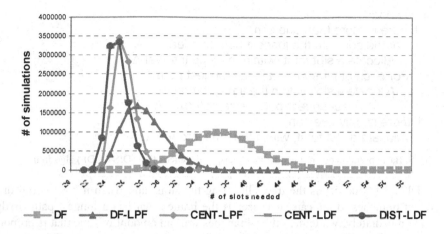

Fig. 2. Histograms of the number of simulations for each TDMA frame size, for the second set of slot allocation algorithms, showing improvements over simple depth-first (DF).

	Average (slots)	Minimum (slots)	Maximum (slots)
RANDOM	41	26	57
BF	42.1	29	49
DF	36.7	23	58
DSA-AGGR	42.7	29	53
SS-TDMA	36	36	36
DF-LPF	27.9	22	43
CENT-LPF	25.6	22	34
CENT-LDF	24.9	21	33
DIST-LDF	24.9	21	33

Table 1. Number of slots obtained by the allocation algorithms.

The explanation for these results is similar to that of the DF-LPF strategy: when we allocate firstly the branches that lead to larger distances from the sinks, we are cascading the slots in a such a way that the hop distances for the farthest nodes are minimized, while the nodes that are closer to the sink, and placed in adjacent branches, can reutilize the slots that are used in those larger branches, without demanding for many extra slot numbers.

With these results in mind, a distributed largest-distances-first strategy (DIST-LDF) was developed, which was proved to provide the same results as the centralized CENT-LDF. Its pseudo-code is listed in Fig.3.

At any node:
  If there is more than one son:
    For the son with the longest path to a leaf:
      Allocate a slot for it, within the time interval Δt;
    For each other son *i* not in the longest path:
      Allocate a slot, within the time interval =
        $c *$ (size-longest-path - size-path(i)) $* \Delta t$;
  If there is only one son:
    Allocate a slot for it, within the time interval Δt;

Fig. 3. Basic pseudo-code of the distributed largest-distances-first (DIST-LDF) algorithm.

DIST-LDF descends the tree, allocating the slots, and when it has several different branches to allocate, it descends the branch that has a longest path firstly and immediately, while the others branches wait an amount of time that is proportional to the difference of the lengths of their paths and the length of the longest path. In this way, longest paths are allocated in advance, reserving slots for them before the smaller branches. Intuitively, in order for the allocations of longer distance branches not to be disturbed by the allocations of shorter branches, the former have to be scheduled sufficiently in advance.

Referring to Fig.3, Δt represents the time needed to allocate a slot in a real implementation distributed slot allocation protocol. Constant c has shown to generate the same results of the centralized algorithm, when it takes values greater or equal then 5. For lower values, DIST-LDF performance degraded progressively into higher values for the TDMA frame size. When constant c is lower than 5, some shorter distance branches do not wait for a sufficiently large delay, and begin to allocate slots for themselves, while longer distance branches are also allocating their slots, and these concurrent actions are not separated enough in space. Therefore, the shorter distance branches can allocate slots that can't be used by longer distance branches, resulting in larger TDMA frames. Or, in other words, longer distance branches are not scheduled sufficiently in advance. On the other hand, if we increase the value for c much beyond that of 5, we do not improve further the behavior of the DIST-LDF algorithm, because the allocation of longer distance branches is already being performed at distances in a way that they cannot be affected anymore by the allocations of shorter distance branches. Dimensioning of constant c for some specific network is, however, a matter for future research.

Although DIST-LDF presents the best results among the considered slot allocation strategies, it requires each node to know the length of the branches that are rooted at their children, which represents an important disadvantage. This information has to be propagated in the network tree, from the leaves to the sink, after the tree construction process, which is a procedure that results in a certain extra amount of overhead. Note, however, that the complexity of DIST-LDF, in terms of the number of visited nodes, seems to be intuitively smaller than that of DF, as DIST-LDF does not need to backtrack in the tree structure, when it full allocates a sub tree. DIST-LDF is an always-forwarding allocating distributed discipline. Therefore, it is also expected that DIST-LDF can achieve smaller execution times than DF. However, these two last observations need to be assessed by future research.

5 Conclusions and Future Work

In most alarm-driven WSN applications (e.g., intrusion detection in restricted areas), traffic can be characterized as very sporadic, but the generation of an alarm report demands an immediate response to the event, which makes this kind of traffic very delay-sensitive. Low latencies and low duty-cycles can be simultaneously accomplished by using TDMA protocols. Cascading of the slots from a given node to the sink can result in low latencies, while TDMA protocols can achieve low duty-cycles, as each node need only to be awake in its slots. Since this kind of applications do not need high throughputs, and it is also desirable to have the same delay bound for all the nodes in the network, we defined a new problem, which is that of allocating slots for all the nodes of the networks, such data can be always transmitted in a single TDMA frame, whatever is the place of the node in the network. However, such unique TDMA must also have the smallest possible size (problem that we designated as the Minimum Single Frame Size – MSFS – problem).

In this paper, several TDMA slot allocation strategies were comparatively evaluated with respect to the goal of minimizing the single TDMA frame size. The simulation results have shown that a breadth-first slot allocation strategy behaves poorly than depth-first, and that an informed depth-first strategy, that visits the longest-path first, improves significantly the results when compared with blind depth-first. It was also shown that a largest-distances-first slot allocation algorithm will produce the smallest single TDMA frame sizes, and the smallest range of values, among all the scheduling algorithms that were considered. A distributed version (DIST-LDF) of this algorithm was implemented, which was able to obtain the same results as its centralized counterpart.

For future work, the authors intend to investigate if these disciplines also minimize the latency of the convergecast for the more general case of transmission done in several frames, and to develop new slot allocation algorithms that can even exceed the DIST-LDF algorithm performance.

Acknowledgments   The work described in this paper is based on results of IST FP6 project UbiSec&Sens. UbiSec&Sens receives research funding from the European Community's Sixth Framework Programme. Apart from this, the European Commission has no responsibility for the content of this paper.

The information in this document is provided as is and no guarantee or warranty is given that the information is fit for any particular purpose. The user thereof uses the information at its sole risk and liability.

References

1. G. Lu, B. Krishnamachari, C. S. Raghavendra, "An Adaptive Energy-Efficient and Low-Latency MAC for Data Gathering in Wireless Sensor Networks", in Proceedings of the 18th International Parallel and Distributed Processing Symposium (IPDPS 2004), Santa Fe, NM, USA, April 2004.
2. I. Chlamtac, S. Kutten; "Tree-based Broadcasting in Multihop Radio Networks", IEEE Transactions on Computers, Volume C-36, No. 10, Oct. 1987.
3. I. Rhee, A. Warrier, J. Min, L. Xu, "DRAND: Distributed Randomized TDMA Scheduling for Wireless Ad-hoc Networks", the 7th ACM International Symposium on Mobile Ad Hoc Networking and Computing (MobiHoc'2006), Florence, Italy, May 2006.
4. V. Annamalai, S.K.S. Gupta, L. Schwiebert, "On Tree-Based Convergecasting in Wireless Sensor Networks", in the Proceedings of the IEEE Wireless Communications and Networking (WCNC 2003), New Orleans, LA, USA, March 2003.
5. S. Upadhyayula, V. Annamalai, S.K.S. Gupta, "A low-latency and energy-efficient algorithm for convergecast in wireless sensor networks", in Proceedings of IEEE Global Telecommunications Conference (GLOBECOM '03), San Francisco, CA, USA, January 2003.
6. S.S. Kulkarni and M.(U.) Arumugam, "SS-TDMA: A Self-Stabilizing MAC for Sensor Networks", Sensor Network Operations, IEEE Press, 2005.
7. M.S. Pan, Y.-C. Tseng, "Quick convergecast in ZigBee beacon-enabled tree-based wireless sensor networks", Computer Communications, Vol. 31, Issue 5, pp. 999-1011, Elsevier, 25 March 2008.
8. K. L. Bryan, T. Ren, L. DiPippo, T. Henry, V. Fay-Wolfe, "Towards Optimal TDMA Frame Size in Wireless Sensor Networks", University of Rhode Island, Technical Report, TR-xxx, March 2007.
9. G. Lu, B. Krishnamachari, "Minimum latency joint scheduling and routing in wireless sensor networks", Ad Hoc Networks, Vol. 5, Issue 6, pp. 832-843, Elsevier, August 2007.
10. J. Mao, Z. Wu, X. Wu, "A TDMA scheduling scheme for many-to-one communications in wireless sensor networks", Computer Communications, Vol. 30, Issue 4, pp. 863-872, Elsevier, February 2007.
11. J. Polastre, J. Hill, D. Culler, "Versatile Low Power Media Access for Wireless Sensor Networks", in Proceedings of the 2nd ACM SenSys Conference, pp. 95-107, Baltimore, MD, USA, November. 2004.
12. T. Rappaport, "Wireless Communications: Principles and Practice", 2nd Edition, Prentice Hall, 2002.
13. T. H. Cormen, C. E. Leiserson, R. L. Rivest, "Introduction to Algorithms", The MIT Press, 2000.

Balancing Between Power Optimization and Iub Efficiency in MBMS Enabled UMTS Networks

Antonios Alexiou[1, 2], Christos Bouras[1, 2] and Vasileios Kokkinos[1, 2]

[1] Computer Engineering and Informatics Dept., Univ. of Patras, Greece

[2] Research Academic Computer Technology Institute, Greece
University of Patras, Rio Campus, 26500 Rio, Patras, Greece

alexiua@cti.gr, bouras@cti.gr, kokkinos@cti.gr

Abstract Multicast transmission is one of the major goals for Universal Mobile Telecommunication System (UMTS) that motivated the 3rd Generation Partnership Project (3GPP) to launch the Multimedia Broadcast/Multicast Service (MBMS) framework. MBMS is a key framework that constitutes a significant step towards the so-called Mobile Broadband by efficiently utilizing network and radio resources, both in the core network and more importantly, in the UMTS Terrestrial Radio Access Network (UTRAN). One of most important problems that MBMS is currently facing is the assignment of the appropriate transport channel for the transmission of MBMS data. This paper proposes an alternative solution to the problem of efficient transport channel selection. In particular, we introduce a cost-based scheme for the efficient radio bearer selection that minimizes the delivery cost of the multicast data. In our approach, the telecommunication cost over the most crucial interfaces of UMTS is calculated and based on this cost, the appropriate radio bearer is selected.

1 Introduction

One of the key aspects of MBMS defined in the 3GPP specifications is power control, since the available power of the base station is limited [1]. Another important challenge for MBMS is the need for optimization of data transmission over the UTRAN interfaces. Efficient mechanisms in MBMS should deal with a major aspect of MBMS traffic. This aspect is the selection of the appropriate transport channel for the transmission of MBMS traffic to multicast users after calculating the power requirements of each channel and the traffic load over the UTRAN interfaces.

Current approaches indicate that MBMS traffic can be provided in each cell by either multiple Point-to-Point (PTP) channels or by a single Point-to-Multipoint (PTM) channel. MBMS specifications deal with this issue with the introduction of MBMS Counting Mechanism of UMTS [2]. According to this mechanism, the

Please use the following format when citing this chapter:

Alexiou, A., Bouras, C. and Kokkinos, V., 2008, in IFIP International Federation for Information Processing, Volume 284; *Wireless and Mobile Networking*; Zoubir Mammeri; (Boston: Springer), pp. 355–368.

decision on the threshold between PTP and PTM bearers is operator dependent, although it is proposed that it should be based on the number of serving MBMS users. Nevertheless, the MBMS Counting Mechanism provides a non realistic approach because mobility and current location of the mobile users are not taken into account; while on the other hand the base station's transmission power is not considered.

The inefficiencies of the MBMS Counting Mechanism motivated novel approaches, indicating that the assignment of the radio bearer should be performed in order to minimize the power requirements of the base stations [3]. A study under these assumptions is presented in [1]. However, this work considers only the air interface of the UMTS network and does not take into account other crucial interfaces of the UMTS network. Moreover, this work does not consider the enhancements that High Speed Downlink Packet Access (HSDPA) technology can provide by increasing data rates and decreasing power requirements, which however are considered in [4].

The fact that the Iub interface capacity is limited, stresses the need for considering this interface when selecting the most efficient radio bearer for the transmission of the MBMS data. Under this prism, in this paper we analytically present the multicast mode of MBMS and propose a novel approach that calculates the cost over the most crucial interfaces of the UMTS network during MBMS transmissions; and based on this calculation, allows the efficient transport channel assignment. The goal achieved by this work is twofold. At a first level, due to the fact that the MBMS Counting Mechanism is an open issue for 3GPP, our approach constitutes a more realistic and adaptive to dynamic wireless environments approach, by employing a cost-based switching criterion when selecting transport channel for MBMS transmissions. At a second level, our approach contributes to Radio Resource Management mechanism of UMTS by presenting a novel framework for MBMS that optimally utilizes power and network resources.

The paper is structured as follows: Section 2 provides an overview of the UMTS and MBMS architecture. Section 3 presents a cost analysis method for the evaluation of the MBMS multicast mode; while Section 4 examines the results of the analysis. Finally, some concluding remarks and planned next steps are described in Section 5.

2   UMTS and MBMS Architecture

A UMTS network consists of two land-based network segments: the Core Network (CN) and the UTRAN (Fig. 1). The CN is responsible for switching/routing voice and data connections, while the UTRAN handles all radio-related functionalities. The CN consists of two service domains: the Circuit-Switched (CS) and the Packet-Switched (PS) service domain. The PS portion of the CN in UMTS consists of two kinds of General Packet Radio Service (GPRS) Support Nodes (GSNs), namely Gateway GSN (GGSN) and Serving GSN

(SGSN). An SGSN is connected to GGSN via the Gn interface and to UTRAN via the Iu interface. UTRAN consists of the Radio Network Controller (RNC) and the Node B. Node B constitutes the base station and provides radio coverage to one or more cells. Node B is connected to the User Equipment (UE) via the Uu interface and to the RNC via the Iub interface [5].

3GPP is currently standardizing MBMS. The major modification compared to the GPRS platform is the addition of a new entity called Broadcast Multicast - Service Center (BM-SC) (Fig. 1). The BM-SC communicates with the existing UMTS/GSM networks and external Public Data Networks [6].

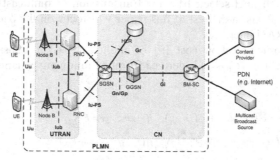

Fig. 1. UMTS and MBMS architecture

Regarding the transmission of the MBMS packets over the UTRAN interfaces, it may be performed on common (Forward Access Channel - FACH), on dedicated (Dedicated Channel - DCH) or on shared channels (High Speed-Downlink Shared Channel - HS-DSCH) [5], [7].

3   Cost Analysis of the MBMS Multicast Mode in UTRAN

As performance metric for our analysis, we consider the transmission cost for packet delivery only over the UTRAN interfaces and not the delivery cost over the interfaces of the CN. In order to justify our choice, we briefly summarize the five steps occurred for the delivery of the multicast packets to the users of the multicast group.

With multicast, the packets are forwarded only to those Node Bs that have multicast users. Firstly, the BM-SC receives a multicast packet and forwards it to the GGSN that has registered to receive the multicast traffic. Secondly, GGSN receives the multicast packet and by querying its multicast routing lists, it determines which SGSCs have multicast users residing in their respective service areas. Thirdly, the destination SGSNs receive the multicast packets; and having queried their multicast routing lists, determine which RNCs should receive the multicast packets. The process of multicast packet delivery continues with the transmission of the multicast data over the UTRAN interfaces. Once the destination RNCs receive the multicast packet, they send it to the Node Bs that have established the appropriate radio bearers for the multicast data transmission.

Finally, the users receive the packets on the appropriate radio bearers either by PTP channels, transmitted to individual users separately, or by PTM channels, transmitted to all members in the cell [8].

At this point, we have to mention that the process of packets' transmission in the CN is independent of the transport channel that is assigned for the transmission of the multicast data over the UTRAN interfaces. This in turn means that the cost for the transmission of multicast packets from BM-SC to RNC is independent of the transport channel that will be assigned in UTRAN. On the other hand, the packet delivery cost over UTRAN interfaces strongly depends on the transport channel selected for the transmission of multicast traffic to mobile users. The analysis in the rest of this paper will focus on the packet delivery cost over the UTRAN interfaces.

The telecommunication cost [9] of multicast packet transmission over the UTRAN interfaces (C_{UTRAN}) is derived from the following equation [10]:

$$C_{UTRAN} = \begin{cases} c_i\left(D_{rb}+p_b\right)+c_w\left(D_{FACH}\right), & \text{if} \quad channel = FACH \\ c_i\left(N_{UE}\cdot\left(D_{rb}+p_b\right)\right)+c_w\left(\sum_{i=1}^{N_{UE}}D_{DCH}(i)\right), & \text{if} \quad channel = DCH \\ c_i\left(\frac{N_{UE}}{2}\cdot\left(D_{rb}+p_b\right)\right)+c_w\left(D_{HS-DSCH}\right), & \text{if} \quad channel = HS-DSCH \end{cases} = c_i\cdot D_{Iub}+c_w\cdot D_{Uu} \quad (1)$$

where N_{UE} represents the total number of multicast users in the cell, D_{rb} is the transmission cost of packet delivery over the Iub interface (RNC - Node B), p_b is the processing cost of multicast packet delivery at Node B, D_{DCH}, D_{FACH}, $D_{HS-DSCH}$ are the transmission costs of packet delivery over the Uu interface with DCH, FACH and HS-DSCH respectively and c_i and c_w are the weights of Iub and Uu respectively (where $c_i + c_w = 1$). According to equation (1) the total telecommunication cost of every channel consists of the transmission cost over the Iub interface plus the cost over the Uu interface, after multiplying each cost with an appropriate weight.

Parameter C_{UTRAN} is calculated for each cell and for each transport channel in a cell separately and these calculations are performed in the RNC. Based on these calculations, the RNC selects for the transmission of the MBMS data, the transport channel that ensures the lowest cost over the UTRAN interfaces (i.e. the transport channel that generates the smallest value for parameter C_{UTRAN}).

3.1 Cost over the Iub Interface

One of the significant operational expenses in UMTS networks is the Iub transmission between the RNC and Node Bs. The fact that the capacity of the Iub interface is limited indicates that this interface should be included in our analysis. In general, PTM transmissions bring benefit in Iub capacity compared to PTP transmissions. In PTP transmissions a dedicated Iub capacity for each user is required, whereas in PTM transmissions only a single Iub capacity allocation is required. The Iub allocation is performed per base station, according to Release 7 3GPP specifications [5].

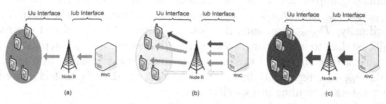

Fig. 2. MBMS transmissions over Iub and Uu with: (a) FACH, (b) DCH, (c) HS-DSCH

Regarding the cost over the Iub interface, when FACH is employed as transport channel, each multicast packet is sent once over the Iub interface and then the packet is transmitted to the UEs that are served by the corresponding Node B (Fig. 2a). On the other hand, when DCHs are used for the transmission of the multicast packets, each packet is replicated over the Iub as many times as the number of multicast users that the corresponding Node B serves (Fig. 2b). In HSDPA, the Iub efficiency is improved by a factor of 2 compared to that of Wideband Code Division Multiple Access (WCDMA) (Fig. 2c). This is a significant improvement, which basically means that twice as many user bits can be transmitted through the same Iub with HSDPA compared to Release 99 WCDMA. This improvement mainly comes from fast dynamic sharing of the HSDPA Iub bandwidth allocated between active users [7].

Fig. 2 depicts that PTM transmissions bring benefit in Iub capacity, while on the other hand DCH has increased Iub capacity requirements compared to HS-DSCH in PTP transmissions. As the Iub capacity is limited, Fig. 2 indicates that the packet delivery cost over the Iub interface should also be taken into account when selecting the most efficient radio bearer for the transmission of the MBMS data.

As far as equation (1) is concerned, as presented and analyzed in our previous work [10], the packet transmission cost in any segment of the UMTS network depends on two parameters: the number of hops between the edge nodes of this network segment and the capacity of the link of the network segment. This means that $D_{rb} = l_{rb}/k_{rb}$, where k_{rb} represents the capacity factor of the link between the RNC and Node B and l_{rb} the hops between these two nodes. Moreover, for the cost analysis and without loss of generality, we assume that the distance between the RNC and Node B is 1 hop and the capacity factor of this link is 0.5. Therefore, the value for parameter D_{rb} is set to 2. We have also estimated the value of parameter p_b that represents the processing cost of packet delivery at Node B. This value is set to 1, as in [10].

3.2 Cost over the Uu Interface

According to equation (1), C_{UTRAN} depends firstly on the population of the multicast group within a cell and secondly on the transport channel that is used. D_{DCH}, D_{FACH} and $D_{HS-DSCH}$ represent the cost over the Uu interface. More specifically, D_{DCH}, represents the cost of using a single DCH to transmit the multicast data to a single multicast user of the network, D_{FACH} represents the cost of using a FACH channel to serve all multicast users residing in a specific cell, while $D_{HS-DSCH}$ represents the cost of using a HS-DSCH that is shared to the multicast users residing in a specific cell.

In order to calculate the costs over the Uu interface, we will follow an approach that reflects the most recent specifications and requirements of 3GPP to consider the power consumption during MBMS transmissions [3]. Therefore, in our analysis, the fundamental factor that determines the transmission cost over the Uu interface is the amount of Node B's transmission power when using HS-DSCH, DCH or FACH transport channels. To this direction, we will first examine the power profile of each transport channel; and then, we will define the exact cost introduced by Uu interface during MBMS multicast transmission.

3.2.1 HS-DSCH Power Profile

HS-DSCH is a rate controlled rather than a power controlled transport channel. Although there are two basic modes for allocating HS-DSCH transmission power [7], in this paper we will focus on a dynamic method in order to provide only the required, marginal amount of power so as to satisfy all the multicast users. Two major measures for HSDPA power planning are: the HS-DSCH Signal-to-Interference-plus-Noise Ratio (SINR) metric and the Geometry factor (G). SINR for a single-antenna Rake receiver is calculated as in (2):

$$SINR = SF_{16}\frac{P_{HS-DSCH}}{pP_{own} + P_{other} + P_{noise}} \tag{2}$$

where $P_{HS-DSCH}$ is the HS-DSCH transmission power, P_{own} is the own cell interference experienced by the mobile user, P_{other} the interference from neighboring cells and P_{noise} the Additive White Gaussian Noise. Parameter p is the orthogonality factor ($p=0$: perfect orthogonality), while SF_{16} is the spreading factor of 16.

There is a strong relationship between the HS-DSCH allocated power and the obtained MBMS cell throughput. This relationship can be disclosed in the three following steps. Initially, we have to define the target MBMS cell throughput. Once the target cell throughput is set, the next step is to define the way that this throughput relates to the SINR. Finally, we can describe how the required HS-DSCH transmission power ($P_{HS-DSCH}$) can be expressed as a function of the SINR value and the user location (in terms of G) as in equation (3) [7]:

$$P_{HS-DSCH} \geq SINR[p - G^{-1}]\frac{P_{own}}{SF_{16}} \tag{3}$$

3.2.2 DCH Power Profile

The total downlink transmission power allocated for all MBMS users in a cell that are served by multiple DCHs is variable. It mainly depends on the number of serving users, their distance from the base station, the bit rate of the MBMS session and the experienced signal quality, E_b/N_0, for each user. Equation (4) calculates the total DCH power required for the transmission of the data to n users in a specific cell [11].

$$P_{DCH} = \frac{P_P + \sum_{i=1}^{n} \frac{(P_N + x_i)}{\frac{W}{(E_b/N_0)_i R_{b,i}} + p} L_{p,i}}{1 - \sum_{i=1}^{n} \frac{p}{\frac{W}{(E_b/N_0)_i R_{b,i}} + p}} \tag{4}$$

where P_{DCH} is the base station's total transmitted power, P_P is the power devoted to common control channels, $L_{p,i}$ is the path loss, $R_{b,i}$ the ith user transmission rate, W the bandwidth, P_N the background noise, p is the orthogonality factor and x_i is the interference observed by the ith user given as a function of the transmitted power by the neighboring cells P_{Tj}, $j=1,...K$ and the path loss from this user to the jth cell L_{ij}.

3.2.3 FACH Power Profile

A FACH essentially transmits at a fixed power level since fast power control is not supported in this channel. FACH is a PTM channel and must be received by all users throughout the part of the cell that the users are found. Table 1 presents the FACH transmission power levels obtained for various cell coverage areas [12]. Depending on the distance between the user with the worst path loss and the Node B, the RNC adjusts the FACH transmission power in one of the ten levels presented in Table 1, so as to ensure a reliable reception of the MBMS data. The FACH transmission power levels presented in Table 1 correspond to the case of a 64 Kbps MBMS service, where no Space Time Transmit Diversity (STTD) is assumed. In addition, Transmission Time Interval (TTI) is set to 80 ms and Block Error Rate (BLER) target is 1% [12].

Table 1. FACH Tx power levels

Cell coverage (%)	Required Tx power (W)
10	1.4
20	1.6
30	1.8
40	2.0
50	2.5
60	3.0
70	3.6
80	4.8
90	6.4
100	12.0

3.2.4 Calculation of the Cost over the Uu Interface

In this section we will present the procedure for calculating the D_{DCH}, D_{FACH} and $D_{HS\text{-}DSCH}$ costs. The mechanism for this procedure, the block diagram of which is illustrated in Fig. 3, runs at the RNC. According to Fig. 3, the procedure can be divided into three operation phases. These are: the parameter retrieval phase, the cost calculation phase and the event scheduling phase.

The parameter retrieval phase is responsible for retrieving the parameters of the existing MBMS users (through uplink channels) in each cell. These parameters are the distance of each UE from the Node B and the E_b/N_0 (or SINR for the HS-DSCH case) requirement per UE. In order to retrieve this information, the RNC broadcasts a message to the UEs belonging to a specific MBMS group and each user of the group responds to this message by indicating its location and its experienced signal quality. The MBMS bit rate service is assumed to be already known (in the BM-SC).

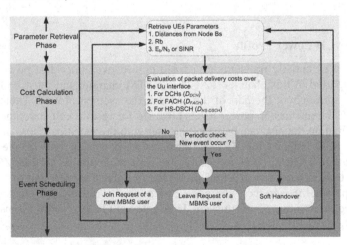

Fig. 3. Calculation of packet delivery cost over the Uu interface

The cost calculation phase substantially processes the data received from the parameter retrieval phase. During this phase, the required cost to be allocated for each cell is computed. The computation is based on the assumption that the transmission of the multicast data over the UTRAN interfaces can be performed with:

- Multiple DCHs (DCHs case).
- FACH with such power to serve the worst path loss user (FACH Dynamic case).
- HS-DSCH (HS-DSCH case).

In other words, the telecommunication cost is computed, assuming that all UEs in a cell could be served with the above three possible ways. For the DCHs case, the computation takes into account the parameters defined in the parameter retrieval phase and calculates the required cost (D_{DCH}) as in equation (4). For the FACH Dynamic case, the cost (D_{FACH}) is computed depending on the user with the worst path loss and according to Table 1, as described in section 3.2.3. Finally, for the HS-DSCH case, the cost ($D_{HS\text{-}DSCH}$) is computed as in equation (3).

The algorithm enters the event scheduling phase, only if one of the following three different events occurs during a MBMS session: a join request from a new MBMS user, a leave request from an existing MBMS user or a handover. The algorithm handles these three events with the absolutely same way, since the parameters of all the users are updated in regular time intervals.

The above description refers to a dynamic model, in the sense that the UEs are assumed to be moving throughout the topology. The parameter retrieval phase is triggered at regular time intervals so as to take into account the users' mobility and the three events of the event scheduling phase. Therefore, the D_{DCH}, D_{FACH} and $D_{HS\text{-}DSCH}$ costs must be computed periodically at a predetermined frequency rate. This periodic computation inserts a further complexity for RNC, as this information is carried in uplink channels. Moreover, a certain bandwidth fraction must be allocated for the transmission of this information in the uplink channel, thus resulting to a capacity reduction.

4   Performance Evaluation

This section presents analytical simulation results for the performance evaluation of our approach. The main assumptions that were used in our simulations are presented in Table 2 and refer to a macro cell environment [5], [13]. In addition, no STTD is assumed, while BLER target is set to 1%.

Our goal is to demonstrate and highlight the advantages of our approach through a mathematical analysis, which however totally simulates the macro cell environment. To this direction, we examine certain scenarios indicative of the way that our mechanism works and how the appropriate channels are assigned.

One point that needs attention is that the total cost computed from equation (1) is a positive number, which however does not have units. According to equation

364 Wireless and Mobile Networking

(1), each channel is associated with a cost and by comparing the corresponding costs, the mechanism assigns the most appropriate transport channel.

Table 2. Simulation assumptions

Parameter	Value
Cellular layout	18 hexagonal grid cells
Sectorization	3 sectors/cell
Site-to-site distance	1 Km
Maximum BS Tx power	20 W (43 dBm)
Other BS Tx power	5 W (37 dBm)
CPICH power	2 W
Common channel power	1 W (30 dBm)
Propagation model	Okumura Hata
Multipath channel	Vehicular A (3km/h)
Orthogonality factor	0.5
E_b/N_0 target	5 dB

4.1 *Scenario 1: Balancing between Power Optimization and Iub Efficiency*

This section describes the role of weights c_i and c_w in equation (1). These weights define which UTRAN interface (Iub or Uu) plays a more significant role in the calculation of the C_{UTRAN}. In general, high values for weight c_i indicate that the transport channel selection is determined based mainly on the cost over Iub interface.

Fig. 4 presents how the total cost for the transmission of a 64 Kbps MBMS service is changing as the c_w increases from 0 to 100%. In the particular scenario, a group of 6 users located at a fixed distance from Node B (35% cell coverage) receive the MBMS service. The small number of users and the relatively small area that needs to be covered regularly would have favored the use of multiple DCHs. However, as it appears from Fig. 4 for small weights of wireless channel, DCH has the highest cost. This occurs because even if the use of multiple DCHs has lower power requirements than FACH or HS-DSCH for the specific user distribution, the small value of c_w (high value of c_i) makes the cost for packet replication over Iub the dominant term in equation (1). As the weight increases (transmission power plays a more important role), the cost for DCH remains lower than the cost of FACH and HS-DSCH. In the following scenarios, the value of c_w is set to 0.9. This high value of c_w is selected to reflect the fact that power is a limited resource and in parallel, to meet the 3GPP requirements for reducing power requirements during MBMS transmissions.

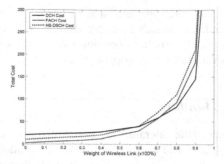

Fig. 4. Costs vs. Weight of wireless link

4.2 *Scenario 2: Join and Leave Requests*

The second scenario examines how the join and leave requests by MBMS users are handled by the mechanism. According to this scenario, the UEs appear in random initial positions and then move randomly throughout the cell, while the number of serving users varies during the simulation. More specifically, the number of users that receive a 64 Kbps MBMS service initially increases, reaching 35 UEs at simulation time 175 sec. For the following 80 seconds, the number of users remains constant. From simulation time 255 sec the number of users is decreasing and finally, at the end of the simulation only 6 UEs receive the 64 Kbps MBMS service (Fig. 5).

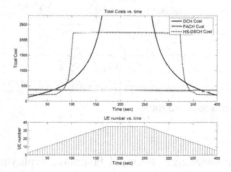

Fig. 5. Costs vs. Time for successive join and leave requests

The algorithm presented in the previous sections that runs at the RNC will force the Node B to select, at each instant, the channel with the lowest telecommunication cost over the UTRAN interfaces. Thus, in the beginning of the simulation when the number of UEs is small, the most efficient channel is the DCH. The increase in the number of UEs causes a switch from DCHs to HS-DSCH at simulation time 30 sec (when the UE population is 7). An additional increase in the number of UEs results to a switch from HS-DSCH to a single

FACH (at simulation time 80 sec when the UE population is 17), with transmission power high enough to cover the UE with the worst path loss. A further increase in the UE number does not involve any change. The decrease in the number of UEs causes the exact opposite results.

4.3 *Scenario 3: Handover*

This scenario presents the operation of the mechanism during handover. Each Node B in the topology has to serve a number of randomly moving UEs with initial positions as in Fig. 6. However, Node B1 initially serves eight UEs, four of which will follow a predefined route so that handover will take place. More specifically, as shown in Fig. 6, UE1 and UE2 will move towards Node B2, while UE3 and UE4 towards Node B3.

Fig. 7 depicts the telecommunication cost over the UTRAN interfaces for the Node Bs under study when DCH, FACH and HS-DSCH are used. The three Node Bs under study, in other words, the three Node Bs that participate in the process of handover are: Node B1, Node B2 and Node B3. The algorithm running at the RNC will command each Node B to select, at each instant, the transport channel that inserts the lowest telecommunication cost.

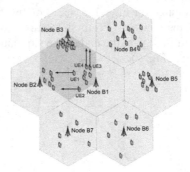

Fig. 6. UEs' initial locations and routes

The small UE population in Node B1 favors the deployment of DCHs. Totally, 4 UEs leave its area and this is obvious by the four abrupt decrements in DCHs cost (Fig. 7a). The FACH and HS-DSCH costs remain high, until the 4 UEs leave the cell (simulation time 255 sec), when an abrupt decrement in their costs is observed. This happens because after the UEs leave the cell, the FACH and HS-DSCH will only have to serve UEs close to Node B1 (Fig. 6). Nevertheless, even if the 4 UEs leave the cell, multiple DCHs should be deployed as the cost in this case remains lower (Fig. 7a).

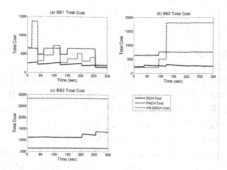

Fig. 7. Costs vs. Time during handover

On the other hand, a decrement in Node B1's costs is followed by a simultaneous increment in another Node B's costs. For example, at simulation time 122 sec, UE2 leaves the coverage area of Node B1 and enters the coverage area of Node B2 (Fig. 6). The DCH and HS-DSCH costs in Fig. 7b increase because in both cases, Node B2 will have to employ one more PTP connection for the new user.

It is worth mentioning, that during the simulations the appropriate channel was selected independently of the UE number and location. The corresponding costs over the UTRAN interfaces were compared and the channel with the lowest cost was selected. This fact makes our approach more powerful and more resistant in changes.

5 Conclusions and Future Work

In this paper, we presented an overview of the MBMS multicast mode and motivated by the fact that the Iub capacity is limited, we introduced a power/cost based scheme for the efficient radio bearer selection that: firstly, minimizes the delivery cost of the multicast data over the UTRAN interfaces and secondly, reduces the power requirements during MBMS transmissions. Our approach considers all the basic functionalities of the two 3GPP approaches (TS 25.346 [2] and TR 25.922 [3]) and incorporates several enhancements. Contrary to TS 25.346, our approach considers users' mobility and utilizes a dynamic scheme for switching between channels. Contrary to TR 25.922, both PTP channels (HS-DSCH and DCH) are supported. Finally, contrary to TS 25.346 and TR 25.922, our approach supports FACH dynamic power allocation in order to reduce power consumption during PTM transmissions.

The step that follows this work is to expand our approach in order to provide an efficient session assignment scheme when multiple MBMS sessions run simultaneously in the network. At a second level we plan to study the complexity that the mechanism inserts in RNCs due to its dynamic and periodic nature.

References

1. Alexiou, A., Bouras, C., Rekkas, E.: A Power Control Scheme for Efficient Radio Bearer Selection in MBMS. The 8th IEEE 21st International Symposium on World of Wireless, Mobile and Multimedia Networks (WoWMoM) (2007)
2. 3GPP, TS 25.346 V8.1.0. Introduction of the Multimedia Broadcast Multicast Service (MBMS) in the Radio Access Network (RAN); Stage 2, (Release 8)
3. 3GPP, TR 25.922 V7.1.0. Technical Specification Group Radio Access Network; Radio resource management strategies (Release 7)
4. Alexiou, A., Bouras, C., Kokkinos, V., Rekkas, E.: Efficient Assignment of Multiple MBMS Sessions in B3G Networks. 2008 IEEE 68th Vehicular Technology Conference (VTC2008 Fall) (to appear)
5. Holma, H., Toskala, A.: WCDMA for UMTS: HSPA Evolution and LTE. 4th edition, John Wiley & Sons (2007)
6. 3GPP, TS 22.146 V8.3.0. Technical Specification Group Services and System Aspects; Multimedia Broadcast/Multicast Service; Stage 1 (Release 8)
7. Holma, H., Toskala, A.: HSDPA/HSUPA for UMTS: High Speed Radio Access for Mobile Communications. John Wiley & Sons (2006)
8. Alexiou, A., Antonellis, D., Bouras, C., Papazois, A.: An Efficient Multicast Packet Delivery Scheme for UMTS. The 9th ACM/IEEE International Symposium on Modeling, Analysis and Simulation of Wireless and Mobile Systems (MSWiM 2006) pp. 147-150
9. Ho, J., Akyildiz, I.: Local anchor scheme for reducing signaling costs in personal communications networks. IEEE/ACM Transactions on Networking, Vol. 4, No. 5 (1996) pp. 709–725
10. Alexiou, A., Bouras, C.: Multicast in UMTS: Evaluation and Recommendations. Wireless Communications and Mobile Computing Journal. Wiley InterScience (2006) (in press)
11. Perez-Romero, J., Sallent, O., Agusti, R., Diaz-Guerra, M.: Radio Resource Management Strategies in UMTS. John Wiley & Sons (2005)
12. 3GPP, TS 25.803 V6.0.0. S-CCPCH performance for MBMS (Release 6)
13. 3GPP, TR 101.102 V3.2.0. Universal Mobile Telecommunications System (UMTS); Selection procedures for the choice of radio transmission technologies of the UMTS (UMTS 30.03 version 3.2.0)

Downlink Macrodiversity in Cellular Network – A Fluid Analysis

Jean-Marc Kelif[1] and Eitan Altman[2]

[1] France Telecom Research and Development Issy Moulineaux, France
[2] INRIA Sophia Antipolis, France

jeanmarc.kelif@orange-ftgroup.com, eitan.altman@sophia.inria.fr

Abstract This paper proposes an analytical study of the downlink macrodiversity. Considering two macrodiversity links, we first show that the downlink macrodiversity induces a specific load in the cell. We establish an explicit expression of this one, and show that macrodiversity increases the total cell's load. The network's fluid analysis we propose enables to calculate the load of a cell and to quantify the impact of macrodiversity. We show that macrodiversity decreases the capacity of a cell. We generalize the analysis, considering a macrodiversity with a great number of base stations of the network.

1 Introduction

The studies related to macrodiversity were mainly done for the uplink [7] [8]. Hanly [7] described macrodiversity as a scheme in which the cellular structure of a wireless communication network is removed and user is jointly decoded by all receivers in the network. Hiltunen and de Bernardi [4] developed a downlink analysis of the macrodiversity to estimate a CDMA network's capacity. Their analysis considers the macrodiversity use to maintain the SIR target of mobiles in soft/softer handover with two base stations. It is well known that downlink macrodiversity induces an extra load that can be considered as the "price" for obtaining the macrodiversity gain. In this paper we demonstrate why there is an extra load. We give its analytical expression and quantify with a high accuracy the impact of macrodiversity. Afterward, we propose a model which allows calculating analytically that extra load. This model considers the network as a continuum of base stations and *allows calculating the influence of any mobile* in a cell, *whatever its position*. For clarity of presentation, this paper is focused on CDMA networks. However, the analysis we develop can be used for other technologies such as OFDMA (see remark at the end of the section 2.1).

The paper is organized as follows. In Section 2 we introduce the interference factor f_i^{DL} which characterizes the "weight" of the network, on a given cell. We

Please use the following format when citing this chapter:

Kelif, J.-M. and Altman, E., 2008, in IFIP International Federation for Information Processing, Volume 284; *Wireless and Mobile Networking*; Zoubir Mammeri; (Boston: Springer), pp. 369–382.

show that mobiles in macrodiversity induce a positive specific load L_{MD}. In Section 3, we express the cell's load, using a fluid model of the network [9][11]. This approach considers the network as a *continuum*. It can be applied to any frequency reuse 1 networks, such as OFDMA or CDMA ones. In Section 4, we establish the macrodiversity decreases a cell's capacity. In Section 5, we generalize the macrodiversity analysis to a whole network, and show it always induces a decrease of the capacity. In Section 6 we conclude.

2   Cellular network Analysis

2.1   *Network analysis*

We use the model similar to [4]. Let us consider a mobile connected to the base station b of a network of N_{BS} base stations, each BS_j defining a cell j. We express that the *Signal to Interference Ratio (SIR)* received by a mobile has to be at least equal to a minimum threshold target value γ_i [4] [5]. Each mobile uses only one service. Using the equation of the transmitting traffic channel power [4] for the downlink, the following condition has to be satisfied:

$$\frac{P_{ib}\, g_{ib}}{\alpha I_{\text{int}} + I_{ext} + Noise} \geq \gamma_i \tag{2.1}$$

where P_{ib} is the useful transmitting power coming from the base station b towards the mobile i belonging to the base station b, and g_{ib} is the pathloss between the base station b and the mobile i, I_{int} is the interferences due to the common channels and the traffic channels of the other mobiles located in the cell b, and I_{ext} is the interferences due to the other base stations of the network, γ_i represents the level of the signal to interference ratio target for the service used by the mobile i for the downlink, *Noise* stands for the level of noise floor at the mobile receiver, and α the orthogonality factor, and $g_{j,i}$ the pathloss between the mobile i and the base station j. Introducing P_b the total transmitting power of the base station b, including the common channels assumed as orthogonal, and $\beta_i = \frac{\gamma_i}{1+\alpha\gamma_i}$. For each mobile i belonging to the cell b, we define the parameter f_i^{DL}, as the ratio between the total power P_{ext} received by the mobile i coming from the other base stations of the network to the total power P_{int} received by its serving base station b:

$$f_i^{DL} = \frac{P_{est}}{P_{\text{int}}} = \frac{1}{P_b g_{ib}} \sum_{j=1,j\neq b}^{N_{BS}} P_j g_{ij} \tag{2.2}$$

We express from (2.1) the minimum needed traffic channel transmitting power as:

$$P_{ib}g_{ib} = \beta_i(\alpha P_b g_{ib} + f_i^{DL} P_b g_{ib} + Noise) \tag{2.3}$$

Remark
Though our analysis is focused on CDMA networks, the model we develop is still valid for cellular technologies without internal interference, providing that $I_{int} = 0$. It can be applied, in particular, to frequency reuse 1 networks based on other technologies, such as OFDMA.

2.2 Downlink macrodiversity analysis

Base station transmitting power
Our approach is inspired by [4]. The downlink *macrodiversity* allows a mobile to use the signals received from more than one base station to reach the requested SIR target. We establish the analytical expression of the cell's load, taking into account the macrodiversity with two base stations, and show that the macrodiversity *always increases* the load. A mobile i in macrodiversity is connected to two base stations b and l. b is defined to be the base station with larger SIR. We express that the power control tries to maintain the SIR target γ_i.

We denote $\gamma_{i,l}$ and $\gamma_{i,b}$ the SIR received by mobile i coming from base stations l and b, and we assume that:

$$\Omega_i = \frac{\gamma_{i,l}}{\gamma_{i,b}} \le 1 \tag{2.4a}$$

is a constant. The SIR target is:

$$\gamma_i = \gamma_{i,b} + \gamma_{i,l} \tag{2.4b}$$

Considering a mobile belonging to the BS b and in macrodiversity with the BS l, and introducing $\kappa_i = \dfrac{\gamma_i}{1+\Omega_i(1+\gamma_i)+\alpha\gamma_i}$ (2.4c), the expression (2.3) becomes, for a mobile i in macrodiversity:

$$P_{ib} = \kappa_i(\alpha P_b + f_i^{DL} P_b + Noise/g_{ib}) \tag{2.4}$$

Let there be N mobiles in a cell b, M among them are in macrodiversity with the BS l. As a consequence, in the macrodiversity zone we can consider M mobiles belonging to the BS b and P mobiles belonging to the BS l in macrodiversity with b. These last ones also receive a signal from the BS b. Denoting P_{CCH} the power dedicated to the common channels, the total transmitting power of the base station b can be expressed as the sum of all the transmitting powers channels:

$$P_b = \sum_{i=1}^{N-M} P_{ib} + \sum_{j=1}^{M} P_{jb} + \sum_{k=1}^{P} P_{kb} + P_{CCH} \qquad (2.5)$$

Hypothesis

For a homogeneous repartition of mobiles in the macrodiversity zone, we can assume that $M=P$. And statistically, due to the homogeneity of the mobiles repartition, the total power dedicated to the mobiles M should be the same as the total power dedicated to the mobiles P. So we can write:

$$\sum_{j=1}^{M} P_{jb} = \sum_{k=1}^{P} P_{kb} \qquad (2.6)$$

The expression (2.5) can be rewritten:

$$P_b = \sum_{i=1}^{N-M} P_{ib} + 2\sum_{j=1}^{M} P_{jb} + P_{CCH} \qquad (2.7)$$

The power P_{CCH} dedicated to common channels is assumed as proportional to the power of the base station so we have $P_{CCH} = \varphi P_b$. Denoting:

$$A = \sum_{i}^{N-M} \beta_i \, Noise/g_{ib} + 2\sum_{j}^{M} \kappa_j \, Noise/g_{jb} \qquad (2.8a)$$

and

$$L = \sum_{i=1}^{N-M} \beta_i (\alpha + f_i^{DL}) + 2\sum_{j=1}^{M} \kappa_j (\alpha + f_j^{DL}) \qquad (2.8b)$$

the total transmitting power of BS b can be deduced from (2.4) and (2.7) and written as:

$$P_b = \frac{A}{1 - \varphi - L} \qquad (2.8)$$

When the number of mobiles in a cell increases, the parameter L increases too. Consequently the transmitting power of BS b increases. L represents the total load of the cell.

Remarks:

The authors of [4] assumed all links within the active set have the same transmit power. This condition is stronger than our statistical hypothesis $(M=P)$. Furthermore, in [4] the authors consider another strong assumption: all the interference factors have the same value. We *consider the exact values* of this parameter: this one varies with the position of the mobile in the cell.

2.3 Macrodiversity load

Each mobile in the cell induces a specific load. To analyze the macrodiversity effect, we need to express that one considering mobiles either in macrodiversity or not. The cell's load L (2.8a) can be expressed as:

$$L = L_{DL} + L_{MD} \tag{2.9}$$

The first term:

$$L_{DL} = \sum_{i=1}^{N} \beta_i (\alpha + f_i^{DL}) \tag{2.10}$$

takes into account *all the mobiles* of the cell. It represents the cell's load, for the downlink, *in a case where there is no macrodiversity.* When a mobile is *not in macrodiversity,* we notice, from (2.4a), that $\Omega_i = 0$ and $\kappa_i = \beta_i$. Introducing:

$$\sigma_i = \frac{\Omega_i}{1 + \alpha \gamma_i} \tag{2.10a}$$

we can write:

$$\kappa_i = \beta_i \left(1 - \frac{\sigma_i}{1 + \sigma_i}\right) \tag{2.10b}$$

We can express:

$$L_{MD} = \sum_{j=1}^{M} \beta_j \left(\frac{1 - \sigma_j}{1 + \sigma_j}\right)(\alpha + f_j^{DL}) \tag{2.11}$$

This term represents an *extra load* due to the fact that M mobiles among N *are in macrodiversity.* Since $0 \leq \sigma_j = \dfrac{\Omega_j}{1 + \alpha \gamma_j} \leq 1$ (2.12), the load L_{MD} is positive.

Expressing the total transmitting power of a BS, our analysis explicitly shows the macrodiversity induces a specific positive load L_{MD} in the cell, increasing its total load. The consequence of this increase is to *decrease* the capacity (number of mobiles, throughput) of the cell. Considering the analytical expression of L_{MD}, our analysis moreover allows to *identify* the parameters which have an explicit influence on that macrodiversity *extra load*: The QoS characterized by β_i, the base stations transmitting powers (interference factor f_i^{DL}) and the term $\dfrac{1 - \sigma_j}{1 + \sigma_j}$ characterizes the powers received from the base stations with which a mobile is in macrodiversity. It appears interesting to calculate analytically this extra load. In this aim, we need to express analytically the parameters contributing to L_{MD}, and particularly the downlink interference factor f_i^{DL}. Hereafter we propose an analytical approach which allows to calculate L_{MD}.

3   Analytical fluid model

The key modelling step of the model we propose consists in replacing a given fixed finite number of transmitters (base stations or mobiles) by an equivalent continuum of transmitters which are distributed according to some distribution function. We denote it a fluid model [9] [11]. We consider a traffic characterised by a mobile density ρ_{MS} and a network by a base station density ρ_{BS}. For a homogeneous network, the downlink interference factor only depends on the distance r between the BS and the mobile. We denote it f_r. From [9] [11], we have:

$$f_r = \frac{\rho_{BS} \cdot 2\pi}{(\eta + 2)r^{\eta}} \cdot \left[(R - r)^{\eta+2} - (2R_c - r)^{\eta+2} \right] \tag{3.1}$$

3.1 Load model with macrodiversity

Using the analytical expression of the interference factor (3.1), and the expressions (2.9) (2.10) and (2.11), we aim to express hereafter the load L of the cell. The parameters γ_i β_i and κ_i , which characterize the QoS of the mobiles, depend on the service used by the mobile i. We assume that these parameters may also depend on the distance r of the mobile from its serving BS b and write them γ_r β_r κ_r. The parameters Ω_i and σ_i can be written Ω_r and σ_r. Considering that mobiles use one service we can drop the index i. In fact, the providers have the choice to modify the mobiles' QoS for them to be admitted in the cell. And this modification may depend on the position of the mobile. The expression of the total transmitting power of BS b, considering the mobiles located at distances r from the base station b is given by (2.8) .From (2.8a) and (2.8b), we have :

$$A = \sum_{r < R_{th}} N_r \beta_r \frac{Noise}{g_{b,r}} + 2 \sum_{r \geq R_{th}} N_r \kappa_r \frac{Noise}{g_{b,r}} \tag{3.2}$$

and

$$L = \sum_{r < R_{th}} N_r \beta_r (\alpha + f_r^{DL}) + 2 \sum_{r \geq R_{th}} N_r \kappa_r (\alpha + f_r^{DL}) \tag{3.3}$$

where N_r represents the number of mobiles located at a distance r from the BS b, R_{th} is a threshold distance defining the macrodiversity zone: If $r < R_{th}$ a mobile is not in macrodiversity, and he is in macrodiversity otherwise. We notice moreover that mobiles at a given distance r have the *same values* of interference factor f_r in our analytical model. Considering the network (base stations and mobiles) as a continuum of transmitters characterized by a base station density ρ_{BS} and a mobile density ρ_{MS}, we can replace the discrete summations (3.2) and (3.3) by continuous ones and express the load L with integrals. Considering a macrodiversity zone with *one* neighbor (figure 1, base stations b and l), the expression of the cell's load (3.3) can be rewritten as:

$$L = \int_{-\frac{\pi}{6}}^{+\frac{\pi}{6}} \int_{0}^{R_{th}} \rho\beta_r(\alpha+f_r)r.drd\theta + 2\int_{-\frac{\pi}{6}}^{+\frac{\pi}{6}} \int_{R_{th}}^{R_c} \rho\kappa_r(\alpha+f_r)r.drd\theta \tag{3.4}$$

In a network, it is currently assumed that a cell b is surrounded by 6 cells (figure 1). Considering there is a macrodiversity zone with each one (figure 1) and assuming all the macrodiversity zones are identical (figure 1) (homogeneous network), we can write the loads expressions (2.10) and (2.11) as:

$$L_{DL} = 2\pi \int_{0}^{R_c} \rho\beta_r(\alpha+f_r)r.dr \tag{3.5}$$

and

$$L_{MD} = 2\pi \int_{R_{th}}^{R_c} \left(\frac{1-\sigma_r}{1+\sigma_r}\right)\rho\beta_r(\alpha+f_r)rdr \tag{3.6}$$

We showed (Section 2) that the analytical expression of L_{MD} enables to determine the parameters which have an influence on the extra load due to the macrodiversity: the QoS, the BS transmitting powers and the term $\left(\frac{1-\sigma_r}{1+\sigma_r}\right)$.

Another parameter explicitly appears, highlighted by the fluid model: the macrodiversity size' zone characterized by R_{th}.

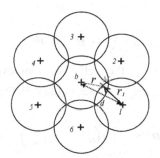

Fig. 1. Cell b sharing macrodiversity zones with its 6 neighbours

4   Admission control analysis

4.1   General Analysis

For the downlink, we express that the power of the base station P_b is limited to a maximum value P_{max}: the call admission control is based on the probability P^{DL} to satisfy the following relation: $P^{DL} = \Pr[P_b > P_{max}]$ which can be expressed, using (2.8):

$$P^{DL} = \Pr\left(L > 1 - \varphi - \frac{A}{P_{max}}\right) \tag{4.1}$$

The cell load L is expressed by (2.9) (3.5) and (3.6). To analyze the admission control, we first need to calculate analytically the expressions (3.5) and (3.6) of L_{DL} and L_{MD}. In a general case, the QoS dependency with the position of the mobile (β_r) in the cell depends on the strategies of the provider: different strategies can be adopted, and for each one that dependency may be different. We will adopt a strategy where the QoS offered to the mobiles do not vary with the position of the mobiles ($\beta_r = \beta$, and $\sigma_r = \sigma$) and write from (3.5) and (3.6):

$$L_{DL} = 2\pi\rho\beta\int_0^{R_c}(\alpha + f_r)rdr \tag{4.2}$$

and

$$L_{MD} = 2\pi\rho\beta\int_{R_{th}}^{R_c}\left(\frac{1-\sigma}{1+\sigma}\right)(\alpha + f_r)rdr \tag{4.3}$$

We introduce the downlink average interference factor F_{DL} for the whole cell as:

$$F_{DL} = \frac{1}{S}\int_0^{R_c}\int_0^{2\pi} f_r\, rdrd\theta \tag{4.4a}$$

and

$$A_{DL} = \frac{1}{S}\int_0^{R_c}\int_0^{2\pi} r^{1-\eta}\, drd\theta \tag{4.4b}$$

where S is the surface of the cell. We moreover introduce the parameter Considering $n^{MS} = \rho_{MS}\pi R_c^2$ mobiles in the cell, the expression (4.1) can thus be written:

$$P^{DL} = \Pr\left(n^{MS} > n_{DL}^{th}\right) \tag{4.5}$$

where:

$$n_{DL}^{th} = \frac{1-\varphi}{\beta(\alpha + F_{DL})} \tag{4.6}$$

and as long as long as the *Noise* is very low, i. e.:

$$\frac{A_{DL}\,Noise}{P_{max}(\alpha + F_{DL})} \ll n_{DL}^{th} \tag{4.7}$$

The downlink interference factor analytical expression (3.1) takes into account the network's size. We denote $c_1 = \dfrac{2R_c}{R} = \dfrac{2R_c}{(2N_R + 1)R_c} = \dfrac{2}{2N_R + 1}$. This parameter represents the relative dimensions of the network compared to the distance between two localisations of BS. N_R represents the number of rings of cells around the studied one. Considering $\rho_{BS} = \dfrac{1}{\pi R_c^2}$, we obtain, from (4.4a) and (3.1):

$$F_{DL} = \frac{-2^{\eta+4}}{(2+\eta)} \int_0^1 x^{1-\eta} \left[\left(1 - \frac{x}{2}\right)^{\eta+2} - c_1^{-2-\eta}(1 - c_1 \frac{x}{2})^{\eta+2} \right] dx \qquad (4.8)$$

and we notice that F_{DL} is positive due to $\eta < -2$. The expression of F_{DL} does not explicitly depend on the size of a cell, but only on its relative dimension to the network's one characterized by the parameter c_1. As we can observe (Table 1) the average interference factors are limited; they tend to an asymptotic value, when the network's dimension increases. For high size networks, *i.e.* $N_R \to \infty$, F_{DL} does no more depend on the network's size: $F_{DL} = \dfrac{-4}{(2+\eta)} \int_0^1 x^{1-\eta} (2-x)^{\eta+2} \, dx$. As a consequence, for a homogeneous network the number of mobiles per cell *does not depend* on the size of the cell. It partially depends on the environment characterized by the pathloss factor η, the SIR target, the orthogonal factor α and the power ratio dedicated to the common channels φ.

4.2 Macro diversity impact

We introduce the downlink average interference factor for the macrodiversity zone:

$$F_{MD} = \frac{1}{S} \int_{R_{th}}^{R_c} \int_0^{2\pi} \left(\frac{1-\sigma}{1+\sigma} \right) f_r \, rdr.d\theta \qquad (4.9a)$$

We moreover introduce the parameters:

$$\Gamma_{MD} = \frac{1}{S} \int_{R_{th}}^{R_c} \int_0^{2\pi} \left(\frac{1-\sigma}{1+\sigma} \right) \alpha rdr.d\theta \qquad (4.9b)$$

and

$$A_{MD} = \frac{1}{S} \int_{R_{th}}^{R_c} \int_0^{2\pi} r^{1-\eta} \, drd\theta \qquad (4.9c)$$

We can write (4.1) as:

$$P^{DL} = \Pr\left(n^{MS} > n^{th}\right) \qquad (4.10)$$

where:

$$n^{th} = \frac{1-\varphi}{\beta(\alpha + F_{DL} + F_{MD} + \Gamma_{MD})} \qquad (4.11)$$

and as long as long as the *Noise* is very low, i.e.:

$$\frac{(A_{DL} + A_{MD})Noise}{P_{max}(\alpha + F_{DL} + F_{MD} + \Gamma_{MD})} \ll n^{th} \tag{4.12}$$

The macrodiversity consequence is to decrease the term n^{th} which represents the limit capacity of the cell.

5   Macrodiversity generalization

For the downlink, we express that the useful power received by a mobile belonging to the base station b comes from N_{MD} base stations of the network. Considering that any mobile is in macrodiversity with *all the base stations* of the network, $N_{MD} = N_{BS}$, the expression (2.1) is thus rewritten as:

$$\frac{P_{ib}g_{ib} + \sum_{l \neq b}^{N_{BS}} P_{il}g_{il}}{\alpha(P_b - P_{ib})g_{ib} + \sum_{l \neq b}^{N_{BS}} (P_l - P_{il})g_{il} + N_{th}} \geq \gamma \tag{5.1}$$

Where P_{il} is the useful transmitting power coming from the base station l towards the mobile i belonging to the base station b, and g_{il} is the path loss between the base station l and the mobile i, P_l is the total transmitting power of the base station l

$$P_{ib}g_{ib} + \sum_{l \neq b}^{N_{BS}} P_{il}g_{il} = \gamma \left(\alpha(P_b - P_{ib})g_{ib} + \sum_{l \neq b}^{N_{BS}} (P_l - P_{il})g_{il} + N_{th} \right) \tag{5.2}$$

Denoting:

$$\mu = \frac{1+\gamma}{1+\alpha\gamma} \tag{5.2b}$$

(we drop the indexes i and *DL*), we can write:

$$P_{ib} = \beta(\alpha P_b + f_i P_b + N_{th}/g_{ib}) - \mu \frac{1}{g_{ib}} \sum_{l \neq b}^{N_{BS}} P_{il}g_{il} \tag{5.3}$$

In our analysis, each base station of the network contributes to the useful power received by any mobile belonging to any base station. Due to the fact that the base stations transmitting powers are limited, and that the mobiles number in the network is great, it is reasonable to consider a limitation of the available transmitting powers P_{il} dedicated to the macrodiversity. Moreover, considering the great distances between the other base stations of the network and the mobile i belonging to the base station b, we can assume that the base stations use the maximum power (denoted P) available for the transmitting power P_{il} We notice an analogy with the expression (2.2): we can write, when all the base stations transmitting powers are identical: $P_l=P_b$ for $l = 1...N_{BS}$, and when all the transmitting powers P_{il} equal P:

$$\frac{1}{g_{ib}}\sum_{l\neq b}^{N_{BS}} P_{il}g_{il} = P\frac{1}{g_{ib}}\sum_{l\neq b}^{N_{BS}} g_{il} = Pf_i \qquad (5.4)$$

These last assumptions can be verified if the network is homogeneous, or when base stations manage a maximum number of mobiles. The total transmitting power of BS b can thus be written as:

$$P_b = \sum_{i=1}^{N} P_{ib} + \sum_{j\neq b}^{N_{BS}}\sum_{i=1}^{N} P + P_{CCH} \qquad (5.5a)$$

or

$$P_b = \sum_{i=1}^{N} P_{ib} + N(N_{BS}-1)P + P_{CCH} \qquad (5.5b)$$

and finally:

$$\sum_{i=1}^{N} P_{ib} = \sum_{i=1}^{N} \beta(\alpha P_b + f_i P_b + N_{th}/g_{ib}) - \mu\sum_{i=1}^{N} Pf_i \qquad (5.6a)$$

Considering that the power P is a fraction of the total power P_b, we can write, $P=\varepsilon P_b$, and when:

$$P_{cch}=\varphi P_b \quad \sum_{i=1}^{N} P_{ib} = N\beta\alpha P_b + (\beta - \mu\varepsilon)P_b\sum_{i=1}^{N} f_i + \sum_{i=1}^{N} \beta N_{th}/g_{ib} \qquad (5.6b)$$

and $P_b = N\beta\alpha P_b + (\beta - \mu\varepsilon)P_b\sum_{i=1}^{N} f_i + \sum_{i=1}^{N} \beta N_{th}/g_{ib} + N(N_{BS}-1)\varepsilon P_b + \varphi P_b$

So we have:

$$P_b\left(1-\varphi- N\beta\alpha - (\beta - \mu\varepsilon)\sum_{i=1}^{N} f_i - N(N_{BS}-1)\varepsilon\right) = \sum_{i=1}^{N} \beta N_{th}/g_{ib} \qquad (5.6c)$$

Using our analytical model we can write: $\sum_{i=1}^{N} f_i$ as $\int_{0}^{R_c}\int_{0}^{2\pi} \rho_{MS} f_r \, rdrd\theta$

Denoting:

$$F = \frac{1}{S_{cell} S_{Network}} \int_0^{R_c} \int_0^{2\pi} \frac{2\pi}{(\eta+2)r^{\eta}} \cdot \left[(R-r)^{\eta+2} - (2R_c - r)^{\eta+2} \right] r dr d\theta \qquad (5.7)$$

we can write $P_b \left(1 - \varphi - N_{MS}\beta\alpha - (\beta - \mu\varepsilon)N_{MS}N_{BS}F - N_{MS}(N_{BS}-1)\varepsilon\right) = \sum_{i=1}^{N} \beta N_{th}/g_{ib}$ and

express P_b as:

$$P_b = \frac{\sum_{i=1}^{N} \beta N_{th}/g_{ib}}{1 - \varphi - N_{MS}\left(\beta\alpha - (\beta - \mu\varepsilon)N_{BS}F - (N_{BS}-1)\varepsilon\right)} \qquad (5.8)$$

The denominator has to be positive:
$$1 - \varphi - N_{MS}\left(\beta\alpha - (\beta - \mu\varepsilon)N_{BS}F - (N_{BS}-1)\varepsilon\right) > 0$$

So the cell capacity is given by:

$$N_{MS} = \frac{1 - \varphi}{\beta\alpha + (\beta - \mu\varepsilon)N_{BS}F + (N_{BS}-1)\varepsilon} \qquad (5.9)$$

We denote $N_{1,MS}$ the cell capacity without macrodiversity, *i.e.* $\varepsilon=0$:

$$N_{1,MS} = \frac{1 - \varphi}{\beta\alpha + \beta N_{BS}F} \qquad (5.10)$$

Does the macrodiversity increase the capacity of a cell? To answer that question we compare (4.9) and (4.10):

$$\frac{1-\varphi}{\beta\alpha + (\beta - \mu\varepsilon)N_{BS}F + (N_{BS}-1)\varepsilon} > \frac{1-\varphi}{\beta\alpha + \beta N_{BS}F} \quad \text{which can be written as}$$

$\beta\alpha + (\beta - \mu\varepsilon)N_{BS}F + (N_{BS}-1)\varepsilon < \beta\alpha + \beta N_{BS}F$ and finally, denoting

$$N_{BS,th} = \frac{1}{1 - \mu F} \qquad (5.11)$$

we conclude that macrodiversity increases the capacity only if we have:

$$N_{BS} < N_{BS,th} \qquad (5.12)$$

For $\eta=-3$, $R_c = 1$, $R = 10$, we obtain F= 0.72% .

For $\alpha=0.7$ and $\gamma=-16$dBm (voice service), we have $N_{BS,th} = 1.007$. The downlink macrodiversity *decreases* the capacity of a cell. We can observe that result whatever the values of F. The loss of capacity due to macrodiversity is Loss = N_{1MS}-N_{MS}

$$\text{Loss} = \frac{1-\varphi}{\beta\alpha + \beta N_{BS} F} - \frac{1-\varphi}{\beta\alpha + (\beta - \mu\varepsilon)N_{BS} F + (N_{BS} - 1)\varepsilon}$$

$$= (1-\varphi)\frac{(-\mu\varepsilon)N_{BS} F + (N_{BS} - 1)\varepsilon}{(\beta\alpha + \beta N_{BS} F)(\beta\alpha + (\beta - \mu\varepsilon)N_{BS} F + (N_{BS} - 1)\varepsilon)}$$

Figures 2 and 3 show the loss of capacity in term of mobile number (figure 2: orange curve) and loss percentage of cell capacity (figure3: violet curve) as a function of the percentage of power ε dedicated to each link for the macrodiversity. The red curve shows the total transmitting power of a base station, dedicated to mobiles in macrodiversity.

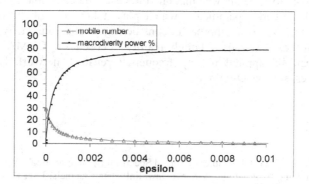

Fig. 2. Macrodiversity impact on the cell capacity vs percentage of transmitting power

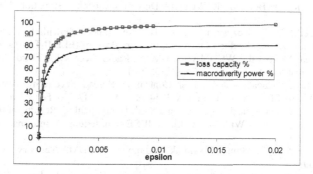

Fig. 3. Macrodiversity impact on the loss of capacity vs percentage of transmitting power

Cancellation of the other cell interferences

We notice from (4.6b) that the term f_i vanishes for $\beta = \mu\varepsilon$, as if the interferences felt by a mobile, due to the other base stations of the network, were *balanced* by the fraction of their transmitting powers dedicated to that mobile. Since

$\beta = \dfrac{\gamma}{1+\alpha\gamma}$ and $\mu = \dfrac{1+\gamma}{1+\alpha\gamma}$, we have $\varepsilon = \dfrac{\gamma}{1+\gamma}$ The cell capacity $N_{1,MS}$ can be written:

$$N_{1,MS} = \frac{1-\varphi}{\beta\alpha} \qquad (5.13)$$

6   Conclusion

In this paper, we established an explicit expression of the load L_{MD} due to mobiles in macrodiversity, and showed that one increases the cell's load. We identified the traffic and network's parameters which play a key role in the cell's load. We finally generalized the approach, considering a macrodiversity with a great number of base stations. Though mainly focused on CDMA networks, our analysis can be applied to any frequency reuse 1 network based on other technologies, such as OFDMA.

References

1. A. J. Viterbi, CDMA Principles of Spread Spectrum Communication, Wesley, 1995.
2. T. Bonald and A. Proutiere, Wireless Downlink Data Channels: User Performance and Cell Dimensioning, ACM Mobicom 2003
3. Jaana Laiho, Achim Wacker Tomas Novosad, "Radio network planning and optimisation for UMTS"
4. Hiltunen, K., De Bernardi, R. WCDMA Downlink capacity estimation, VTC 2000, p. 992-996
5. F. Baccelli, B. Błaszczyszyn, and F. Tournois (2003) Downlink admission/congestion control and maximal load in CDMA networks, in Proc. of IEEE INFOCOM'03
6. H. Holma A. Toskala, WCDMA for UMTS, Radio Access for Third Generation Mobile Communications. John Wiley & Sons, Ltd.,2001.
7. S.V Hanly,., "Capacity and Power Control in Spread Spectrum Macrodiversity Radio Networks", IEEE Trans. on Comm., vol. 44, NO. 2, pp.247-256, Feb. 1996
8. D. Aktas, M. N. Bacha, J. S. Evans, and S. V. Hanly, Scaling Results on the Sum Capacity of Cellular Networks With MIMO Links, IEEE transactions on information theory, vol 52, n°7, July 2006
9. J-Marc Kelif and E. Altman, Downlink fluid model for CDMA Networks, VTC 2005 Stockholm
10. P. Jacquet, "Geometry of information propagation in massively dense adhoc networks," in Proc. ACM MobiHOC, Roppongi Hills, Japan, May 2004, pp. 157–162.
11. J-Marc Kelif, M. Coupechoux, and P. Godlewski, Spatial Outage Probability for Cellular Networks, Globecom 2007, Washington

Multiple Cell Partitions for Increasing the CDMA-Based Cell Capacity

Ardian Ulvan[1] , Diogo Ribeiro[2] and Robert Bestak[1]

[1]Czech Technical University in Prague, Technicka 2 166 27, Praha 6, Czech Republic
ulvana1, bestar1[@fel.cvut.cz]

[2]Instituto Superior Técnico de Lisboa, Av. Rovisco Pais, 1049-001 Lisboa, Portugal
dpbr@mega.ist.utl.pt

Abstract This paper investigates the impact of cell partitioning in cell capacity of CDMA-based system. We examine the implementation of four partitions per cell as well as the influence of various height of the base station transceiver antenna to the system. We contemplated the urban area as the target, therefore the COST-231 Walfisch – Ikegami is applied as the propagation model. Calculations on the capacity of cell, the link budget (and MAPL) and the radius of each partition, depending on the height of the base station transceiver antenna, are made. The results show that the capacity increases as the number of partitions increases; the height of the base station transceiver affects the radius of the partitions.

1 Introduction

The conventional method for cellular planning is based on multi-cell configuration. The topology has a base transceiver station (BTS) that serves areas divided in cells or several BTS covering the whole area. However, in this method, to avoid the co-channel interference, each adjacent cell needs to use different frequencies. In practice, the spacing has to be more than just adjacent cells, around 7 frequencies are often used per planning. Thus, to increase the capacity, the number of frequency channels would have to be increased. Since frequency is a precious resource and in most cities the growth of traffic tends to concentrate in certain area only, this method becomes very inefficient.

The use of CDMA-based systems in this work is due to its potential concerning capacity increase and frequency spectrum management. However, since this type of systems are strongly influenced by interference between users or even the one that comes from base transceiver stations, the way to improve capacity is to control this sources of interference. These two types are called inter-user interference and co-channel interference. This paper describes the use of cell partition as an alternative solution for CDMA-based cellular planning.

In this paper we analyze the effect of increasing the number of partitions and varying the BTS's antenna height.

Please use the following format when citing this chapter:

Ulvan, A., Ribeiro, D. and Bestak, R., 2008, in IFIP International Federation for Information Processing, Volume 284; *Wireless and Mobile Networking*; Zoubir Mammeri; (Boston: Springer), pp. 383–394.

Resorting to a variable number of partitions, an existing cell is divided into 4 partitions, being scaled in radius as well as in frequency. In order to determine the radius of each partition, it's required the calculation of link budget, which provides the maximum allowable path loss (MAPL) and the usage of a propagation model, which is in this case the Walfisch – Ikegami. After having all of this data, it's possible to determine the maximum capacity of the cell.

The paper is organized as follows: the definition of the cell partition for improving cell capacity, frequency planning and channel allocation scheme for partitioned cell, link budget and cell radius calculations are discussed in Section II. Section III proposes three and four partitions topology in each cell that are used in or simulation scenarios. In Section IV we discussed the results of total capacity of the system and compared them with the capacity of conventional frequency planning. Finally, section V and VI concludes the work and assign our future work.

2   Cell Capacity

2.1 Variable number of partitions

Increasing the cell capacity by using 2-partition topology was carried out by [1]. However, the used of two different frequencies for inner and outer cell seems have low complexity in term of interference. Additionally, the cell radius which is influenced by antenna altitude was not considered yet. This paper intends to determine the complexity by increase the number of partitions and analyze what happens to the total capacity of the cell. A cell is divided into four partitions, all of them with a radius disparity that is scaled between them. The way to perform the scaling of radius is to vary the height of the antennas and the transmitting power of each BTS [5]. So, the scheme of one cell is shown in figure 1.a below.

If this cell is spanned throughout a whole coverage area, the frequencies within each partition have to be alternated, and so, for a 3 and 4 partitions scheme, we have a frequency planning for each partitions as can be seen on figure 1.b.

Note that in this figure each colour corresponds to one different frequency, so the goal of not having boundaries with common frequencies on each side is achieved.

The frequency planning is the key to improve the capacity of the system. Each partition within the cell, have a different frequency not to cause interference between the partitions. It means that with three partitions we have a frequency reuse factor of three, with four partitions, a reuse factor of four, and so on. To maximize the capacity of each cell, one has to minimize the interference, since CDMA is an interference limited technology. When a mobile station moves to the cell's boundary, the interference from neighboring cells increase considerably. The worst case for the forward link occurs at the boundary of three cells where powers received from two adjacent cells are almost equal to that from the given cell. Taking this fact into consideration, the goal of the frequency planning is to avoid the existence of cell boundaries with the same frequency in each of the outer partitions that compose this boundary, which yield the distribution in figure 1.b for a 3 cell partition scheme, and in figure 1.c for a 4 cell partition topology.

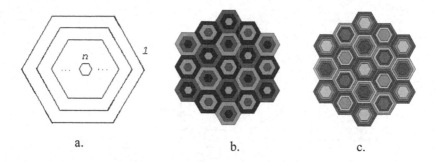

a.   b.   c.

Fig.1. Schematic representation of a cell containing n partitions (a) and frequency planning for a scheme with 3 and 4 partitions per cell (b, c)

Accordingly as it is mentioned, each partition is designed to use different frequencies. The outer most partition always includes the coverage of the other ones, consequently there are as many frequencies as the number of partitions in the outer most cell. However, there is no interference since all of the frequencies are different.

Concerning the traffic allocation process it becomes slightly different from the one without partitions. The traffic allocation process is always prioritised to the inner most cell. If a mobile station (MS) is in the inner most cell coverage, the allocation of channel is served by its frequency and the connection is held by the inner most cell's radio base station (RBS). On the other hand, if there are no idle channels in the inner most cells, the connection is relocated to the next partition (the second smallest in radius) and the system tries to establish the connection here. If it is not possible as well, the system tries the next partitions in an orderly fashion from the smallest to the biggest radius partition, until the connection is established or rejected. The rejection can be due to all of the radio base stations not having idle traffic channels or the mobile station moved farther away than the radius of the outer most cells. When the connection is established, it is served by the frequency of the partition where an idle channel has been found. In figure 2, it is shown the algorithm of traffic channel allocation in a cell with an indefinite number of partitions.

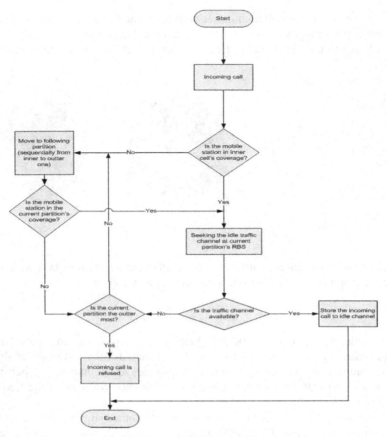

Fig. 2. Channel allocation algorithm for an indefinite number of partitions

2.2 CDMA Considerations

In CDMA systems the W^{64} of Walsh code generates 1 pilot channel, 1 synchronization channel, 7 paging channels and 55 traffic channels. To allow enough bandwidth for data and for bandguard, the 55 traffic channels can be served by 1.25 MHz of bandwidth. The capacity of the system, which is represented by the number of users that the system can support, with a single cell topology is [6]:

$$N = 1 + \frac{W/R}{E_b/N_0} - (\eta/S) \tag{1}$$

In above equation it was considered the background thermal noise, η, which has to be taken into account in the spread bandwidth.

2.3 Link Budget

To determine the radius, it needs to be known the *link budget,* this allows the calculation of the total losses and gains on the transmission link. It is known that the signal in receiver can be detected if the following condition is reached [5]:

$$\left(P_{tr}\right)_{dBm} + \left(Gains\right)_{dB} - \left(Losses\right)_{dB} > (Min.\ required\ power$$

$$for\ detection\ at\ the\ receiver)_{dBm}$$

The result of the link budget calculation is a cell's *MAPL* (Maximum Allowable Path Loss). This calculation is employed in both directions: the *reverse link* and the *forward link.* The *MAPL* for reverse and forward link is described in the following equations, respectively [2]:

$MAPL_R$ = Total mobile transmitter EIRP (dBm) - Receiver

sensitivity (dBm) + Rx Antenna Gain (dBi) - Rx Cable Loss (dB)

− Body Loss (dB) - Fade Margin (dB) - Building Penetration

Loss (dB) + Diversity Gain (dB)

$MAPL_F$ = Total mobile transmitter EIRP (dBm) - Receiver

sensitivity (dBm) + Rx Antenna Gain (dBi) - Rx Cable Loss (dB)

− Body Loss (dB) - Fade Margin (dB) - Building Penetration

Loss (dB)

The results attained for the link budget calculations are as follow.

Table 1. Results of Link Budget Calculation for a cell with three partitions.

	Unit	Outer Cell	Medium Cell	Inner Cell
BTS's Maximum transmitting power	dBm	35.00	30.00	25.00
MAPL	dB	133.81	128.81	123.8

Table 2. Results of Link Budget Calculation for a cell with four partitions

	Unit	Outer Cell	2nd tier Cell	3rd tier Cell	Inner Cell
BTS's Maximum transmitting power	dBm	40.00	35.00	30.00	25.00
MAPL	dB	138.81	133.81	128.81	123.81

2.4 Cell Partition's radius

By using the MAPL, it is possible to calculate the radius of a desired cell/partition using propagation models that are adequate for the environment where the cells/partitions are inserted. We consider the COST 231 propagation model, suitable for urban and dense urban areas.

To determine the cell radius, accurate data of the street and building altitude is required. The cell radius is assumed to be less than 5 km and the antenna elevation less than 70m and more than the average building height. The model employed here consists in several equations with restriction and conditions that are to be used combined. So, mathematical descriptions of the model are [3] [4]:

$$L = L_0 + L_{rts} + L_{msd} \tag{2}$$

note:

L = *path loss (dB), L_0=free space loss (dB), L_{rts} = roof-top-street diffraction and scatter loss, L_{msd} = multi-screen diffraction loss.*

$$L_0 = 32,4 + 20.\log(r) + 20.\log(f) \tag{3}$$

$$L_{rts} = -16,9 - 10.\log(w) + 10.\log(f) + 20.\log(\Delta_{mobile}) + L_{street} \tag{4}$$

$$for\ \Delta_{mobile} > 0$$

$$L_{rts} = 0 \quad for\ \Delta_{mobile} \leq 0 \tag{5}$$

$$L_{street} = -10 + 0,354\phi \quad for\ 0 \leq \phi < 35 \tag{6}$$

$$L_{street} = 2,5 + 0,075(\phi - 35) \quad for\ 35 \leq \phi < 55 \tag{7}$$

$$L_{street} = 4,0 - 0,114(\phi - 55) \quad for \ 55 \le \phi \le 90 \tag{8}$$

note:

h_{roof}= average of roof building altitude (m), h_{mobile}=antenna altitude for MS(m), h_{BTS}= antenna altitude for BTS(m), Δ_{mobile}=h_{roof} h_{mobile} (m), Δ_{BTS}=h_{BTS}-h_{roof} (m), w= average of street width (m), ϕ= road orientation concerning to direct radio path (degree).

$$L_{msd} = L_{med} + k_a + k_r \log(r) + k_f \log(f) - 9\log(b) \tag{9}$$

where:

$$L_{med} = -18\log(1 + \Delta_{BTS}) \quad for \Delta_{BTS} > 0 \tag{10}$$

$$L_{med} = 0 \qquad for \ \Delta_{BTS} \le 0 \tag{11}$$

$$k_a = 54 \qquad for \ \Delta_{BTS} > 0 \tag{12}$$

$$k_a = 54 - 0,8\Delta_{BTS} \ for \ r \ge 0,5 \ and \ \Delta_{BTS} \le 0 \tag{13}$$

$$k_a = 54 - 1,6\Delta_{BTS}r \ for \ r < 0,5 and \Delta_{BTS} \le 0 \tag{14}$$

$$k_r = 18 \quad for \ \Delta_{BTS} > 0 \tag{15}$$

$$k_r = 18 - 15\frac{\Delta_{BTS}}{h_{roof}} \quad for \ \Delta_{BTS} \le 0 \tag{16}$$

$$k_f = -4 + 0,7\left(\frac{f}{925} - 1\right) \tag{17}$$

for urban and suburban area

$$k_f = -4 + 1,5\left(\frac{f}{925} - 1\right) \tag{18}$$

for dense urban area

note:

b is the average interbuilding distance (m), k_a and k_r are the correction constants of antenna altitude, kf is the adaptation constant for diverse building density.

In this paper, the height of the BTS antenna will be varied, so the results for the radiuses will be dependent of it. In figure 3.a and 3.b, the results of the calculations are explicit for a 3 and 4 partitions scheme, respectively:

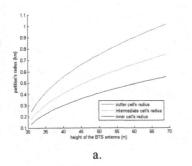

a.

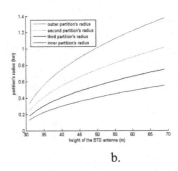

b.

Fig. 3. Variation of the several partitions' radiuses with the height of the BTS antenna for 3 (a) and 4-partitions topology (b).

3   Cell Capacity with 3 and 4 Partitions Topology

The equation (1) allows the calculation for the capacity in a single-cell scheme. With a multipartitional topology per cell some other considerations have to be taken into account. However, when the cell partition is done, a different frequency is used for each of the resulting cells and since they do not interfere with one another, it's possible to calculate the capacity individually for each of these. Afterwards, all of the capacities are summed to yield the final result. So, the total capacity of the cell with the partitions is be given by:

$$N_{total} = \sum_{i=1}^{n} N_i \qquad (19)$$

where N_{total} is the total capacity of the cell with the partitions and N_i is the capacity of the ith partition. Due to this separation principle, for an arbitrary partition of the cell, the S/I ratio is given as:

$$SNR = \frac{P_t \cdot (1/N) \cdot r^{-\alpha}}{P_t \cdot \left(1 - \frac{1}{N}\right) \cdot r^{-\alpha} + \sum_{k=1}^{3} \sum_{j=1}^{6} P_{kj} \cdot L_{kj}^{-\alpha}} \qquad (20)$$

then

$$N_i = \frac{P_i \cdot r_i^{-\alpha} \cdot \left(1 + \frac{S}{I}\right)}{\frac{S}{I} \cdot \left(P_i \cdot r_i^{-\alpha} + \sum_{k=1}^{3} \sum_{j=1}^{6} P_{kj} L_{kj}^{-\alpha}\right)} \qquad (21)$$

where

$$\frac{S}{I} = \frac{E_b/I_0}{W/R} = \frac{E_b/I_0}{G_P} \qquad (22)$$

In the above equations S/I is the signal to interference ratio, P_i is the transmitted EIRP of the partition (Watt), r_i is the radius of the partition (km), P_{kj} is the transmitted power of neighbour cells (Watt), L_{kj} is the distance between neighbour base station to MS (km), α is the path loss exponent and N_i is the i [th] partition capacity (number of users).

4   Results for the Traffic Capacity

Using all of the mentioned equations, the results from the link budget calculation and the radiuses for each partition, are dependent of the height of each BTS. It is now possible to determine the total capacity of the system. This capacity is calculated for 3 and 4 partitions and depends on the BTS's antenna height. Figures 4.a and 4.b show the results of the capacity per partition per cell. In figure 4.c we can see the total capacity of the resulting cell. Tables 3 and 4 are the results for the capacity attained when using the conventional method and 2 partitions per cell topology.

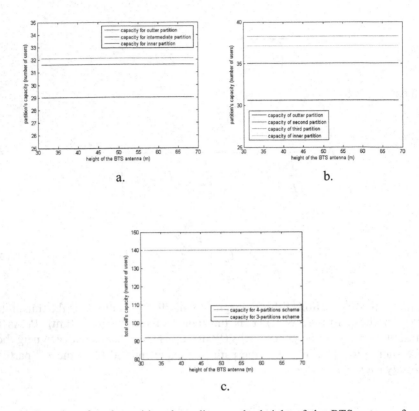

Fig. 4. Capacity of each partition depending on the height of the BTS antenna for 3-partitions scheme (a), 4-partitions scheme (b) and total cell's capacity for a topology with 3 and 4 partitions per cell.

Table 3. Results for calculation and simulation of capacity using conventional method (2 frequencies).

	Unit	RBS 1	RBS 2
BTS's EIRP	dBm	45	45
Frequency	MHz	1967.50	1966.25
Antenna altitude	m	50	50
MAPL	dBm	130.8	130.8
Cell radius	Km	0.75	0.75
Traffic capacity	users	29	29

Table 4. Results for calculation and simulation of capacity using a topology with 2 partitions per cell.

	Unit	Inner cell	Outer cell
BTS's EIRP	dBm	34	45
Frequency	MHz	1967.50	1966.25
Antenna altitude	m	40	50
MAPL	dBm	123.8	130.8
Cell radius	Km	0.36	0.75
Traffic capacity	users	45	35

5   Conclusions

Obtained results show that the cell capacity can be increased by using cell partitions. Furthermore, the capacity is increased linearly with the number of partitions used per cell. In case of 3 partitions the total cell capacity is increased to 92 users; and in case of 4 partitions per cell it is increased to 140 users. Using the conventional method, the capacity is only 58 users per cell and with 2 partitions per cell 80 users. The CDMA-based systems are indeed interference dependent. It implies that the only parameter affecting the capacity is the interference among users or caused by another BTS which is emitting using the same frequency. Concerning the capacity for each partition inside the cell, simulation results show that the inner cell has a very high capacity comparatively to the others.

The increase in the number of partitions has also the great advantage of allowing an effective frequency planning, since more frequencies are allowed to be used, and one can choose in which partition the capacity is to be increased.

6   Further Work

As discussed, the increase of the number of partitions increases the capacity in CDMA-based systems. However, increasing the number of partitions brings some drawbacks. The use of n-frequencies per cell, corresponding to n-partitions per cell, will lead to hard-handoff when the mobile station is leaving the coverage area from inside to outside of the cell. The hard handoff can lead to a degradation of the quality of service as well as the grade of service, which are two very important parameters that specify the minimum conditions for an acceptable conversation.

Acknowledgement

This research work was supported by grant of Czech Ministry of Education, Youth and Sports No. MSM6840770014.

References

1. Ulvan, A (2006) Increasing the CDMA-based Cell Capacity for Urban Area With Cell Partition. In Research in Telecommunication Technology. Proceeding, Vol.1, pp 176 – 181. ISBN 80-8070-637-9.
2. Kim, W. S. and Prabhu, V. K (1998) Enhanced Capacity in CDMA System with Alternate Frequency Planning. IEEE International Conference on Communication. Vol. 2, pp 972-978. ISBN 0-7803-4788-9.
3. Hecker, A., Neuland, M. and Kuerner, T. (2006) Propagation models for high sites in urban areas. Advance in Radio Science, Vol 4, pp 345-349.
4. Hecker, A., and Kuerner, T. (2005) Analysis of Propagation Models for UMTS Ultra High Sites in Urban Area. IEEE 16th International Symposium on Personal, Indoor and Mobile Radio Communications (PIMRC), Vol 4, pp 2337 – 2341. ISBN 9783800729098.
5. Rappaport, T. S. (1996) Wireless communications principles and pratice", Prentice Hall PTR.
6. Ericsson Academy (2006) CDMA2000 RF Engineering Workshop.

Location Management in Civil Emergency Wireless Communication

Dora Maros

Budapest Tech, Hungary
maros.dora@kvk.bmf.hu

Abstract The prompt availability of location information is very important in emergency situations (e.g. accidents, natural or technological disasters etc), when people need help immediately. The precise identification of the caller's position in a mobile network is the foundation of rescue operations. The paper presents technical questions and some solutions in the context of determining and identifying the caller's geographical position in emergency cases, and it rather highlights some practical problems instead a presentation of a scientific solution.

1 Preface

Many challenges and considerations need to be addressed in defining and establishing the functional capabilities to support civil emergency communications in telecommunications networks [10]. One of these capabilities is the location management in the mobile networks.

Services based on user location in mobile networks are called *Location Based Services (LBS)*. Many GSM/UMTS operators support LBS all around the world, mainly in commercial applications. In case of commercial LBS, the information, that the network sends to the user (e.g. the text of an SMS) depends on terminal geographical position. LBS is either a pull or a push type of service. In ETSI/GSM LBS is called "Location Related Service". Another terminology is used related to the service concepts: *LoCation Services (LCS)*. LCS is a service concept in systems (e.g. GSM or UMTS) standardization. LCS specifies all the necessary network elements and entities, their functionalities, interfaces as well as communication messages, by implementing the positioning functionality in a cellular network. Note that LCS does not specify any location based (value added) services except locating emergency calls. There are four categories in use for locating services. These are the Commercial, the Internal, the Emergency and the Lawful Intercept LCS. The Commercial LCS (or Value Added Services) will typically be associated with an application that provides a value-added service through the knowledge of the user's location. The Internal LCS is developed to support internal network operations, for example location assisted handover or traffic and cov-

Please use the following format when citing this chapter:

Maros, D., 2008, in IFIP International Federation for Information Processing, Volume 284; *Wireless and Mobile Networking*; Zoubir Mammeri; (Boston: Springer), pp. 395–406.

erage measurement. The Emergency LCS supports the identification of user location in case of emergency calls. In this service, the location of the caller is provided to the emergency service provider to assist them in the response. This service may be mandatory in some jurisdictions. In the United States, for example, this service is mandated for all mobile voice subscribers. The Lawful Intercept LCS supports various legally required or sanctioned services.

The determination of user location in the network is based on the capabilities of terminal and network elements and procedures. There are different types of measuring methods, and it is very important, that the method we choose should meet the requirements of the actually used applications. For example in normal (e.g. a simple speech service) calls the location information relates to MSC Service Area and Location Area. In emergency situation (e.g. emergency call of an accident) this is not enough, the emergency organizations need more accurate (some 10 meters) geographical positioning information to find, for example, the car on the route or along the highway, in case nobody can inform them by phone of the place of accident. Using mobile phones in case of emergency is another way, for the authorities or disaster managing organizations to send warning messages to people who are in danger, for example after an explosion in a chemical factory, or in extraordinary weather conditions, e.g. hurricanes, tornadoes, high wind and rain storms. Civil warning applications also need location information of the subscribers to identify the cell where they actually are, unless the network can't manage to send SMS or CBS to the people being in danger.

Understanding how we can get the location of the users and how we can manage these data in the network information systems, we need to identify some basic concepts:

- *Target:* a person/handset whose geographical position we need.
- *Source of location measuring:* a network element where the location information originated. There are two types of sources: network originated or terminal originated sources. Sometimes a hybrid solution is used.
- *Location measurement system*: this system controls the measurement procedures, collects and evaluates measurement data from different network devices.
- *LBS-provider:* a company or organization, that uses location information of its users to send different types of information to their terminals.

Network based/mobile assisted techniques use mobile network elements to identify the geographical position of the user's terminal. The handset measures some simple transmission parameters (received signal level, timing advance), detects and sends back some identities (like CGI). Network based methods are independent of the users' terminal capabilities, it does not affect the handset.

Mobile based/network assisted techniques require specific hardware/software installations in the mobile phone to measure location. In this case, the handset determines its position, measuring some predefined parameters or GPS coordinates and it sends the measurement reports to the network for further processing.

Hybrid techniques are the different combinations of two of the above techniques. These techniques give the best accuracy of the three.

2 Regulations, Standards

Regulations and standards can describe and lay down the technical and administrative rules of the realizations of the given requirements. The concept of Emergency Telecommunications (EMTEL) addresses a broad spectrum of providing telecommunication services in emergency situations. This is operating in cooperation with the telecommunications industry in the major national and international standard bodies. ITU and ETSI have been identified that address various issues related to the development of effective and comprehensive standards for LCS and the Emergency Telecommunications Services (ETS). EMTEL related standardization work takes place across ETSI's technical committees, projects and partnership projects. EMTEL issued three documentations that are to connect civil emergency wireless communications [3]. These are:

- *TS 102 182:* Requirements for communications from authorities to citizens during emergencies (civil warning)
- *TR 102 444:* Suitability of SMS and CBS for Emergency Messaging
- *TS 102 180*: Requirements for communications of citizens with authorities/organizations in case of distress (emergency call handling)

3 Location Management without LCS

When a subscriber terminates a call (speech, data, SMS etc.) the system must know its location in the GSM/UMTS network. To determine user location in mobile network, we have to know the generic geographical structure of the network, as well as Public Land Mobile Network (PLMN), MSC/VLR Service Area, Location Area and cell. As the mobile subscriber moves within GSM network, the system must know where the subscriber is located. The administration of user location information takes place in HLR and VLR. HLR, that stores the MSC/VLR Service Area code (VLR address) where the mobile was last registered. Location Area Code (LAC) is used for administration of mobile subscriber location within MSC/VLR Service Area. LAC is always stored in Visitor Location Register.

Let us suppose that the mobile is in standby mode. The mobile is connected to serving BTS continuously listening to its broadcast channel (BCCH). When attaching to a new cell it is possible that the mobile recognizes a new Location Area Code on BCCH channel (if MS enters into a cell which is in the same location area where the previous was, LAI does not change). As the location information has a great importance, the network must be informed about this change. At this point the mobile sends a location updating request message toward the MSC (see Fig. 1).

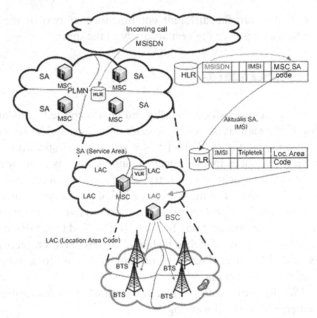

Fig. 1. Location management in case of normal calls (without LCS)

4 Location Management with LCS

When LCS is used, the system has to determine the location information of the terminal more accurately than in the case of normal calls, when the system only knows LAC. In LCS the location information is more complex and gives more accurate data. To support this new concept, new system functions are applied in the GSM/UMTS networks [1]. These two functions are the Serving Mobile Location Center (SMLC) and the Gateway Mobile Location Center (GMLC). SMLC controls the location measurement procedures GMLC receives the LCS service request from LCS clients, and transmits location data from the network. GMLC also supports the routing info request from HLR, when the system determines the serving MSC/VLR Area of the user (Fig. 2.).

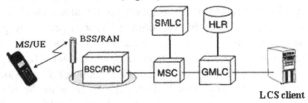

SMLC (Serving Mobile Location Center)
GMLC (Gateway Mobile Location Center)

Fig. 2. Network elements for LCS

Fig. 3 and Fig 4 show the network and terminal based location measurement procedures. For better understanding we pull together the network element in one box that are part of the location measurement procedures (BSC/RNC+SMLC).

The network based procedure starts when an LCS client sends a request to GMLC. The GMLC gets the routing info (the identity of the serving MSC) from HLR, and it sends a location info determination request to the serving MSC. As we saw the MSC's VLR stores the actual LAC and BSC or RNC sends a paging message to the user. When the paged terminal returns its answer, the security procedures start under the control of MSC. When the security procedures are successful (e.g. user is authenticated by IMSI) MSC starts the location measurement procedures [8]. When the procedures are finished, the system sends location data to the LCS client. When a terminal based procedure is used, the MS/UE initiates the LCS procedure. First it sends a service request to MSC, and after its security functions, the MSC enables the starting of the measurement procedures. When the procedures are finished, the measurement report is sent to the MSC, GMLC and LCS client.

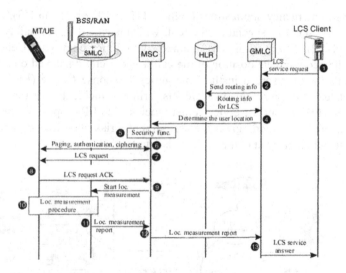

Fig. 3. Network based location determination signalling procedure

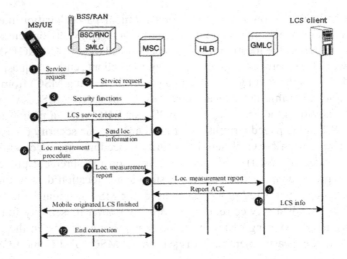

Fig. 4. Terminal based location identification signalling procedure

In case of emergency applications (calling 112 in EU or 911 in US), the LCS information is sent to a special LCS client, which is called Public Safety Answering Point (PSAP). PSAP is directly connected to Emergency Call Centres (ECC), where the geographical position of the caller is directly displayed on a map on the operator's monitor screen in the Emergency Response Centre (ERC). The calls may relate to an injury, traffic accidents, criminal incidents that threaten the law and order, fires or social services emergencies. The ERC operator finds out what has happened and where, gives the assignment a risk classification and then notifies to send help needed to the accident scene.

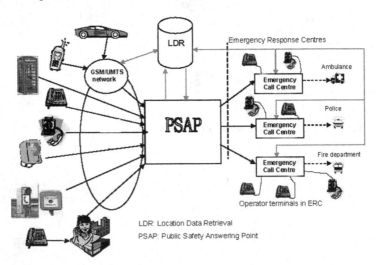

Fig. 5. Location management in case of emergency calls [4]

The member countries of the European Commission are obliged to use E112 in their communication networks (Commission Recommendation 2003/558/EC) [2]. E112 is a location-enhanced emergency call services, which means that the location information of the caller is automatically and immediately transmitted when the call set-up (speech) is completed. In ETSI TS 102 180 the documentation recommends possible network architecture for E112 as shown on Fig. 5. This concept is between two new network functions, telecommunication networks and ECCs. Public Safety Answering Point (PSAP), and Location Data Retrieval (LDR). As the location information can originate from different types of communication networks and terminals (wired, wireless, public, private, etc.), first of all every emergency call is routed to PSAP [4]. When the call is terminated to PSAP, PSAP sends a location information request message toward LDR. Hence the LDR is connected to mobile telecommunication providers SMLCs, the location information will be sent directly to LDR, and then to PSAP. The procedure has to be very fast because the call and location information must receive them practically at the same time in ECC. So, when the operator picks up the phone in ERC and starts the oral connection, he/she can see the geographical location of the caller on his/her computer terminal screen.

5 Geographical Position Measurement Methods and their Accuracy

There are many methods for measuring the geographical location of the terminal/user:

Cell Identification with CGI: Cell Identification is based on Cell Global Identity (CGI): The accuracy of this method can be a few hundred meters (except in UMTS indoor picocell where it is 10-50 m) in urban areas, but in suburban areas and rural zones it can be as poor as 32 km (GSM) and 20 km (in UMTS).

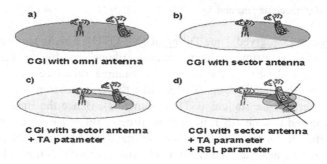

Fig. 6. Accuracy of geographical position using CGI and other parameters [7]

The accuracy depends on the known range of the particular network base station and the type of the antenna. It is also a problem that in UMTS Terrestrial Radio Access Network (UTRAN) the User Equipment (UE) can connect parallel with two or more base stations (its called macro diversity). In this case, two or more CGI are active at the same time. Fig. 6. shows four different methods when CGI is applied. The most inaccurate method is using an omni-directional antenna. (Fig. 6/a) but using a sector antenna, the serving area is smaller (Fig. 6./b), so the possible location of the user is smaller too. The accuracy is increasing when the mobile measures the Timing Advance parameter on an active downlink channel (Fig. 6./c). The mobile sends back TA to the Base Station, thus the network calculates the distance of the terminal to the Base Station. The distance accuracy of this method is about 50 meters, but the possible area (dark grey area) depends on the cell size. The most accurate method is called E-CGI (Fig. 6/d), when the Received Signal Level (RSL) on the downlink dedicated channel is also measured by the mobile phone [9]. In this case the area where the mobile is located is an area about 500 meters in diameter.

Time Difference Of Arrival (TDOA) and Time Of Arrival (TOA): In TDOA technology the network determines the signal transmission time difference and the distance from the mobile phone to each base station. The TOA is similar to TDOA, but this method uses the absolute time of arrival at a certain base station rather than the difference between two stations.

Angle of arrival (AOA): AOA technique locates the user at the point where the lines along the angles from each base station intersect. To determine this point a reference direction is used (see. Fig. 7.). The calculation of angles is originated from measuring the time delay from the antennas.

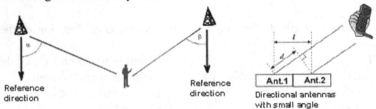

Fig. 7. AOA measuring method

Enhanced Observed Time Difference (E-OTD): This is similar to TDOA, but the position is estimated by the mobile phone, not by the base station. The measuring is based on the hiperbolyc triangle rule (see Fig. 8.). During the procedure, the mobile terminal measures the time difference of sending signals from different base stations (GTD parameters). Hence the Base Stations are not synchronized to each other, there is no time of reference for exact calculation. A new network function has to be used to make this synchronization; this is called Location Management Unit (LMU). The precision of this method depends on the number of available LMUs in the network.

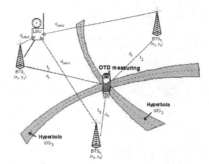

Fig. 8. E-OTD measurement method with LMU

Assisted-GPS: GPS-based technology, which uses a network ground station to eliminate GPS errors caused by the atmosphere or topography (Fig. 9.). The method uses differential GPS technique: the built in GPS receiver determines the GPS coordinates and gets some more GPS reference data from the ground Station through SMLC.

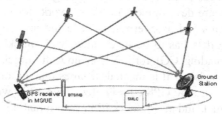

Fig. 9. A-GPS application with SMLC

The efficiency of different location measurement techniques depends not only on the accuracy and terminal capabilities, the importance being where it is used. For example the GPS based technologies do not work inside buildings or tunnels, but the enhanced accuracy technologies also are problematic indoor and outdoor urban areas, where the multipath spreading causes serious fading problems in the receiver. We can say that the better accuracy and more complicated method we use, the application in practice decreases. The main problem with E112 calls is that it is not clearly defined in relevant documentations which of the location measurement method is the best and most efficient in this case. If we examine the possible methods again, we can see that the answer is not simple, there are many factors that have to be considered. These are:

- software/hardware capabilities of mobile phones
- software/hardware capabilities of the network
- where the emergency call is originated from (outdoor, indoor, urban , suburban, rural, forest, mountain, sea etc.)
- is the caller able to give more information about his/her location or not

what kind of help he/she needs, etc.

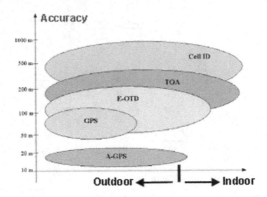

Fig. 10. Accuracy and application of location determination technologies

Considering the factors above, we can say that for emergency calls nowadays the operators use network based measurement methods mainly. Generally CGI identification is used, sometimes E-CGI. Using TOA and TDOA the operator needs further software development in the network, for using E-OTD or A-GPS, the network elements and user terminals need further capabilities. In emergency cases, the location data has to be determined very quickly, that is why the CGI identification is (reading CGI form VLR) now the quickest if the procedure is automatic (1-2 seconds). If it is manual, it takes much more time. Later when the user terminals can measure GPS coordinates, the A-GPS will be the most efficient method for very quick and accurate location determination.

6 Location Management in Civil Warning Systems using SMS and CBS

When SMS or CBS is used in civil warning applications [6], two main aspects have to be considered:
- How many people are affected?
- Haw large is the affected area?

Sending a SMS (a warning message or an instruction) can only target specific MS's and so its suitability to reach large numbers of MS's within a reasonable time frame and geographical area is limited. The Cell Broadcast Service allows text messages to be broadcasted to all MS's in a particular cell area, or all MS's in a selected group of geographical locations (e.g. a given region). The GSM BSC/BTS within the range 2 s to 32 minutes may repeatedly broadcast text messages periodically. In a UMTS environment, the highest repetition rate is 1 second. Fig. 11. and Fig. 12. show the network aspects of two applied solutions [5]. When SMS is applied, the system first identifies the MSISDN number of each user in the given cell (cell where the warning message should be sent). Normally, the SMS sending procedure is same as a speech call (regarding location management), but in warning applications, the LAC information is not enough (the is many cells with the same LAC), CGI is needed. It is done, by filtering the users from VLR database by CGI. This procedure is time consuming and depends on the number of users records in VLR (some hundreds thousand). The messages are stored in SMSC and the speed sending SMS from SMC to MSC is about 100-200 SMS per seconds [11]. When CBS is used, the operator enters CGI values and text messages to the Network Management System (NMS), selects the repetition time, and starts the broadcasting procedure. If a Cell Broadcast Centre is used in the network, the procedure is quicker and more efficient because in CBC it is possible to make a list of CGIs or messages and the procedure automatically manages to broadcast CBS messages.

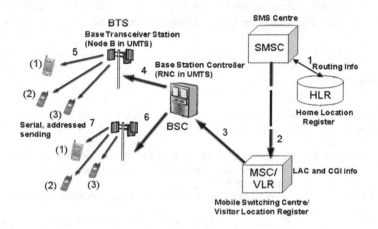

Fig. 11. SMS sending procedure

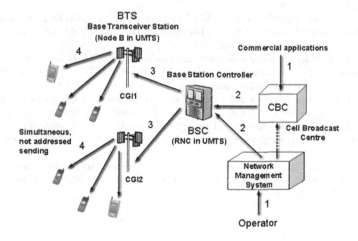

Fig. 12. CBS sending procedure

7 Summary

The accurate and quick determination of user location in the mobile network in emergency situations is very important for rescue operations and for saving lives. There are different types of measurement methods, and it is very important, that the method we choose should meet the requirements of the actually used application. In civil wireless emergency communication two main fields are defined by regulations: emergency calls and sending warning messages through mobile networks. These two applications need different location management procedures and location determination solutions. As this field of telecommunication is less known and less applied in EU countries and in other parts of the World, standardisation bodies, national authorities and rescue organisations should cooperate to develop more efficient and widely usable common civil emergency telecommunication solutions.

References

1. ETSI TS 123 171 V3.11.0 (2004-03) Technical Specification Universal Mobile Telecommunications System (UMTS); Location Services (LCS); Functional description; Stage 2 (UMTS), www.etsi.org
2. Commission Recommendation 2003/558/EC of 25 July 2003 on the processing of caller location information in electronic communication networks for the purpose of location-enhanced emergency call services (OJ L 189, 25.7.2003, p.12)
3. ETSI SR 002 299: „Emergency communication; Collection European Regulatory Framework (http://www.etsi.org)
4. ETSI TS 102 180: Requirements for communication of citizens with authorities/organizations in case of distress (emergency call handling), (http://www.etsi.org)
5. ETSI TS 102 182: Requirements for communications from authorities to citizen during emergencies (http://www.etsi.org)
6. ETSI TR 102 444: Suitability of SMS and CBS for Emergency Messaging (http://www.etsi.org)
7. GSM Association, Permanent Reference Document (PRD) SE 23. Title: Location Based Services, January 2003., (http://www.gsmworld.com)
8. Tibor Wührl: Test calls in universal telecommunication networks, 13. Telecommunication and information networks seminar and exhibition. Siófok (Hungary); 25-26-27. szeptember 2002. p247-252, (presented in Hungarian language)
9. Tibor Wührl: Data collection and transmission via radio interface, Conference on innovation, BMF-HTI 16. nov. 2006., ISBN:978-963-7154-57-7 (presented in Hungarian language)
10. Dora Maros: Questions of national and international regulation of the operation of the telecommunication networks in emergency and disaster cases, PhD Thesis, Zrínyi Miklós Defence Universit, Hungary, 2006.
11. Dr. Dora Maros: Technical and regulation questions of SMS and CBS based civil warning systems supported by public telecommunication networks. Case Study for Ministry of Economics and Transport Hungary, 2007.

Dynamic Connectivity Analysis of ABF-based Ad-hoc Networks

Fei Liu and Geert Heijenk

University of Twente, P.O. Box 217,
7500 AE Enschede, The Netherlands

{fei.liu, geert.heijenk}@utwente.nl[1]

Abstract This paper evaluates the performance of a context discovery protocol using attenuated Bloom filters while nodes appear, disappear, and are temporary unreachable in ad-hoc networks through analytical analysis. Further we verified obtained results with simulation analysis. The analytical results are most accurate when node density is high. Further, we discover that adding a node generates less traffic than removing a node in our protocol. Some proposals are given to reduce the traffic generated by propagating updates due to removing a node.

1 Introduction

Context-aware ad-hoc networks adapt their behavior, based on the context in which they operate. For this purpose, nodes use information from context sources. To discover these sources, a context discovery protocol is needed. Ad-hoc networks are severely limited in resources, such as communication bandwidth, energy usage, and processing power. To save communication resources, we have proposed to perform context discovery using attenuated Bloom filters (ABFs) [8]. We have proven that using ABFs can well save the traffic compared with conventional approaches in realistic situations.

Another important feature of ad-hoc networks is dynamics in connectivity. In this paper, we present an investigation of the impact of network dynamics on our ABF-based discovery protocol through an analytical approach. In general, three categories of causes of network dynamics can be identified: nodes may be mobile; battery-supplied devices might exhaust their batteries; the quality of the wireless transmissions might be varying due to varying propagation conditions.

Because of the random position and movement of the nodes, it is too complex to quantify the network traffic in a mobile environment mathematically. Thus, simulation is a good approach to study this problem. [5] has examined the net-

[1] This work is part of the Freeband AWARENESS project (http://awareness.freeband.nl). Freeband is sponsored by the Dutch government under contract BSIK 03025.

Please use the following format when citing this chapter:

Liu, F. and Heijenk, G., 2008, in IFIP International Federation for Information Processing, Volume 284; *Wireless and Mobile Networking*; Zoubir Mammeri; (Boston: Springer), pp. 407–420.

work traffic generated by updating the ABFs while nodes are moving in a low density network, and the reach-ability of the required services through simulations. In this paper, we present an analytical modeling of the dynamics due to the limited battery-supply and unstable transmission quality in very high density networks. First, we will consider node disappearance and appearance. When a node is powered off, it disappears from the network. After it switches on again, it joins the network again. We quantify the network load through analytical study and verify obtained results with simulations. Further, we observe a special case where the packets transmitted by a node get lost for certain time due to the poor propagation conditions. In this scenario, the node is considered as disappearing and reappearing in the network. We obtain simulation results for various packet loss periods.

This paper is structured as follows. Section 2 gives a brief introduction of the ABF-based context discovery protocol for ad-hoc networks. Section 3 introduces discusses related work, the assumptions we use in our analysis, and an approximation for the basic notion of i-hop node degree. Section 4 presents the analysis of network traffic when nodes appear and disappear in the network, or when a series of consecutive advertisement packets are lost. Section 5 concludes the study and discusses the future work.

2   ABF-based Ad-hoc network

2.1 Attenuated Bloom filters (ABF)

Bloom filters [3] have been proposed in 1970s to represent a set of information in a simple and efficient way. They use b independent hash functions to code the information. The hash results are over a range $\{1..w\}$, where w denotes the width of the filter. In the filter, which has a length of w bits, every bit is set to 0 by default. Only the bit positions associated with the hash results will be set to 1. The resulting Bloom filter can be used to query the existence of certain information. If all the bit positions related to the hash results of the queried information are 1 in the filter, the information exists with small chance of false positive.

Attenuated Bloom filters (ABFs) are layers of basic Bloom filters. We use ABFs to represent information regarding the presence of context sources on a hop-distance basis [8]. The ith layer of an ABF ($0 \le i < d-1$) aggregates all information about context sources i hops away. The depth of the ABF, d, also stands for the total propagation range of the information. Note that context sources reachable in i hops may also be reachable via longer paths. As a result, hash results at larger i will often be repeated in lower layer j ($j>i$).

Fig.1 exemplifies the context aggregation operation for a node with two neighbors. Each node has an ABF with 8 bits width ($w=8$) and the depth of 3 ($d=3$). The node uses two hash functions ($b=2$) to encode its local context sources "temperature" and "humidity" into $\{2,8\}$ and $\{2,5\}$ respectively. If we set the corresponding bit positions, we can obtain *filter_local* as shown in Fig.1. When the node receives the incoming filters *filter_in[1,..]* and *filter_in[2,..]* from its neighbors, it shifts the received filters one layer down and discards the last layer. *filter_in[1,..]'* and *filter_in[2,..]'* are obtained. We perform a logical OR operation on each set of corresponding bits of *filter_local, filter_in[1,..]'*, and *filter_in[2,..]'*. *filter_out* can be obtained as the ABF that the node broadcasts to its neighbors. This filter contains the local information of the node on layer 0; one hop neighbors' information on layer 1; and two hop neighbors' information on layer 2.

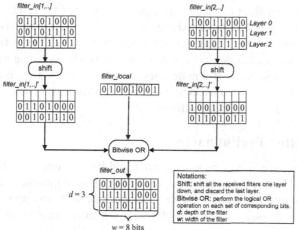

Fig. 1. An example of ABF aggregation

2.2 Protocol specification

Our ABF-based context discovery protocol distinguishes 3 phases [9]: context exchange, context query, and context update and maintenance.

Context exchange: every node stores two kinds of ABFs: incoming ABFs for each neighbor and an aggregated outgoing one with all local and neighboring information. When a new node joins the network, it will broadcast an ABF with only the local information first. Any node receiving this ABF will update its outgoing ABF with the new information and broadcast it. Once the newly joined node receives the neighboring information, it updates its outgoing ABF and broadcasts it. Every neighboring node will aggregate this update into its outgoing ABF as well. If there is any change in the outgoing ABF, the updated ABF will be broadcast to the network. After the exchange of ABFs, every node will have a clear view of the context information present within d hops.

Context query: whenever a query is generated in a node, the node first looks for presence of the information locally. If the required information is not available locally, it will hash the query string and check it against the stored neighboring ABFs. If there is no match, the query will be discarded. If there is any match, a query message will be uni-casted to that neighbor with a *hop-counter* set to d. The neighbor will perform the same action. It checks the query against the locally available context sources. If there is any match, a response message will be sent back to the querying node. If nothing matches, it will check the stored neighboring ABFs. Whenever there is a match, the query will be propagated to that node with the *hop-counter* decreased by 1. When the *hop-counter* equals 0, the query will stop spreading. If a node receives the same query multiple times, as identified by a unique query ID, the query will simply be dropped.

Context update and maintenance: if there is no change in the context sources offered by a node, a keep-alive message will be sent out periodically. A keep-alive message is a short message with a *generation-id* of the last broadcasted ABF from this node. A node can identify the freshness of the stored ABFs by comparing *generation-id*s. Once it notices the *generation-id* is different from that of the stored ABF for this neighbor, an update request is sent out. The neighbor replies back with its latest ABF. If a node does not receive keep-alive messages from a certain neighbor for two consecutive *keep-alive period*s, it considers the node has left and removes its neighbor's information.

3   Modeling Preliminaries

In this section, we introduce related work and background knowledge regarding graph theory. Further, we introduce our modeling assumptions, and the important notion of the multi-hop node degree. We conclude with an approximation of the mean multi-hop node degree, which is an essential component of our further analysis.

3.1 Related graph theory

Networks can be represented as a graph $G=G(V,E)$, where nodes are vertices (V), while links between nodes are edges (E). The degree of a vertex can be defined as the number of edges incident to it. If each vertex has degree of at least k, the graph can be called k-connected. Random geometric graphs [10] and unit disk graphs [4] are often used to model wireless ad-hoc networks. In ad-hoc networks, nodes are only directly connected to each other if they are within each others vicinity. The vicinity of those wireless nodes mostly depends on the geographic distance and transmission power. In both of the graph types mentioned above, vertices are connected, only if the distance between them is at most a threshold r (referred to as the communication range of wireless nodes). Both graphs are considered to be among the most realistic methods to model wireless ad-hoc networks. A random geometric graph is a graph in which the vertices or edges are associated with geometric objects or configurations. In a random geometric graph, vertices are placed random uniformly and independently in a geographic area, while in unit disk graph there is no specific restriction for vertices distributions. In here, we assume nodes are uniformly distributed in the network. Therefore, in this paper, we analyze ad-hoc networks with random geometric graph theory.

Using graph theory can help us to analyze some specific network characteristics. Most studies have been done in the area of node degree and connectivity. [4]

has discussed the connectivity problems of unit disk graph. [2] has investigated the relationship between required range r, node density, and almost certainly k-connected networks, assuming random geometric graphs. The results provide the principles to choose practical values of those parameters for simulations and design. [6] has shown that the degree distribution in wireless ad-hoc networks, modeled as a random geometric graph, is binomial for low values of the mean degree.

Besides using graph theory, some other approaches have also been used to investigate the connectivity problems in ad-hoc networks. [1] has examined the connectivity of a certain number of mobile nodes within a certain area by using a stochastic activity model. However, the study is limited to low density networks due to the limitation of the stochastic model. Besides this analytical analysis, some studies have been done by means of simulation [11] and test bed [7].

3.2 Multi-hop node degree

The current research of connectivity mostly focuses on the following two major questions: (1) how to achieve a k-connected network; (2) what is the degree distribution of a node. For instance, [6] has studied the degree distribution of one node in ad-hoc networks through a combination of analytical modeling and simulation. It is binomial for low value of the mean degree. Therefore, by given network density and communication range, we can obtain the distribution of number of direct neighbors one node has.

However, we have not found any research describing the degree distribution multiple hops away. In here, we define the i-hop node degree to be the number of nodes one node can reach within exactly i number of hops, but not fewer than that. Let us observe the neighbors of one node. Let N_i denote the i-hop node degree. For a random geometric graph, the distribution of N_i can be derived from N_{i-1}, conditioned on the position and the number of the nodes reachable in i-1 hops. Theoretically, we can derive N_i in this way. However, the formula is going to be too complex to calculate. We cannot obtain the exact distribution formula for more than one hop. Therefore, we will take a step back and observe the upper bound of this problem.

3.3 Modeling assumptions

As we mentioned above, we model our network based on random geometric graph, where nodes are uniformly distributed in a certain area. To observe the entire network as one graph, we assume the graph is connected, which implies that no node is isolated. For a given node density n, total number of nodes Num, and the probability that the network has no isolated node p_c, we can obtain the minimum communication range r_0 for which there is no node isolated in the network [2]:

$$r_0 \geq \sqrt{\frac{-\ln\left(1 - p_c^{1/Num}\right)}{n\pi}}. \tag{1}$$

In our model, we abstract from the fact that communication between two nodes is subject to various kinds of time- and place-dependent propagation effects, which would imply that the communication range is also varying with time and place. Therefore, we fix the communication range for each node to r. To simplify our analysis, and to achieve with high probability a network without isolated nodes, we assume a very high-density network.

3.4 i-hop communication range

In line with our assumptions, a node can reach all the nodes located within the circle with the radius of r whose center is the position of the node A as shown in Fig. 2a. Node B, which is located within the annulus R_2 with outer circle radius $2r$ and the inner circle radius r, will reach the center node A, if and only if there is a node C located within the intersection area S_{AB} of the communication range of A and B, as shown in Fig. 2a. Because the distance between A and B is between r and $2r$, the intersection of circle A and B S_{AB} is between 0 and $\frac{2}{3}\pi r^2 - \frac{\sqrt{3}}{2}r^2$.

Since we have assumed that nodes are uniformly distributed in the network, the number of nodes located in the intersection area S_{AB} fits the Poisson distribution with $\lambda_{AB} = S_{AB} \cdot n$. We set the probability that there is at least one node located in the area S_{AB} as $P(N_{AB}>0)$, which is also the probability of having a path between A and B. This probability equals 1 minus the probability that no node is located in the area S_{AB}:

$$P(B \text{ is a 2-hop neighbor of } A \mid B \text{ is in } R_2) = P(N_{AB} > 0) = 1 - P(N_{AB} = 0). \tag{2}$$

Since the number of nodes is Poisson distributed, formula (2) can be rewritten as:

$$P(N_{AB} > 0) = 1 - e^{-\lambda_{AB}} = 1 - e^{-S_{AB} \cdot n} \quad \left(0 < S_{AB} < \frac{2}{3}\pi r^2 - \frac{\sqrt{3}}{2}r^2\right). \tag{3}$$

We can observe that if n is sufficiently large, $P(N_{AB}>0)$ goes to 1. This implies that with almost 100% probability there is a path between node A and B if the node density is sufficiently high:

$$\lim_{n \to \infty} P(B \text{ is a 2-hop neighbor of } A \mid B \text{ is in } R_2) \to 1. \tag{4}$$

Let us now have a look at node F in Fig. 2b, which is located within the annulus R_3 with outer circle radius $3r$ and the inner circle radius $2r$. Node F can reach the center node A, if and only if there is at least one node E located within the communication range of node F, and that node has a connection to node A. Therefore, the probability that node F is a 3-hop neighbor of A can be derived as:

$$P(F \text{ is a 3-hop neighbor of } A \mid F \text{ is in } R_3)$$
$$= P(\exists E : d(E,F) \le r \wedge E \text{ is a 2-hop neighbor of } A \mid F \text{ is in } R_3). \tag{5}$$

From Fig. 2b, we can observe that if node E is located outside ring R_2, the probability that E is a 2-hop neighbor of A is 0. Moreover, when the network density goes to infinite, from formula (4), we can obtain:

$$\lim_{n \to \infty} P\big(F \text{ is a 3 - hop neighbor of } A \mid F \text{ is in } R_3\big)$$

$$\to \lim_{n \to \infty} P\big(\exists E : d(E,F) \le r \wedge E \text{ is in } R_2 \mid F \text{ is in } R_3\big) \cdot \tag{6}$$

Since n goes to infinite, we have:

$$\lim_{n \to \infty} P\big(\exists E : d(E,F) \le r \wedge E \text{ is in } R_2 \mid F \text{ is in } R_3\big) \to 1. \tag{7}$$

In a similar way, we can deduce the formula for the probability of node X located in R_i is a i-hop neighbor node A as:

$$\lim_{n \to \infty} P\big(X \text{ is a i - hop neighbor of } A \mid X \text{ is in } R_i\big)$$

$$\to \lim_{n \to \infty} P\big(\exists Y : d(Y,X) \le r \wedge Y \text{ is } (i-1)\text{- hop neighbor of } A \mid X \text{ is in } R_i\big) \ . \tag{8}$$

$$\to \lim_{n \to \infty} P\big(\exists Y : d(Y,X) \le r \wedge Y \text{ is in } R_{i-1} \mid X \text{ is in } R_i\big) \to 1$$

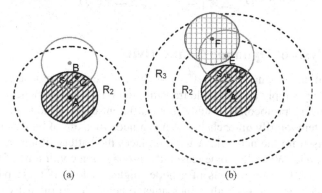

(a)   (b)

Fig. 2. (a) A and B are connected through C; (b) A and F are connected through E and D.

This shows that in a high-density network, when node X is located in R_i, X is an i-hop neighbor of A with almost 100% probability. Therefore, we assume a high density network in this paper. This implies that with very high probability, the network is connected. Further, adding or removing a node in the network will not influence the length of the shortest path between any two other nodes in the network. Formula (8) shows that in a high-density network, the probability of any node located in R_i being node A's i-hop neighbor goes to 1. That implies the i-hop communication range of node A goes to ir in a high-density network, which can be represented as:

$$\lim_{n \to \infty} \big(i \text{ - hop communcation range of } A\big) \to ir . \tag{9}$$

Therefore, in this paper we can use ir as our approximate i-hop communication range of node A with the assumption of a high-density network. The accuracy of this approximation depends on the actual network density, being highest at very high density.

3.5 Mean multi-hop node degree

We define the number of nodes that can be reached within i hops, but not fewer than i hops, as random variable N_i. Given formula (8), those nodes are located in the annulus with outer circle radius as ir and the inner circle radius as $(i-1)r$ in high density networks. The expected value of N_i can be written as:

$$\lim_{n \to \infty} E[N_i] = \begin{cases} 1 & i = 0 \\ n\pi r^2 \left(i^2 - (i-1)^2\right) = (2i-1)n\pi r^2 & (i > 0) \end{cases} \tag{10}$$

The total number of reachable nodes in i hops can be derived as $Totalnumofnodes_i = \sum_{j=0}^{i} N_j$. The expected total reachable nodes in i hops can be derived as:

$$\lim_{n \to \infty} E[Totalnumofnodes_i] = \lim_{n \to \infty} E\left[\sum_{j=0}^{i} N_j\right] = \lim_{n \to \infty} \sum_{j=0}^{i} E[N_j] = 1 + n\pi r^2 i^2. \tag{11}$$

4   Analysis of Dynamic Connectivity

In this section, we analyze the effect of dynamic connectivity, e.g., due to the limited battery supply and unstable transmission on the performance of our ABF-based discovery protocol. We study three different cases: a node disappears, appears, or is temporarily unreachable. When a node runs out of battery for instance, it disappears from the network. After it replaces the battery, it appears again as a brand new node. When for some reason the propagation conditions of the wireless medium are bad, some packets of a node might get lost. If these packets are a number of consecutive keep-alive messages, other nodes in the network will consider this node disappeared. After some time, the propagation conditions may improve so that the nodes packet will be received again. As a result, it reappears in the network. We will quantify the extra traffic load caused by those three different cases through an analytical approach and verify with the results from simulation.

Our model has been implemented with the discrete event simulator OPNET Modeler version 11.5. We observe the node density influence on the traffic load in all three experiments below. We place 25, 61, 100, 125, 150 nodes randomly into a $1700 \times 1700 m^2$ area with 300 meters communication range, r, for every node. Note that the 61 nodes scenario can generate networks that are 1-connected graphs with 90% probability (see formula (1)). Therefore, we consider the 25 nodes scenario as a low density network, and the 150 nodes scenario as a high-density network. We expect that simulation results obtained for this high-density network are close to our analytical analyses, as this analysis was based on the assumption of a very high node density. The node, which disappears, or appears, or is temporarily unreachable, is located in the center of the area to avoid border effects. For each parameter setting of the simulations introduced below, 30 independent runs will be done to calculate a 90% confidence interval.

Some basic ABF parameters are set as follows: number of hash functions per service, $b = 10$; ABF width, $w = 1024$ bits; ABF depth, $d = 3$; number of context sources advertised per node, $s = 1$.

4.1 Node disappearance

We start the analysis with the case of one node disappearing from the network. We assume that a node disappears at the moment the network has reached the stable state, i.e. all ABFs are up-to-date at the moment the node disappears. Possible reasons for node disappearance are insufficient battery supply, entering deep power saving mode, system shut down, un-functional antenna, system crash, etc. The absence of node A will be discovered by its direct neighbors when no keep-alive messages have been received for two consecutive keep-alive periods. Since the keep-alive period is unsynchronized, one of the direct neighbors B will notice this first. This node will remove the incoming ABF from node A. As a result, the representation of node A's context sources will be removed from layer 1 of B's outgoing ABF. For ease of explanation we will write that a node is advertised (or removed), where we actually mean that the context sources of a node are advertised (or removed). Since the other direct neighbors of A have advertised A in layer 1 of their ABF, node B will continue to advertise A in layer 2 of its ABF. As a matter of fact, we duplicate the local context sources of each node to every lower layer from layer 2 in the advertisement and maintenance phase of our protocol. This is because in a very high density network, if a path exists to a node, there are always longer paths to the same node. By duplicating a node's context sources to all lower layers in the ABF, we avoid that extra advertisements are exchanged to announce these longer path. So in the situation above, node B will still think that it can reach the services of node A via other neighbors. Therefore, those absent services are only removed from Layer 1 of the outgoing ABF from B.

There are two kinds of nodes that are the direct neighbor of B: direct neighbors of A and two-hop neighbors of A. The other direct nodes which receive this information will not take any action since they still think there are other routes to. As the last direct neighbor of A notices the disappearance of node A, it will realize that it cannot reach the absent services within one or two hops. It will start sending out an updated ABF with layer 1 and layer 2 cleaned up. Nodes which are two-hop neighbors of A that receive the updated ABF from direct neighbors of A will also take no action, until all their direct neighbors which are also the direct neighbors of A notice the absence of A. Only then these nodes will realize there is no path to A with 2 hops. They will send out an ABF with layer 2 cleaned up (Note that these two-hop neighbors do not have node A's information on layer 1). This clean up will be spread till $(d-1)$-hop neighbors based in a similar way.

It is a very complex procedure to clean up the services. Every node i-hop away has to clean up $(d-i)$ layers in total. It will clean up layer j $(i \leq j \leq d-1)$ once it realizes there is no route to the service within j hops. Every node cleans up the service layer by layer. Only the last node in the ith hop that realizes the absent service will clean up two layers at once. When removing the context sources of node A from the ABF at a certain layer, there is a slight chance that no changes to the ABF are required, because the bits that would have to be set to zero have to remain one, as they also represent other context sources in other nodes. This is the same property that causes a false positive when querying context sources. In [8] we have already defined and derived this probability. We use $P_{fp,i}$ to represent the false positive probability of layer i. [8] has proved that

$$P_{fp,i} \approx \left(1 - e^{\frac{-bx_i}{w}}\right)^{b} \tag{12}$$

where x_j denotes the total number of i layers context sources in layer i, with $x_i = s \cdot \left(1 + n\pi r^2 i^2\right)$. $P_{fp,i}$ is the probability that no changes have to be made to layer i of an ABF, upon the disappearance of node A, provided that node A has only one context source advertised. If node A advertises s context sources, the probability that no changes have to be made to layer i is raised to the power s, i.e. $P^s_{fp,i}$. Therefore, we can derive the expected number of clean-up updates while one node disappears, $E[N_{updates\text{-}disa}]$, as:

$$
E[N_{updates-disa}] \approx \sum_{i=1}^{d-2}\left((E[N_i]-1)\cdot\sum_{j=i}^{d-1}\left(1-P^s_{fp,j}\right)+\sum_{j=i+1}^{d-1}\left(1-P^s_{fp,j}\right)\right)+E[N_{d-1}]\cdot\left(1-P^s_{fp,d-1}\right)
$$

$$
\approx \sum_{i=1}^{d-1}E[N_i]\cdot\sum_{j=i}^{d-1}\left(1-\left(1-e^{\frac{-bx_j}{w}}\right)^{sb}\right)-\sum_{j=2}^{d-1}\left(1-\left(1-e^{\frac{-bx_j}{w}}\right)^{sb}\right) \tag{13}
$$

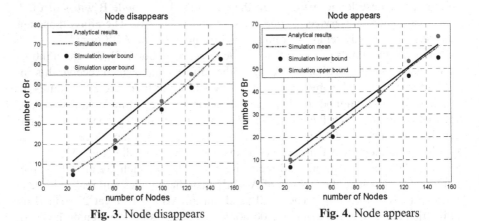

Fig. 3. Node disappears   **Fig. 4.** Node appears

We verify the results of this approximation with simulations. In here, we study the traffic load generated by one node disappearance under different network density see Fig.3. We found that the analytical results are slightly higher than the simulation results. This is because our analytical analysis is based on the assumption of a very high density network, so that the i-hop node degree is slightly overestimated. In that respect, our analysis provides an upper bound to the expected number of updates. In our scenarios, there are fewer nodes involved in updating and more nodes clean up more than one layer of filter at once. This results in fewer update packets sent out than we estimate in formula (13). We also observe that the higher the network density, the smaller difference there is between analytical and simulation analysis as we expected from our assumption.

4.2 Node appearance

In this section, we consider the scenario that one new node appears in the network. The reason could be that the node just switches on. We assume that the new node is familiar with the standardized format and hash functions of attenuated Bloom filters used in the current network. However, the node does not have knowledge about nodes and context sources in the network. First of all, this node will broadcast its filter (size of $w \times d$ bits) with its local services. The direct neighbors who receive this filter will update theirs. Those new filters will be broadcasted around. The new node waits for a short moment, till it receives all the neighbors' replies. It aggregates all incoming filters, updates its own filter and broadcasts it. Note that, the network is assumed to have a high node density, which means that the appearance of the new node will not generate any shorter path between any pair of existing nodes. Therefore, for any node up to d-1 hops away from the new node, only the appearance of the new node will be added into the existing filters. Further, since the local information is duplicated to every layer of the ABF before it is sent out, there will not be a loop between neighbors to add the information layer by layer. After the initial broadcast, every node, including the new one, will only update once. The expected number of updates can be quantified as the total number of nodes within range plus one:

$$E\left[N_{update-a}\right] = E\left[Totalnumofnodes_{d-1}\right]+1 = 2 + n\pi\left(r \cdot (d-1)\right)^2 \qquad (14)$$

We observe the traffic load generated by one node appearing in networks with various densities. We expected fewer broadcasts to be generated in the simulation than in the analytical study. Because the node density is not infinitely high, there are fewer nodes in reach than we expected in the analytical study. However, it turns out that the load is quite accurately predicted by the analytical model. This is because in a very high density network as we assumed, one nodes' appearance will not generate new shortest paths between any pair of nodes. In the lower density networks we simulated, quite some nodes update more than once, because extra new indirect neighbors are discovered due to the appearance of one node. Interestingly, as shown in Fig 4, we found that the number of extra updates compensates the number of extra nodes we estimated in the analytical study. Of course, the higher the network density is, the more accurately the i-hop node degree is approximated, and fewer new neighbors are discovered due to one node appearance.

4.3 Packet loss

In this section, we study the situation when some packets of a node get lost, due to unfavorable propagation conditions. If at least two keep-alive messages from a node are lost consecutively, the other neighbors of the node consider the node disappeared. They start cleaning up their ABFs as we described in Section 4.1. After some time, the transmission quality of the node gets better, and keep-alive messages will be received again. The neighbors think there is a new node appearing in the network. The actions as addressed Section 4.2 will be taken. Here, we assume that the packet loss only occurs in one direction, i.e., we assume the node can still receive packets from its neighbors. Therefore, it keeps updated information of the neighbors. This is a slight difference from the scenario in Section 4.2. In Section 4.2, the appearing node does not have any knowledge about the network. Therefore, in here, one update less is generated than in section 4.2. The number of updates generated in this scenario, N_{packet_loss}, can be obtained as:

$$N_{packet\_loss} = N_{update-disa} + N_{updates-a} - 1 \qquad (15)$$

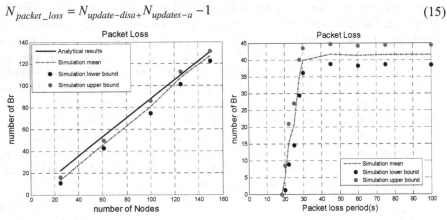

Fig. 5. Effect of Packet loss   **Fig. 6.** Effect of Packet loss periods

We compared this with simulation results in networks of various densities, as shown in Fig.6. The keep-alive period, i.e. the time between two consecutive keep-alive messages is distributed uniformly in the interval [15, 17] seconds. Packet loss period is 45 sec, which guarantees at least two continuous keep-alive messages are lost. Simulation results are slightly lower than analytical results. All the reasons we mentioned above in Section 4.1 and 4.2 influence the results of this experiment as well. We also did an experiment to study the effect of different packet loss periods, which is shown in Fig.6. We use the 61-node scenario. We vary the packet loss period from 18sec to 100 sec. When there is only one packet lost, there is no update needed in the network, since nodes are only considered disappeared if no keep-alive messages have been received for two keep-alive periods. When there are at least two packets lost consecutively, updates are generated. When reappearance period is between 20 and 45 sec, some of the nodes notice the node disappearance, but the node reappears before its information has been removed from the network totally. The longer the period is, the more updates can be done before the reappearance of the node. Therefore, the number of updates is growing in this period. After 45 sec period, the number of packets generated is almost constant. This is because the nodes have enough time to complete the updates for disappearance within this time period.

4.4 Summary and discussion

We have derived analytical expressions for the number of additional broadcasts in an ad-hoc network using ABF-based context discovery. These expressions approximate the expected number of additional broadcasts, in case the network density is sufficiently high. From the comparisons above, we observed that analytical the formulas are indeed more accurate for higher density network. This fits our hypothesis. The higher the network density is, the more accurate our approximation of the i-hop node degree. Further, since the proposed protocol automatically duplicates the Bloom filter representing its own context sources to all lower layers of the ABF, the appearance of a new node can be handled in a single pass of advertisement. No advertisements have to go up and down to propagate the availability of indirect paths to the new node into the lower layers of the ABF. However, in the case of removal of a node, multiple passes are needed to remove its representation completely from all ABFs. Removal of context sources has to be done layer by layer, as the equivalent of duplication cannot be performed. Therefore, adding a node generates less traffic than removing a node.

An important issue to improve the performance of ABF-based ad-hoc networks in dynamic environments is to reduce the traffic while removing context sources. One of the possible solutions to improve the protocol is to be more conservative when adding information regarding new context sources to the ABFs. We could add certain policies to restrict adding new context sources, based on the quality level of the source, such as stability, bandwidth, and distance, etc. Only "good quality" and "valuable" information will be added into ABFs. By restricting incoming information, we can reduce the traffic for removing context sources that are most probably not used during their presence. In section 4.2, we have studied the update traffic caused by node appearance without outdated information which needs to be cleaned up. However, in reality this is not always the case. Nodes might appear in an environment where its advertised services may still be present somewhere in some of the ABFs, especially in the case when a node is moving. Based on our study, we found it is mathematically unachievable to quantify the update traffic load caused by this type of clean up. We can consider a moving node as a more complex action, which extends the actions of nodes appearing and disappearing.

5   Conclusions and Further Work

In this paper, we have extended the performance analysis of ABF-based ad-hoc networks to a dynamic environment where nodes appear and leave the network, or are temporarily unreachable due to poor propagation conditions. We have used random geometric graphs to model our network topology. In order to be able to approximate the i-hop node degree accurately, we assume that the network density is very high. The study has been done analytically to quantify the update traffic caused by a node appearing, disappearing, or being temporarily unreachable. We verify the analytical results with simulations. The analytical formulas give more accurate results when the network density is higher. We discovered that it is easier to add context information than to remove it. Especially, in the case when context information moves out of the range of some nodes but still can be reached by other nodes, there are many dynamic parameters, such as node positions and network topology, needed to compute the exact network traffic. This part of work cannot be done analytically.

In the experiments, we observed that there is much less traffic generated by adding context information than removing. Therefore, reducing broadcast traffic for removing context sources is an important topic of further study.

References

1. T. Albero, V. Sempere, J. Mataix, "A Study of Mobility and Research in Ad Hoc Networks Using Stochastic Activity Networks", in *Proc. of the 2nd Conference on Next Generation Internet Design and Engineering, 2006, NGI '06*, Valencia, Spain, April 2006.
2. C. Bettstetter, "On the Minimum node Degree and Connectivity of a Wireless Multihop Networks", in *Proc. of the 3rd ACM International Symposium on Mobile Ad Hoc Networking and Computing, MOBIHOC'02*, EPF Lausanne, Switzerland, June 2002.
3. B. H. Bloom, "Space/Time Trade-offs in Hash Coding with Allowable Errors", *Communications of the ACM 13(7)*: 422-426.
4. B. Clark, C. Colbourn, D. Johnson, "Unit Disk Graphs", *Discrete Metematics*, vol. 86, no. 1-3, pp. 165-177, December 1990.
5. P.T.H. Goering, G.J. Heijenk, B. Haverkort, R. Haarman, "Effect of Mobility on Local Service Discovery in Ad-Hoc", in *Proc. of Performance Engineering Workshop*, 2007, Berlin, Germany, September, 2007.
6. R. Hekmat, P. Van Mieghem, "Degree Distribution and Hopcount in Wireless Ad-hoc Networks", in *Proc. of the 11th IEEE ICON2003*, Sydney, Austrilia, September 2003.
7. V. Lenders, J. Wagner, M. May, "Analyzing the impact of mobility in Ad Hoc Networks", in *Proc. of the 2nd international workshop on Multi-hop ad hoc networks: from theory to reality 2006, REALMAN2006*, Florence, Italy, May, 2006.
8. F. Liu, G. Heijenk, "Context Discovery Using Attenuated Bloom filters in Ad-hoc Networks", in *Journal of Internet Engineering*, 2007, Vol. 1, No. 1, pp. 49-58.
9. F. Liu, P. Goering, G. Heijenk, "Modeling Service Discovery in Ad-hoc Networks", in Proc. of *the 4th ACM International Workshop on Performance Evaluation of Wireless Ad Hoc, Sensor, and Ubiquitous Networks, PE-WASUN 2007* , Chania, Crete Island, October 2007.
10. M. Penrose, "Random Geometric Graphs", *Oxford University Press Inc.*, 2003.
11. D. Trajanov, S. Filiposka, M. Efnuseva, A. Grnarov, "Ad Hoc Networks Connection Availability Modeling", in Proc. Of *the 1st ACM international workshop on Performance evaluation of wireless ad hoc, sensor, and ubiquitous networks, PE WASUN'04*,Venice, 2004.

Impact of Mobility on Epidemic Broadcast in DTNs

Francesco Giudici, Elena Pagani and Gian Paolo Rossi

Information Science and Communication Department, Università degli Studi di Milano, Italy, e-mail: {fgiudici,pagani,rossi}@dico.unimi.it

Abstract The broadcast diffusion of messages in Delay Tolerant Networks (DTNs) is heavily dependent on the mobility of the nodes, since protocols must rely on contact opportunities among devices to diffuse data. This work is the first effort of studying how the dynamics of nodes affect both the effectiveness of the broadcast protocols in diffusing the data, and their efficiency in using the network resources. The paper describes three simple self-adaptive control mechanisms that keep the broadcast overhead low, while ensuring high node coverage. Those mechanisms characterize a family of protocols able to achieve some awareness about the surrounding environment, and to use this knowledge in order to improve performances. Simulation results allow to identify the winning mechanisms to diffuse messages in DTNs under different conditions.

1 Introduction

The mobile nodes of a delay and disruption tolerant network, or DTN [6], experiment intermittent connectivity, network partitions and poor radio link quality. So far, in such a critical scenario, the research mainly focused on the problem of providing unicast communications (e.g., [5, 12, 13, 1, 18]). By contrast, the one-to-all communication scheme has not received the same attention despite the fact that its service is strategic to support protocols at both application and routing levels. For instance, a broadcast service is required to diffuse scoped advertisements – e.g. about available services or events – and summaries [14], to support podcasting [15], to upload software patches or new parameter settings – e.g. in environmental observation systems – or to diffuse acknowledgements, or cure, packets [9]. In a DTN, broadcast can be designed by adopting one of the gossip-based mechanisms that have been proposed in the literature in a few slightly different alternatives by starting from the following basic scheme: when a node has in its cache a message m to diffuse, it forwards m to one or more (and possibly all) neighbors it happens to encounter while moving. The forwarding, elsewhere called infection or epidemic, can be either performed periodically [17] or whenever the contact occurs [21]. Infection can continue up to the message life time or up to a given hop/copy count. It is easy to show [8] that this simple PUSH-based algorithm provides an effective broadcast service, by achieving a node coverage arbitrarily close to 1 with a low latency, but fails in doing this ef-

Please use the following format when citing this chapter:

Giudici, F., Pagani, E. and Rossi, G.P., 2008, in IFIP International Federation for Information Processing, Volume 284; *Wireless and Mobile Networking;* Zoubir Mammeri; (Boston: Springer), pp. 421–434.

ficiently. The inefficient use of the network resources seriously limits the practical use of the protocol. This is mainly motivated by the fact that nodes perform epidemic forwarding with a very limited knowledge about the state of the encountered nodes and, as a consequence, they often happen to forward the message to already infected nodes. There are several, growing levels of knowledge a node can achieve about the neighbors state and to approximate the global system state. They range from zero knowledge, as for the sketched stateless PUSH-based algorithm [21] and for the SA-BCAST described in [8], to full knowledge, which can be approximated by maintaining some log of encounters and by enabling the log exchange among encountering nodes, [16].

The primary focus in the design of a deployable, i.e. both efficient and effective, broadcast protocol is to increase the node likelihood of delivering the message only to uninfected nodes. However, whatever is the followed approach to achieve efficiency, the performances of the algorithms are greatly influenced by the mobility patterns that nodes follow, [2], and a mechanism properly working when nodes move according to the random waypoint model may be totally useless when they move according to a different mobility model. The comparative analysis of the effects of mobility on DTN protocols deserves more attention and, as far as we know, has never been applied to broadcast. This paper moves into this research track and provides some interesting contributions to understand broadcast delivery over DTNs under different mobility conditions. Firstly, the paper defines a family of broadcast protocols obtained by starting from the above mentioned PUSH-based forwarding protocol and by leveraging its behaviors through the incremental introduction of autonomic and adaptive mechanisms whose purpose is the improvement of the node awareness about the level of infection in the neighborhood. Secondly, the performances of the different mechanisms are analyzed in 3 different mobility models: the classical random way point, RWP, mobility model [2], the swarm mobility model [10], SWR, and the aggregation model, AGG, in which nodes move throughout aggregation points according to some spatial or functional mobility law. The main contribution of the paper is twofold: (*i*) it identifies and characterizes the winning mechanisms to diffuse messages in DTNs under different conditions; (*ii*) it is the first attempt to move toward the design of an autonomic and situational algorithm able of autonomously deriving the mobility context the node is moving through, and adapting its parameters accordingly in order to optimize performances.

2 System and Mobility Models

2.1 System Model

The scenario we consider in this paper includes people walking in a limited urban area, such as a *campus area*, and equipped with wireless portable devices. No base stations are assumed and the communication between a source *s* and a destination

d may eventually occur through either direct contact, when, for instance, node d moves into the range of s, or indirect contact, when one or more relaying nodes help to create the multi-hop path towards the destination and the last of them finally enters the range of d. The devices have a unique identifier ID, are not required to have positioning capabilities on board and, to meet resource saving requirements, are supposed to adopt a short radio range to communicate. This latter point, together with the fact that devices can be sparsely distributed over a large area, makes high the probability of network partitions and link disruption. Throughout the paper we only assume that each mobile device, or node, periodically broadcasts a *beacon* message in its radio cell. Beacons are used to discover other devices in the neighborhood and their content is limited to the device identifier. In such a scenario, people mobility might follow either a Random Waypoint model [2] or a more structured motion, as described in the next subsection.

2.2 Mobility Models

A great deal of research is currently ongoing in order to characterize mobility models suitable for opportunistic networks. Mobility could be extracted from traces of movements of nodes in real settings; several traces are for instance provided by the CRAWDAD community [4]. The use of traces with simulators creates, however, some problems. Their timescale is hardly scaled to the simulation time and they generally model the specific behavior of a given mobility scenario thus loosing the generality required during the protocol design phase. Traces are more likely useful during the validation process than during the design and performance analysis phase.

In this work, we analyze how three basic movement models affect the performance of the epidemic protocols described in sec.3. The models are: Random Waypoint (RWP), aggregation (AGG) and swarm (SWR). The classical RWP model is not realistic, but it is simple, often provided within network simulators, and the most commonly used in the literature. In the AGG model, a node moves toward an aggregation point (ap), chosen from a set according to a certain probability distribution P_{AGG}, and once there it pauses for a time t_{AGG} before selecting the next ap. This model reproduces mobility of users who may group in interest points according to some spatial or functional rule. Parameters of this model are also the number and position of aps over the area, the speed range $[v_{min}, v_{max}]$ and the radius of the aps. The arrival point of a node inside an ap can be determined according to a Gaussian distribution centered at the center of the ap and with standard deviation σ_{AGG}. In the SWR model, nodes move in a coordinated way. Each swarm has a logical center, which moves toward a destination chosen randomly. Once there, the nodes in the swarm stop for a pause time t_{SWR} before moving to a new destination. Each swarm has a number of nodes determined by a probability distribution with mean μ_{SWR} and standard deviation σ_{SWR}. Nodes in a swarm move randomly around its logical center, within maximum distance d_{SWR}. If the regions of two swarms overlap, nodes in the intersection may choose to migrate to the other swarm according to a probability M_{SWR}.

The RWP model reproduces sporadic encounters of two (or a few) nodes. The AGG model reproduces the encounters of many nodes, with nodes experiencing relevant neighborhood changes every time they enter an *ap*. The SWR model reproduces nodes maintaining the same neighborhood for a long time, with sporadic encounters with other (groups of) nodes. Analyzing these three basic models allows to bring into evidence the effects each of them separately has on message diffusion. However, mobility of people in an opportunistic scenario is more likely modeled by the combination of the above three patterns. At the best of our knowledge, the research community has not yet produced a synthetic model that addresses these issues or adopts statistical distributions inferred from real traces [4].

Whatever is the adopted mobility model, it should be assumed that the following *mobility assumption* applies: when a contact occurs, the reciprocal speed is such that the two nodes can set up a communication channel and a significant amount of data is exchanged before they become disconnected. This assumption is reasonable according to results achieved by observations reported in [19, 11], but can be occasionally violated in our simulations.

3 A Family of Broadcast Protocols for DTNs

Given a general DTN scenario as described in the previous section, purpose of this paper is the comparative analysis of a family of topology-independent broadcast protocols under different mobility conditions. Protocols are obtained by the incremental introduction of adaptive and situational mechanisms that progressively augment the protocol capability to adapt to changing conditions. Purpose of the paper is the evaluation of the role played by the different mechanisms and parameter settings to ensure broadcast *effectiveness*, i.e. the capability of the protocol to eventually achieve node coverage arbitrarily close to 1, and *efficiency*, i.e. the capability of the protocol to keep the generated broadcasts-per-message as close as possible to $O(n \ln n)$ [3]. Each broadcast message m is supposed to have a *"scope"* that is defined by the source and specified through a *lifetime*; when this time expires, a node deletes the copy of m and stops its diffusion. In the following, we assume long lived messages to better understand the broadcast behavior independently of other constraints.

The basic broadcast protocol to start with is represented by the above mentioned PUSH-based algorithm: a node p, holding a message m, starts a forwarding of m with probability $Prob_p = 1$ whenever a node enters its radio range. We indicate this protocol with the name P-BCAST. It is possible to improve P-BCAST behaviors by adding some autonomic capability that extracts an approximation of global state from locally observed data.

The first improvement of P-BCAST is to let p start the forwarding of m when the percentage of neighborhood change with respect to the previous diffusion exceeds a threshold *Nth*. To this purpose, each node maintains a local view of the neighborhood changes by exploiting the underlying beaconing. To avoid broadcast storms, the nodes in range adopt a random mechanism that desynchronizes transmissions and suppresses duplicates. This way, p, and the nodes in range of p, control the duplicate generation and maximize the probability of infecting new nodes by adopting a membership-driven infection. This *reactive* mechanism is supposed not to be influential when moving according to RWP in sparse conditions, which is very close to model a single encounter scenario; by contrast, it should positively affect performances when moving according to AGG.

A second, *adaptive* mechanism can be adopted to let a node p to be able to tune the value of $Prob_p$ according to the delivery status of m in the area where p is moving. In fact, when most nodes in the neighborhood have delivered m, p should reduce the probability $Prob_p$ of a new diffusion accordingly, and vice versa. In a zero knowledge paradigm, the node p is unable to achieve this type of knowledge; however, p can derive the symptoms of the delivery status from sensing the events generated by its encounters. The number of received duplicates of m is the first of these symptoms; it reveals that other encounters have delivered m and is helpful to decrease, according to a given function $\mathscr{F}$, the local value of $Prob_p$. In [8], it has been shown that this simple mechanism works properly to limit the number of duplicates under high coverage conditions and, with the addition of some further control mechanism, it is also able to promptly increase $Prob_p$ when p moves from a covered area to another where m has not been widely delivered. Both the *reactive* and the *adaptive* mechanisms are part of a new protocol that we will call self-adaptive broadcast, or SA-BCAST.

In [8], the authors have observed that SA-BCAST is unable to terminate before the message lifetime expires. This is intuitively motivated by observing that the algorithm has to ensure a drip feed of message transmissions to manage node joins and temporary partitions. A non-terminating protocol has severe effects on the efficiency that can be only mitigated by adding more knowledge to the nodes about their neighborhood. The introduction of an encounters' history can provide the extra information required and moves the protocol from a zero-knowledge paradigm to a full knowledge one.

To verify the benefits of a history-based algorithm, we implemented the following simple mechanism: each node maintains a *history* of the nodes to which it forwarded m and from which it received a duplicate. In order to speed up the learning process, we allow the *history* exchange among encounters by piggybacking it on m. If a node p encounters a node it has in the local history, then p suppresses the message forwarding. The history mechanism can be added to both the above mentioned protocols to obtain HP-BCAST and HSA-BCAST.

The described mechanisms lead to a family of broadcast protocols whose behavior has been mainly designed to properly work under both RWP and AGG mobility models. By contrast, the SWR mobility generates some new issues that deserve specific attention. In fact, with this setting, we will show in the next section that the 100% coverage is hard to reach, while a high number of duplicates might be generated. In order to achieve high effectiveness while maintaining an acceptable efficiency, a mechanism of *local duplicate suppression* has been added to HP-BCAST (thus obtaining LP-BCAST) and HSA-BCAST (LSA-BCAST). When a beacon from a new neighbor is received, a node *p* sets a timer slightly larger than the beacon period. When the timer expires, the message is sent with the history, *including all the nodes that are new neighbors.* If another infected node with the timer set receives this message, it schedules its own transmission only if it has new neighbors not included in the history. This way, diffusion is not prevented for nodes that connect two swarms or two different groups in a swarm, but multiple infections of the same nodes are avoided. The local suppression mechanism leads to obtain the complete family of protocols shown in fig.1.

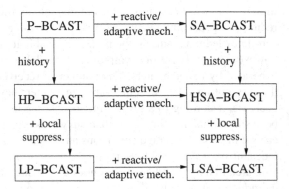

Fig. 1 Family of adaptive protocols

4 Performance Evaluation

4.1 Simulated Conditions and Performance Indexes

We implemented the described protocols in the framework of the GloMoSim [20] simulation environment. The simulation setting considers a system of 50 nodes sparsely distributed over a 1000×1000 m. area. Nodes move at a speed in $[1,2]$ m/s, thus reproducing a pedestrian environment. They are equipped with a low power 802.11 radio device with 10 m. communication range and DCF at the MAC layer. Beaconing is performed every 1 sec.; after 3 missing beacons, the corresponding neighbor is removed from the neighbor list.

The simulations run different values of *Nth* and two different functions $\mathscr{F}$: a linearly decreasing function (or Lin10) and an inverse exponential function (or InvExp). When an infected node *p* receives a duplicate from a node that is infected from less than 3 min., then *p* sets $Prob_p$ to MAXP= 1. Otherwise, $Prob_p$ is either decremented of 0.1 or halved in line with functions Lin10 or InvExp, respectively. $Prob_p$ has a lower bound defined by MINP= 0.01. We consider long lived broadcasts, with simulations lasting up to 6 hours. All simulation results are averaged over 50 simulations performed with variable random seed. The mobility models are provided by BonnMotion [7]; in order to allow movements to reach a steady state, the first 1000 sec. of the traces are not considered for the measures. The parameters of the different mobility models are presented in the next subsections.

Performance indexes are the *coverage*, i.e. the percentage of nodes infected, the *duplicate messages* (a message is a duplicate if it is received by an already infected node), and the *target ratio* $T = (msgrecv - dups)/msgrecv$, with *msgrecv* the total number of messages received and *dups* the total number of duplicates among them. T is a measure of efficiency in using the network resources. Of course, T is optimized by $dups = 0$ and is affected by the number of the encounter nodes and by the progress of the infection in the neighborhood. In fact, packets are broadcast to the nodes in range, let us say k; so that, for any message sent, we count $msgrec = k$ and the *dups* value depends on the level of infection among the k nodes.

4.2 Random Waypoint vs. Aggregation Model

In the measurements presented in this section, the pause time for the RWP model is 0. With AGG, we performed experiments with a number of *aps* variable from 3 to 10, uniformly distributed in the area . A node stops in an *ap* for 10 minutes. The next *ap* is chosen according to a uniform probability distribution. The distance of a node from the *ap* center is determined by σ_{AGG} in $[0, 15]$, and follows the probability distribution reported in Table 1.

Table 1 Distribution of distance of nodes from *ap* center

σ	68.3%	99.0%	99.7%
0	0 m.	0 m.	0 m.
5	5 m.	12.9 m.	15 m.
10	10 m.	25.8 m.	30 m.
15	15 m.	38.7 m.	45 m.

When switching to the AGG model, SA-BCAST fruitfully uses the contact opportunities in *aps* to speed up the infection (fig.2). The collateral effect is that SA-BCAST, although able of smoothing down the generated traffic as soon as a high coverage is reached (fig.2), is too aggressive in diffusing when nodes are in an *ap*, thus generating a high number of duplicates (fig.3). Some improvements can be achieved with a more stringent $\mathscr{F}$, as shown in fig.3 for $\sigma_{AGG} = 10$. With $Nth > 100$ some contact opportunities may be missed, thus further reducing traffic; coverage is anyway achieved, although with a higher latency, thanks to the existence of multiple relays. The number of *aps* also has impact: when it tends to ∞, the RWP and AGG models coincide. By contrast, with 3 *aps* we observed more duplicates, because

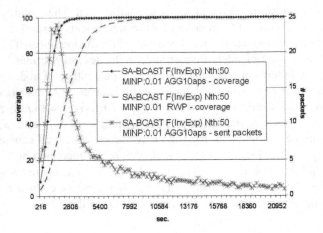

Fig. 2 Coverage and number of generated packets vs. time for SA-BCAST in either the RWP or the AGG model, with $\sigma_{AGG} = 10$

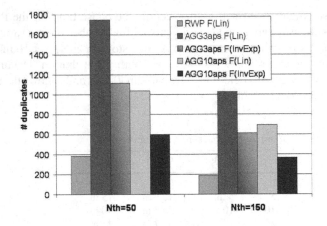

Fig. 3 Cumulative number of duplicates after 6 hours, for different mobility models, $\mathscr{F}$, Nth, with $\sigma_{AGG} = 10$

(*i*) nodes are more dense in *ap*s, and (*ii*) there is a higher probability of encounters during movements between two *ap*s, which are used for dissemination.

An interesting aspect is shown in fig.4, where the network coverage is reported for a single simulation; in order to emphasize the behavior, with $\mathscr{F} = \mathsf{InvExp}$ the $Prob_p$ is decreases by dividing the current value by 20. With 10 *ap*s, where encounters during movements are more sporadic, coverage increases in steps, which correspond to relevant membership changes in the *ap*s. Steps become less high with the progress of the simulation, because the probability of entering an *ap* with already infected nodes increases. This behavior is much more evident for $Prob_p$ decreasing more quickly. It confirms that SA-BCAST, although nodes are unaware of being either in an *ap* or on the road, allows to effectively exploit node density to increase the coverage. However, this is achieved at the expenses of efficiency. The size of the aggregation area also has impact (fig.5): with a larger σ_{AGG}, nodes in an *ap* are not all in mutual communication range. When a node enters in an *ap*, the messages exchanged do not affect all nodes and, at the same time, reduce $Prob_p$ thus preventing excessive diffusion. Yet, efficiency is still far from that achieved in the RWP model. The lesson learnt is thus that:

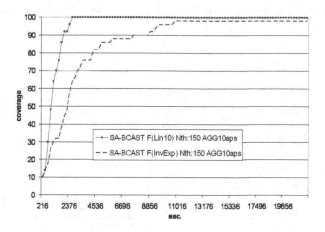

Fig. 4 Progress of coverage vs. time in a single simulation, with $\sigma_{AGG} = 10$

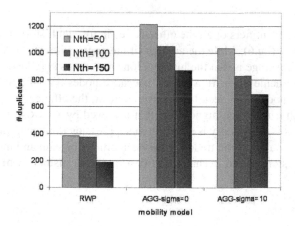

Fig. 5 Cumulative number of duplicates after 6 hours for SA-BCAST with $\mathscr{F}$ =Lin10, variable *Nth* and mobility model, and 10 *ap*s

- with sporadic encounters, monitoring both the neighborhood and the infection state allows to guarantee both effectiveness and efficiency; but,
- in aggregation points, slowing down diffusion when duplicates are received is a late reaction. Moreover, when the nodes are all infected, encounters in densely populated regions generate a large amount of useless traffic, due to the lack of knowledge about the system state. The need of a stop condition is much more evident.

We then measured the performance achieved with HP-BCAST and HSA-BCAST. In our measures, we assume that each node has enough memory to record up to 50 encounters. The history actually implements a stop condition because, when

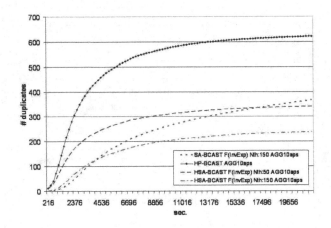

Fig. 6 Cumulative number of generated duplicates vs. time with and without history, in AGG model with $\sigma_{AGG} = 10$

each node has the identifiers of all the other nodes in its own history, no message is anymore generated (fig.6), while the number of messages with SA-BCAST diverges. Its effect on the coverage is that the history alone (HP-BCAST) reduces the latency; this effect is also achieved in HSA-BCAST because nodes are able to react to the encounter with a node never seen before. By contrast, the efficiency achieved with HSA-BCAST with *ap*s is even higher than that achieved by SA-BCAST in the RWP model (fig.7), that is, the history is effective in suppressing duplicate transmissions. We are currently analyzing the trade-off between efficiency gain and memory overhead for history storage and exchange, in case a partial history is maintained or exchanged.

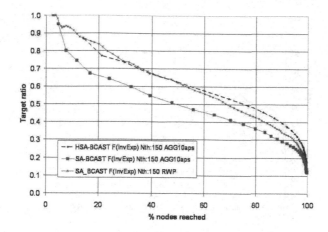

Fig. 7 Target ratio vs. coverage with and without history, in RWP and AGG model with $\sigma_{AGG} = 10$

4.3 Aggregation vs. Swarm Model

The SWR model used in the experiments has pause time of 10 minutes, $\sigma_{SWR} = 1.73$, μ_{SWR} of 4 or 15, $d_{SWR} = 15$ m., and $M_{SWR} = 0.2$. With this model, coverage can be incremented when two swarms partially overlap, one of which has already been infected. On the other hand, once a swarm has been infected, the nodes belonging to it should refrain from transmitting again till the swarm membership does not change. Hence, better performance is achieved with Nth low, which promptly detects swarm overlapping. In fig.8, the performance of SA-BCAST is reported for $\mathscr{F} =$ Lin10; with $\mathscr{F} =$ InvExp the coverage achieved is worse. Yet, in the latter case a lower number of duplicates is generated (fig.9). Hence, the InvExp function has been adopted for experiments with HSA-BCAST and LSA-BCAST.

The local suppression mechanism does not provide benefits in the aggregation model. However, in the SWR model (figs.8 and 9) it is able to improve both coverage and – above all – efficiency. This derives from the small delay before diffusing: if two swarms A and B are overlapping, such that nodes in A own m while nodes in B do not, an infected node in swarm A is likely to observe a sequence of new neighbors appearing at a short interval one after another. One "late" transmission allows to infect more new neighbors at one time. At the same time, the history mechanism allows infection propagation in swarm B: the newly infected nodes in the intersection have empty histories. They see all their neighbors in swarm B as not being in their histories, thus starting message diffusion. This repeats recursively till the whole swarm B is infected.

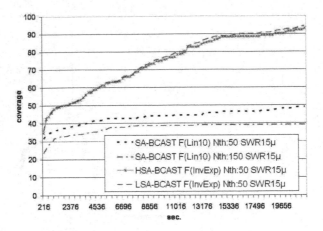

Fig. 8 Coverage vs. time for different protocols

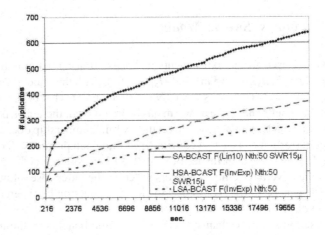

Fig. 9 Cumulative number of duplicates vs. time for different protocols

5 Conclusions and Future Work

A family of protocols – adopting different mechanisms to adapt the infection aggressiveness – has been measured in different mobility models. The AGG model brings into evidence the importance of maintaining some knowledge about the system in order to improve the usage of resources and approximate a stop condition, in highly mobile but not too sparse environments. The SWR model emphasizes the need of both suppressing duplicates when no changes in the neighborhood occur, and being prompt in diffusing when partitions happen to be merged.

Our future work is developing in three directions. We are analyzing the trade-off between performance obtained and the amount of knowledge maintained and exchanged. We are designing a dynamically adaptive protocol that monitors neighborhood in order to estimate the mobility model it currently is in, in order to dynamically change its own diffusion policy. We are developing a *hybrid* mobility model, in which nodes can assume and alternate several possible human behaviors, in order to (*i*) reproduce a realistic environments for an accurate evaluation of the diffusion protocols, and (*ii*) test the adaptive algorithm under deployment.

Acknowledgements This work has been partially funded by the Italian Ministry of University and Research in the framework of the "Context-Aware RouTing Over Opportunistic Networks (CARTOON)" PRIN Project.

References

1. Burgess, J., Gallagher, B., Jensen, D., Levine, B.N.: MaxProp: Routing for Vehicle-Based Disruption-Tolerant Networks. In: Proc. IEEE INFOCOM (2006).
2. Camp, T., Boleng, J., Davies, V.: A Survey of Mobility Models for Ad Hoc Network Research. In: Wireless Communication and Mobile Computing (WCMC): Special issue on Mobile Ad Hoc Networking: Research, Trends and Applications, 2(5), pp. 483-502 (2002).
3. Cooper, D.E., Ezhilchelvan, P., Mitrani, I.: High Coverage Broadcasting for Mobile Ad-hoc Networks. In: Proc. NETWORKING 2004, Lecture Notes in Computer Science, vol. 3042, pp. 100-111 (2004).
4. CRAWDAD – A Community Resource for Archiving Wireless Data At Dartmouth. http://crawdad.cs.dartmouth.edu/
5. Davis, J.A., Fagg, A.H., Levine, B.N.: Wearable computers as packet transport mechanisms in highly-partitioned ad-hoc networks. In: Proc. 5th IEEE Intl. Symp. on Wearable Computers (2001).
6. Delay Tolerant Networking Research Group. http://www.dtnrg.org/wiki
7. de Waal, C., Gerharz, M.: BonnMotion – A mobility scenario generation and analysis tool. http://web.informatik.uni-bonn.de/IV/Mitarbeiter/dewaal/BonnMotion/
8. Giudici, F., Pagani, E., Rossi, G.P.: Stateless and self-adaptive broadcast in delay and disruption tolerant networks. Technical Report, Università degli Studi di Milano (2008).
9. Harras, K.A., Almeroth, K.C., Belding-Royer, E.M.: Delay Tolerant Mobile Networks (DTMNs): Controlled Flooding in Sparse Mobile Networks. In: Proc. IFIP Networking (2005).
10. Hong, X., Gerla, M., Pei, G., Chiang, C.: A group mobility model for ad hoc wireless networks. In: Proc. 2nd ACM international Workshop on Modeling, Analysis and Simulation of Wireless and Mobile Systems, pp. 53-60 (1999).
11. Hui, P., Chaintreau, A., Scott, J., Gass, R., Crowcroft, J., Diot, C.: Pocket switched networks and human mobility in conference environments. In: Proc. ACM SIGCOMM Workshop on Delay Tolerant Networking (2005).
12. Jones, E.P.C., Li, L., Ward, P.A.S.: Practical routing in delay-tolerant networks. In: Proc. ACM SIGCOMM Workshop on Delay-tolerant networking (WDTN), pp. 237-243 (2005).
13. Juang, P., Oki, H., Wang, Y., Martonosi, M., Peh, L., Rubenstein, D.: Energy-efficient computing for wildlife tracking: Design tradeoffs and early experiences with Zebranet. In: Proc. ASPLOS (2002).

14. Lee, U., Magistretti, E., Zhou, B., Gerla, M., Bellavista, P., Corradi, A.: MobEyes: Smart Mobs for Urban Monitoring with a Vehicular Sensor Network. In: IEEE Wireless Communications, 13(5) (2006).
15. Lenders. V., Karlsson, G., May, M.: Wireless Ad Hoc Podcasting. In: Proc. 4th IEEE Conf. SECON, pp. 273-283 (2007).
16. Lindgren, A., Doria, A., Schelen, O.: Probabilistic routing in intermittently connected networks. In: Proc. 1st Intl. Workshop on Service Assurance with Partial and Intermittent Resources (SAPIR), Lecture Notes in Computer Science, Vol. 3126, pp. 239-254 (2004).
17. Montresor, A., Jelasity, M., Babaoglu, O.: Gossip-based Aggregation in Large Dynamic Networks. In: ACM Transactions on Computer Systems, 23(3), pp.219-252 (2005).
18. Spyropoulos, T., Psounis, K., Raghavendra, C.S.: Single-copy routing in intermittently connected mobile networks. In: Proc. 1st IEEE SECON, pp. 235-244 (2004).
19. Su, J., Chin, A., Popinova, A., Goely, A., de Lara, E.: User Mobility for Opportunistic Ad-Hoc Networking. In: Proc. 6th IEEE Workshop on Mobile Computing Systems and Applications (2004).
20. UCLA Parallel Computing Laboratory: GloMoSim – Global Mobile Information Systems Simulation Library. University of California at Los Angeles. http://pcl.cs.ucla.edu/projects/glomosim/
21. Vahdat, A., Becker, D.: Epidemic Routing for Partially Connected Ad Hoc Networks. Technical Report CS-200006, Duke University (2000).

Supporting Adaptive Real-time Mobile Communication with Multilayer Context Awareness

Ruwini Kodikara[1], Christer Åhlund[2] and Arkady Zaslavsky[1]

[1] Centre for Distributed Systems & Software Engineering, Monash University, Australia
{piyangae, a.zaslavsky}@infotech.monash.edu.au

[2] Division of Mobile Networking & Computing, Luleå University of Technology, Sweden
christer.ahlund@ltu.se

Abstract   Real time mobile communication is challenging due to the inherent limitations of mobile networks. On the other hand the stringent quality of service requirements of real time traffic is highly in demand. Our first contribution is the generic context aware architecture for adaptive real time applications. Adaptation is based on the awareness of context parameters from different layers of the existing protocol stack which involves context exchange among the neighboring layers as well as non-neighboring layers. The architecture comprises of context representation, context acquisition, cross-layer context exchange and context management. Our second contribution is the mobility aware, adaptive Multi-homed Mobile IP. Simulation of adaptive M-MIP was carried out as a proof of concept. Simulation demonstrated that adaptation to mobility was able to decrease Mobile IP handover latency. Further, the results show that the quality of service of real time traffic can be enhanced by using context aware adaptive MIP. The simulation involved with various speeds ranging from pedestrian scenarios to vehicular scenarios. Results are analyzed with variable data rates. The evaluations show that performance of the proposed solution is better compared to conventional MIP in terms of packet loss and throughput of real time traffic.

1 Introduction

Layer standardization is vital as the foundation of internetworking computers. It is still applied and functions efficiently in static wired networks. It enables standardization of the system design and implementation hence reduces design complexity. Moreover, the layered approach assures interoperability between different systems and ease maintenance because of modularity. By maintaining layers independent of the others, controlled interaction among them can be guaranteed.

Though strict layered approach functioned as an elegant solution for internetworking static wired networks, it is not adequate for efficient functionality of wireless networks. Inherent broadcast nature of wireless medium and interdepen-

Please use the following format when citing this chapter:

Kodikara, R., Åhlund, C. and Zaslavsky, A., 2008, in IFIP International Federation for Information Processing, Volume 284; *Wireless and Mobile Networking;* Zoubir Mammeri; (Boston: Springer), pp. 435–446.

dency between overlapping connectivity pairs restrict the efficiency of media applications. Moreover, the dynamic nature of network topology due to random movements of nodes adds extra complexity. Further, there are stringent resource constraints in wireless networks in terms bandwidth, energy and available battery power and computation capabilities of hosts. Utilization of network bandwidth and other limited resources have to be managed efficiently. The long distance communication is forced through multi-hop. Routing is complicated and needs interaction among other applications.

The applications should be managed and adapted to dynamic nature to improve performance. Especially resource hungry applications like real-time media should be managed dynamically. Moreover, next generation situation and context aware applications necessitate the adaptation. This adaptation may range from application adaptation to channel adaptation. In application adaptation, running applications adapt to the lower layer conditions such as dynamic network conditions. In channel or lower layer adaptations, lower layer entities or protocols adapt to meet application quality of service requirements. Cross layer interaction was proposed in the literature as a solution to avoid bottlenecks of the strict layered protocol design in wireless networks. On the other hand there are some controversial arguments about cross layer interactions in wireless networks [4]. Kawadia and Kumar [4] argue that once the layers are broken through cross layer interactions, it affects not only to the layer concerned but also to the other parts of the system. Moreover, they discuss the fact that cross-layer design causes several adaptation loops which are parts of different protocols interacting with each other. Finally, [4] was concluded with the fact that cross layer interaction should be exercised with appropriate caution. This raises the research challenge of designing cross layer interactions without complete redesign and replacement of the system, without unintended interactions and with carefully examined dependency relationships.

We argue that the existing strict layered architecture itself is not sufficient to support the next generation context aware, adaptive wireless communications due above discussed facts. On the other hand we agree to the fact that full cross layering by loose coupling of protocol stack destroy the concept of modularity and hence the interoperability of various systems. We propose that cross layering should be used without breaking the modularity of the protocol stack to balance these two extremities. We believe that cross layer interaction is still a promising paradigm for wireless networks if it is carefully and appropriately designed. Furthermore, we present the argument that cross layer architecture should be designed using proper design considerations to ensure the generality, modularity, maintainability and efficient operation.

Section 2 of this paper analyses the related work. Section 3 presents our cross layer context aware architecture, which is called Context Aware Architecture for Adaptive Real-time Mobile Communications (CA3RM-com). Section 4 discusses the evaluation of a scenario in the simulation setup. The simulation scenarios, topologies control variables of the simulation and results analysis is presented in this section. Finally section 5 concludes the paper.

2 Background

There were different cross layer architectures proposed in the past. Some proposed frameworks or architectures tailored towards specific requirements, which are non-generic in design goals. We consider, only the architectures, which are based on a generic design in this section.

Wang and Rgheff [12] suggest a mechanism called CLASS for direct signaling between non-neighboring layers. Internal message format of CLASS is light-weighted, but the external information flow is based on standard ICMP and TCP/IP headers so external messaging is not flexible and not synchronized with the internal messaging format proposed in CLASS. CLASS proposal violates the concept of layered protocol stack by direct signaling among layers for performance objectives.

Cross layer architecture in MobileMan [6] project adds another stack component called network status which is accessible by each layer. They recommend existing stack replacing the standard protocol layer, with a redesigned network-status-oriented protocol, so that the protocol can interact with network status. This design supports the local and global adaptation to all network functions through the network status. Authors mention that non-cross layer optimized protocols can still function within the framework they propose. But this framework can't be equally applied for protocols which are not network-status-oriented. Even for network-status-oriented protocols there is a need of redesigning.

The GRACE (Global Resource Adaptation through CoopEration) project [9] considers four different layers which are the network layer, the application layer, the hardware layer, and the operating system layer all connected through a resource manager. GRACE differentiates between two kinds of adaptations, global and local. The admission process and resource reservation process is costly for new applications entering in to the system. Further, global adaptation they defined requires hardware and software reconfiguration which is a bottleneck.

CrossTalk [8] is a cross-layer architecture in which locally available information is used to influence protocol behavior, and it also establishes a global view of the network according to one or multiple metrics like energy level, communication load or neighbor degree. The CrossTalk architecture consists of two data management entities. One entity is for the organization of locally available information. The other data-management entity is for network wide global view. To produce the global view, CrossTalk provides a data dissemination procedure. Establishing a global view and data dissemination is costly and complex. Application of CrossTalk to individual protocol requirements, for instance adaptation to mobility is not obtainable. Information in relation to whether CrossTalk handles conflicting global or local optimizations which may lead to overall system performance degradation is not presented.

In ECLAIR [11] a tuning layer (TL) for each layer, provides an interface to read and update the protocol data-structures. TLs are used by Protocol Optimizers

(POs), which contain cross-layer feedback algorithms. It is based on registering and notification process. ECLAIR doesn't support global context and adaptation. This solution mainly discusses the optimization or context manipulation in a particular protocol. For the proposed system to work the protocols and applications should have the strict structural differentiation that the ECLAIR solution is based on. Moreover the protocol optimization functionalities are carried out in individual performance optimizers, in which there is no central control. This could lead to conflicting optimizations and hence ultimate system performance degradation.

3 CA3RM-Com Architecture

3.1 Design Considerations

CA3RM-com is the context aware architecture we propose, which facilitates the context aware adaptation. The architectural is based on several design goals.

CA3RM-com is generic and can facilitate context aware adaptation for any protocol or application in the protocol stack. This architecture is not specifically tailored to a particular adaptation or application domain. Any entity in a layer of the protocol stack can subscribe to the LAYER LENA of ConEx [5] to request context. Since it is generic it can be used and extended in wide range of adaptations ranging from application adaptation to channel adaptation.

CA3RM-com attempts to achieve a balanced solution of performance benefits with a minimum and tight coupling in the protocol stack. Cross layer exchange can be achieved through subscriptions without changes to the existing stack. So, another important feature is the uninterrupted operation to the existing protocol stack for non cross layer functionalities. Interested protocols and applications can subscribe and register for context. CA3RM-com architecture can be easily and dynamically enabled/disabled.

CA3RM-com is an event driven system. Once a particular context is available in the system it is notified to entire set of interested entities who has subscribed. The architecture is based on event notifications to enable quick responsiveness to the events that are triggering. Context exchange in CA3RM-com is event driven rather than a context storing and querying system. It is an integral and important feature of a context aware adaptive system to ensure the delivery of most current context to the subscribers rather than obsolete context.

CA3RM-com architecture supports the context exchange within the mobile host which enables the local adaptation as well as global adaptation to the network wide contextual data [5]. Global context exchange is achieved through a specific node acts as the Global Event Notification Agent (GENA) in the network. GENA is the tentatively elected node in a situation of an ad hoc network. Internal and External messaging is synchronized. Another important feature in CA3RM-com architecture is the context delivery based on interest. Only interested protocols can subscribe to acquire the context in contrast to a context/message push system where the context is delivered to all the relevant entities.

CA3RM-com architecture facilitates flexible adaptation. It supports context awareness in three categories of adaptations. Protocols and applications can perform "Entity Executed" adaptations through either subscribing to context parameters or to adaptation itself. This way, interested entities can make individual functionalities efficient and adaptive through subscriptions. "System Executed" adaptations are used to force adaptations to achieve system performance. Moreover, the conflicting adaptations are handled in the system to avoid performance degradations that can cause by contradictory adaptations.

3.2 Modules of the Architecture

CA3RM-com architecture and its modules and components are shown in Fig 1.

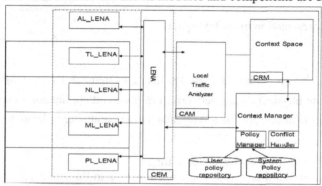

Fig 1. CA3Rm-Com Architecture.

Every context aware solution comprises of a mechanism to represent context, in this architecture it is called Context Representation Module (CRM). CA3Rm-Com architecture exploits extended version of Context Space [7] to represent context used for adaptive real time communication in mobile networks. Fig 2 shows the representation of context parameters and performance parameters in Euclidian vector space for a given problem domain. These set of parameters corresponds to a situation and represented by situation vector. Combination of context and performance parameters which form the context vector could be static and/or dynamic. Context vector corresponding to a given situation at time t v_t, can be represented as a vector consists of a set of context parameters (cp) and set of performance parameters (pp) as shown in Equation 1.

$$v_t = (\sum_{i=1}^{n} a_i cp_{xit} + \sum_{i=1}^{m} b_i pp_{it}) \qquad (1)$$

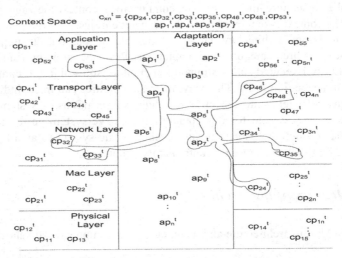

Fig 2. Context representation in context space.

Where, a_i, b_i are scalars. x indicates the layer number 1 to 5, which represent the indicate physical, mac, network, transport, and application layers of the practical protocol stack. cp_{xnt} is the nth adaptation parameter at layer x at time t.

pp_{nt} is the nth performance parameter at time t.

So, context vector at time t, can be written as shown in Equation 2.

$$v_t = (a_1.cp_{11t} + ... + a_n cp_{5nt} + b_1.pp_{1t} + ... + b_m pp_{mt}) \qquad (2)$$

Context exchange across the protocol stack and the network is carried out through the Context Exchange Module (CEM) which is called ConEx [5]. ConEx is an event driven context exchange framework in which context delivery is based on subscriptions.

Context acquisition is accomplished through the Local Traffic Analyzer which sniffs the packets flow through the protocol stack. ConEx exchanges context via this Context Acquisition Module (CAM).

Context Management Module (CMM) executes two major tasks. Firstly Context Manager (CM) ensures that the context aware adaptations are based on predefined user and system policies through the Policy Manager (PM). Secondly CMM controls context aware adaptations to avoid unintended conflicts that may arise by uncontrolled adaptations. This is done through the Conflict Handler (CH).

Two main categories of adaptation are considered in the CA3RM-com architecture as illustrated in Fig 3. They are "Entity Executed" adaptations and "System Executed" adaptations. The term "entity" is referred to as any protocol or application throughout the discussion.

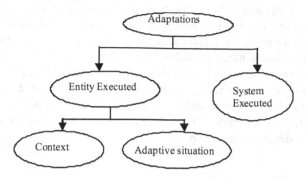

Fig 3. Categorization of adaptations supported.

In "Entity Executed" adaptations the entity which is interested in the adaptation subscribes to the architecture to execute adaptation. Entity executed adaptation can be achieved through two types of subscriptions. In one type of subscription, the entity requests particular context parameters in order to make the adaptation decision based on its own rules and conditions. In the other type of entity executed adaptation, entity make the subscription to an adaptive situation, where the policy manager executes the policies related to the adaptation and notifies the adaptation decision to the relevant entity. In "System Executed" adaptations, the entity is not involved in subscriptions but the context manager forces the adaptation to the entity based on system and user defined policies, which enable control and administration of the system.

4 Simulations

4.1 Scenario

A scenario is considered, where a traveling businessman engaged in a videoconference in his PDA at the office and is wandering around in the office buildings continuing the video conference he already initiated. It is essential to maintain uninterrupted ongoing session while moving from one network coverage area to another network coverage area. In this situation his mobility pattern could be predicted inside buildings and it could be unpredicted and random outside. This maintenance of the ongoing session is necessary with both the predicted and unpredicted mobility patterns. Moreover, the delay jitter, delay and packet loss should be minimized to achieve the quality of video conference. Later on, he would drive to his business site situated at another location. A situation is assumed where he travels by car, while continuing his business conferences. In this situation his mobility pattern is predicted on the road. As he crosses the intersections of highways the mobility pattern can become unpredicted.

In the scenario discussed above, there is a need of maintaining uninterrupted ongoing videoconference with guaranteed quality of service while moving. Mobile IP (MIP) is a promising network layer mobility management solution but its agent discovery and movement detection delays are significant for real-time data communication. The motivation of the simulation work is to minimize the handover latency in Mobile IP to cater for the quality of service requirements of real time applications depending on the situation awareness. Here we apply context aware adaptation to multi-homed mobile IP (M-MIP), based on this scenario. We discuss the simulation in detail in the section.

4.2 Evaluation

Context vector discussed in section 3 is used in context aware adaptive multi-homed mobile IP handover decision. Context parameters used were Constant Bit Rate (CBR) traffic at application layer, Relative Network Load (RNL) metric, frequency and Signal to Noise Ratio (SNR) of received Agent Advertisements (AA) in MIPV4 or Binding Updates (BU) in MIPV6, Round Trip Time (RTT) delay, jitter of BUs at network layer, radio receiver SNR threshold at mac sub layer. The performance parameters used in simulation were packet loss and throughput of CBR traffic.

The context aware adaptive MIP approach minimizes the overall handover latency by improving two phases of MIP layer-3 handover. The agent discovery / address configuration phase is improved by multi-homing. Movement detection phase was improved by proactive movement detection. Hence the total MIP handover latency is minimized by decreasing the agent discovery delay and movement detection delay. We use Multi-homed MIP [2] in evaluation. Gate Way (GW) selection based on RNL metric [1] is used, when ore than one candidate networks are available. In brief, If Mobile Node (MN) is multi-homed in an overlapping coverage area the RNL metric selects least congested GW as the default gateway. Agent advertisement frequency, RTT delay and jitter are used as context parameters. Proactive movement detection algorithm is based SNR of received Agent Advertisements (AA) in multi-homed MIPV4 or Binding Updates of multi-homed MIPV6. In addition to the SNR AA/BU at network layer, SNR threshold at mac sub layer are used as context parameters. This proactive move detection is beneficial over conventional unreachability detection in which the MN waits till AA/BU timeout. The detailed discussion of proactive move detection and its algorithms are beyond the scope of this paper.

The discussed scenario was simulated in a wireless set up. We present the simulation of the proposed solution which was carried out using the network simulator Glomosim [3] in this section. Agent advertisements in the MIP were sent every half a second and MN registers every third advertisement with the Home Agent (HA). Time out for bindings used was three times the agent advertisement time. Simulation was carried out for 200 seconds. CBR traffic flows were sent from MN to Corresponding Node (CN) every 3MS. Results for different data rates with different packet sizes were simulated. Scenarios of pedestrian speeds and vehicular speeds with varying data rates were simulated and the results are analyzed. Simulations of two approaches were examined to compare the performance of the proposed solution. Pure M-MIP approach, which does not use context exchange for handover decision is called WithOut ConEx (WOConEx) approach. SNR based movement predicted approach uses context for handover decision and is based on ConEx architecture hence referred to as the ConEx (ConEx) approach. Simulation was carried out for both approaches and results are compared. Results are presented as mean value of multiple simulations with different seeds to use normal distribution. Results are presented with 90% confidence level.

The network topology shown in Fig 4 was used to simulate various moving speeds of the MN. Results of two major speed categories were examined and analyzed. One is the pedestrian speeds. The other simulation was carried out to represent a vehicular network, where mobile node was moved with vehicular speeds.

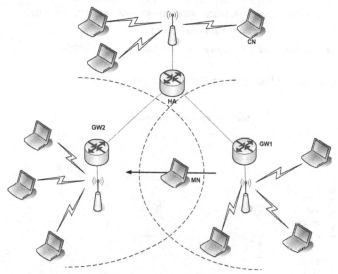

Fig 4. Network topology used in speed analysis.

Fig 5 and Fig 6 represent the results of simulations carried out in situations where MN moves in walking speed. The speeds tested are from 2m/s to 4 m/s. 2m/s represented as MP1_S2, 3m/s represented as MP1_S3, and 4m/s represented as MP1_S4 in the graphs.

Fig 5 shows the packet loss rate of CBR traffic for variable mobility speeds in the range of walking speeds. In the "WOConEx" approach, there is a delay for move detection since the MN waits till agent advertisement timeouts or registration timeouts. Due to the delay of move detection in "WOConEx" a considerable packet loss is noticed. In "ConEx" the move detection delay is zero since the movement is detected before loosing the current network attachment. So the packet loss rate is zero in "ConEx". The graph in Fig 6 shows the throughput of CBR traffic for variable data rates where the mobility speed is in the range on walking speed. Due to the packet loss during the handover in this approach, the throughput is lower. There is a significant decrease in throughput as the speed increases.

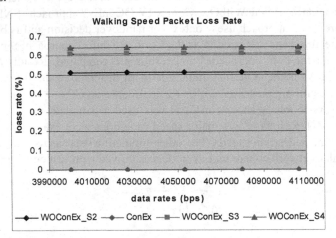

Fig 5. Walking Speed Packet Loss Rates Analysis.

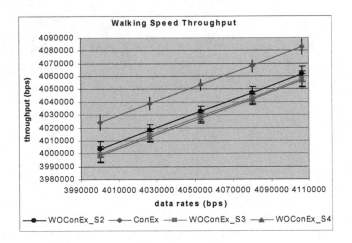

Fig 6. Walking Speed Throughput Analysis

The graphs in Fig 7 and Fig 8 show the packet loss rate and throughput of CBR traffic for variable mobility speeds in the range of vehicular speeds. Explanation of reason for increased packet loss and decreased throughput at higher speeds of WOConEx and the way it was avoided in ConEx solution are similar to the explanation discussed in the sub section of walking speeds.

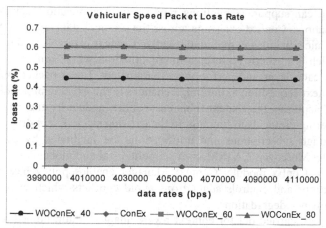

Fig 7. Walking Speed Packet Loss Rates Analysis

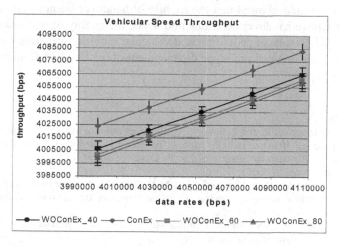

Fig 8. Walking Speed Throughput Analysis

Moreover, there is a significant increase in the packet loss as the speed increases. This is due to faster cell edge crossing of the default gateway. As the speed increases this happens quicker and in "WOConEx" approach should either increase the agent advertisement frequency through agent solicitations or thought more frequent binding updates to overcome the problem of increased packet loss, with the additional cost of the additional overhead. In "ConEx" approach, this is avoided by detecting network detachment before the cell edge is passed.

5 Conclusions

We have discussed CA3RM-Com, the generic context aware architecture proposed for adaptive real time communications in mobile networks. The architecture is flexible and can support adaptations ranging form application adaptations to channel adaptations. Context exchange across the protocol stack enables the adaptation to dynamic situations in mobile networks. Context is represented using context space which is a generic representation of situations which consists of context parameters at each layer and performance parameters. Local packet analyzer is utilized in context acquisition to minimize changes to the existing protocols during the process of acquiring the context. This ensures the modularity and capability of non-cross layering protocols to function in the existing stack. Event driven context exchange through subscriptions and notifications are facilitated by context exchange module. Moreover, CA3RM-com supports local and global context awareness through it ConEx module. Context Manager enables policy based system driven adaptations and controls adaptations avoid conflicts which would consequence performance degradations.

Simulation was carried out for context aware adaptive multi-homed mobile IP which enables adaptive handover based various context and performance parameters. Simulation results showed that the mobile IP handover latency can be minimized with adaptive handover decisions and hence the quality of real time traffic can be improved. Results of pedestrian and vehicular mobility scenarios were analyzed. Performance oriented prototype development of the CA3RM-Com architecture is in ongoing.

References

1. Ahlund, C., Brännström, R. and Zaslavsky, A., Running variance metric for evaluating performance of wireless IP networks in the MobileCty testbed. in First International Conference on Testbeds and Research Infrastructures for the Development of Networks and Communities, 2005. Tridentcom. , (2005).
2. Åhlund, C., Brännström, R. and Zaslavsky, A., M-MIP: extended mobile ip to maintain multiple connections to overlapping wireless access networks. in International Conference on Networking (ICN 2005), (April 2005).
3. Glomosim, Global Mobile Information Systems Simulation Library, http://pcl.cs.ucla.edu/projects/glomosim/
4. Kawadia, V. and Kumar, P.R. A cautionary perspective on cross-layer design. IEEE Wireless Communications, 12 (1). 3 - 11.
5. Kodikara, R., Zaslavsky, A. and Åhlund, C., ConEx: Context Exchange in MANETs for Real time multimedia. in fifth International Conference on Networking (ICN'06), (2006), 70 - 78.
6. M.Conti and al., "Cross-Layering in Mobile Ad Hoc Network Design," IEEE Comp. 48–51.
7. Padovitz, A., Loke, S.W. and Zaslavsky, A., Towards a Theory of Context Spaces. in Work shop on Context Modeling and Reasoning (CoMoRea), at 2nd IEEE International Conference onPervasive Computing and Communication (PerCom), (March 2004)
8. R.Winter, J.H.Schiller, N.Nikaein and CBonnet CrossTalk: cross-layer decision support based on global knowledge. IEEE Communications Magazine, vol. 44 (1). 93 - 99.
9. S.V.Adve and al., e., "The Illinois GRACE Project: Global Resource Adaptation through Cooperation,". in SHAMAN, (June 2002).
10. VoIP Service Level FAQ, http://www.voip-news.com/faq/voip-service-level-faq/
11. V.T.Raisinghani and S.Iyer Cross-layer feedback architecture for mobile device protocol stacks. IEEE Communications Magazine, vol. 44 (1). 85 - 92.
12. Wang, Q. and M.A., A.-R., Cross-layer signalling for next-generation wireless systems. in (WCNC 2003) IEEE Wireless Communications and Networking,(16-20 March 2003).

Path Selection of SCTP Fast Retransmission in Multi-homed Wireless Environments

Yuansong Qiao[1,2], Enda Fallon[1], John Murphy[3], Liam Murphy[3] and Austin Hanley[1]

[1] Applied Software Research Centre, Athlone Institute of Technology, Ireland

[2] Institute of Software, Chinese Academy of Sciences, China

[3] Performance Engineering Laboratory, University College Dublin, Ireland
{ysqiao, efallon}@ait.ie, {j.murphy, Liam.Murphy}@ucd.ie, ahanley@ait.ie

Abstract In heterogeneous wireless network environments, network connections of a device may have a significant differential. This paper studies the effect of path bandwidth differential on the performance of fast retransmission strategies in Multi-homing environments. It identifies that fast retransmission on an alternate path may cause receive buffer blocking when path bandwidth differential is significant and the receive buffer is limited. A theoretical model is proposed for selecting retransmission path during the fast retransmission phase, which is based on receive buffer and path conditions. The model is verified through simulations with various path differentials.

1 Introduction

Multi-homing technologies, where a host can be addressed by multiple IP addresses, are increasingly being considered by developers implementing mobile applications. An enabling factor reinforcing this adoption is the trend towards mobile devices supporting a hybrid of networking capabilities such as 802.11 and UMTS. The characteristics of mobile environments, with the possibility of frequent disconnections and fluctuating bandwidth, pose significant issues for mobile application developers and therefore the path redundancy offered by multi-homing protocols has a clear attraction.

There is a significant standardization effort focusing on mobility and Multi-homing at various layers in the OSI stack. This is illustrated by the interest in tech-

† The authors wish to recognize the assistance of Enterprise Ireland through its Innovation Partnership fund in the financing of this Research programme.

Please use the following format when citing this chapter:

Qiao, Y., Fallon, E., Murphy, J., Murphy, L. and Hanley, A., 2008, in IFIP International Federation for Information Processing, Volume 284; *Wireless and Mobile Networking*; Zoubir Mammeri; (Boston: Springer), pp. 447–458.

nologies such as Media Independent Handover Framework (IEEE 802.21) [1], Mobile IP (MIP) [2], IP layer Multi-homing (SHIM6) [3], Datagram Congestion Control Protocol (DCCP) [4] and SCTP Dynamic Address Reconfiguration [5]. While it is possible to implement mobility at the network layer and the application layer, it is the Transport Layer through a technology such as SCTP [6] which enables an end-to-end and user centric implementation of mobility and at the same time provides transparent switch over services to the application layer.

Stream Control Transmission Protocol (SCTP) is a reliable TCP-friendly transport layer protocol defined by IETF, which was originally designed for signalling data. Due to its attractive features such as multi-homing and multi-streaming, SCTP has received much attention from the network community. SCTP support link backup through transmitting and receiving data from multiple IP addresses. It sends new data to the primary address and lost data could be transmitted to the current address or to an alternate address. SCTP continually monitors path availability. If the primary address fails, it will switch over to an alternate address.

This paper discusses the performance of SCTP retransmission policies in mobile environments where the paths used in an SCTP association have a significant transmission differential. According to path selection strategies during the fast retransmission phase, two retransmission policies have been proposed in [7]. They are:

FRtxOnAlt - fast retransmission on an alternate path.

FRtxOnSame - fast retransmission on the same path.

FRtxOnSame is a safe solution undoubtedly because it returns to single path scenarios, while FRtxOnAlt may benefit by exploring multi-homing features. The basic idea behind FRtxOnAlt is that it assumes sending data on different paths is similar to sending data on a single path with network anomalies, such as reordering or delay spikes. This paper studies the effects of path bandwidth differential and a limited receive buffer on the performance of the two retransmission strategies. The features of WLAN, 3G and GPRS are considered because they are broadly used in the current Internet.

This paper identifies and illustrates FRtxOnAlt may cause receive buffer blocking which degrades performance significantly. It presents a theoretical model for selecting retransmission path based on receive buffer size and path bandwidth differential.

This paper is organized as follows. Section 2 summarizes related work. Section 3 illustrates the simulation setup. Section 4 describes the SCTP performance degradation problem in detail. Section 5 proposes a theoretical model for analyzing receiving buffer blocking problem and presents suggestions about implementation of the model. The conclusions are presented in Section 6.

2 Related Work

Stream Control Transmission Protocol (SCTP) [6] originated as a protocol called Multi-Network Datagram Transmission Protocol (MDTP). The motivation for MDTP arose from the fact that TCP had inherent weaknesses in relation to the control of telecommunication sessions. MDTP was designed to transfer call control signalling on "carefully engineered" networks [8]. When one analyses the origins of SCTP it is interesting to note that its initial target environment was vastly different from that experienced in current day mobile networks. Given its origin as a fixed line oriented protocol, and in particular a protocol designed towards links with roughly equivalent transmission capabilities, the transition towards a mobile enabled protocol has raised a number of design issues. Many related works have raised issues in relation to the design of SCTP.

In [9] two SCTP stall scenarios are presented, the authors identify that the stalls occur as a result of SCTP coupling the logic for data acknowledgment and path monitoring. In [7] different SCTP retransmission policies are investigated for a lossy environment, a retransmission strategy which sends the fast retransmission packets on the same path and the timeout retransmission packets on an alternate path are suggested. In [10] SCTP is extended for Concurrent Multi-path Transfer (CMT-SCTP) while in [11] the authors identify that a finite receiver buffer will block CMT-SCTP transmission when the quality of one path is lower than others. Several retransmission policies are studied which can alleviate receiver buffer blocking. In [12] the authors focus on making SCTP more robust to packet reordering and delay spikes.

3 Simulation Setup

The simulations focus on the situation where a mobile node has a fixed GPRS or 3G connection along with various high bandwidth connections and analyze the SCTP performance degradation. The high bandwidth connection is set to the primary path in SCTP. All simulations in this paper are carried out by running Delaware University's SCTP module [13, 14] for NS-2.

The simulation topology is shown in Fig. 1. Node S and Node R are the SCTP sender and receiver respectively. Both SCTP endpoints have two addresses. R1,1, R1,2, R2,1 and R2,2 are routers. It is configured with no overlap between the two paths. As only the effect of bandwidth is considered in this paper the loss rate is set to zero. Node S begins to send 20MB ftp data to Node R at the 5th second. The MTU of each path is 1500B. The queue lengths of bottleneck links in both paths are 50 packets. The queue lengths of other links are set to 10000 packets. The bandwidth of the secondary path bottleneck link is 36Kbps or 384Kbps, the delay is 300ms. The bandwidth of the primary path bottleneck link changes from

36Kbps to 30Mbps, the delay is a constant 50ms. SCTP parameters are all default except those mentioned. Initially the receiver window is set to 1MB. The initial slow start threshold is set large enough to ensure that the full primary path bandwidth is used. Only one SCTP stream is used and the data is delivered to the upper layer in order.

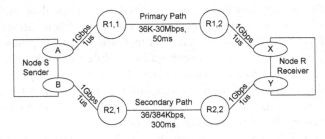

Fig. 1. Simulation network topology.

4 A Case Study for Receive Buffer Blocking

This section describes the FRtxOnAlt performance issues in detail for the simulation configuration where the primary path bandwidth is 10Mbps and the secondary path bandwidth is 36Kbps. Node S starts to send 20MB data to Node R at the 5th second. The initial slow start threshold is 350KB. The data transmission time for retransmission on the secondary path and retransmission on the primary path are 38.1697s and 18.1355s respectively. The secondary path affects the performance dramatically in this situation.

The simulation results for FRtxOnAlt are shown in Fig. 2. The sending process begins in slow start mode. From A to B (Fig. 2a), 68 packets are dropped on the primary path because of congestion. At C (Fig. 2b,2c), the sender finds the packets lost by duplicate SACKs, and it reduces the congestion window by half to 147534B. From C to E (Fig. 2b), the sender sends lost packets on the secondary path using the fast retransmission algorithm. Within these retransmitted packets, 18 are lost as a result of the queue of the secondary path being full due to its low bandwidth. These 18 lost packets will be retransmitted again on the primary path after their retransmission timeout.

The queuing delay of the secondary path is very large (Fig. 2b). This delay is in proportion to the retransmission packet number since the data enqueuing interval is shorter than the data sending time. In this simulation, the 68 packets are enqueued on the secondary path in 6.761304s-6.579304s=182ms (E-C), whereas the time for sending one packet on the secondary path is 1500B/36Kb=333.3ms. At D (Fig. 2a), the primary outstanding data size is less than the congestion window, so the sender begins to send new data on the primary path at a speed of around

147534B per RTT (around 100ms). At F (Fig. 2a,2d), the receiver window maintained at the sender side drops to 292B and at this moment only the first retransmitted packet is received on the secondary path. Since SCTP provides ordered delivery of data, the receiver can not deliver the received data to upper layer. It takes 0.664396s (F-C) from the beginning of the fast retransmission phase to fill the receiver's buffer. After point F, the sender can only send new data chunks on the primary path after it receives a SACK from the secondary path even though the cwnd of the primary path is not fully used. Then the sender will recover from this blocking situation after all packets transmitted on the secondary path are received.

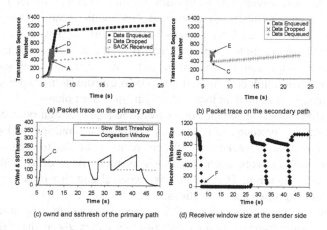

(a) Packet trace on the primary path   (b) Packet trace on the secondary path

(c) cwnd and ssthresh of the primary path   (d) Receiver window size at the sender side

Fig. 2. Retransmission on the secondary path. A: 6.414934s, B: 6.575737s, C: 6.579304s, D: 6.658611s, E: 6.761304s F: 7.24370s.

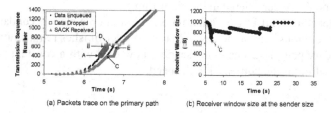

(a) Packets trace on the primary path   (b) Receiver window size at the sender size

Fig. 3. Retransmission on the primary path. A: 6.414934s, B: 6.575737s, C: 6.579304s, D: 6.699467s, E: 6.740312s.

As a comparison with FRtxOnAlt, the simulation results for retransmission on the primary path are shown in Fig. 3. Fig. 3a shows the packets trace on the primary path. The sender starts transmission at the 5th second in slow start mode. From A to B, 68 packets are dropped as a result of the sending speed reaching the maximum bandwidth. At C, the sender finds the packets lost by duplicate SACKs, and the congestion window is reduced by half. From C to E, each dropped packet is fast retransmitted on the primary path immediately when the sender receives 4 consecutive loss reports for it. After D, the sender begins to transmit new data because the outstanding data size is smaller than the congestion window size. At C (Fig. 3b), the receiver window size maintained in the sender side drops to the lowest point 701996KB.

4.1 Result Analysis

The above tests illustrate that FRtxOnAlt becomes inefficient when the secondary path has a relatively low bandwidth and the receiver's buffer is finite. The sender injects large numbers of packets into a path with uncertain condition during fast retransmission. Then the receiver's buffer is filled up when the receiver is waiting for the retransmitted packets arrival from the secondary path. It is important to note that slow start phase happens not only in the beginning stage but also after a transmission timeout. Furthermore, fast retransmission can be triggered for many reasons, such as random loss, not only in slow start phase.

This performance degradation comes from the SCTP design rationale. SCTP is not a load sharing protocol, so it does not send data on multiple paths simultaneously. It assumes sending data on different paths is similar to sending data on a single path with network anomalies, such as reordering, delay spikes. Consequently, it adopts current TCP's congestion control and fast retransmission algorithms without significant modifications.

In single path configurations, network anomalies exist but happen randomly. In multi-homed environments, besides network anomalies, the paths differences are usually constants. Every time an alternate path is used, it will affect performance, and therefore performance degradation occurs frequently. Accordingly, path differences should be considered in the algorithm.

If the receiver's buffer is infinite, retransmission on a slow secondary path will not decrease throughput obviously. After the sender finishes retransmitting data on the secondary path, it can continue sending new data with a constant speed which is an estimation of the bottleneck link speed.

5   Modelling Receive Buffer Blocking

This section analyzes the relationship between receive buffer blocking and bandwidth difference to provide method for path selection during the fast retransmission phase.

The symbols used for this section are listed as follows:

B1 – Bandwidth of the primary path;
R1 – RTT of the primary path;
Q1 – Queue length of the primary path;
B2 – Bandwidth of the secondary path;

R2 – RTT of the secondary path;

Q2 – Queue length of the secondary path;

A – Receive buffer size;

W – Data length which has been sent on the primary path at the beginning moment of the fast retransmission phase; suppose these data has been received or lost when the fast retransmit occurs.

V1 – Data arriving rate from the primary path;

V2 – Receive buffer releasing rate when the retransmitted data arrives at the receive;

D1 – The delay between the moment for the sender entering the fast retransmit phase and the moment the sender starting to transmit new data on the primary path.

cwnd1_Final – Congestion window size before the sender enters the fast retransmit phase.

cwnd1_Pevious – Congestion window size of the last second round before the sender enters the fast retransmit phase.

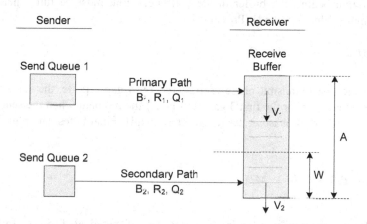

Fig. 4. Model for receive buffer blocking

Suppose the receive buffer size is large enough to fully use the bandwidth in the bottleneck link. When the sender enters the fast retransmit phase, W bytes data has been transmitted on the primary path. The sender will fast retransmit lost data on the secondary path. As the congestion window of the primary path has been decreased, the sender will wait for D1 seconds before transmitting data one the primary path. In order to avoid receive buffer blocking, W bytes data should be released before the data arrived from the primary path fills up the receive buffer. The first data packet transmitted on each path takes half of the path RTT to arrive at the receiver. The following packets arrive at the speed of V1 and V2 for the primary and secondary path respectively. Therefore, the relationship of these variables could be described as (1):

$$\frac{W}{V_2} + \frac{R_2}{2} \leq \frac{A}{V_1} + \frac{R_1}{2} + D_1 \tag{1}$$

Next, we need to estimate the variables in (1). In the slow start phase, the final transmission round of the sender begins from the first lost packet is detected. The congestion window size is cwnd1_Final. The congestion window size before the final RTT round is cwnd1_Previous. As the receiver uses delayed acknowledgements, the congestion window grows by 50% every RTT round. Therefore:

$$cwnd1\_Final = \frac{3}{2} cwnd1\_Previous \tag{2}$$

In the final transmission round before the fast retransmit phase begins, cwnd1_Previous bytes data arrives at the receiver and cwnd1_Previous/2 bytes data is dropped by network. Consequently, at the moment when the final transmission round begins, the buffer in the bottleneck link must be full. Therefore the maximum value for cwnd1_Previous is:

$$cwnd1\_Pevious \leq B_1 R_1 + Q_1 \tag{3}$$

As the fast retransmit phase is triggered by 4 gap reports, the sender sends 3 new data packets for the first 3 gap reports. At the moment when the sender enters the fast retransmit phase, it has transmitted cwnd1_Final bytes data plus 3 packets (4):

$$W \leq \frac{3}{2}(B_1 R_1 + Q_1) + 3 \times MTU \tag{4}$$

The receive buffer releasing rate can be estimated as follows. In the final transmission round before the fast retransmit phase, the sender transmits 1.5×cwnd1_Pevious bytes data and 0.5×cwnd1_Pevious bytes data are lost evenly. Consequently, 3 packets are released for every packet received on the secondary path. Since the data arriving rate of the secondary path equals to the secondary path bandwidth, the receive buffer releasing rate is 3 times of the secondary path bandwidth (5).

$$V_2 = 3B_2 \tag{5}$$

When the sender enters the fast retransmit phase, the congestion window is reduced by half. The transmission speed of the primary path can be estimated as in (6).

$$V_1 \leq \min(B_1, \frac{cwnd1\_Final/2}{R_1})$$

$$(6)$$

Since the primary path congestion window of the sender is reduced by half when the sender enters the fast retransmit phase, the sender need to wait for half of the congestion window data being acknowledged before sending new data. The waiting time is greater than half of the primary path RTT because the queue at the bottleneck link is full and the end to end RTT is greater than the path RTT (7).

$$D_1 > \frac{R_1}{2}$$

$$(7)$$

Substitute (4), (5), (6) and (7) into (1), receive buffer blocking can be avoid if (8) is satisfied.

$$B_2 > \frac{B_1 R_1 + Q_1 + 2 \times MTU}{\frac{2A}{B_1} + (2R_1 - R_2)}$$

$$(8)$$

5.1 Verification of the Model

Two groups of simulations are executed for the fixed secondary path bandwidths of 36Kbps and 384Kbps. The primary path bandwidth changes from 36Kbps to 30Mbps in both tests. The simulation topology is shown in Fig. 1. The initial slow start threshold is 1MB. 20MB data is transmitted via FTP. For each path configuration, the data transmission time for retransmission on the secondary path and retransmission on the primary path are computed. The data transmission time and the percentage change of two retransmission strategies for the 36Kbps secondary path bandwidth are shown in Table 1. The same results for the 384Kbps secondary path bandwidth are shown in Table 2. The percentage change P is calculated as in (9).

$$P = \frac{RtxOnSec - RtxOnPri}{RtxOnSec} \times 100\%$$

$$(9)$$

Table 1. Data Transmission Time for Primary Paths of Various Bandwidths and Secondary Path of 36kbps.

Primary Bandwidth	FRtxOnAlt (s)	FRtxOnSame (s)	Percentage Change (%)
30 Mbps	40.7766	9.02946	77.85
25 Mbps	40.821	9.06883	77.78
20 Mbps	30.0813	9.76529	67.53
15 Mbps	40.1722	12.8919	67.90
10 Mbps	38.1697	18.1355	52.48
5 Mbps	49.0648	34.1332	30.43
2 Mbps	91.5079	83.8049	8.41
1 Mbps	167.976	166.792	0.70
900 kbps	185.301	185.241	0.03
800 kbps	207.632	208.307	-0.32
512 kbps	324.038	325.116	-0.33
384 kbps	431.673	433.298	-0.37
36 kbps	4596.8	4617.78	-0.45

Table 2. Data Transmission Time for Primary Paths of Various Bandwidths and Secondary Path of 384kbps.

Primary Bandwidth	FRtxOnAlt (s)	FRtxOnSame (s)	Percentage Change (%)
30 Mbps	24.1781	9.02946	62.65
25 Mbps	25.577	9.06883	64.54
20 Mbps	21.841	9.76529	55.28
15 Mbps	18.7894	12.8919	31.38
10 Mbps	26.4738	18.1355	31.49
6Mbps	29.0827	28.6448	1.50
5.1Mbps	33.5139	33.4865	0.08
5 Mbps	34.0862	34.1332	-0.13
2 Mbps	83.5958	83.8049	-0.25
1 Mbps	166.252	166.792	-0.32
512 kbps	324.014	325.116	-0.34
384 kbps	431.673	433.298	-0.37
36 kbps	4591.13	4617.78	-0.58

The results show that when the primary path bandwidth is below a certain threshold, approximately 900Kbps for the 36Kbps secondary path and 5.1Mbps for the 384Kbps secondary path, retransmission on the secondary path can improve performance. When the primary path bandwidth is above this threshold, retransmission on the secondary path will decrease performance significantly. Higher primary bandwidth will suffer more performance degradation because the higher bandwidth will retransmit more data on the secondary path during congestion, and therefore the receiver buffer blocking time will be longer. Retransmission on the primary path will increase performance for this situation.

Equation (8) can be verified by the simulation results in Table I & Table II. According to (8), when the secondary path bandwidth is 36kbps, the primary path bandwidth should be less than 801.6kbps to avoid receive buffer blocking. Table I shows that this threshold is between 800kbps and 900kbps. When the secondary path bandwidth is 384kbps, the primary path bandwidth should be less than 4.86Mbps according to (8) and it is between 5Mbps and 5.1Mbps according to Table II.

The results of (8) are less than the simulation results in Table I and II because equation (5) underestimates the receive buffer releasing rate (V2) when the retransmitted data arrives at the receiver. In the final transmission round before the fast retransmit phase starts, if the lost data size of the primary path is less than cwnd1_Final/3, the receive buffer releasing speed will be greater than 3 times of the secondary path bandwidth.

5.2 Implementation of the Model

This section presents some suggestions for implementing (8). The primary path bandwidth could be estimated through the bandwidth estimation algorithm in Westwood TCP [15]. The primary path RTT could come from the SCTP internal RTT measurement. The queue length in the primary path bottleneck link could be estimated from the maximum RTT and the minimum RTT. Suppose the minimum RTT is the transmission time for a null system and the maximum RTT is the transmission time for a full-loaded system, the estimated queue length is the product of the primary path bandwidth and the difference of the maximum and minimum RTT. The secondary path RTT can be acquired from SCTP internal RTT measurement. The secondary path bandwidth can be estimated from local link information or from active detection, such Packet-Pair Bandwidth Estimation (PPBE) [16].

6 Conclusions and Future Work

This paper studies the effects of path bandwidth difference on the fast retransmission strategies performance in a heterogeneous context. It illustrates that fast retransmission on an alternate path will decrease performance when the bandwidth of the secondary path is relatively low. The transmission will be blocked in this scenario due to packet re-ordering filling the receiver's buffer. A model for estimating receive buffer blocking is proposed, which is based on path bandwidth, delay and receive buffer size. An implementation suggestion is given for using the model in path selection during the fast retransmit phase.

We plan to implement the receive buffer blocking model in SCTP for helping path selection and study path selection algorithms in experimental wireless and mobile environments.

References

1. Dutta, A., Das, S., Famolari, D., Ohba, Y., Taniuchi, K., Kodama, T., Schulzrinne, H.: 'Seamless Handoff across Heterogeneous Networks - An 802.21 Centric Approach', Proc. IEEE WPMC 2005, Aalborg Denmark, September 2005.
2. C. Perkins Ed., "IP Mobility Support for IPv4", IETF RFC 3344, August 2002.
3. E. Nordmark, M. Bagnulo, "Shim6: Level 3 Multihoming Shim Protocol for IPv6", IETF draft, Feb. 2008, http://www.ietf.org/internet-drafts/draft-ietf-shim6-proto-10.txt.
4. E. Kohler, M. Handley, S. Floyd, "Datagram Congestion Control Protocol (DCCP)", IETF RFC 4340, Mar. 2006.
5. R. Stewart, Q. Xie, M. Tuexen, S. Maruyama, M. Kozuka, "Stream Control Transmission Protocol (SCTP) Dynamic Address Reconfiguration", IETF RFC 5061, Sep. 2007.
6. R. Stewart, Q. Xie, K. Morneault, C. Sharp, H. Schwarzbauer, T. Taylor, I. Rytina, M. Kalla, L. Zhang and V. Paxson, "Stream Control Transmission Protocol", IETF RFC 2960, Oct. 2000.
7. Caro Jr., P. Amer and R. Stewart, "Retransmission Schemes for End-to-end Failover with Transport Layer Multihoming", GLOBECOM 2004, November 2004.
8. R. Stewart and Q. Xie, "Stream Control Transmission Protocol (SCTP), A Reference Guide", Addison-Wesley, ISBN 0-201-72186-4, Jan. 2006.
9. J. Noonan, P. Perry, S. Murphy and J. Murphy, "Stall and Path Monitoring Issues in SCTP", Proc. of IEEE Infocom, Conference on Computer Communications, Barcelona, April 2006.
10. J. Iyengar, K. Shah and P. Amer, "Concurrent multipath transfer using sctp multihoming", SPECTS'04, San Jose, USA, July 2004.
11. J. Iyengar, P. Amer and R. Stewart, "Receive buffer blocking in concurrent multipath transfer", IEEE Globecom 2005, St. Louis, Nov. 2005.
12. S. Ladha, S. Baucke, R. Ludwig and P. Amer, "On Making SCTP Robust to Spurious Retransmissions", ACM Computer Communication Review, 34(2), Apr. 2004.
13. Caro   and   J.   Iyengar,   "ns-2   SCTP   module,   Version   3.5", http://www.armandocaro.net/software/ns2sctp/.
14. UC Berkeley, LBL, USC/ISI, and Xerox Parc, "ns-2 documentation and software, Version 2.29", Oct. 2005, www.isi.edu/nsnam/ns.
15. C. Casetti, M. Gerla, S. Mascolo, M. Sanadidi and R.Wang, "TCP Westwood: Bandwidth Estimation for Enhanced Transport over Wireless Links", ACM Wireless Networks, 2002, 8:467-479.
16. R.L. Carter and M.E. Crovella, "Measuring Bottleneck Link Speed in Packet-Switched Networks", Performance Evaluation, 1996, 27: 297–318.

Towards the Use of Models for Autonomic Network Management

N. Van Wambeke, F. Armando, C. Chassot, K. Guennoun, K. Drira and E. Exposito

LAAS-CNRS - Université de Toulouse

Toulouse, France
{van.wambeke, armando, chassot, kguennou, khalil, exposito }@laas.fr

Abstract This paper presents a model-based framework to support the automated and adaptive deployment of communication services for QoS. The application domain targets cooperative group activities applied to military emergency operation management systems. Various models are introduced to represent the different levels of cooperation (applicative/middleware/transport). The adaptation decision process relies on structural model transformations while its enforcement is based on the dynamic composition of micro-protocols and software components. Automated deployment is performed both at the transport (i.e. UDP-TCP level) and middleware level. The architecture to support automated network management based on these models is introduced and illustrated.

1 Introduction

Cooperative group activities using wireless mobile communicating systems constitute an increasingly evolving application domain. It is likely to be one of the most important directions that may enable reliable and efficient human and machine-to-machine cooperation under the current networking systems and software, and may deeply shape their future deployment. Such activity-support systems have to deal with dynamically evolving activity-level requirements under constantly changing network-level unpredictable constraints. Maintaining reliable connectivity and QoS in such a communication context is difficult. Adaptive service provisioning should help the different provisioning actors to achieve this goal and constitutes a challenge for different research communities.

Ad hoc solutions are not likely to be applicable to solve such a complex problem. Providing a basic framework for automated services and QoS deployment may constitute an important contribution towards solving such a problem.

Please use the following format when citing this chapter:

Van Wambeke, N., Armando, F., Chassot, C., Guennoun, K., Drira, K. and Exposito, E., 2008, in IFIP International Federation for Information Processing, Volume 284; *Wireless and Mobile Networking*; Zoubir Mammeri; (Boston: Springer), pp. 459–470.

Aiming to answering this problem, we propose a model-based framework for adaptability management. Our framework has been elaborated in the context of network management systems with service provisioning at the transport and network layers of the TCP/IP stack as the final objectives.

Our approach provides, refines and exploits different models, each one representing a different point of view on the context. The models that represent other aspects of communication are automatically generated from higher level models representing the cooperation requirements and the communication constraints. Our research efforts have been developed to cover communication at the transport layer as well as the network layer.

Our paper is organized as follows. Section 2 describes related work. Section 3 describes the different models of the framework. Section 4 presents an architecture to support the use of these models for automated network adaptation management as well as an example of their use in response to a change of collaboration. This architecture is currently under study and development within the European NETQoS Project. Section 5 provides conclusions and future works.

2   Related Work

2.1 Classification of Context Adaptation Solutions

This section studies and classifies the main facets of adaptation: its objectives, techniques and properties.

Adaptation Objectives

Adaptation targets several objectives depending on the context in which it takes place. QoS aspects such as access bandwidth issues in roaming scenarios are considered in [7]. End to end QoS optimization for the Best Effort Internet makes heavy use of adaptation techniques [1]. Security in wireless networks, such as firewalls activation and deactivation, can also benefit from adaptability [10]. Resources optimization related to device power, computation or storage capability are presented in [9].

Adaptation Techniques

Application layer – Reference [14] addresses adaptation of video streaming applications for the Best-Effort Internet. The proposed techniques are based on two mechanisms: an applicative congestion control (rate control, rate-adaptive video encoding) and time aware error control with FEC.

Middleware layer – Reflexive architectures such as OpenORB or Xmiddle [2] are good supports for adaptation as they allow run-time modification of the architecture.

Transport layer - TCP's congestion control is a well-known adaptation example. In [1] various types of mobile applications in wireless Internet are studied. Adaptation consists in parameterization of congestion control mechanisms using context information. In [5, 6] the architectural adaptation of transport protocols by dynamic composition of protocol modules are presented, these approaches are detailed in section 2.2.

Network layer - [4] addresses QoS-aware routing problems within mobile networks. In [10], dynamic provision of IP services for military wired/wireless networks is considered. In a policy-based networking management context, the need for self-adaptation is considered in [12], using a learning-based approach.

MAC layer - The solutions handle connection and access QoS problems for mobile users using different terminals and roaming. [7] provides a solution for optimizing the handover latency but the other QoS requirements are not considered.

Adaptation Properties

The adaptation is *behavioral* when a service can be modified without modifying its structure. TCP and protocols in [1] provide behavioral adaptation. This easy to implement approach limits adaptability because the components have to be recompiled to be extended. Adaptation can not be performed during run-time.

The adaptation is *architectural* when the services' structure can be modified. The replacement components can be implemented following a plug and play approach where the new component has the same interfaces as the replaced one.

Finally, adapting components can be distributed or centralized. In the first case, adaptation is *vertical* as changes are local. In the second case, it is horizontal and synchronization between adapting peers has to be managed.

2.2 Dynamically Configurable Protocol Architectures and Model based Adaptation

Dynamically configurable protocol architectures are based on the *protocol module* concept [6]. A protocol is then viewed as the composition of various protocol modules in order to provide a given service. These architectures can be classified depending on their internal structure: the event based model and the hierarchical model. The Enhanced Transport Protocol (ETP) [5] follows a hybrid approach combining both models.

These protocol architectures are a good choice for *self-adaptation* as they provide *run-time* architectural reconfiguration. The modules composing them can change during communication. This *run-time* architectural adaptation raises many problems such as: (1) synchronization of peers; and (2) the choice of the best composition.

Adaptation management still remains a complex problem, particularly when it is required at several layers (Transport, Middleware ...) simultaneously [8]. In such cases, the need to ensure coherency of the adaptation choices, both within and between layers clearly appears.

Informal methods lead to suboptimal solutions, often specific to a problem. This is due, in part to the complexity of the problem. To overcome these limitations, graph based formal approaches are appropriate to coordinate architectural adaptation at different layers of the stack. In [3], we illustrate this approach by using graph based models and graph transformation rules. In the present paper, we complement this initial work by an architecture to manage these models.

3   The Proposed Model-based Framework

The framework is composed of three main models: **the Connection Model, the Cooperation Model** and **the Adaptive Deployment Model (ADM)**. The communication context is captured by the **Connection Model** while the **Cooperation Model** captures the activity cooperation context. The relationships between these models presented hereafter are summarized on Figure 1.

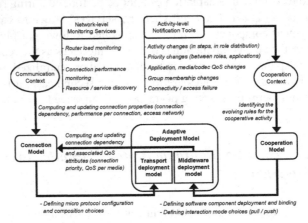

Fig. 1. Relationship between context elements and framework models

3.1   General Overview of the Framework Models

The activity requirements are derived from the cooperation context and captured by the **Cooperation Model** which captures the changes occurring at the activity level. These include modifying activity phases, role distribution, modifying priorities between roles and applications, modifying QoS parameters of applications, media and codecs, dynamic group membership, and access and connectivity failures.

The communication context includes connection dependencies, connection performances and the characteristics of the access network which are captured by the **Connection Model**. This model expresses the connection dependencies and the associated Quality of Service (QoS) attributes including connection priority and per media QoS parameters. The communication context changes are monitored by a set of network-level monitoring services. Changes occurring at this level include router load, routing choices, connection performances, and resource and service discovering.

The **Adaptive Deployment Model (ADM)** is generated from the above two context models. It is composed of two sub-models, the **Middleware Deployment Model** and the **Transport Deployment Model (TDM)**.

The **Middleware Deployment Model (MDM)** represents the different software components supporting the information exchange between the different actors of the cooperative activity. Such components are event producers, event consumers, and channel managers interacting following the publish/subscribe paradigm or simple clients and servers interacting through direct message exchange. The different bindings of information requesters to information providers and the different interaction modes are also elements of the **MDM**. These elements can change for adaptability purposes at runtime.

The **Transport Deployment Model (TDM)** is deduced from the **Connection Model** and the **Middleware Deployment Model**. It represents the transport level decisions. In the case of dynamically configurable protocol architectures, the different protocol modules as well as their configurations are represented.

3.2 Framework Instantiation Example

In order to illustrate the use of the previously presented models, their application to Military Emergency Operation (MEO) management is presented in the next paragraphs.

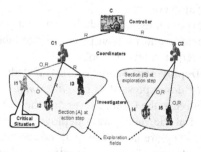

Fig. 2. Example of cooperations in MEO

3.2.1 Application context: Military emergency operation management

We consider the context of Military Emergency Operation (MEO) management systems (see Figure 2) which involve structured groups of communicating actors that cooperate to manage a given crisis. The cooperating actors have roles and use communication devices with unequal communication, processing, energy and storage resources. Devices are fixed or mobile, and communicate through wired and/or wireless networks.

Cooperation is based on data exchange between members: Observation data (O) and Report data (R) are produced periodically or immediately after a particular event. An activity controller supervises the teams, receives the coordinator reports summarizing the current situation and mission progress. According to actions and objectives assigned by the controller, a coordinator manages a team of investigators by giving orders and assigning tasks to be performed.

Investigators explore the field; they observe, analyze and submit reports of the situation to coordinators. For each team, two phases are considered. During the exploration phase (section B), investigators communications have the same priority. The action phase (section A) corresponds to the discovery of a critical situation. The investigator who discovers it is given high priority for communications.

3.2.2 Description of the elaborated models

In the context presented above, the various models introduced in our approach are detailed in the following paragraphs. As a summary, Figure 3 provides a global view of the elaborated models, their relationship as well as the different techniques used for automating their implementation.

The **Cooperation Model** (CoopM) is deduced from the cooperation context which is subject to changes, e.g. from one phase of the activity to another. When such changes happen, *reconfiguration rules* are used to automate the model's adaptation. These rules are written as *graph transformation* rules introduced in [3].

The CoopM involves (1) characterizing all valid configurations as a graph grammar, (2) describing valid configurations, (3) defining all possible structural changes at the cooperation level as graph transformation rules. This formally provides the valid reconfiguration rules and actions to be performed in reaction to changes in the cooperation context.

For cooperation level graphs, node labels represent actor identifiers, cooperation roles, hosting devices, and mission phases. Edge labels represent exchanged data, priority, and the required level of QoS.

The **Middleware Deployment Model** (MDM) is deduced from the CoopM using model *refinement rules* expressed as *graph-grammar* productions. It supports two architectural paradigms: the Client/Server and the Publish/Subscribe.

For graphs handled at the middleware deployment level, nodes represent the deployment elements. They are labeled by parameters such as type (e.g. P/C/G on Figure 4), and hosting devices. Edges are labeled by related communication characteristics such as QoS and priorities.

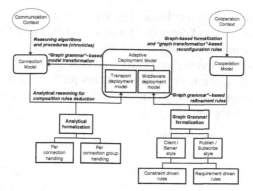

Fig. 3. Techniques for automated model adaptation in the framework

Refinement from the CoopM into the MDM is implemented using extended *edNCE graph grammars* [11]. The system allows the generation of all the deployment configurations with respect to a given cooperation model. On the other hand, it also allows automatic conformance verification of dynamically evolving cooperation and deployment instance models.

The **Connection Model (ConnM)** is deduced from the MDM following a set of model transformation rules expressed as *graph-grammar productions*.

The connections are represented by graph nodes as first level elements of the **ConnM**. Dependant connections are immediate neighbors in the graph.

In practice, a dependency relationship means that the two connections share at least one common resource, such as access networks or routers. The higher the dependency degree is, the more it will be suitable to coordinate the connections to improve their performance. Dependency also results from topology properties such as sharing of the sending and/or receiving hosts, or *n* common routers. Such information may be useful to *estimate* the probability of a common bottleneck when its presence cannot be determined by the monitoring services.

Node labels, such as (c1, R, QoS_R, high, AN_{MC1}, AN_{MC}, $Perf_{c1}$) on Figure 4 represent, respectively, the the connection id, the transported data type, the QoS required, the priority of the connection, the access network of the sender and the receiver, and the observed performances (i.e. delay, loss rate).

Edge labels refine the dependency degree between each pair of dependant connections, using values deduced from the MDM and monitoring information.

The **Transport Deployment Model (TDM)** is built in two stages. First, a *per-connection* decision is taken. This decision is based on reasoning procedures that take the **ConnM** as input and output the protocol modules composition to be used in a dynamically configurable transport protocol in order to optimize the QoS. This approach of our work detailed in [13]. Then, a *per-group of connections* decision is taken in order to consider dependency and priority properties. This decision refines the compositions and adds modules for managing priorities.

The reasoning process is based on two models, the *composition model* and the *decision model*. The composition model is used to define the *conditions* of the validity of the assembled protocol modules. By such, it reduces the size of the set of potential composition candidates for the reasoning process. The decision model is used to guide the process of choosing a composition among all the valid ones in order to maximize the overall user perceived efficiency (i.e. the required QoS). In previous works [13], we have shown that this problem is equivalent to a multi-criteria optimization problem given a proper formal description of the candidate protocol modules composition.

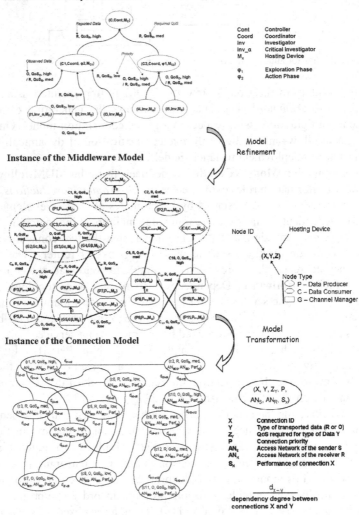

Fig. 4. Example of refinement and transformations from the Cooperation Model to the Connection Model

4   Implementing an Architecture to Support Model based Adaptation

In this section, the details and benefits of using the previously introduced models in the provisioning process is described in the context of the NETQoS IST project which addresses the problem of QoS management using a policy-based approach.

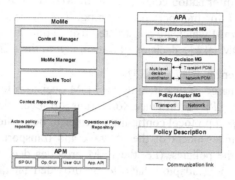

Fig. 5. General NETQoS architecture

The general architecture of the NETQoS system distinguishes four main entities (see Figure 5):

The *Policy Description* is used to specify the actor-level policies, the operational policies, etc. The *Automated Policy Adaptor* (APA) does not provide QoS by itself, but decides upon and dispatches operational policies. It is responsible for the provisioning process in which the models are used. The *Actor Preference Manager* (APM) provides NETQoS GUI/API allowing users to define policies. These policies (e.g. requirements, preferences, profile, quality reporting...) may be expressed before or during the communications. This information is used by the APA as input to the **CoopM**. The *Monitoring and Measurement* (MoMe) captures context evolution, (e.g. evolving actor's policies, end systems/network resource change). This information is used by the APA as input to the **ConnM**.

4.1   Models for the Automated Policy Adaptor (APA)

The APA decides, dispatches, and adapts the operational policies that take into account the actors dynamic requirements as well as the evolving context. It is composed of three main components. The *Policy Decision Manager* (PDM) is in charge of the decision process. This process is based on the use of the models presented in section 3. The *Policy Enforcement Manager* (PEM) is in charge of the deployment of the policies decided by the PDM on the policy enforcement points.

The *Policy Adaptation Manager* (PAM) is in charge of the adaptation, individually or by groups, when the communication or the cooperation context changes. The following paragraphs detail the three APA components implementation.

Policy decision manager (PDM)
The PDM decides an optimal set of policies to be settled at the Network and/or at the Transport level to satisfy the set of actor-level policies. This *provisioning* is performed using information contained on the **MDM** for network provisioning as well as the **TDM** for transport provisioning. The models are derived from the **CoopM and ConnM** which are constructed using context monitoring information. Each time the PDM takes a decision, it transmits it to the PEM presented below.

Policy enforcement manager (PEM)
The PEM is in charge of dispatching the PDM decisions to the actual policy enforcement point (PEP). For instance, for a transport level adaptation, the PEM dispatches the transport protocol configuration rules to be applied on the end nodes.

The PEM is independent of the network and transport technologies that are used to enforce the policies, (i.e. the PEM provides decisions in a generic language). Consequently, adaptors have to be provided on the PEP themselves to translate the generic PEM rules into specific technology-dependant rules.

Policy adaptation manager (PAM)
The PAM is in charge of the adaptation when the context changes. It may decide to adapt the policy by re-creating a completely new one or simply amending the one in place.

The PAM mainly acts when it receives alarms from the MoMe component informing it that the communication or cooperation contexts have changed. It performs adaptation by applying the *graph-grammar* transformations to the actual **Connection and Cooperation Models** and re-generating derived (**MDM, TDM ...**) models.

4.2 Example: Model Based Adaptation

In this section, the Military Emergency Operations context presented in section *3.2.1* is used to illustrate the adaptation steps that take place on the models constructed by the APA when the cooperation goes from the exploration step to the action step. This adaptation corresponds to the discovery of a critical situation by one of the investigators taking place in the activity.

For instance on the **MDM** presented on Figure 6a, the investigators M_1 and M_2 are in the exploration step. Two channels are implemented: each one is in charge of a specific (data, priority) couple. Assuming a mobile participant is allowed to host only one event service component, the two channel managers (CMs) are deployed on participants M_1 and M_2.

When an investigator discovers a critical situation, the policies/preferences change and MoMe component informs the APA of this event. The APA then modifies the **Cooperation Model** according to the user's preferences. In this case, the user has specified that in exploration step, each investigator reports directly to its coordinator while in the action step, the investigator who discovered a critical situation reports to both his direct coordinator as well as his fellow investigators.

To support the changes of the **Cooperation Model** when the mission goes from the exploration step (step 1) to the action step (step 2), several adaptation actions are performed on the **MDM**. These actions lead to different possible architectures, one of them is illustrated on Figure 6b.

Architecture transformation is guided by rules that consider not only changes of the **Cooperation Model**, but also changes of resource-oriented parameters such as machines' energy and storage/computation capacity. For instance, in the action step, four CM are implemented: one per (data, priority) couple. In order to save energy, two CM are deployed on the controller's machine M_3, and only one CM is deployed on each of the investigators' machine M_1 and M_2. Such transformation may also be caused by resources parameters only. In such cases, a "good" transformation should have no impact on the upper **Cooperation Model**.

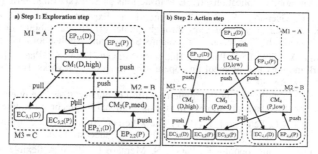

Fig.6 Graph transformations from exploration step to action step – MDM

This new **MDM** is used to automatically update the **Connection Model**, both models will then be used to adapt the policy in place and deploy the updated decision on the different network and transport PEP resulting in optimized QoS to all users in this new step of their mission.

5   Conclusion and Perspectives

In this paper, different models have been elaborated and implemented to help automating adaptive deployment for QoS management. Different points of view have been considered to capture the influence of the cooperation as well as the communication contexts. The interest of our approach resides in its capacity to support the full automation of the network management tasks in evolving contexts.

An architecture that uses these models in the context of automated policy based network management has been presented. This architecture allows activity-level requirement to be expressed by the user and have the system behave accordingly. The use of the models in the decision process has been illustrated in the context of simple Military Emergency Operations.

Extending the work presented here, future work includes the implementation and benchmarking of the NETQoS architecture. Scalability issues as well as convergence speed of the decision algorithms have to be addressed.

Acknowledgments: Part of this work is done in the context of the EU IST FP6 NETQoS (STREP) project and by a French DGA (Direction Générale de l'Armement) grant.

References

1. Akan O B, Akyildiz I F (2004) ATL: An adaptive transport layer suite for next-generation wireless Internet. IEEE Journal on Selected Areas in Communications 5:802–817.
2. Capra L, Emmerich W, Mascolo C (2003) Carisma: Context-aware reflective middleware system for mobile applications. IEEE Transactions on Software Engineering 10:929–945.
3. Chassot C, Guennoun K, Drira K, Armando F, Exposito E, Lozes A (2006) Towards autonomous management of QoS through model driven adaptability in communication-centric systems. Int Transactions on Systems Science and Applications 3:255–264.
4. DaSilva L A, Midkiff S F, Park J S, Hadjichristofi G C, Davis N J, Phanse K S, Lin T (2004) Network mobility and protocol interoperability in ad hoc networks. IEEE Communications Magazine 11:88–96.
5. Exposito E J (2003) Design and implementation of quality of service oriented transport protocol for multimedia applications. PhD thesis, National Polytechnic Institute of Toulouse.
6. Hutchinson N C, Peterson L L (1991) The x-kernel: An architecture for implementing network protocols. IEEE Transactions on Software Engineering 1:64–76.
7. Kaloxylos A, Lampropoulos G, Passas N, Merakos L (2006) A flexible handover mechanism for seamless service continuity in heterogeneous environments. Computer Communications 6:717–729.
8. Landry R, Grace K, Saidi A (2004) On the design and management of heterogeneous networks: A predictability-based perspective. IEEE Communications Magazine, 11:80 – 87.
9. Marshall I, Roadknight C (2001) Provision of quality of service for active services. Computer Networks 1:75–85.
10. Perez G, Skarmeta A G (2004) Policy-based dynamic provision of IP services in a secure vpn coalition scenario. IEEE Communications Magazine 11:118 – 124.
11. Rozenberg G (1997) Handbook of Graph Grammars and Computing by Graph Transformation, World Scientific Publishing, ISBN 981-02-2884-8
12. Samaan N, Karmouch A (2005) An automated policy-based management framework for differentiated communication systems. IEEE Journal on Selected Areas in Communications 12:2236-2248.
13. Van Wambeke N, Armando F, Chassot C, Exposito E (2008) A model-based approach for self-adaptive Transport protocols. Comput Commun. doi: 10.1016/j.comcom.2008.02.026.
14. Wu D, Hou Y T, Zhu W (2001) Streaming video over the internet: Approaches and directions. IEEE Transactions on Circuits and Systems for Video Technology 11:282-301

Improved Lightweight Mutual Authentication Protocol for RFID Systems

Győző Gódor and Mátyás Antal

Győző Gódor and Mátyás Antal
Department of Telecommunication, Budapest University of Technology and Economics,
Magyar Tudósok körútja 2., Budapest, Hungary H-1117, e-mail: godorgy@hit.bme.hu

Abstract The usage of the RFID technology is becoming more and more widespread, however, the systems are quite vulnerable regarding security aspects. The authentication protocols developed for computer networks are not suitable for RFID use, because the tags have very limited memory and computing capacity. New solutions are needed, which requires less operations and fewer messages. The lightweight protocols are one of the currently known methods for this purpose, but the proposed algorithms do not satisfy all of the security requirements. In this paper we introduce our lightweight authentication protocol, which provides prevention against all known attack schemes. We provide a full security analysis and prove the correctness of our solution with formal verification using GNY logics.

1 Introduction

The potential uses of radio frequency identification is nearly endless: logistics, entrance systems, medical applications, measuring traffic, etc. However, radio based identification implies new types of problems - just like in mobile communication and wireless networks - since the radio channel that carries the signals are accessible by everyone who is nearby, thus providing a chance to eavesdrop or attack it. One of the most important problems to solve is to allow the communicating parties to identify and authorize each other in a secure manner, which means they can be sure that the other one is indeed who she says to be.

RFID systems consist of three main functional units: the items to be identified are called tags, the device with which the tags are communicating is called a reader and the back-end, which controls the readers and has access to the database.

Tags are usually very small devices that contain a simple processing unit, a small amount of ROM and/or RAM and a small sized coiled antenna. Tags may be equipped with an own power source, i. e. a battery, in which case

Please use the following format when citing this chapter:

Gódor, G. and Antal, M., 2008, in IFIP International Federation for Information Processing, Volume 284; *Wireless and Mobile Networking*; Zoubir Mammeri; (Boston: Springer), pp. 471–482.

they are so called active tags. In contrast, passive tags, since they do not have any source of power, are capable of communicating only if a reader has initiated a connection beforehand. The amount of energy needed for memory operations, calculations and transmitting the reply message is retrieved from the radio waves emitted by the reader. This means that this type of tags have very limited capabilities regarding the number and complexity of calculations as well as the length of the reply messages. The main goal is to implement a communication protocol between the tag and the reader which allows the parties to exchange data securely, whilst it does not require the tag to be too complex to keep its production cost reasonably low.

The back-end can command a reader to retrieve the identification number stored in an RFID tag. The reader acts very similarly to a simple optical bar code reader in a sense that it forwards every data received from its radio interface to the back-end on a secure, standardized channel, i.e. RS-232 or Ethernet. The identification number read from a tag is processed by the back-end. Its task is to carry out authentication: to check if the ID provided can be found in the database and, depending on the application of RFID, verify if the tag is allowed to use the service, etc. The back-end may be anything from a simple PC to an enormous cluster of servers. When discussing lightweight authentication protocols we suppose the back-end has (at least compared to the tags) unlimited computational capacity. Naturally, in larger systems the back-end may easily become the bottleneck, thus we must take its performance and scalability into consideration as well.

2 Security Requirements of an RFID System

Since the communication between the tags and the reader takes place on a radio channel, practically anyone can eavesdrop the identification number sent by the tags or the requests issued by the reader. Moreover, it is quite possible that an adversary impersonates a reader and requests tag A to give out her identification number. In the possession of that information, he can later personate tag A by demonstrating its ID to a legal reader. If this happened in a supermarket, the worst case would be that someone bought a plasma TV at the price of a soft drink. But if an attacker was able to authorize himself as a government agent and got into a top secret area, it would possibly mean the end of someone's job. Nevertheless it is desirable that a tag gives out its identity only if it has made certain that the reader was authentic and not being an attacker trying to get valuable information. Besides that the reader should authenticate the tag as well.

The messages sent by the tag during the authentication process can be seen by anyone, thus it is very important that an attacker should not be able to gain any valuable information from these. This criteria is fulfilled if the transmitted data on the channel is completely undistinguishable from random bits.

Since there can be possibly more than thousands of RFID tags in a system, their production price should be kept very low. This leads to the fact that they cannot be equipped with tamperproof memory chips, which would ensure that no data can be read out without permission. But it is desirable that even if the attacker knows the identity of a tampered tag, he will still not be able to find a connection between the previous and current transactions of the tag. This property of tags is called untraceability. Untraceability can be achieved if tags do not reveal their identity to the reader directly, but use a unique identification number in each transaction, which is only known by the reader and themselves.

A proper authentication protocol should ensure that:

- tags' and reader's messages cannot be eavesdropped
- tags are not traceable
- in case a tag is tampered no connection can be found to its previous transactions
- messages cannot be replayed
- man-in-the-middle type of attacks are prevented
- messages cannot be interleaved between different protocol runs
- denial of service attacks are prevented
- no-one can impersonate the tags or the reader
- messages sent by the tags are undistinguishable from random bits

3 Related Work

Protocols that require low computing capacity, such as carrying out simple bit operations and/or calculating one-way hash functions are called lightweight protocols. Because of the relatively low production price of tags running lightweight protocols, they are likely to become popular among consumer goods. There were several solutions, e.g. the Hash Lock Scheme [3] and the Extended Hash-chain Scheme [4] that aimed at fulfilling the security requirements shown in the previous section. The first one fails to prevent the traceability of tags, since the ID is constant between transactions. The latter one does not provide protection against man-in-the-middle attacks, since an adversary can easily stand between the tag and the reader catching and forwarding messages without being noticed. Also the tags need a good random number generator to make random numbers unpredictable which is very hard to implement on a CPU with low capacity.

Luo, Chan and S. Li proposed a new scheme, the Lightweight Mutual Authentication Protocol [1], based on Ohkubo's hash chain [2] and simple XOR operations that provided mutual authentication for the tags and the back-end. The motivation for using mutual authentication is to ensure that the back-end, and thus the reader itself, is authentic before transferring the tag's ID to the back-end, whilst the back-end can verify whether the tag is an authentic one in the system. To achieve backward privacy, which means that secret values used in previous transactions cannot be recovered even if a tag gets compromised, Ohkubo proposed a hash chain of length n. In the ith transaction the tag sends $a_i = G(s_i)$ to the reader and renews its secret by calculating $s_{i+1} = H(s_i)$, where s_i is determined recursively and G and H are hash functions.

The RFID tag stores an initial s_0 secret value as well as its ID, which can be loaded into its memory during production. To ensure that the tag remains untraceable by a third party who keeps track of the secret values, it is periodically changed after every transaction. For this purpose a s_i secret value is used for the ith transaction as the input for the hash chain and get the a_i output after n rounds of the one-way hash function G in order to maintain backward privacy.

In that scheme the tags have three readable/writeable memory blocks denoted by W_1, W_2 and W_3. Also there is a separate memory block reserved for keeping track of the c_i transaction counter. The back-end stores the s_0 secret value, the current values of the W_1, W_2 and W_3 blocks as well as the tag's ID. The messages of the protocol run can be seen on Figure 1.

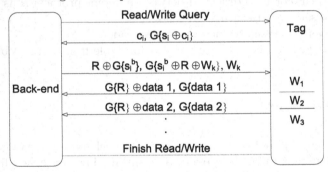

Fig. 1 Luo, Chan and S. Li's Lightweight Mutual Authentication Protocol

The main problem of the proposed scheme is that an adversary can easily replay the second message sent by the tag, thus impersonating it without being noticed. The reason why the protocol does not prevent replay attacks is because the back-end does not use any challenge to ensure the freshness of the tag's response.

Also, because in order to authenticate a tag the back-end needs to calculate hash c_i times for every tag in its database, it can easily become the performance bottleneck in the system. It is desirable to lower the number of required hash operations.

4 Improved Lightweight Mutual Authentication Protocol

Our proposed improvement for the above protocol can be seen on Figure 2.

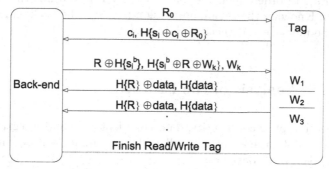

Fig. 2 Improved Lightweight Mutual Authentication Protocol

Instead of Ohkubo's hash chain, we use a simple iterative hash in every transaction. In the beginning let the secret value be s_0, which can be loaded into the tag during production. After a successful authentication, s_{i+1} is calculated by hashing s_i.

In the ith transaction a challenge (R_0) is sent by the back-end, which enables it to verify whether the tag has responded recently. The tag calculates the XOR value of the transaction counter (c_i), the current secret value (s_i) and the back-end's challenge. The tag sends the transaction counter and the hash value of the XOR's output. The challenge is needed to prevent adversaries from replaying the tag's message at a later time.

Given c_i, the back-end does an exhaustive search to find the tag's current secret value in its database, for which $H(s_i^b \oplus c_i \oplus R_0) = H(s_i \oplus c_i \oplus R_0)$, where s_i^b is derived from s_{i-1}^b by hashing. Because of the cryptographic hash function's preimage collision resistant property described in Rogaways's and Shrimpton's work [6], this holds if and only if $s_i^b = s_i$. If it finds a match in the database, it means the tag is authentic.

For mutual authentication the back-end still has to prove it knows the tag's current secret value. Also it is desirable to share a common random session number that can later be used by the parties to send encrypted data. Let this random number be denoted by R. The back-end's response consists of three parts: $R \oplus H(s_i^b)$, $H(s_i^b \oplus R \oplus W_k)$ and W_k.

The tag starts to decipher the message by calculating the XOR of $H(s_i)$ and the first part of the received message ($R \oplus H(s_i^b)$), thus it learns the random number R^t. It authenticates the back-end if and only if both $R^t = R$ and $s_i = s_i^b$ hold.

By the end of the protocol run the parties also agreed on which W_k memory block to read/write in the current transaction. The integrity of W_k is ensured by bounding it with s_i in the second part of the back-end's reply.

Also the tag may transfer encrypted data to the back-end by sending $G(R) \oplus data_i$. In order to ensure data integrity it also sends the hash value of the data. Knowing the R random session number, the back-end can easily decipher the message and check its integrity.

5 Security Analysis of the Protocol

When analyzing protocol security, data confidentiality and integrity, protection against well-known attacks as well as the requirements stated in Section 2 should be taken into consideration.

Data confidentiality and integrity   the tags store no valuable system data except for their s_i secret value and the W_1, W_2 and W_3 memory blocks. This means that even if an adversary manages to compromise a tag, she will not be able to obtain any more information than what is stored in its memory. Since the messages sent and received by tags are transferred in hashed form, no information can be learnt by eavesdropping. Data integrity is ensured by adding the hash value of the data to the end of each message.

Tag anonymity   the tag's messages are undistinguishable from random bits by a third party, because of the H hash function. Since no private data is sent in clear, tags remain anonymous towards any third party.

Untraceability of tags   in the ith transaction $H(s_i \oplus c_i \oplus R_0)$ is sent by the tag, where s_i is changed after a successful read or write and is unknown by third parties. To find a connection between s_i and s_k, where $0 \leq k < i$, an adversary would have to find the preimage of hash function H at least twice, which is known to be a hard problem. This holds even if the attacker manages to tamper a tag and learns the data stored in the tag's memory (eg. the current secret value: s_i).

Prevention of replay attacks   the back-end uses a challenge in the first message to ensure the freshness of the tag's response. The adversary would have to wait until the same R_0 is chosen by the back-end for which she already has the response. If R_0 has a large entropy (and it can be assumed because it is generated by the back-end which has enough resources to generate such a R_0 random number), this is very unlikely to happen. The same holds if an attacker tries to replay messages between different protocol runs.

Prevention of man-in-the-middle attacks   the second and the third messages of the protocol renders it impossible for an adversary to carry out the attack. Both the secret value and the random session number is transferred in a hashed form or is XOR-ed to a hash value. In order to stand between the two parties and manipulate the messages without being discovered she would have to recover s_i from $H(s_i \oplus c_i \oplus R_0)$, which is not possible because the H hash function is preimage resistant.

Prevention of impersonating the parties   the attacker has to know the common secret value s_i in order to impersonate any of the parties. Since the protocol never reveals s_i, and because H is preimage resistant, it is ensured that no-one will be able to impersonate the tag or the reader.

6 Verification of the Protocol's Correctness

6.1 GNY Rules Used For Verification

The postulates used for the proof can be found in [5], the lack of space prevents the authors to communicate them in this paper. Throughout the deduction we always use the same notation as the authors of GNY logics.

In that article $(I3)$ postulate does not cover the case when such a formula is hashed which contains the S secret indirectly through an F function. So let us introduce a new postulate for this case and extend the GNY logics with the following:

$$(I3b) \quad \frac{P \triangleleft \star H\left(F\left(X,S\right)\right), P \ni F\left(X,S\right), P \models P \stackrel{S}{\leftrightarrow} Q, P \models \sharp(F\left(X,S\right))}{P \models Q \hspace{-0.3em}\sim\hspace{-0.3em} F\left(X,S\right), P \models Q \hspace{-0.3em}\sim\hspace{-0.3em} H\left(F\left(X,S\right)\right)}$$

6.2 Notation

To make the protocol verification more readable, let us introduce the following standard GNY logics notations:

$A : T$
$B : B$
$K_i : s_i$
$K'_i : s_i^b$
$N_a : R_0$
$N_b : R$
$H(X) : G(X)$

6.3 Idealization of messages

The idealized Improved Lightweight Mutual Authentication Protocol's messages can be written in GNY logics in the following form:

$(Ideal1)\ B \rightarrow\ A : \star N_a$
$(Ideal2)\ A \rightarrow\ B : \star c_i, \star H\left(\star F\left(\star F\left(N_a, \star c_i\right), \star K_i\right)\right)$, where $K_i = H^{c_i}\left(K_0\right)$
$(Ideal3)\ B \rightarrow\ A : \star F\left(\star N_b, \star H\left(\star K'_i\right)\right), \star H\left(\star F\left(\star F\left(\star W_k, \star N_b\right), \star K'_i\right)\right), \star W_k$

$$(\ (Ideal4) \ A \rightarrow \ B : \star F \left(H \left(N_b \right) \right), data), \star H \left(data \right) \ )$$

6.4 Assumptions

The following statements are believed to be true prior to the protocol's run:

(A1) $B \ni K_0$

(A2) $B \ni N_a$

(A3) $B \ni N_b$

(A4) $B \ni W_k$

(A5) $B \models B \xleftrightarrow{K_i} A$

(A6) $B \models \sharp(N_a)$

(A7) $B \models \sharp(N_b)$

(A8) $A \ni K_0$

(A9) $A \ni c_i$

(A10) $A \models B \xleftrightarrow{K_i} A$

(A11) $A \models \sharp(c_i)$

(A12) $A \models B \ Z\Rightarrow \sharp(N_b)$

(A13) $A \models B \models \sharp(N_b)$

6.5 Aims

The main aim of the protocol is to provide mutual authentication. This consists of the following two aims:

1st **aim**: the back-end ensures that the tag knows the K_i secret.

(C1) $B \models A \ni K_i$

2nd **aim**: the tag ensures that the back-end also knows the K_i secret.

(C2) $A \models B \ni K_i$

6.6 Proof

We will deduce the aims from the idealized protocol messages using the assumptions we made. It can be seen during the deduction that no third parties are able to learn the K_i secrets at any time during or after the protocol run.

After receiving the 1st message:

$$(M1) \ A \triangleleft \star N_a$$

Using the $(T1)$ postulate:

$$(D1) \ A \triangleleft N_a$$

From this using the $(P1)$ rule we get:

$$(D2) \ A \ni N_a$$

After receiving the 2nd message:

$$(M2)\ B \lhd (\star c_i, \star H\left(\star F\left(\star F\left(N_a, \star c_i\right), \star K_i\right)\right))$$

Using rule $(T2)$:

$$(D3)\ B \lhd \star c_i$$

Using $(T1)$ postulate:

$$(D4)\ B \lhd c_i$$

From this using he $(P1)$ rule we get:

$$(D5)\ B \ni c_i$$

$$(A1)\ B \ni K_0$$

Using $(A1)$ and the $(P4)$ rule c_i times in a row we get:

$$(D6)\ B \ni H^{c_i}(K_0), \text{which means } B \ni K_i$$

$$(A2)\ B \ni N_a$$

From assumption $(A2)$ and statement $(D6)$ using the $(P2)$ possession rule:

$$(D7)\ B \ni F(N_a, c_i)$$

From statements $(D6)$ and $(D7)$ using $(P2)$ postulate:

$$(D8)\ B \ni F\left(F\left(N_a, c_i\right), K_i\right)$$

$$(A6)\ B \models \sharp(N_a)$$

From $(D7)$ using $(A6)$ and $(F1)$ we get:

$$(D9)\ B \models \sharp(N_u, c_i)$$

From statement $(D9)$ using $(F1)$ freshness rule:

$$(D10)\ B \models \sharp(F(N_a, c_i))$$

From $(D10)$ using $(F1)$ again:

$$(D11)\ B \models \sharp(F(N_a, c_i), K_i)$$

From $(D11)$ statement using $(F1)$ rule once again:

$$(D12)\ B \models \sharp(F(F(N_a, c_i), K_i))$$

From $(D8)$ and $(D12)$ statements using $(F10)$ we get:

$$(D13)\ B \models \sharp(H(F(F(N_a, c_i), K_i)))$$

From message $(M2)$ using $(T2)$ postulate:

$$(D14)\ B \lhd \star H\left(\star F\left(\star F\left(N_a, \star c_i\right), \star K_i\right)\right)$$

From statements $(D8)$, $(D12)$ and $(D14)$ using the $(A5)$ assumption and the $(I3b)$ postulate with which the GNY logics were extended above (having $X = F(N_a, c_i)$, $S = K_i$ substituted) we get:

$$(D15)\ B \models A \hspace{-0.3em}\sim\hspace{-0.3em} F(F(N_a, c_i), K_i)$$

From $(D12)$ and $(D15)$ statements and the $(I6)$ rule:

$$(D16)\ B \models A \ni F\left(F\left(N_a, c_i\right), K_i\right)$$

From $(D2)$ statement using assumption $(A9)$, postulate $(P2)$ and the rationality rule:

$$(D17)\ B \models A \ni F\left(N_a, c_i\right)$$

From statements $(D16)$ and $(D17)$ using the $(P5)$ postulate and the rationality rule:

$$(D18)\ B \models A \ni K_i$$

Notice that statement $(D18)$ is the same as our $(C1)$ aim, which means that the tag is authenticated by the back-end indeed.

After receiving the 3rd message:

$$(M3)\ A \triangleleft \star F\left(\star N_b, \star H\left(\star K_i'\right)\right), \star H\left(\star F\left(\star F\left(\star W_k, \star N_b\right), \star K_i'\right)\right), \star W_k$$

Using the $(T2)$ being told rule:

$$(D19)\ A \triangleleft \star F\left(\star N_b, \star H\left(\star K_i'\right)\right)$$

$$(D20)\ A \triangleleft \star H\left(\star F\left(\star F\left(\star W_k, \star N_b\right), \star K_i'\right)\right)$$

$$(D21)\ A \triangleleft \star W_k$$

$$(A8)\ A \ni K_0$$

From assumption $(A8)$ using the $(P4)$ postulate c_i times in a row we get:

$$(D22)\ A \ni H^{c_i}\left(K_0\right), azaz\ A \ni K_i$$

From statement $(D22)$ using $(P4)$ again:

$$(D23)\ A \ni H\left(K_i\right)$$

From $(D19)$ and $(D23)$ using the $(P5)$ postulate:

$$(D24)\ A \ni N_b$$

From $(D21)$ using $(T1)$:

$$(D25)\ A \triangleleft W_k$$

From $(D25)$ using the $(P1)$ postulate:

$$(D26)\ A \ni W_k$$

From statements $(D24)$ and $(D26)$ using $(P2)$ we get:

$$(D27)\ A \ni F\left(W_k, N_b\right)$$

From statements $(D22)$ and $(D24)$ using the $(P2)$ postulate again:

$$(D28)\ A \ni F\left(F\left(W_k, N_b\right), K_i\right)$$

$$(A12)\ A \models B\ Z \Rightarrow \sharp(N_b)$$

$$(A13)\ A \models B \models \sharp(N_b)$$

From assumptions $(A12)$ and $(A13)$ using the $(J1)$ jurisdiction rule:

$$(D29)\ A \models \sharp(N_b)$$

From $(D29)$ using $(F1)$:

$$(D30)\ A \models \sharp(W_k, N_b)$$

From $(D30)$ using $(F1)$ again:

$$(D31)\ A \models \sharp(F(W_k, N_b))$$

From $(D31)$ using $(F1)$ once again:

$$(D32)\ A \models \sharp(F(W_k, N_b), K_i)$$

From statement $(D32)$ using $(F1)$:

$$(D33)\ A \models \sharp(F(F(W_k, N_b), K_i))$$

From statements $(D20)$, $(D28)$ and $(D33)$, the $(A10)$ assumption and the $(I3b)$ postulate from the extended GNY logics (having $X = F(W_k, N_b)$, $S = K_i$ substituted) we get:

$$(D34)\ A \models B \vdash F(F(W_k, N_b), K_i)$$

From statements $(D33)$ and $(D34)$ using $(I6)$:

$$(D35)\ A \models B \ni F(F(W_k, N_b), K_i)$$

From assumptions $(A3)$ and $(A4)$ using the $(P2)$ postulate:

$$(D36)\ A \models B \ni F(W_k, N_b)$$

And finally from statements $(D35)$ and $(D36)$ using $(P5)$ we get:

$$(D37)\ A \models B \ni K_i$$

Notice that the $(D37)$ statement is the same as our $(C2)$ aim, which means the back-end is authenticated by the tag. Since both of our aims, $(C1)$ and $(C2)$ are fulfilled, it is proved that the improved protocol provides mutual authentication between the tags and the back-end.

7 Future Work and Conclusions

We have seen that authentication is really important in RFID systems, because of the public radio communication. Passive tags have a very limited CPU capacity, thus it has become obvious that lightweight protocols are the only suitable solutions for this problem. A number of RFID authentication protocols exist, but every one of them had their security issues. We chose an existing protocol that needed some improvement to prevent against well known reply attacks, but was still simple enough to suit passive tags. We analyzed the secureness and then formally verified the correctness of our protocol.

The proposed protocol still has weaknesses that need further studies:

Desynchronization attacks   when the 3rd message is blocked by an adversary, the back-end advances in the hash-chain but the tag does not, which leads to different secret values at the two parties. Even if a 4th confirmation message is inserted to let the back-end know that the tag has successfully run the protocol, it can still be blocked, etc. This is known as The Byzantine Generals Problem [7].

Problems with database error   when the back-end's database is corrupted for some reason and it needs to be rolled back to a previous state, tags that were authenticated since the last save will be desynchronized and this will render them completely unusable. Further studies are needed to find a way to let the parties get resynchronized.

The protocol presented in this paper still needs improvements, thus our future work is to eliminate these vulnerabilities. After addressing these issues this work may provide the RFID industry a good starting point in making their products more secure.

Acknowledgements This paper was made in the frame of Mobile Innovation Centre's integrated project Nr. 1.1., supported by the National Office for Research and Technology (Mobile 01/2004 contract).

References

1. Luo, Z., Chan, T., Li, J. S.: A Lightweight Mutual Authentication Protocol for RFID Networks. Proc. of the 2005 IEEE International Conference on e-Business Engineering (ICEBE'05), IEEE (2005)
2. Ohbuko, M., Suzuki, K., Kinoshita, S.: Cryptographic Approach to "Privacy-Friendly" Tag. RFID Privacy Workshop@MIT (2003)
3. Weis, S. A., Sarma, S. E., Rivest, R. L., Engels, D. W.: Security and Privacy Aspects of Low-Cost Radio Frequency Identification Systems. Security in Pervasive Computing, LNCS 2802 (2004) 201–212
4. Ohbuko, M., Suzuki, K., Kinoshita, S.: Hash-Chain Based Forward-Secure Privacy Protection Scheme for Low-Cost RFID. Proceedings of the 2004 Symposium on Cryptography and Information Security(SCIS2004), Vol. 1 (Jan. 2004) 719–724
5. Gong, L., Needham, R., Yahalom, R.: Reasoning about belief in cryptographics protocols. Proceedings 1990 IEEE Symposium on Research in Security and Privacy, IEEE Computer Society Press (1990) 234–248
6. Rogaway, P. and Shrimpton, T.: Cryptographic hash-function basics: Definitions, implications, and separations for preimage resistance, second-preimage resistance, and collision resistance. In Bimal Roy and Willi Meier, editors, Lecture Notes in Computer Science. Springer-Verlag Heidelberg, (2004) 371–388
7. Lamport, L., Shostak, R., Pease, M.: The Byzantine Generals Problem. ACM Transactions on Programming Languages and Systems, Vol. 4., No. 3 (July 1982) 382–401

Author Index